MapArt.com

Contents

City QuickFinder

Abbotsford	63		41	Saanich	41
	64	Langley	62	Seattle (WA)	30
Aberdeen (WA)	52		63		31
	63	Mission	63	Sechelt	91
Bellingham (WA)	52	Nanaimo	60	Sidney	50
Burnaby	62		59	Sooke	40
Chilliwack	64	New Westminster	62	South Surrey	62
Comox	88	North Delta	62	Squamish	92
Coquitlam	67	North Vancouver	61	Surrey	62
Courtenay	88		62	Tofino	55
Duncan	49	Parksville	58	Vancouver	61
Esquimault	41		59		62
Everett (WA)	36	Port Coquitlam	62	Vernon	159
Fernie	111	Port Moody	62		160
Hope	65	Qualicum Beach	58	Victoria	41
Kamloops	173	Richmond	61		
Langford	40		62		

© Copyright 2021
MapArt Publishing Corporation
70 Bloor Street East • Oshawa, Ontario • L1H 3M2
phone: (905) 436-2525
email: info@mapart.com

Questions or Comments? Contact us at info@mapart.com
Image(s) used under license from Shutterstock.com:
Cover photo; Golf photo page 234

MapArt and the MapArt logo are trademarks of © MapArt Publishing Corporation (Oshawa)

Compiled, reproduced and lithographed in Canada. Every effort has been made to ensure the accuracy of this publication; however, since inconsistencies and frequent changes occur in this type of work the publishers cannot be responsible for any variations from the printed information but would appreciate notification should any be discovered. Reproducing or recording of maps, text or any other material in this publication, by photocopying, by electronic storage and retrieval, or by any other means is prohibited without written permission of the publisher.

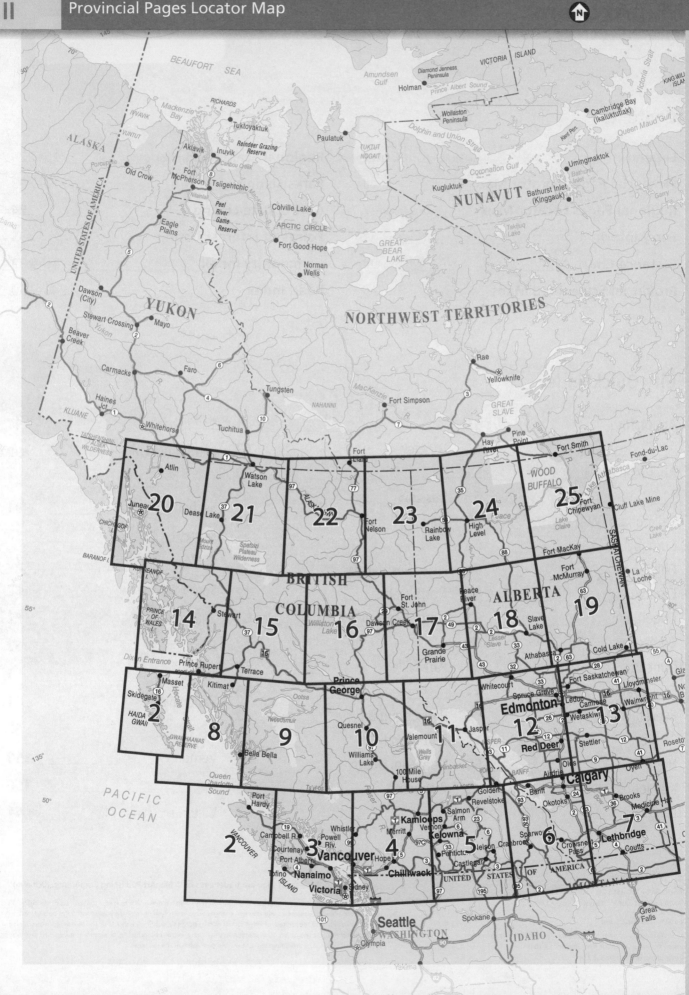

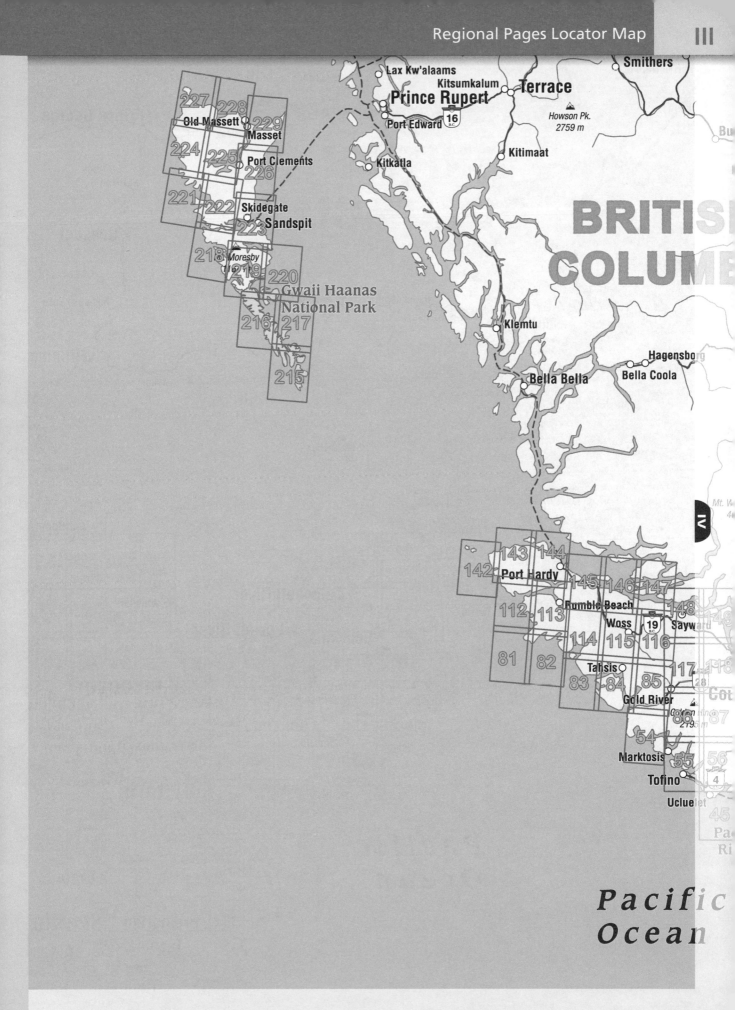

Smithers

Lax Kw'alaams
Kitsumkalum
Prince Rupert   Terrace
Port Edward   16 B.C.   Howson Pk.
2759 m

227 228 229
Old Massett   Kitimaat
Masset   Kitkatla

224 225 Port Clements
226   BRITISH
COLUMB

221 222
Skidegate
223 Sandspit

218 Moresby
116 219 220
Gwaii Haanas
National Park   Klemtu

216 217   Hagensborg
Bella Coola
Bella Bella

215   IV   Mt. W
4

142 143 144
Port Hardy

145 146 147
112 113 Rumble Beach   148
Woss 19 B.C. Sayward 149
114 115 116
81 82 Tahsis   117 118
83 84 85   28   Côt
Gold River   87
86 2193 m
54   Marktosis 55 56
Tofino   4
Ucluelet   45
Pa
Ri

Pacific
Ocean

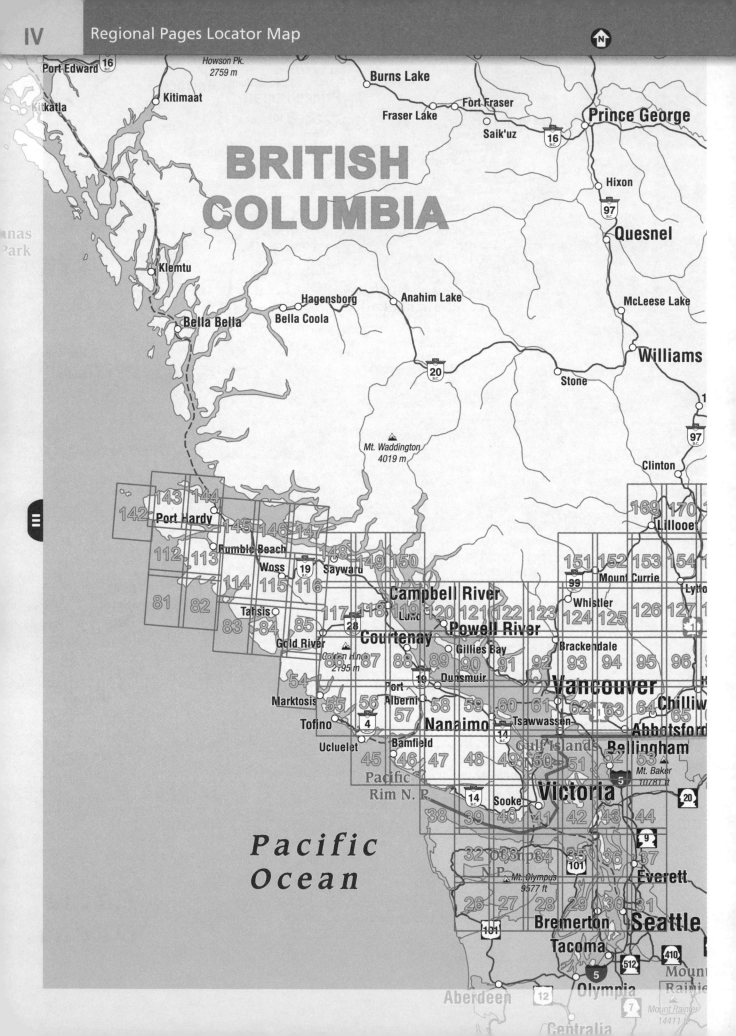

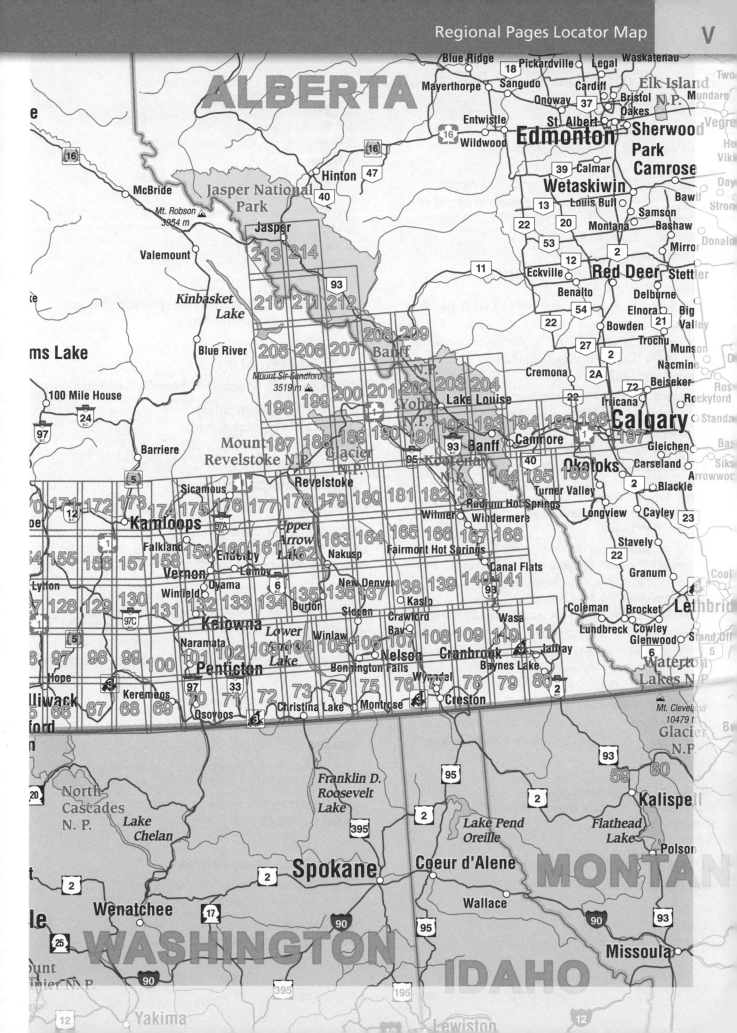

British Columbia Ferry Information

BC Ferries

Metro Vancouver - Vancouver Island

Metro Vancouver - Vancouver Island
- Vancouver (Tsawwassen) ▶ Victoria (Swartz Bay)
- Vancouver (Tsawwassen) ▶ Nanaimo (Duke Point)
- West Vancouver (Horseshoe Bay) ▶ Nanaimo (Departure Bay)

Saanich Inlet
- Brentwood Bay ▶ Mill Bay

Sunshine Coast
- West Vancouver (Horseshoe Bay) ▶ Sunshine Coast (Langdale)
- Sechelt Peninsula (Earls Cove) ▶ Powell River (Saltery Bay)
- Powell River (Westview) ▶ Comox (Little River)
- Bowen Island (Snug Cove) ▶ West Vancouver (Horseshoe Bay)
- Langdale ▶ Gambier Island ▶ Keats Island

Southern Gulf Islands
- Bowen Island ▶ West Vancouver (Horsehoe Bay)
- Chemainus ▶ Thetis Island ▶ Penelakut Island
- Crofton ▶ Salt Spring Island (Vesuvius Bay)
- Nanaimo Harbour ▶ Gabriola Island
- Victoria (Swartz Bay) - Gulf Island Terminals: Salt Spring Island (Fulford Harbour, Long Harbour), Pender Island (Otter Bay), Saturna Island (Lyall Harbour), Mayne Island (Village Bay), Galiano Island (Sturdies Bay)

Northern Gulf Islands
- Buckley Bay ▶ Denman Island ▶ Hornby Island
- Campbell River ▶ Quadra Island (Quathiaski Cove/Heriot Bay) ▶ Cortes Island (Whaletown)
- Port McNeill ▶ Alert Bay ▶ Sointula
- Powell River (Westview) ▶ Texada Island (Blubber Bay)

Inside Passage / Mid Coast / Bella Coola / Haida Gwaii
- Port Hardy ▶ Bella Bella ▶ Klemtu ▶ Prince Rupert
- Ocean Falls ▶ Shearwater ▶ Bella Bella
- Prince Rupert ▶ Skidegate
- Skidegate ▶ Alliford Bay

Discovery Coast
- Port Hardy ▶ Bella Bella ▶ Shearwater ▶ Klemtu ▶ Ocean Falls ▶ Bella Coola

1-888-223-3779 (in North America)
(250) 386-3431 (outside North America)
www.bcferries.com

BC Ministry of Transportation and Infrastructure
- Adams Lake
- Arrow Park
- Barnston Island
- Big Bar
- Francois Lake
- Glade
- Harrop
- Kootenay Lake
- Little Fort
- Lytton
- McLure
- Needles
- Upper Arrow Lake
- Usk

www2.gov.bc.ca/gov/content/transportation/passenger-travel/water-travel/inland-ferries

Black Ball Ferry Line
- Victoria, British Columbia ▶ Port Angeles, Washington

(360) 457-4491 (Washington)
(250) 386-2202 (British Columbia)
www.cohoferry.com

Clipper Navigation Inc.
- Victoria, British Columbia ▶ Seattle, Washington

(360) 448-5000 (Washington)
(250) 382-8100 (British Columbia)
www.clippervacations.com/clipper-ferry

False Creek Ferries
- Maritime Museum ▶ Aquatic Centre ▶ Granville Island ▶ David Lam Park ▶ Stamp's Landing ▶ Spyglass Place ▶ Yaletown ▶ Plaza of Nations ▶ Village/Science World

(604) 684-7781
www.granvilleislandferries.bc.ca

SeaBus
- Waterfront Station (Vancouver) ▶ Lonsdale Quay (North Vancouver)

(604) 953-3333
www.translink.ca

Washington State Ferries
- Sidney, British Columbia ▶ San Juan Islands, Washington ▶ Anacortes, Washington

(206) 464-6400
www.wsdot.wa.gov/ferries

Always check with Terminals for extra or delayed departures. Schedules are subject to change without notice. Most routes load vehicles in order of arrival, however, some routes require reservations.

British Columbia Distance Chart

	Abbotsford	Banff	Burnaby	Calgary	Chilliwack	Coquitlam	Edmonton	Hope	Kamloops	Kelowna	Lake Louise	Langley	Maple Ridge	Merritt	Nanaimo	New Westminster	North Delta	Osoyoos	Penticton	Pitt Meadows	Port Moody	Princeton	Revelstoke	Richmond	Saanich	Salmon Arm	Seattle (WA)	Sicamous	Sidney	Surrey	Tacoma (WA)	Vancouver	Vernon	Victoria	View Royal	White Rock
White Rock	40	820	47	944	74	40	1132	25	326	362	763	25	39	243	124	35	30	370	390	36	42	256	537	40	114	434	184	464	93	25	238	52	414	118	118	0
View Royal	158	936	122	1060	190	127	1248	241	442	478	879	134	139	359	104	113	107	486	506	136	125	372	653	103	6	550	296	580	26	112	217	114	530	6	0	118
Victoria	158	936	123	1061	191	128	1248	242	443	478	880	135	139	359	111	113	107	487	506	136	130	373	654	103	5	550	297	581	27	113	211	115	531	0	6	118
Vernon	378	430	432	555	343	425	841	292	117	51	374	392	408	180	522	425	427	176	116	413	427	215	147	450	528	60	553	75	507	419	607	442	0	531	530	414
Vancouver	70	848	16	972	102	32	1160	153	354	390	791	55	45	271	82	21	31	398	418	39	28	285	565	17	111	462	229	492	90	36	283	0	442	115	114	52
Tacoma (WA)	242	1044	275	1153	266	268	1324	317	519	554	956	236	267	435	321	269	262	479	541	264	270	449	729	273	214	626	54	656	237	258	0	283	607	211	217	238
Surrey	46	824	17	949	76	18	1136	129	331	366	768	31	25	247	118	8	6	375	394	22	19	261	541	29	108	438	202	468	87	0	258	36	419	113	112	25
Sidney	133	911	98	1036	165	103	1223	216	418	453	855	109	114	334	130	88	82	462	481	111	100	348	628	78	23	525	272	555	0	87	237	90	507	27	26	93
Sicamous	427	356	481	480	392	474	767	341	139	125	299	441	457	225	572	474	477	250	190	462	476	311	73	499	577	31	602	0	555	468	656	492	75	581	580	464
Seattle (WA)	189	959	222	1131	213	215	1271	364	465	501	902	183	214	381	301	215	208	457	519	211	217	395	676	220	292	573	0	602	272	202	54	229	553	297	296	184
Salmon Arm	397	386	450	511	362	444	798	311	109	111	330	411	427	194	541	443	446	236	176	432	446	281	104	469	547	0	573	31	525	438	626	462	60	550	550	434
Saanich	155	933	119	1057	187	124	1245	238	439	475	876	131	136	356	109	110	103	483	503	133	122	369	650	100	0	547	292	577	23	108	214	111	528	5	6	114
Richmond	72	855	28	980	110	37	1167	160	362	397	799	56	53	278	110	22	23	406	425	43	34	292	573	0	100	469	220	499	78	29	273	17	450	103	103	40
Revelstoke	500	283	554	408	465	547	655	414	212	197	227	515	530	298	645	547	550	323	263	536	549	384	0	573	650	104	676	73	628	541	729	565	147	654	653	537
Princeton	220	667	273	792	185	267	980	134	174	162	611	234	250	90	364	266	269	114	112	255	269	0	384	292	369	281	395	311	348	261	449	285	215	373	372	256
Port Moody	54	831	15	956	86	4	1144	137	338	374	775	39	20	254	104	17	24	382	402	14	0	269	549	34	122	446	217	476	100	19	270	28	427	130	125	42
Pitt Meadows	38	816	28	941	71	12	1128	122	323	358	760	23	8	239	119	22	30	367	386	0	14	255	536	43	133	432	244	462	111	22	264	39	413	136	136	36
Penticton	352	545	405	670	317	399	956	266	238	63	489	366	381	153	496	398	401	63	0	386	402	112	263	425	503	176	519	190	481	384	541	418	116	506	506	390
Osoyoos	333	605	387	730	298	380	1017	248	298	123	549	348	363	214	478	380	383	0	63	367	382	114	323	406	483	236	457	250	462	375	479	398	176	487	486	370
North Delta	54	832	18	957	89	25	1144	137	338	374	776	39	31	255	112	8	0	383	401	30	24	269	550	23	103	446	208	477	82	6	262	31	427	107	107	30
New Westminster	54	829	10	954	84	16	1142	135	336	371	773	36	28	252	100	0	8	380	398	22	17	266	547	22	110	443	215	474	88	8	269	21	425	113	113	36
Nanaimo	149	927	96	1052	182	111	1239	233	434	469	871	134	124	350	0	100	112	478	496	119	104	364	645	110	109	541	301	572	130	118	321	82	522	111	104	124
Merritt	206	550	360	705	171	253	892	121	87	127	524	221	236	0	350	252	255	214	153	239	254	90	298	278	356	194	381	225	334	247	435	271	180	359	359	243
Maple Ridge	38	813	34	937	67	18	1125	125	319	355	756	27	0	236	124	28	31	363	381	8	20	250	530	59	136	427	214	457	114	25	267	45	408	139	139	39
Langley	18	797	44	922	52	37	1110	103	304	339	741	0	27	221	134	36	39	348	366	23	39	234	515	56	131	411	183	441	109	31	236	55	392	135	134	25
Lake Louise	726	57	780	182	691	773	469	640	438	423	0	741	756	524	871	773	776	549	489	760	775	611	227	799	876	330	902	768	855	768	956	791	374	880	879	763
Kelowna	325	480	379	605	290	372	891	239	167	0	423	339	355	127	469	371	374	123	63	358	374	162	197	397	475	111	501	125	453	366	554	390	51	478	478	52
Kamloops	289	495	343	620	254	336	807	204	0	167	438	304	319	87	434	336	338	298	238	323	338	174	212	362	439	109	465	139	418	331	519	354	117	443	442	326
Hope	88	698	142	822	54	135	1010	0	204	239	640	103	125	121	233	135	137	248	266	122	137	134	414	160	238	311	364	341	216	129	317	153	292	242	241	125
Edmonton	1095	415	1149	299	1060	1142	0	1010	807	891	469	1110	1125	892	1239	1142	1144	1017	956	1128	1144	980	695	1167	1245	798	1271	797	1223	1136	1324	1160	841	1248	1248	1132
Coquitlam	52	830	17	954	84	0	1142	135	336	372	773	37	18	253	111	16	25	380	399	12	4	267	547	37	124	444	215	474	103	18	268	32	425	128	127	40
Chilliwack	38	748	92	872	0	84	1060	54	254	290	691	52	67	171	182	84	89	298	317	71	86	185	465	110	187	362	213	392	165	76	266	102	343	191	190	74
Calgary	906	125	960	0	872	954	299	822	620	605	182	922	937	705	1052	954	957	730	670	941	956	792	408	980	1057	511	1131	480	1036	949	1153	972	555	1061	1060	944
Burnaby	59	836	0	960	92	17	1149	142	343	379	780	44	34	360	96	10	18	387	405	28	15	273	554	28	119	450	222	481	98	17	275	16	432	123	122	47
Banff	783	0	836	125	748	830	415	698	495	480	57	797	813	550	927	829	832	605	545	816	831	667	283	855	933	386	959	356	911	824	1044	848	430	936	936	820
Abbotsford	0	783	59	906	38	52	1095	88	289	325	726	18	38	206	149	54	54	333	352	38	54	220	500	72	155	397	189	427	133	46	242	70	378	158	158	40

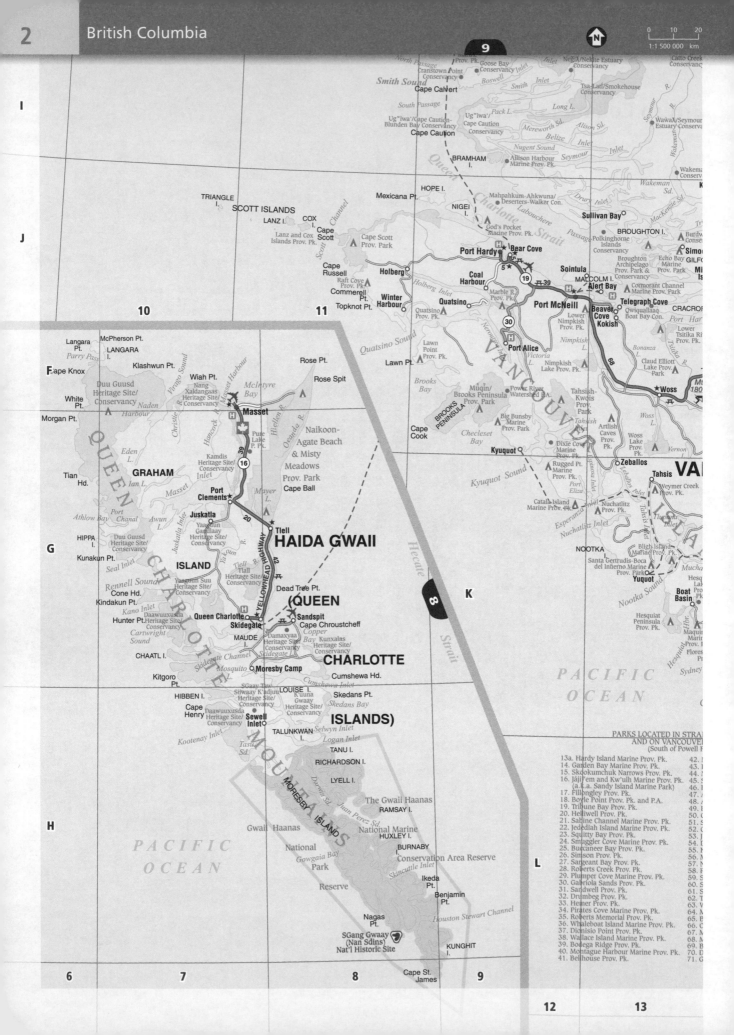

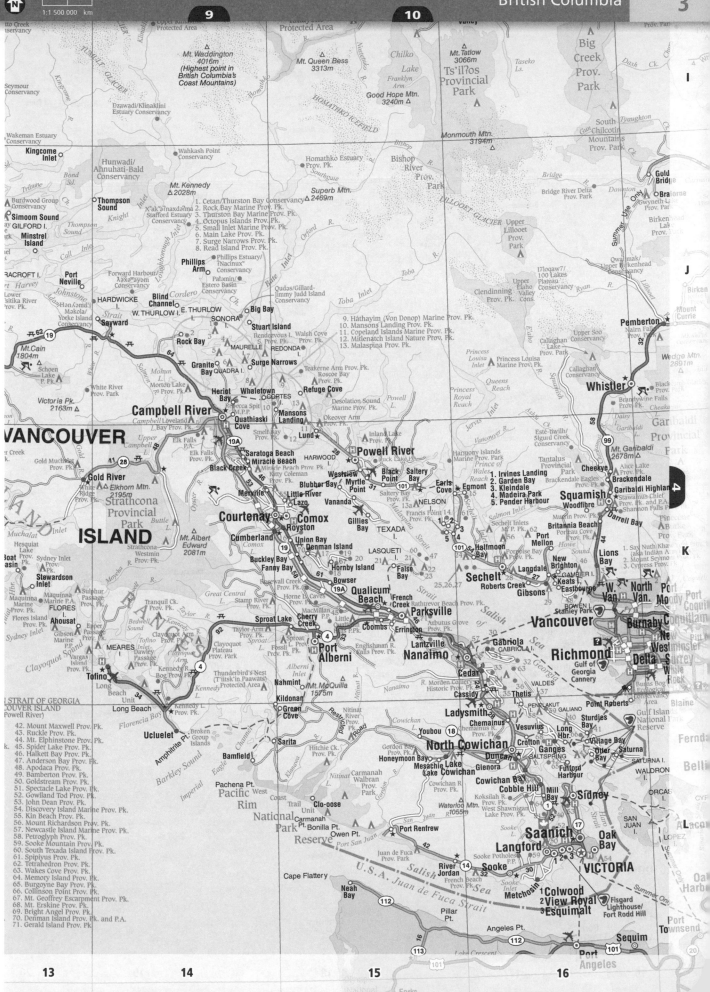

1:1 500 000 km
0 10 20

1. Cetan/Thurston Bay Conservancy
2. Rock Bay Marine Prov. Pk.
3. Thurston Bay Marine Prov. Pk.
4. Octopus Islands Prov. Pk.
5. Small Inlet Marine Prov. Pk.
6. Main Lake Prov. Pk.
7. Surge Narrows Prov. Pk.
8. Read Island Prov. Pk.

9. Háthayim (Von Donop) Marine Prov. Pk.
10. Mansons Landing Prov. Pk.
11. Copeland Islands Marine Prov. Pk.
12. Mitlenatch Island Nature Prov. Pk.
13. Malaspina Prov. Pk.

1. Irvines Landing
2. Garden Bay
3. Kleindale
4. Madeira Park
5. Pender Harbour

42. Mount Maxwell Prov. Pk.
43. Ruckle Prov. Pk.
44. Mt. Elphinstone Prov. Pk.
45. Spider Lake Prov. Pk.
46. Halkett Bay Prov. Pk.
47. Anderson Bay Prov. Pk.
48. Apodaca Prov. Pk.
49. Bamberton Prov. Pk.
50. Goldstream Prov. Pk.
51. Spectacle Lake Prov. Pk.
52. Gowlland Tod Prov. Pk.
53. John Dean Prov. Pk.
54. Discovery Island Marine Prov. Pk.
55. Kin Beach Prov. Pk.
56. Mount Richardson Prov. Pk.
57. Newcastle Island Marine Prov. Pk.
58. Petroglyph Prov. Pk.
59. Sooke Mountain Prov. Pk.
60. South Texada Island Prov. Pk.
61. Spipiyus Prov. Pk.
62. Tetrahedron Prov. Pk.
63. Wakes Cove Prov. Pk.
64. Memory Island Prov. Pk.
65. Burgoyne Bay Prov. Pk.
66. Collinson Point Prov. Pk.
67. Mt. Geoffrey Escarpment Prov. Pk.
68. Mt. Erskine Prov. Pk.
69. Bright Angel Prov. Pk.
70. Denman Island Prov. Pk. and P.A.
71. Gerald Island Prov. Pk.

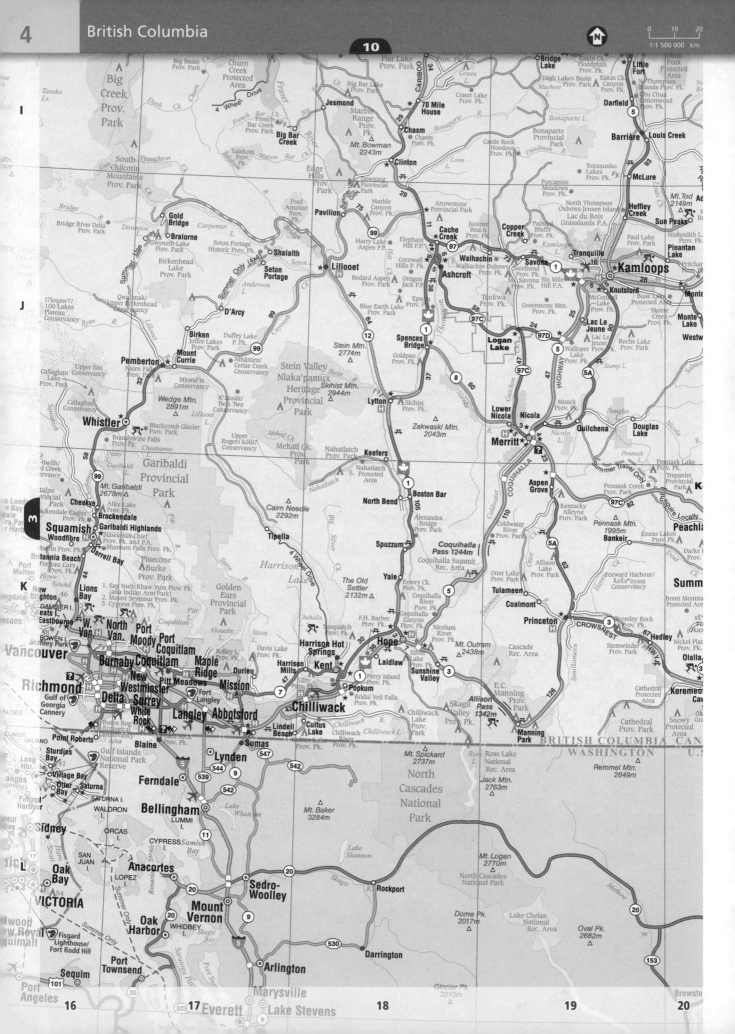

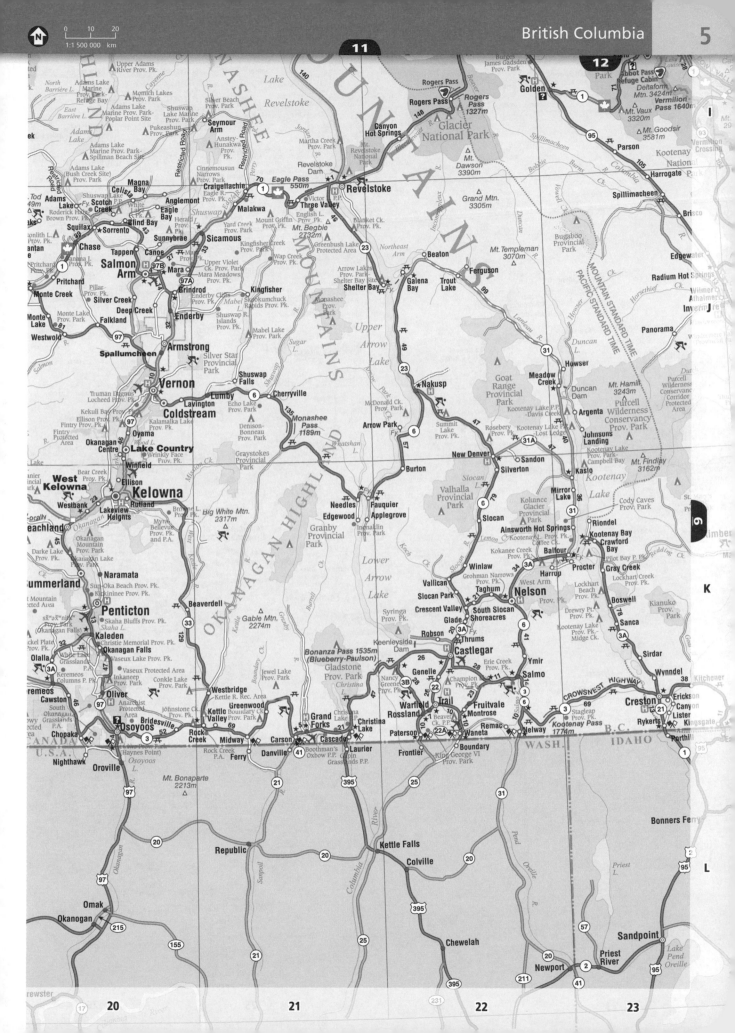

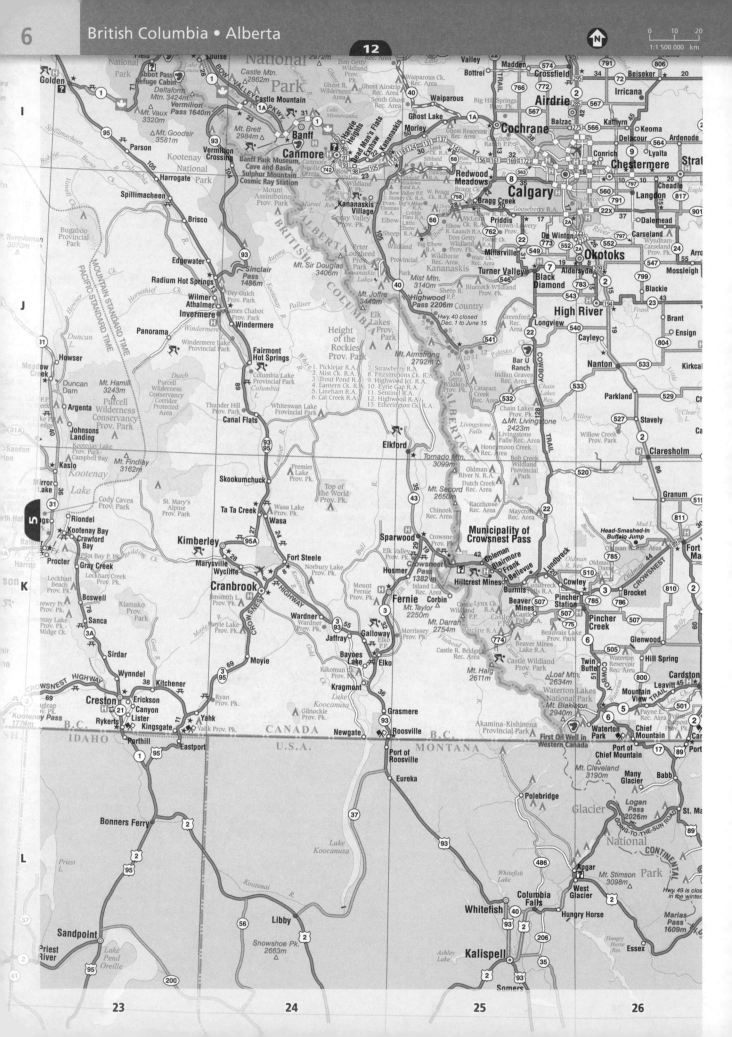

N

0   10   20

1:1 500 000 km

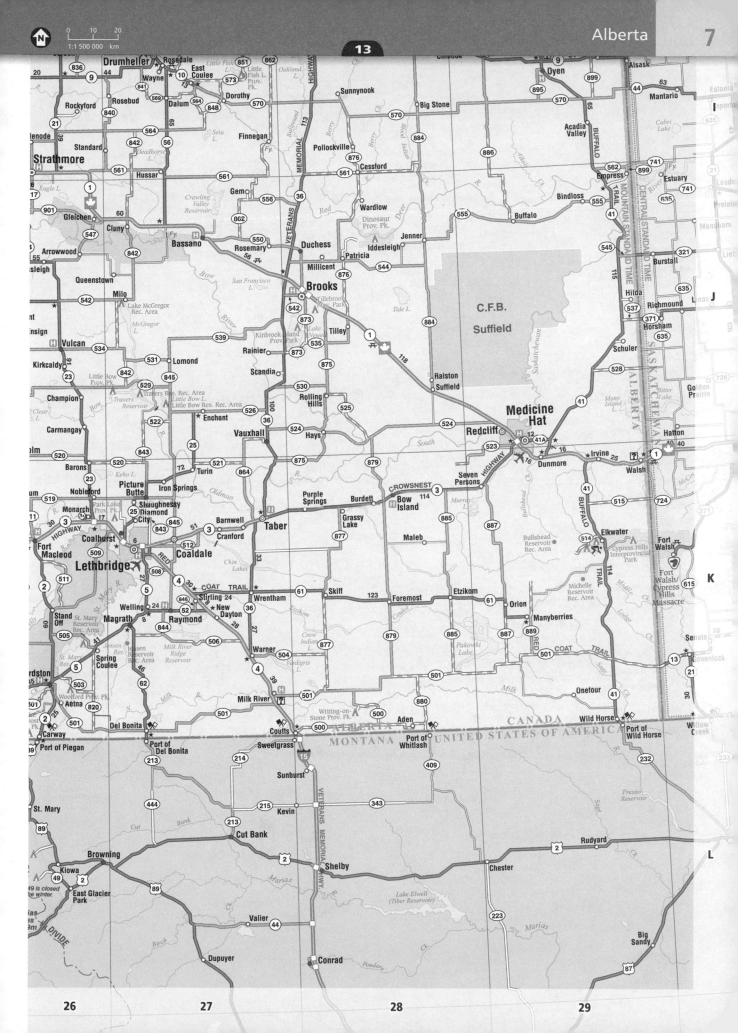

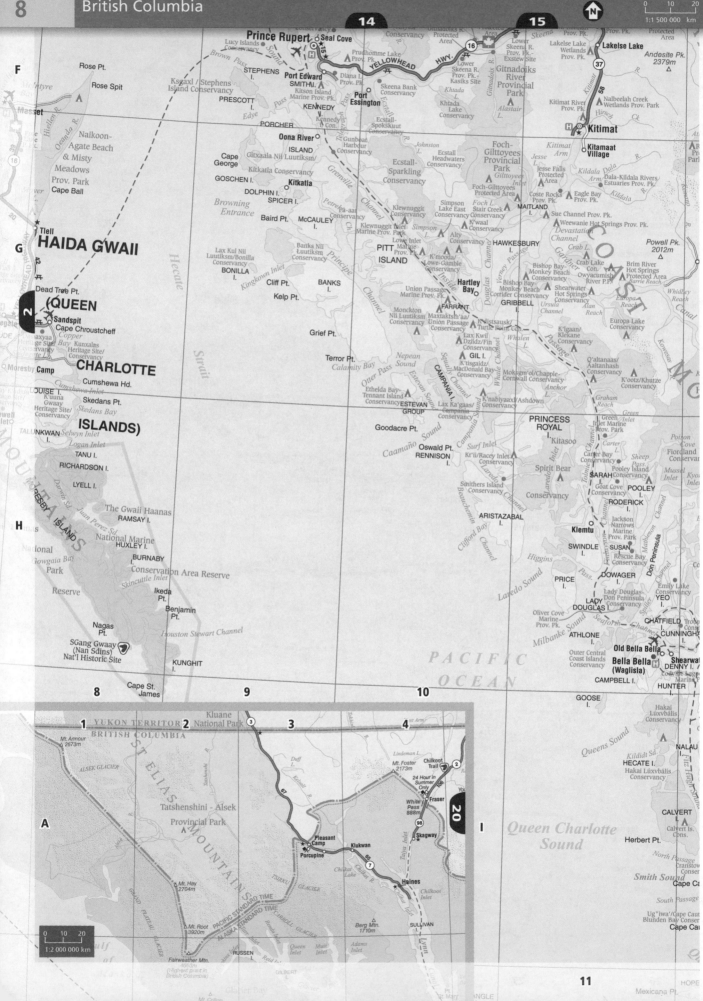

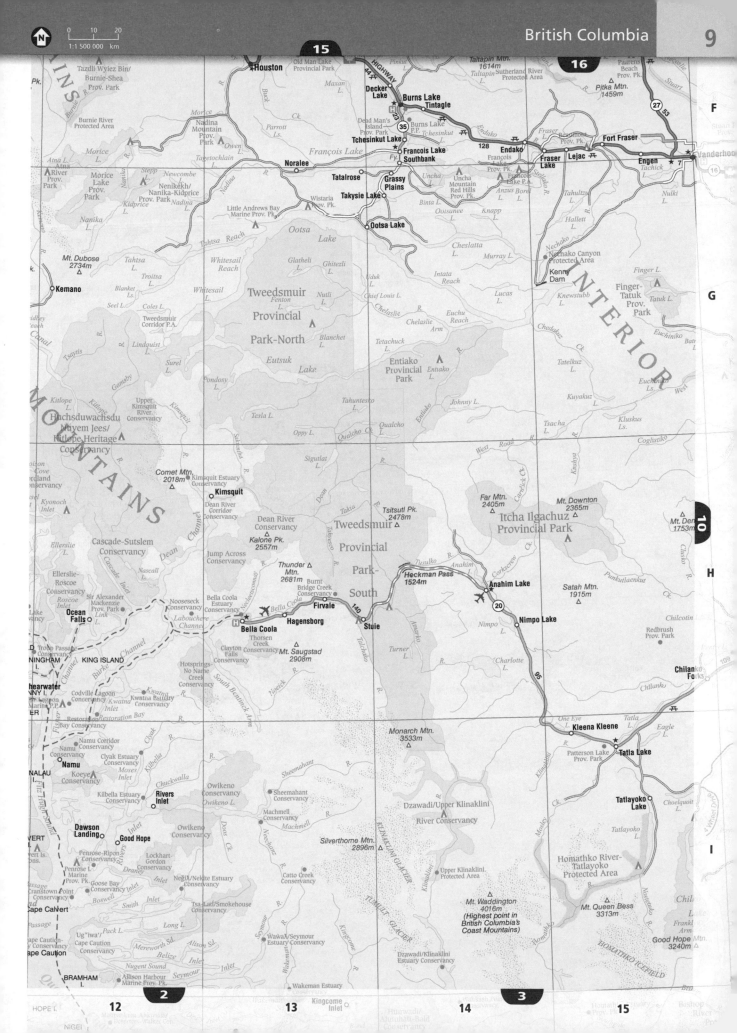

15

16

1:1 500 000 km

N

Tazdli Wyiez Bin/ Burnie-Shea Prov. Park

Houston

Old Man Lake Provincial Park

Pinkut

Taltapin Mtn. 1614m

Paarens Beach Prov. Pk.

Pitka Mtn. 1459m

27 53

F

Burnie River Protected Area

Nadina Mountain Prov. Park

Parrott Ls.

Decker Lake

Burns Lake

Tintagle

Sutherland River Protected Area

Stuart

Vanderhoof

Morice

Atna Pk.

Atna River Prov. Park

Morice Lake Prov. Park

Nenikëkh/ Nanika-Kidprice Prov. Park

Kidprice

Nanika

Owen L.

Tagetochlain L.

Dead Man's Island Prov. Park

Burns Lake P.P.

Tchesinkut Lake

François Lake

Noralee

23

35

Tchesinkut

Endako

128

Endako

Francois Lake Prov. Pk.

Fraser Lake

Lejac

Engen

Fort Fraser

16

7

Tatalrose

Francois Lake Southbank

Grassy Plains

Uncha L.

Uncha Mountain Red Hills Prov. Pk.

Anzus Borel L.

Francois Lake P.P.

Tachick L.

Nulki L.

G

Stepp

Newcombe

Wistaria Prov. Pk.

Takysie Lake

Little Andrews Bay Marine Prov. Pk.

Binta L.

Ootsa Lake

Ootsa

Lake

Ooisunee L.

Knapp L.

Hallett L.

Stellako R.

Tahultzu L.

Mt. Dubose 2734m

Tahtsa L.

Troitsa L.

Whitesail Reach

Glatheli L.

Ghitezli L.

Cheslatta L.

Murray L.

Nechako

Nechako Canyon Protected Area

Finger L.

Finger-Tatuk Prov. Park

Tatuk L.

Kemano

Blanket Ls.

Seel L.

Coles L.

Tweedsmuir

Whitesail L.

Fenton L.

Nutli L.

Uduk L.

Chief Louis L.

Intata Reach

Lucas L.

Kenny Dam

Knewstubb L.

INTERIOR

Euchiniko L.

Euchiniko Ls.

Kitlope Conservancy

Tweedsmuir Corridor P.A.

Provincial

Park-North

Blanchet L.

Chelaslie L.

Chelaslie Arm

Tetachuck L.

Cheduba Ck.

Tatelkuz L.

Kuyakuz L.

Euchu Reach

Bat L.

West

Huchsduwachsdu Nuyem Jees/ Kitlope Heritage Conservancy

Lindquist L.

Surel L.

Eutsuk

Lake

Pondosy L.

Entiako Provincial Park

Entiako L.

Johnny L.

Tsacha L.

Kluskus Ls.

MOUNTAINS

Kitlope

Tsaytis R.

Gamsby R.

Upper Kimsquit River Conservancy

Kimsquit R.

Sakumtha R.

Tesla L.

Tahuntesko L.

Oppy L.

Qualcho Ck.

Qualcho L.

Entiako R.

Coglistiko R.

Keshyu L.

Poison Cove fjordland Conservancy

Kyonoch Inlet

Comet Mtn. 2018m

Kimsquit Estuary Conservancy

Sigutlat L.

West Road

Corlick Ck.

Far Mtn. 2405m

Mt. Downton 2365m

Itcha Ilgachuz Provincial Park

Mt. Dent 1753m

Chisko R.

10

H

Ellerslie L.

Cascade-Sutslem Conservancy

Nascall L.

Dean Channel

Kimsquit

Dean River Corridor Conservancy

Dean R.

Takia R.

Tsitsutl Pk. 2478m

Tweedsmuir

Punkutlaenkut Ck.

Ellerslie-Roscoe Conservancy

Roscoe Inlet

Sir Alexander Mackenzie Prov. Park

Link L.

Nooseseck Conservancy

Jump Across Conservancy

Kalone Pk. 2557m

Thunder Mtn. 2681m

Provincial

Park-

South

Tulsuko R.

Heckman Pass 1524m

Anahim L.

Anahim Lake

Satah Mtn. 1915m

20

Redbrush Prov. Park

Chilcotin R.

Chilanko Forks

Labouchere Channel

Burnt Bridge Creek Conservancy

Firvale

140

Stuie

Nimpo L.

Nimpo Lake

Chlunko R.

Ocean Falls

Codville Lagoon Conservancy

Kwatna Inlet

Bella Coola Estuary Conservancy

Bella Coola

Hagensborg

Thorsen Creek Conservancy

Clayton Falls Conservancy

Mt. Saugstad 2908m

Turner L.

Charlotte L.

95

One Eye L.

Kleena Kleene

Tatla L.

Eagle L.

Shearwater

Kwatna Estuary Conservancy

Restoration Bay Conservancy

Restoration Bay

Hotsprings No Name Creek Conservancy

Poweck R.

South Bentinck Arm

Talchako R.

Monarch Mtn. 3533m

Patterson Lake Prov. Park

Tatla Lake

Namu Corridor Conservancy

Namu Conservancy

Namu

Koeye Conservancy

Clyak Estuary Conservancy

Moses Inlet

Kilbella R.

Chuck L.

Chuckwyalla R.

Sheemahant R.

Owikeno Conservancy

Sheemahant Conservancy

Dzawadi/Upper Klinaklini River Conservancy

Tatlayoko Lake

Choelquoit L.

Kilbella Estuary Conservancy

Rivers Inlet

Owikeno L.

Machmell Conservancy

Machmell R.

Neechanz R.

KLINAKLINI GLACIER

Klinaklini R.

Tatlayoko L.

Homathko River-Tatlayoko Protected Area

I

Dawson Landing

Good Hope

Penrose-Ripon Conservancy

Penrose I. Marine Prov. Pk.

Lockhart-Gordon Conservancy

Draney Inlet

NeɁa/Nekite Estuary Conservancy

Nekite Inlet

Doos Ck.

Catto Creek Conservancy

Silverthorne Mtn. 2896m

Upper Klinaklini Protected Area

Mt. Waddington 4016m (Highest point in British Columbia's Coast Mountains)

Mt. Queen Bess 3313m

Good Hope Mtn. 3240m

Cape Calvert

Goose Bay Conservancy

Boswell Inlet

Smith Inlet

Tsa-Latl/Smokehouse Conservancy

Seymour R.

WawaɁ/Seymour Estuary Conservancy

Kingcome R.

TUMULT GLACIER

Dzawadi/Klinaklini Estuary Conservancy

HOMATHKO ICEFIELD

Cape Caution Conservancy

Ug"iwa'/ Cape Caution Conservancy

Cape Caution

Pack L.

Long L.

Mereworth Sd.

Belize Inlet

Nugent Sound

Allison Sd.

Wakeman Sd.

Kingcome Inlet

BRAMHAM I.

Allison Harbour Marine Prov. Pk.

Wakeman Estuary

NIGEI

12

2

13

14

3

15

HOPE I.

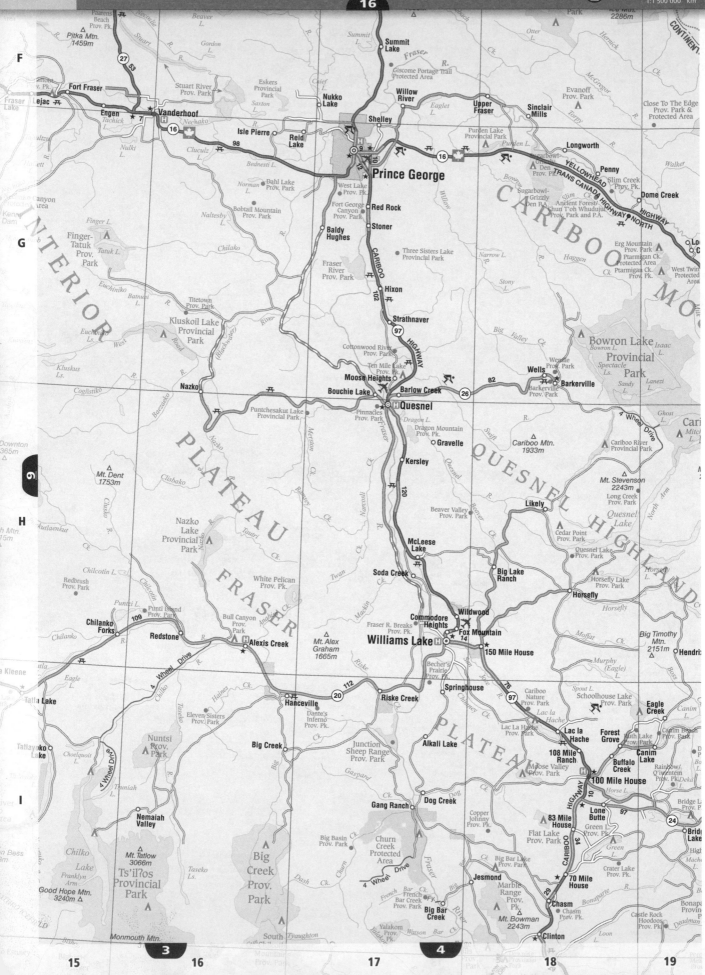

0 10 20
1:1 500 000 km

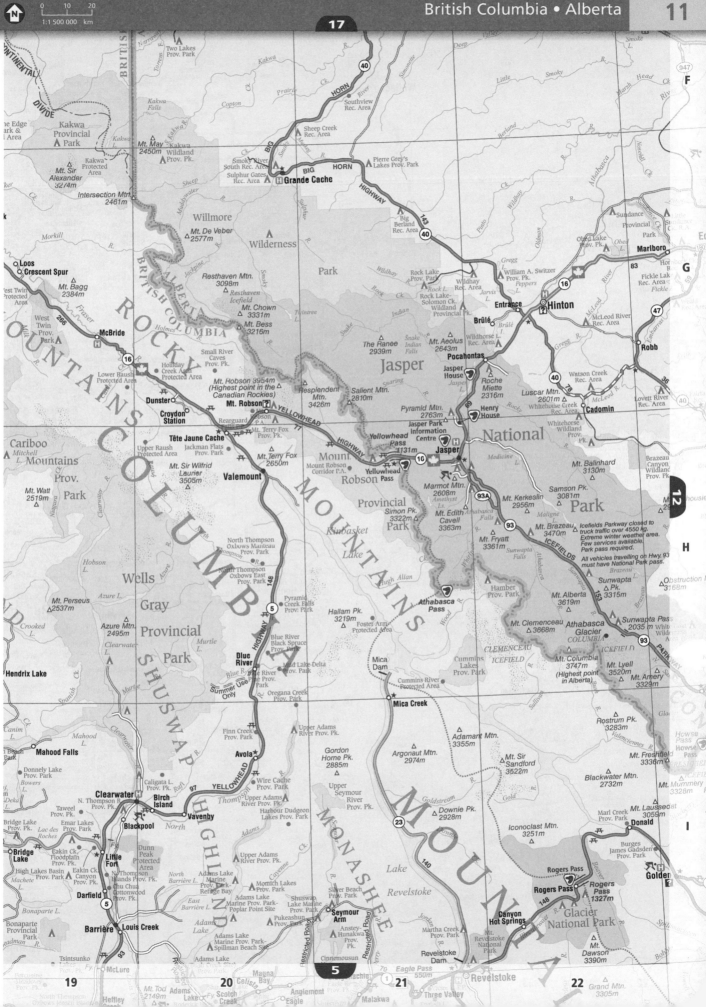

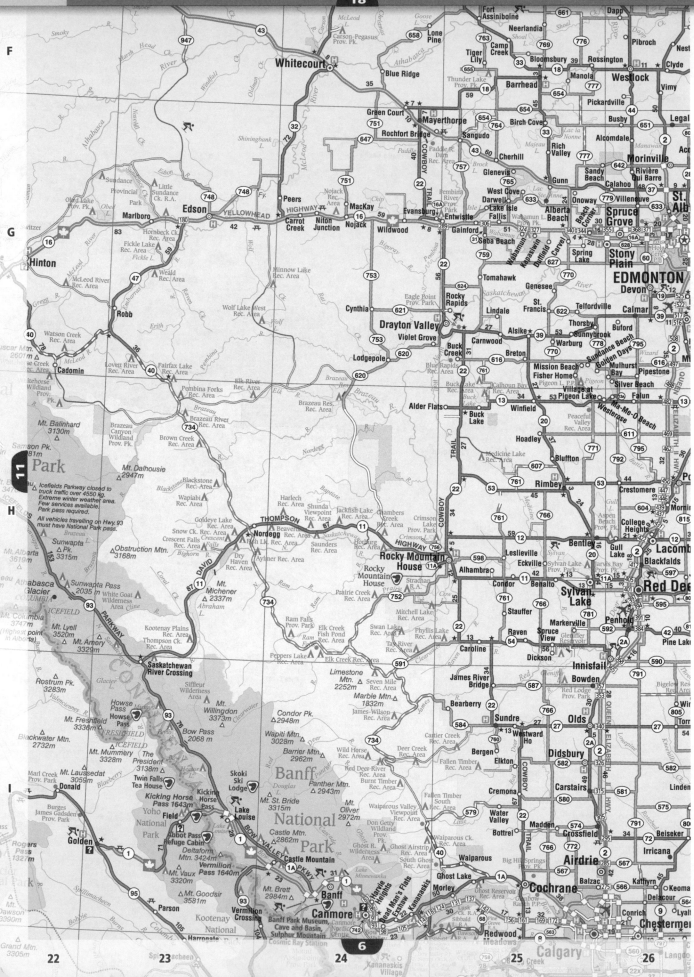

1:1 500 000 km

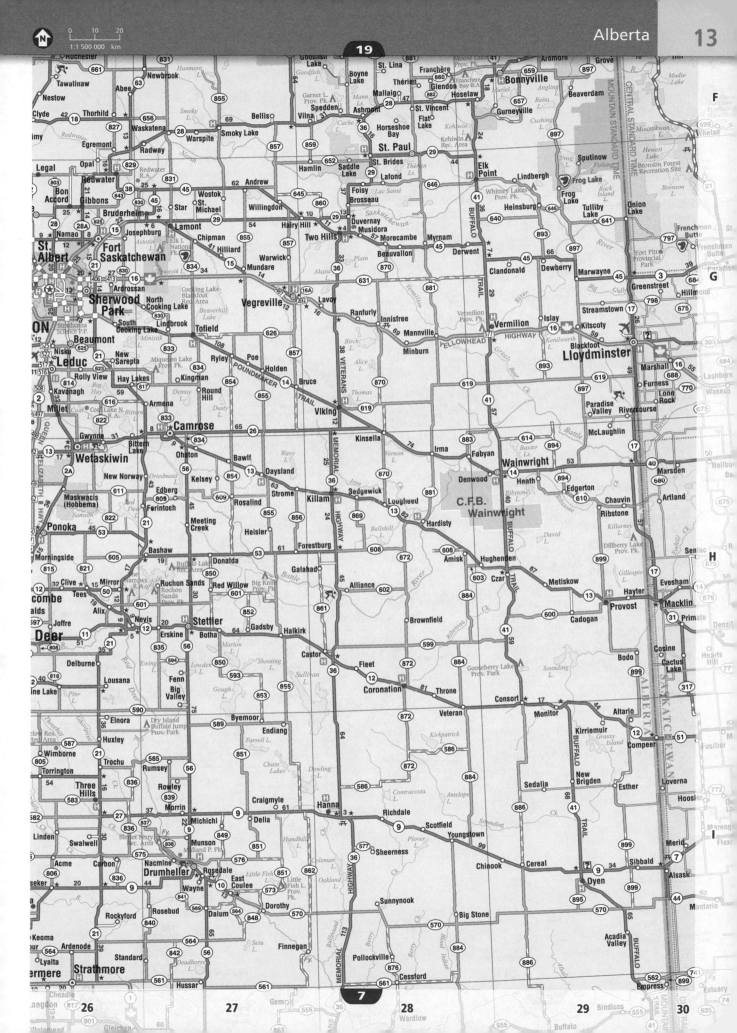

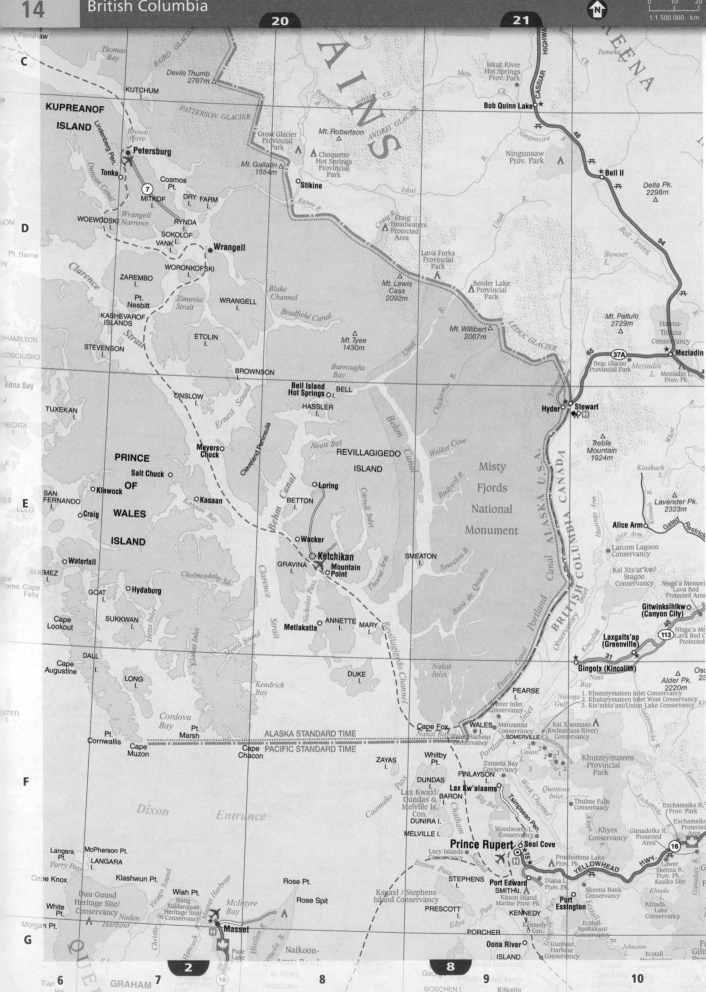

C

Thomas
Bay

Fanshaw

Devils Thumb
2767m

KUTCHUM

KUPREANOF
ISLAND

Baird Glacier

PATTERSON GLACIER

Brown
Cove

Lindenberg Pen.

Petersburg

Tonka

Cosmos
Pt.

MITKOF

DRY FARM

Duncan Canal

7

Great Glacier
Provincial
Park

Mt. Gallatin
1554m

Stikine

AINS

Mt. Robertson

ANDREI GLACIER

Porcupine

Schulze Ck.

Choquette
Hot Springs
Provincial
Park

Iskut River
Hot Springs
Prov. Park

CASSIAR HIGHWAY

Bob Quinn Lake

Tumeka

SKEENA

More Ck.

Ningunsaw
R.

Ningunsaw
Prov. Park

48

Bell II

Delta Pk.
2298m

94

D

Pt. Barrie

Clarence

WOEWODSKI I.

Wrangell
Narrows

RYNDA

SOKOLOF I.

VANK I.

WORONKOFSKI I.

Wrangell

ZAREMBO
I.

Pt.
Nesbitt

Zimovia
Strait

WRANGELL
I.

Blake
Channel

Bradfield Canal

Craig R.

Iskut R.

Katete R.

Craig
Headwaters
Protected
Area

Lava Forks
Provincial
Park

Mt. Lewis
Cass
2092m

Unuk R.

Mt. Willibert
2067m

LEDUC GLACIER

Schwatka

Border Lake
Provincial
Park

Bowser
L.

Mt. Pattulo
2729m

65

37A

Hanna-
Tintina
Conservancy

Meziadin

E

Edna Bay

HAMILTON

KOSCIUSKO

KASHEVAROF
ISLANDS

Strait

STEVENSON
I.

ETOLIN
I.

BROWNSON
I.

Burroughs
Bay

ONSLOW
I.

Ernest Sound

Bell Island
Hot Springs

HASSLER

BELL
I.

Mt. Tyee
1430m

Behm Canal

Chickamin R.

Walker Cove

Bear Glacier
Provincial Park

Meziadin
L.

Meziadin L.
Prov. Pk.

Hyder

Stewart

Treble
Mountain
1924m

White R.

Kinskuch R.

E

Edna Bay

TUXEKAN
I.

PRINCE

Meyers
Chuck

Cleveland Peninsula

Neets Bay

REVILLAGIGEDO

ISLAND

Carroll Inlet

Rudyerd B.

Misty

Fjords

National

Monument

ALASKA U.S.A.

Lavender Pk.
2323m

Alice Arm

Kinskuch R.

SAN
FERNANDO
I.

OF

Salt Chuck

Klawock

Kasaan

Kasaan Bay

Loring

BETTON
I.

WALES

Craig

Behm Canal

Wacker

Ketchikan

ISLAND

Nicholas Pass.

GRAVINA
I.

Mountain
Point

Thorne Arm

SMEATON
I.

Smeaton B.

Boca de Quadra

Portland Canal

BRITISH COLUMBIA CANADA

Larcom Lagoon
Conservancy

Ksi Xts'at'kw/
Stagoo
Conservancy

Nisga'a Memorial
Lava Bed
Protected Area

Gitwinksihlkw
(Canyon City)

Laxgalts'ap
(Greenville)

Nisga'a Me
Lava Bed
Protected

95

113

SUEMEZ
I.

Cape
Felix

Waterfall

GOAT
I.

Hydaburg

SUKKWAN
I.

Cape
Lookout

Cholmondeley Sd.

Clarence

Strait

Hetta Inlet

Klakas Inlet

Metlakatla

ANNETTE
I.

MARY
I.

DUKE
I.

Revillagigedo Channel

Nakat
Inlet

Observatory Inlet

Gingolx (Kincolith)

Alder Pk.
2220m

Osc

31

Kincolith R.

DALL
I.

Cape
Augustine

LONG
I.

Kendrick
Bay

Cordova
Bay

Pt.
Marsh

Cape
Muzon

PEARSE
I.

WALES
I.

Cape Fox

Nakat Bay

Nass
Bay

Nasoga
Gulf

Portland

Hastings Arm

Kinskuch R.

Nasoga Inlet

1. Khutzeymateen Inlet Conservancy
2. Khutzeymateen Inlet West Conservancy
3. Kts'mkta'ani/Union Lake Conservancy

Ksi X'anmaas
(Kwinamass River)
Conservancy

F

STER

Pt.
Cornwallis

DALL
I.

Langara
Pt.

McPherson Pt.

LANGARA
I.

Parry Pass

Cape Knox

Klashwun Pt.

White
Pt.

Duu Guusd
Heritage Site/
Conservancy

Nang
Xaldangaas
Heritage Site/
Conservancy

ALASKA STANDARD TIME

Cape
Chacon

ZAYAS
I.

Whitby
Pt.

DUNDAS
I.

Lax Kwaxl/
Dundas &
Melville Is.
Con.

DUNIRA I.

MELVILLE I.

PACIFIC STANDARD TIME

WALES
Harbour

Zumtela Bay
Conservancy

FINLAYSON
I.

BARON
I.

Chatham
Sound

Big Bay

Manzanita
Con.

SOMERVILLE
I.

Lax Kw'alaams

Work Channel

Tsimpsean Pen.

Quottoon
Inlet

Union
L.

Khutzeymateen
Provincial
Park

Thulme Falls
Conservancy

Khyex
Conservancy

Exchamsiks R.
Prov. Park

Exchamsiks R.
Protected
Area

16

G

Morgan Pt.

Tian
Hd.

QUEEN

Christie Passage

Virago Sound

Wiah Pt.

Naden
Harbour

Masset Harbour

McIntyre
Bay

Rose Pt.

Rose Spit

Ksgaxl /
Stephens
Island Conservancy

Lucy Islands
Conservancy

Masset

Pure
Lake

Hiellen R.

Yakan R.

Naikoon-
Agate Beach
& Misty
Meadows
Prov. Park

PRESCOTT
I.

PORCHER

Edye
Pass

Oona River

ISLAND

Telegraph
Passage

Brown Pass

STEPHENS
I.

SMITH I.

KENNEDY
I.

Prince Rupert

Seal Cove

Port Edward

Kitson Island
Marine Prov. Park

Port Essington

Skeena R.

Prudhomme Lake
Prov. Pk.

Diana L.
Prov. Pk.

Skeena Bank
Conservancy

YELLOWHEAD

HWY.

Lower
Skeena R.
Prov. Pk.-
Kasiks Site

Khtada
L.

Khtada
Lake
Conservancy

Ecstall-
Spokskuut
Conservancy

Gunboat
Harbour
Conservancy

Johnston
L.

Ecstall
Headwaters

16

GRAHAM

6   7   2   8   8   9   10

16

Dixon

Entrance

Blake R.

Masset Inlet

Naden R.

DOLPHIN I.

GOSCHEN I.

Kitkatla

Georgetown

Fo
Giltr
Prov.

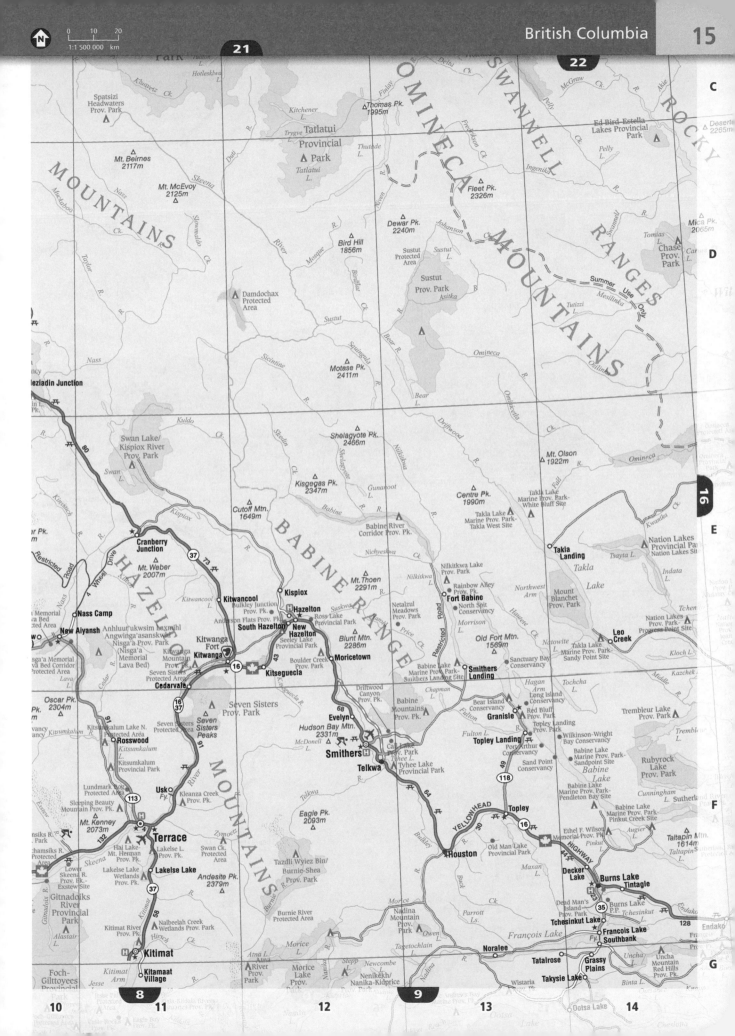

0   10   20
1:1 500 000 km

21

22

C

OMINECA   *SWANNELL*

Spatsizi
Headwaters
Prov. Park

Thomas Pk.
1995m

Ed Bird-Estella
Lakes Provincial
Park

Deser
2265m

Tatlatui
Provincial
Park

*Tatlatui
L.*

Mt. Beirnes
2117m

Fleet Pk.
2326m

D

Mt. McEvoy
2125m

MOUNTAINS

Dewar Pk.
2240m

Mica Pk.
2065m

Bird Hill
1856m

Sustut
Protected
Area

*Chase
Prov.
Park*

RANGES

Damdochax
Protected
Area

Sustut
Prov. Park

ROCKY

Summer Use
Only

Meziadin Junction

Motase Pk.
2411m

MOUNTAINS

80

Swan Lake/
Kispiox River
Prov. Park

Shelagyote Pk.
2466m

Mt. Olson
1922m

Omineca

16

E

Kisgegas Pk.
2347m

Centre Pk.
1990m

Takla Lake
Marine Prov. Park-
White Bluff Site

Nation Lakes
Provincial Park
Nation Lakes Site

Cranberry
Junction

Cutoff Mtn.
1649m

37   73

Takla
Landing

Takla

Mt. Weber
2007m

BABINE

Babine River
Corridor Prov. Pk.

Takla Lake
Marine Prov. Park-
Takla West Site

Lake

Mt. Thoen
2291m

Nilkitkwa Lake
Prov. Park

HAZELTON

Kitwancool   Kispiox

Bulkley Junction
Prov. Pk.

Rainbow Alley
Prov. Pk.

Mount
Blanchet
Prov. Park

Nass Camp

Hazelton

Netalzul
Meadows
Prov. Pk.

Fort Babine

North Spit
Conservancy

New Aiyansh

Anderson Flats Prov. Pk.

Nation Lakes
Prov. Park-
Progress Point Site

Anhluut'ukwsim Laxmihl
Angwinga'asanskwit
Nisga'a Prov. Park
(Nisga'a
Memorial
Lava Bed)

South Hazelton   New
Hazelton

Ross Lake
Provincial Park

Morrison

Old Fort Mtn.
1569m

Leo
Creek

Kitwanga
Fort

Seeley Lake
Provincial Park

Takla Lake
Marine Prov. Park-
Sandy Point Site

Kitwanga

Blunt Mtn.
2286m

Moricetown

43

Boulder Creek
Prov. Park

Sanctuary Bay
Conservancy

Nation Lakes
Prov. Pk.

Seven Sisters
Protected Area

Kitseguecla

Babine Lake
Marine Prov. Park-
Smithers Landing Site

Smithers
Landing

Cedarvale

*Hagan
Arm*   Long Island
Conservancy

Oscar Pk.
2304m

Seven Sisters
Prov. Park

Driftwood
Canyon
Prov. Pk.

68

Babine
Mountains
Prov. Pk.

Chapman L.

Bear Island
Conservancy

Trembleur Lake
Prov. Park

Kitsumkalum Lake N.
Protected Area

Seven
Sisters
Peaks

Evelyn

Red Bluff
Prov. Pk.

Granisle

Rosswood

Kitsumkalum
Provincial Park

Hudson Bay Mtn.
2331m

Topley Landing
Prov. Pk.

Wilkinson-Wright
Bay Conservancy

*Babine
Lake*

Rubyrock
Lake
Prov. Park

Topley Landing

McDonell
L.

Smithers

Call Lake
Prov. Park

Port Arthur
Conservancy

Babine Lake
Marine Prov. Park-
Sandpoint Site

Lundmark Bog
Protected Area

Telkwa

Tyhee
L.

Tyhee Lake
Provincial Park

Sand Point
Conservancy

118

Babine Lake
Marine Prov. Park-
Pendleton Bay Site

*Cunningham
L.*

Sleeping Beauty
Mountain Prov. Pk.

113

Mt. Kenney
2073m

132

Terrace

Eagle Pk.
2093m

64

YELLOWHEAD

Topley

Ethel F. Wilson
Memorial Prov. Pk.

Babine Lake
Marine Prov. Park-
Pinkut Creek Site

F

Hai Lake-
Mt. Herman
Prov. Pk.

Lakelse L.
Prov. Pk.

Swan Ck.
Prov. Park

49

30

16

HIGHWAY

Augier L.

Taltapin Mtn.
1614m

Lakelse Lake

Old Man Lake
Provincial Park

Decker
Lake

44

Taltapin
L.

Usk
Fy.

Kleanza Creek
Prov. Pk.

Tazdli Wyiez Bin/
Burnie-Shea
Prov. Park

Houston

Maxan
L.

Burns Lake

Tintagle

Gitnadoiks
River
Provincial
Park

37

Andesite Pk.
2379m

Burnie River
Protected Area

58

Kitimat River
Prov. Pk.

Nalbeelah Creek
Wetlands Prov. Pk.

Nadina
Mountain
Prov.
Park

Dead Man's
Island P.P.

Burns Lake

35

Tchesinkut Lake

128

Francois Lake
Fy.

Lower
Skeena
Prov. Pk.-
Exstew Site

Morice
L.

Francois Lake
Southbank

Kitimat

Morice
Lake
Prov.
Park

François Lake

Tatalrose

Grassy
Plains

Uncha
L.

Uncha
Mountain
Red Hills
Prov. Pk.

Kitamaat
Village

Kitimat
Arm

Morice
River
Prov.

Noralee

Takysie Lake

G

Foch-
Gilttoyees
Provincial

8   *11*   *12*   *9*   *13*   *14*

10   11   12   13   14

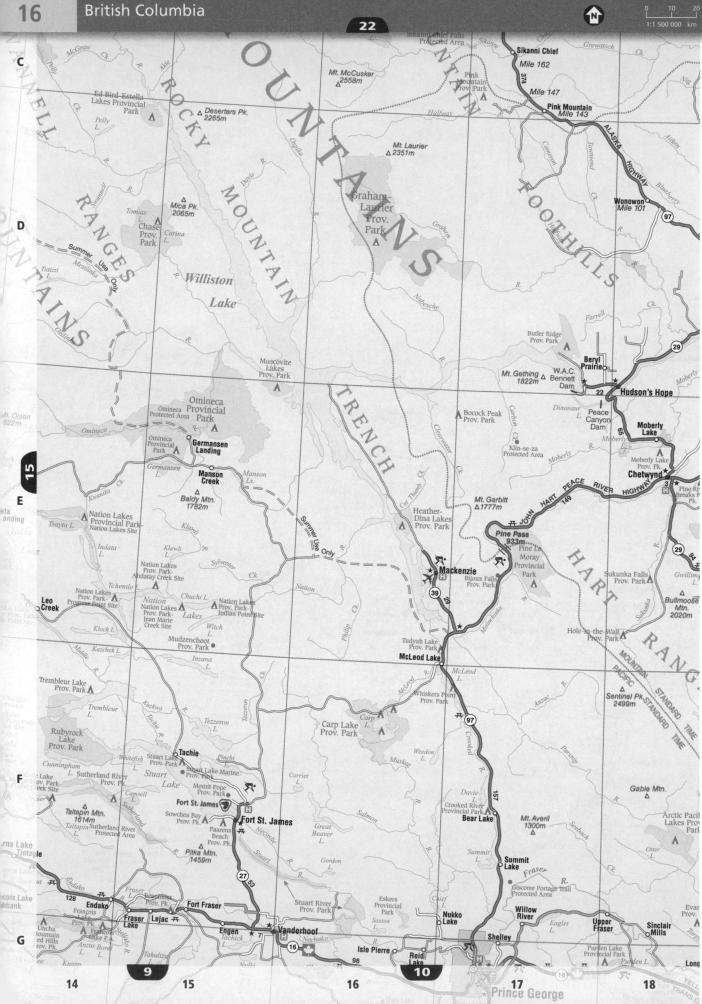

N

1:1 500 000 km

0   10   20

C

D

E

15

F

G

McGraw Ck.

ROCKY

Ed Bird-Estella
Lakes Provincial
Park

Deserters Pk.
2265m

Mt. McCusker
2558m

Mt. Laurier
2351m

Graham-
Laurier
Prov.
Park

Sikanni Chief Falls
Protected Area

Pink
Mountain
Prov. Park

Sikanni Chief
Mile 162

374   Mile 147

Pink Mountain
Mile 143

Halfway

ALASKA   HIGHWAY

Wonowon
Mile 101

97

MOUNTAIN

MOUNTAINS

FOOTHILLS

RANGES

Tomias
L.

Chase
Prov.
Park

Mica Pk.
2065m

Carina

Williston

Lake

Swannell R.

Mesilinka

Summer
Use
Only

Tutizzi
L.

Ospika R.

Davis

Muscovite
Lakes
Prov. Park

Butler Ridge
Prov. Park

Farrell

Beryl
Prairie

Mt. Gething
1822m

W.A.C.
Bennett
Dam

22   Hudson's Hope

29

Mt. Olson
922m

Omineca
Provincial
Park

Omineca
Protected Area

Omineca
Provincial
Park

Germansen
Landing

Germansen L.

Manson
Creek

Manson
Ls.

Bocock Peak
Prov. Park

Klin-se-za
Protected Area

Dinosaur
L.

Peace
Canyon
Dam

65

Moberly
Lake

Moberly Lake
Prov. Pk.

Chetwynd

3

Pine-Ri
Breaks P
Pk.

TRENCH

Kwanika

Baldy Mtn.
1782m

Nation Lakes
Provincial Park
Nation Lakes Site

Indata
L.

Klawli
L.

Klawli
R.

Sylvester

Ck.

Summer
Use
Only

Nation

Cut Thumb
Ck.

Heather-
Dina Lakes
Prov. Park

Mt. Garbitt
1777m

JOHN HART PEACE RIVER HIGHWAY

149

Pine Pass
933m

Pine Le
Moray
Provincial
Park

Sukunka Falls
Prov. Park

29   94

Gwillim
L.

HART

Leo
Creek

Tsayta L.

Nation Lakes
Prov. Park-
Ahdatay Creek Site

Chuchi L.

Tchentlo
L.

Nation

Lakes

Nation Lakes
Prov. Park-
Progress Point Site

Nation Lakes
Prov. Park-
Jean Marie
Creek Site

Nation Lakes
Prov. Park-
Indian Point Site

Witch
L.

Mudzenchoot
Prov. Park

Kloch L.

Philip
Ck.

Mackenzie

Bijoux Falls
Prov. Park

39   29

Misinchinka

Hole-in-the-Wall
Prov. Park

Bullmoose
Mtn.
2020m

RANG

Trembleur Lake
Prov. Park

Trembleur
L.

Rubyrock
Lake
Prov. Park

Kazchek L.

Inzana
L.

Kazkwa
R.

Tezzeron
L.

Tudyah Lake
Prov. Park

McLeod Lake

McLeod
L.

Whiskers Point
Prov. Park

Anzac R.

Sentinel Pk.
2499m

PACIFIC STANDARD

MOUNTAIN STANDARD TIME

Taltapin Mtn.
1614m

Taltapin
Sutherland River
Protected Area

Cunningham
L.

Sutherland River
Prov. Pk.

Sutherland R.

Camsell
L.

Stuart
Lake

Tachie

Stuart Lake
Prov. Park

Stuart Lake Marine
Prov. Park

Pinchi
L.

Mount Pope
Prov. Park

Fort St. James

Carrier
L.

Carp Lake
Prov. Park

Carp
L.

Weedon
L.

Muskeg
L.

McLeod
R.

Crooked
R.

157

Davie
L.

Crooked River
Provincial Park

Bear Lake

Mt. Averil
1300m

Gable Mtn.

Arctic Pacific
Lakes Prov
Park

F

ns Lake
Tintagle

Sowchea Bay
Prov. Pk.

Paarens
Beach
Prov. Pk.

Pitka Mtn.
1459m

27   53

Stuart R.

Necastle
L.

Great
Beaver
L.

Salmon
R.

Gordon
L.

Summit
L.

Summit
Lake

Fraser
R.

Giscome Portage
Trail
Protected Area

128   Endako

Francois
Lake
Prov. Pk.

Fraser
Lake

Lejac

Engen

Vanderhoof

7

16

Stuart River
Prov. Park

Eskers
Provincial
Park

Saxton
L.

Nukko
Lake

Willow
River

Shelley

Upper
Fraser

Sinclair
Mills

Purden Lake
Provincial Park

Purden L.

Lon

cois Lake
hbank

Uncha
d Hills
G.P.A.

Anzus Bore

Isle Pierre

Reid
Lake

Chief
L.

Eaglet
L.

16

Evan
Prov.
Pk.

9

14   15   16   10   17   18

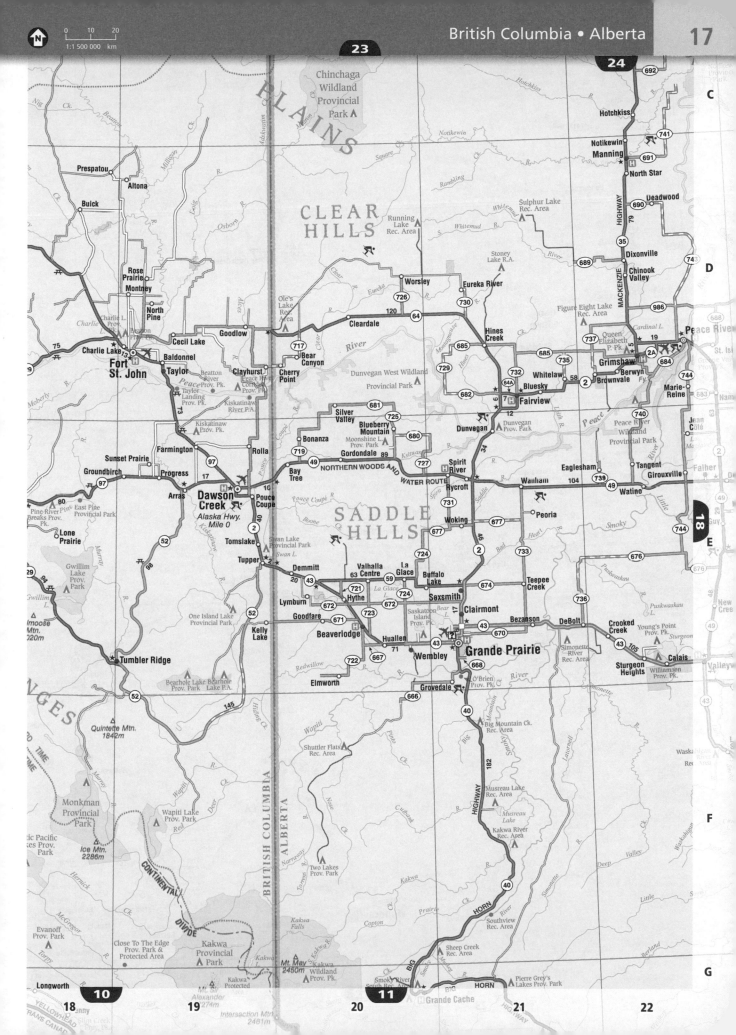

N
0 10 20
1:1 500 000 km

PLAINS

Chinchaga
Wildland
Provincial
Park

23

24

692

C

Hotchkiss

741

Notikewin
Manning
691

North Star

CLEAR
HILLS

Prespatou

Altona

Buick

Running
Lake
Rec. Area

Sulphur Lake
Rec. Area

690

Deadwood

79

35

Dixonville

Chinook
Valley

743

D

Rose
Prairie

Montney

North
Pine

Worsley

726

Eureka River

730

689

Figure Eight Lake
Rec. Area

986

688

Peace River

Charlie L.
Prov.

Goodlow

Cleardale

120

64

Hines
Creek

737

Queen
Elizabeth
P. Pk.

19

5

2A

684

744

75

Charlie Lake

Cecil Lake

717

Bear
Canyon

Clear

River

685

729

735

685

732

Whitelaw

58

2

Grimshaw

Berwyn
Brownvale

Marie-
Reine

883

Fort
St. John

Baldonnel

Taylor

Clayhurst

Cherry
Point

Dunvegan West Wildland
Provincial Park

682

64A

Bluesky

12

6

H

Fairview

740

Jean
Côté

73

Silver
Valley

681

725

Blueberry
Mountain

680

Dunvegan

Dunvegan
Prov. Park

34

Peace

Peace River
Wildland
Provincial Park

Farmington

Rolla

719

Bonanza

Moonshine L.
Prov. Park

Gordondale

89

727

Spirit
River

Eaglesham

Tangent
Girouxville

Sunset Prairie

97

49

NORTHERN WOODS AND WATER ROUTE

Rycroft

Wanham

104

739

49

Watino

Groundbirch

Progress

17

Bay
Tree

731

Woking

Peoria

744

80

Arras

Dawson
Creek

16

Pouce
Coupe

SADDLE
HILLS

677

677

2

Smoky

18

E

Lone
Prairie

Alaska Hwy.
Mile 0

2

724

46

733

676

876

52

Tomslake

Swan Lake
Provincial Park

Valhalla
Centre

La
Glace

Buffalo
Lake

674

Teepee
Creek

Tupper

2

Demmitt

20

63

59

43

721

Hythe

724

Sexsmith

736

Lymburn

672

672

Clairmont

43

Bezanson

DeBolt

Crooked
Creek

Young's Point
Prov. Pk.

43

105

Goodfare

671

723

17

Saskatoon
Island
Prov. Park

670

Calais

52

Kelly
Lake

H

Beaverlodge

Huallen

43

H

Grande Prairie

Simonette
River
Rec. Area

Sturgeon
Heights

Williamson
Prov. Pk.

29

Tumbler Ridge

722

667

71

Wembley

668

O'Brien
Prov. Pk.

Grovedale

666

40

Big Mountain Ck.
Rec. Area

48

49

BRITISH COLUMBIA

ALBERTA

Quintette Mtn.
1842m

145

182

Shuttler Flats
Rec. Area

Musreau Lake
Rec. Area

F

Monkman
Provincial
Park

Ice Mtn.
2286m

Two Lakes
Prov. Park

Musreau
Lake

Kakwa River
Rec. Area

HIGHWAY

CONTINENTAL DIVIDE

Kakwa
Provincial
Park

Mt. May
2450m

Kakwa
Wildland
Provincial Pk.

40

HORN

Southview
Rec. Area

Longworth

10

11

21

22

18

19

20

Grande Cache

G

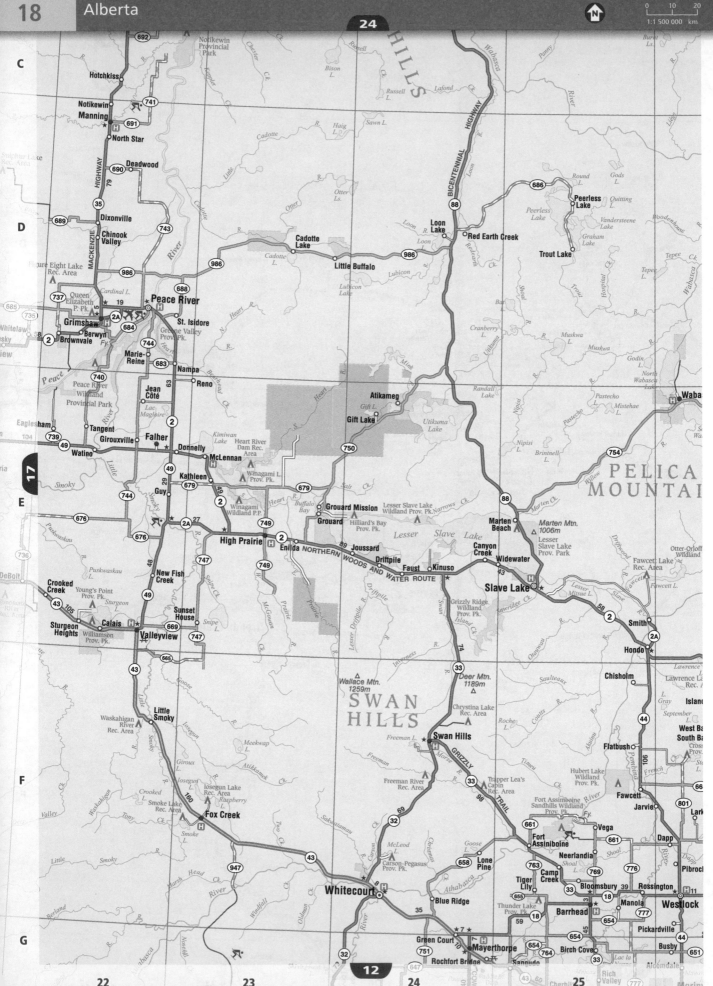

N

| 0 | 10 | 20 |

1:1 500 000 km

24

C

Hotchkiss
Notikewin Provincial Park
692
741
Notikewin
Manning
691
North Star
HIGHWAY 79
690 Deadwood
35
689 Dixonville
Chinook Valley
743

Russell L.
Bison L.
Cadotte
Sawn L.
Haig L.
Otter Ls.
Loon L.
Loon
Loon Lake
88
986
Red Earth Creek

Round L.
Gods L.
686
Peerless Lake
Quitting L.
Peerless Lake
Vandersteene Lake
Trout Lake
Graham Lake
Tepee L.

BICENTENNIAL HIGHWAY

D

685
737
Queen Elizabeth P. Pk.
Grimshaw
2A
684
Berwyn
Brownvale
735
58
2
Whitelaw
esky
view

Cardinal L.
Peace River
688
St. Isidore
Greene Valley Prov. Pk.
744
Marie-Reine
683
Nampa
Reno

986
986
Cadotte Lake
Little Buffalo
Lubicon L.
Lubicon Lake

Bat L.
Cranberry L.
Muskwa L.
Godin L.
North Wabasca Lake
Wabasca
H
Mistehae L.
Pastecho L.

Peace River Wildland Provincial Park
740
739
104
Eaglesham
Jean Côté
Lac Magloire
63
2
Tangent
Girouxville
Falher
49
Watino
Donnelly
McLennan

Heart River
Atikameg
Gift L.
Gift Lake
750

Utikuma Lake

PELICAN MOUNTAINS

Nipisi L.
Brintnell L.
Pastecho R.
754

17

Smoky
744
676
676
DeBolt
736
Puskwaskau
Crooked Creek
43
105
Sturgeon Heights
Williamson Prov. Park
Calais
H
Valleyview
669
747
665
43

Kimiwan Lake
Winagami L. Prov. Pk.
Kathleen
679
49
Guy
2A
27
749
New Fish Creek
747
Sunset House
Snipe L.

Winagami Wildland P.P.
Buffalo Bay
Grouard Mission
Grouard
Hilliard's Bay Prov. Pk.
89
High Prairie
H
2
Enilda
NORTHERN WOODS AND WATER ROUTE
Joussard
Driftpile
Faust
Kinuso

Lesser Slave Lake
Lesser Slave Lake Wildland Prov. Pk.
Marten Beach
Marten Mtn. 1006m
Canyon Creek
Widewater
43
H
Slave Lake

Lesser Slave Lake Prov. Park
Fawcet Lake Rec. Area
Otter-Orloff Wildland
Fawcett L.

E

Marten R.
88
Willow R.

Driftpile R.
Swan R.
74
Inverness L.
Grizzly Ridge Wildland Prov. Pk.
Sawridge Ck.
58
2
Smith
Lesser Mitsue L.
Mitsue L.
2A
Hondo

Lawrence L.
Lawrence Lake Rec. A.
Chisholm
Gray L.
September L.
Island
West Ba
South Ba
Cross Prov.
44
Flatbush
106
French R.
66

F

Fox Creek
160
947
43
32
Smoke Lake Rec. Area
Iosegun Lake Rec. Area
Raspberry L.
Iosegun L.
Giroux L.
Meekwap L.
Little Smoky
Waskahigan River Rec. Area

Wallace Mtn. 1259m
SWAN HILLS
Deer Mtn. 1189m
Chrystina Lake Rec. Area
Roche L.
33
33
Swan Hills
H
Freeman L.
Freeman River Rec. Area
98
GRIZZLY TRAIL
Trapper Lea's Cabin
Fort Assiniboine Sandhills Wildland Prov. Pk.
69
Carson-Pegasus Prov. Pk.
32
658
Lone Pine
McLeod L.
Goose L.
Athabasca R.
Fort Assiniboine
661
661
Neerlandia
Vega
Dapp
Hubert Lake Wildland Prov. Pk.
Fawcett
Jarvie
801
Lark
66

G

Whitecourt
H
8
Blue Ridge
35
947
32
12
647
Green Court
10
751
Rochfort Bridge
Sangudo
764
Mayerthorpe
H
7
59
Thunder Lake Prov. Pk.
655
Tiger Lily
763
Camp Creek
Bloomsbury
33
39
18
Barrhead
H
18
Manola
654
45
654
654
Birch Cove
777
Pickardville
44
Busby
651
Westlock
H
11
Pibroch
769
776
Rossington
H
Moriny
757
642
Glenevis
Cherhill
777
Rich Valley
Sandy Beach
Lac la
Aldmote

22
23
24
25

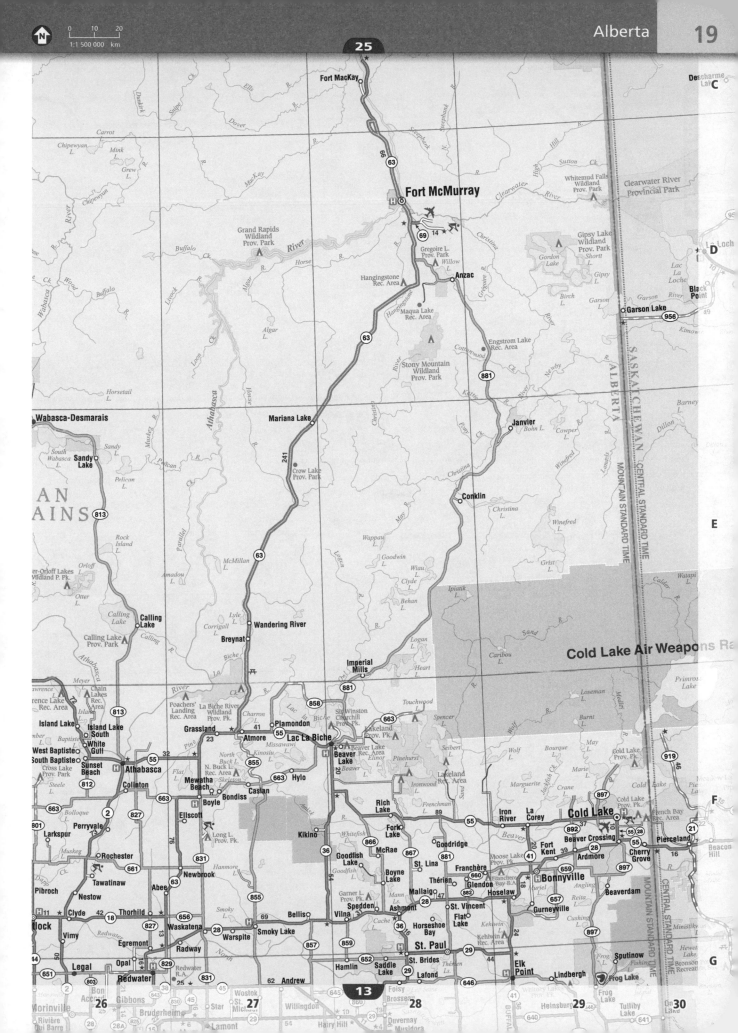

N
0   10   20
1:1 500 000 km

25

13

Descharme L.

Fort MacKay

63

Fort McMurray

69   14

Gregoire L.
Prov. Park
Willow
Hangingstone
Rec. Area   Anzac

Grand Rapids
Wildland
Prov. Park

Maqua Lake
Rec. Area

63   Stony Mountain
Wildland
Prov. Park   881

Engstrom Lake
Rec. Area

Gipsy Lake
Wildland
Prov. Park

Gordon
Lake   Shortt

Gipsy
L.

Garson L.

Lac
La
Loche

Black
Point

Garson Lake   956   49

Clearwater River
Provincial Park

Whitemud Falls
Wildland
Prov. Park

Wabasca-Desmarais   Mariana Lake   Janvier

Sandy
Lake

South
Wabasca
L.

241   Crow Lake
Prov. Park

813   Conklin   Christina
L.

Winefred
L.

Cold Lake Air Weapons Ra

Calling   Calling
Lake   Lake

813   63   McMillan
L.

Wandering River
Breynat

Calling Lake
Prov. Park

Ipiatik
L.

Imperial
Mills   881

Poachers'
Landing
Rec. Area   La Biche River
Wildland
Prov. Pk.   858   Sir Winston
Churchill
Prov. Pk.   663   Lakeland
Prov. Pk.

Island Lake   Grassland   41   Plamondon
Island Lake
South
White
Gull   23   Atmore   55   Lac La Biche

West Baptiste
South Baptiste   32   855   663   Hylo

Sunset
Beach   Beaver
Lake
Rec. Area
Elinor   Pinehurst   Lakeland
Rec. Area

Athabasca   Mewatha
Beach   Casian
Bondiss   Beaver
Lake
Rec. Area

Colinton   663   Boyle   663

812   Ellscott

663   827   Kikino   Rich
Lake

Perryvale   Long L.
Prov. Pk.

Larkspur   Fork
Lake   Iron
River   La
Corey   Cold Lake

801   Whitefish
L.   55   Fort
Kent   892

Rochester   661   831   36   Goodfish
Lake   866   McRae   867   Goodridge   881   Beaver Crossing   Piercland   21

Tawatinaw   Newbrook   63   St. Lina   Franchère   660   Ardmore   897   Cherry
Grove

Pibroch   Nestow   855   Boyne
Lake   Therien   659   Glendon   Bonnyville

Clyde   42   Thorhild   Mallaig   147   882   Hoselaw   657   Gurneyville   Beaverdam

lock   11   Bellis   Spedden   Ashmont   St. Vincent   Reita
656   69   Vilna   Flat
Lake

Vimy   Waskatena   28   Smoky Lake   36   Horseshoe
Bay   Kehiwin

Egremont   857   859   652   St. Paul   29   Elk   Sputinow
Radway   Hamlin   Saddle
Lake   St. Brides   Point   Lindbergh

Legal   Opal   829   62   Andrew   Lafond   646   Frog Lake

Redwater   803   831

2   Bon   Gibbons   Star   Willingdon   Foisy   Heinsburg   29   Tulliby
Accord   St.   Brosseau
Morinville   Bruderheim   Mich   Hairy Hill   Duvernay
Lamont   Musidora

26   27   28   29   30

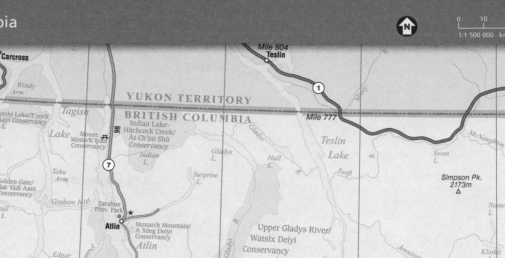

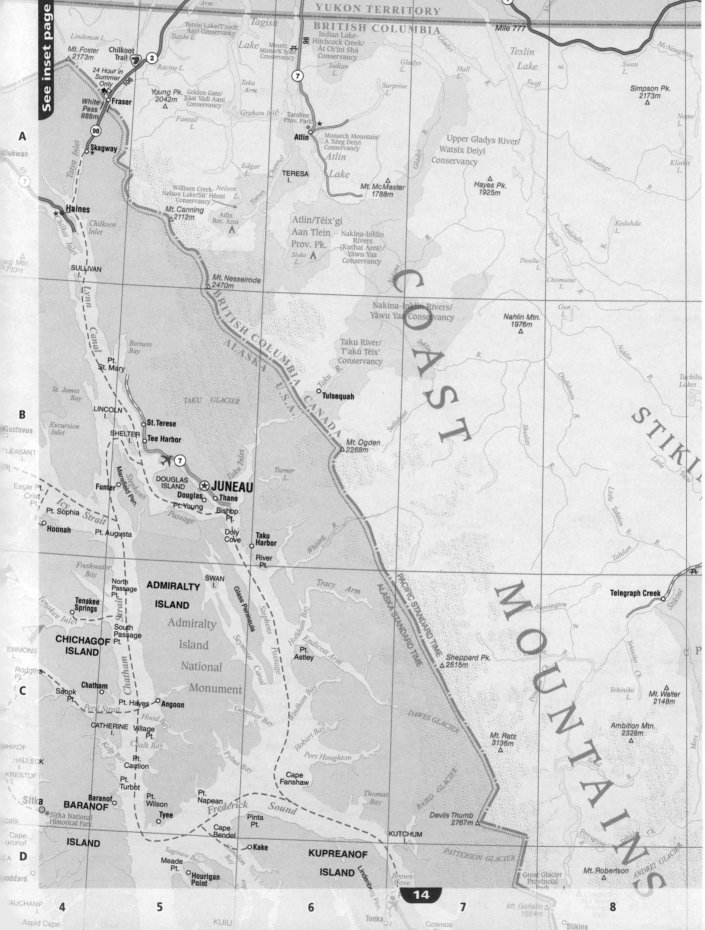

N

0   10   20
1:1 500 000   km

See inset page 8

YUKON TERRITORY

BRITISH COLUMBIA

Mile 804
Teslin

Mile 777

★ **Carcross**

Bennett Lake

West Arm

Windy Arm

1

McNaughton

Tagish Lake

Teslin Lake

Swan

Simpson Pk. 2173m

Tutshi Lake/T'ooch' Aayi Conservancy

Tutshi L.

Indian Lake-Hitchcock Creek/ Åt Ch'ini Shà Conservancy

Noone

Racine L.

Mt. Minto/K'iyán Conservancy

Gladys

Hall L.

Mt. Foster 2173m

Chilkoot Trail

2

Indian L.

Gladys R.

Klinkit L.

Young Pk. 2042m

Golden Gate/ Xáat Yadi Aani Conservancy

7

Surprise L.

Upper Gladys River/ Watsix Deiyi Conservancy

Jennings R.

24 Hour in Summer Only

106

Graham Inlet

Tarahne Prov. Park ★

Monarch Mountain/ A Xéeg Deiyi Conservancy

Hayes Pk. 1925m

Kedahda R.

White Pass 888m

Fraser

Fantail L.

Atlin

Mt. McMaster 1788m

A

98

Skagway ★

Edgar L.

TERESA I.

Atlin Lake

Kedahda L.

7

Taiya Inlet

Mt. Canning 2112m

Willison Creek-Nelson Lake/Sit' Héeni Conservancy

Nelson L.

Atlin/Téix'gi Aan Tlein Prov. Pk.

Nakina-Inklin Rivers (Kuthai Area)/ Yàwu Yaa Conservancy

Disella R.

Chismaina R.

Ujukwan

Haines ★

Chilkoot Inlet

Atlin Rec. Area

Sloko L.

Gun R.

rg Mtn. 710m

Chilkat Inlet

SULLIVAN I.

Mt. Nesselrode 2470m

Nakina-Inklin Rivers/ Yàwu Yaa Conservancy

Nahlin Mtn. 1976m

Nahlin R.

Lynn Canal

Berners Bay

Taku River/ T'akú Téix' Conservancy

Tachilta Lakes

Pt. St. Mary

Inklin R.

Dudidontu R.

St. James Bay

TAKU GLACIER

Taku R.

Sutlahine R.

Sheslay R.

Little Tahltan R.

Gustavus

B

LINCOLN I.

Tulsequah

Little Trapper L.

PLEASANT I.

Excursion Inlet

St. Terese

Mt. Ogden 2268m

SHELTER I.

Tee Harbor

Tahltan R.

Turner L.

7

Eagle Pt.

Funter

Stephens Pen.

Mansfield Pen.

DOUGLAS ISLAND

⊛ **JUNEAU**

Crist Pt.

Pt. Sophia

Douglas • **Thane**

Whiting R.

Hoonah

Icy Strait

Pt. Young

Bishop Pt.

Passage

Pt. Augusta

Doty Cove

Taku Harbor

River Pt.

Freshwater Bay

North Passage Pt.

ADMIRALTY

SWAN I.

Tracy Arm

Telegraph Creek

Stikine R.

Tenakee Inlet

Tenakee Springs

Chatham Strait

ISLAND

Glass Peninsula

Stephens Passage

Burrington R.

South Passage Pt.

Admiralty

Hobbium Bay

PACIFIC STANDARD TIME

ALASKA STANDARD TIME

Sheppard Pk. 2515m

EMMONS I.

Island

Seymour Canal

Endicott Arm

Pt. Astley

Rodgers I.

National

Pt. Caution

CHICHAGOF ISLAND

Gambier Bay

Windham Bay

Yehiniko L.

Mt. Walter 2148m

C

Saook Pt.

Chatham

Peril Strait

Pt. Hayes

Monument

Hood Bay

Angoon

Port Houghton

DAWES GLACIER

Ambition Mtn. 2328m

SHIKOF I.

CATHERINE I.

Village Pt.

Chaik Bay

Pybus Bay

Hobart Bay

Mt. Ratz 3136m

HALLECK I.

Kelp Bay

Pt. Turbot

Thomas Bay

KRESTOF I.

Baranof

Pt. Wilson

Pt. Napean

Cape Fanshaw

BAIRD GLACIER

Devils Thumb 2767m

Sitka

BARANOF

Sitka National Historical Park

Tyee

Frederick Sound

Pinta Pt.

Cape Bendel

KUTCHUM

D

Cape urunof

ISLAND

Saginaw Bay

Kake

KUPREANOF

PATTERSON GLACIER

Mt. Robertson

ANDREI GLACIER

Doddard

Meade Pt.

Hourigan Point

ISLAND

Lindenberg Pen.

Great Glacier Provincial

AUCHAMP

Aspid Cape

KUIU

Tenka

Brown Cove

14

Cosmos

Mt. Gallain 1854m

Stikine

4   5   6   7   8

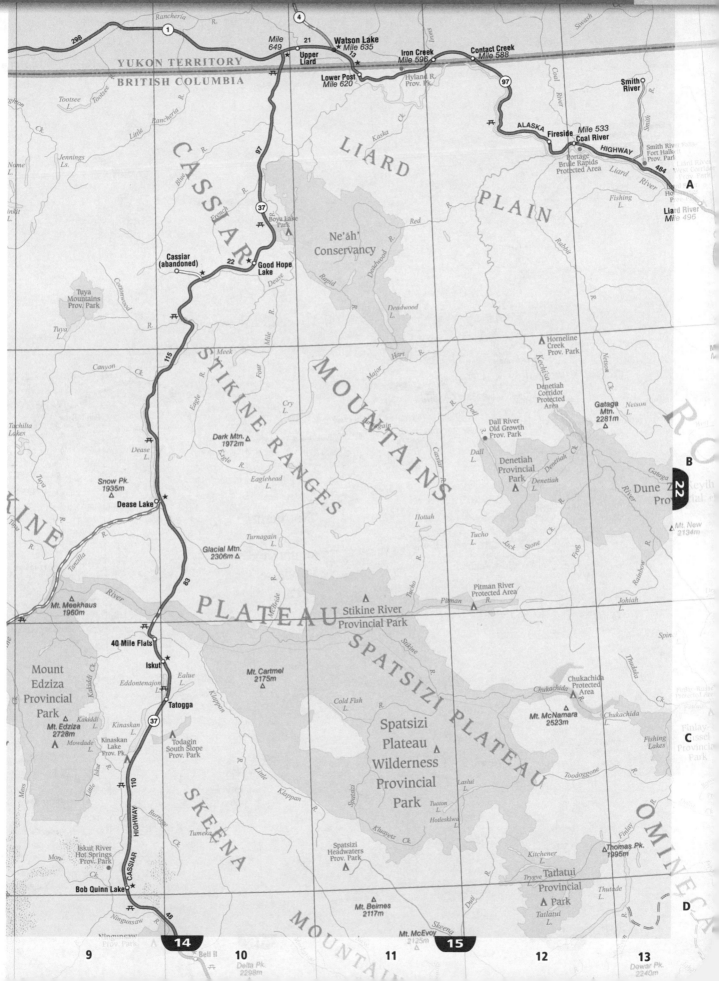

N
0 10 20
1:1 500 000 km

298
1
Rancheria R.

4
21
Mile 649
Watson Lake
Mile 635
13
Iron Creek
Mile 596
Contact Creek
Mile 588

YUKON TERRITORY
BRITISH COLUMBIA

Upper Liard
Lower Post Mile 620
Hyland R. Prov. Pk.

97
Smith River

ALASKA
Fireside Mile 533
Coal River
HIGHWAY

484
Smith River Falls - Fort Halkett Prov. Park
Liard River West Corridor Prov. Park

Tootsee L.
Tootsee R.

Portage Brule Rapids Protected Area
Liard River

A
Liard River Mile 496

CASSIAR

Jennings Ls.
Name L.

97

Blue R.

37
Boya Lake Park

Ne'āh' Conservancy

Deadwood R.
Red R.

Fishing L.

Linkit L.

Cassiar (abandoned)
22
Good Hope Lake

Dease R.

Rapid R.

Deadwood L.

Horneline Creek Prov. Park

Tuya Mountains Prov. Park
Cottonwood R.
Tuya L.
Tuya R.

Mile R.

Kechika R.
Nelson R.

Gataga Mtn. 2281m

B
Dune Z Keyih Prov.

22

STIKINE RANGES

115

Meek R.
Four R.
Eagle R.

Canyon Ck.

Tiachilta Lakes

Dease L.

Dark Mtn. 1972m

Cry L.

Major Hart R.

Denetiah Corridor Protected Area

Dall River Old Growth Prov. Park

Gataga R.

Snow Pk. 1935m

Eagle R.
Eaglehead L.

Dease Lake

Cassiar R.

Dall L.

Denetiah Provincial Park
Denetiah L.

Mt. New 2134m

STIKINE MOUNTAINS

Tuya R.

Turnagain R.

Glacial Mtn. 2306m

Hottah L.

Tucho L.

Jack Stone Ck.

Frog R.

Rainbow R.

Johiah L.

PLATEAU

Mt. Meekhaus 1960m

Tancilla River

83

McBride R.

Stikine River Provincial Park

Pitman R.

Pitman River Protected Area

Spin

40 Mile Flats

Iskut

Ealue L.
Eddontenajon L.

Mt. Cartmel 2175m

Stikine R.

Chukachida Protected Area

Thudaka

Mount Edziza Provincial Park

Kakiddi Ck.

Tatogga

37

Klappan R.

Cold Fish L.

Spatsizi Plateau Wilderness Provincial Park

Chukachida R.

Mt. McNamara 2523m

Chukachida R.

Finlay sel Prov Park

C

Mt. Edziza 2728m

Kinaskan L.

Kinaskan Lake Prov. Pk.
Mowdade L.

Todagin South Slope Prov. Park

Little Klappan R.

Spatsizi R.

Laslui L.

Tuaton L.

Toodoggone R.

Fishing Lakes

SKEENA

Iskut R.

110

Tumeka L.
Burrage Ck.

Hotlesklwa Ck.

K'hayetz Ck.

Kitchener L.

Thomas Pk. 1995m

Iskut River Hot Springs Prov. Park

CASSIAR HIGHWAY

More R.

Spatsizi Headwaters Prov. Park

Trygve L.
Tatlatui Provincial Park
Tatlatui L.

Bob Quinn Lake

48

Ningunsaw R.

OMINECA

Thutade L.

D

14

Ningunsaw Prov. Park

Bell II

Delta Pk. 2298m

MOUNTAINS

Mt. Beirnes 2117m

Mt. McEvoy 2125m

15

Skeena R.

Dall R.

Finlay R.

Dowar Pk. 2240m

9   10   11   15   12   13

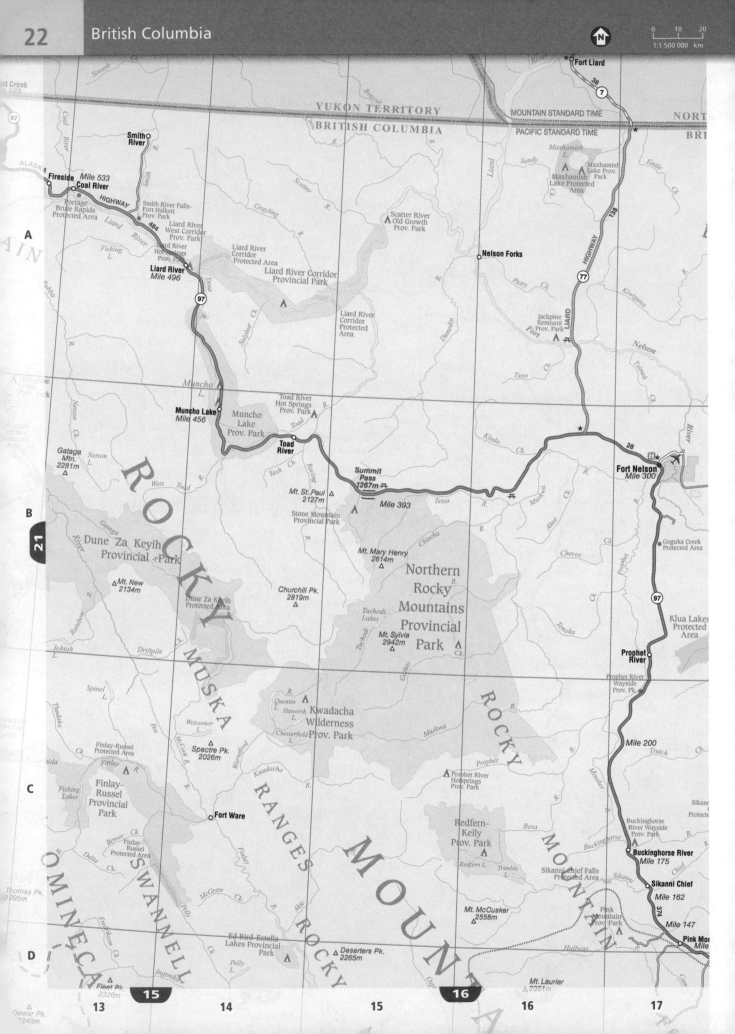

1:1 500 000 km

0 10 20

YUKON TERRITORY

BRITISH COLUMBIA

MOUNTAIN STANDARD TIME

PACIFIC STANDARD TIME

Fort Liard

Smith River

Fireside
Coal River
Mile 533

ALASKA

HIGHWAY

Portage Brule Rapids Protected Area

Smith River Falls-Fort Halkett Prov. Park

Liard River West Corridor Prov. Park

Liard River Hot Springs Prov. Park

Liard River
Mile 496

Liard River Corridor Protected Area

Liard River Corridor Provincial Park

Liard River Corridor Protected Area

Scatter River Old Growth Prov. Park

Maxhamish L.

Maxhamish Lake Prov. Park

Maxhamish Lake Protected Area

Nelson Forks

Jackpine Remnant Prov. Park

Muncho L.

Muncho Lake
Mile 456

Muncho Lake Prov. Park

Toad River Hot Springs Prov. Park

Toad River

Summit Pass
1267m

Mile 393

Fort Nelson
Mile 300

Gataga Mtn.
2281m

Mt. St. Paul
2127m

Stone Mountain Provincial Park

Mt. Mary Henry
2614m

Goguka Creek Protected Area

Dune Za Keyih Provincial Park

Mt. New
2134m

Dune Za Keyih Protected Area

Churchill Pk.
2819m

Northern Rocky Mountains Provincial Park

Mt. Sylvia
2942m

ROCKY

MUSKWA

Prophet River

Prophet River Wayside Prov. Pk.

Klua Lakes Protected Area

Spinel L.

Weissener L.

Spectre Pk.
2026m

Quentin L.

Haworth L.

Kwadacha Wilderness Prov. Park

Chesterfield L.

Mile 200

Finlay-Russel Protected Area

Finlay-Russel Provincial Park

Fishing Lakes

Fort Ware

RANGES

Redfern-Keily Prov. Park

Redfern L.

Trimble L.

Prophet River Hotsprings Prov. Park

Buckinghorse River Wayside Prov. Park

Buckinghorse River
Mile 175

Sikanni Chief Falls Protected Area

Sikanni Chief
Mile 162

OMINECA

SWANNELL

ROCKY

Thomas Pk.
1095m

Ed Bird-Estella Lakes Provincial Park

Deserters Pk.
2265m

Mt. McCusker
2558m

Pink Mountain Prov. Park

Pink Mou
Mile

Fleet Pk.
2326m

Pelly L.

MOUNTA

Mt. Laurier
2351m

Dewar Pk.
2240m

ROCKY MOUNTAIN

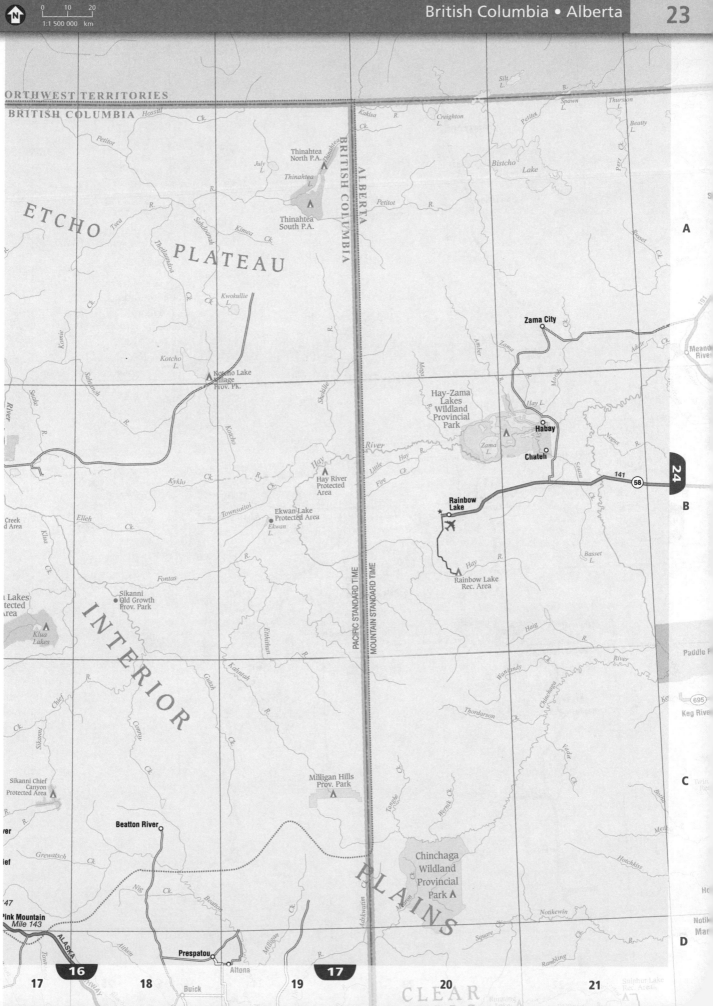

1:1 500 000   km
0   10   20

NORTHWEST TERRITORIES

BRITISH COLUMBIA

Hossill   Ck.

Petitot   R.

Thinahtea
North P.A.

July
L.

Thinahtea
L.

Thinahtea
South P.A.

BRITISH COLUMBIA

ALBERTA

Kakisa

Ck.

Creighton
L.

Petitot

Silt
L.

Thurson
L.

Spawn
L.

Beatty
L.

Perz   Ck.

Bistcho   Lake

Basset   Ck.

Meander
River

ETCHO

PLATEAU

Tsea   R.

Theltwandoa   R.

Sahdoonah   R.

Kimea   Ck.

Kwokullie
L.

Komie   Ck.

Kotcho
L.

Kotcho   R.

Sahtaneh   R.

Snake   R.

River

Kotcho Lake
Village
Prov. Pk.

Zama City

A

Amber   R.

Zama   R.

Adel   Ck.

Hay-Zama
Lakes
Wildland
Provincial
Park

Hay L.

Negus   R.

Hay

River

Shekilie   R.

Kyklo   Ck.

R.

Ck.

Little   R.

Hay   R.

Fire   Ck.

Zama
L.

Habay

Chateh

Sousa   R.

141

58

24

B

Creek
d Area

Elleh   Ck.

Klua   Ck.

Townsoitoi   R.

Ekwan Lake
Protected
Area

Ekwan
L.

Hay River
Protected
Area

Fontas   R.

Etchihun   R.

PACIFIC STANDARD TIME

MOUNTAIN STANDARD TIME

Rainbow
Lake

Rainbow Lake
Rec. Area

Hay   R.

Basset
L.

Paddle F

n Lakes
tected
Area

Klua
Lakes

Sikanni
Old Growth
Prov. Park

INTERIOR

Chief   Ck.

Conroy   Ck.

Kahntah   R.

Gnah   R.

Wonandy   Ck.

Thordarson   R.

Chinchaga   R.

River

Vodar   R.

695

Keg River

Sikanni   Ck.

Sikanni Chief
Canyon
Protected Area

C

Milligan Hills
Prov. Park

Wemik   Ck.

Tanghe   Ck.

Meir   R.

ver

ief

Beatton River

Grewatsch   Ck.

Nig   Ck.

Beatton   R.

Milligan   R.

Adskwatim   R.

PLAINS

Chinchaga
Wildland
Provincial
Park

Notikewin   R.

Hotchkiss   R.

Ho

Pink Mountain
Mile 143

ALASKA HIGHWAY

Town   R.

Atkien   R.

Prespatou

Altona

Buick

17

16

18

Buick

19

17

Square   Ck.

Rambling   R.

20

CLEAR
HILLS

Burning

21

Notik
Mar

D

Notil
Sulphut Lake
Rec. Area

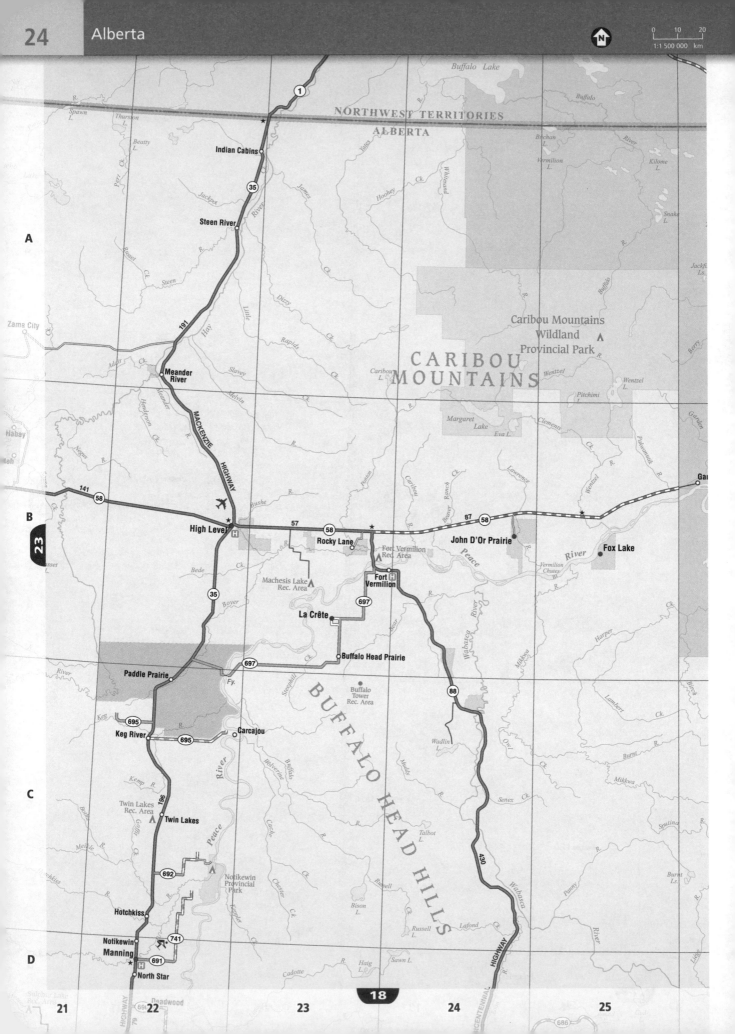

NORTHWEST TERRITORIES
ALBERTA

Buffalo Lake

Buffalo

Caribou Mountains
Wildland
Provincial Park

CARIBOU
MOUNTAINS

Indian Cabins

Steen River

Meander
River

Zama City

Habay

141 58

MACKENZIE HIGHWAY

High Level

57

58

Rocky Lane

Fort Vermilion
Rec. Area

87 58

John D'Or Prairie

Fox Lake

Peace   River

Machesis Lake
Rec. Area

Fort
Vermilion

697

La Crête

Buffalo Head Prairie

Paddle Prairie

697

Buffalo
Tower
Rec. Area

88

Keg River

695

695

Carcajou

BUFFALO HEAD HILLS

196

Twin Lakes
Rec. Area

Twin Lakes

692

430

Notikewin
Provincial
Park

Hotchkiss

741

Notikewin

Manning

North Star

691

23

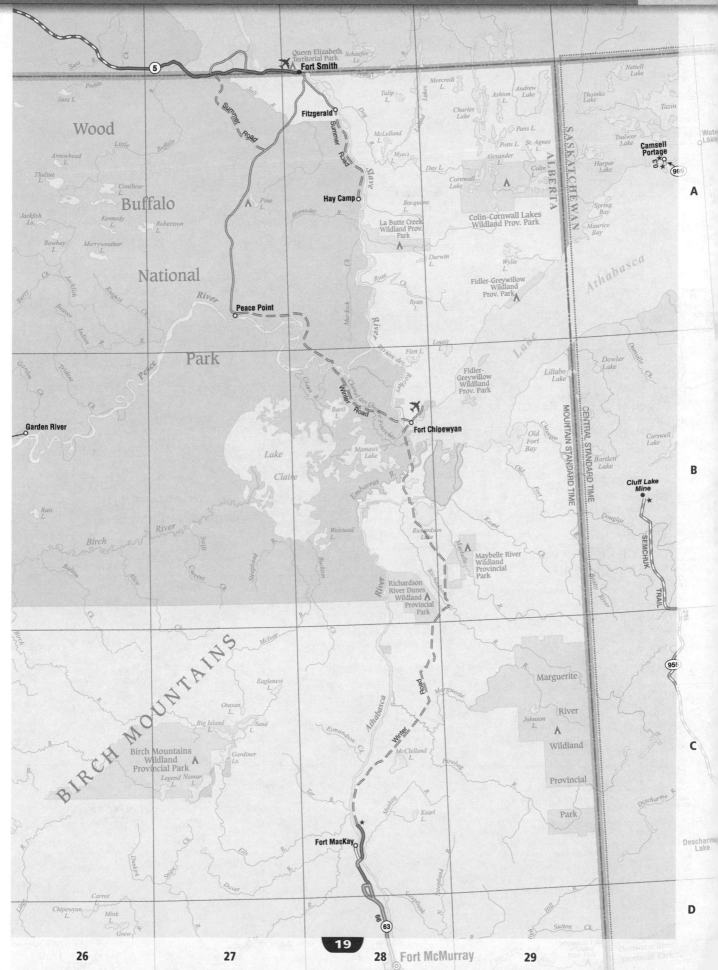

Wood

Buffalo

National

Park

BIRCH MOUNTAINS

Queen Elizabeth Territorial Park
Fort Smith
Fitzgerald
Hay Camp
Peace Point
Garden River
Fort Chipewyan
Fort MacKay
Fort McMurray

SASKATCHEWAN
ALBERTA

Colin-Cornwall Lakes Wildland Prov. Park

La Butte Creek Wildland Prov. Park

Fidler-Greywillow Wildland Prov. Park

Fidler-Greywillow Wildland Prov. Park

Maybelle River Wildland Provincial Park

Richardson River Dunes Wildland Provincial Park

Marguerite River Wildland Provincial Park

Birch Mountains Wildland Provincial Park

Camsell Portage

Cluff Lake Mine

MOUNTAIN STANDARD TIME
CENTRAL STANDARD TIME

SEMCHUK TRAIL

Summer Road
Winter Road

Slave River
Peace River
Birch River
Athabasca River

Lake Claire
Mamawi Lake
Lake Athabasca

26   27   28   29

A

B

C

D

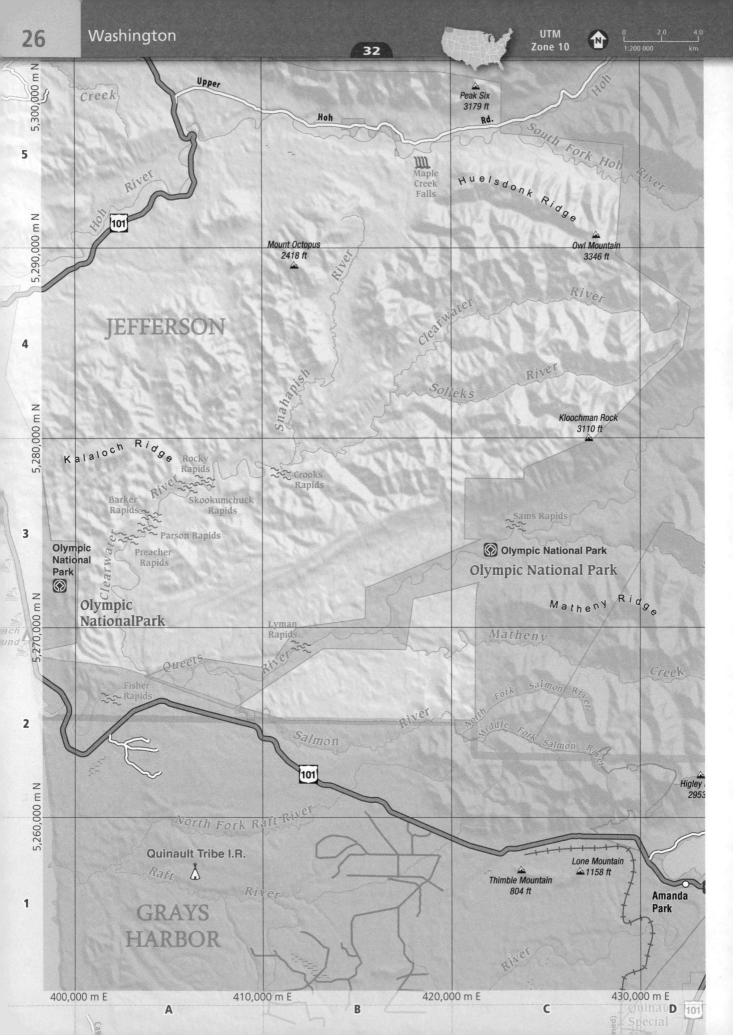

Upper

Hoh

Creek

Peak Six
3179 ft

Rd.

Maple
Creek
Falls

Huelsdonk Ridge

South Fork Hoh

River

Hoh

River

River

Hoh

101

Mount Octopus
2418 ft

Owl Mountain
3346 ft

JEFFERSON

Clearwater

River

River

Snahapish

Solleks

River

Kalaloch Ridge

Rocky
Rapids

Crooks
Rapids

Kloochman Rock
3110 ft

River

Barker
Rapids

Skookumchuck
Rapids

Sams Rapids

Olympic National Park

Parson Rapids

Olympic National Park

Olympic
National
Park

Clearwater

Preacher
Rapids

Matheny Ridge

Olympic
NationalPark

Lyman
Rapids

Matheny

Queets

River

Creek

Fisher
Rapids

North Fork Salmon River

River

Middle Fork Salmon River

Salmon

101

Higley
2953

North Fork Raft River

Quinault Tribe I.R.

Lone Mountain
1158 ft

Raft

Thimble Mountain
804 ft

Amanda
Park

River

GRAYS
HARBOR

River

101

Quinault
Special

5,300,000 m N

5,290,000 m N

5,280,000 m N

5,270,000 m N

5,260,000 m N

5

4

3

2

1

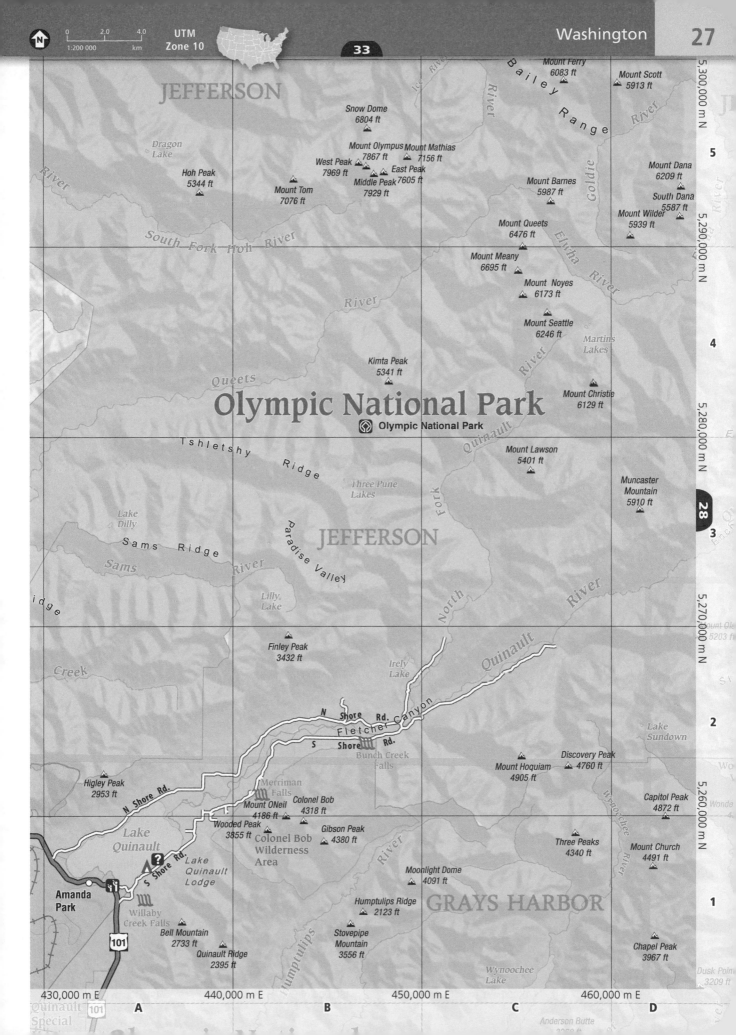

JEFFERSON

Dragon
Lake

Hoh Peak
5344 ft

River

South Fork Hoh River

Snow Dome
6804 ft

Mount Olympus   Mount Mathias
7867 ft   7156 ft
West Peak
7969 ft   East Peak
           7605 ft
Middle Peak
7929 ft

Mount Tom
7076 ft

Mount Ferry
6083 ft

Mount Scott
5913 ft

Bailey Range

Goldie River

Ice River

Mount Dana
6209 ft

South Dana
5587 ft
Mount Wilder
5939 ft

Mount Barnes
5987 ft

Mount Queets
6476 ft

Mount Meany
6695 ft

Mount Noyes
6173 ft

Mount Seattle
6246 ft

Elwha River

Martins
Lakes

River

Kimta Peak
5341 ft

Queets

Mount Christie
6129 ft

Olympic National Park

Olympic National Park

Quinault

Tshletshy   Ridge

Three Pune
Lakes

Mount Lawson
5401 ft

Muncaster
Mountain
5910 ft

28

JEFFERSON

Lake
Dilly

Sams   Ridge

Sams

River

Paradise Valley

Lilly
Lake

North   Fork

Quinault   River

ridge

Creek

Finley Peak
3432 ft

Irely
Lake

Lake
Sundown

N Shore Rd.

Fletcher Canyon

S Shore Rd.
Bunch Creek
Falls

Mount Hoquiam
4905 ft

Discovery Peak
4760 ft

Wynoochee River

Capitol Peak
4872 ft

Higley Peak
2953 ft

N Shore Rd.

Merriman
Falls

Mount ONeil
4186 ft
Wooded Peak
3855 ft

Colonel Bob
4318 ft

Gibson Peak
4380 ft

Colonel Bob
Wilderness
Area

River

Moonlight Dome
4091 ft

Three Peaks
4340 ft

Mount Church
4491 ft

Lake
Quinault

S Shore Rd.

Lake
Quinault
Lodge

Amanda
Park

Willaby
Creek Falls

Bell Mountain
2733 ft

Quinault Ridge
2395 ft

101

Humptulips

Humptulips Ridge
2123 ft

Stovepipe
Mountain
3556 ft

Wynoochee
Lake

GRAYS HARBOR

Chapel Peak
3967 ft

Dusk Point
3209 ft

5,300,000 m N

5

5,290,000 m N

4

5,280,000 m N

3

5,270,000 m N

2

5,260,000 m N

1

101

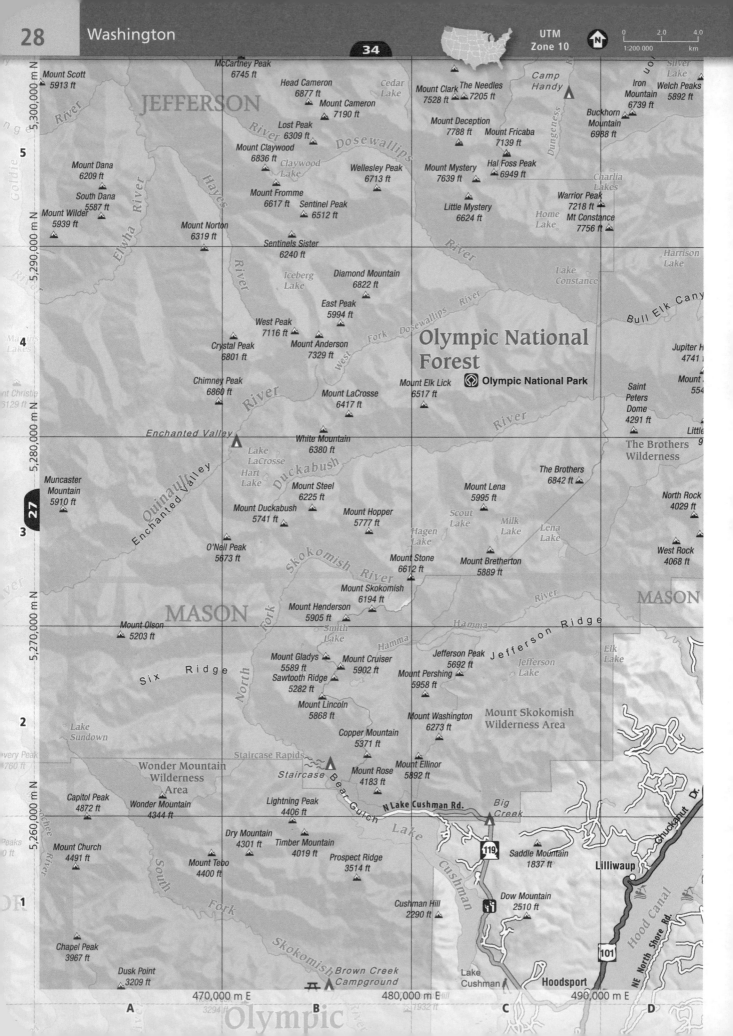

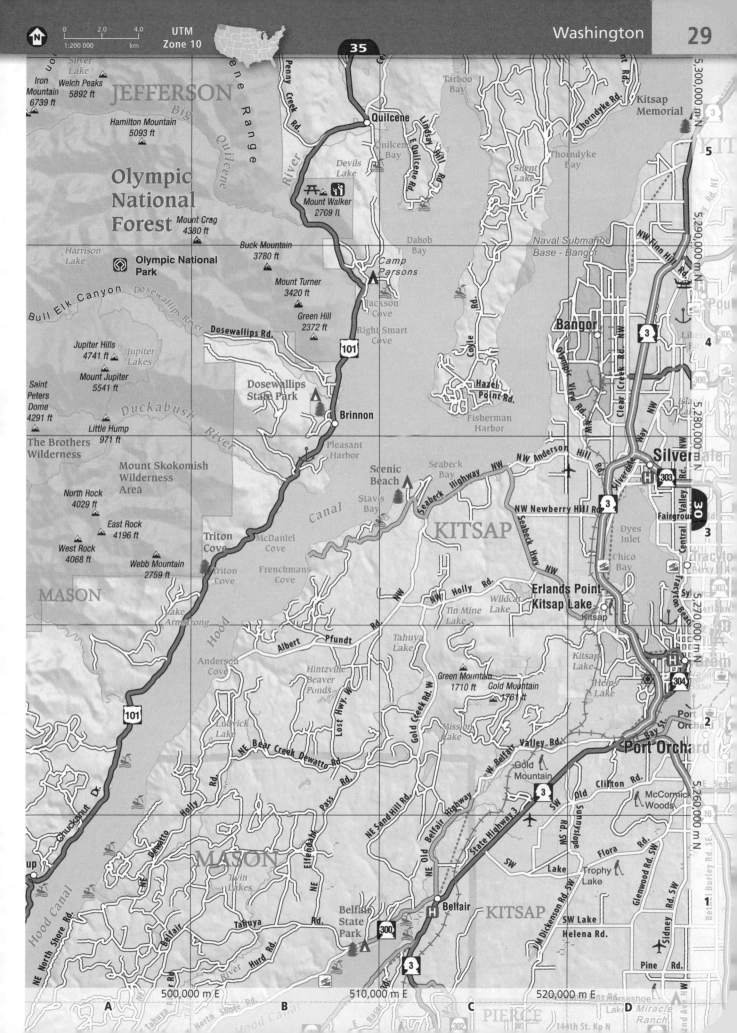

N

UTM
Zone 10

1:200 000

0   2.0   4.0
km

JEFFERSON

Silver
Lake

Iron
Mountain
6739 ft

Welch Peaks
5892 ft

Hamilton Mountain
5093 ft

Big

ene Range

Quilcene

Penny Creek Rd.

River

35

Quilcene

Tarboo
Bay

Kitsap
Memorial

KIT

Olympic
National
Forest

Mount Crag
4380 ft

Devils
Lake

Quilcene
Bay

E Quilcene Rd.

Lindsay Hill Rd.

Shent
Lake

Thorndyke
Bay

Thorndyke Rd.

5

Mount Walker
2709 ft

Buck Mountain
3780 ft

Dabob
Bay

Thorndike
Bay

Harrison
Lake

Olympic National
Park

Dosewallips River

Mount Turner
3420 ft

Green Hill
2372 ft

Camp
Parsons

Jackson
Cove

Right Smart
Cove

Naval Submarine
Base - Bangor

NW Finn Hill Rd.

Pou

Olympic View Rd.

Bangor

3

Liberty
Ba

305

4

Bull Elk Canyon

Dosewallips Rd.

101

Coyle Rd.

308

Island
Lake

Jupiter Hills
4741 ft

Jupiter
Lakes

Hazel
Point Rd.

NW

Clear Creek Rd. NW

Duckabush River

Mount Jupiter
5541 ft

Dosewallips
State Park

Brinnon

Hazel
Point

Fisherman
Harbor

Silverdale Way NW

Silverdale

H

303

30

Saint
Peters
Dome
4291 ft

Little Hump
971 ft

Pleasant
Harbor

Seabeck
Bay

NW Anderson Hill

3

Fairgrou

Central Valley

3

The Brothers
Wilderness

Scenic
Beach

Stavis
Bay

Seabeck Highway NW

KITSAP

NW Newberry Hill Rd.

Dyes
Inlet

Tracyto
Bexly H

Mount Skokomish
Wilderness
Area

North Rock
4029 ft

Canal

Seabeck Hwy NW

Chico
Bay

303

303

Syl

East Rock
4196 ft

Triton
Cove

McDaniel
Cove

NW Holly Rd.

Wildcat
Lake

Erlands Point
Kitsap Lake

Kitsap

H

West Rock
4068 ft

Webb Mountain
2759 ft

Triton
Cove

Frenchmans
Cove

Tin Mine
Lake

NW

304

Naval
Base

MASON

Lake
Armstrong

Hood

Albert

Pfundt

Tahuya
Lake

Holly Rd.

Helps
Lake

Kitsap
Lake

Port
Orchard

2

Anderson
Cove

Hintzville
Beaver
Ponds

Green Mountain
1710 ft

Gold Mountain
1761 ft

Mission
Lake

Bay St.

Port Orchard

Ludvick
Lake

Gold Creek Rd. W

Lost Hwy. W

Valley Rd.

Clifton Rd.

McCormick
Woods

16

101

NE Bear Creek Dewatto Rd.

Rd.

Pass Rd.

NW Belfair

Gold
Mountain

3

SW

Old

Sunnyslope Rd. SW

Flora
Lake

Chuckanut Dr.

Dewatto

NE

Holly

Elfendahl

NE Sand Hill Rd.

NE Old Belfair Highway

State Highway 3

SW

Rd. SW

Trophy
Lake

Glenwood Rd. SW

Sedt

MASON

Twin
Lakes

JM Dickenson Rd. SW

SW Lake

Sidney Rd. SW

up

Belfair
State
Park

Belfair

H

KITSAP

Helena Rd.

Bet

Burley Rd. SE

Hood Canal

NE North Shore Rd.

Belfair

Tahuya

River

Hurd Rd.

300

3

SW Lake
Helena Rd.

Pine Rd.

Horseshoe
Lake

Miracle
Ranch

Tahuya

North Shore Rd.

144th St. Kp N

302

PIERCE

2nd Ave NE

500,000 m E

510,000 m E

520,000 m E

A

B

C

D

5,300,000 m N

5,290,000 m N

5,280,000 m N

5,270,000 m N

5,260,000 m N

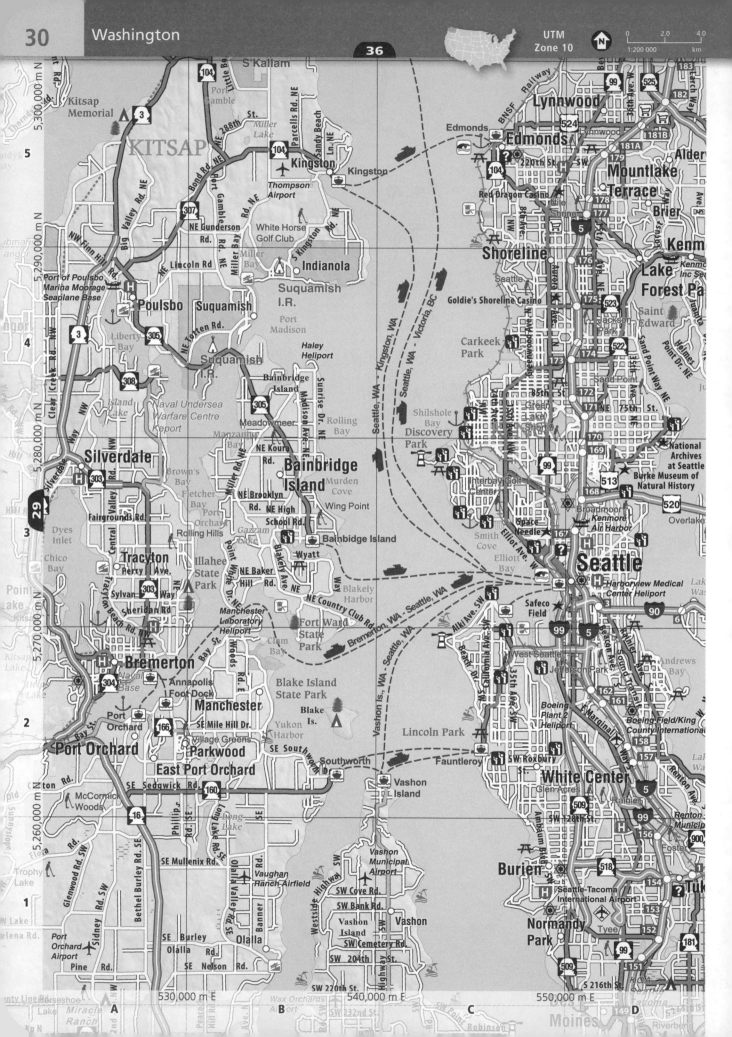

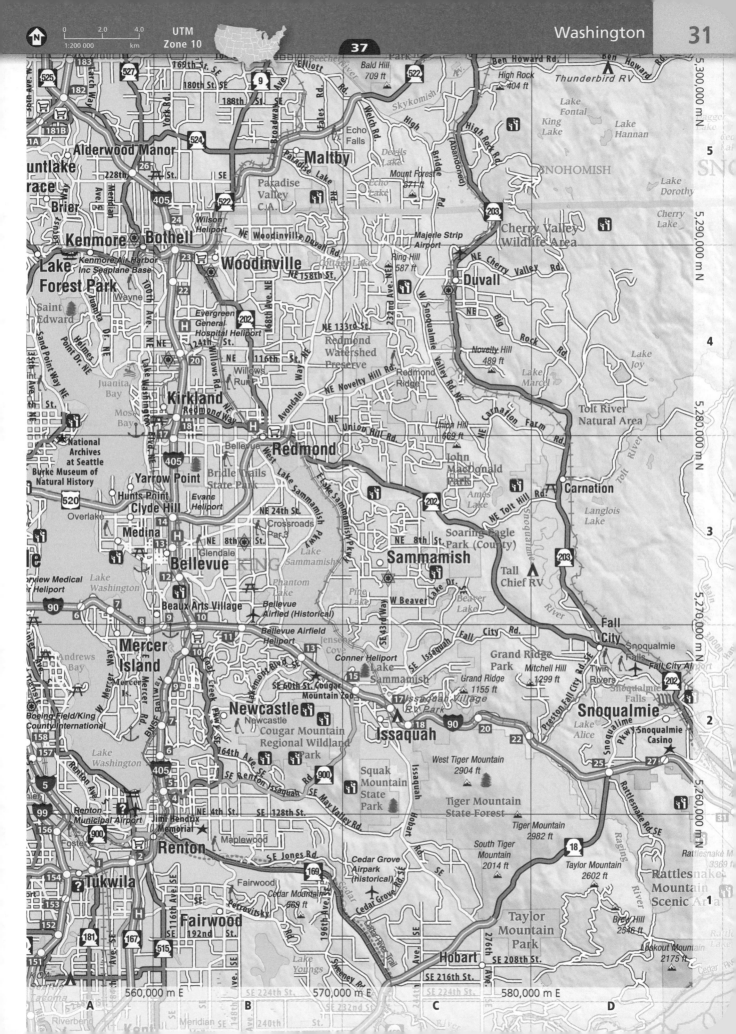

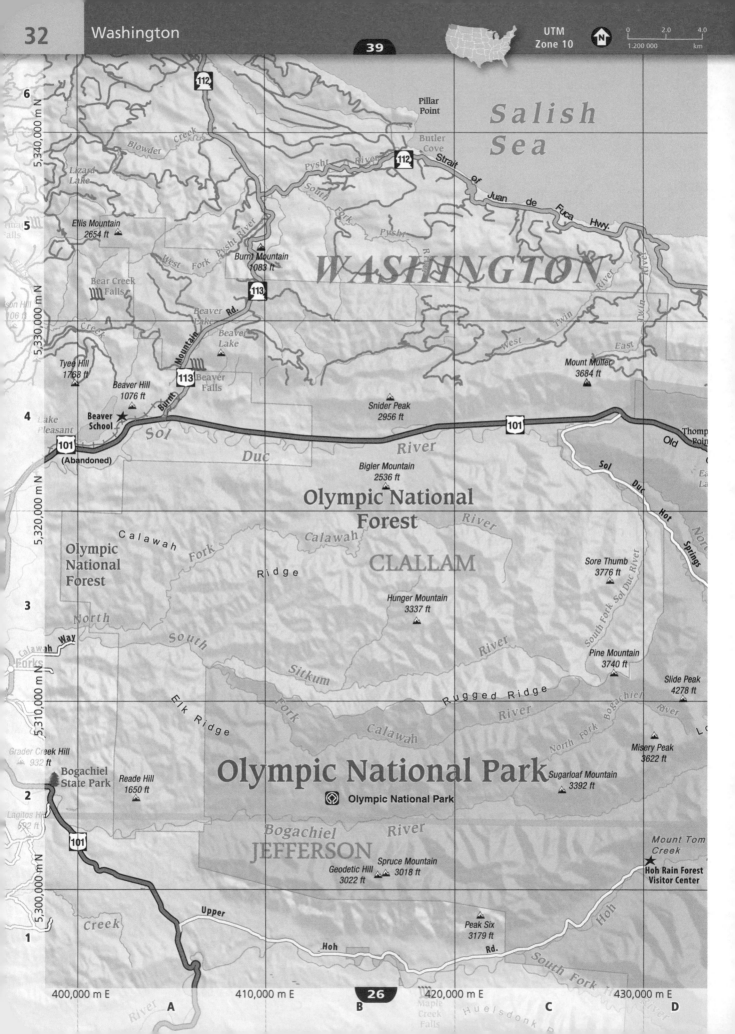

39

UTM
Zone 10

1:200 000

0   2.0   4.0
km

6

5,340,000 m N

5

5,330,000 m N

4

5,320,000 m N

3

5,310,000 m N

2

5,300,000 m N

1

Pillar
Point

*Salish
Sea*

Butler
Cove

112

Strait *of* *Juan* *de* *Fuca* Hwy.

112

Blowder *Creek*

Lizard
Lake

Ellis Mountain
2654 ft

Pysht *River*

South *Fork*

Burnt Mountain
1083 ft

Pysht

WASHINGTON

River

Twin

River

Twin

Bear Creek
Falls

113

Beaver Lake Rd.

Mount Muller
3684 ft

Creek

Tyee Hill
1768 ft

Mountain

Beaver
Lake

Beaver Hill
1076 ft

113

Beaver
Falls

West

East

Snider Peak
2956 ft

101

Burnt

Lake
Pleasant

Beaver
School

Sol

Duc

River

101

Thomp...
Poin...

Old

Sol

Duc

Hot

Springs

North

101
(Abandoned)

Bigler Mountain
2536 ft

**Olympic National
Forest**

Calawah

River

East
La...

Olympic
National
Forest

Calawah

Fork

Ridge

CLALLAM

Hunger Mountain
3337 ft

South Fork Sol Duc River

Sore Thumb
3776 ft

North

Way

South

Sitkum

River

Pine Mountain
3740 ft

Slide Peak
4278 ft

Calawah

Forks

Elk Ridge

Fork

Calawah

Rugged *Ridge*

River

North Fork Bogachiel

River

Misery Peak
3622 ft

L...

Grader Creek Hill
932 ft

Bogachiel
State Park

Reade Hill
1650 ft

Olympic National Park

Olympic National Park

Sugarloaf Mountain
3392 ft

Mount Tom
Creek

Lagitos Hi...
5.2 ft

101

Bogachiel *River*

JEFFERSON

Geodetic Hill
3022 ft

Spruce Mountain
3018 ft

Hoh Rain Forest
Visitor Center

Upper

Creek

Hoh

Rd.

Peak Six
3179 ft

Hoh

South Fork

400,000 m E   410,000 m E   420,000 m E   430,000 m E

A   B   C   D

River

Maple
Creek
Falls

Huelsdonk *R...*

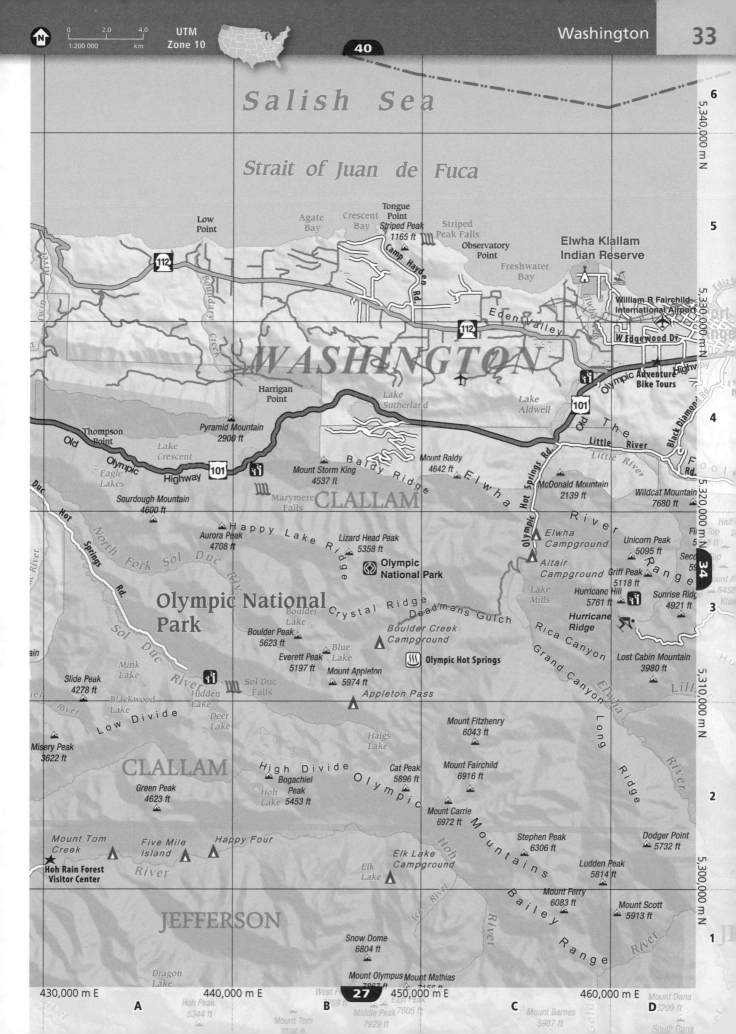

N

| 0 | 2.0 | 4.0 |
1:200 000   km

UTM
Zone 10

40

Salish Sea

Strait of Juan de Fuca

Low
Point

Agate
Bay

Crescent
Bay

Tongue
Point
Striped Peak
1165 ft

Striped
Peak Falls

Camp Hayden Rd.

Observatory
Point

Freshwater
Bay

Elwha Klallam
Indian Reserve

112

William R Fairchild
International Airport

112

Eden Valley

W Edgewood Dr

WASHINGTON

Harrigan
Point

Lake
Sutherland

Lake
Aldwell

101

Olympic Adventure
Bike Tours

Old

Thompson
Point

Pyramid Mountain
2900 ft

The

Little   River

Little River

Black Diamond Rd.

Foot

Olympic

101

Lake
Crescent

Highway

Eagle
Lakes

Mount Storm King
4537 ft

Baldy Ridge

Mount Baldy
4642 ft

Elwha

Hot Springs Rd.

Olympic

River

McDonald Mountain
2139 ft

Rd.

Wildcat Mountain
7680 ft

Range

Sourdough Mountain
4600 ft

Marymere
Falls

CLALLAM

Happy Lake Ridge

Aurora Peak
4708 ft

Lizard Head Peak
5358 ft

**Olympic
National Park**

Elwha
Campground

Unicorn Peak
5095 ft

Altair
Campground

Griff Peak
5118 ft

Lake
Mills

Hurricane Hill
5761 ft

Sunrise Ridge
4921 ft

**Olympic National
Park**

Crystal Ridge

Deadmans Gulch

Boulder
Lake

Boulder Peak
5623 ft

Boulder Creek
Campground

Blue
Lake

Olympic Hot Springs

Rica Canyon

Grand Canyon

**Hurricane
Ridge**

Lost Cabin Mountain
3980 ft

Everett Peak
5197 ft

Mount Appleton
5974 ft

Appleton Pass

Mink
Lake

Slide Peak
4278 ft

Hidden
Lake

Sol Duc
Falls

Low Divide

Deer
Lake

Haigs
Lake

Mount Fitzhenry
6043 ft

Long

Ridge

Lillia

Blackwood
Lake

River

CLALLAM

High Divide

Cat Peak
5896 ft

Mount Fairchild
6916 ft

Misery Peak
3622 ft

Green Peak
4623 ft

Bogachiel
Peak
5453 ft

Hoh
Lake

Olympic

Mount Carrie
6972 ft

Mountains

Stephen Peak
6306 ft

Dodger Point
5732 ft

Mount Tom
Creek

Five Mile
Island

Happy Four

Elk Lake
Campground

Hoh

Ludden Peak
5814 ft

**Hoh Rain Forest
Visitor Center**

River

Elk
Lake

Bailey Range

Mount Ferry
6083 ft

Mount Scott
5913 ft

JEFFERSON

Snow Dome
6804 ft

Ice

River

Dragon
Lake

West P

27

Mount Olympus Mount Mathias
7867 ft   7156 ft

Hoh Peak
5344 ft

Mount Tom
7076 ft

Middle Peak
7929 ft

East Peak
7605 ft

Mount Barnes
5987 ft

Mount Dana
8209 ft

South Dana

North Fork Sol Duc Riv

Sol Duc River

5,340,000 m N — 6

5,330,000 m N — 5

5,320,000 m N — 4

34

5,310,000 m N — 3

5,300,000 m N — 2

1

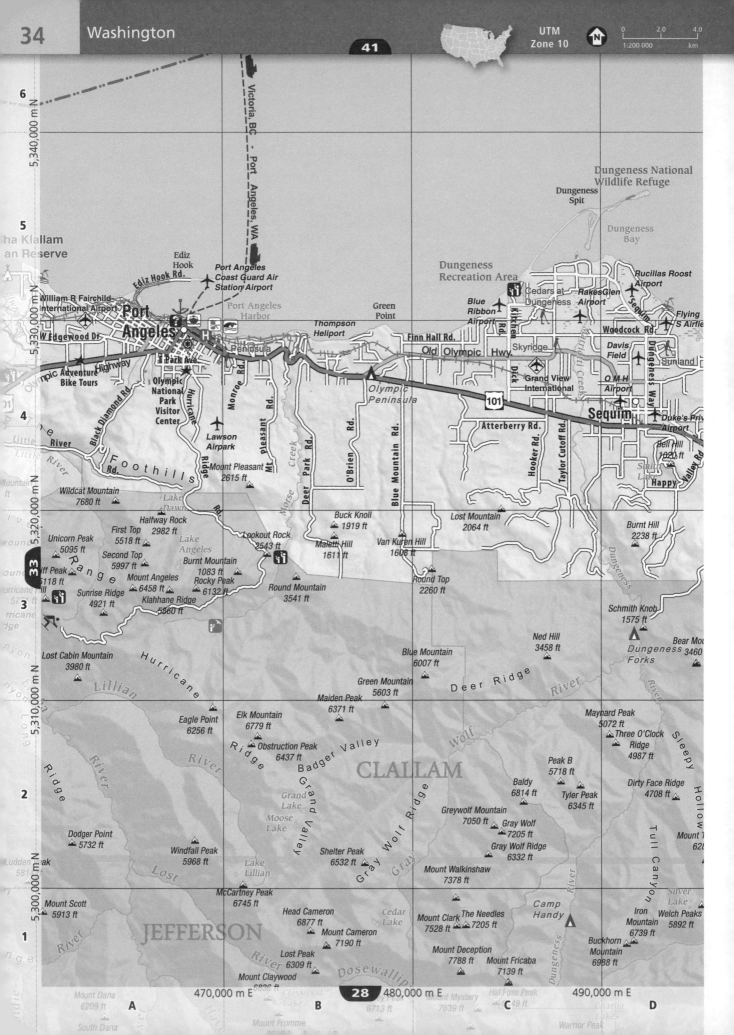

6
N

5,340,000 m N

5

5,330,000 m N

4

5,320,000 m N

3

5,310,000 m N

2

5,300,000 m N

1

ha Klallam
an Reserve

Dungeness National
Wildlife Refuge

Dungeness
Spit

Dungeness
Bay

Dungeness
Recreation Area

Ediz
Hook

Port Angeles
Coast Guard Air
Station Airport

Ediz Hook Rd.

William R Fairchild
International Airport

W Edgewood Dr

Port Angeles
Harbor

Port
Angeles

Peninsula

Olympic Adventure
Bike Tours

Highway

Park Ave

Olympic
National
Park
Visitor
Center

Monroe Rd.

Hurricane Ridge

Lawson
Airpark

Thompson
Heliport

Green
Point

Finn Hall Rd.

Old Olympic Hwy.

Blue
Ribbon
Airport

Cedars at
Dungeness

RakesGlen
Airport

Rucillas Roost
Airport

Flying
S Airfie

Woodcock Rd.

Skyridge

Kitchen Dick Rd.

Grand View
International

Davis
Field

O M H
Airport

Olympic
Peninsula

101

Sequim

Duke's Priv
Airport

sequim

Dungeness Way

Marlotti Creek

Atterberry Rd.

Hooker Rd.

Taylor Cutoff Rd.

Bell Hill
1920 ft

Smith
Lake

Happy

Mt Pleasant Rd.

Foothills
Rd.

Black Diamond Rd.

e River

Little
Mountain
ft

Little
River

Wildcat Mountain
7680 ft

Halfway Rock
First Top 2982 ft
5518 ft

Unicorn Peak
5095 ft

Second Top
5997 ft

ff Peak
5118 ft

Mount Angeles
6458 ft

Sunrise Ridge
4921 ft

Klahhane Ridge
5860 ft

Burnt Mountain
1083 ft
Rocky Peak
6132 ft

Lake
Dawn

Lake
Angeles

Lookout Rock
2543 ft

Deer Park Rd.

O'Brien Rd.

Blue Mountain Rd.

Mount Pleasant
2615 ft

Morse Creek

Buck Knoll
1919 ft

Maletti Hill
1611 ft

Van Kuren Hill
1608 ft

Lost Mountain
2064 ft

Burnt Hill
2238 ft

Round Mountain
3541 ft

Round Top
2260 ft

Schmith Knob
1575 ft

Dungeness

Lost Cabin Mountain
3980 ft

Range

Hurricane

Lillian

nyon

nyog

Long

Ned Hill
3458 ft

Blue Mountain
6007 ft

Green Mountain
5603 ft

Deer Ridge

River

Dungeness
Forks

Bear Mou
3460

Maiden Peak
6371 ft

Eagle Point
6256 ft

Elk Mountain
6779 ft

Obstruction Peak
6437 ft

Ridge

Badger Valley

Grand Valley

CLALLAM

Wolf

Maynard Peak
5072 ft

Three O'Clock
Ridge
4987 ft

Peak B
5718 ft

Baldy
6814 ft

Tyler Peak
6345 ft

Dirty Face Ridge
4708 ft

Sleepy Hollow

Tull Canyon

Mount T
628

Grand
Lake

Moose
Lake

Gray Wolf Ridge

Greywolf Mountain
7050 ft

Gray Wolf
7205 ft

Gray Wolf Ridge
6332 ft

Dodger Point
5732 ft

Windfall Peak
5968 ft

Lake
Lillian

Shelter Peak
6532 ft

Gray

Mount Walkinshaw
7378 ft

Silver
Lake

Ludden
ak
581

McCartney Peak
6745 ft

Cedar
Lake

Camp
Handy

Iron
Mountain
6739 ft

Welch Peaks
5892 ft

Mount Scott
5913 ft

JEFFERSON

Head Cameron
6877 ft

Mount Cameron
7190 ft

Lost Peak
6309 ft

Mount Claywood
6836 ft

Mount Clark
7528 ft

The Needles
7205 ft

Mount Deception
7788 ft

Mount Fricaba
7139 ft

Buckhorn
Mountain
6988 ft

River

River

River

Dosewallip

Dungeness

Mount Dana
6209 ft

South Dana

470,000 m E

Claywood
Lake

Mount Fromme

28

Mount Mystery
6713 ft

480,000 m E

Hal Foss Peak
7639 ft

Warrior Peak

Charlia
Lakes

490,000 m E

A   B   C   D

33

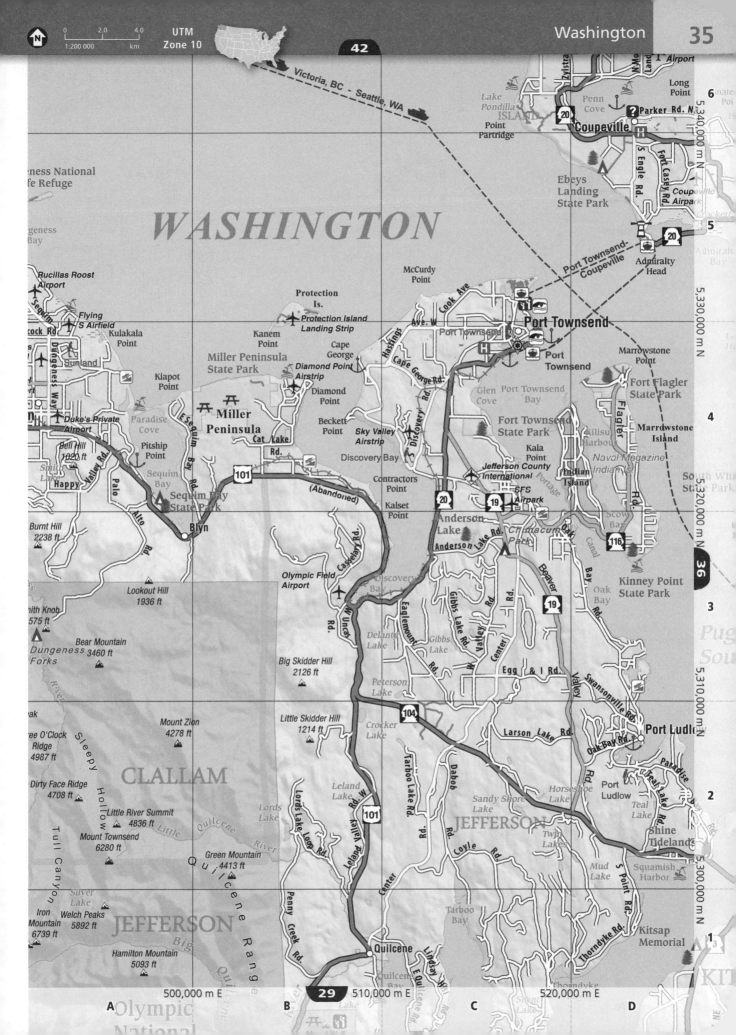

N
1:200 000

0   2.0   4.0
km

UTM
Zone 10

42

Victoria, BC – Seattle, WA

WASHINGTON

Olympic National

CLALLAM

JEFFERSON

500,000 m E   510,000 m E   520,000 m E

29

A   B   C   D

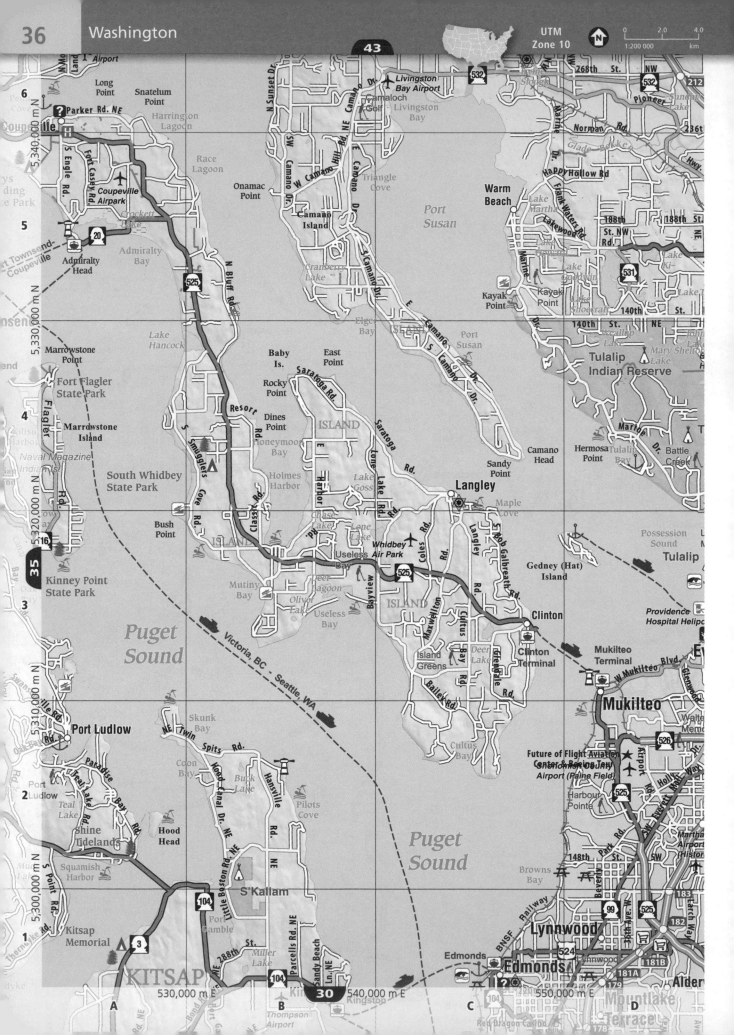

43

532

UTM
Zone 10

N

1:200 000

0   2.0   4.0
km

212

532

NW

Pioneer

Sundae Lake

236th

Airport

Long
Point

Snatelum
Point

Parker Rd. NE

Coupeville

S Engle Rd.

Fort Casey Rd.

Coupeville
Airpark

Crockett
Lake

20

Admiralty
Head

Admiralty Bay

N Bluff Rd.

525

Harrington
Lagoon

Race
Lagoon

Onamac
Point

W Camano Dr.

Camano Dr.

N Sunset Dr.

Camano
Island

E Camano Dr.

Camaloch
Golf

Livingston
Bay Airport

Livingston
Bay

Triangle
Cove

268th   St.

Warm
Beach

Lake
Martha

Happy Hollow Rd

Frank Waters Rd.

188th
St. NW

188th   St.

Lakewood
Rd.

Lake
Ki-

531

Marine

Lake
Goodwin

140th

140th   St.   NE

Port
Susan

Cranberry
Lake

S Camano Dr.

Elger
Bay

ISLAND

Port
Susan

S Lamby Dr.

E Camano   Dr.

Kayak
Point

Kayak
Point

Lake
Shoecraft

St.

Tulalip
Indian Reserve

Lake

Mary Shelter
Lake

John

5,340,000 m N

5,330,000 m N

6

5

4

Fort Flagler
State Park

Marrowstone
Point

Marrowstone
Island

Naval Magazine
Indian Is.

South Whidbey
State Park

Lake
Hancock

Smugglers Cove Rd.

Resort Rd.

Baby
Is.

Rocky
Point

Dines
Point

Honeymoon
Bay

Holmes
Harbor

Saratoga Rd.

E Harbor Rd.

ISLAND

Saratoga

Lake
Goss

Lone Lake Rd.

Saratoga   Rd.

East
Point

Port
Susan

Sandy
Point

Camano
Head

Hermosa
Point

Battle
Creek

Marine Dr.

Tulalip
Bay

5,320,000 m N

35

16

Kinney Point
State Park

Flagler Rd.

Bush
Point

Classat. Rd.

ISLAND

Chase
Lake

Useless
Bay

Whidbey Air Park

Lone
Lake

Bayview

Coles   Rd.

Langley Rd.

Maxwelton   Rd.

Langley

Maple
Cove

Bob Galbreath Rd.

Gedney (Hat)
Island

Possession
Sound

Tulalip

525

3

Puget
Sound

Victoria, BC — Seattle, WA

Mutiny
Bay

Oliver
Lake

Deer Lagoon

Useless
Bay

Bayview

ISLAND

Island
Greens

Cultus   Rd.

Deer
Lake

Bailey Rd.

Clinton

Clinton
Terminal

Glendale

Providence
Hospital Helipod

Mukilteo
Terminal

Mukilteo

W Mukilteo   Blvd.

E

Blvd.

Walter

Glenwood

526

5,310,000 m N

2

Port Ludlow

Port
Ludlow

Teal
Lake

Shine
Tidelands

Paradise Bay Rd.

Squamish
Harbor

Port Ludlow

Hood
Head

S Point Rd.

Skunk
Bay

Twin   Spits   Rd.

Coon
Bay

Buck
Lake

Hood Canal Dr. NE

Hansville   Rd.   NE

NE

Pilots
Cove

Cultus
Bay

Puget
Sound

Browns
Bay

148th

Future of Flight Aviation
Center & Boeing Jay
Airport (Paine Field)

Harbour
Pointe

Park Rd.

Beverly

Holly   Dr.

Martha
Airport
(Historic)

525

5,300,000 m N

1

Kitsap
Memorial

3

S Point Rd.

Little Boston Rd. NE

Port
Gamble

S'Kallam

104

NE 288th   St.

Miller
Lake

Parcells Rd. NE

Sandy Beach Ln. NE

104

30

Kingston

Thompson
Airport

Edmonds

BNSF   Railway

524

Edmonds

Lynnwood

99

Lynnwood

181B

181A

179

183

525

182

Alder

Mountlake
Terrace

A

530,000 m E

B

540,000 m E

C

104

550,000 m E

D

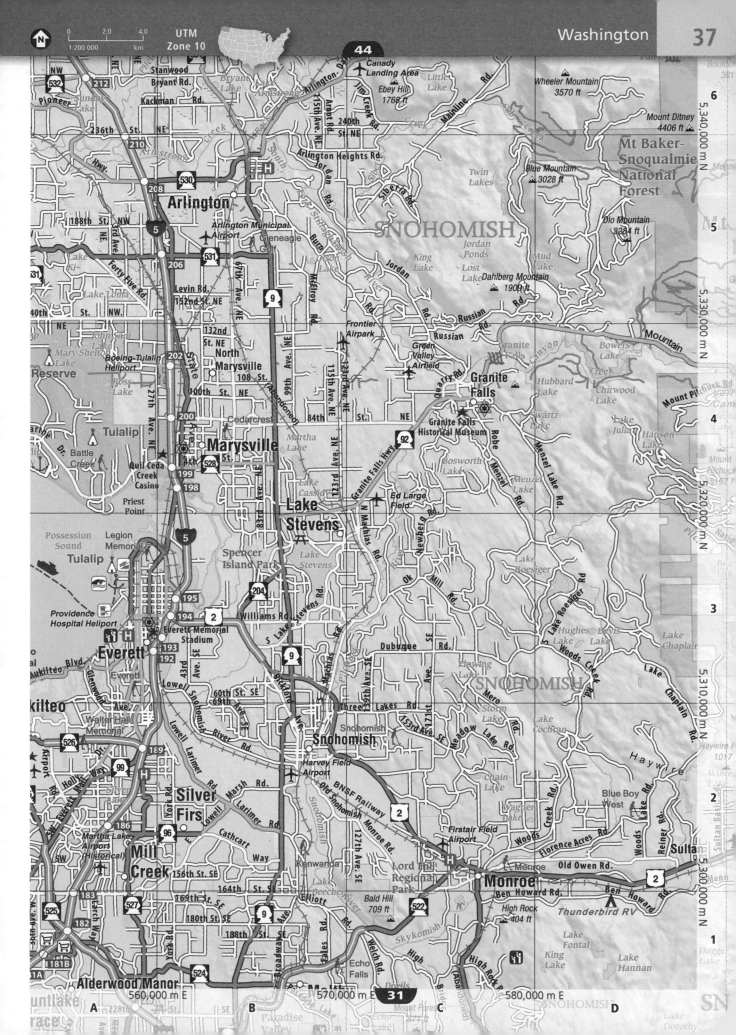

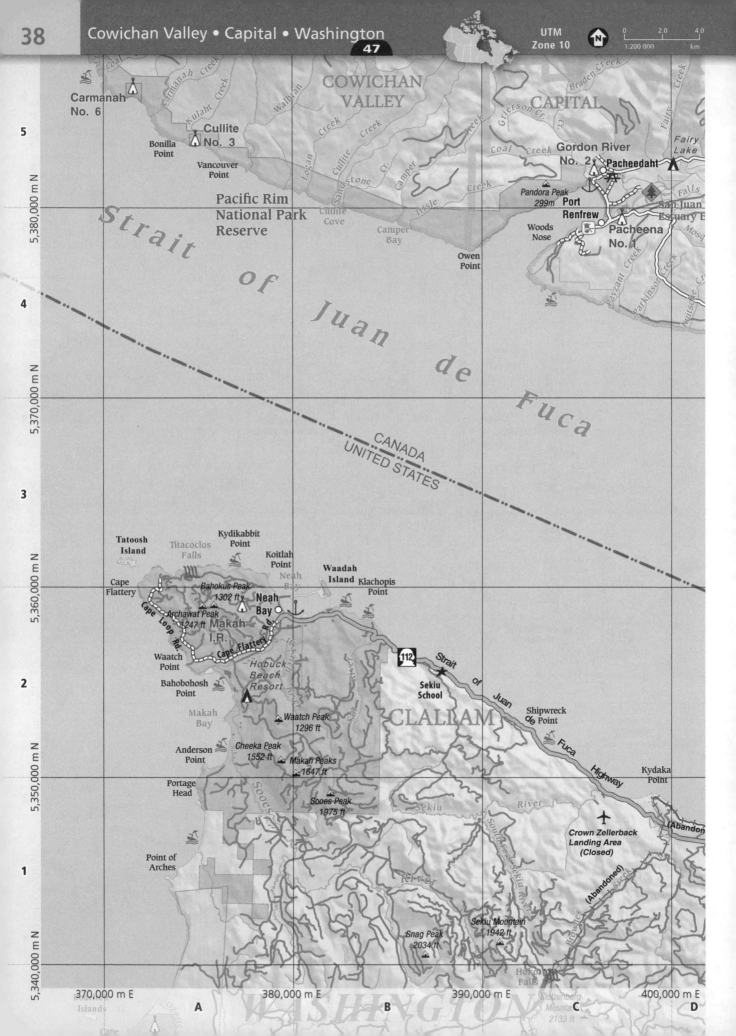

Strait of Juan de Fuca

COWICHAN VALLEY

CAPITAL

Carmanah
No. 6

Bonilla
Point

Cullite
No. 3

Vancouver
Point

Gordon River
No. 2

Pacheedaht

Fairy
Lake

Pandora Peak
299m
**Port
Renfrew**

San Juan
Estuary

Pacheena
No. 1

Pacific Rim
National Park
Reserve

Cullite
Cove

Camper
Bay

Woods
Nose

Owen
Point

CANADA
UNITED STATES

Tatoosh
Island

Titacoclos
Falls

Kydikabbit
Point

Koitlah
Point

Waadah
Island

Klachopis
Point

Cape
Flattery

Bahokus Peak
1302 ft

Neah
Bay

Neah
Bay

Cape Loop Rd.

Archawat Peak
1247 ft
**Makah
I.R.**

Cape Flattery Rd.

112

Strait

Waatch
Point

Hobuck
Beach
Resort

Sekiu
School

of

Bahobohosh
Point

Makah
Bay

Juan

Shipwreck
Point

CLALLAM

Anderson
Point

Waatch Peak
1296 ft

de

Fuca

Kydaka
Point

Cheeka Peak
1552 ft

Makah Peaks
1647 ft

Highway

Portage
Head

Sooes Peak
1975 ft

Crown Zellerback
Landing Area
(Closed)

(Abandon

Point of
Arches

Sooes

River

(Abandoned)

Sekiu Mountain
1942 ft

Snag Peak
2034 ft

Hoko
Falls

370,000 m E   380,000 m E   390,000 m E   400,000 m E

A   **B**   **C**   **D**

5,380,000 m N

5,370,000 m N

5,360,000 m N

5,350,000 m N

5,340,000 m N

5

4

3

2

1

WASHINGTON

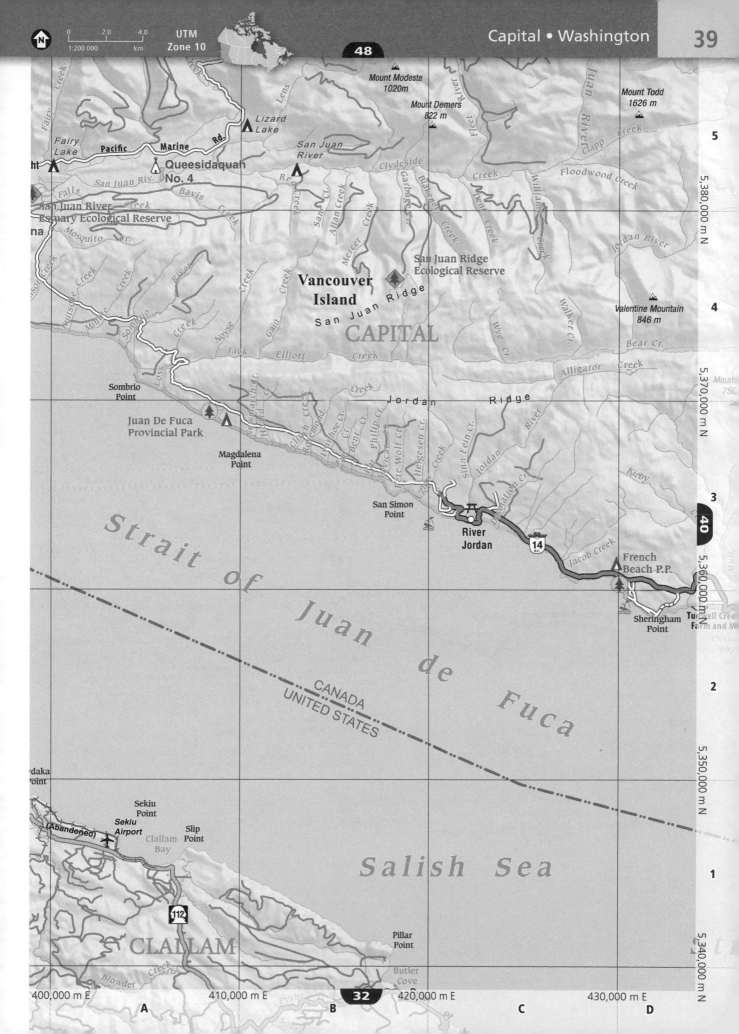

N

0   2.0   4.0
1:200 000   km

UTM
Zone 10

48

Fairy Creek

Mount Modeste
1020m

Mount Demers
822 m

Mount Todd
1626 m

Lens Creek

Lizard
Lake

San Juan
River

5

ght

Fairy
Lake

Pacific   Marine   *Rd.*

Queesidaquah
No. 4

San Juan Riv.

Bavis

Red Creek

Clydeside

San Cr.

Allan Creek

Blakeney Creek

Garbage Cr.

Creek

Mem Creek

Williams Creek

Floodwood Creek

Juan River

Clapp Creek

5,380,000 m N

Falls

San Juan River
Estuary Ecological Reserve

Creek

na

Mosquito Cr.

Twilssle Creek

Minto Creek

Sombrio River

Creek

River

Noyse Creek

Gain Creek

**Vancouver
Island**

San Juan Ridge

San Juan Ridge
Ecological Reserve

Wye Cr.

Walker Cr.

Valentine Mountain
846 m

Bear Cr.

4

CAPITAL

Jack Creek

Elliott Creek

Creek

Jordan   Ridge

Sinn Fein Cr.

Jordan River

Alligator   Creek

Moun
756

5,370,000 m N

Sombrio
Point

Juan De Fuca
Provincial Park

Magdalena
Point

Loss Creek

Mountalich Cr.

Hard Cr.

Clinch Creek

Ivedemord

Tahoe Cr.

Ci.

Bent Cr.

Vica Cr.

Phillip Cr.

Pete Wolf Cr.

Helgesen Cr.

Uglg Creek

Jordan

Kirby Creek

San Simon
Point

River
Jordan

14
B.C.

Jacob Creek

French
Beach P.P.

3

40

5,360,000 m N

Strait

Sheringham
Point

Tu *ell Cree*
rm and M

*Orver
Bay*

of

2

Juan

CANADA
UNITED STATES

5,350,000 m N

ydaka
Point

de

Sekiu
Point

*Sekiu
Airport*

(Abandoned)

Slip
Point

Clallam
Bay

Fuca

Salish   Sea

1

112

Pillar
Point

CLALLAM

Blower   Creek

Butler
Cove

5,340,000 m N

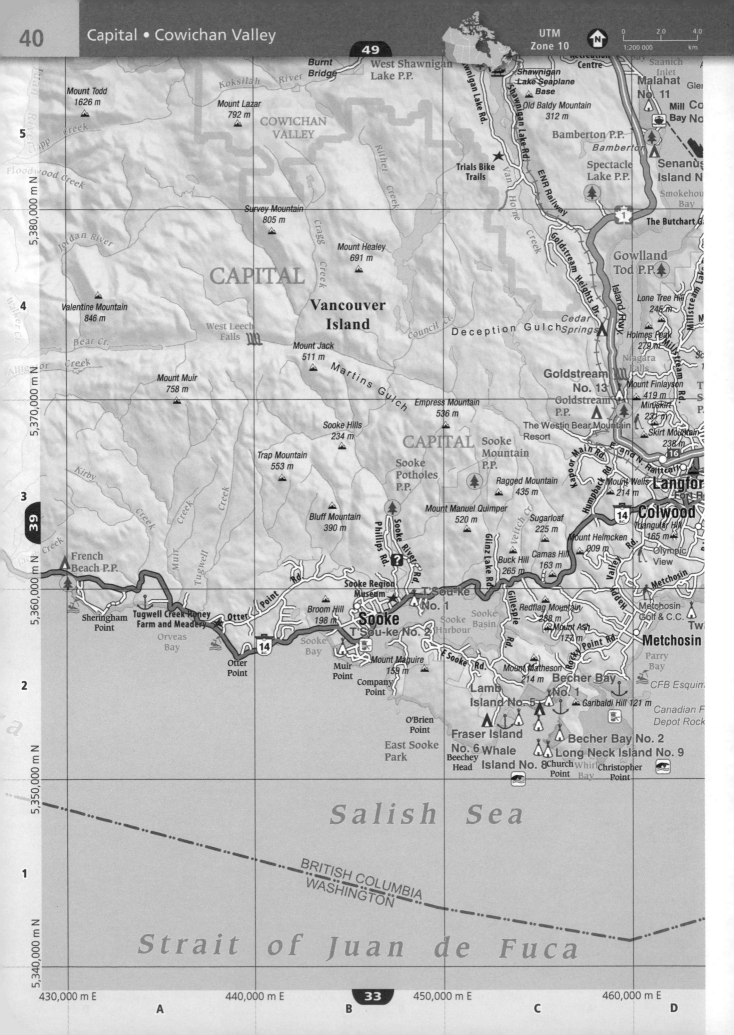

UTM
Zone 10

1:200 000

km

49

Burnt
Bridge

West Shawnigan
Lake P.P.

Malahat
No. 11

Mill Co
Bay No

Mount Todd
1626 m

Koksilah River

Mount Lazar
792 m

COWICHAN
VALLEY

Shawnigan
Lake Seaplane
Base

Old Baldy Mountain
312 m

Bamberton P.P.

Bamberton

Spectacle
Lake P.P.

Senanus
Island N

Smokehou
Bay

Trials Bike
Trails

Survey Mountain
805 m

Craggy Creek

Rithet Creek

ENR Railway

Van Horne

Shawnigan Lake Rd.

The Butchart G

Mount Healey
691 m

CAPITAL

Goldstream Heights Dr.

Cedar
Springs

Gowlland
Tod P.P.

Lone Tree Hill
245 m

Holmes Peak
279 m

Millstream Lake

Valentine Mountain
846 m

**Vancouver
Island**

West Leech
Falls

Council Cr.

Deception Gulch

Niagara
Falls

Goldstream
No. 13

Mount Finlayson
419 m

Mount Muir
758 m

Mount Jack
511 m

Martins Gulch

Empress Mountain
536 m

Goldstream
P.P.

Miniskirt
231 m

Skirt Mountain
238 m

Sooke Hills
234 m

CAPITAL

Sooke
Mountain
P.P.

The Westin Bear Mountain
Resort

16

Mount Wells
214 m

Trap Mountain
553 m

Sooke
Potholes
P.P.

Mount Manuel Quimper
520 m

Ragged Mountain
435 m

Kemp
oor
Main
Rd.

Humpback Rd.

E and N. Railtrail

Langfor

Fort R

Bluff Mountain
390 m

Phillips Rd.

Sooke River Rd.

Sugarloaf
225 m

Mount Helmcken
209 m

14
B.C.

Colwood

Triangular Hill
165 m

Buck Hill
265 m

Camas Hill
163 m

Olympic
View

39

Jamie Creek

French
Beach P.P.

Glinz Lake Rd.

Veitch Cr.

Metchosin

Sheringham
Point

Tugwell Creek Honey
Farm and Meadery

Otter
Point

Sooke Region
Museum

T'Sou-ke
No. 1

Redflag Mountain
288 m

Metchosin
Golf & C.C.

Tw

Orveas
Bay

Broom Hill
198 m

Sooke

T'Sou-ke No. 2

Sooke
Harbour

Sooke
Basin

Mount Ash
177 m

Metchosin

Otter
Point

14
B.C.

Sooke
Bay

Gillespie Rd.

Parry
Bay

Muir
Point

Mount Maguire
159 m

E Sooke Rd.

Mount Matheson
214 m

Becher Bay

No. 1

CFB Esquim

Company
Point

Lamb
Island No. 5

Garibaldi Hill 121 m

Canadian F
Depot Rock

O'Brien
Point

East Sooke
Park

Fraser Island
No. 6

Whale
Island No. 8

Beechey
Head

Becher Bay No. 2

Long Neck Island No. 9

Church
Point

Whirl
Bay

Christopher
Point

S a l i s h   S e a

BRITISH COLUMBIA
WASHINGTON

S t r a i t   o f   J u a n   d e   F u c a

33

430,000 m E   440,000 m E   450,000 m E   460,000 m E

A   B   C   D

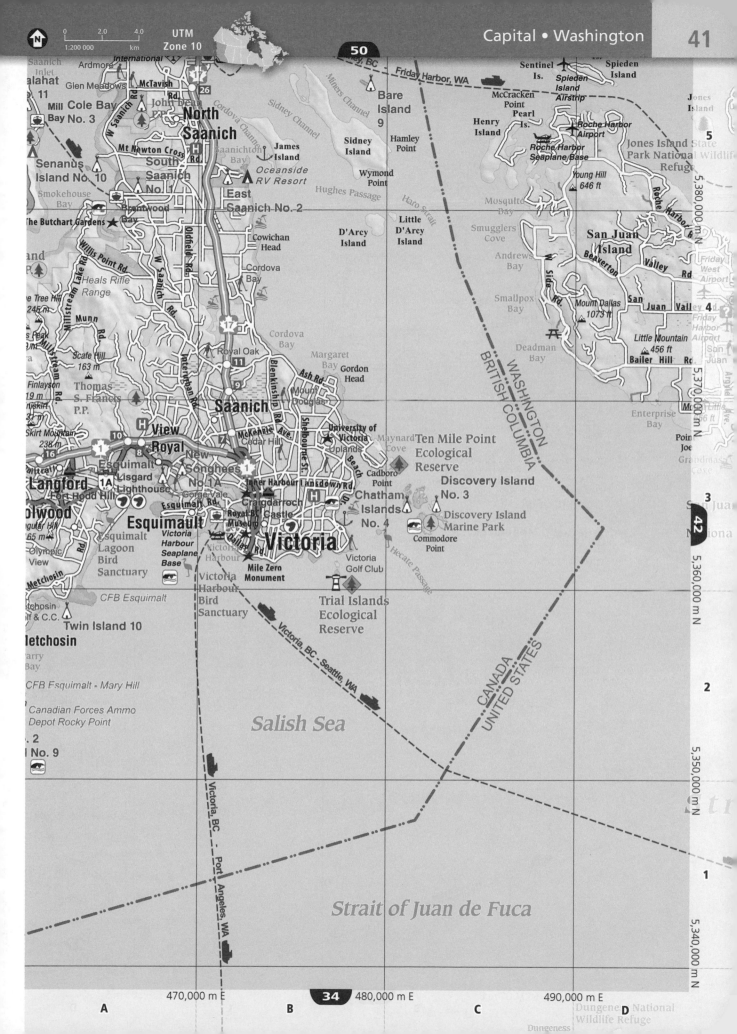

N

0   2.0   4.0
1:200 000   km

UTM
Zone 10

50

Friday Harbor, WA

Sentinel Is.

Spieden Island

Spieden Island Airstrip

Spieden Island

McCracken Point

Pearl Is.

Roche Harbor Airport

Jones Island

Ardmore

International

Glen Meadows

McTavish

17

26

Miners Channel

Bare Island 9

Henry Island

Roche Harbor

Roche Harbor Seaplane Base

Jones Island State Park National Wildlife Refuge

5

Mill Cole Bay Bay No. 3

Cole Bay

North Saanich

John Dean P.P.

Sidney Channel

Sidney Island

Hamley Point

Young Hill 646 ft

Senanus Island No. 10

Mt Newton Cross Rd

South Saanich No. 1

Saanichton Bay

James Island

Oceanside RV Resort

Wymond Point

Mosquito Bay

San Juan Island

5,380,000 m N

Smokehouse Bay

Brentwood Bay

East Saanich No. 2

Hughes Passage

Smugglers Cove

Beaverton

The Butchart Gardens ★

Cowichan Head

D'Arcy Island

Little D'Arcy Island

Andrews Bay

Mount Dallas 1073 ft

Valley Rd

4

Willis Point Rd.

Heals Rifle Range

Cordova Bay

Haro Strait

Smallpox Bay

W Side Rd

San Juan Valley

Friday West Airport

Tree Hill 245 m

Munn Rd

Deadman Bay

Little Mountain 456 ft

Bailer Hill Rd

Friday Harbor Airport

San Juan

Peak m

Scafe Hill 163 m

Cordova Bay

Margaret Bay

Gordon Head

WASHINGTON

BRITISH COLUMBIA

Enterprise Bay

5,370,000 m N

Finlayson Rd

17

Royal Oak

Ash Rd

Mount Douglas

Point Joe

Thomas S. Francis P.P.

11

Blenkinsop Rd

Sheliourne St

Grandma Cove

Skirt Mountain 238 m

9

Saanich

McKenzie Ave.

University of Victoria

Uplands

Maynard Cove

Ten Mile Point Ecological Reserve

San Juan National

3

1

10

View Royal

8

Cedar Hill

Beach

Cadboro Point

Discovery Island No. 3

42

1

16

Esquimalt

7

New Songhees No.1A

1

Inner Harbour

Lansdowne Rd

Chatham Islands No. 4

Discovery Island Marine Park

Langford

1A

Lisgard Lighthouse

Gorge Vale

Esquimalt Rd

Craigdarroch Castle

H

Commodore Point

5,360,000 m N

olwood

Fort Rodd Hill

Esquimalt

Royal BC Museum

Victoria

ngular Hill 65 m

Esquimalt Lagoon Bird Sanctuary

Victoria Harbour Seaplane Base

Dallas Rd

Victoria Harbour

Victoria Golf Club

Hecate Passage

Olympic View

Metchosin

CFB Esquimalt

Victoria Harbour Bird Sanctuary

Mile Zero Monument

Trial Islands Ecological Reserve

tchosin olf & C.C.

Twin Island 10

Victoria, BC · Seattle, WA

etchosin

arry Bay

CANADA

UNITED STATES

2

CFB Esquimalt - Mary Hill

Canadian Forces Ammo Depot Rocky Point

Salish Sea

. 2

No. 9

Victoria, BC

Port Angeles, WA

5,350,000 m N

1

Strait of Juan de Fuca

5,340,000 m N

A

470,000 m E

34

480,000 m E

B

C

490,000 m E

D

Dungeness National Wildlife Refuge

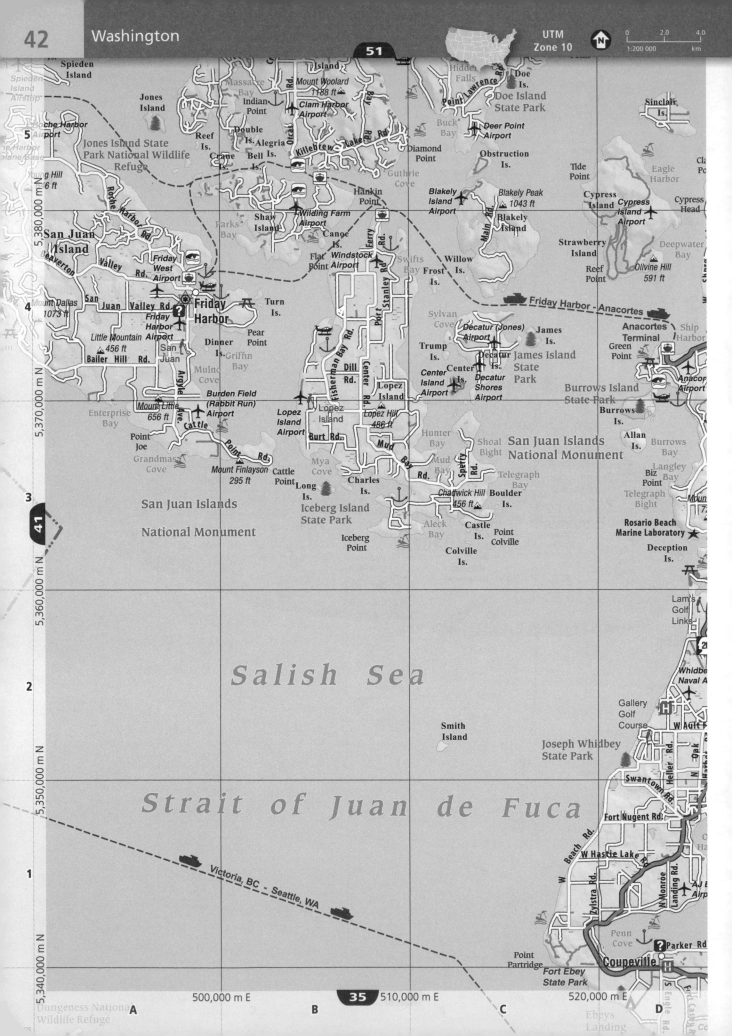

UTM
Zone 10

51

1:200 000

0   2.0   4.0
km

Spieden
Island

Spieden
Island
Airstrip

Jones
Island

Massacre
Bay

Island

Mount Woolard
1188 ft

Clam Harbor
Airport

Indian
Point

Point Lawrence Rd.

Hidden
Falls

Doe
Is.

Doe Island
State Park

Sinclair
Is.

5

Boche Harbor
Airport

Young Hill
6 ft

Jones Island State
Park National Wildlife
Refuge

Reef
Is.

Double
Is.

Alegria

Crane
Is.

Bell
Is.

Killebrew

Orcas

Lake Rd.

Buck
Bay

Diamond
Point

Deer Point
Airport

Obstruction
Is.

Tide
Point

Eagle
Harbor

Cla
Po

5,380,000 m N

Roche Harbor Rd.

Guthrie
Cove

Hankin
Point

Blakely
Island
Airport

Blakely Peak
1043 ft

Blakely
Island

Cypress
Island

Cypress
Island
Airport

Cypress
Head

San Juan
Island

Beaverton

Valley
Rd.

Friday
West
Airport

Shaw
Island

Wilding Farm
Airport

Parks
Bay

Canoe
Is.

Flat
Point

Windstock
Airport

Ferry Rd.

Swifts
Bay

Willow
Is.

Frost
Is.

Strawberry
Island

Reef
Point

Deepwater
Bay

Olivine Hill
591 ft

4

Mount Dallas
1073 ft

San

Juan

Valley Rd.

Friday
Harbor
Airport

Friday
Harbor

Turn
Is.

Port Stanley Rd.

Sylvan
Cove

Decatur (Jones)
Airport

James
Is.

Anacortes
Terminal

Ship
Harbor

Little Mountain
456 ft

Bailer Hill   Rd.

San
Juan

Dinner
Is.

Pear
Point

Griffin
Bay

Fisherman Bay Rd.

Dill
Rd.

Center Rd.

Lopez
Island

Trump
Is.

Center
Is.

Center
Is.

Decatur
Is.

Decatur
Shores
Airport

James Island
State
Park

Green
Point

Anacor
Airport

5,370,000 m N

Enterprise
Bay

Argyle Ave.

Mount Little
656 ft

Burden Field
(Rabbit Run)
Airport

Cattle

Lopez
Island
Airport

Lopez
Island

Burt Rd.

Lopez Hill
486 ft

Mud

Center
Island
Airport

Hunter
Bay

Shoal
Bight

San Juan Islands
National Monument

Burrows Island
State Park

Burrows
Is.

Allan
Is.

Burrows
Bay

Langley
Bay

Biz
Point

Telegraph
Bight

Mou
7

Point
Joe

Grandma's
Cove

Mount Finlayson
295 ft

Point

Cattle
Point

Long
Is.

Rd.

Mya
Cove

Charles
Is.

Mud
Bay

Sperry

Mud
Bay
Rd.

Rd.

Telegraph
Bay

Rosario Beach
Marine Laboratory

3

San Juan Islands

National Monument

5,360,000 m N

41

Iceberg Island
State Park

Iceberg
Point

Chadwick Hill
456 ft

Aleck
Bay

Boulder
Is.

Castle
Is.

Point
Colville

Deception
Is.

Colville
Is.

Lam's
Golf
Links

2

Salish Sea

Whidbe
Naval A

Gallery
Golf
Course

W Ault F

5,350,000 m N

Smith
Island

Joseph Whidbey
State Park

Swantown

Heller   Rd.

Oak

N

Strait of Juan de Fuca

Fort Nugent Rd.

W Beach Rd.

W Hastie Lake

N Monroe
Landing Rd.

Zylstra Rd.

1

Victoria, BC - Seattle, WA

Penn
Cove

Parker   Rd.

Coupeville

5,340,000 m N

Dungeness National
Wildlife Refuge

500,000 m E

35

510,000 m E

Point
Partridge

Fort Ebey
State Park

520,000 m E

Ebeys
Landing

A   **B**   **C**   **D**

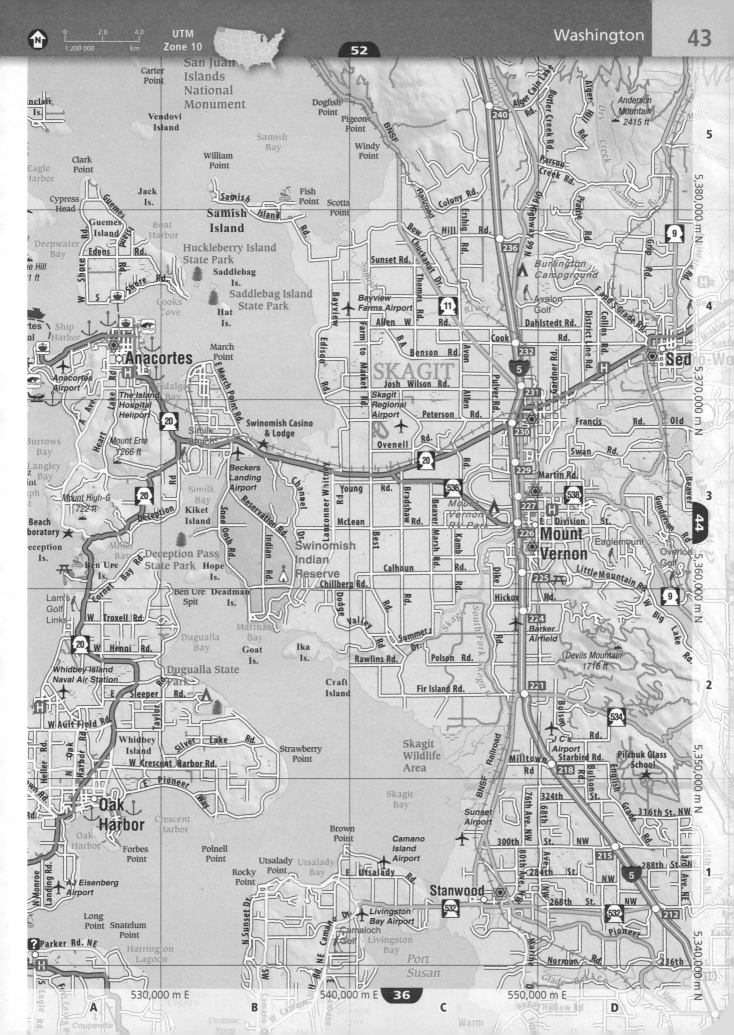

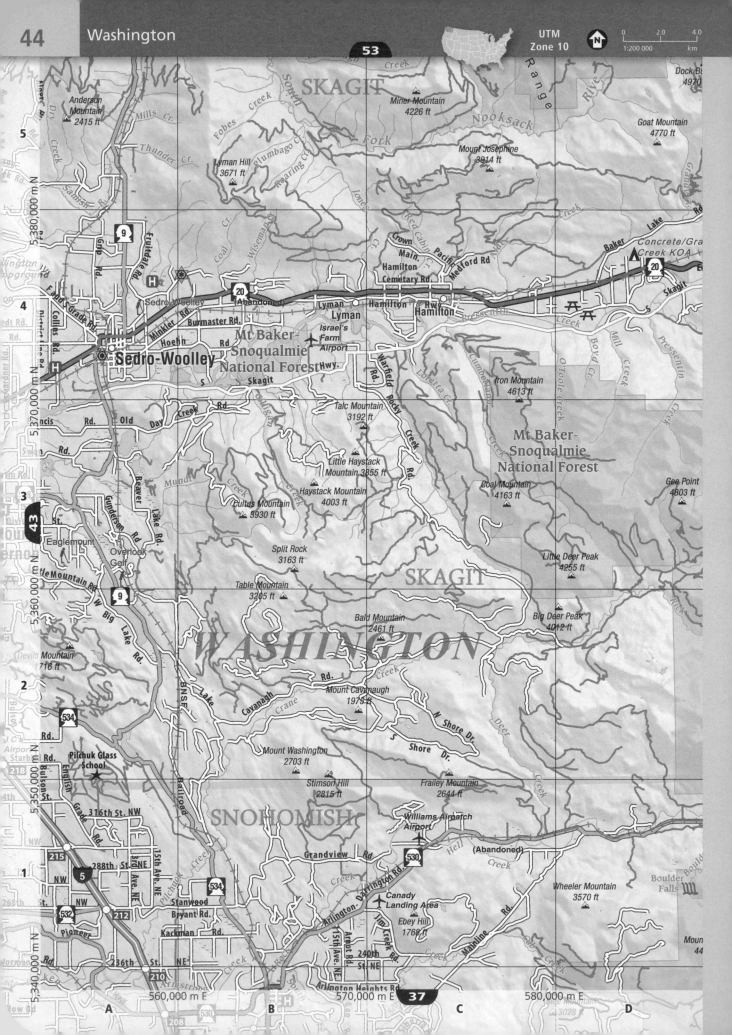

53

UTM
Zone 10

0   2.0   4.0
1:200 000   km

SKAGIT

Dock Bu
4970

Anderson
Mountain
2415 ft

Miner Mountain
4226 ft

Goat Mountain
4770 ft

Mount Josephine
3914 ft

Lyman Hill
3671 ft

Baker
Lake

Concrete/Gra
Creek KOA

20

9

20
(Abandoned)

Sedro-Woolley

Burmaster Rd.

Hoehn

Lyman

Lyman

Hamilton

Crown
Main.

Hamilton
Cemetary Rd.

Medford Rd.

Hamilton

Hwy.

Skagit

**Mt Baker-
Snoqualmie
National Forest**

Israel's
Farm
Airport

Skagit

Hwy.

Warfield

Rd.

Rocky

Iron Mountain
4613 ft

Sedro-Woolley

Minkler
Rd.

Francis

Rd.

Old

Day

Rd.

Creek

Rd.

Rd.

Talc Mountain
3192 ft

Creek

Rd.

Little Haystack
Mountain 3855 ft

Haystack Mountain
4003 ft

**Mt Baker-
Snoqualmie
National Forest**

Gee Point
4803 ft

43

St.

Eaglemount

Gunderson
Rd.

Overlook
Golf

Cultus Mountain
3930 ft

Coal Mountain
4163 ft

9

Beaver

Lake
Rd.

Split Rock
3163 ft

Little Deer Peak
4255 ft

Devils Mountain
716 ft

Mountain Rd.

W
Big
Lake
Rd.

Table Mountain
3205 ft

SKAGIT

Big Deer Peak
4012 ft

WASHINGTON

Bald Mountain
2461 ft

534

Rd.

BNSF

Lake

Rd.

Cavanagh

Crane

Creek

Mount Cavanaugh
1973 ft

N Shore Dr.

Deer

218

English

Bulson St.

Pilchuk Glass
School

Railroad

Mount Washington
2703 ft

S
Shore
Dr.

215

5

288th

316th St. NW

15th
Ave. NE

Grade

Pilchuck

Rd.

SNOHOMISH

Stimson Hill
2815 ft

Frailey Mountain
2644 ft

Williams Airpatch
Airport

(Abandoned)

Boulder
Falls

532

212

Pioneer

Stanwood

Bryant Rd.

Kackman

534

Rd.

Grandview

Rd.

530

Canady
Landing Area

Arlington

Darrington Rd.

Hell

Creek

Rd.

Mainline

Wheeler Mountain
3570 ft

Mou
44

240th
St. NE

15th
Ave. NE

Ebey Hill
1768 ft

Jim
Creek
Rd.

236th

St.

NE

210

Arlington Heights Rd.

37

208

530

560,000 m E

570,000 m E

580,000 m E

A   B   C   D

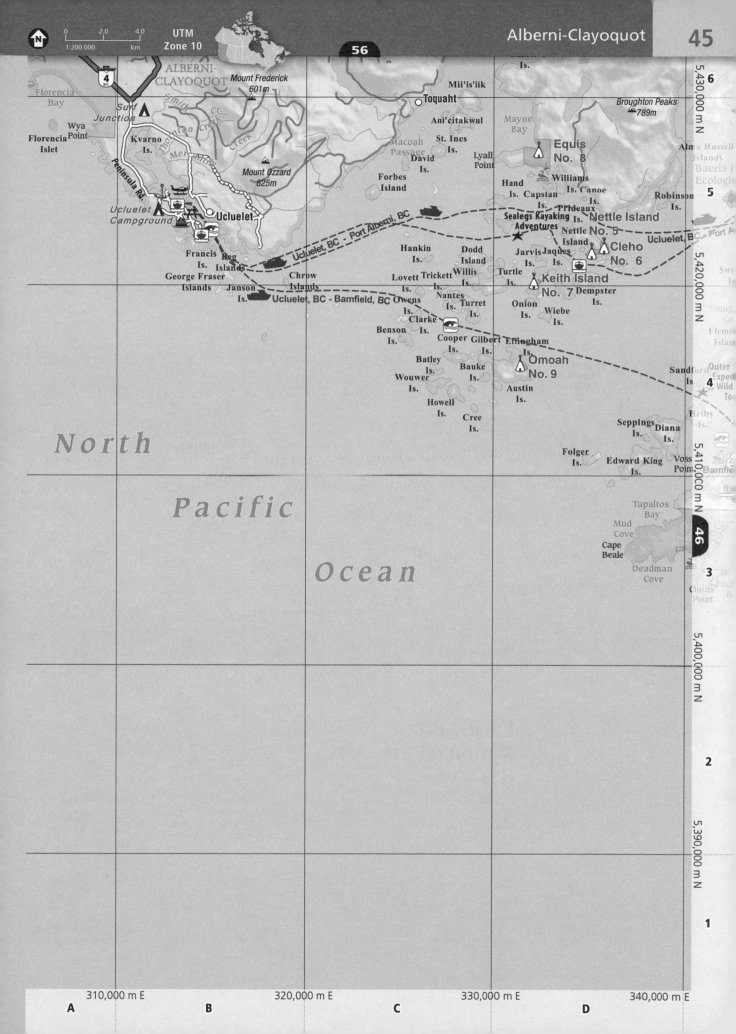

UTM
Zone 10

1:200 000

56

North

Pacific

Ocean

ALBERNI-CLAYOQUOT

Mount Frederick
601m

Florencia
Bay

Surf
Junction

Wya
Point

Florencia
Islet

Kvarno
Is.

Mount Ozzard
625m

Peninsula Rd.

Ucluelet
Campground

Ucluelet

Francis
Is.   Beg
Islands

George Fraser
Islands   Janson
Is.

Chrow
Islands

Ucluelet, BC - Bamfield, BC

Ucluelet, BC - Port Alberni, BC

Mii'is'iik

Toquaht

Ani'eitakwul

St. Ines
Is.

Macoah
Passage

David
Is.

Forbes
Island

Lyall
Point

Mayne
Bay

Broughton Peaks
789m

Equis
No. 8

Hand
Is.   Capstan
Is.   Williams
Is.   Canoe
Is.

Alma Russell
Islands

Baeria
Ecologi

Robinson
Is.

Prideaux
Is.

Sealegs Kayaking
Adventures

Nettle Island

Nettle No. 5
Island

Ucluelet, BC   Port A

Cleho
No. 6

Jaques
Is.

Jarvis
Is.

Hankin
Is.

Dodd
Island

Willis
Is.

Turtle
Is.

Keith Island

Lovett
Is.   Trickett
Is.

Nantes
Is.

Owens
Is.

Clarke
Is.

Benson
Is.

Cooper
Is.

Turret
Is.

Gilbert
Is.

Bauke
Is.

Onion
Is.

Wiebe
Is.

Dempster
Is.

No. 7

Sandford
Is.

Effingham
Is.

Omoah
No. 9

Austin
Is.

Batley
Is.

Wouwer
Is.

Howell
Is.

Cree
Is.

Seppings
Is.

Folger
Is.

Edward King
Is.

Diana
Is.

Voss
Point

Helby
Is.

Outer
Exped
Wild
To

Bamfic

Tapaltos
Bay

Mud
Cove

Cape
Beale

Deadman
Cove

46

Clutus
Point

5,430,000 m N

5,420,000 m N

5,410,000 m N

5,400,000 m N

5,390,000 m N

310,000 m E   320,000 m E   330,000 m E   340,000 m E

A   B   C   D

6

5

4

3

2

1

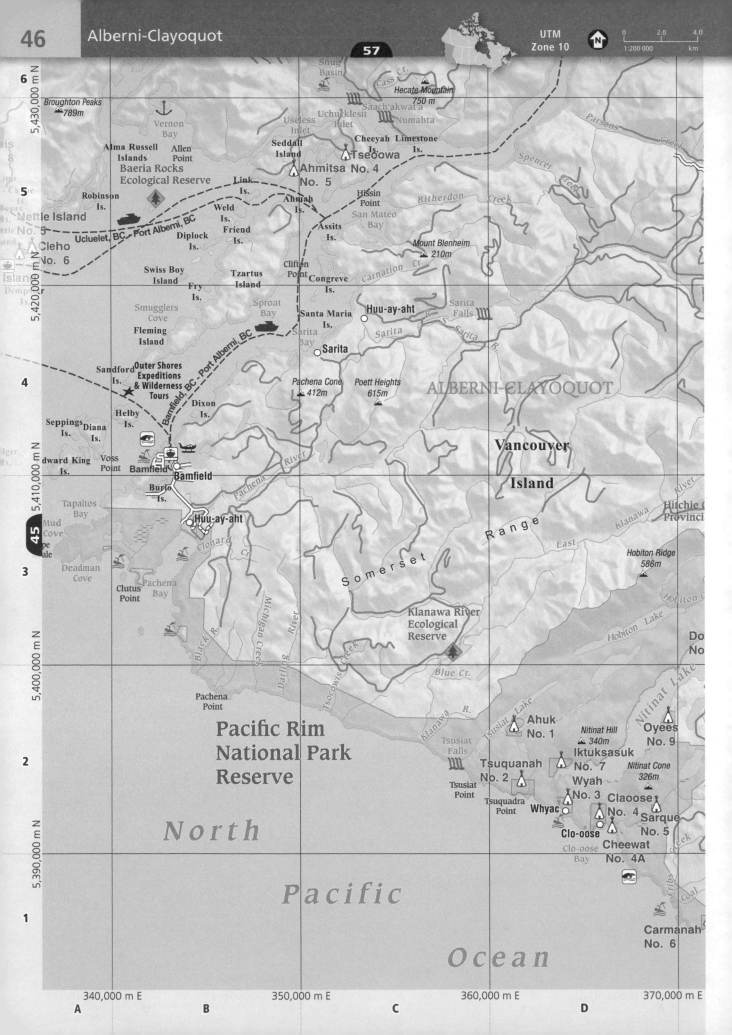

57

6

5,430,000 m N

Broughton Peaks
▲789m

Snug
Basin

Cass Cr.

Hecate Mountain
750 m

Saach'akwat'a
Numahta

Parsons

Creek

Vernon
Bay

Uchucklesit
Inlet

Useless
Inlet

Seddall
Island

Cheeyah
Is.

Limestone
Is.

Tseoowa

Ritherdon

Creek

Spencer

Creek

Alma Russell
Islands

Allen
Point

Baeria Rocks
Ecological Reserve

Ahmitsa No. 4
No. 5

5

5,426,000 m N

Robinson
Is.

Link
Is.

Ahmah
Is.

Hissin
Point

San Mateo
Bay

Mount Blenheim
210m

Cr.

Nettle Island

Ucluelet, BC - Port Alberni, BC

Weld
Is.

Cleho
No. 6

Diplock
Is.

Friend
Is.

Assits
Is.

Dempster
Is.

Swiss Boy
Island

Fry
Is.

Tzartus
Island

Clifton
Point

Congreve
Is.

Carnation

Sarita
Falls

Island

5,420,000 m N

Smugglers
Cove

Sproat
Bay

Santa Maria
Is.

Huu-ay-aht

Sarita R.

Sarita
Bay

Sarita

Sarita R.

Fleming
Island

Sandford
Is.

Outer Shores
Expeditions
& Wilderness
Tours

Dixon
Is.

Pachena Cone
▲412m

Poett Heights
615m

ALBERNI-CLAYOQUOT

4

Bamfield, BC - Port Alberni, BC

Seppings
Is.

Diana
Is.

Helby
Is.

Vancouver

Iger
Is.

dward King
Is.

Voss
Point

Bamfield

River

Island

5,410,000 m N

Bamfield

Pachena

Burlo
Is.

River

Tapaltos
Bay

Huu-ay-aht

Range

Klanawa

River

Hitchie
Provinci

Mud Cove
pe
ale

45

Clonard

Cr.

Somerset

East

Hobiton Ridge
586m

3

Deadman
Cove

Clutus
Point

Pachena
Bay

Michigan Creek

Klanawa River
Ecological
Reserve

Hobiton Lake

Do
No

5,400,000 m N

Black R.

Darling River

Tsocowis Creek

Blue Cr.

Pachena
Point

Klanawa R.

Tsusiat Lake

Nitinat Lake

Pacific Rim
National Park
Reserve

Tsusiat
Falls

Tsusiat
Point

Ahuk
No. 1

Nitinat Hill
▲340m

Oyees
No. 9

2

Tsuquanah
No. 2

Iktuksasuk
No. 7

Nitinat Cone
326m

Tsuquadra
Point

Wyah
No. 3

Claoose
No. 4

Sarque
No. 5

North

Whyac

Clo-oose

Cheewat
No. 4A

5,390,000 m N

Clo-oose
Bay

Pacific

Cribs

Coal

1

Carmanah
No. 6

Ocean

340,000 m E

350,000 m E

360,000 m E

370,000 m E

A   B   C   D

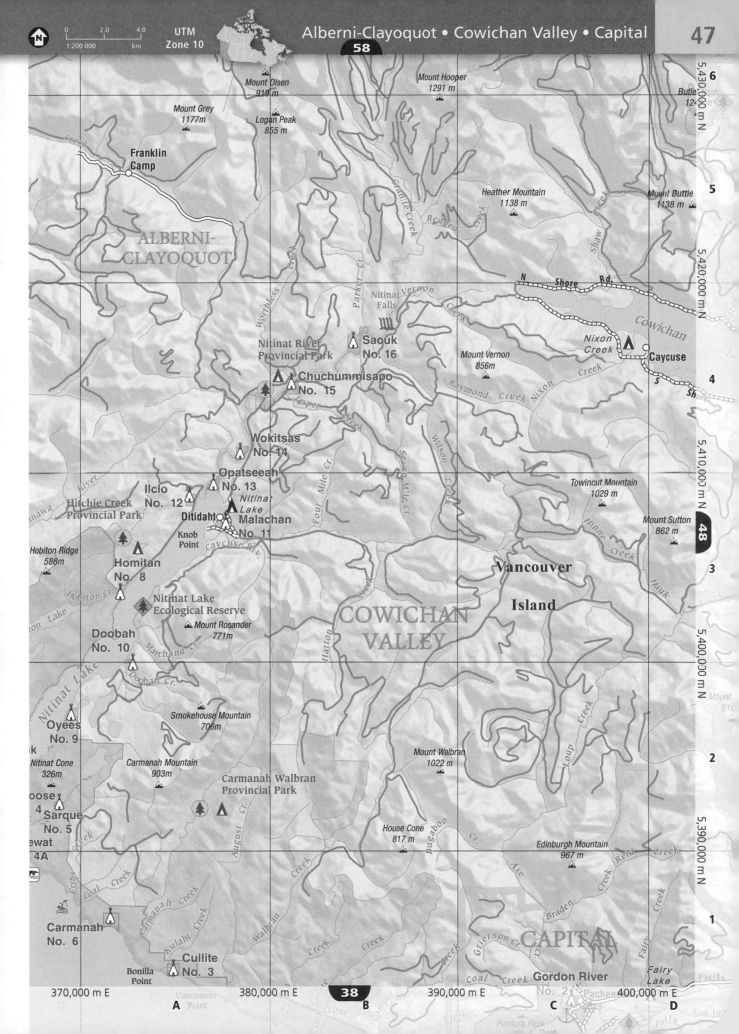

UTM
Zone 10

0   2.0   4.0
1:200 000   km

5,430,000 m N

6

Mount Olsen
919 m

Mount Hooper
1291 m

Butle
124

Mount Grey
1177m

Logan Peak
855 m

Heather Mountain
1138 m

Mount Buttle
1138 m

5

Franklin
Camp

ALBERNI-
CLAYOQUOT

5,420,000 m N

N   Shore   Rd.

Cowichan

Nitinat Vernon
Falls

Nixon
Creek

Caycuse

Saouk
No. 16

Mount Vernon
856m

Nitinat River
Provincial Park

Chuchummisapo
No. 15

Raymond Creek

4

5,410,000 m N

Wokitsas
No. 14

Towincut Mountain
1029 m

48

Opatseeah
No. 13

Ilclo
No. 12

Nitinat
Lake

Mount Sutton
862 m

Hitchie Creek
Provincial Park

Ditidaht

Malachan
No. 11

Knob
Point

Vancouver

3

Hobiton Ridge
586m

Homitan
No. 8

Island

5,400,000 m N

Nitinat Lake
Ecological Reserve

Mount Rosander
771m

COWICHAN
VALLEY

Doobah
No. 10

Nitinat Lake

Smokehouse Mountain
706m

Oyees
No. 9

Mount Walbran
1022 m

2

Nitinat Cone
326m

Carmanah Mountain
903m

Carmanah Walbran
Provincial Park

oose

Sarque
No. 5

House Cone
817 m

Edinburgh Mountain
967 m

5,390,000 m N

ewat
4A

Carmanah
No. 6

Bonilla
Point

Cullite
No. 3

CAPITAL

1

Gordon River

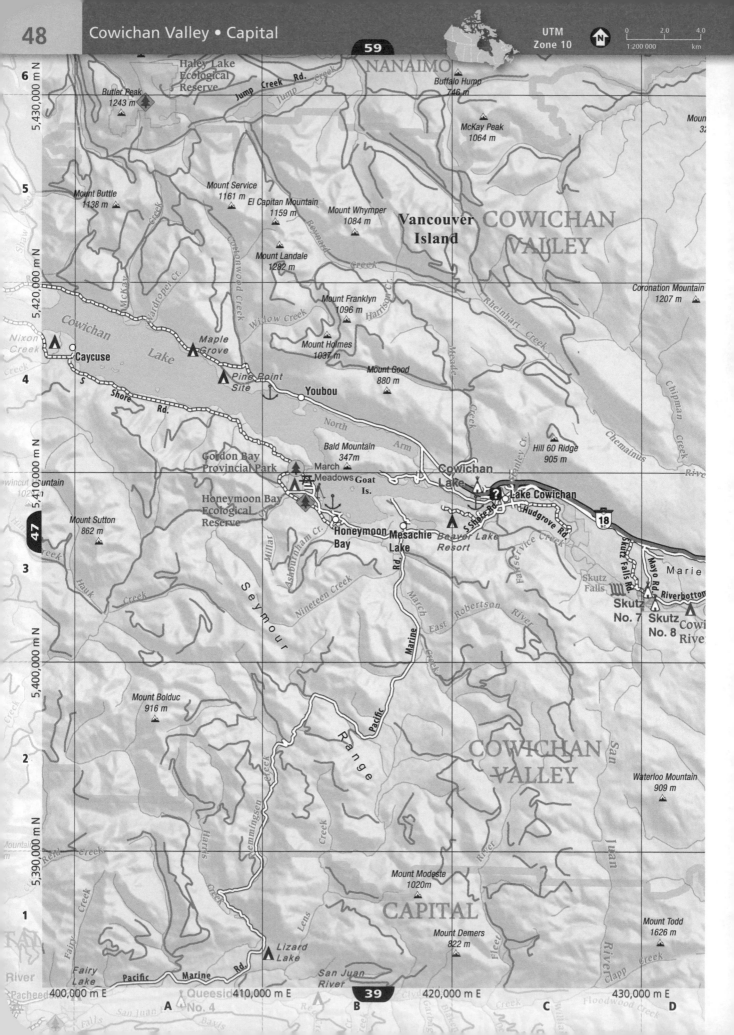

UTM
Zone 10

1:200 000

0   2.0   4.0
km

59

NANAIMO

Haley Lake
Ecological
Reserve

Jump Creek Rd.

Buffalo Hump
746 m

Butler Peak
1243 m

McKay Peak
1064 m

Mount
32

6

5,430,000 m N

Mount Service
1161 m

El Capitan Mountain
1159 m

Mount Whymper
1084 m

Vancouver
Island

COWICHAN
VALLEY

5

Mount Buttle
1138 m

Mount Landale
1282 m

Coronation Mountain
1207 m

McKay Creek

Cottonwood Creek

Widow Creek

Reynard Creek

Harrison Cr.

Rheinhart Creek

Mount Franklin
1096 m

Chipman Creek

Chemainus

5,420,000 m N

Nixon
Creek

Cowichan
Lake

Maple
Grove

Mount Holmes
1037 m

Mount Good
880 m

Caycuse

Pine Point
Site

Youbou

North

Arm

Hill 60 Ridge
905 m

River

4

S Shore Rd.

Bald Mountain
347m

Stanley Cr.

Cowichan
Lake

47

Gordon Bay
Provincial Park

March
Meadows

Goat
Is.

Lake Cowichan

Hudgrove Rd.

18
BC

5,410,000 m N

Mount Sutton
862 m

Honeymoon Bay
Ecological
Reserve

Honeymoon
Bay

Mesachie
Lake

Beaver Lake
Resort

Fairservice Creek

Skutz
Falls Rd.

Mayo Rd.

Marie

3

Mount
1020m

Ashburnham Cr.

Millar

Nineteen Creek

Marine Rd.

East Robertson River

Skutz
Falls

Skutz
No. 7

Riverbottom

Skutz
No. 8

Cowi
River

5,400,000 m N

Seymour

Mount Bolduc
916 m

Pacific

Range

COWICHAN

VALLEY

San Juan

Waterloo Mountain
909 m

2

Hemmingsen Creek

Harris Creek

Lens Creek

Marine

Fleet

River

5,390,000 m N

Fairy
Lake

River

Pacheed

Pacific   Marine   Rd.

Lizard
Lake

San Juan
River

Mount Modeste
1020m

CAPITAL

Mount Demers
822 m

Mount Todd
1626 m

Clapp Creek

1

400,000 m E

Queeside
No. 4

410,000 m E

39

420,000 m E

430,000 m E

A

B

C

D

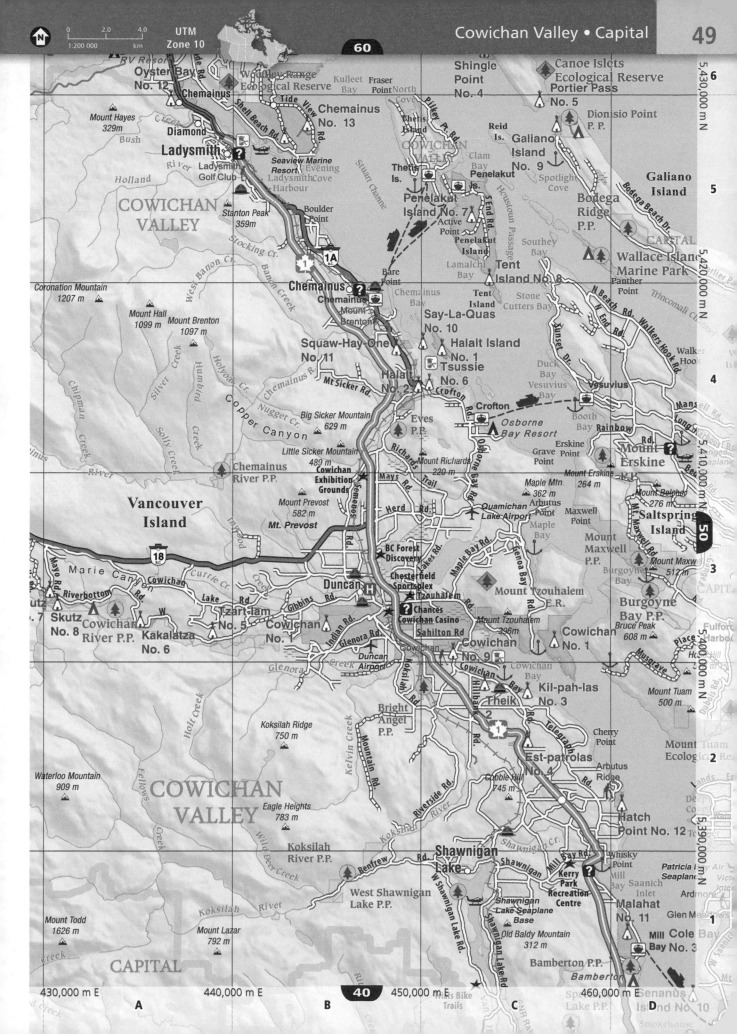

UTM
Zone 10

N

1:200 000
km
0   2.0   4.0

60

COWICHAN VALLEY

Oyster Bay No. 12
RV Resort
Chemainus
Mount Hayes 329m
Diamond
Ladysmith
Ladysmith Golf Club
Seaview Marine Resort
Ladysmith Cove
Holland
Shell Beach Rd.
Tide View Rd.
Woodley Range Ecological Reserve
Kulleet Bay
Fraser Point
North Cove

Chemainus No. 13
Shingle Point No. 4
Canoe Islets Ecological Reserve
Portier Pass
No. 5

Thetis Island
COWICHAN
Dionisio Point P.P.
Galiano Island No. 9
Galiano Island
Bodega Ridge P.P.
CAPITAL

Stanton Peak 359m
Boulder Point
Stuart Channel
Thetis Is.
Penelakut Is.
Clam Bay
Penelakut
Spotlight Cove
Bodega Beach Dr.

Coronation Mountain 1207 m
Mount Hall 1099 m
Mount Brenton 1097 m
West Banon Cr.
Banon Creek
Stocking Cr.
1
1A
BC
Chemainus
Chemainus
Mount Brenton
Bare Point
Penelakut Island No. 7
Active Point
Penelakut Island
Lamalchi Bay
Chemainus Bay
Tent Island No. 8
Houstoun Passage
Southey Bay
Wallace Island Marine Park
Panther Point

Chipman Creek
Silver Creek
Humbird Creek
Solly Creek
Holyoak Cr.
Copper Canyon
Nugget Cr.
Chemainus R.
Mt Sicker Rd.
Squaw-Hay-One No. 11
Halalt No. 2
Say-La-Quas No. 10
Halalt Island No. 1
Tsussie No. 6
Crofton
Tent Island
Stone Cutters Bay
Duck Bay
Vesuvius Bay
Vesuvius
Sunset Dr.
N Beach Rd.
N End Rd.
Walkers Hook Rd.
Trincomali Channel
Walker Hook

Big Sicker Mountain 629 m
Little Sicker Mountain 489 m
Eves P.P.
Mount Richards 220 m
Crofton
Osborne Bay Resort
Booth Bay
Rainbow
Grave Point
Erskine Point
Maple Mtn. 362 m
Mount Erskine 264 m
Mount Erskine P.P.
Mount Belcher 276 m

Chemainus River P.P.
Cowichan Exhibition Grounds
Mays Rd.
Richards Trail
Herd Rd.
Quamichan Lake Airport
Arbutus Point
Maxwell Point
Maple Bay
Saltspring Island
Mount Maxwell
Mount Maxwell P.P.
Burgoyne Bay
Mount Maxwell 512 m

Vancouver Island

Mount Prevost 582 m
Mt. Prevost
18
BC
Marie Canyon
Currie Cr.
Cowichan Lake
Duncan
BC Forest Discovery
Chesterfield Sportsplex
Mount Tzouhalem
Genoa Bay
Mount Tzouhalem E.R.
Bruce Peak 608 m
Burgoyne Bay P.P.
Cowichan No. 1

50
BC

Mayo Rd.
Skutz No. 7
Riverbottom Rd.
Skutz No. 8
Cowichan River P.P.
Kakalatza No. 6
Tzart-lam No. 5
Glenora Rd.
Gibbins Rd.
Indian Rd.
Cowichan No. 1
Chances Cowichan Casino
Sahilton Rd.
Tzouhalem
Cowichan No. 9
Cowichan Bay
Mount Tzouhalem 396 m
Cowichan No. 1
Mount Tuam 500 m

Duncan Airport
Glenora Creek
Cowichan
Kil-pah-las No. 3
Cowichan Bay
Holt Creek

Koksilah Ridge 750 m
Bright Angel P.P.
Kelvin Creek
Theik
Est-patrolas No. 4
Cherry Point
Mount Tuam Ecologica[l]

Waterloo Mountain 909 m
COWICHAN VALLEY
Eagle Heights 783 m
Mountain Rd.
Riverside Rd.
Cobble Hill 745 m
Arbutus Ridge
Hatch Point No. 12

Koksilah River P.P.
Renfrew Rd.
Shawnigan Lake
Shawnigan Cr.
Shawnigan
Mill Bay Rd.
Whisky Point
Patricia Seaplane

Mount Todd 1626 m
Mount Lazar 792 m
Koksilah River
West Shawnigan Lake P.P.
Shawnigan Lake Seaplane Base
Kerry Park Recreation Centre
Old Baldy Mountain 312 m
Malahat No. 11
Glen Meadows
Mill Bay No. 3
Cole Bay
Bamberton P.P.
Bamberton
CAPITAL

430,000 m E
440,000 m E
450,000 m E
460,000 m E

A   B   C   D

40

5,430,000 m N
5,420,000 m N
5,410,000 m N
5,400,000 m N
5,390,000 m N

6   5   4   3   2   1

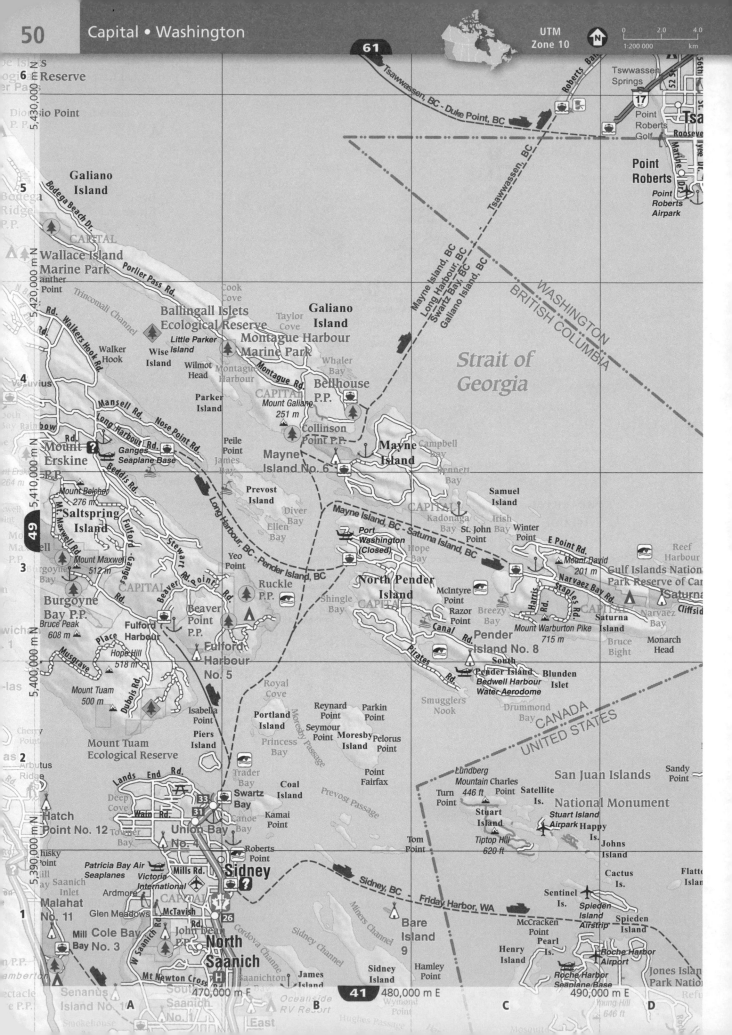

UTM Zone 10

61

1:200 000

Tsawwassen, BC - Duke Point, BC

Tsawwassen Springs

17

Point Roberts Golf

Roosevelt

Point Roberts

Point Roberts Airpark

Galiano Island

Bodega Beach Dr.

CAPITAL

Wallace Island Marine Park

Panther Point

Porlier Pass Rd.

Trincomali Channel

Galiano Island

Cook Cove

Taylor Cove

Ballingall Islets Ecological Reserve

Little Parker Island

Wise Island

Walkers Hook Rd.

Walker Hook

Wilmot Head

Mansell Rd.

Montague Harbour

Montague Rd.

Montague Harbour Marine Park

Whaler Bay

Bellhouse P.P.

Mayne Island, BC

Long Harbour, BC

Swartz Bay, BC

Galiano Island, BC

WASHINGTON

BRITISH COLUMBIA

Strait of Georgia

Parker Island

Mount Galiano 251 m

Nose Point Rd.

Collinson Point P.P.

Mayne Island

Campbell Bay

Mount Erskine P.P.

Ganges Seaplane Base

Beddis Rd.

Peile Point

James Bay

Mayne Island No. 6

Kennett Bay

Mount Belcher 276 m

Long Harbour, BC - Pender Island, BC

Prevost Island

Samuel Island

Mayne Island, BC - Saturna Island, BC

CAPITAL

Kadonaga Bay

St. John Bay

Irish Point

Winter Point

49

Saltspring Island

Mt. Maxwell Rd.

Fulford - Ganges Rd.

Diver Bay

Ellen Bay

Port Washington (Closed)

Hope Bay

E Point Rd.

Reef Harbour

Mount Maxwell 512 m

Stewart Rd.

Yeo Point

Ruckle P.P.

Shingle Bay

North Pender Island

McIntyre Point

Mount David 201 m

Gulf Islands National Park Reserve of Can

Saturna

Burgoyne Bay

Bruce Peak 608 m

Beaver Point Rd.

Beaver Point P.P.

Razor Point

Breezy Bay

Harris Rd.

Staples Rd.

Saturna Island

Narvaez Bay

Cliffside

Place

Hope Hill 518 m

Fulford Harbour

Fulford Harbour No. 5

Canal

Mount Warburton Pike 715 m

Bruce Bight

Monarch Head

Musgrave

Dubois Rd.

Pirates Rd.

Pender Island No. 8

Mount Tuam 500 m

Isabella Point

Royal Cove

Reynard Point

Parkin Point

Smugglers Nook

South Pender Island

Bedwell Harbour Water Aerodome

Blunden Islet

Drummond Bay

Mount Tuam Ecological Reserve

Piers Island

Portland Island

Seymour Point

Moresby Island

Pelorus Point

CANADA

UNITED STATES

Princess Bay

Moresby Passage

Point Fairfax

Cherry Point

Arbutus Ridge

Trader Bay

Coal Island

Prevost Passage

Lundberg Mountain

Turn Point

Charles Point

Satellite Is.

San Juan Islands

Sandy Point

Lands End Rd.

Swartz Bay

Kamai Point

33

31

Deep Cove

Wain Rd.

Hatch Point No. 12

Canoe Bay

Tom Point

Stuart Island

Tiptop Hill 620 ft

National Monument

Stuart Island Airpark

Happy Is.

Johns Island

Patricia Bay Air Seaplanes

Mills Rd.

Union Bay No. 4

Roberts Bay

Sidney

Sidney, BC

Cactus Is.

Flatte Islan

Victoria International

Ardmore

26

Glen Meadows

McTavish Rd.

CAPITAL

Friday Harbor, WA

Sentinel Is.

Spieden Island Airstrip

Spieden Island

Malahat No. 11

North Saanich

41

Bare Island 9

Henry Island

Pearl Island

Roche Harbor Airport

Jones Island

Mill Bay No. 3

Cole Bay

John Dean P.P.

H

Mt Newton Cross

Saanichton

James Island

Sidney Island

Hamley Point

Roche Harbor Seaplane Base

Young Hill 646 ft

470,000 m E

480,000 m E

490,000 m E

Senanus Island

South Saanich

Oceanside RV Resort

Wymond Point

A

B

C

D

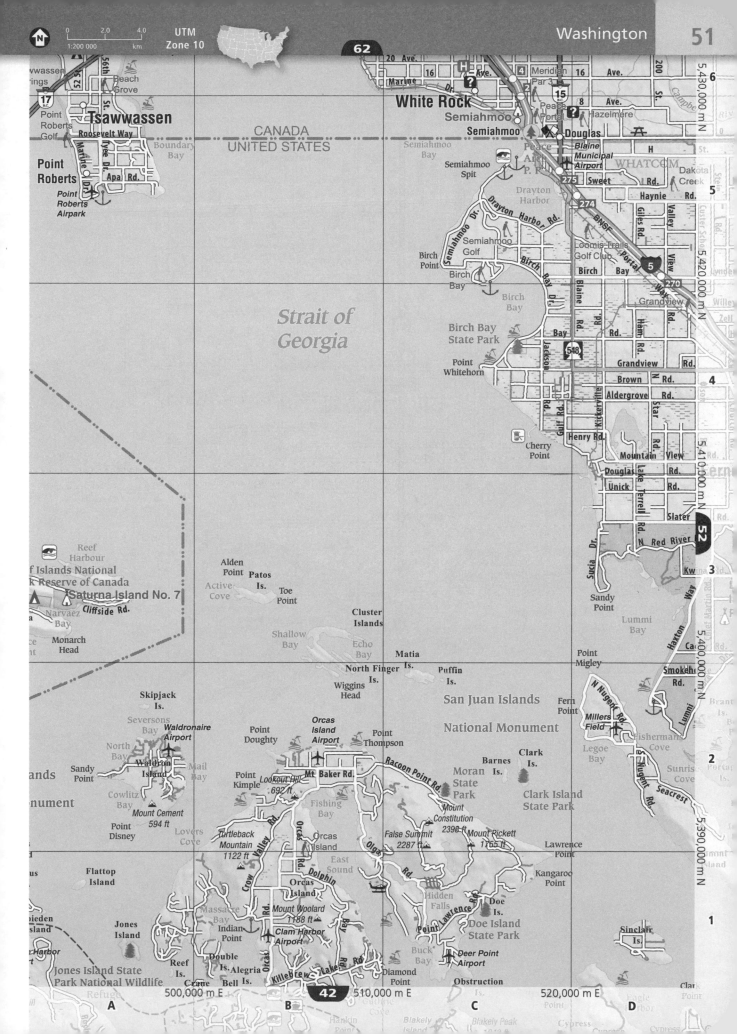

N

0   2.0   4.0
1:200 000   km

UTM
Zone 10

Tsawwassen

wassen
rings

Beach
Grove

**Point
Roberts**

Point
Roberts Golf

Roosevelt Way

Marble Dr.

Tyee Dr.

Apa Rd.

Point
Roberts
Airpark

Boundary
Bay

CANADA
UNITED STATES

*Strait of
Georgia*

20 Ave.

62

16   Ave.

Marine   Dr.

White Rock

Semiahmoo

Semiahmoo

Semiahmoo
Bay

Semiahmoo
Spit

Semiahmoo   Dr.

Drayton   Harbor   Rd.

Drayton
Harbor

Semiahmoo
Golf

Birch
Point

Birch
Bay

Birch
Bay

Birch Bay Dr.

**Birch Bay
State Park**

Point
Whitehorn

Cherry
Point

Meridian
Par 3

4

16   Ave.

Ave.

15

Peace
Portal

Hazelmere

Douglas

Peace
Arch
P. P.

Blaine
Municipal
Airport

275

274

BNSF

Portal   Way

5

270

Sweet   Rd.

Haynie   Rd.

Loomis Trails
Golf Club

Birch   Bay

Blaine   Rd.

Grandview

Bay   Rd.

548

Jackson   Rd.

Gulf   Rd.

Kickerville   Rd.

Henry Rd.

WHATCOM

Dakota
Creek

5

Grandview   Rd.

Brown   N   Rd.

Aldergrove   Rd.

Star   Rd.

Mountain   View

Douglas   Rd.

Unick   Rd.

Lake Terrell   Rd.

Slater   Rd.

52

N   Red   River

Kwina

Sucia   Dr.

Sandy
Point

Lummi
Bay

Point
Migley

Haxton   Way

Smokeho
Rd.

Lummi

5,430,000 m N

5,420,000 m N

5,410,000 m N

5,400,000 m N

5,390,000 m N

Custer Scho

Giles Rd.

Valley

View

Ham   Rd.

5

4

3

2

**Reef
Harbour**

f Islands National
k Reserve of Canada

Saturna Island No. 7

Cliffside   Rd.

Narvaez
Bay

Monarch
Head

Alden
Point

Active
Cove

Patos
Is.

Toe
Point

Shallow
Bay

Echo
Bay

Cluster
Islands

North Finger
Is.

Wiggins
Head

Matia
Is.

Puffin
Is.

San Juan Islands

National Monument

Fern
Point

Point
Migley

Legoe
Bay

Millers
Field

Fisherman
Cove

Sunris
Cove

**Skipjack
Is.**

Seversons
Bay

Waldronaire
Airport

North
Bay

Sandy
Point

**Waldron
Island**

Mail
Bay

Cowlitz
Bay

Mount Cement
594 ft

Point
Disney

Lovers
Cove

Point
Doughty

Orcas
Island
Airport

Point
Thompson

Point
Kimple

Lookout Hill
692 ft

Mt. Baker Rd.

Racoon Point Rd.

Fishing
Bay

Barnes
Is.

Clark
Is.

**Moran
State
Park**

Mount
Constitution
2398 ft

False Summit
2287 ft

Mount Rickett
1765 ft

**Clark Island
State Park**

Lawrence
Point

Kangaroo
Point

Crow Valley   Rd.

Orcas   Rd.

Olga   Rd.

Turtleback
Mountain
1122 ft

**Orcas
Island**

East
Sound

Dolphin   Bay   Rd.

Orcas
Island

Mount Woolard
1188 ft

Indian
Point

Clam Harbor
Airport

Killebrew Lake   Rd.

Hidden
Falls

Point   Lawrence   Rd.

Doe
Is.

**Doe Island
State Park**

Buck
Bay

Deer Point
Airport

Flattop
Island

Massacre
Bay

Jones
Island

Double
Is.

Reef
Is.

Alegria

Bell   Is.

Crane

Diamond
Point

Obstruction

Sinclair
Is.

nds

nument

Flattop
Island

s

eden
sland

Harbor

**Jones Island State
Park National Wildlife**

Refuge

500,000 m E

42

510,000 m E

B

520,000 m E

C

D

A

1

Hankin
Point

Blakely
Point

Blakely Peak

Cypress

Clark
Point

Eagle
Harbor

Cypress

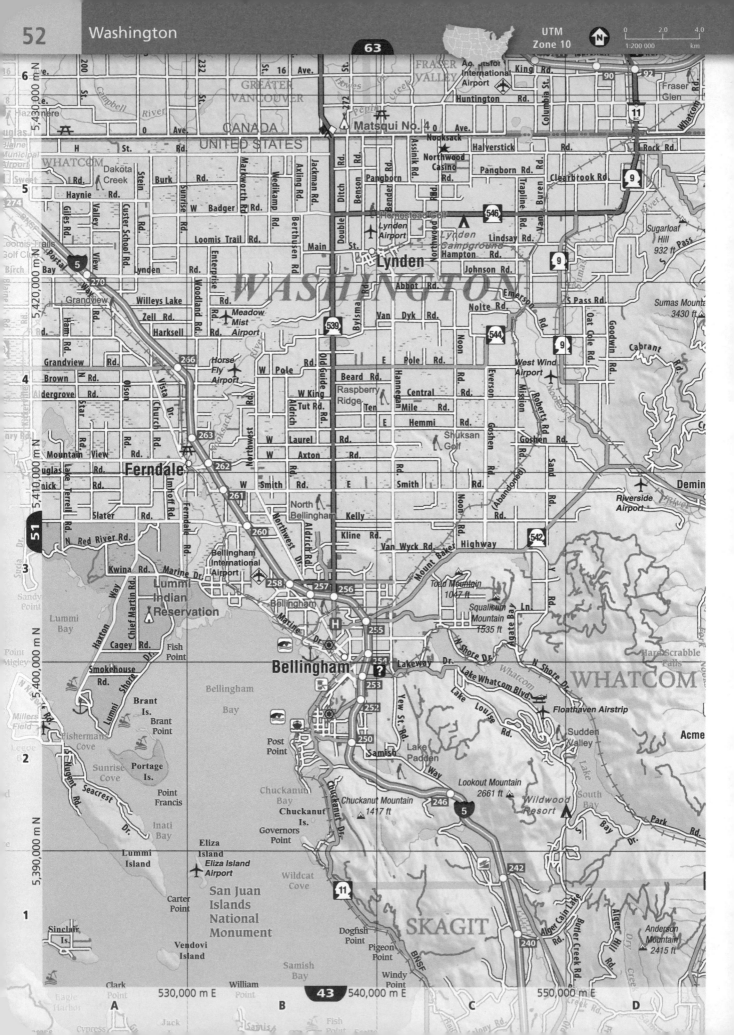

63

GREATER
VANCOUVER

FRASER
VALLEY

CANADA
UNITED STATES

WHATCOM

Matsqui No. 4

King Rd.

Huntington

Fraser
Glen

Nooksack

Northwood
Casino

Halverstick

Rock Rd.

Pangborn

Pangborn Rd.

Clearbrook Rd.

Sugarloaf
Hill
932 ft

Sumas
Pass

Dakota
Creek

Haynie
Rd.

Burk
Rd.

Badger

Loomis Trail Rd.

Homestead Golf

Lynden
Airport

Lynden
Campground

Lindsay Rd.

Sumas Mountain
3430 ft

LYNDEN

WASHINGTON

Main
St.

Hampton
Rd.

Johnson Rd.

Grandview

Willeys Lake

Meadow
Mist
Airport

Abbot Rd.

Byrsma Rd.

Van
Dyk
Rd.

Nolte Rd.

Emerson Rd.

Zell Rd.

Harksell
Rd.

539

Pole
Rd.

544

9

Grandview Rd.

256

Horse
Fly
Airport

W Pole

Beard Rd.

West Wind
Airport

Cabrant

Brown Rd.

Raspberry
Ridge

Central

Goodwin Rd.

Aldergrove Rd.

W King

Tut Rd.

Ten

Mile Rd.

Hemmi

Shuksan
Golf

Goshen

263

W Laurel Rd.

Rd.

Goshen Rd.

Mountain View

262

W Axton Rd.

Sand

Riverside
Airport

Demin

Ferndale

261

W Smith Rd.

E Smith Rd.

51

260

North
Bellingham

Kelly Rd.

Van Wyck Rd.

Highway

542

Slater Rd.

Kline Rd.

N Red River Rd.

Kwina Rd.

Marine Dr.

Bellingham
International
Airport

258

257

256

Mount Baker Highway

Toad Mountain
1047 ft

Squalicum
Mountain
1535 ft

Hare Scrabble
Falls

3

**Lummi
Indian
Reservation**

Lummi
Bay

Chief Martin Rd.

Smokehouse
Rd.

Cagey Rd.

Fish
Point

Bellingham

255

254

253

Lakeway Dr.

N Shore Dr.

Lake Whatcom Blvd.

Floathaven Airstrip

WHATCOM

Point
Migley

Brant Is.

Brant
Point

Bellingham
Bay

H

252

Yew St. Rd.

Lake Louise

Sudden
Valley

Acme

2

Millers
Field

Fisherman
Cove

Sunrise
Cove

Portage
Is.

Point
Francis

Post
Point

250

Samish

Lake
Padden

Way

Lookout Mountain
2661 ft

Wildwood
Resort

South
Bay

Seacrest Dr.

Inati
Bay

Chuckanut
Bay

Chuckanut
Is.

Chuckanut Mountain
1417 ft

246

5

Park Rd.

Lummi
Island

Eliza
Island

Eliza Island
Airport

Governors
Point

Wildcat
Cove

242

1

Sinclair
Is.

Carter
Point

Vendovi
Island

San Juan
Islands
National
Monument

Dogfish
Point

SKAGIT

240

Alger Cain Lake

Anderson
Mountain
2415 ft

Clark
Point

William
Point

43

Windy
Point

Samish
Bay

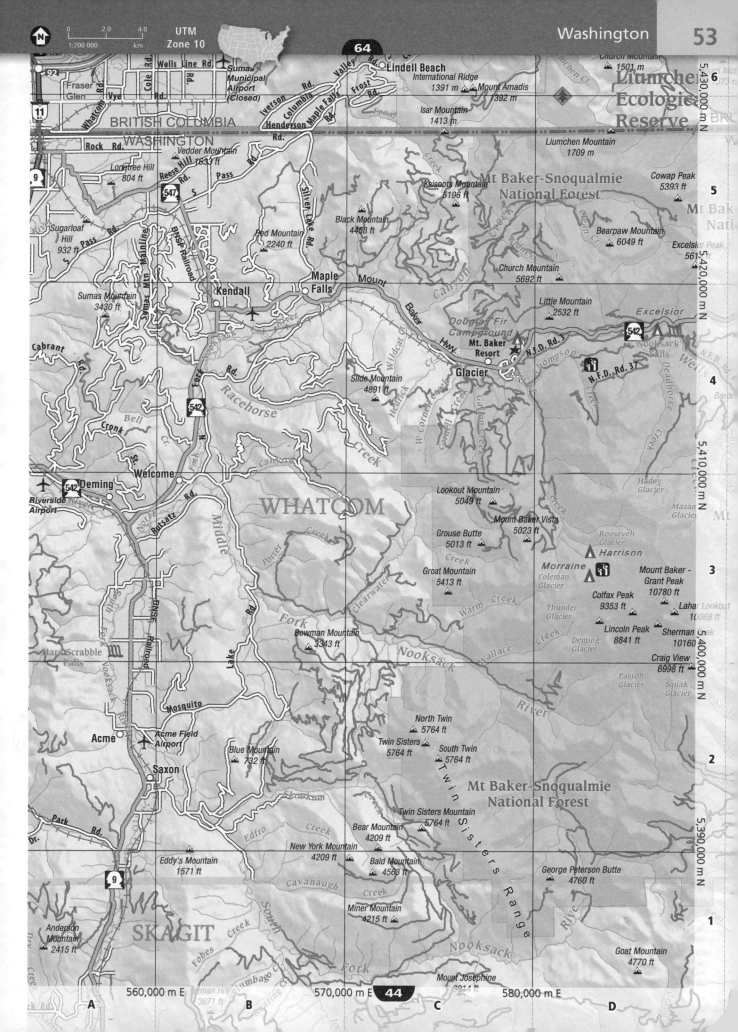

N

1:200 000

0   2.0   4.0
km

64

92

Wells Line Rd.

Sumas
Municipal
Airport
(Closed)

Lindell Beach

International Ridge
1391 m   Mount Amadis
1392 m

Church Mountain
1501 m

Liumchen
Ecological
Reserve

Fraser
Glen

Vye

Cole

Rd.

Whatcom

Iverson   Rd.

Columbia

Maple Falls Rd.

Valley   Rd.

Frost   Rd.

Isar Mountain
1413 m

11
B.C.

BRITISH COLUMBIA

Henderson   Rd.

Liumchen Mountain
1709 m

WASHINGTON

9

Rock   Rd.

Longtree Hill
804 ft

Reese Hill   Rd.

Vedder Mountain
1633 ft

Pass   Rd.

Silver Lake Rd.

Kaisoots Mountain
5196 ft

Mt Baker-Snoqualmie
National Forest

Cowap Peak
5393 ft

5

547

Sugarloaf
Hill
932 ft

Pass   Rd.

BNSF Railroad

Red Mountain
2240 ft

Black Mountain
4458 ft

Church Mountain
5692 ft

Bearpaw Mountain
6049 ft

Mt Bak
Nati

Excelsior Peak
561

Cabrant   Rd.

Sumas Mtn Mainline

Sumas Mountain
3430 ft

Kendall

Maple
Falls

Mount

Baker

Hwy.

Douglas Fir
Campground

Mt. Baker
Resort

N.F.D. Rd. 3

Little Mountain
2532 ft

Excelsior

542

N.F.D. Rd.

Nooksack
Falls

Wells

Racehorse   Rd.

Fork

Nooksack

542

Slide Mountain
4891 ft

Wildcat Cr.

Hedrick Cr.

Glacier

Thompson Cr.

N.F.D. Rd. 37

Deadhorse

Creek

Bell
Cr.

Cronk

N. Fork

Canyon

Creek

W Corner Creek

Cornell Creek

Galena Creek

Hadey
Glacier

Mazama
Glacier

Mt

Welcome

Deming

542

Riverside
Airport

Butsatz

Middle   Fork Nooksack   River

WHATCOM

Porter   Creek

Clearwater   Creek

Lookout Mountain
5049 ft

Grouse Butte
5013 ft

Mount Baker Vista
5023 ft

Harrison

Roosevelt
Glacier

Morraine
Coleman
Glacier

Thunder
Glacier

Colfax Peak
9353 ft

Mount Baker -
Grant Peak
10780 ft

Lahar Lookout
10068 m

Hare Scrabble
Falls

BNSF Railroad

North Fork Nooksack River

Lake   Rd.

S. Fork

Bowman Mountain
3343 ft

Nooksack

Groat Mountain
5413 ft

Warm   Creek

Wallace   Creek

Deming
Glacier

Lincoln Peak
8841 ft

Sherman
10160

Craig View
6998 ft

3

Easton
Glacier

Squak
Glacier

Acme

Acme Field
Airport

Blue Mountain
732 ft

River

North Twin
5764 ft

Twin Sisters
5764 ft

South Twin
5764 ft

Saxon

Shuksan   Creek

Twin   Sisters   Range

Twin Sisters Mountain
5764 ft

Mt Baker-Snoqualmie
National Forest

2

Park   Rd.

Dr.

Edfro   Creek

Bear Mountain
4209 ft

New York Mountain
4209 ft

Bald Mountain
4563 ft

George Peterson Butte
4760 ft

Eddy's Mountain
1571 ft

Cavanaugh   Creek

Anderson
Mountain
2415 ft

9

SKAGIT

South Fork   Creek

Miner Mountain
4215 ft

Nooksack

Goat Mountain
4770 ft

1

560,000 m E   44   570,000 m E   580,000 m E

Mount Josephine

A   B   C   D

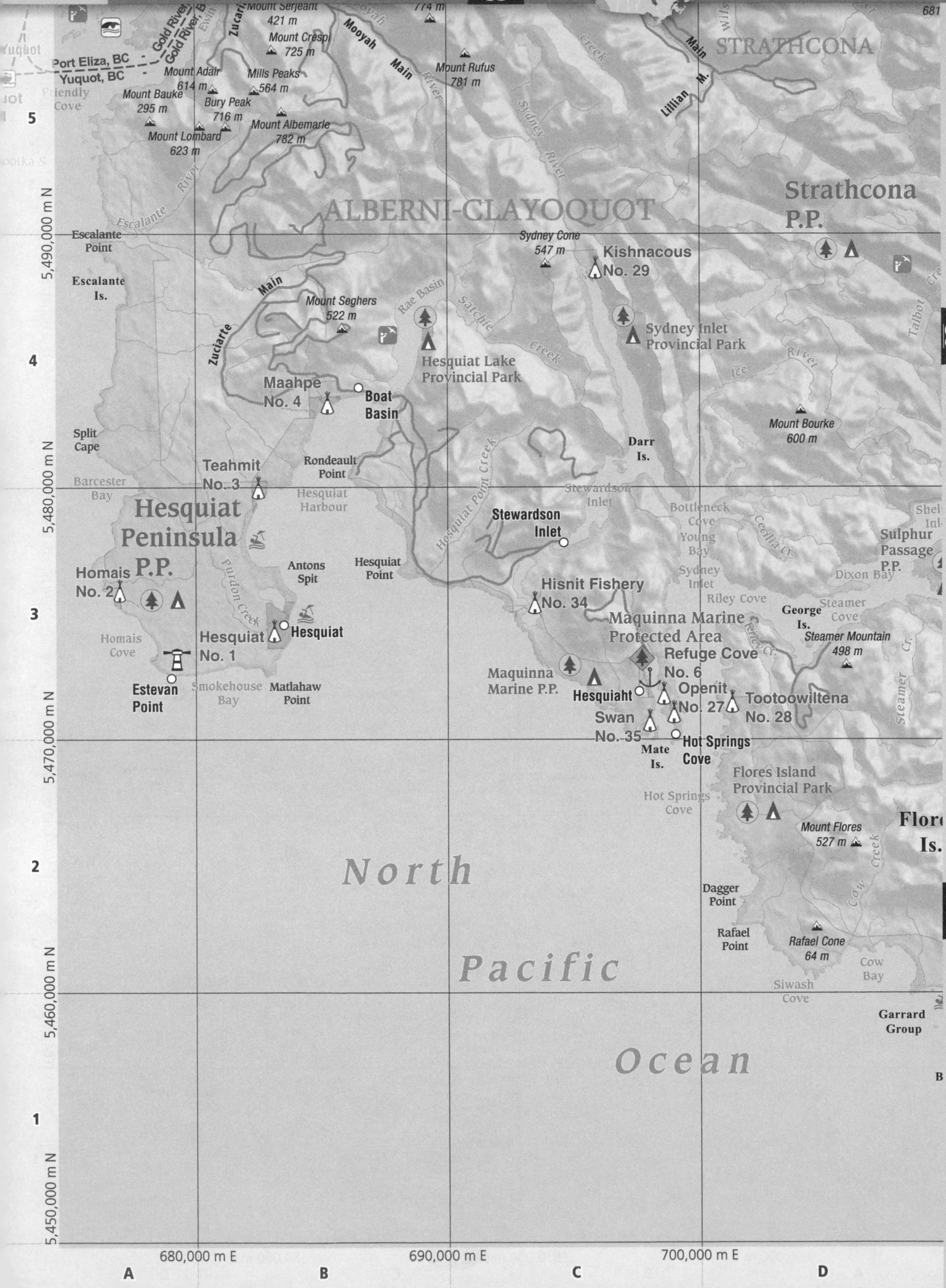

85

STRATHCONA

681

Gold River, B
Gold River, B

Mount Serjeant
421 m
Mount Crespi
725 m

774 m

Mooyah Main

Mount Rufus
781 m

Lillian M.

Mount Adair
614 m
Mills Peaks
564 m

Port Eliza, BC
Yuquot, BC
Friendly
Cove

Mount Bauke
295 m
Bury Peak
716 m

5

Mount Lombard
623 m
Mount Albemarle
782 m

Nootka S.

ALBERNI-CLAYOQUOT

Strathcona
P.P.

5,490,000 m N

Escalante
Point

Escalante
Is.

Sydney Cone
547 m
Kishnacous
No. 29

Mount Seghers
522 m

Rae Basin

Sydney Inlet
Provincial Park

4

Zuciarte   Main

Hesquiat Lake
Provincial Park

Satchie   Creek

Mount Bourke
600 m

Ice   River

Talbot

86

Maahpe
No. 4
Boat
Basin

5,480,000 m N

Split
Cape

Teahmit
No. 3

Rondeault
Point

Darr
Is.

Stewardson
Inlet

Barcester
Bay

Hesquiat
Harbour

Hesquiat Point Creek

Sulphur
Passage
P.P.

Hesquiat
Peninsula
P.P.

Hesquiat
Point

Stewardson
Inlet

Bottleneck
Cove
Young
Bay
Sydney
Inlet

Shel
Inl

Dixon Bay

Homais
No. 2

Antons
Spit

Hisnit Fishery
No. 34

Riley Cove

George
Is.
Steamer
Cove

3

Homais
Cove

Hesquiat
No. 1
Hesquiat

Purdon Creek

Maquinna Marine
Protected Area

Steamer Mountain
498 m

5,470,000 m N

Estevan
Point

Smokehouse
Bay

Matlahaw
Point

Maquinna
Marine P.P.

Hesquiaht

Refuge Cove
No. 6
Openit
No. 27

Tootoowiltena
No. 28

Swan
No. 35
Mate
Is.

Hot Springs
Cove

Flores Island
Provincial Park

Flore
Is.

Hot Springs
Cove

Mount Flores
527 m

N

o

r

t

h

Dagger
Point

2

P

a

c

i

f

i

c

Rafael
Point

Rafael Cone
64 m

Cow
Bay

55

5,460,000 m N

Siwash
Cove

Garrard
Group

O

c

e

a

n

B

1

5,450,000 m N

680,000 m E   690,000 m E   700,000 m E

A   B   C   D

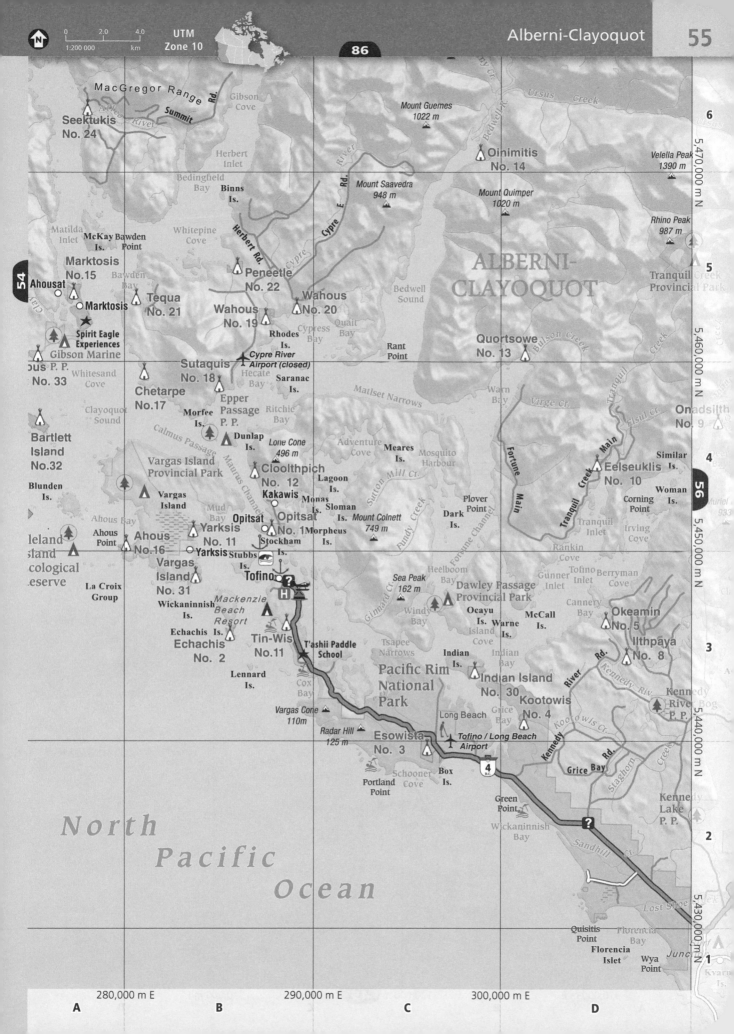

N

0   2.0   4.0   UTM
1:200 000   km   Zone 10

86

6

MacGregor Range

Gibson
Cove

Summit

Seektukis
No. 24

Mount Guemes
1022 m

Oinimitis
No. 14

Velella Peak
1390 m

5,470,000 m N

Herbert
Inlet

Binns
Is.

Bedingfield
Bay

Mount Saavedra
948 m

Mount Quimper
1020 m

Rhino Peak
987 m

Matilda
Inlet

Whitepine
Cove

McKay Bawden
Is. Point

ALBERNI-
CLAYOQUOT

5

Marktosis
No.15

Peneetle
No. 22

Bawden
Bay

Wahous
No. 20

Tranquil Creek
Provincial Park

54

Ahousat

Marktosis

Tequa
No. 21

Wahous
No. 19

Bedwell
Sound

5,460,000 m N

Spirit Eagle
Experiences

Rhodes
Is.

Cypress
Bay

Quait
Bay

Rant
Point

Quortsowe
No. 13

Gibson Marine

Cypre River
Airport (closed)

ous P. P.
No. 33

Whitesand
Cove

Sutaquis
No. 18

Hecate
Bay

Saranac
Is.

Matlset Narrows

Warn
Bay

Virge Cr.

On adsilth
No. 9

Chetarpe
No.17

Morfee
Is.

Epper
Passage
P. P.

Ritchie
Bay

Clayoquot
Sound

Calmus Passage

Dunlap
Is.

Lone Cone
496 m

Adventure
Cove

Meares
Is.

Mosquito
Harbour

Fortune
Main

Similar
Is.

Eelseuklis
No. 10

4

Bartlett
Island
No.32

Vargas Island
Provincial Park

Cloolthpich
No. 12

Lagoon
Is.

Sutton Mill Cr.

Plover
Point

Woman
Is.

Corning
Point

56

5,450,000 m N

Blunden
Is.

Kakawis

Monas
Is.

Sloman
Is.

Mount Colnett
749 m

Dark
Is.

Vargas
Island

Opitsat

Opitsat
No. 1

Morpheus
Is.

leland
sland
cological
eserve

Ahous
Point

Ahous
No.16

Yarksis
No. 11

Stockham
Is.

Fortune Channel

Heelboom
Bay

Tofino
Inlet

Berryman
Cove

La Croix
Group

Vargas
Island
No. 31

Yarksis

Stubbs
Is.

Tofino

Sea Peak
162 m

Gunner
Inlet

Rankin
Cove

Gitmard Cr.

Wickaninnish
Is.

Mackenzie
Beach
Resort

H

Windy
Bay

Dawley Passage
Provincial Park

Ocayu
Is.

McCall
Is.

Cannery
Bay

Okeamin
No. 5

3

Echachis Is.

Tin-Wis
No.11

T'ashii Paddle
School

Tsapee
Narrows

Warne
Is.

Island
Cove

Ilthpaya
No. 8

Echachis
No. 2

Lennard
Is.

Cox
Bay

Pacific Rim
National
Park

Indian
Is.

Indian
Bay

Indian Island
No. 30

Rd.

Kennedy River

Kennedy
Rive
P. P.

Vargas Cone
110m

Kootowis
No. 4

5,440,000 m N

Radar Hill
125 m

Esowista
No. 3

Long Beach

Tofino / Long Beach
Airport

Grice
Bay

Kootowis Cr.

Grice Bay

Staghorn Creek

North

Pacific

Ocean

Portland
Point

Schooner
Cove

Box
Is.

4
B.C.

Green
Point

Wickaninnish
Bay

?

Sandhill Cr.

Kennedy
Lake
P. P.

Lost Shoe

2

5,430,000 m N

Quisitis
Point

Florencia
Bay

Florencia
Islet

Wya
Point

Junc

Kyaru
Is.

1

280,000 m E   290,000 m E   300,000 m E

A   B   C   D

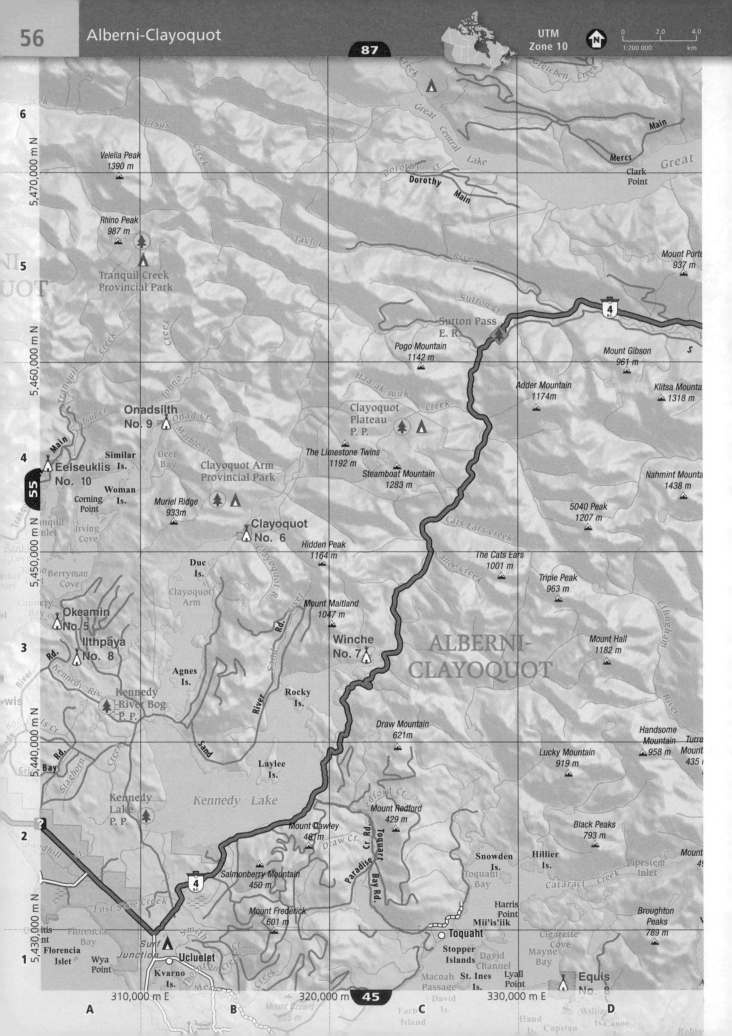

6

Velella Peak
1390 m

Great Central Lake

Dorothy Main

Mercs

Clark Point

Great

Ursus Creek

Rhino Peak
987 m

Taylor

River

Mount Porte
937 m

5,470,000 m N

5

Tranquil Creek
Provincial Park

Sutton Cr.

Sutton Pass
E. R.

4

Mount Gibson
961 m

S

5,460,000 m N

Pogo Mountain
1142 m

Haa-ak-suuk

Creek

Adder Mountain
1174m

Klitsa Mounta
1318 m

Onadsilth
No. 9

Onad Cr.

Clayoquot
Plateau
P. P.

Marble Cr.

Deer Bay

The Limestone Twins
1192 m

Steamboat Mountain
1283 m

Nahmint Mounta
1438 m

4

Similar
Is.

Eelseuklis
No. 10

Clayoquot Arm
Provincial Park

Woman
Is.

Corning
Point

Muriel Ridge
933m

5040 Peak
1207 m

55

Tranqu

Irving
Cove

Clayoquot R.

Clayoquot
No. 6

Hidden Peak
1164 m

Cats Ears Creek

The Cats Ears
1001 m

Triple Peak
963 m

Effingham

5,450,000 m N

Berryman
Cove

Duc
Is.

Clayoquot
Arm

Canoe Creek

Cannery
Bay

Okeamin
No. 5

Mount Maitland
1047 m

Mount Hall
1182 m

3

Ilthpaya
No. 8

Rd.

Kennedy Riv.

Agnes
Is.

Winche
No. 7

ALBERNI-
CLAYOQUOT

Kennedy
River Bog
P. P.

Rocky
Is.

River

5,440,000 m N

Rd.

Bay

Sand

Draw Mountain
621m

Handsome
Mountain

Turre
Mount
435

Laylee
Is.

Lucky Mountain
919 m

958 m

2

Kennedy
Lake
P. P.

Kennedy   Lake

Mount Dawley
461m

Draw Cr.

Mount Redford
429 m

Black Peaks
793 m

Mount
45

Snowden
Is.

Hillier
Is.

Ripestem
Inlet

Mount
4

5,430,000 m N

Lost Shoe Creek

Salmonberry Mountain
450 m

Paradise

Toquart Bay Rd.

Toquahi
Bay

Cataract

Creek

Florencia
Bay

Mount Frederick
601 m

Smith

Harris
Point

Mii'is'iik

Broughton
Peaks
789 m

V

Florencia
Islet

Florencia
Bay

Surf
Junction

Ucluelet

Toquaht

Stopper
Islands

Cigarette
Cove
Mayne
Bay

1

Wya
Point

Kvarno
Is.

Thornton

St. Ines
Is.

Lyall
Point

Equis
No.

Mount Ozzard
625 m

Macoah
Passage

David
Channel

David
Is.

Hand
Is.

Willia
Is.Canoe

310,000 m E

B

320,000 m E

45

C

330,000 m E

D

A

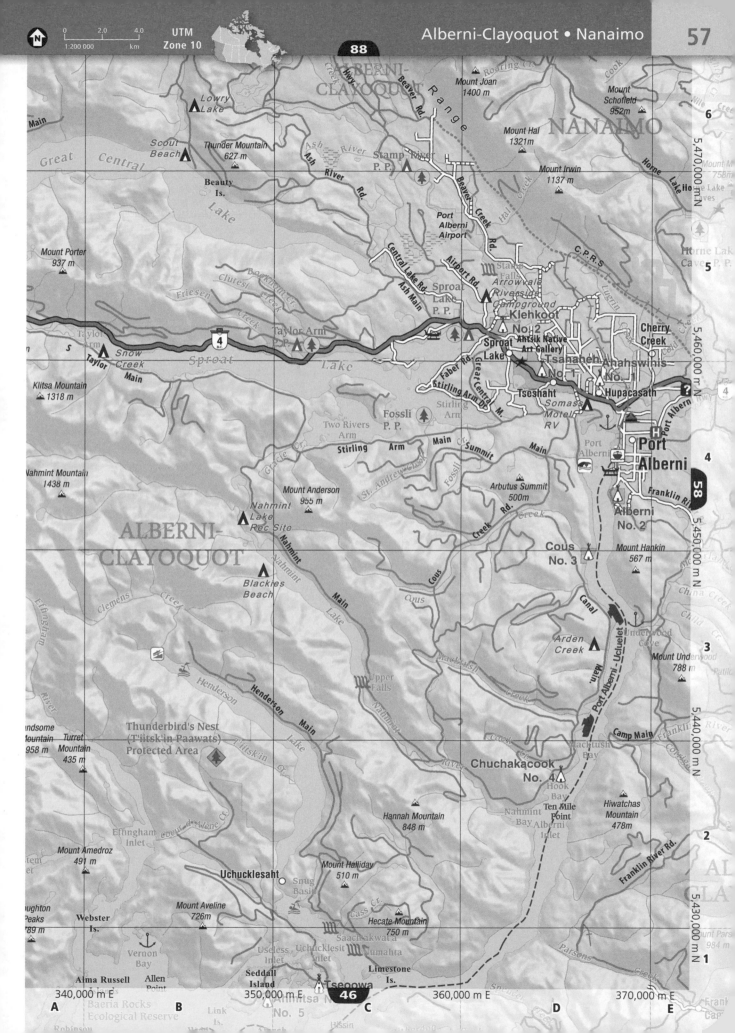

UTM
Zone 10

0   2.0   4.0
1:200 000   km

88

ALBERNI-
CLAYOQUOT

NANAIMO

Mount Joan
1400 m

Mount
Schofield
952m

Mount Hal
1321m

Roaring Cr.

Mount Irwin
1137 m

Horne Lake Caves

Horne Lake Caves
P. P.

6

5,470,000 m N

Lowry
Lake

Scout
Beach

Thunder Mountain
627 m

Beauty
Is.

Great   Central   Lake

Mount Porter
937 m

Stamp River
P. P.

Port Alberni
Airport

Stamp River

Ash   River

Ash   River   Rd.

Beaver Creek   Rd.

C.P.R.S

Stokes
Falls

Arrowvale
Riverside
Campground

Sproat
Lake
P. P.

Klehkoot
No. 2

Sproat
Lake

Ahtsik Native
Art Gallery

Tsahaheh
No. 1

Cherry
Creek

Ahahswinis
No. 1

Hupacasath

5,460,000 m N

5

Friesen   Cr.

Clutesi

Bookham Cr.

Central Lake Rd.

Ash Main

Taylor Arm
P. P.

Taylor Arm

Taylor

Snow
Creek

Main

4
B.C.

Sproat   Lake

Faber Rd.

Stirling Arm Dr.

Great Central   M.

Tseshaht
No. 1

Somass
Motel
RV

Port Alberni

?

**Port
Alberni**

H

Klitsa Mountain
1318 m

Fossli
P. P.

Stirling
Arm

Main   Cr.

Summit

Main

Port
Alberni

4

Nahmint Mountain
1438 m

Two Rivers
Arm

Stirling   Arm

Mount Anderson
955 m

St. Andrew Creek

Gracie   Cr.

Fossli   Creek

Arbutus Summit
500m

Creek   Rd.

Cous   Creek

Creek

Franklin Riv

58

Alberni
No. 2

Mount Hankin
567 m

5,450,000 m N

3

ALBERNI-
CLAYOQUOT

Nahmint
Lake
Rec Site

Blackies
Beach

Clemens   Creek

Nahmint

Main

Nahmint   Lake

Cous

Cous

Blackjack Cr.

Cous   Creek

Cous
No. 3

Arden
Creek

Canal

Underwood
Cove

Mount Underwood
788 m

China   Creek

Child   Cr.

Effingham   River

Henderson

Henderson   Main

Nahmint

Upper
Falls

Port Alberni-Ucluelet   Main

Camp Main

Franklin

3

Handsome
Mountain
958 m

Turret
Mountain
435 m

Thunderbird's Nest
(T'iitsk'in Paawats)
Protected Area

T'iitskin Cr.

coeur d'Alene   Cr.

Hannah Mountain
848 m

Macktush
Bay

Chuchakacook
No. 4

Hook
Bay

Nahmint
Bay   Alberni
Inlet

Ten Mile
Point

Hiwatchas
Mountain
478m

Franklin River Rd.

Consu ga

Franklin   River

2

Mount Amedroz
491 m

Effingham   Inlet

Uchucklesaht

Snug
Basin

Mount Halliday
510 m

Cass   Cr.

AL
CLA

Broughton
Peaks
789 m

Webster
Is.

Mount Aveline
726m

Hecate Mountain
750 m

Mount Parso
984 m

1

5,430,000 m N

Alma Russell

Allen
Point

Vernon
Bay

Seddall
Island

Uchucklesit
Inlet

Tseqowa

Limestone
Is.

Parsons   Creek

Frank
Cap

46

Baeria Rocks
Ecological Reserve

Link
Is.

Nahmitsa I
No. 5

Robinson

NANAIMO

Mount
Schofield
952m

Nile   Creek

Main

19
B.C.

Nile   Cr.

Qualicum
Bay

Shalom RV
Park

Stevens

Passage

Beach - Lasqueti Island

NANAIMO

Qualicum
Bay

Qualicum

Qualicum

Dunsmuir

Creek

Mount Mark
758m

Horne Lake

Hunts   Caves

Horne Lake
Caves

Horne   Lake   Rd.

Fish   Hatchery Rd.

Arrowsmith
Country
Club

19A
B.C.

Dashwood

Riverside Resort
Motel

Eaglecrest

Milner Gardens
& Woodland

C.P.R.S

Lugrin

Cook

Thames

Horne   Lake

Shady Ln.

Qualicum

Cr.

Spider Lake
P. P.

Kinkade

Meadowood Way

Little

Qualicum

Cr.

? Qualicum
Beach

Claymore Rd. W

Qualicum
Beach

19A
B.C.

Qualicum Beach
Airport

Pheasant
Glen

Morningstar

Park

Horne Lake
Caves P. P.

Mount Horne
744 m

Mount Wesley
760 m

Wesley   Ridge

4
B.C.

Little
Qualicum
Falls

Lockwood

Whisky

Coombs
Country
Campground

19
B.C.

French

Cherry
Creek

Cherry
Creek

C.P.R.S

Cameron   Lake

Macmillan
P. P.

Cameron

Little Qualicum
Falls P. P.

Whisky
Creek

Whiskey
Creek
Campground

Hilliers

Pratt Rd.

Grafton   Rd.

4A
B.C.

Coombs

Errington

Brrington

Tsahaheh
No.

Ahahswinis
No.

Hupacasath

?

4
B.C.

Port Alberni Hwy

Cameron   River   Rd.

Wesley

Creek

Mount Cokely
1460 m

Lockwood   Main

NANAIMO

Fisher   Rd.

Swane

Englishman
River Falls
P. P.

Port
Alberni

Port
Alberni

Franklin River Rd.

Stokes

Yellows

Cr.

Cameron

River

Copy Cr.

Main

Rd.

Mount Arrowsmith
1499 m

Englishman   River   Main

Alberni
No. 2

Mount Hankin
567 m

McFarland Cr.

McLaughlin   Ridge

McQuillanCr.

Dehwiuz

River

Marshall Cr.

57

Cous
No. 3

China   Creek

Child Cr.

Arden
Cr.

Mount Underwood
788 m

Patlicant Mountain
1027 m

Underwood
Cove

Douglas Peak
1281 m

McKinlay Peak
1066 m

Mount McQuillan
1422 m

Father &
Son Lake

Mount Moriarty
1163 m

Labour Day
Lake

Rockyrun Cr.

Port Alberni - Ucluelet

Canal

Camp Main

Franklin   River

Museum

Cowichan Creek

Creek

Limestone Mountain
1169 m

Green
Creek

Ritters Cr.

Hiwatchas
Mountain
478m

Franklin   River   Rd.

ALBERNI-
CLAYOQUOT

Mount Spencer
1127 m

COWICHAN
VALLEY

Sadie

Green
Mountain
1284

Rush

Mount Olsen
919 m

Mount Hooper
1291 m

Mount Parsons
984 m

Logan Peak
855 m

Mount Grey
1177 m

5,470,000 m N

5,460,000 m N

5,450,000 m N

5,440,000 m N

5,430,000 m N

Heather Mountain

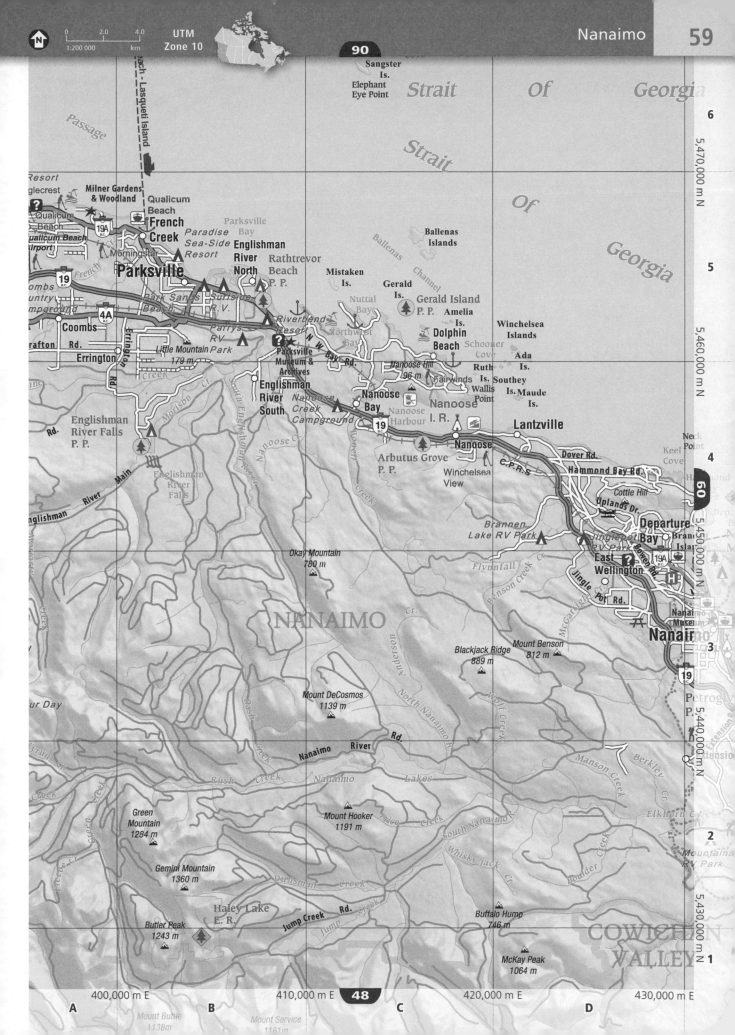

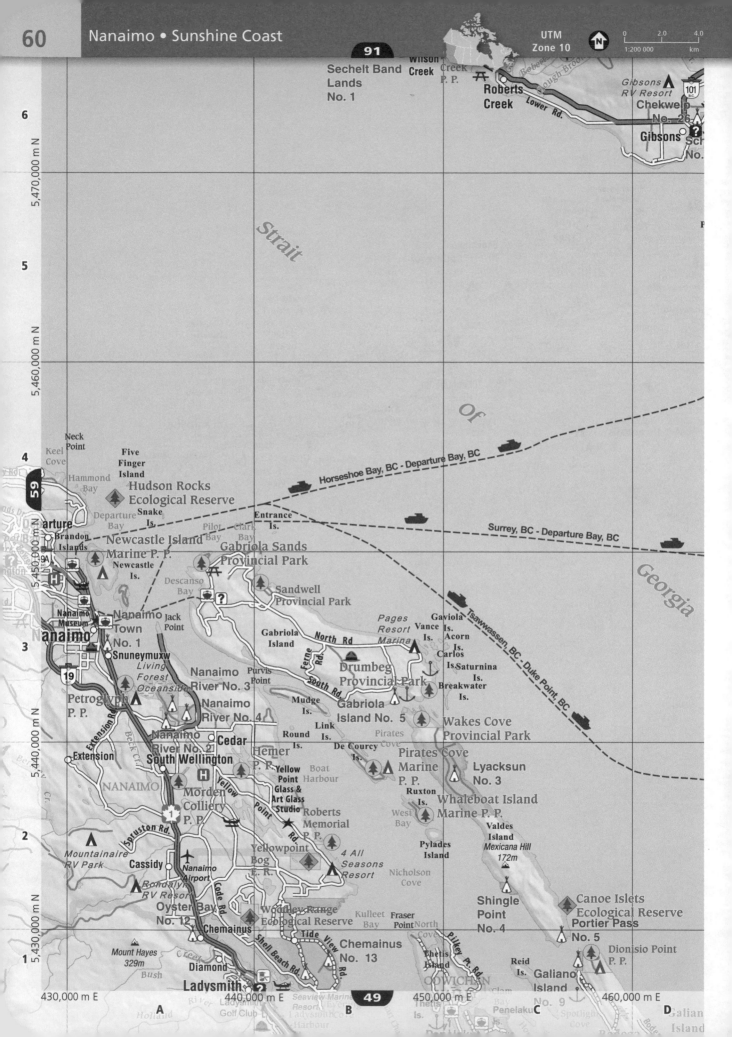

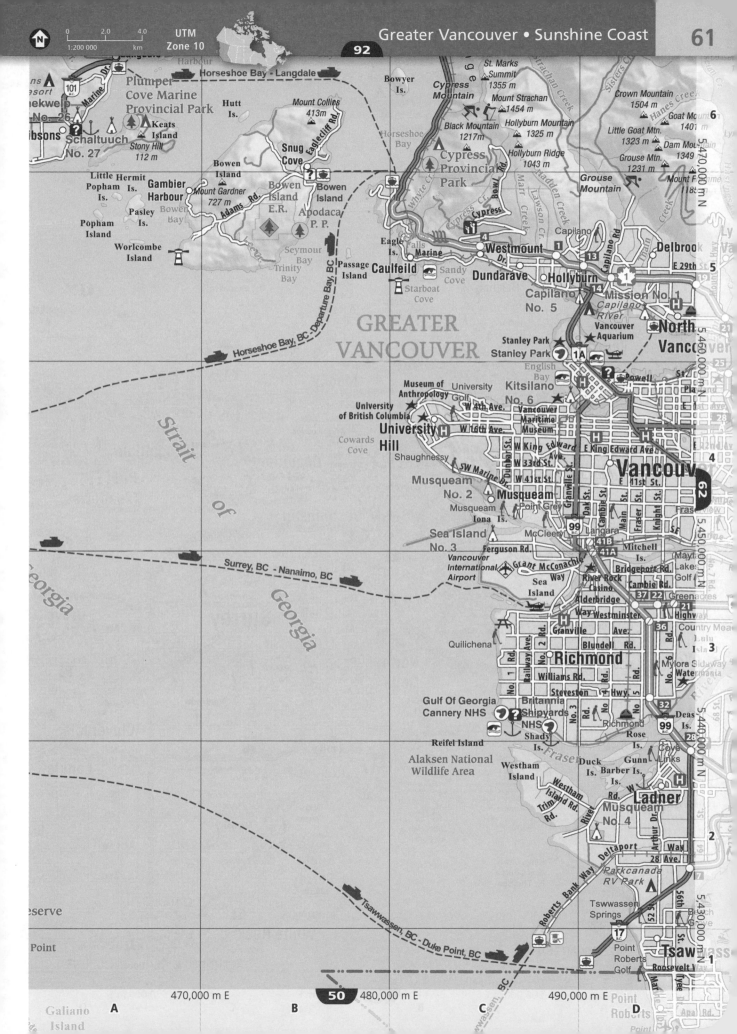

N

0	2.0	4.0

1:200 000   km

UTM
Zone 10

92

Horseshoe Bay - Langdale

Plumper
Cove Marine
Provincial Park

101

Gibsons

Schaltuuch
No. 27

Keats
Island

Stony Hill
112 m

Hutt
Is.

Bowyer
Is.

Mount Collins
413m

Snug
Cove

Little Hermit
Popham Is.
Is.

Gambier
Harbour

Mount Gardner
727 m

Bowen
Island

Bowen
Bay

Pasley
Is.

Popham
Island

Bowen
Island
E.R.

Bowen
Island

Apodaca
P.P.

Worlcombe
Island

Seymour
Bay

Trinity
Bay

Passage
Island

Caulfeild

Starboat
Cove

Eagle
Is.

Marine

Westmount

Dundarave

Sandy
Cove

St. Marks

Cypress
Mountain

Summit
1355 m

Mount Strachan
1454 m

Black Mountain
1217m

Hollyburn Mountain
1325 m

Cypress

Provincial
Park

Hollyburn Ridge
1043 m

Cypress

Falls

Hollyburn

Capilano

Crown Mountain
1504 m

Little Goat Mtn.
1323 m

Goat Mount
1401

Dam Mou
1349

Grouse Mtn.
1231 m

Grouse
Mountain

Mount F
1185

Delbrook

E 29th

Capilano
No. 5

Mission No. 1

Capilano
River

North
Vanco

GREATER
VANCOUVER

Horseshoe Bay, BC

Museum of
Anthropology

University
Golf

Univerity
of British Columbia

University
Hill

Cowards
Cove

Shaughnessy

Strait

of

Georgia

Surrey, BC - Nanaimo, BC

Georgia

Stanley Park
Stanley Park

English
Bay

Powell

Kitsilano
No. 6

Vancouver
Maritime
Museum

W 4th Ave.

W 10th Ave.

Vancouver
Aquarium

W King Edward

E King Edward Ave

W 33rd St.

W 41st St.

SW Marine Dr.

Musqueam
No. 2

Musqueam

Point Grey

Musqueam
Iona Is.

Sea Island
No. 3

Ferguson Rd.

Vancouver
International
Airport

Sea
Island

Grant McConachie Way

Vancouv

E 11th St.

Granville St.

Oak St.

Cambie St.

Main St.

Fraser St.

Knight St.

Langara

Mitchell
Is.

River Rock
Casino

Bridgeport Rd.

Cambie Rd.

Greenacres

Quilichena

Railway Ave.

No. 2 Rd.

Granville Ave.

Blundell Rd.

Richmond

Williams Rd.

Steveston

Gulf Of Georgia
Cannery NHS

Britannia
Shipyards

NHS

No. 1 Rd.

No. 3 Rd.

No. 4 Rd.

No. 5 Rd.

Hwy.

Westminster

Alderbridge
Way

Country Mea
Lulu
Isla

Mylora Sidaway
Watermania

Richmond
Rose
Is.

Shady
Is.

Deas
Is.

Reifel Island

Alaksen National
Wildlife Area

Westham
Island

Westham
Island Rd.

Trim
Rd.

Duck
Is.

Gunn
Is.

Barber
Is.

Cove
Links

Ladner

Musqueam
No. 4

Fraser River

Deltaport Way

28 Ave.

Parkcanada
RV Park

Tsawwassen
Springs

Point
Roberts
Golf

Tsaw

Roosevelt W

Arthur Dr.

56th St.

17

52 St.

Galiano
Island

Point

reserve

Point

Tsawwassen, BC - Duke Point, BC

470,000 m E

50

480,000 m E

490,000 m E

Point
Roberts

A   B   C   D

5,470,000 m N

5,460,000 m N

5,450,000 m N

5,440,000 m N

5,430,000 m N

6

5

4

3

2

1

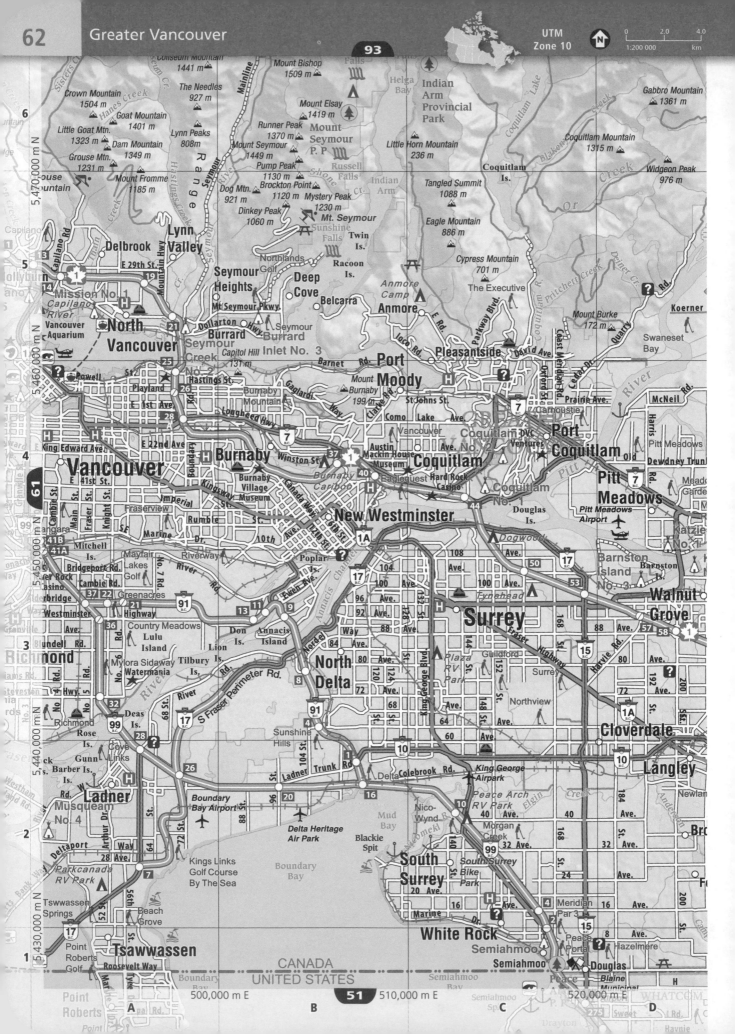

93

Coliseum Mountain
1441 m
The Needles
927 m

Crown Mountain
1504 m

Mount Bishop
1509 m

Mount Elsay
1419 m

Goat Mountain
1401 m

Little Goat Mtn.
1323 m

Dam Mountain
1349 m

Lynn Peaks
808 m

Runner Peak
1370 m

Mount Seymour
1449 m

Grouse Mtn.
1231 m

Mount Fromme
1185 m

Pump Peak
1130 m

Brockton Point

Dog Mtn.
921 m

Mystery Peak
1230 m

Dinkey Peak
1060 m

Mt. Seymour

Lynn
Valley

Delbrook

E 29th St.

Seymour
Heights

Deep
Cove

Belcarra

Mt Seymour Pkwy.

Dollarton

Mission No. 1

Capilano
River

Vancouver
Aquarium

North
Vancouver

Burrard

Seymour
Creek

Capitol Hill

Seymour
Burrard
Inlet No. 3

Barnet   Rd.

Hastings St.

Gaglardi

Mount
Burnaby
199 m

Mount
Seymour
P.P.

Russell
Falls

Indian
Arm

Twin
Is.

Racoon
Is.

Indian
Arm
Provincial
Park

Helga
Bay

Tangled Summit
1088 m

Anmore
Camp

Anmore

Pleasantside

Port
Moody

St Johns St.

Como Lake   Ave.

Eagle Mountain
886 m

Cypress Mountain
701 m

The Executive

Mount Burke
172 m

Coquitlam
Is.

Gabbro Mountain
1361 m

Coquitlam Mountain
1315 m

Widgeon Peak
976 m

Swaneset
Bay

Koerner

Prairie Ave.

McNeil

Harris

Pitt Meadows

Dewdney Trun

Vancouver
Golf

Coquitlam   DVC
Ventures

Port
Coquitlam

Coquitlam

Austin
Mackin House
Museum

Hard Rock
Casino

Coquitlam
No. 1

Douglas
Is.

Pitt Meadows
Airport

Pitt
Meadows

Meado
Garde

Katzie
No. 1

Vancouver

Burnaby

Burnaby
Mountain

King Edward Ave.

E 22nd Ave.

E 41st St.

Winston St.

Burnaby
Village
Museum

Lougheed Hwy.

New Westminster

Cariboo

Eaglequest

Barnston
Island

Barnston
Island
No. 3

Walnut
Grove

Imperial

Fraserview

Rumble

10th

Poplar
Is.

104

100

96

92

88

84

80

Surrey

Guildford

Surrey

Northview

Cloverdale

Langley

Mitchell
Is.

Mayfair
Lakes
Golf

River

Bridgeport Rd.

Cambie Rd.

Greenacres

Don
Is.

Lion
Is.

Annacis
Island

Tilbury
Is.

North
Delta

108

100

50

53

Fynehead

168

15

Harvie   Rd.

88

Ave.

57

58

192

72

200

Richmond

Westminster

Country Meadows

Lulu
Island

Mylora Sidaway

Watermania

Country

S Fraser Perimeter Rd.

72

68

64

60

144

St.

152
St.

148
St.

Plaza
RV
Park

184

Blundell Rd.

Richmond
Rose
Is.

Gunn
Is.

Barber Is.
Is.

Deas
Is.

Sunshine
Hills

120

Ladner Trunk Rd.

Delta

Colebrook   Rd.

King George
Airpark

Peace Arch
RV Park

Elgin

40

1A

Cloverdale

Langley

Newlan

Ladner

Musqueam
No. 4

Boundary
Bay Airport

Delta Heritage
Air Park

Blackie
Spit

Mud
Bay

Nico-
Wynd

Morgan
Creek

99

32 Ave.

140

32   Ave.

168

Br

Fo

Deltaport

Parkcanada
RV Park

Kings Links
Golf Course
By The Sea

Boundary
Bay

South
Surrey

South Surrey
Bike
Park

20 Ave.

24

Tsawwassen
Springs

Beach
Grove

White Rock

Semiahmoo

Marine

16

Meridian
Par 3

Peace
Portal

Hazelmere

8   Ave.

Point
Roberts
Golf

Roosevelt Way

Tsawwassen

CANADA
UNITED STATES

Boundary
Bay

Semiahmoo

Semiahmoo

Douglas

Blaine
Municipal

WHATCOM

Point
Roberts

500,000 m E

51   510,000 m E

520,000 m E

A   B   C   D

61

99

41B
41A

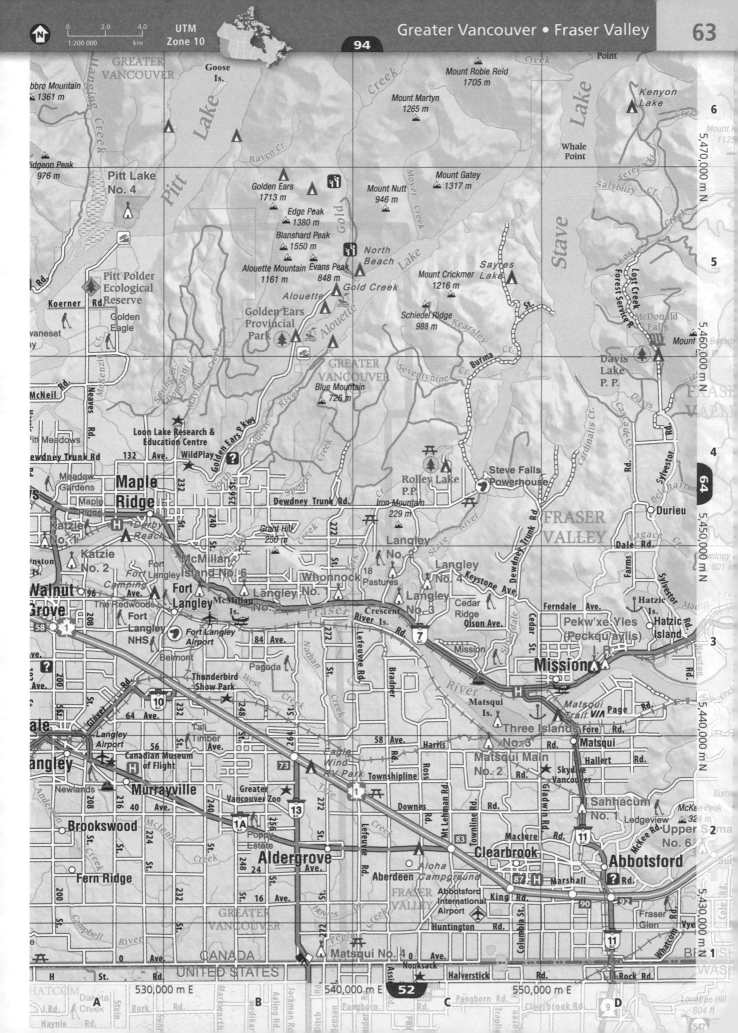

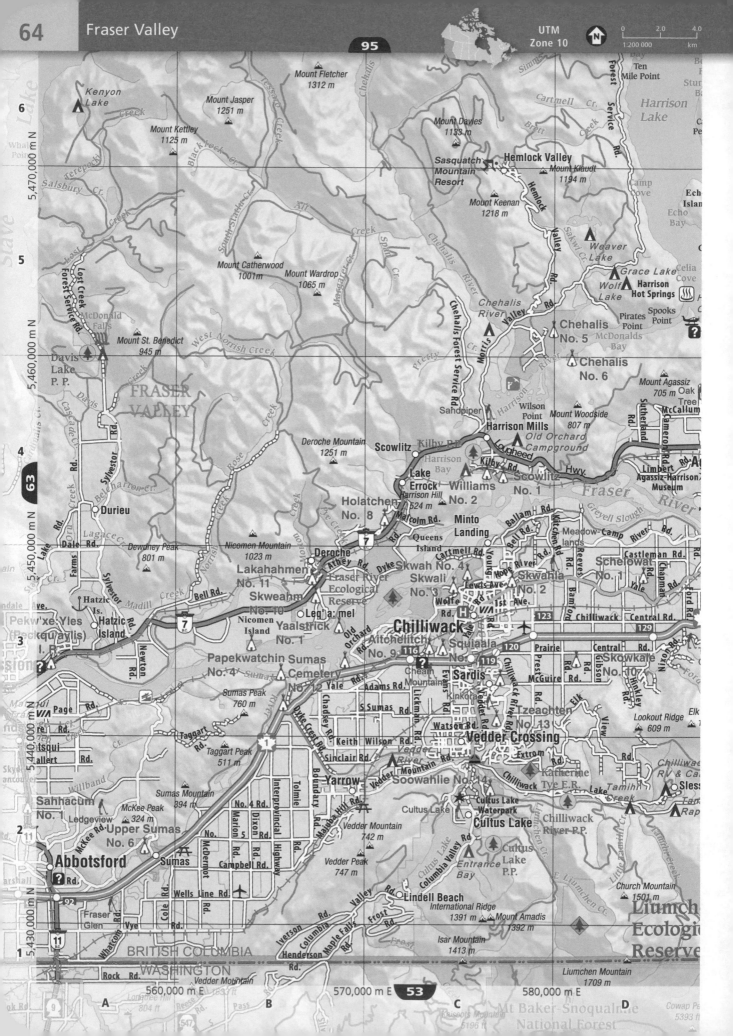

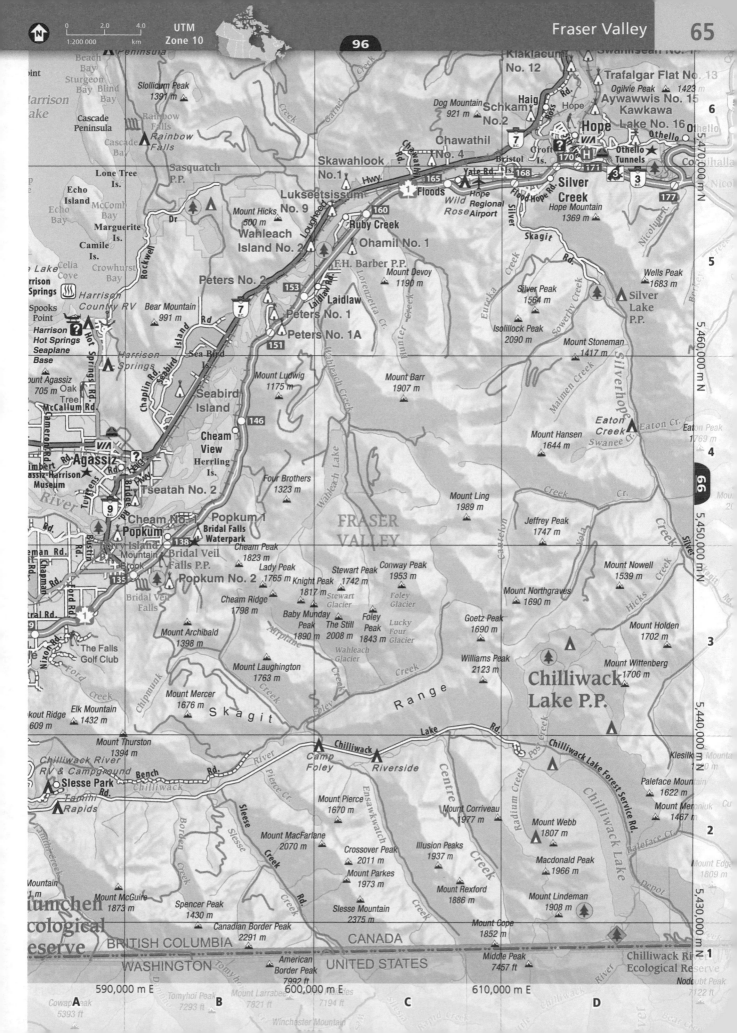

UTM
Zone 10

1:200 000

96

7

N

590,000 m E

600,000 m E

610,000 m E

A

B

C

D

1

2

3

4

5

6

5,470,000 m N

5,460,000 m N

5,450,000 m N

5,440,000 m N

5,430,000 m N

66

Beach
Bay

Sturgeon
Bay

Blind
Bay

Harrison
Lake

point

Peninsula

Slollicum Peak
1391 m

Cascade
Peninsula

Rainbow
Falls

Rainbow
Falls

Cascade
Bay

Lone Tree
Is.

Sasquatch
P.P.

Echo
Island

McComb
Bay

Marguerite
Is.

Camile
Is.

Crowhurst
Bay

Celia
Cove

Lake

Harrison
Springs

Spooks
Point

Harrison
Hot Springs
Seaplane
Base

Harrison
County RV

Harrison
Springs

Echo
Bay

Mount Agassiz
705 m

Oak
Tree
McCallum

Rd.

Cameron

Agassiz-Harrison
Museum

Agassiz

VIA

River

Tseatah No. 2

Cheam No. 1

Popkum

Cherry Island

Mountain

Bridal Falls
Waterpark

Popkum No. 2

Bridal Veil
Falls

Bridal Veil
Falls P.P.

Cheam
View

Herrling
Is.

Seabird
Island

Sea Bird
Is.

Peters No. 1A

Peters No. 1

Peters No. 2

Laidlaw

Wahleach
Island No. 2

Lukseetsissum
No. 9

Mount Hicks
500 m

Skawahlook
No. 1

Ruby Creek

Ohamil No. 1

F.H. Barber P.P.

Floods

Chawathil
No. 4

Skawam
No. 2

Dog Mountain
921 m

Klaklacum
No. 12

Trafalgar Flat No. 13

Ogilvie Peak   1423 m

Aywawwis No. 15

Kawkawa
Lake No. 16

Hope

Haig

Bristol
Is.

Crofts
Is.

Othello
Tunnels

Silver
Creek

Hope Mountain
1369 m

Hope
Regional
Airport

Wild
Rose

Mount Devoy
1190 m

Mount Barr
1907 m

Silver Peak
1564 m

Wells Peak
1683 m

Silver
Lake
P.P.

Isolillock Peak
2090 m

Mount Stoneman
1417 m

Mount Hansen
1644 m

Eaton
Creek

Swanee

Eaton Peak
1769 m

Eaton Cr.

Mount Ludwig
1175 m

Cheam
Peak
1823 m

Lady Peak
1765 m

Knight Peak
1817 m

Stewart Peak
1742 m

Conway Peak
1953 m

Mount Ling
1989 m

Jeffrey Peak
1747 m

Mount Nowell
1539 m

Mount Northgraves
1690 m

Goetz Peak
1690 m

Mount Holden
1702 m

Williams Peak
2123 m

Mount Wittenberg
1706 m

Chilliwack
Lake P.P.

Stewart
Glacier

Foley
Glacier

Lucky
Four
Glacier

Baby Munday
Peak
1890 m

The Still
2008 m

Foley
Peak
1843 m

Wahleach
Glacier

Cheam Ridge
1798 m

Mount Archibald
1398 m

Mount Laughington
1763 m

Mount Mercer
1676 m

Elk Mountain
1432 m

Lookout Ridge
609 m

The Falls
Golf Club

Mount Thurston
1394 m

Chilliwack River
RV & Campground

Slesse Park

Tamihi
Rapids

Bench

Camp
Foley

Chilliwack

Riverside

Mount Pierce
1670 m

Mount MacFarlane
2070 m

Crossover Peak
2011 m

Mount Parkes
1973 m

Slesse Mountain
2375 m

Spencer Peak
1430 m

Canadian Border Peak
2291 m

American
Border Peak
7992 ft

Illusion Peaks
1937 m

Mount Corriveau
1977 m

Mount Webb
1807 m

Macdonald Peak
1966 m

Mount Rexford
1886 m

Mount Lindeman
1908 m

Mount Cope
1852 m

Middle Peak
7457 ft

Paleface Mountain
1622 m

Mount Meroniuk
1467 m

Klesilkwa

Chilliwack Lake

Chilliwack Lake Forest Service Rd.

Chilliwack River
Ecological Reserve

Nodoubt Peak

Skagit   Range

FRASER
VALLEY

Four Brothers
1323 m

McGuire
1873 m

Sumas Mountain
Ecological
Reserve

BRITISH COLUMBIA

WASHINGTON

CANADA

UNITED STATES

Tomyhoi Peak
7293 ft

Mount Larrabee
7821 ft

7194 ft

Cowap Peak
5393 ft

7122 ft

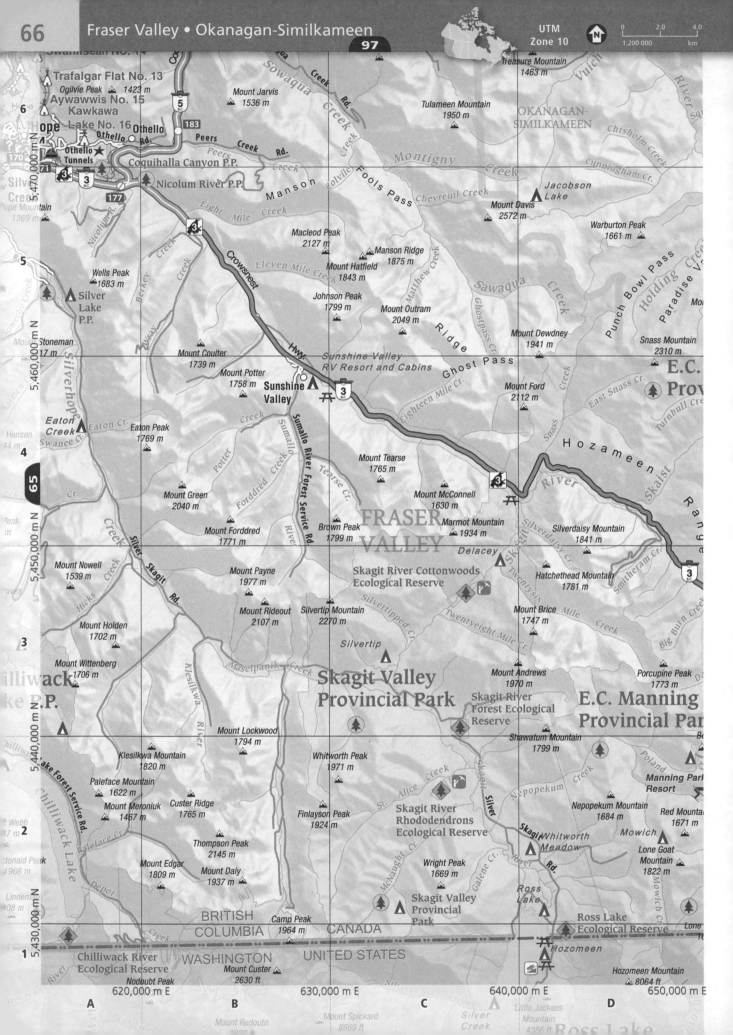

Treasure Mountain
1463 m

Swamsean No. 14

Trafalgar Flat No. 13
Ogilvie Peak   1423 m
Aywawwis No. 15
Kawkawa
Lake No. 16   Othello
Hope   Othello
Othello   Rd.
Othello
Tunnels

Mount Jarvis
1536 m

Tulameen Mountain
1950 m

OKANAGAN-
SIMILKAMEEN

Peers   Creek
Peers   Creek   Rd.
Coquihalla Canyon P.P.

Nicolum River P.P.

Manson   Creek

Eight   Mile   Creek

Crowsnest

Colville   Creek

Fools Pass

Montigny   Creek

Chevreuil Creek

Mount Davis
2572 m

Jacobson
Lake

Warburton Peak
1661 m

Silver
Creek
Hope Mountain
1369 m

Wells Peak
1683 m

Silver
Lake
P.P.

Mount
Stoneman
17 m

Macleod Peak
2127 m

Manson Ridge
1875 m

Mount Hatfield
1843 m

Eleven Mile Creek

Johnson Peak
1799 m

Mount Outram
2049 m

Matthew Creek

Ghospass Cr.

Sawaqua   Creek

Ridge

Mount Dewdney
1941 m

Punch Bowl Pass

Holding Creek

Paradise V

Snass Mountain
2310 m

E.C.
Prov

Eaton
Creek

Hansen
14 m

Swanee   Cr.

Eaton Cr.

Mount Coulter
1739 m

Mount Potter
1758 m

Sunshine
Valley

Sunshine Valley
RV Resort and Cabins

Ghost Pass

Eighteen Mile Cr.

Mount Ford
2112 m

East Snass Cr.

Turnbull Cre

Eaton Peak
1769 m

Potter   Creek

Forddred   Creek

Sumallo   River   Forest   Service   Rd.

Sumallo   River

Tearse Cr.

Mount Tearse
1765 m

Hozameen   River

Skaist   Range

Peak
m

Mount Green
2040 m

Mount Forddred
1771 m

Brown Peak
1799 m

Mount McConnell
1630 m

Marmot Mountain
1934 m

Silverdaisy Mountain
1841 m

FRASER
VALLEY

65

Mount Nowell
1539 m

Silver   Creek

Skagit   Rd.

Mount Payne
1977 m

Skagit River Cottonwoods
Ecological Reserve

Delacey

Silvertipped Cr.

Twentysix

Hatchethead Mountain
1781 m

Silverdaisy Cr.

Mount Brice
1747 m

aves

Hicks   Creek

Mount Holden
1702 m

Mount Rideout
2107 m

Silvertip Mountain
2270 m

Silvertipped Cr.

Twentyeight Mile Cr.

Skagit   River

Big Burn Creek

Mount Wittenberg
1706 m

Klesilkwa   River

Maselpanik   Creek

Silvertip

Skagit Valley
Provincial Park

Mount Andrews
1970 m

Skagit River
Forest Ecological
Reserve

E.C. Manning
Provincial Par

Porcupine Peak
1773 m

illiwack
ke P.P.

Mount Lockwood
1794 m

Whitworth Peak
1971 m

Shawatum Mountain
1799 m

Webb
7 m

Chilliwack   Lake   Forest   Service   Rd.

Klesilkwa Mountain
1820 m

Paleface Mountain
1622 m

Paleface Cr.

Mount Meroniuk
1467 m

Custer Ridge
1765 m

St. Alice   Creek

Skagit River
Rhododendrons
Ecological Reserve

Finlayson Peak
1924 m

Skagit   Silver

Nepopekum   Creek

Manning Park
Resort

Nepopekum Mountain
1684 m

Red Mounta
1671 m

donald Peak
1966 m

Thompson Peak
2145 m

Mount Edgar
1809 m

Mount Daly
1937 m

McNaught   Cr.

Wright Peak
1669 m

Skagit   River

Galene Cr.

Whitworth
Meadow

Mowich

Lone Goat
Mountain
1822 m

Lindeman
08 m

Depot   Creek

Camp Peak
1964 m

BRITISH
COLUMBIA

CANADA

Skagit Valley
Provincial
Park

Ross
Lake

Ross Lake
Ecological Reserve

Lone

Chilliwack River
Ecological Reserve

WASHINGTON

UNITED STATES

Hozomeen

Hozomeen Mountain
8064 ft

Nodoubt Peak

Mount Custer
2630 ft

Mount Redoubt

Mount Spickard
8969 ft

Silver   Creek

Little Jackass
Mountain
4336 ft

Ross Lake

620,000 m E   630,000 m E   640,000 m E   650,000 m E
A   B   C   D
5,470,000 m N   5,460,000 m N   5,450,000 m N   5,440,000 m N   5,430,000 m N
6   5   4   3   2   1

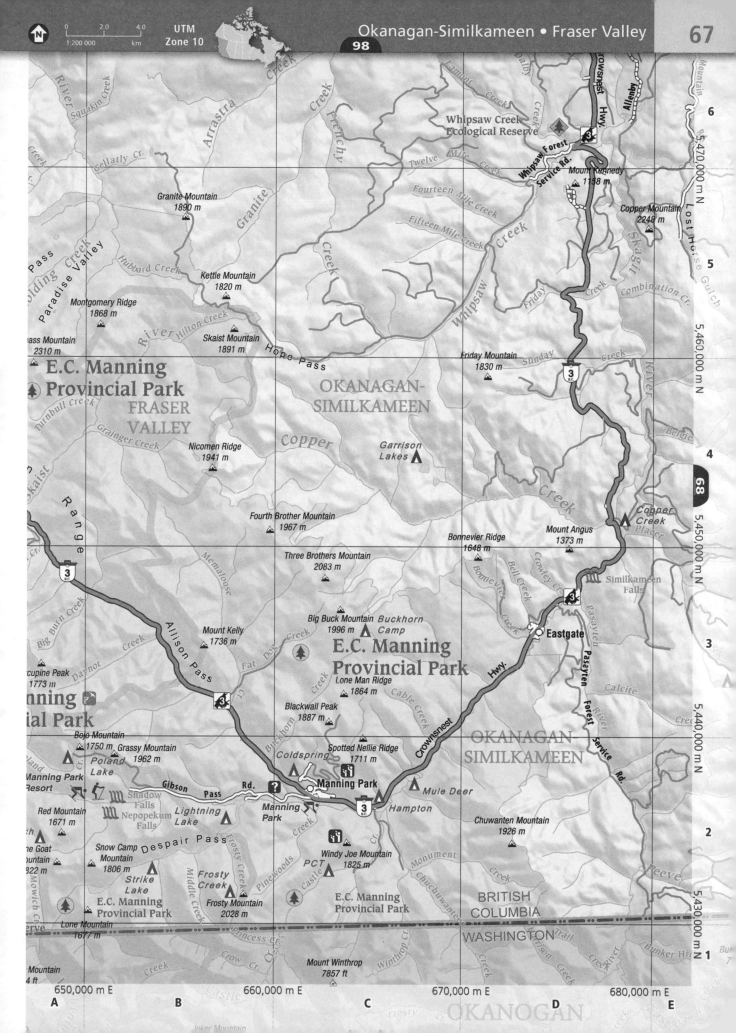

0   2.0   4.0
km

650,000 m E
660,000 m E
670,000 m E
680,000 m E

5,470,000 m N
5,460,000 m N
5,450,000 m N
5,440,000 m N
5,430,000 m N

A   B   C   D   E

6
5
4
3
2
1

Squakin Creek
Arrastra Creek
Creek
Frenchy Creek
Lamont Creek
Dalby
Crowsnest Hwy
Allenby
Mountain

Whipsaw Creek
Ecological Reserve

Whipsaw Forest
Service Rd.

Mount Kennedy
1158 m

Copper Mountain
2248 m

Lost Horse Gulch

River
Gellatly Cr.

Granite Mountain
1890 m

Granite Creek

Twelve Mile Creek

Fourteen Mile Creek

Fifteen Mile Creek

Whipsaw Creek

Skagit

Golding Pass
Paradise Valley

Hubbard Creek

Kettle Mountain
1820 m

Friday Creek

Combination Cr.

Nass Mountain
2310 m

River
Hilton Creek

Montgomery Ridge
1868 m

Skaist Mountain
1891 m

Hope Pass

Friday Mountain
1830 m

Sunday Creek

3
B.C.

Bergie

E.C. Manning
Provincial Park

FRASER
VALLEY

Turnbull Creek

Grainger Creek

Nicomen Ridge
1941 m

OKANAGAN-
SIMILKAMEEN

Copper

Garrison
Lakes

Creek

68

Skaist Range

Fourth Brother Mountain
1967 m

Bonnevier Ridge
1648 m

Mount Angus
1373 m

Copper
Creek
Placer

3
B.C.

Memaloose Creek

Three Brothers Mountain
2083 m

Bonnevier Creek

Bell Creek

Crowley Cr.

Similkameen
Falls

3
B.C.

Porcupine Peak
1773 m

Daynor Creek

Allison Pass

Mount Kelly
1736 m

Fat Dog Creek

Big Buck Mountain
1996 m

Buckhorn
Camp

E.C. Manning
Provincial Park

Pasayten

Similkameen Falls

Eastgate

Big Burn Creek

Buckhorn Creek

Cable Creek

Lone Man Ridge
1864 m

Calcite Creek

Manning
ial Park

Bojo Mountain
1750 m

Grassy Mountain
1962 m

Blackwall Peak
1887 m

Spotted Nellie Ridge
1711 m

Crowsnest Hwy.

OKANAGAN
SIMILKAMEEN

Pasayten River

Poland
Lake

Coldspring

Forest

Manning Park
Resort

Gibson Pass Rd.

?

Manning Park

Mule Deer

Service Rd.

Red Mountain
1671 m

Shadow
Falls
Nepopekum
Falls

Lightning
Lake

Manning
Park

Hampton

3
B.C.

Chuwanten Mountain
1926 m

ne Goat
ountain
922 m

Snow Camp
Mountain
1806 m

Despair Pass

Strike
Lake

Frosty Creek

Middle Creek

Frosty Creek

Pinewoods

Castle Creek

Windy Joe Mountain
1825 m

PCT

Monument Creek

chuchuwanten Creek

Creek

Reeve

Mowich Creek

E.C. Manning
Provincial Park

Frosty Mountain
2028 m

E.C. Manning
Provincial Park

BRITISH
COLUMBIA

Lone Mountain
1677 m

Princess Cr.

Crow Cr.

Castle Cr.

WASHINGTON

Trail

Bunker Hill

Mountain
4 ft

Mount Winthrop
7857 ft

Winthrop Creek

Frosty Cr.

OKANOGAN

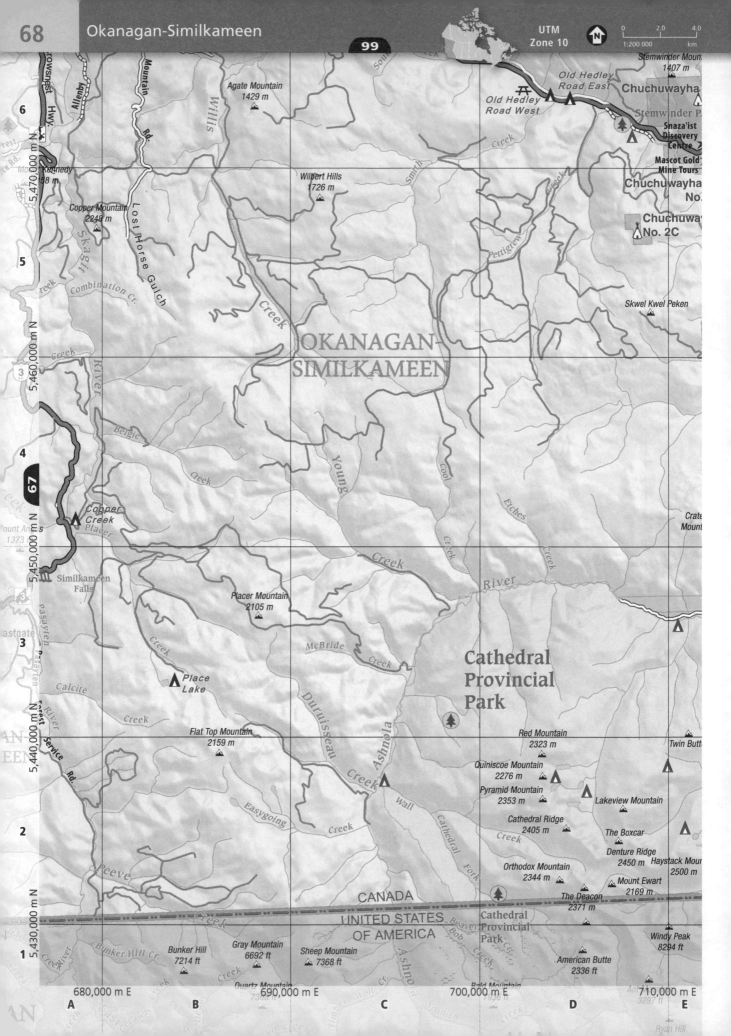

UTM
Zone 10

1:200 000

0   2.0   4.0
km

**OKANAGAN-
SIMILKAMEEN**

**Cathedral
Provincial
Park**

Agate Mountain
1429 m

Wilbert Hills
1726 m

Stemwinder Mountain
1407 m

Old Hedley
Road East

Old Hedley
Road West

Chuchuwayha

Stemwinder P.

Snaza'ist
Discovery
Centre

Mascot Gold
Mine Tours

Chuchuwayha
No.

Chuchuwayha
No. 2C

Skwel Kwel Peken

Kennedy
98 m

Copper Mountain
2248 m

Mount Ames
1373 m

Copper
Creek
Placer

Similkameen
Falls

Placer Mountain
2105 m

Place
Lake

McBride

Flat Top Mountain
2159 m

Red Mountain
2323 m

Twin Butte

Quiniscoe Mountain
2276 m

Pyramid Mountain
2353 m

Lakeview Mountain

Cathedral Ridge
2405 m

The Boxcar

Orthodox Mountain
2344 m

Denture Ridge
2450 m

Haystack Mountain
2500 m

Mount Ewart
2169 m

The Deacon
2371 m

Crater
Mountain

**CANADA
UNITED STATES
OF AMERICA**

Cathedral
Provincial
Park

Windy Peak
8294 ft

Bunker Hill
7214 ft

Gray Mountain
6692 ft

Sheep Mountain
7368 ft

American Butte
2336 ft

Quartz Mountain

Bald Mountain

680,000 m E   690,000 m E   700,000 m E   710,000 m E

A   B   C   D   E

5,470,000 m N
5,460,000 m N
5,450,000 m N
5,440,000 m N
5,430,000 m N

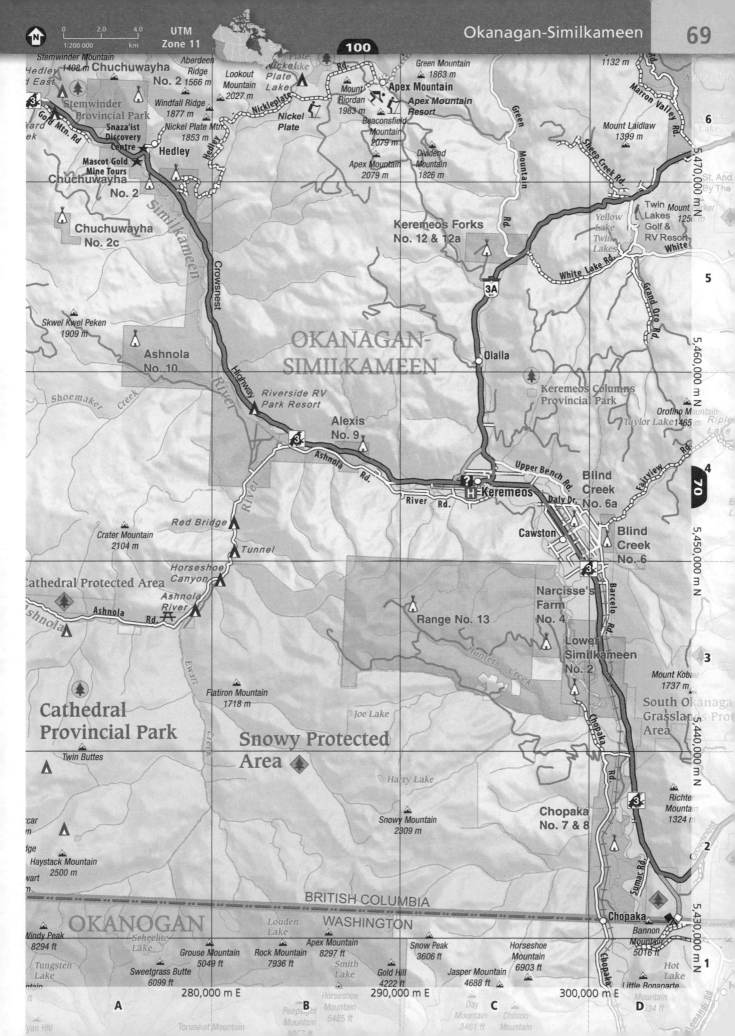

100

N

0   2.0   4.0
km

Stemwinder Mountain
1408 m **Chuchuwayha**
Hedley **No. 2** 1566 m
d East

Aberdeen
Ridge
1566 m

Lookout
Mountain
2027 m

Plate
Nickelake
Plate
Lake
Nickleplate

**Nickel
Plate**

Mount
Riordan
1983 m

Green Mountain
1863 m

Apex Mountain

**Apex Mountain
Resort**

Beaconsfield
Mountain
2079 m

1132 m

Marron Valley Rd.

Mount Laidlaw
1399 m

6

Stemwinder
Provincial Park

Windfall Ridge
1877 m

Nickel Plate Mtn.
1853 m

Apex Mountain
2079 m

Dividend
Mountain
1826 m

St. And
By The

Gold
Mtn. Rd.

**Snaza'ist
Discovery
Centre**

Hedley

Sheep Creek Rd.

5,470,000 m N

Mascot Gold
Mine Tours

**Chuchuwayha
No. 2**

Hedley Rd.

**Keremeos Forks
No. 12 & 12a**

Yellow
Lake

Twin
Lakes

Mount
1256 m

Twin
Lakes
Golf &
RV Resort

White

**Chuchuwayha
No. 2c**

Similkameen

Crowsnest

3A
B.C.

White Lake Rd.

Grand Oro Rd.

5

Skwel Kwel Peken
1909 m

**Ashnola
No. 10**

Green
Mountain

**OKANAGAN-
SIMILKAMEEN**

Olalla

Keremeos Columns
Provincial Park

Orofino Mountain
Taylor Lake 1465 m

Riple
Lake

Shoemaker   Creek

Highway

River

Riverside RV
Park Resort

**Alexis
No. 9**

Ashnola   Rd.

3

Fairview Rd.

**Blind
Creek
No. 6a**

70

4

5,460,000 m N

Red Bridge

River   Rd.

H Keremeos

Upper Bench Rd.

Daly Dr.

Barcelo Rd.

5,450,000 m N

Crater Mountain
2104 m

Tunnel

Cawston

**Blind
Creek
No. 6**

Cathedral Protected Area

Horseshoe
Canyon

Ashnola
River

Ashnola   Rd.

**Narcisse's
Farm
No. 4**

Mount Kobau
1737 m

3

Ashnola

Range No. 13

**Lower
Similkameen
No. 2**

South Okanaga
Grasslan s Pro
Area

Ewart

Creek

Flatiron Mountain
1718 m

**Cathedral
Provincial Park**

Joe Lake

Hunters   Creek

Chopaka Rd.

5,440,000 m N

**Snowy Protected
Area**

Twin Buttes

Harry Lake

**Chopaka
No. 7 & 8**

3

Richter
Mountain
1324 m

2

car
m

Snowy Mountain
2309 m

Sumac Rd.

Crowsnest

Haystack Mountain
2500 m
wart
m

BRITISH COLUMBIA

Chopaka

Bannon
Mountain
5016 ft

5,430,000 m N

OKANOGAN   **WASHINGTON**

Louden
Lake

Hot
Lake

Windy Peak
8294 ft

Scheelite
Lake

Grouse Mountain
5049 ft

Rock Mountain
7936 ft

Apex Mountain
8297 ft

Snow Peak
3606 ft

Horseshoe
Mountain
6903 ft

Chopaka

Little Bonaparte
334 ft

1

Tungsten
Lake

Sweetgrass Butte
6099 ft

Smith
Lake

Gold Hill
4222 ft

Jasper Mountain
4688 ft

Horseshoe
Mountain
5485 ft

Day
Mountain
3461 m

Chilson
Mountain

Tonasket Mountain

Peepsight
Mountain

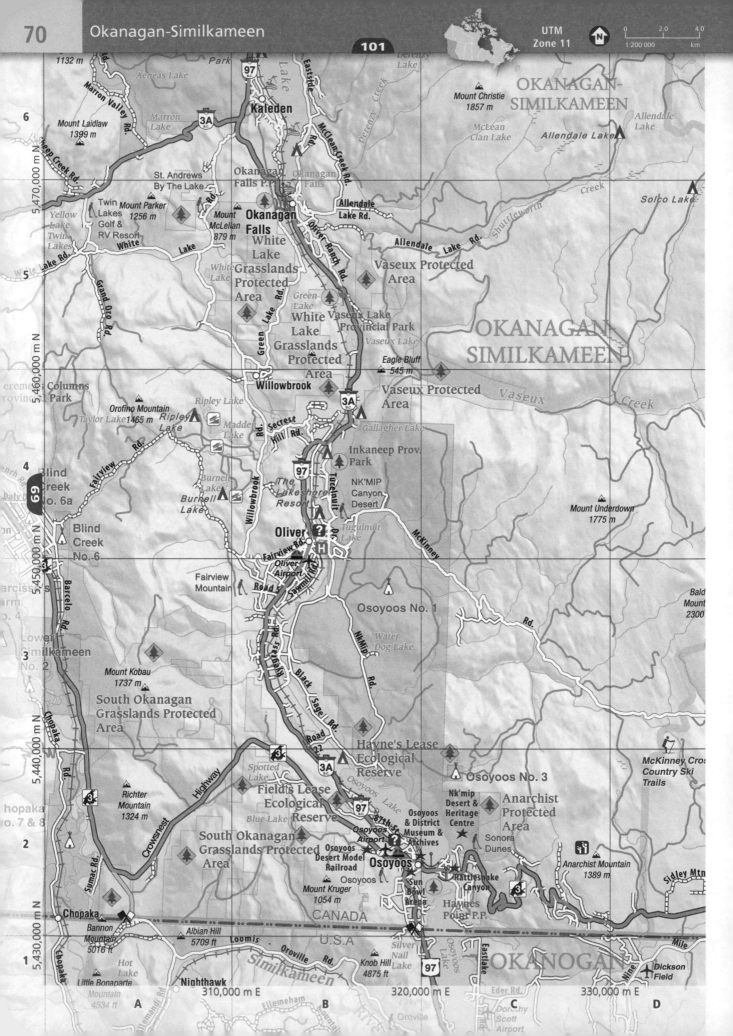

OKANAGAN-
SIMILKAMEEN

Mount Christie
1857 m

McLean
Clan Lake

Allendale Lake

Allendale
Lake

6

1132 m

Park

Aeneas Lake

Marron Valley Rd.

Marron
Lake

Mount Laidlaw
1399 m

Eastside

Lake

McClean Creek Rd.

Derenzy
Lake

Derenzy Creek

Creek

Solco Lake

97
B.C.

3A
B.C.

Kaleden

Deep Creek Rd.

Yellow
Lake

5,470,000 m N

St. Andrews
By The Lake

Okanagan
Falls P.P.

Okanagan
Falls

Allendale
Lake Rd.

Allendale   Lake   Rd.

Shuttleworth

Twin
Lakes
Golf &
RV Resort

Mount Parker
1256 m

Mount
McLellan
879 m

Okanagan
Falls

Oliver Ranch Rd.

5

Twin
Lakes

White   Lake   Rd.

White

Lake

White
Lake

White
Lake
Grasslands
Protected
Area

Green
Lake

Vaseux Protected
Area

OKANAGAN

White Lake Rd.

Green
Lake

White
Lake
Grasslands
Protected
Area

Vaseux Lake
Provincial Park

Vaseux Lake

SIMILKAMEEN

Grand Oro Rd.

Columns
rovincial Park

Willowbrook

Eagle Bluff
545 m

Vaseux

Creek

4

Orofino Mountain
1465 m

Taylor Lake

Ripley Lake

Ripley
Lake

Madden
Lake

Secrest
Hill   Rd.

3A
B.C.

Gallagher Lake

Vaseux Protected
Area

Vaseux

Blind
Creek
No. 6a

69

Fairview   Rd.

Burnell
Lake

Burnell
Lake

Willowbrook Rd.

The
Lakeshore
Resort

97
B.C.

Inkaneep Prov.
Park

NK'MIP
Canyon
Desert

Tuc-el-nuit

Mount Underdown
1775 m

5,450,000 m N

arciss's
arm
o. 4

3

Blind
Creek
No. 6

Oliver

?

H

Tuc-el-nuit
Lake

McKinney

Lower
Similkameen
No. 2

Barcelo   Rd.

Fairview Rd.

Oliver
Airport

Fairview
Mountain

Road 5

Sawmill Rd.

Osoyoos No. 1

Rd.

Bald
Mount
2300

3

Fairview
Mountain

Bigtail Rd.

Black   Sage   Rd.

Water
Dog Lake

NkMip   Rd.

Mount Kobau
1737 m

South Okanagan
Grasslands Protected
Area

Road
22

Hayne's Lease
Ecological
Reserve

2

Chopaka Rd.

W

3

Richter
Mountain
1324 m

Spotted
Lake

3A
B.C.

Osoyoos   Lake

Osoyoos No. 3

Nk'mip
Desert &
Heritage
Centre

Anarchist
Protected
Area

McKinney Cros
Country Ski
Trails

hopaka
o. 7 & 8

Highway

Crowsnest

Fields Lease
Ecological
Reserve

Blue Lake

97
B.C.

87th St.

Osoyoos
Airport

?

Osoyoos
& District
Museum &
Archives

Sonora
Dunes

Anarchist Mountain
1389 m

Sidley Mtn

Sumac Rd.

South Okanagan
Grasslands Protected
Area

Osoyoos
Desert Model
Railroad

Osoyoos

Osoyoos

Rattlesnake
Canyon

3
B.C.

5,430,000 m N

Chopaka

Bannon
Mountain
5016 ft

Albian Hill
5709 ft

Loomis

Mount Kruger
1054 m

Sun
Bowl
Arena

Haynes
Point P.P.

Haynes
Point P.P.

Sidley Mtn

1

Chopaka

Hot
Lake

Little Bonaparte
Mountain
4534 ft

Nighthawk

310,000 m E

Oroville   Rd.

Similkameen

CANADA
U.S.A.

Knob Hill
4875 ft

Silver
Nail
Lake

97

320,000 m E

Oroville

Eder Rd.

OKANOGAN

Dickson
Field

Nine   Mile

330,000 m E

A   B   C   D

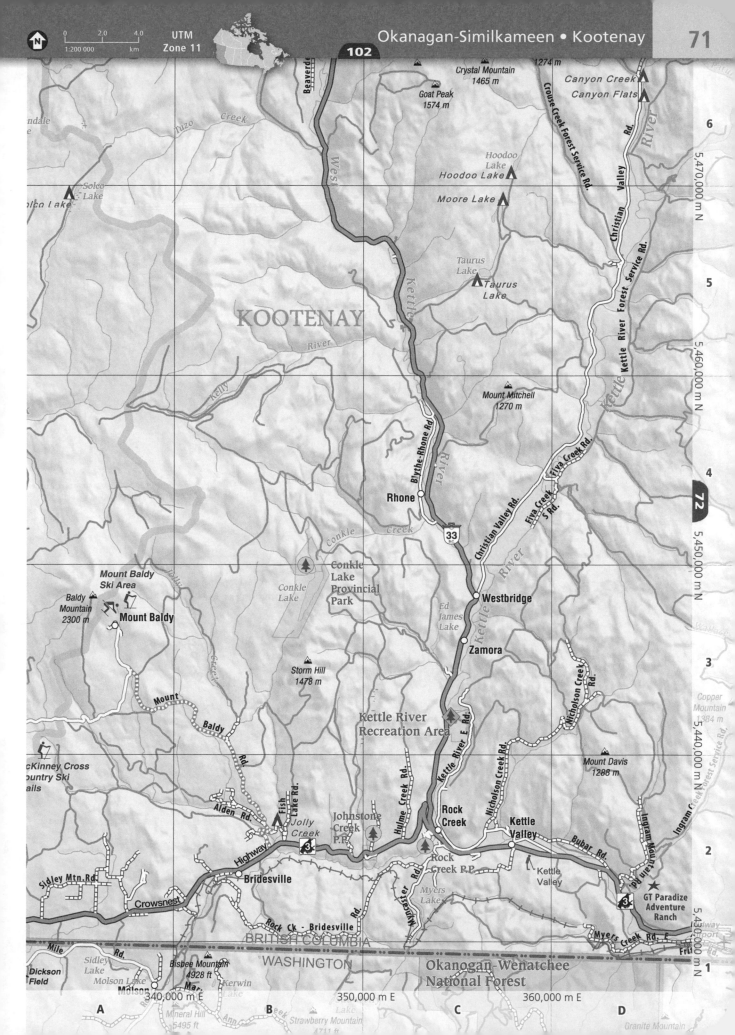

N

| 0 | 2.0 | 4.0 |
| 1:200 000 | | km |

UTM
Zone 11

102

6

5,470,000 m N

Beaverde

Crystal Mountain
1465 m

1274 m

Goat Peak
1574 m

Canyon Creek

Canyon Flats

Crouse Creek Forest Service Rd.

Solco
Lake

olco Lake

Hoodoo
Lake

Hoodoo Lake

Moore Lake

West

Tuzo

Creek

Christian Valley

Kettle River Forest Service Rd.

River

5

5,460,000 m N

KOOTENAY

Kettle

River

Taurus
Lake

Taurus
Lake

Mount Mitchell
1270 m

Kettle

River

72

4

5,450,000 m N

Kelly

Blythe-Rhone Rd.

Rhone

Conkle

Creek

33
B.C.

Christian Valley Rd.

Fiva Creek Rd.

Fiva Creek
S Rd.

Mount Baldy
Ski Area

Baldy
Mountain
2300 m

Mount Baldy

Conkle
Lake
Provincial
Park

Conkle
Lake

Ed
James
Lake

Westbridge

Kettle

River

Zamora

Nicholson Creek
Rd.

Copper
Mountain
1384 m

3

5,440,000 m N

McKinney Cross
ountry Ski
ails

Jolly

Creek

Mount

Baldy

Rd.

Storm Hill
1478 m

Kettle River
Recreation Area

Kettle River E Rd.

Hulme Creek Rd.

Nicholson Creek Rd.

Mount Davis
1288 m

Ingram Creek Forest Service Rd.

Alden Rd.

Fish Lake Rd.

Jolly
Creek

Johnstone
Creek
P.P.

Rock
Creek

Kettle
Valley

Bubar Rd.

Ingram Mountain Rd.

2

5,430,000 m N

Sidley Mtn. Rd.

Highway

3

Bridesville

Crowsnest

Rock Ck - Bridesville

Rock Creek P.P.

Myers
Lakes

Mcmaster Rd.

Kettle
Valley

Kettle
Valley

3

GT Paradize
Adventure
Ranch

Myers Creek Rd. E

Frit

way
port

Mile

Rd.

Sidley
Lake

Molson Lake

Dickson
Field

Molson

Bisbee Mountain
4928 ft

Kerwin

Mar.

BRITISH COLUMBIA

WASHINGTON

Okanogan-Wenatchee
National Forest

Mineral Hill
5495 ft

Strawberry Mountain

Ann

Lake

Granite Mountain

340,000 m E

350,000 m E

360,000 m E

A

B

C

D

1

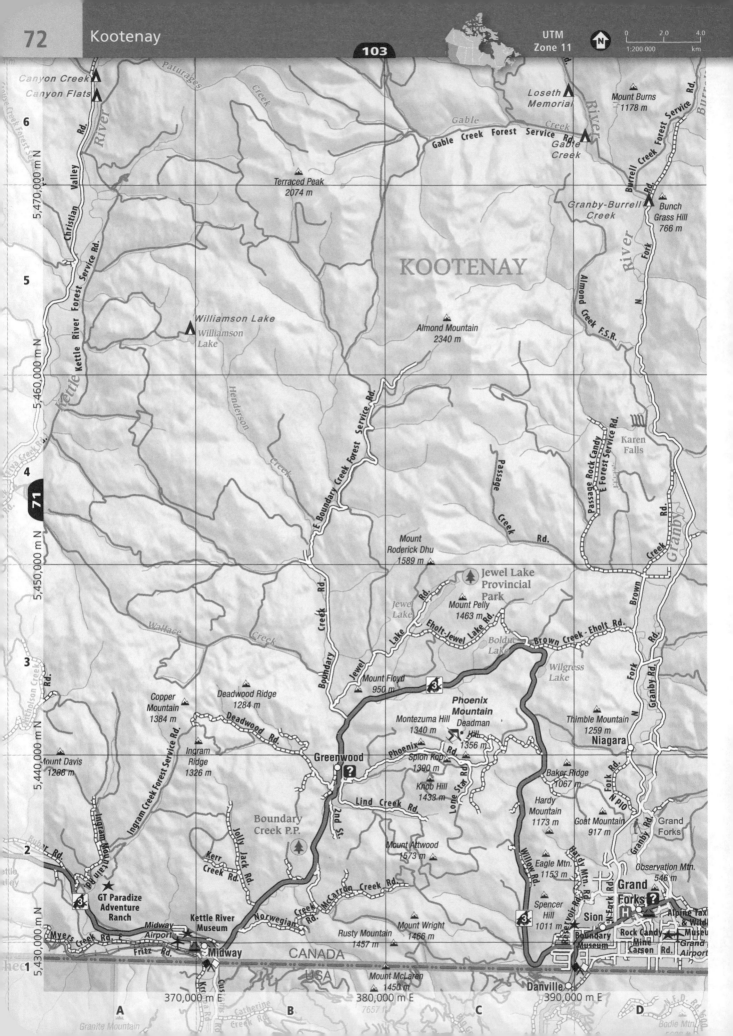

103

UTM Zone 11

1:200 000

0   2.0   4.0
km

KOOTENAY

Canyon Creek
Canyon Flats

Loseth Memorial

Mount Burns 1178 m

Gable Creek Forest Service Rd.
Gable Creek

Granby-Burrell Creek

Bunch Grass Hill 766 m

Terraced Peak 2074 m

Williamson Lake
Williamson Lake

Almond Mountain 2340 m

Karen Falls

Passage Creek Rd.

Mount Roderick Dhu 1589 m

Jewel Lake Provincial Park

Mount Pelly 1463 m

Brown Creek - Eholt Rd.

Eholt-Jewel Lake Rd.

Bolduc Lake

Wilgress Lake

Mount Floyd 950 m

Phoenix Mountain

Montezuma Hill 1340 m

Deadman Hill 1356 m

Thimble Mountain 1259 m

Niagara

Copper Mountain 1384 m

Deadwood Ridge 1284 m

Deadwood Rd.

Greenwood

Phoenix Rd.

Spion Kop 1390 m

Baker Ridge 1067 m

Mount Davis 1288 m

Ingram Ridge 1326 m

Knob Hill 1433 m

Hardy Mountain 1173 m

Goat Mountain 917 m

Grand Forks

Boundary Creek P.P.

Lind Creek Rd.

Mount Attwood 1573 m

Eagle Mtn. 1153 m

Observation Mtn. 546 m

Kerr Creek Rd.

Jolly Jack Rd.

2nd St.

Grand Forks

GT Paradize Adventure Ranch

Spencer Hill 1011 m

Sion

Midway Airport

Kettle River Museum

Norwegian Creek Rd.

McCarron Creek Rd.

Mount Wright 1466 m

Rock Candy Mine Carson Rd.

Myers Creek Rd. E.

Fritz Rd.

Midway

Rusty Mountain 1457 m

CANADA

USA

Boundary Museum

Grand Airport

Mount McLaren 1450 m

Danville

370,000 m E   380,000 m E   390,000 m E

5,470,000 m N
5,460,000 m N
5,450,000 m N
5,440,000 m N
5,430,000 m N

71

A   B   C   D

6
5
4
3
2
1

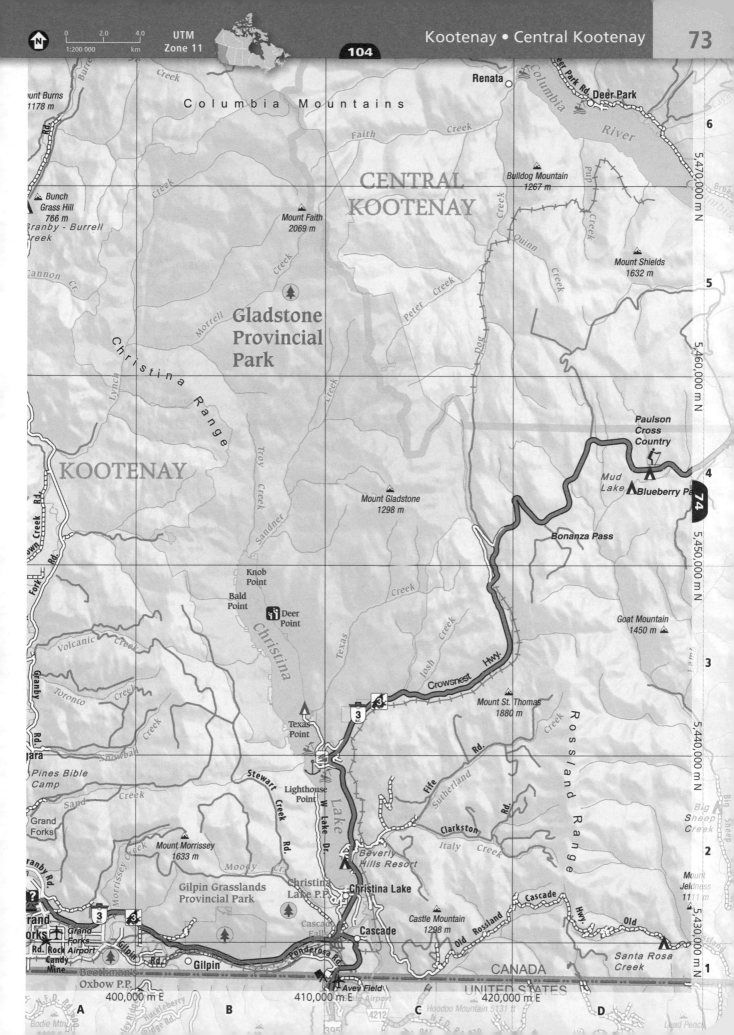

UTM
Zone 11

1:200 000

0   2.0   4.0
km

104

Columbia Mountains

CENTRAL
KOOTENAY

Renata

Deer Park Rd.

Deer Park

Columbia

River

6

Faith   Creek

Bulldog Mountain
1267 m

Mount Faith
2069 m

Quinn   Creek

Pup   Creek

Mount Shields
1632 m

5

Gladstone
Provincial
Park

Peter Creek

Morrell

Dog   Creek

Paulson
Cross
Country

Christina Range

Troy   Creek

Mud
Lake

Blueberry Pa

74

KOOTENAY

Sandner

Mount Gladstone
1298 m

Bonanza Pass

4

Knob
Point

Creek

Goat Mountain
1450 m

Bald
Point

Christina

Deer
Point

Texas

Josh   Creek

Crowsnest   Hwy.

3

Mount St. Thomas
1880 m

Rossland Range

Texas
Point

Rd.

Big
Sheep
Creek

Stewart

Lighthouse
Point

Creek

Fife

Sutherland

Clarkston

Rd.

Mount
Jeldness
1111 m

2

Pines Bible
Camp

Sand   Creek

Snowball

Italy   Creek

Mount Morrissey
1633 m

Moody   Cr.

Beverly
Hills Resort

Grand
Forks

Gilpin Grasslands
Provincial Park

Christina
Lake P.P.

Christina Lake

Cascade

Castle Mountain
1298 m

Old Rossland

Cascade   Hwy.

Old

Granby Rd.

Grand
Forks

Rock Airport

Gilpin   Rd.

Gilpin

Cascade
Falls

Ponderosa Rd.

Cascade

CANADA

Santa Rosa
Creek

1

Candy
Mine

Boothman's
Oxbow P.P.

Avey Field

UNITED STATES

4212   Hoodoo Mountain 5131 ft

A   B   C   D

400,000 m E   410,000 m E   420,000 m E

Deer Park

6

Columbia River

Pine Ridge
1657 m

Cayuse Creek

Tulip Creek

Ladybird Mountain
2027 m

Norns Creek

Ladybird Creek

Goose Cr.

Pass Creek Rd.

Pass Valley

Syringa Prov. Park

Broadwater Rd.

Syringa Provincial Park

Shields Point

River

Sentinel Mountain
1523 m

3

Mount Shields
1632 m

5

N 5,470,000 m N

Columbia River

Broadwater Rd.

Arrow Lakes Dr.

Robson

Pass Creek Fairgrounds

Raspberry

Kinnaird

Brilliant

Castlegar

H

Selkirk College

West Kootenay Airport

Castlegar Golf & RV Park

CENTRAL KOOTENAY

Robson Ridge
1281 m

Crowsnest Hwy.

Gem Hill
1580 m

Doukhobor Discovery Centre

Kootenay Gallery Of Art History & Science

Kinnaird

Ootischenia

Little Bear

N 5,460,000 m N

3 B.C.

3 B.C.

3 B.C.

3 B.C.

Paulson Cross Country

Nancy Greene P.P.

Castlegar Cabins, RV Park & Campground

Blueberry Creek

4

Mud Lake

Blueberry Pass

Mount Neptune
1981 m

Mount Mackie
1978 m

Buckely Rd.

73

Creek

Bonanza Pass

Mount Crowe
1981 m

Genelle

H

3B B.C.

Columbia Rd.

KOOTENAY

Murphy Creek

22 B.C.

Bonnington Range

River

Champion Lakes P.P.

Chan

3

N 5,450,000 m N

Goat Mountain
1450 m

Lamb Creek

Old Glory Mountain
2376 m

3B B.C.

Birchbank

Mount Heinze
1376 m

Bear Creek

BlackJack Ski Club

Big Red Cats Ski

Hanna Creek Rd.

Columbia Ave.

Sunningdale

Fruitva

Beaver Falls

Granite Mountain
1792 m

Red Mountain
1302 m

Trail H

Glenmerry

N 5,440,000 m N

Big Sheep Creek

Big Sheep Creek Rd.

Rossland Historical Museum

?

Rossland

22 B.C.

3B B.C.

Warfield

?

Casino Rd.

3B B.C.

22A B.C.

Montrose

Beaver Creek P.P.

2

Mount Jeldness
1111 m

Record Ridge
1766 m

Cascade Hwy Rd.

Deerpark Hill
1350 m

Redstone Resort

Cherry Ridge
1264 m

Lookout Mountain
1218 m

Lake Mountain
1380 m

22 B.C.

22A B.C.

Station Rd.

Columbia Gardens

Sheppard Creek

Columbia River

Tamarac Mountain
1276 m

Baldy Mountain
1250 m

Old Rossland

N 5,430,000 m N

Santa Rosa Creek

Mount Sophia
1356 m

King George VI P.P.

Paterson

BRITISH COLUMBIA
WASHINGTON

Moraski Mountain
3051 ft

Waneta-Nelway

Seven

1

Frontier

Simons Mountain
3517 ft

Mitchell Mountain
3694 ft

9445

Lead Pencil

A

430,000 m E

Velvet

B

440,000 m E

Grouse Mountain
3409 ft

C

450,000 m E

D

Rossland Range

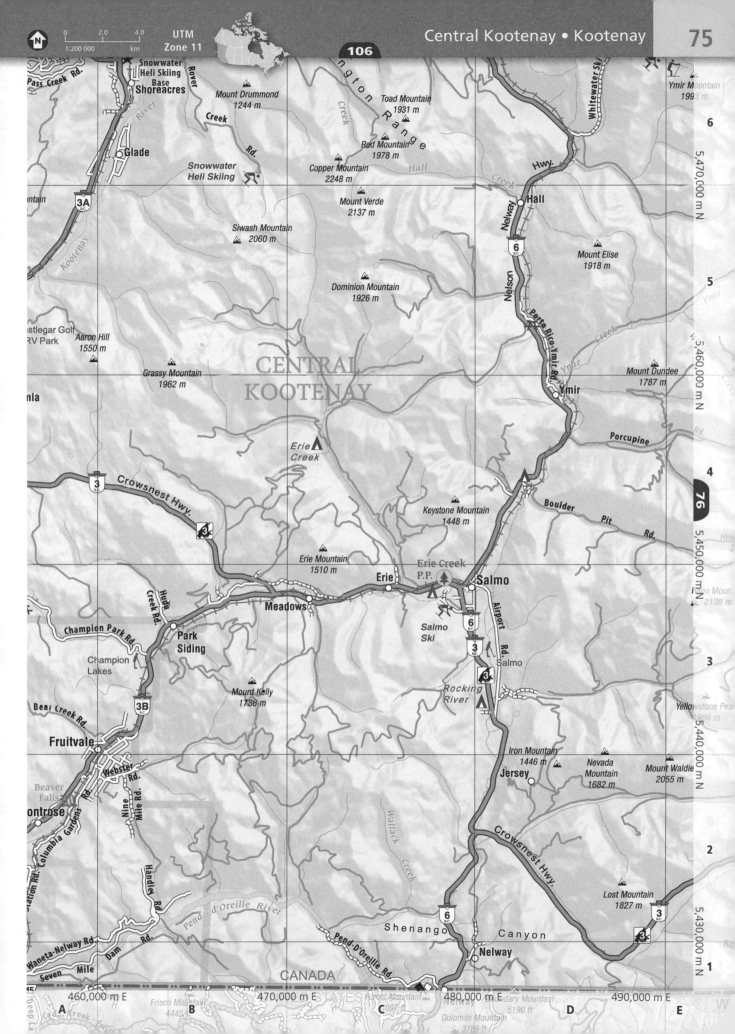

N

0   2.0   4.0
1:200 000   km

UTM
Zone 11

106

Snowwater
Heli Skiing
Base
Shoreacres

Mount Drummond
1244 m

Rover

Creek

Rd.

Glade

Snowwater
Heli Skiing

3A
B.C.

Toad Mountain
1931 m

Red Mountain
1978 m

Copper Mountain
2248 m

Mount Verde
2137 m

Siwash Mountain
2060 m

Hall
Creek

Nelway

Hall

6
B.C.

Nelson

Mount Elise
1918 m

Porto Rico-Ymir Rd.

Ymir
Creek

Mount Dundee
1787 m

Dominion Mountain
1926 m

Ymir

Whitewater Ski

Ymir Mountain
1993 m

6

5

W 5,470,000 m N

5,460,000 m N

Castlegar Golf
RV Park

Aaron Hill
1550 m

Grassy Mountain
1962 m

**CENTRAL
KOOTENAY**

Erie
Creek

Keystone Mountain
1448 m

Boulder

Porcupine

Rd.

Pit

Rd.

Hugo Moun...
2138 m

76

4

W 5,450,000 m N

3
B.C.

Crowsnest Hwy.

3
B.C.

Erie Mountain
1510 m

Erie

Meadows

Erie Creek
P.P.

Salmo

6
B.C.

3
B.C.

Salmo
Ski

Salmo

Airport

Rd.

Hugh

Creek Rd.

Park
Siding

Champion Park Rd.

Champion
Lakes

Mount Kelly
1736 m

3
B.C.

Rocking
River

Iron Mountain
1446 m

Jersey

Nevada
Mountain
1682 m

Mount Waldie
2055 m

Yellowstone Pea...
1996 m

3

W 5,440,000 m N

3B
B.C.

Bear Creek Rd.

Fruitvale

Webster

Rd.

Nine

Mile Rd.

Beaver
Falls

...ontrose

Rd.

...tion Rd.

Columbia Gardens

Handley

Rd.

Dam

Rd.

Waneta-Nelway Rd.

Seven

Mile

Pend-d'Oreille River

Pend-D'Oreille Rd.

Wallack

Creek

Crowsnest Hwy.

Lost Mountain
1827 m

3
B.C.

3
B.C.

2

W 5,430,000 m N

Shenango

Canyon

6
B.C.

Nelway

Nelway

...dary Mountain
5190 ft

1

W 5,420,000 m N

CANADA

Frisco Mountain
4445...

Dolomite Mountain
3789 ft

Forest Mountain...
2097...

A   460,000 m E   **B**   470,000 m E   **C**   480,000 m E   **D**   490,000 m E   **E**

107

UTM
Zone 11

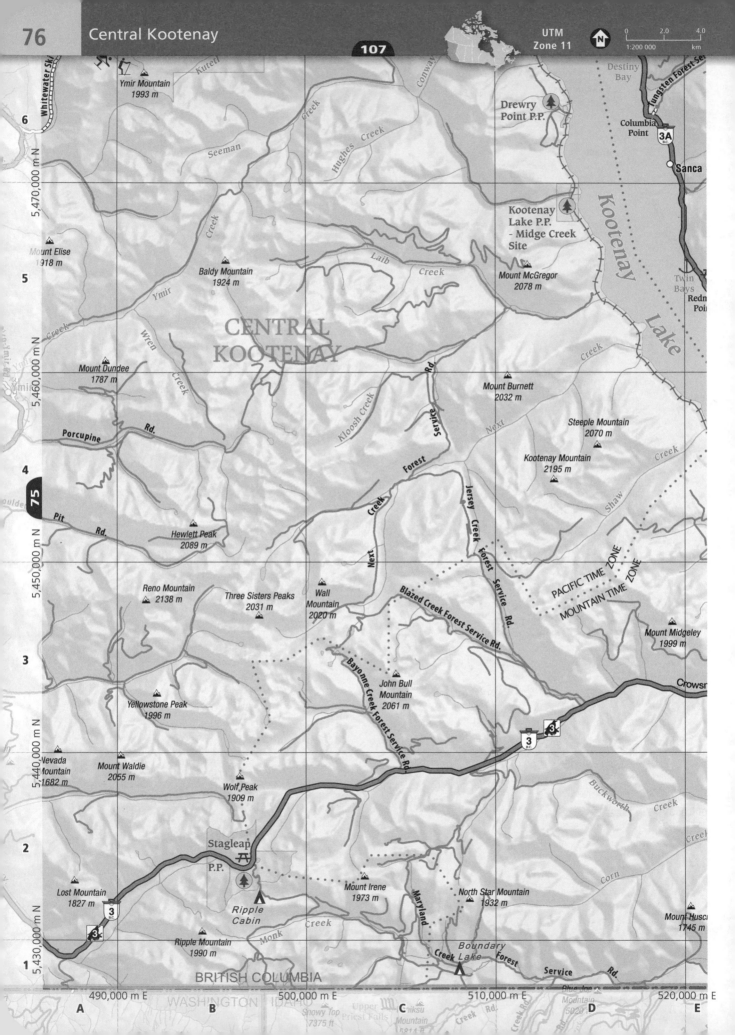

0   2.0   4.0
1:200 000   km

6

Ymir Mountain
1993 m

Whitewater Ski

Kuteel

Creek

Creek

Conway

Destiny
Bay

Tungsten Forest Ser

Drewry
Point P.P.

Columbia
Point

3A
B.C.

Sanca

Seeman

Hughes

Creek

Creek

5,470,000 m N

Mount Elise
1918 m

Laib

Creek

Kootenay
Lake P.P.
- Midge Creek
Site

Kootenay

Lake

Twin
Bays

5

Baldy Mountain
1924 m

Mount McGregor
2078 m

Redn
Poin

Ymir

5,460,000 m N

Mount Dundee
1787 m

CENTRAL
KOOTENAY

Wren

Creek

Kloosh Creek

Mount Burnett
2032 m

Service

Next

Creek

Steeple Mountain
2070 m

Porcupine

Rd.

Forest

Kootenay Mountain
2195 m

Shaw

Creek

4

Pit

Rd.

Hewlett Peak
2089 m

Creek

Jersey

Creek

Forest

Service

Rd.

PACIFIC TIME ZONE

MOUNTAIN TIME ZONE

5,450,000 m N

Reno Mountain
2138 m

Three Sisters Peaks
2031 m

Wall
Mountain
2020 m

Next

Blazed Creek Forest Service Rd.

Mount Midgeley
1999 m

3

Yellowstone Peak
1996 m

Bayonne Creek Forest Service Rd.

John Bull
Mountain
2061 m

Crowsn

Nevada
Mountain
1682 m

Mount Waldie
2055 m

Wolf Peak
1909 m

3
B.C.

3
B.C.

Buckworth

Creek

5,440,000 m N

2

Stagleap
P.P.

Mount Irene
1973 m

North Star Mountain
1932 m

Maryland

Corn

Creek

Lost Mountain
1827 m

*Ripple
Cabin*

Mount Husc
1745 m

3
B.C.

3
B.C.

Ripple Mountain
1990 m

Monk

Creek

Boundary

Forest

1

Boundary
Creek Lake

Service

Rd.

5,430,000 m N

BRITISH COLUMBIA

WASHINGTON IDAHO

Snowy Top
7375 ft

*Upper
Priest Falls*

Chiksu

Mountain

Creek Rd.

Blue Joe

Mountain

490,000 m E

500,000 m E

510,000 m E

520,000 m E

A   B   C   D   E

75

N

0   2.0   4.0
km
1:200 000

UTM
Zone 11

108

**Kianuko
Provincial
Park**

Putnam Peak
2262 m

Jackson Peak
2241 m

6

Sanca

Sanca Creek Forest Service Rd.

3A
B.C.

Sanca Creek

Service Rd.

Kamma Creek Forest

Kamma Creek

Mount Skelly
2228 m

Skelly Creek Forest Service Rd.

Mount O'Neill
2044 m

5

5,470,000 m N

Twin
Bays

Redman
Point

Wooden
Shoe

Kuskonook

Mount Bohan
1986 m

Bohan Creek

Goat River

Cameron Creek

Mount Cowley
1901 m

5,460,000 m N

**CENTRAL
KOOTENAY**

Hall Forest Service Rd.

Leadville Forest Service

CE
OO

Six Mile Creek

Duck
Lake

Kootenay River

Slough

Goat
River
Canyon

Leadville

78

4

5,450,000 m N

3A
B.C.

Channel Rd.

Duck Lake Rd.

Duck Creek

Iron Range Mountain
1715 m

Rd.

Service

ount Midgeley
1999 m

Lower
Kootenay No. 5

Wynndel

Mount Kitchener
1601 m

Uri Rd.

Lakeview

Arrow

Arrow Creek

Lower Kootenay No. 4

Wilson
Rd.

3A
B.C.

Kitchener

3
B.C.

3

Crowsnest Hwy.

Lower
Kootenay
No. 3

Indian
Rd.

Arrow Mountain
1423 m

Rd.

Russell Creek Forest Service Rd.

5,440,000 m N

3
B.C.

Lower
Kootenay No. 2

3
B.C.

Creston
Mountain
1743 m

Nicks Island

Kootenay

Creston
Museum
River Rd.

?

H

Creston

Lower
Kootenay No. 1C

Creston Rd.

S Rd.

Rd.

Erickson Rd.

Canyon

2

Lower
Kootenay
No. 1B

38th St.

36th St.

Lister Rd.

Mount Thompson
1927 m

Creston
No. 1

21
B.C.

Lower
Kootenay

24th St.

Lister

Mount Huscroft
1745 m

Mount Rykert
1719 m

Reclamation Rd.

Lower
Kootenay
No. 1A

20th St.

Canyon Rd.

Airport Rd.

Huscroft

Mission Mountain
6158 ft

Swan Rd.

Sinclair Rd.

4th
St.

1

MOUNTAIN TIME ZONE

PACIFIC

520,000 m E

Canida Peak
5   ft

530,000 m E

Eckhart
International
Airport

Port

540,000 m E

Huscroft Rd.

City Rd.

CANADA

UNITED STATES

550,000 m E

5,430,000 m N

A   B   C   D   E

45

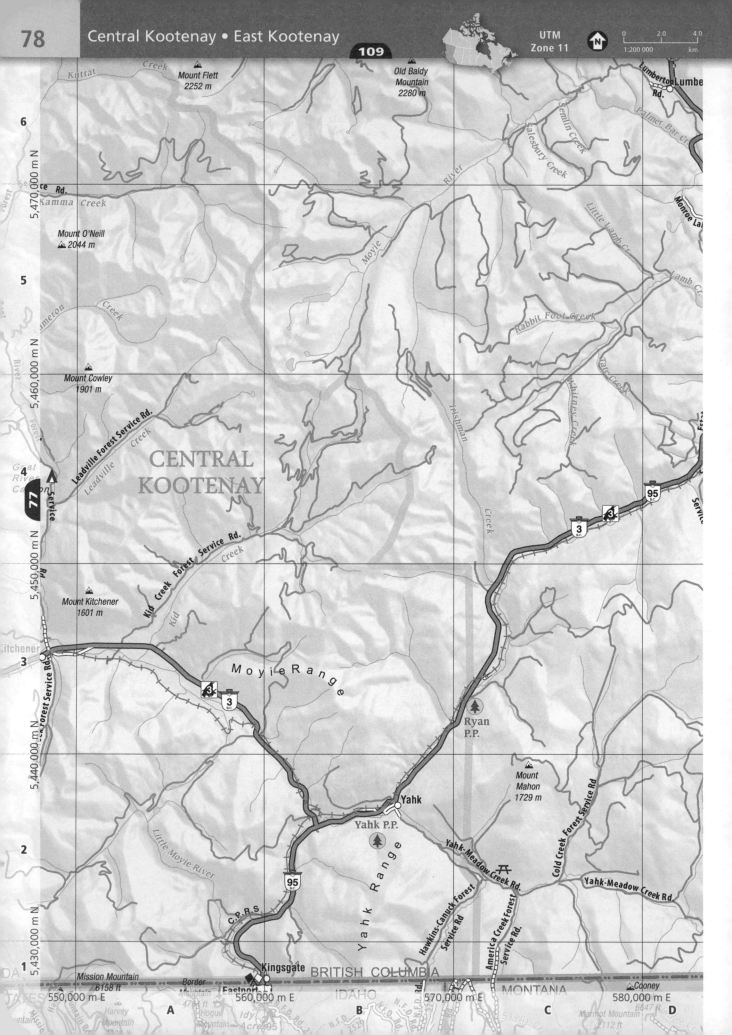

UTM
Zone 11

109

1:200 000

Kuttat Creek

Mount Flett
2252 m

Old Baldy
Mountain
2280 m

Semlin Creek

Salesbury Creek

Lumberton
Rd.
Lumber

6

Rd.

5,470,000 m N

Kamma Creek

Moyie River

Little Lamb Ck.

Monroe La

Mount O'Neill
2044 m

5

5,460,000 m N

Cameron Creek

Creek

Mount Cowley
1901 m

Rabbit Foot Creek

Lamb Cr.

Whitney Creek

Yate Creek

River

Irishman Creek

Leadville Forest Service Rd.

CENTRAL
KOOTENAY

Creek

95
B.C

Service

3
B.C

3
B.C

4

77

Service

Kid Creek Forest Service Rd.

Creek

Creek

5,450,000 m N

Mount Kitchener
1601 m

Kid

Moyie Range

Forest Service Rd.

Kitchener

3

3
B.C

3
B.C

Ryan
P.P.

Mount
Mahon
1729 m

Cold Creek Forest Service Rd

5,440,000 m N

Little Moyie River

Yahk

Yahk P.P.

Yahk-Meadow Creek Rd.

Yahk Range

2

95
B.C

Hawkins-Canuck Forest Service Rd

Yahk-Meadow Creek Rd.

America Creek Forest Service Rd.

C.P.R.S.

1

5,430,000 m N

Mission Mountain
6158 ft

Border
Mountain

Kingsgate

BRITISH COLUMBIA

Eastport

IDAHO

MONTANA

Cooney

Harvey
Mountain

Hogue

Idy
Acres

95

Marmot Mountain
2112 ft

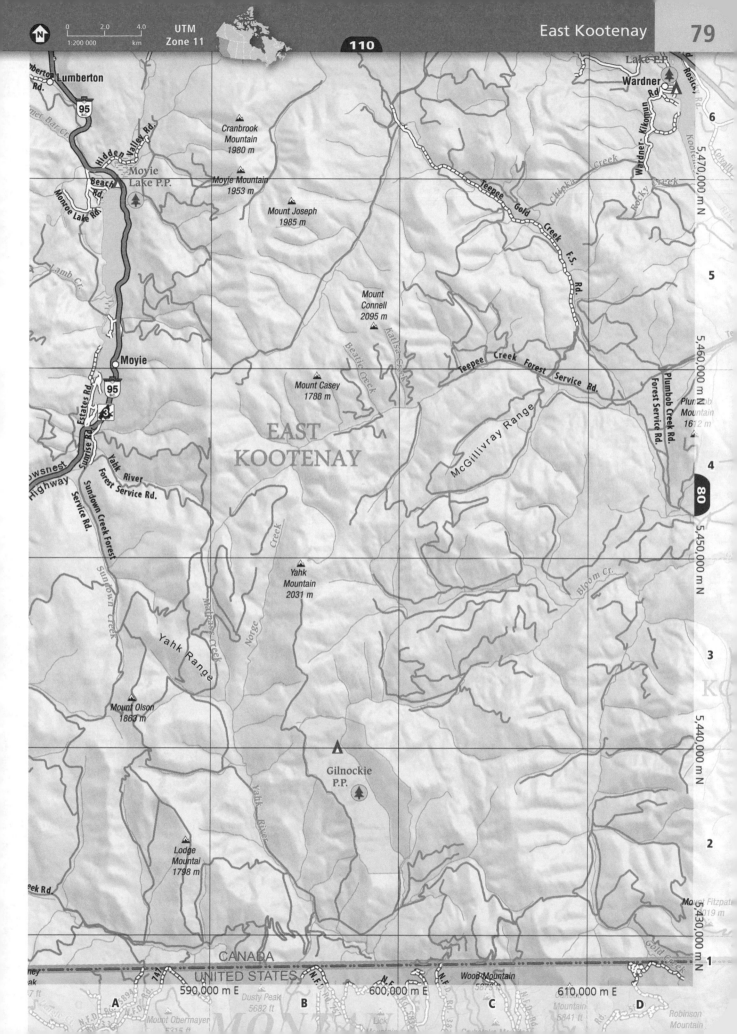

N

0   2.0   4.0
1:200 000   km

UTM
Zone 11

110

CANADA

UNITED STATES

Lumberton Rd.
Lumberton

95
BC

Calmet Bar Cr.

Hidden Valley Rd.

Moyie
Beach
Rd.

Moyie
Lake P.P.

Monroe Lake Rd.

Lamb Cr.

Moyie

95
BC

3
BC

Estates Rd.

Crowsnest
Highway

Sunrise Rd.

Sundown Creek Forest
Service Rd.

Yahk
River
Forest Service Rd.

Sundown Creek

Yahk Range

Mount Olson
1863 m

Lodge
Mountai
1798 m

Creek Rd.

Cranbrook
Mountain
1980 m

Moyie Mountain
1953 m

Mount Joseph
1985 m

EAST
KOOTENAY

Mount Casey
1788 m

Beattie Creek

Matlse Creek

Norge Creek

Yahk
Mountain
2031 m

Mathews Creek

Creek

Yahk River

Gilnockie
P.P.

Mount
Connell
2095 m

Teepee
Gold
Creek
F.S.
Rd.

Chipka
Creek

Teepee Creek Forest Service Rd.

McGillivray Range

Bloom Cr.

Wardner
Rd.
Wardner

Wardner- Kikomun

Lake P.P.

Rosita Rd.

Kootenay

Cohalil

Rocky Creek

Plumbob Creek Rd.
Forest Service Rd.

Plumbob
Mountain
1612 m

KO

Mo nt Fitzpat
019 m

Gold Creek

Dusty Peak
5682 ft

Wood Mountain
5873 ft

N.F.D.

N.F.D.

N.F.D.

590,000 m E

600,000 m E

610,000 m E

A   B   C   D

80

5,470,000 m N

5,460,000 m N

5,450,000 m N

5,440,000 m N

5,430,000 m N

6

5

4

3

2

1

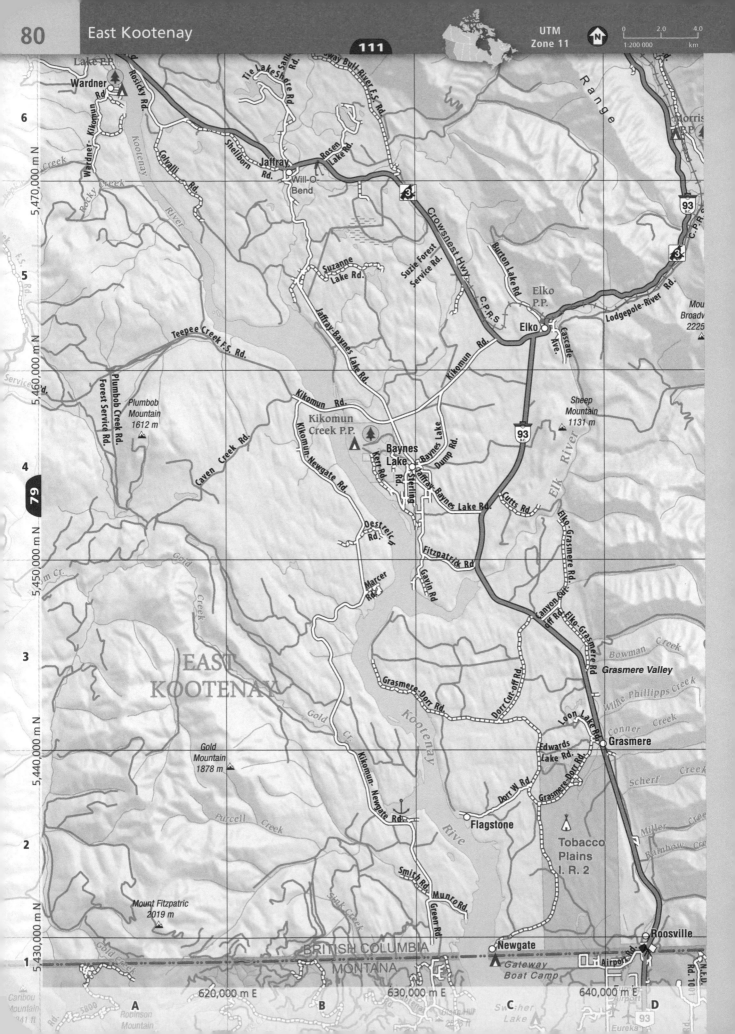

111

UTM
Zone 11

N

1:200 000

0   2.0   4.0
km

EAST KOOTENAY

BRITISH COLUMBIA

MONTANA

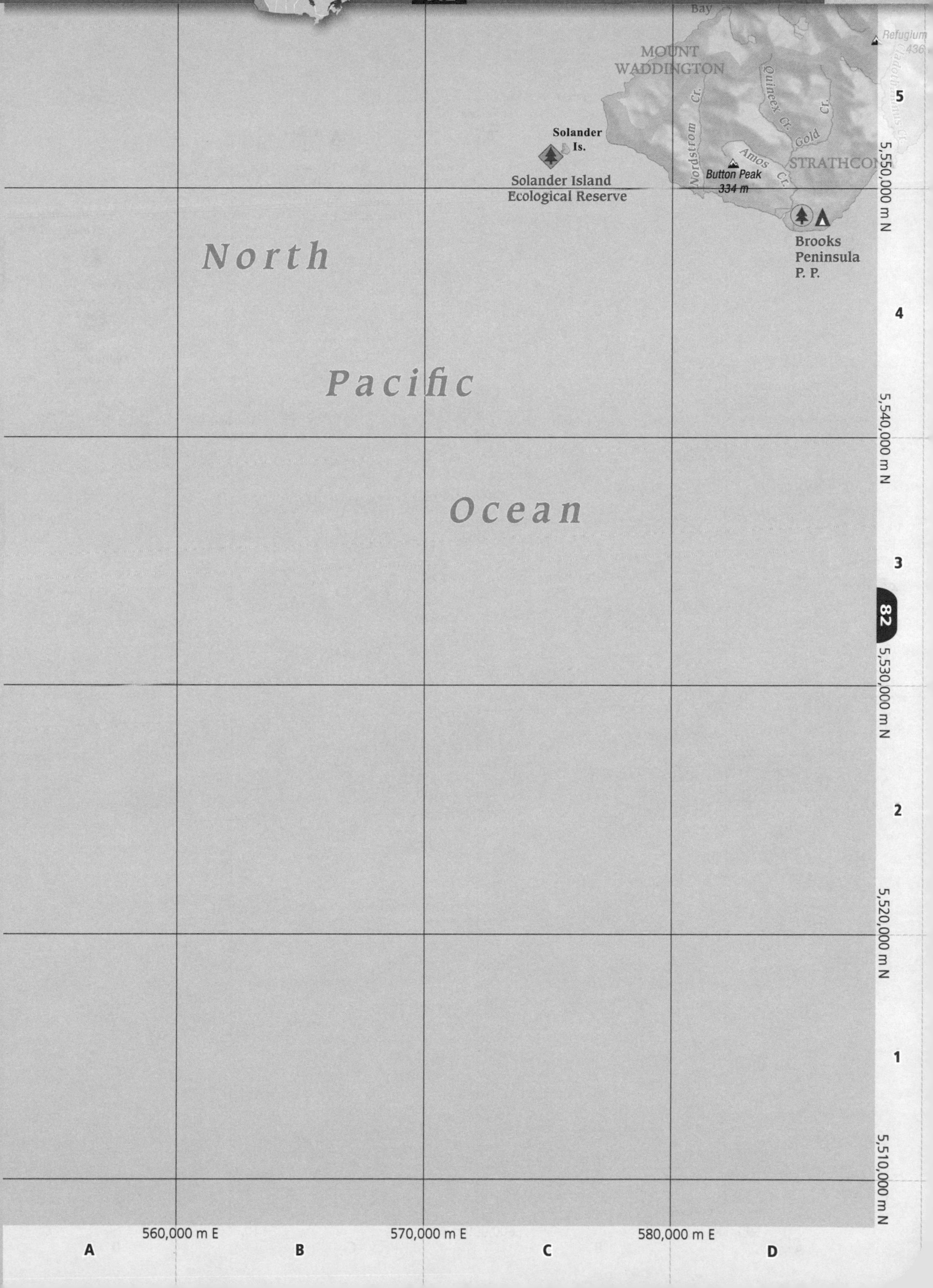

0 2.0 4.0
1:200 000 km

UTM
Zone 9

112

North

Pacific

Ocean

MOUNT
WADDINGTON

Bay

Refugium
436

5

Solander
Is.

Solander Island
Ecological Reserve

Nordstrom Cr.

Button Peak
334 m

Amos Cr.

Quineex Cr.

Gold Cr.

STRATHCON

Cladorhynus Cr.

5,550,000 m N

Brooks
Peninsula
P. P.

4

5,540,000 m N

3

82

5,530,000 m N

2

5,520,000 m N

1

5,510,000 m N

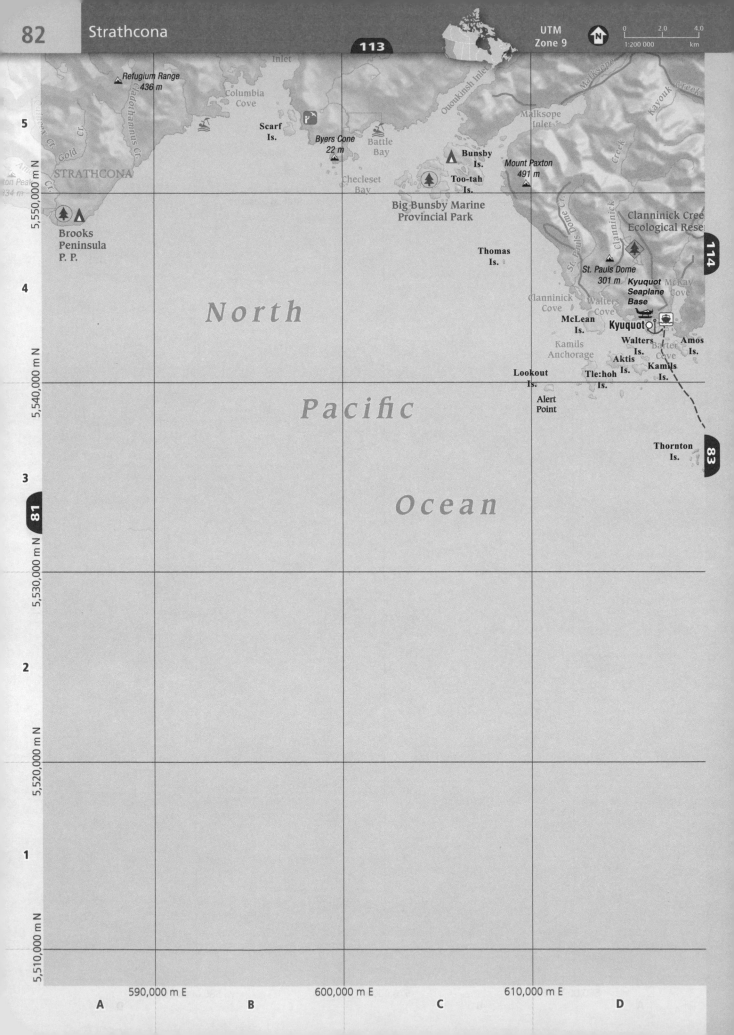

113

UTM
Zone 9

1:200 000

0   2.0   4.0
km

Refugium Range
436 m

Columbia
Cove

Inlet

Ououkinsh Inlet

Malksope

Kayouk Creek

Malksope
Inlet

Scarf
Is.

Byers Cone
22 m

Battle
Bay

Bunsby
Is.

Mount Paxton
491 m

Clanninick Creek
Ecological Reserve

5

STRATHCONA

Gold Cr.

Cladothamnus Cr.

ron Peak
34 m

Checleset
Bay

Too-tah
Is.

**Big Bunsby Marine
Provincial Park**

Clanninick Cr.

Brooks
Peninsula
P. P.

Thomas
Is.

St. Pauls Dome
301 m

**Kyuquot
Seaplane
Base**

4

North

Clanninick
Cove

Walters
Cove

McKay
Cove

**McLean
Is.**

Kyuquot

Amos
Is.

Kamils
Anchorage

**Walters
Is.**

Barter
Cove

Pacific

Lookout
Is.

**Aktis
Is.**

Kamils
Is.

Tle:hoh
Is.

Alert
Point

3

114

83

81

Ocean

Thornton
Is.

2

1

5,550,000 m N

5,540,000 m N

5,530,000 m N

5,520,000 m N

5,510,000 m N

590,000 m E

600,000 m E

610,000 m E

A   B   C   D

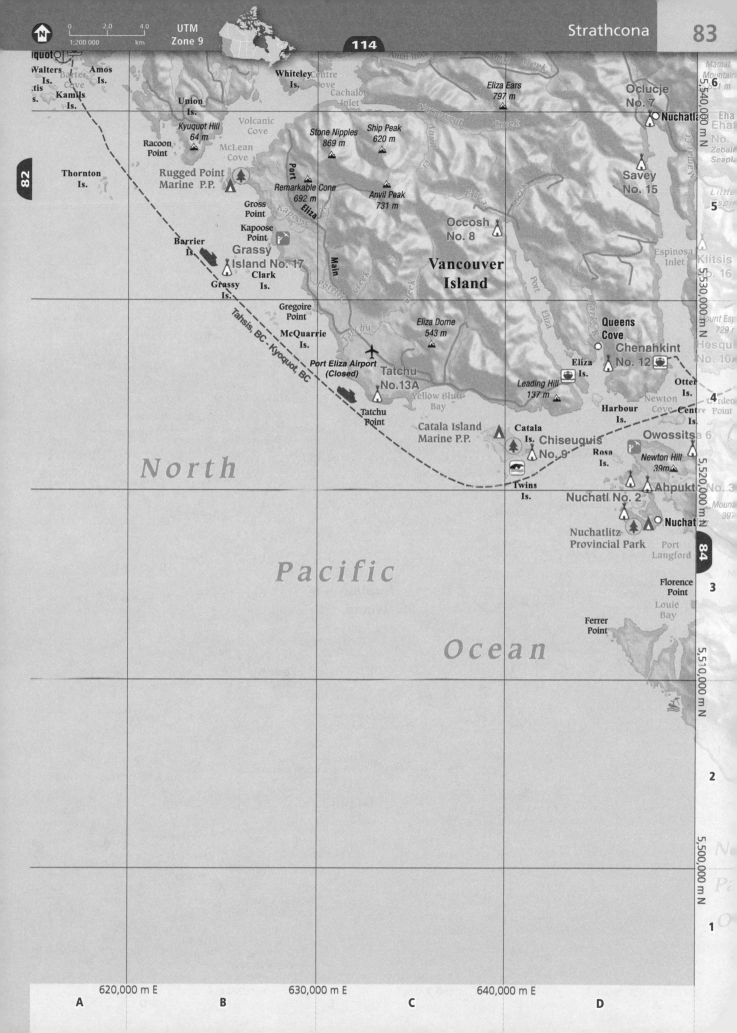

N

0 2.0 4.0
km

114

82

84

North

Pacific

Ocean

**Vancouver
Island**

Walters
Is.
Amos
Is.
Barter
Cove
Kamils
Is.
quot
tis
Is.

Thornton
Is.

Whiteley
Is.
Centre
Cove
Cachalot
Inlet

Eliza Ears
797 m

Oclucje
No. 7

Nuchatla

Mamat
Mountain

Eha
Eha
No.
Zeball
Seapl

Union
Is.

Kyuquot Hill
64 m

Volcanic
Cove

McLean
Cove

Stone Nipples
869 m

Ship Peak
620 m

Savey
No. 15

Racoon
Point

Rugged Point
Marine P.P.

Remarkable Cone
692 m

Anvil Peak
731 m

Occosh
No. 8

Little
spit

Gross
Point

Kapoose
Point

Barrier
Is.

Grassy
Island No. 17

Clark
Is.

Grassy
Is.

Port

Eliza

Main

Port

Eliza

Kapoose

Espinosa
Inlet

Klitsis
16

Gregoire
Point

McQuarrie
Is.

Port Eliza Airport
(Closed)

Tatchu
No.13A

Tatchu
Point

Eliza Dome
543 m

Yellow Bluff
Bay

Catala Island
Marine P.P.

Queens
Cove

Chenahkint
No. 12

Eliza
Is.

Leading Hill
137 m

Harbour
Is.

Catala
Is.

Chiseuquis
No. 9

Rosa
Is.

Newton
Cove

Otter
Is.

Centre
Is.

Owossitsa

Newton Hill
39m

Ahpukt

Nuchatl No. 2

Nuchatlitz
Provincial Park

Nuchat

Port
Langford

Florence
Point

Louie
Bay

Ferrer
Point

Twins
Is.

Mount Esp
729 r

Hesqui
No.10

Garden
Point

No. 3

Mount
397

Tahsis, BC - Kyoquot, BC

5,540,000 m N
6

5,530,000 m N
5

4

5,520,000 m N

5,510,000 m N
3

2

5,500,000 m N
1

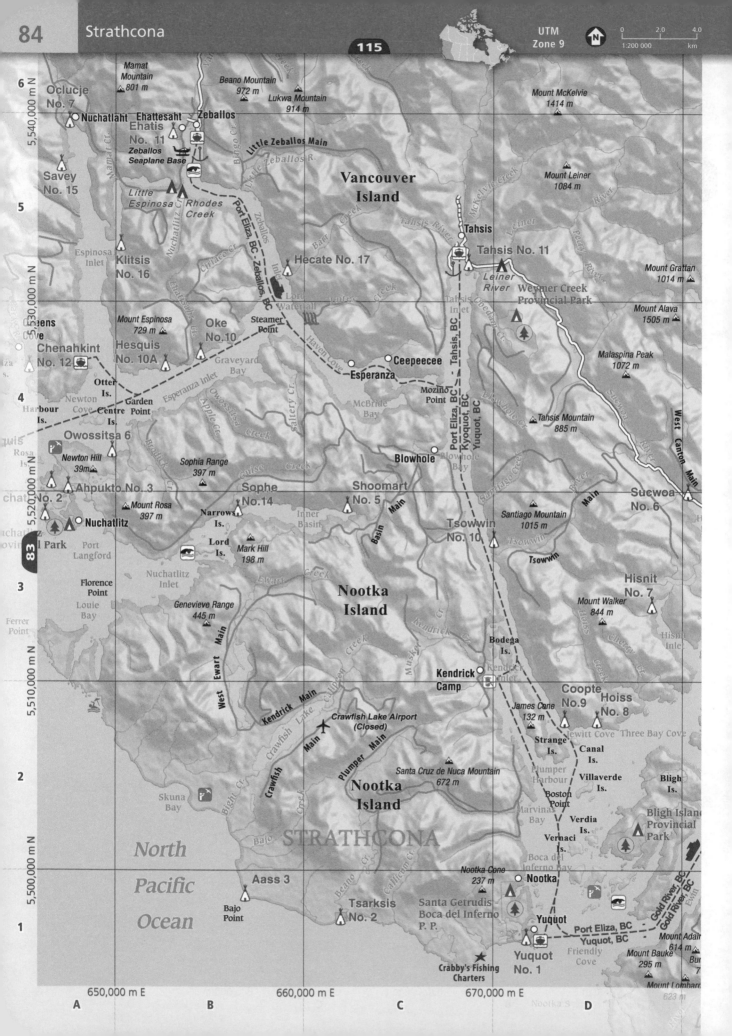

Vancouver Island

Oclucje No. 7

Mamat Mountain 801 m

Beano Mountain 972 m

Lukwa Mountain 914 m

Mount McKelvie 1414 m

Nuchatlaht

Ehattesaht

Zeballos

Ehatis No. 11

Zeballos Seaplane Base

Little Zeballos Main

Little Zeballos R.

Savey No. 15

Little Espinosa

Rhodes Creek

Mount Leiner 1084 m

Espinosa Inlet

Klitsis No. 16

Hecate No. 17

Tahsis

Tahsis No. 11

Mount Grattan 1014 m

Leiner River

Weymer Creek Provincial Park

eens Cove

Mount Espinosa 729 m

Oke No.10

Steamer Point

Lord Waterfall

Mount Alava 1505 m

Chenahkint No. 12

Hesquis No. 10A

Graveyard Bay

Ceepeecee

Esperanza

Mozino Point

Malaspina Peak 1072 m

Otter Is.

Newton Cove

Garden Centre Point

Esperanza Inlet

McBride Bay

Tahsis Mountain 885 m

Harbour Is.

Owossitsa 6

Rosa Is.

Newton Hill 39m

Sophia Range 397 m

West Canton Main

Blowhole

Blowhole Bay

chat No. 2

Ahpukto No. 3

Mount Rosa 397 m

Sophe No.14

Shoomart No. 5

Sucwoa No. 6

chatlitz ovincial Park

Nuchatlitz

Narrows Is.

Inner Basin

Basin Main

Tsowwin No. 10

Santiago Mountain 1015 m

Port Langford

Lord Is.

Mark Hill 198 m

Tsowwin

Hisnit No. 7

Florence Point

Louie Bay

Genevieve Range 445 m

Nootka Island

Mount Walker 844 m

Ferrer Point

Hisnit Inlet

Bodega Is.

Kendrick Camp

Coopte No.9

Hoiss No. 8

Kendrick Lake

Crawfish Lake Airport (Closed)

James Cone 132 m

Jewitt Cove

Three Bay Cove

Strange Is.

Canal Is.

Skuna Bay

Plumper Harbour

Santa Cruz de Nuca Mountain 672 m

Villaverde Is.

Bligh Is.

Nootka Island

Boston Point

Bligh Island Provincial Park

North

STRATHCONA

Marvinas Bay

Verdia Is.

Vernaci Is.

Pacific

Aass 3

Nootka Cone 237 m

Boca del Inferno Bay

Nootka

Gold River, BC

Ocean

Bajo Point

Tsarksis No. 2

Santa Getrudis-Boca del Inferno P.P.

Yuquot

Gold River, BC

Mount Adam 614 m

Yuquot No. 1

Port Eliza, BC

Yuquot, BC

Friendly Cove

Mount Bauke 295 m

Crabby's Fishing Charters

Mount Lombard 623 m

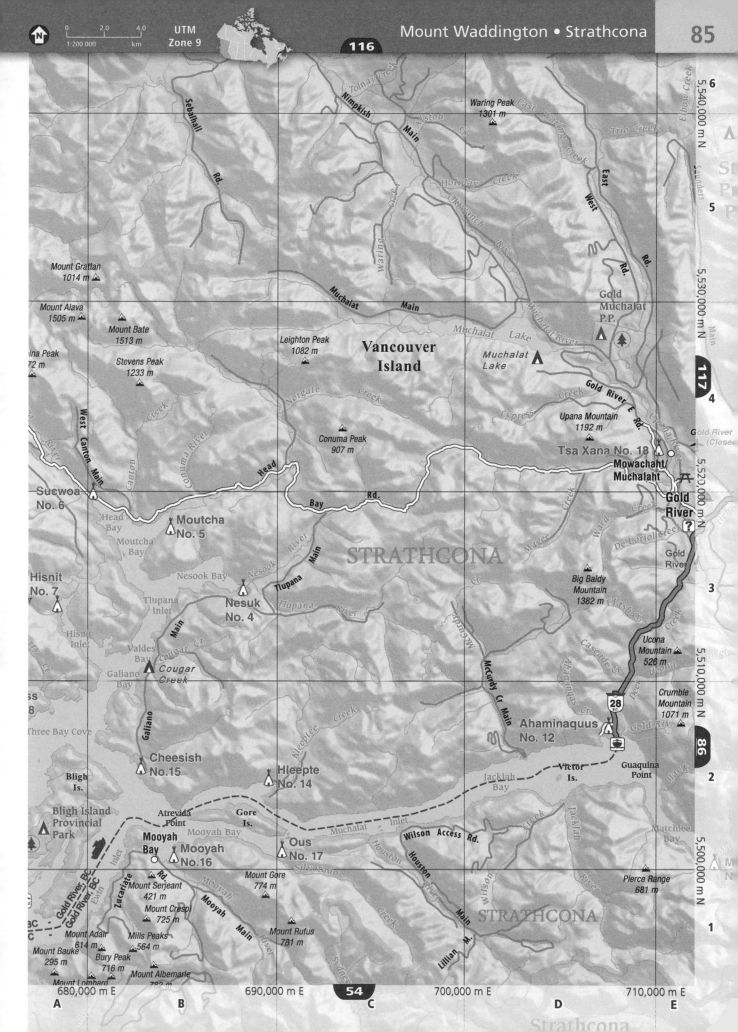

N

1:200 000   0   2.0   4.0
km

UTM
Zone 9

116

6

5,540,000 m N

Tolnay Creek

Nimpkish Main

Sebalhall Rd.

Waring Peak
1301 m

East Waring Creek

Trio Creek

Elbow Creek

St
P
P

Alston Cr.

Holiday Creek

East

West

Rd.

Rd.

Saunders

5

5,530,000 m N

Mount Grattan
1014 m

Ashwood Creek

Oktwanch Riv.

Muchalat

Main

Muchalat Lake

Gold
Muchalat
P.P.

Main

117

Mount Alava
1505 m

Mount Bate
1513 m

Leighton Peak
1082 m

Vancouver
Island

Muchalat
Lake

Gold River E. Rd.

4

5,520,000 m N

na Peak
72 m

Stevens Peak
1233 m

Norgate Creek

Creek

Cypress

Upana Mountain
1192 m

Upana River

Gold River
(Close

West Canton Main

Conuma River

Canton

Creek

Head

Conuma Peak
907 m

Creek

Tsa Xana No. 18

Mowachaht/
Muchalaht

Gold
River

?

Sucwoa
No. 6

Head
Bay

Bay

Rd.

Ward

Creek

De Loriol Creek

Gold
River

3

5,520,000 m N

Moutcha
No. 5

Moutcha
Bay

Nesook Bay

Nesook River

Main

Tlupana

STRATHCONA

Magee

Cr.

Big Baldy
Mountain
1382 m

Flash Cr.

Hisnit
No. 7

Tlupana
Inlet

Nesuk
No. 4

Tlupana River

Hisnit
Inlet

Valdes
Bay

Cougar Cr.

Main

McCurdy

Cr.

Ucona
Mountain
526 m

Cascade Cr.

Ahaminaas Cr.

Ucona River

5,510,000 m N

ss
8

Three Bay Cove

Galiano
Bay

Cougar
Creek

Galiano

Kleeptee

Creek

McCurdy Cr Main

28
BC

Crumble
Mountain
1071 m

Gold Riv.

86

2

Bligh
Is.

Cheesish
No.15

Hleepte
No. 14

Jacklah
Bay

Victor
Is.

Guaquina
Point

Bligh Island
Provincial
Park

Atrevida
Point

Gore
Is.

Mooyah Bay

Muchalat

Inlet

Wilson Access Rd.

Matchlee
Bay

5,500,000 m N

Gold River, BC
Gold River, BC

Zuciarte

Mooyah
Bay

Mooyah
No.16

Ous
No. 17

Silverado

Houston River

Houston

Wilson Cr.

Jacklah River

Rd.

Mount Serjeant
421 m

Mount Crespi
725 m

Mount Gore
774 m

Mooyah Main

Mount Rufus
781 m

STRATHCONA

Pierce Range
681 m

1

Mount Adair
614 m

Mills Peaks
564 m

Mount Bauke
295 m

Bury Peak
716 m

Mount Albemarle
782 m

Mount Lombard

Lillian M.

Sydney Creek

BC
BC
BC

Erwin

680,000 m E   A

690,000 m E   B

54   C

700,000 m E   D

710,000 m E   E

Strathcona

UTM
Zone 10

1:200 000

0   2.0   4.0
km

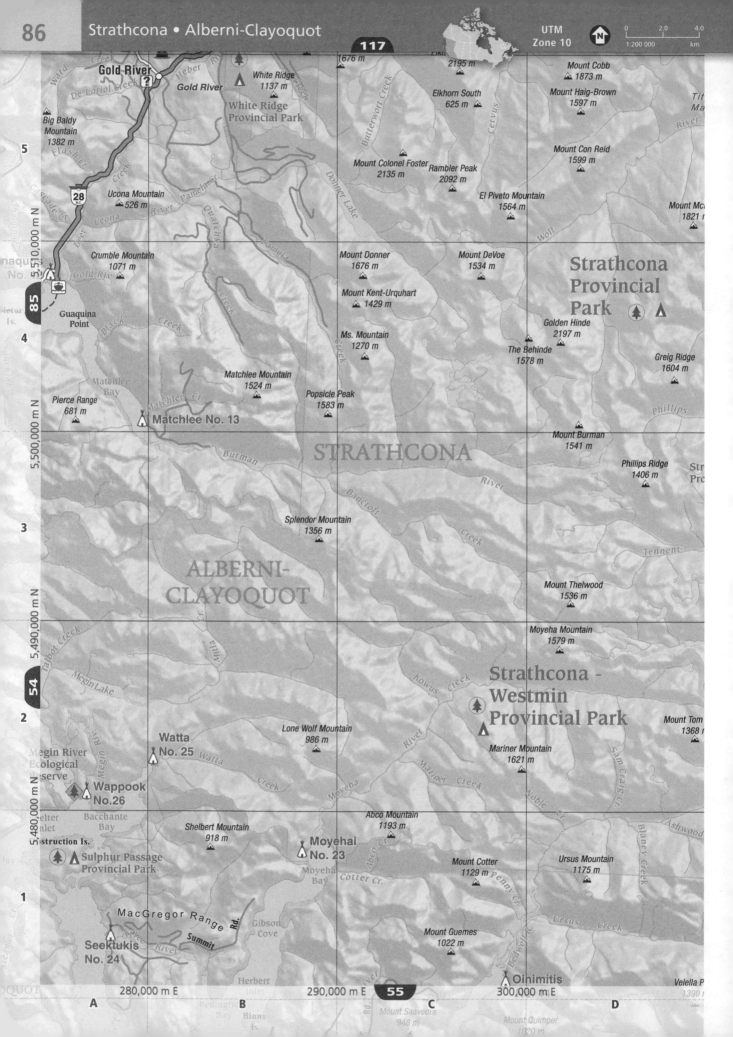

117

Gold River
Gold River

Big Baldy
Mountain
1382 m

White Ridge
1137 m

White Ridge
Provincial Park

1676 m

2195 m

Mount Cobb
1873 m

Mount Haig-Brown
1597 m

Elkhorn South
625 m

Mount Con Reid
1599 m

Ucona Mountain
526 m

Mount Colonel Foster
2135 m

Rambler Peak
2092 m

El Piveto Mountain
1564 m

Mount Mc...
1821 ...

28
BC

Crumble Mountain
1071 m

Mount Donner
1676 m

Mount DeVoe
1534 m

Strathcona
Provincial
Park

Mount Kent-Urquhart
1429 m

Golden Hinde
2197 m

85

Guaquina
Point

Ms. Mountain
1270 m

The Behinde
1578 m

Greig Ridge
1604 m

Matchlee Mountain
1524 m

Pierce Range
681 m

Matchlee
Bay

Matchlee No. 13

Popsicle Peak
1583 m

Mount Burman
1541 m

Phillips Ridge
1406 m

Str
Pro

STRATHCONA

Burman

Splendor Mountain
1356 m

Mount Thelwood
1536 m

ALBERNI-
CLAYOQUOT

Moyeha Mountain
1579 m

54

Megin Lake

Strathcona -
Westmin
Provincial Park

Mount Tom
1368 m

Lone Wolf Mountain
986 m

Mariner Mountain
1621 m

Watta
No. 25

Megin River
Ecological
Reserve

Wappook
No.26

Bacchante
Bay

Abco Mountain
1193 m

Shelbert Mountain
918 m

Moyehai
No. 23

Ursus Mountain
1175 m

Sulphur Passage
Provincial Park

Moyeha
Bay

Mount Cotter
1129 m

1

MacGregor Range

Summit

Gibson
Cove

Mount Guemes
1022 m

Seektukis
No. 24

Oinimitis

Velella P...
1390 ...

280,000 m E   290,000 m E   **55**   300,000 m E

A   B   C   D

Mount Saavedra
948 m

Mount Quimper
1020 m

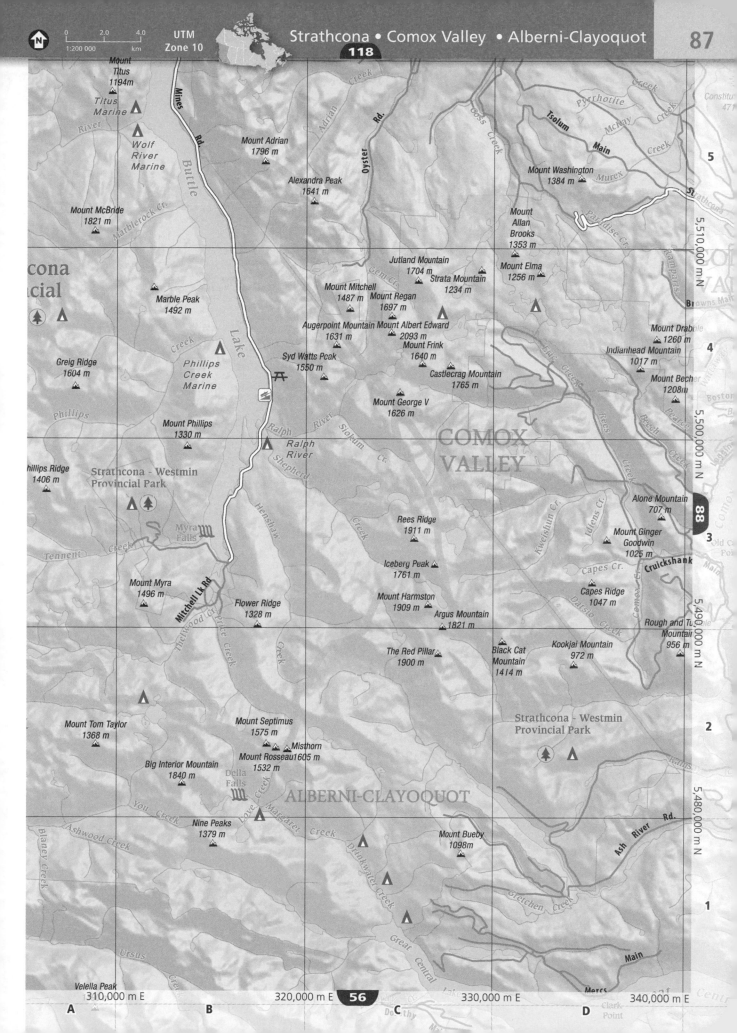

UTM
Zone 10

1:200 000

2.0   4.0
km

5

Mount
Titus
1194m

Titus
Marine

Wolf
River
Marine

Mount Adrian
1796 m

Mount Washington
1384 m

Tsolum

Main

Pyrrhotite

McKay

Mount McBride
1821 m

Marble Peak
1492 m

Alexandra Peak
1641 m

Mount
Allan
Brooks
1353 m

Browns Main

Jutland Mountain
1704 m

Mount Elma
1256 m

Strata Mountain
1234 m

Mount Mitchell
1487 m

Mount Regan
1697 m

Mount Drable
1260 m

4

Greig Ridge
1604 m

Augerpoint Mountain
1631 m

Mount Albert Edward
2093 m

Mount Frink
1640 m

Indianhead Mountain
1017 m

Mount Becher
1208m

Syd Watts Peak
1550 m

Castlecrag Mountain
1765 m

Phillips
Creek
Marine

Mount George V
1626 m

Phillips

Mount Phillips
1330 m

Ralph
River

Slokum
Cr.

COMOX
VALLEY

Phillips Ridge
1406 m

Strathcona - Westmin
Provincial Park

Ralph
River

Shepherd

Alone Mountain
707 m

88

Myra
Falls

Rees Ridge
1911 m

Mount Ginger
Goodwin
1025 m

3

Tennent

Iceberg Peak
1761 m

Capes Cr.

Cruickshank

Mount Myra
1496 m

Flower Ridge
1328 m

Mount Harmston
1909 m

Argus Mountain
1821 m

Capes Ridge
1047 m

Rough and Tumble
Mountain
956 m

The Red Pillar
1900 m

Black Cat
Mountain
1414 m

Kookjai Mountain
972 m

Mount Tom Taylor
1368 m

Mount Septimus
1575 m

Strathcona - Westmin
Provincial Park

2

Big Interior Mountain
1840 m

Misthorn
1605 m

Mount Rosseau
1532 m

Della
Falls

ALBERNI-CLAYOQUOT

Nine Peaks
1379 m

Mount Bueby
1098m

Ash
River
Rd.

Velella Peak

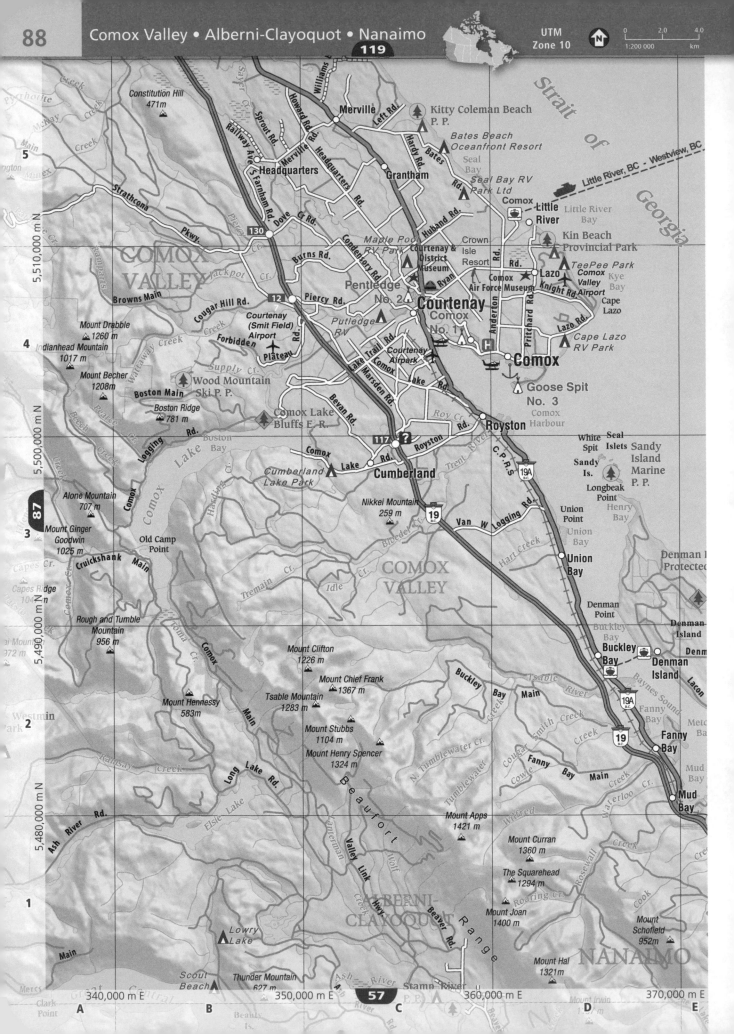

88

Comox Valley • Alberni-Clayoquot • Nanaimo

119

UTM
Zone 10

1:200 000

0   2.0   4.0
km

Strait of Georgia

Constitution Hill
471m

Merville

Kitty Coleman Beach
P. P.

Bates Beach
Oceanfront Resort

Seal
Bay

Seal Bay RV
Park Ltd

Grantham

Comox

Little River, BC – Westview, BC

Little River
Bay

Little
River

Kin Beach
Provincial Park

Headquarters

130

COMOX
VALLEY

Maple Pool
RV Park

Courtenay &
District
Museum

Crown
Isle
Resort

Comox
Air Force Museum

TeePee Park

Lazo

Comox
Valley
Airport

Kye
Bay

Browns Main

12
7

Pentledge
No. 2

Ryan

Cape
Lazo

Mount Drabble
1260 m

Courtenay
(Smit Field)
Airport

Piercy Rd.

Courtenay

Comox
No. 1

Anderton Rd.

Pritchard Rd.

Lazo Rd.

Cape Lazo
RV Park

Indianhead Mountain
1017 m

Forbidden

Putledge
RV

Courtenay
Airpark

Comox

Plateau

Comox
Lake

Lake
Trail
Rd.

Marsden Rd.

Lake
Rd.

Comox

Mount Becher
1208m

Wood Mountain
Ski P. P.

Boston Main

Bevan Rd.

Roy Cr.

Goose Spit
No. 3

Boston Ridge
781 m

Comox Lake
Bluffs E. R.

Comox
Lake

Comox
Lake   Rd.

Royston

Comox
Harbour

White
Spit

Seal
Islets

Sandy
Island
Marine
P. P.

117

Royston

Trent   River

Sandy
Is.

Alone Mountain
707 m

Cumberland
Lake Park

Cumberland

C.P.R.s

19A
B.C.

Longbeak
Point

Henry
Bay

87

Mount Ginger
Goodwin
1025 m

Old Camp
Point

Nikkei Mountain
259 m

19
B.C.

Van W Logging Rd.

Union Point

Union
Bay

Denman I
Protected

Cruickshank   Main

Capes Cr.

Capes Ridge
104 N

Hart Creek

Union
Bay

COMOX
VALLEY

Broeder

Tremain   Cr.

Idle   Cr.

Cr.

Denman
Point

Denman
Island

Rough and Tumble
Mountain
956 m

Buckley
Bay

Buckley
Bay

Denman

i Mount
72 m

Foma   Cr.

Comox

Mount Clifton
1226 m

Buckley
Bay
Main

Tsable   River

19A
B.C.

Denman
Island

Mount Hennessy
583 m

Mount Chief Frank
1367 m

Fanny
Bay

Westmin
ark

Tsable Mountain
1283 m

Smith Creek

Baynes Sound

Mount Stubbs
1104 m

19
B.C.

Fanny
Bay

Mount Henry Spencer
1324 m

N. Tumblewater Cr.

Cougar

Fanny Bay

Fanny
Bay

Main

Ramsay   Creek

Long   Lake   Rd.

Beaufort

Tumblewater

Cowle

Mud
Bay

Main

Elsie Lake   Rd.

Mount Apps
1421 m

Wilfred

Mud
Bay

Ash River Rd.

Valley   Link   Hwy.

Mount Curran
1360 m

Roaring Cr.

Rosewall   Creek

Waterloo   Cr.

Cook   Cr.

ALBERNI-
CLAYOQUOT

Beaver Rd.

The Squarehead
1294 m

Lowry
Lake

Mount Joan
1400 m

Mount
Schofield
952m

Scout
Beach

Thunder Mountain
627 m

Ash   River

Stamp River

Mount Hal
1321m

NANAIMO

Mercs

Clark
Point

Main

P. P. A

Mount Irwin

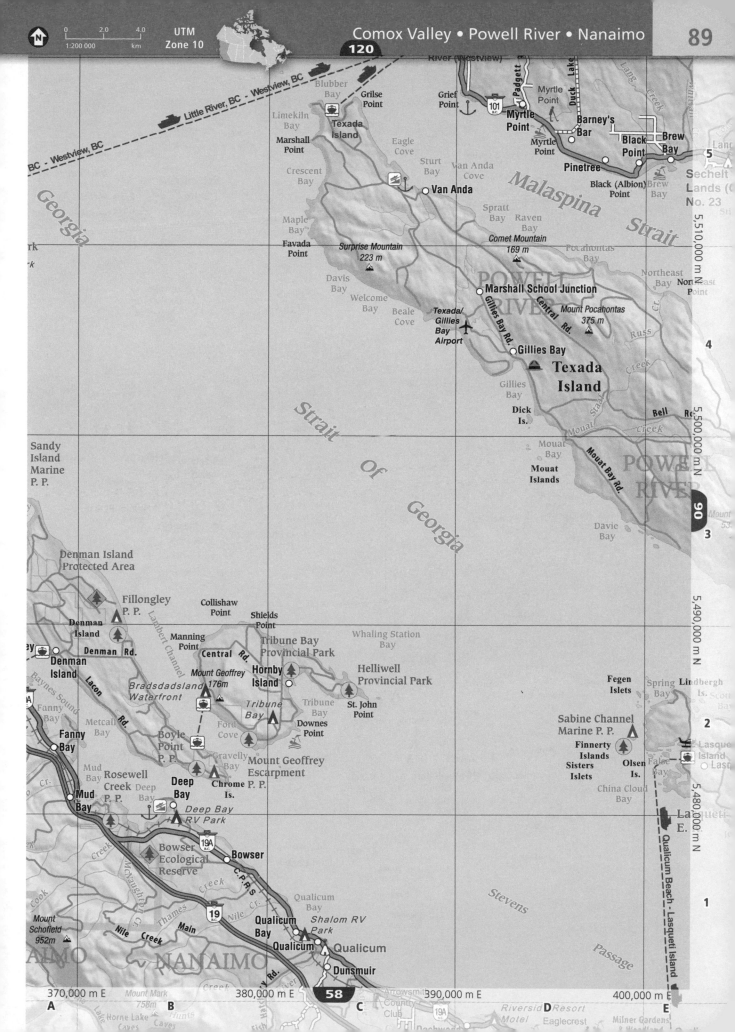

N

| 0 | 2.0 | 4.0 |

1:200 000   km

UTM
Zone 10

120

River (Westview)

BC - Westview, BC

Little River, BC - Westview, BC

BC - Westview, BC

Blubber
Bay

Grilse
Point

Limekiln
Bay

Texada
Island

Marshall
Point

Crescent
Bay

Maple
Bay

Favada
Point

Davis
Bay

Welcome
Bay

Beale
Cove

Grief
Point

101
B.C.

Padgett

Myrtle
Point

Myrtle
Point

Barney's
Bar

Black
Point

Brew
Bay

Pinetree

Black (Albion)
Point

Brew
Bay

Sechelt
Lands (
No. 23

Eagle
Cove

Sturt
Bay

Van Anda
Cove

Van Anda

Malaspina   Strait

Spratt
Bay

Raven
Bay

Comet Mountain
169 m

Pocahontas
Bay

Surprise Mountain
223 m

Marshall School Junction

Mount Pocahontas
375 m

Northeast
Bay

Northeast
Point

5,510,000 m N

Lang

5

A

Texada/
Gillies
Bay
Airport

Gillies Bay Rd.

Central   Rd.

Russ
Cr.

Russ
Creek

4

5,500,000 m N

Gillies
Bay

Gillies Bay

Texada
Island

Bell   Rd.

Dick
Is.

Mouat
Creek

Mouat
Bay

POWER
RIVER

90

Georgia

Sandy
Island
Marine
P. P.

Strait

of

Georgia

Mouat
Bay

Mouat
Islands

Mouat Bay Rd.

Davie
Bay

Mount
53

3

5,490,000 m N

Denman Island
Protected Area

Fillongley
P. P.

Denman
Island

Denman
Island

Denman Rd.

Manning
Point

Lambert Channel

Collishaw
Point

Shields
Point

Tribune Bay
Provincial Park

Central   Rd.

Mount Geoffrey
176m

Hornby
Island

Bradsdadsland
Waterfront

Tribune
Bay

Ford
Cove

Whaling Station
Bay

Helliwell
Provincial Park

Tribune
Bay

Downes
Point

St. John
Point

Fegen
Islets

Spring   Lindbergh
Bay   Is.   Scott
Bay

2

Sabine Channel
Marine P. P.

Finnerty
Islands

Sisters
Islets

Olsen
Is.

Lasqueti
Island

Last

5,480,000 m N

Fanny
Bay

Baynes Sound

Lacon   Rd.

Metcalf
Bay

Fanny
Bay

Boyle
Point
P. P.

Gravelly
Bay

Mount Geoffrey
Escarpment

Mud
Bay   Deep
Bay

Mud
Bay

Rosewell
Creek
P. P.

Deep Bay
RV Park

Chrome
Is.

China Cloud
Bay

False
Bay

Lasqueti
Island

E.

Lasqueti
Is.

19A
B.C.

Bowser
Ecological
Reserve

C.P.R.S.

Bowser

Qualicum
Bay

Stevens

Passage

1

Mount
Schofield
952m

19

Nile   Creek

Main

Nile   Cr.

Qualicum
Bay

Qualicum

Shalom RV
Park

Qualicum

Dunsmuir

Riversid   Resort
Motel   Eaglecrest

Milner Gardens

19A

NAIMO   NANAIMO

Cook   Cr.

McNaughton Cr.

Thames   Creek

Creek

Arrowsmith
Country
Club

Horne Lake
Caves

121

POWELL RIVER

Mount Troubridge
1253 m

Sykes
Is.

Mount Foley
266m

Sydney
Is.

Lois
Point

Lois
Lake

Saltery
Bay P. P.

Saltery
Bay

Culloden
Point

Foley
Head

Saltery Bay, B.C.

Black
Point

Brew
Bay

Lang Bay

101
B.C.

Saltery
Bay P. P.

Powell River
(Saltery Bay)

Fairview
Bay

Cook
Point

Earls Cove, B.C.

Captain
Island

Killam
Bay

(Albion)
Point

Sechelt Band
Lands (Cokqueneets)
No. 23

Stillwater

Thunder
Bay

Mermaid
Cove

Saltery
Bay

Ahlstrom
Point

Nelson
Island (Earl's
Cove)

Sechelt
Terminal

Backeddy
Resort
Marine

Earls
Cove

Black
Point

Thunder
Point

Copper
Is.

Eagle
Is.

Vanguard
Bay

Egmont Rd

Egmont

Strait

Stillwater
Bay

Froland

Ball
Point

Hardy
Is.

Telescope
Passage

Caldwell
Is.

Klein
Lake

McRae
Cove

Evenden
Point

Bishop
Is.

Scotch Fir
Point

Hardy Island
Marine P. P.

Oyster
Is.

Fox
Is.

Marr
Is.

Nelson
Island

Ambrose
Lake Ecological
Reserve

Mount Hallo
1046 m

Northeast
Bay

Northeast
Point

Ballet
Bay

Kelly
Is.

Hidden
Basin

Green
Bay

Billings
Bay

SUNSHINE
COAST

Sechelt Band
Lands
(Saughanaught)
No. 22

Garden
Bay
Marine
P. P.

Spipiyus
Provincial
Park

Cockburn
Bay

Cape
Cockburn

Orchard
Bay

Flat Rock
Bay

Mermaid
Point

Pender Hill
103m

Sechelt
Band
Lands
No. 19

Pender
Harbour

Sechelt Band
Lands No. 18

Bell   Rd.

Malaspina

Martin
Is.

Charles
Is.

Donnely
Landing

Garden Bay

Sechelt Band
Lands

POWELL
RIVER

Mount Grant
676 m

Strait

Francis
Point
E. R.

Francis
Bay

No. 20A

Madeira Park

Mount Davies
533 m

Bobs
Lake

Pope
Landing

89

Francis Point
Provincial Park

Sechelt Band
Lands
No. 24

Harness
Is.

Gerrans
Bay

Bay Rd.

Farrington
Cove

Bill Bay

Shingle
Beach

McNaughton
Point

Dingman
Bay

Secret
Cove

Fegen
Islets

Spring
Bay

Lindbergh
Is.

Bunny
Is.

Cook
Bay

South
Texada
Island
P. P.

Mount Shepherd
743 m

Turnagain
Is.

Smuggler
Cove
Marine
P. P.

Scottie
Bay

Jelina
Is.

West
Point

Sabine

Deep
Bay

North
Thormanby
Is.

Smuggler
Cove

Channel

Tucker
Bay

Jervis
Is.

Paul
Is. Jedediah
Is.

Mount Dick
163 m

Anderson Bay
Provincial Park

Epsom
Point

Halfmoon
Bay

Olsen
Is.

Lasqueti
Island

Main   Rd.

Boho
Is.

Home
Bay

Anderson
Bay

Buccaneer
Bay P. P.

Spy Glass Hill
71m

Simson
Provincial
Park

Lasqueti

Trematon Mountain
161 m

Lasqueti
Island

Jedediah
Island
Marine
P. P.

Bull
Is.

Rabbit
Is.

Upwood
Point

South
Thormanby
Is.

Lasqueti Island
E. R.

Jenkins
Cove

Richardson
Cove

Graveyard
Bay

Boat
Cove

Rouse Bay

Windy Bay

Squitty
Bay

Strait Of Georgia

Bertha
Island

Jenkins
Is.

Young
Point

Squitty Bay
Provincial Park

Tahini
Cove

Sangster
Is.

Elephant
Eye Point

Qualicum Beach - Lasqueti Island

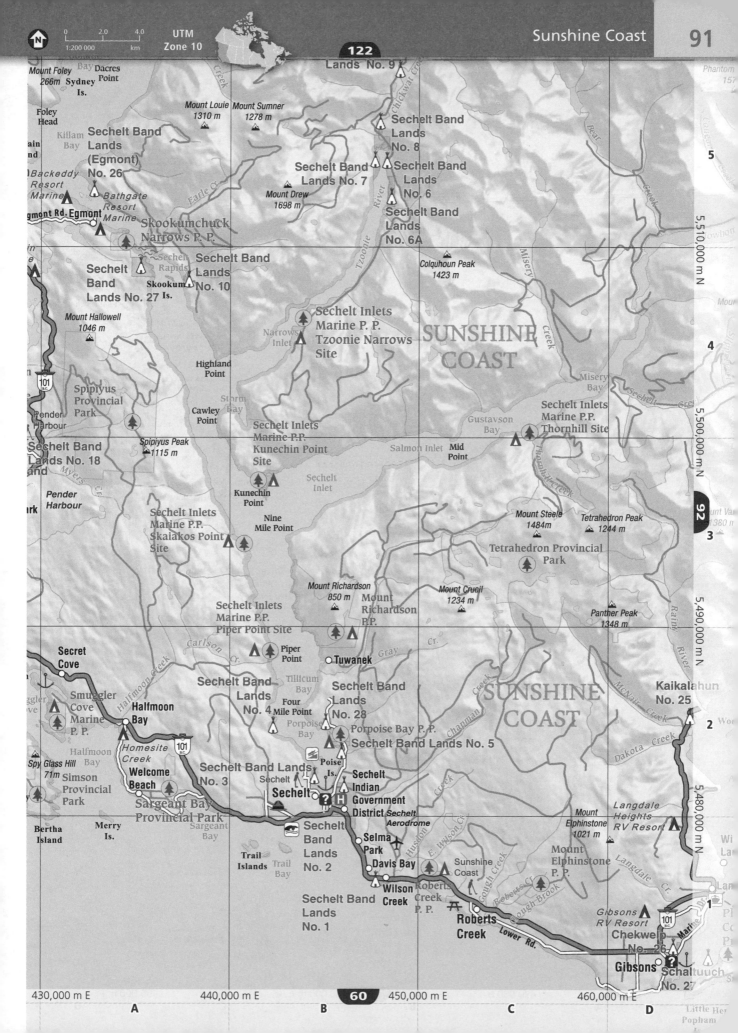

UTM
Zone 10
1:200 000

122

Mount Foley
266m Sydney Point
Is.

Dacres
Point

Foley
Head

Killam
Bay

Mount Louie
1310 m

Mount Sumner
1278 m

Lands No. 9

Sechelt Band
Lands
No. 8

Sechelt Band
Lands
(Egmont)
No. 26

Sechelt Band
Lands No. 7

Sechelt Band
Lands
No. 6

Backeddy
Resort
Marine

Bathgate
Resort
Marine

Mount Drew
1698 m

Sechelt Band
Lands
No. 6A

Egmont Rd. Egmont

Skookumchuck
Narrows P. P.

Sechelt
Rapids

Colquhoun Peak
1423 m

Sechelt
Band
Lands No. 27

Sechelt Band
Lands
No. 10

Skookum
Is.

SUNSHINE
COAST

Mount Hallowell
1046 m

Narrows
Inlet

Sechelt Inlets
Marine P. P.
Tzoonie Narrows
Site

Spipiyus
Provincial
Park

Highland
Point

Misery
Bay

Pender
Harbour

Spipiyus Peak
1115 m

Cawley
Point

Storm
Bay

Sechelt Inlets
Marine P.P.
Kunechin Point
Site

Gustavson
Bay

Sechelt Inlets
Marine P.P.
Thornhill Site

Sechelt Band
Lands No. 18

Salmon Inlet

Mid
Point

Myers

Pender
Harbour

Kunechin
Point

Sechelt
Inlet

Mount Steele
1484m

Tetrahedron Peak
1244 m

Nine
Mile Point

Sechelt Inlets
Marine P.P.
Skaiakos Point
Site

Tetrahedron Provincial
Park

Mount Richardson
850 m

Mount
Richardson
P.P.

Mount Crucil
1234 m

Sechelt Inlets
Marine P.P.
Piper Point Site

Panther Peak
1348 m

Carlson Cr.

Gray
Cr.

Secret
Cove

Piper
Point

Tuwanek

SUNSHINE
COAST

Kaikalahun
No. 25

Smuggler
Cove
Marine
P. P.

Halfmoon
Creek

Halfmoon
Bay

Sechelt Band
Lands
No. 4

Tillicum
Bay

Four
Mile Point

Sechelt Band
Lands
No. 28

Porpoise Bay P.P.
Sechelt Band Lands No. 5

McNair Creek

Spy Glass Hill
71m

Halfmoon
Bay

Homesite
Creek

Porpoise
Bay

Poise
Is.

Dakota Creek

Simson
Provincial
Park

Welcome
Beach

Sechelt Band Lands
No. 3

Sechelt

Sechelt
Indian
Government
District

Sechelt
Aerodrome

Mount
Elphinstone
1021 m

Langdale
Heights
RV Resort

Bertha
Island

Merry
Is.

Sargeant Bay
Provincial Park

Sargeant
Bay

Selma
Park

Sunshine
Coast

Mount
Elphinstone
P.P.

Trail
Islands

Trail
Bay

Sechelt
Band
Lands
No. 2

Davis Bay

Wilson
Creek

Sunshine
Coast

Gibsons
RV Resort

Chekwelp
No. 26

Roberts
Creek P.P.

Roberts
Creek

Lower Rd.

Gibsons

Schaltuuch
No. 27

Sechelt Band
Lands
No. 1

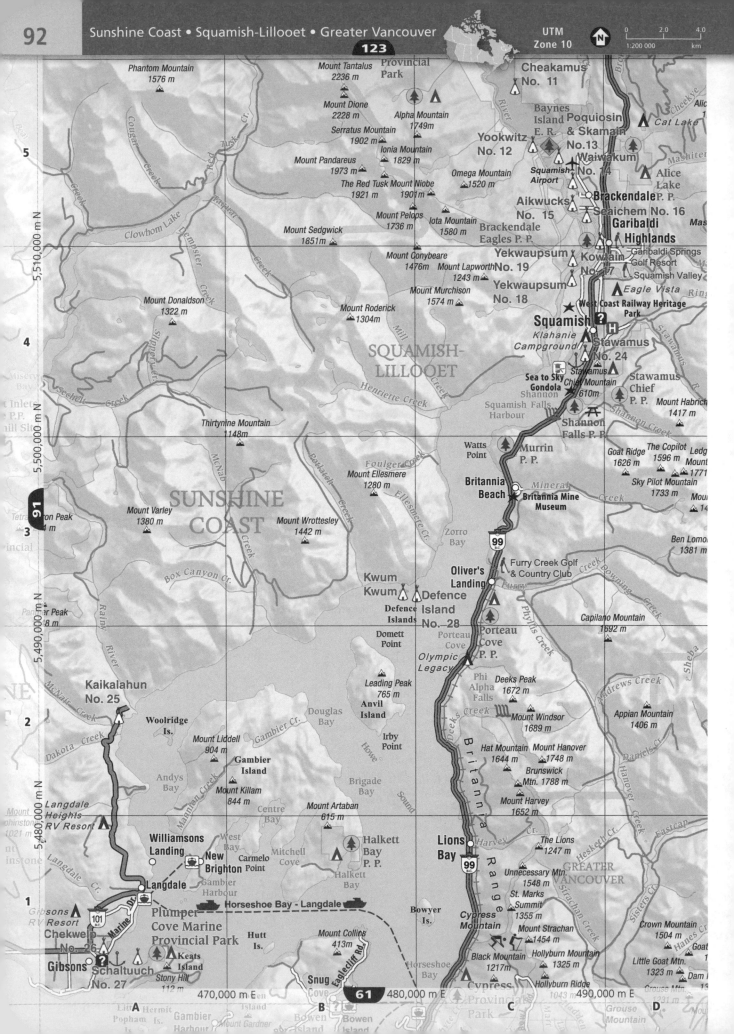

123

Phantom Mountain
1576 m

Mount Tantalus
2236 m

Provincial
Park

Cheakamus
No. 11

Mount Dione
2228 m

Baynes
Island
E. R.

Poquiosin
& Skamain
No.13

Cat Lake

Alpha Mountain
1749m

Serratus Mountain
1902 m

Ionia Mountain
1829 m

Yookwitz
No. 12

Waiwakum
No. 14

Alice
Lake
P. P.

Mount Pandareus
1973 m

Omega Mountain
1520 m

Squamish
Airport

The Red Tusk Mount Niobe
1921 m   1901m

Aikwucks
No. 15

Brackendale

Seaichem No. 16

Garibaldi
Highlands

Mount Pelops
1736 m

Iota Mountain
1580 m

Brackendale
Eagles P. P.

Mount Sedgwick
1851 m

Mount Conybeare
1476m   Mount Lapworth
1243 m

Yekwaupsum
No. 19

Kowtain
No. 17

Garibaldi Springs
Golf Resort

Squamish Valley

Mount Donaldson
1322 m

Mount Murchison
1574 m

Yekwaupsum
No. 18

Eagle Vista

Clowhom Lake

Mount Roderick
1304m

West Coast Railway Heritage
Park

SQUAMISH-
LILLOOET

Squamish

Klahanie
Campground

Stawamus
No. 24

Thirtynine Mountain
1148m

Henriette Creek

Sea to Sky
Gondola

Stawamus
Chief Mountain
610m

Stawamus
Chief
P. P.

Mount Habrich
1417 m

Squamish Falls

Squamish
Harbour

Shannon
Falls P. P.

Mount Ellesmere
1280 m

Watts
Point

Murrin
P. P.

Goat Ridge
1626 m

The Copilot
1596 m

Ledge
Mount
1771

SUNSHINE
COAST

Mount Varley
1380 m

Mount Wrottesley
1442 m

Foulger Creek

Sky Pilot Mountain
1733 m

Britannia
Beach

Mineral

Britannia Mine
Museum

Mou
14

Tetrahedron Peak

Zorro
Bay

Ben Lomo
1381 m

99
B.C.

Box Canyon Cr.

Kwum
Kwum

Oliver's
Landing

Furry Creek Golf
& Country Club

Panther Peak

Defence
Island
No. 28

Defence
Islands

Porteau
Cove
P. P.

Capilano Mountain
1692 m

Domett
Point

Porteau
Cove

Kaikalahun
No. 25

Woolridge
Is.

Leading Peak
765 m

Anvil
Island

Olympic
Legacy

Phi
Alpha
Falls

Deeks Peak
1672 m

Mount Windsor
1689 m

Appian Mountain
1406 m

Douglas
Bay

Irby
Point

Mount Liddell
904 m

Gambier Cr.

Hat Mountain
1644 m

Mount Hanover
1748 m

Andys
Bay

Gambier
Island

Mount Killam
844 m

Brigade
Bay

Brunswick
Mtn. 1788 m

Langdale
Heights
RV Resort

Centre
Bay

Mount Artaban
615 m

Mount Harvey
1652 m

Williamsons
Landing

West
Bay

Carmelo
Point

Mitchell
Cove

Halkett
Bay
P. P.

Lions
Bay

New
Brighton

Gambier
Harbour

Halkett
Bay

99
B.C.

Horseshoe Bay - Langdale

Bowyer
Is.

The Lions
1247 m

GREATER
VANCOUVER

Langdale

Gibsons
RV Resort

Plumper
Cove Marine
Provincial Park

Hutt
Is.

Unnecessary Mtn.
1548 m

Cypress
Mountain

St. Marks
Summit
1355 m

Crown Mountain
1504 m

101
B.C.

Mount Collins
413 m

Mount Strachan
1454 m

Chekwelp
No. 26

Hollyburn Mountain
1325 m

Little Goat Mtn.
1323 m

Gibsons

Schaltuuch
No. 27

Keats
Island

Stony Hill
112 m

Snug
Cove

Black Mountain
1217m

Hollyburn Ridge

61

Horseshoe
Bay

Cypress

Provincial
Park

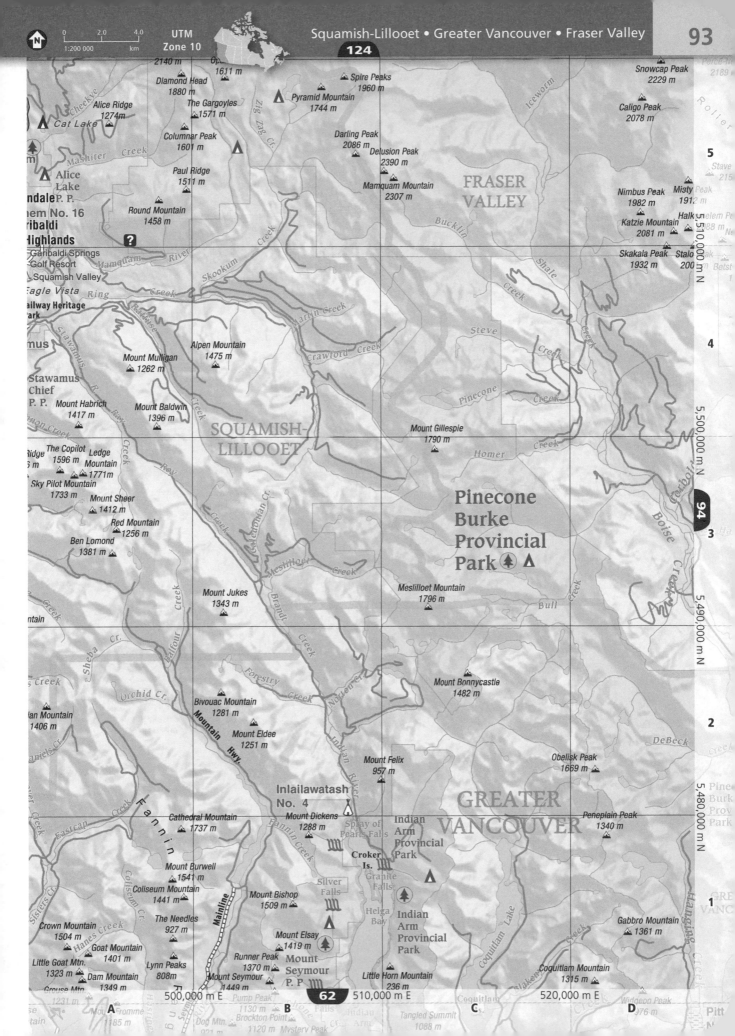

UTM
Zone 10

1:200 000

0   2.0   4.0
km

2140 m
1611 m
Spire Peaks
1960 m

Snowcap Peak
2229 m

2189

Diamond Head
1880 m

Pyramid Mountain
1744 m

Caligo Peak
2078 m

The Gargoyles
1571 m

Alice Ridge
1274m

Columnar Peak
1601 m

Darling Peak
2086 m

Delusion Peak
2390 m

FRASER
VALLEY

Nimbus Peak
1982 m

Misty
Peak
1912 m

Cat Lake

Stave
215

Alice
Lake
P. P.

Paul Ridge
1511 m

Mamquam Mountain
2307 m

Katzie Mountain
2081 m

Halk
88 m

5,510,000 m N

ndale P. P.

hem No. 16

Round Mountain
1458 m

Skakala Peak
1932 m

Stalo
200

ribaldi

Highlands

?

Garibaldi Springs
Golf Resort

Squamish Valley

Eagle Vista

Skookum

Bucklin

Shale

Steve

5

4

ailway Heritage
Park

mus

Mount Mulligan
1262 m

Alpen Mountain
1475 m

Martin Creek

Crawford   Creek

Pinecone

Creek

Stawamus
Chief
P. P.

Mount Habrich
1417 m

Mount Baldwin
1396 m

SQUAMISH-
LILLOOET

Mount Gillespie
1790 m

Homer   Creek

5,500,000 m N

Ridge

The Copilot
1596 m

Ledge
Mountain
1771m

Sky Pilot Mountain
1733 m

Mount Sheer
1412 m

Pinecone
Burke
Provincial
Park

Red Mountain
1256 m

Ben Lomond
1381 m

Meslilloet Mountain
1796 m

Bull

94

3

5,490,000 m N

Mount Jukes
1343 m

Meslilloet

Creek

Brandt   Creek

Sheba   Cr.

Orchid Cr.

Mount Bonnycastle
1482 m

Boise   Creek

dian Mountain
1406 m

Bivouac Mountain
1281 m

Forestry   Creek

Norton   Cr.

DeBeck

2

aniels Cr.

Mount Eldee
1251 m

Mountain   Hwy.

Mount Felix
957 m

Obelisk Peak
1669 m

5,480,000 m N

Inlailawatash
No. 4

Indian River

GREATER
VANCOUVER

Pine
Burk
Prov
Park

Cathedral Mountain
1737 m

Mount Dickens
1288 m

Spray of
Pearls Falls

Indian
Arm
Provincial
Park

Peneplain Peak
1340 m

Eastcap

Fannin   Creek

Croker
Is.

Fannin

Mount Burwell
1541 m

Granite
Falls

GRE
VANC

Coliseum Mountain
1441 m

Mount Bishop
1509 m

Silver
Falls

Helga
Bay

Indian
Arm
Provincial
Park

Gabbro Mountain
1361 m

Sisters Cr.

Coliseum Cr.

Mainline

The Needles
927 m

Crown Mountain
1504 m

Lynn Peaks
808m

Mount Elsay
1419 m

Coquitlam Lake

Coquitlam Mountain
1315 m

1

Goat Mountain
1401 m

Runner Peak
1370 m

Mount
Seymour
P. P.

Little Goat Mtn.
1323 m

Dam Mountain
1349 m

Mount Seymour
1449 m

Little Horn Mountain
236 m

Grouse Mtn.
1231 m

Mou Fromme
1185 m

1130 m
Dog Mtn.
921 m

Brockton Point

Mystery Peak

Indian
Arm

Tangled Summit
1088 m

Pitt

Widgeon Peak
976 m

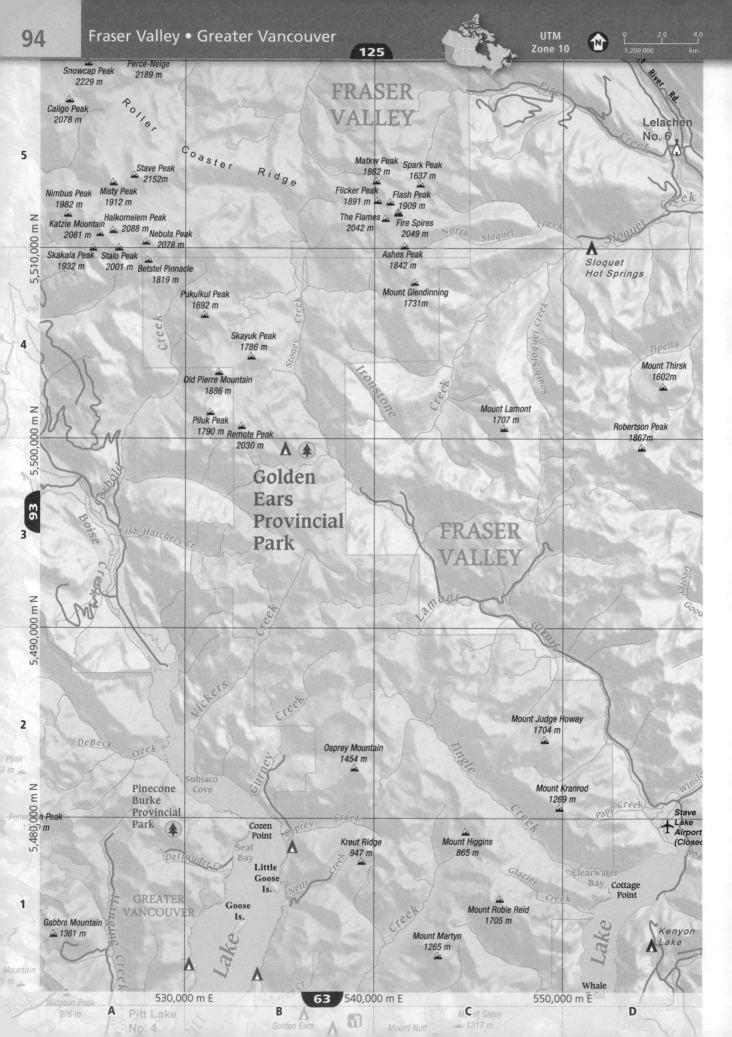

UTM
Zone 10

1:200 000

FRASER VALLEY

Snowcap Peak
2229 m

Perce-Neige
2189 m

Caligo Peak
2078 m

Lelachen
No. 6

Matkw Peak
1862 m

Spark Peak
1637 m

Stave Peak
2152m

Flicker Peak
1891 m

Flash Peak
1909 m

Nimbus Peak
1982 m

Misty Peak
1912 m

The Flames
2042 m

Fire Spires
2049 m

Katzie Mountain
2081 m

Halkomelem Peak
2088 m

Nebula Peak
2078 m

Ashes Peak
1842 m

Sloquet
Hot Springs

Skakala Peak
1932 m

Stalo Peak
2001 m

Betstel Pinnacle
1819 m

Mount Glendinning
1731m

Pukulkul Peak
1692 m

Mount Thirsk
1602m

Skayuk Peak
1786 m

Old Pierre Mountain
1886 m

Mount Lamont
1707 m

Robertson Peak
1867m

Piluk Peak
1790 m

Remote Peak
2030 m

**Golden
Ears
Provincial
Park**

**FRASER
VALLEY**

Mount Judge Howay
1704 m

Osprey Mountain
1454 m

**Pinecone
Burke
Provincial
Park**

Mount Kranrod
1269 m

Stave
Lake
Airport
(Closed

Cozen
Point

Kreut Ridge
947 m

Mount Higgins
865 m

Seal
Bay

Little
Goose
Is.

Clearwater
Bay

Cottage
Point

**GREATER
VANCOUVER**

Goose
Is.

Mount Robie Reid
1705 m

Kenyon
Lake

Gabbro Mountain
1361 m

Mount Martyn
1265 m

Whale

Widgeon Peak
976 m

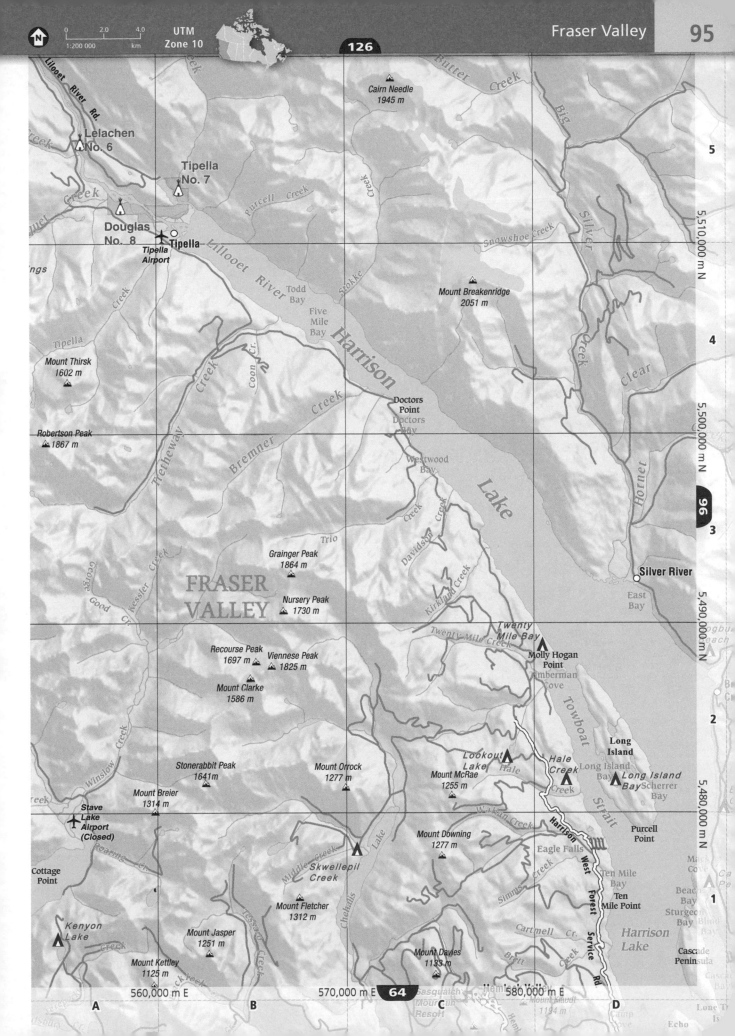

UTM
Zone 10

1:200 000

0   2.0   4.0
km

N

126

Cairn Needle
1945 m

Lelachen
No. 6

Tipella
No. 7

Douglas
No. 8

Tipella Airport

Tipella

Mount Breakenridge
2051 m

Snowshoe Creek

Silver Creek

Clear Creek

5,510,000 m N

5

4

Lillooet River

Todd Bay

Five Mile Bay

Mount Thirsk
1602 m

Robertson Peak
1867 m

Doctors Point

Doctors Bay

Westwood Bay

Hornet

96

3

5,500,000 m N

Bremner Creek

Metheway Creek

Coon Cr.

Harrison

Lake

Trio

Grainger Peak
1864 m

Nursery Peak
1730 m

FRASER
VALLEY

Davidson Creek

Kirkland Creek

Silver River

East Bay

5,490,000 m N

Kessler Creek

George Good Cr.

Recourse Peak
1697 m

Viennese Peak
1825 m

Mount Clarke
1586 m

Twenty-Mile Creek

Twenty
Mile Bay

Molly Hogan
Point

Timberman Cove

2

Long
Island

Winslow Creek

Stonerabbit Peak
1641m

Mount Orrock
1277 m

Mount McRae
1255 m

Lookout
Lake

Hale

Hale
Creek

Long Island
Bay

Long Island
Bay

Scherrer
Bay

5,480,000 m N

Mount Breier
1314 m

Stave
Lake
Airport
(Closed)

Cottage
Point

Skwellepil
Creek

Middle Creek

Chehalis Lake

Mount Downing
1277 m

Wakan Creek

Harrison

West

Forest

Strait

Eagle Falls

Purcell
Point

Ten Mile
Bay

Ten
Mile Point

Harrison

1

Kenyon
Lake

Mount Jasper
1251 m

Mount Fletcher
1312 m

Cartmell Cr.

Simms Creek

Mount Davies
1133 m

Service Rd.

Lake

Beach
Bay

Sturgeon
Bay

Cascade
Peninsula

Mount Kettley
1125 m

Sasquatch
Mountain
Resort

Hemlock Valley

560,000 m E

570,000 m E

64

580,000 m E

A

B

C

D

127

N

0   2.0   4.0
km
1:200 000

Mount Nesbitt
1645 m

No. 5

Shrypttahooks No. 7

Scuzzy Rapids

Paul's No. 6

Boston Bar No. 11

Hell's Gate Airtram

Austin's
Flat No. 3

Six Mile Cr.

Hell's Gate

Fraser

Anderson River

East

Oztius

Tsileuh   Creek

L i l l o o e t

Yelakin
No. 4

Yelakin
No. 4A

Long Tunnel
No. 5A

Long Tunnel No. 5

5

5,510,000 m N

Spuzzum Mountain
1573 m

Chapman's Ba

Teequaloose
No. 3A

Alexandra Bri
Provincial Park

R a n g e s

Teequaloose
No. 3

Skuet No. 6

Spuzzum

Papsilqua No

Papsilqua N

4

Spuzzum Creek

Spuzzum
No. 1

Papsilqua No.

Clear

Creek

Creek

Urquhart   Creek

Spuzzum
No. 1A

Spuzzum
No. 7

5,500,000 m N

Creek

Mount Urquhart
1451 m

Inkawthia Cr.

Saddle
Rock No. 9

Stout
No. 8

Hornet

95

1

3

Silver River

Creek

Sawmill

Creek

Yale No. 21

Yale No. 22

East
Bay

Creek

Yale Historic
Site & Museum
Yale

Yale Garry
Ecological

5,490,000 m N

Mount Fagervik
1693 m

Yale

Creek

?

Kuthlalth

Cogburn
Beach

Cogburn

Settler

Creek

Gordon   Creek

Yale Town No. 1

Mount
Oppenheimer
523 m

Mount Allard
847 m

Bear
Creek

Talc

Creek

Creek

Fraser

Qualark No. 4

Emory Creek
Campground

Emory Creek
Provincial Park

Albert
Flat No. 5

Suka

2

Long
Island

The Old Settler
1671 m

Squeah

Squeah No.

Long Island
Bay

Field Peak
1307 m

Mount Baird
1464 m

Creek

Kaykaip No.

Scherrer
Bay

Bear
Creek

Mount McNair
1405 m

Emory

Dogwood Valley

Stullawheets
No. 8

Dave's   Creek

Purcell
Point

Bear

Choate

Mount Parker
1375 m

FRASER
VALLEY

Zofka Ridge
1068 m

Puckat

Cr.

1

Ten Mile
Bay

Lookout Peak
1233 m

Ruby

Skawahlum No.

Ten
Mile Point

Macs
Cove

Cascade
Peninsula

American   Creek

Puckatholetchin

West   Forest   Service   Rd.

Beach
Bay

Sturgeon
Bay

Blind
Bay

Slollicum Peak
1391 m

Klaklacum
No. 12

Ross   Rd.

Trafalgar

Swahliseah No.

Harrison
Lake

Cascade
Peninsula

Rainbow
Falls

Garnet   Creek

Dog Mountain
921 m

Schkam
No.2

Haig

Hope

Ogilvie Peak

Trafalgar Flat

Aywawwis No.

Kawkawa

Cascade
Falls

7
B.C.

?

VIA

Hope

Lake No. 16

Othello

Rainbow
Falls

Chawathil

65

?
170

Croft

168

Othello
Tunnels

A   590,000 m E   B   600,000 m E   C   610,000 m E   D   3   3

Lone Tree
Is.

Sasquatch
P.P.

Yale Rd. E.

Silver
165   1   168   Hope   Floods

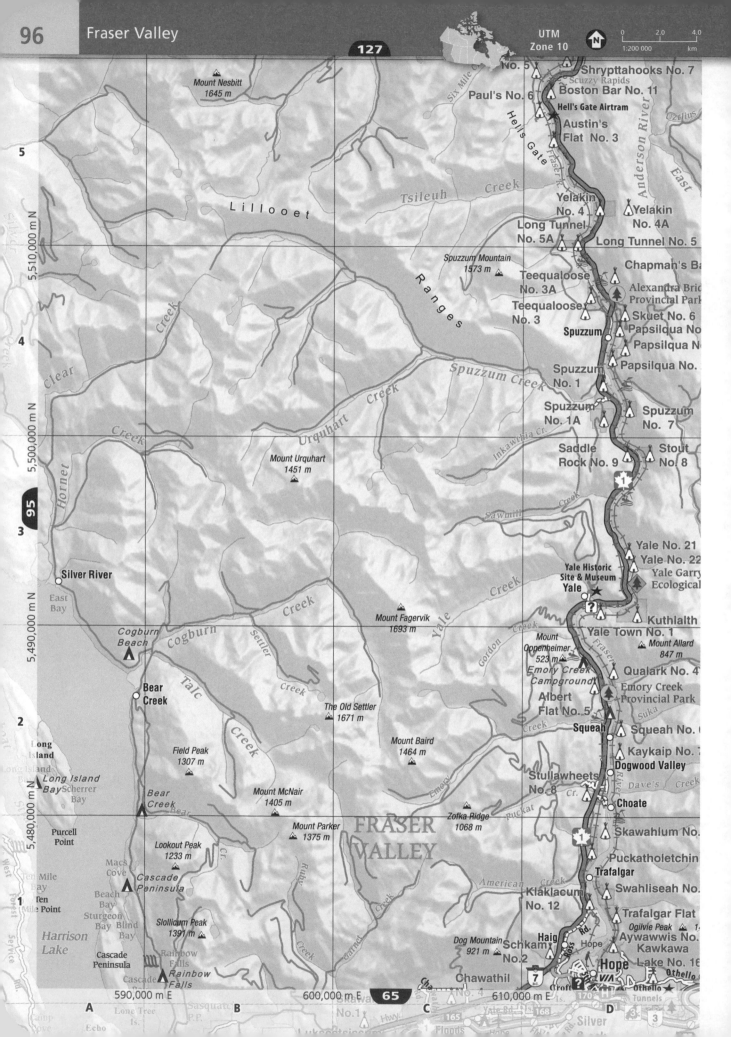

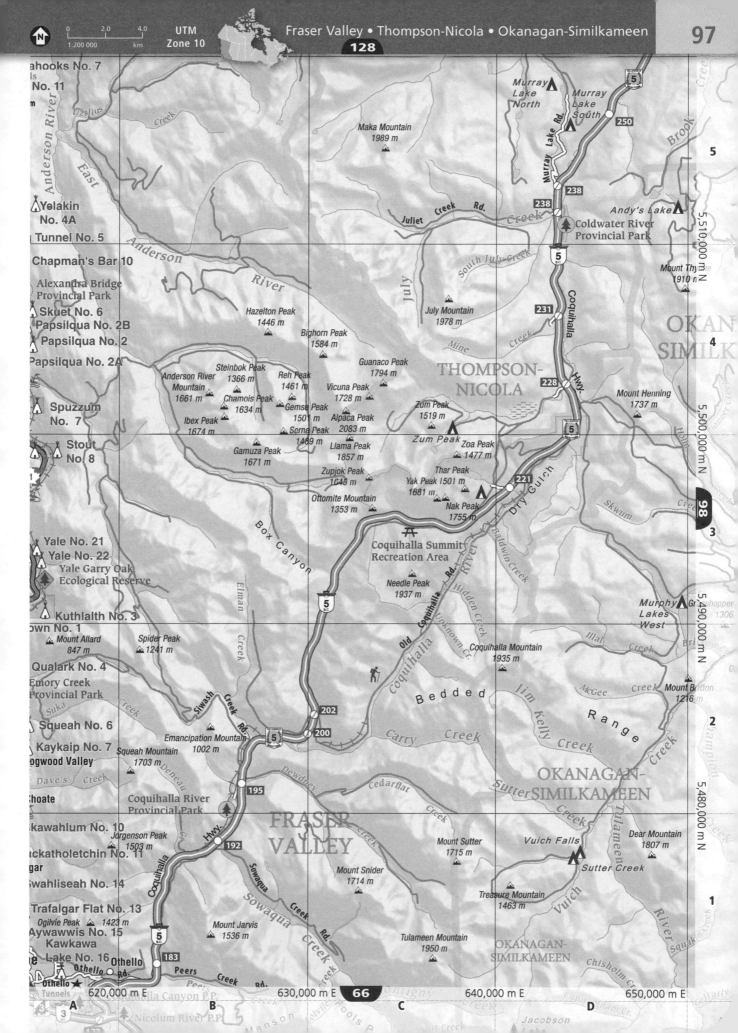

N

| 0 | 2.0 | 4.0 |

1:200 000   km

UTM
Zone 10

Fraser Valley • Thompson-Nicola • Okanagan-Similkameen

128

97

ahooks No. 7
No. 11

Murray
Lake
North

Murray
Lake
South

5

250

Maka Mountain
1989 m

Creek

Brook

5

Juliet Creek Rd.

238

238

Murray Lake Rd.

Andy's Lake

Coldwater River
Provincial Park

Yelakin
No. 4A

Tunnel No. 5

Anderson

River

5
B.C.

Mount Thy
1910 m

Chapman's Bar 10

South July Creek

Coquihalla

Alexandra Bridge
Provincial Park

231

July Mountain
1978 m

Skuet No. 6

Hazelton Peak
1446 m

THOMPSON-
NICOLA

Papsilqua No. 2B

Bighorn Peak
1584 m

Mine Creek

228

Papsilqua No. 2

Papsilqua No. 2A

Steinbok Peak
1366 m

Guanaco Peak
1794 m

Hwy.

Mount Henning
1737 m

Anderson River
Mountain
1661 m

Reh Peak
1461 m

Vicuna Peak
1728 m

5

Chamois Peak
1634 m

Gemse Peak
1501 m

Zum Peak
1519 m

Spuzzum
No. 7

Ibex Peak
1674 m

Alpaca Peak
2083 m

Serna Peak
1469 m

Zum Peak

Zoa Peak
1477 m

Stout
No. 8

Gamuza Peak
1671 m

Llama Peak
1857 m

Thar Peak

Zupjok Peak
1645 m

Yak Peak 1501 m
1681 m

Nak Peak
1755 m

Dry Gulch

221

Skwum

98

Yale No. 21

Ottomite Mountain
1353 m

Yale No. 22

Box Canyon

Yale Garry Oak
Ecological Reserve

Coquihalla Summit
Recreation Area

Baldwin Creek

Kuthlalth No. 3

Needle Peak
1937 m

Elman

Rd.

Murphy
Lakes
West

Gr
1306

own No. 1

Mount Allard
847 m

Spider Peak
1241 m

5
B.C.

Coquihalla

Hidden Creek

Illal

Creek

Qualark No. 4

Unknown Cr.

Coquihalla Mountain
1935 m

McGee

Creek

Mount Britton
1216

Emory Creek
Provincial Park

Siwash Creek

Bedded

Jim Kelly

Range

Squeah No. 6

202

Kaykaip No. 7

Emancipation Mountain
1002 m

5

200

Carry

Creek

Creek

ogwood Valley

Squeah Mountain
1703 m

Dave's Creek

Deneau

Dewdney

Cedarflat

Creek

OKANAGAN-
SIMILKAMEEN

Choate

195

Coquihalla River
Provincial Park

FRASER
VALLEY

Sutter

Creek

kawahlum No. 10

Jorgenson Peak
1503 m

192

Mount Sutter
1715 m

Vuich Falls

Dear Mountain
1807 m

ckatholetchin No. 11

Coquihalla Hwy.

Sowaqua

Sutter Creek

gar

Mount Snider
1714 m

Vuich

wahliseah No. 14

Treasure Mountain
1463 m

Trafalgar Flat No. 13

Sowaqua Creek Rd.

River

Ogilvie Peak 1423 m

Mount Jarvis
1536 m

Aywawwis No. 15

Kawkawa

5
B.C.

Tulameen Mountain
1950 m

OKANAGAN-
SIMILKAMEEN

Lake No. 16 Othello

183

Othello Rd.

Chisholm Cr.

Othello

Tunnels

Peers Creek Rd.

3

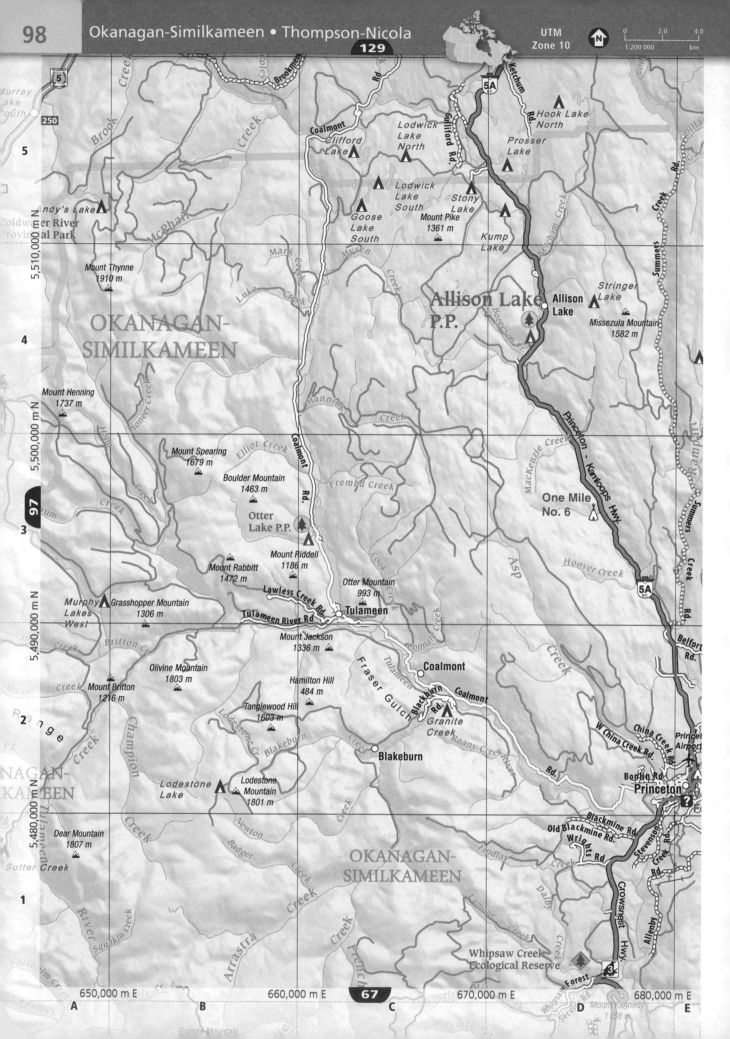

UTM
Zone 10

1:200 000

129

5

250

Brookmere

Coley Creek

Coalmont

Clifford Lake

Lodwick Lake North

Lodwick Lake South

Gulliford Rd.

Hook Lake North

Prosser Lake

Ketchum Rd.

5A

Andy's Lake

Coldwater River Provincial Park

McPhail Creek

Mark Creek

Myren Creek

Goose Lake South

Stony Lake

Mount Pike 1361 m

Kump Lake

Allison Lake P.P.

Allison Lake

Stringer Lake

Missezula Mountain 1582 m

5,510,000 mN

Mount Thynne 1910 m

Luke Creek

Borgeson Cr.

Ketchum Creek

Summers Creek

OKANAGAN-
SIMILKAMEEN

4

Mount Henning 1737 m

Pioneer Creek

Manning Creek

Princeton - Kamloops Hwy.

MacKenzie Creek

5,500,000 mN

Mount Spearing 1679 m

Elliot Creek

Coalmont Rd.

Fremba Creek

One Mile No. 6

Hoover Creek

97

Boulder Mountain 1463 m

Otter Lake P.P.

3

Mount Rabbitt 1472 m

Mount Riddell 1186 m

Cook Creek

Otter Mountain 993 m

Asp Creek

5A

Murphy Lakes West

Grasshopper Mountain 1306 m

Lawless Creek Rd.

Tulameen River Rd

Tulameen

Mount Jackson 1336 m

Aconnati Creek

Belfort Rd.

5,490,000 mN

Britton Cr.

Champion Creek

Olivine Mountain 1803 m

Hamilton Hill 484 m

Fraser Gulch

Tulameen River

Coalmont

Blackburn Rd.

Coalmont Rd.

China Creek

Princ. Airport

2

Range

McGee Creek

Mount Britton 1216 m

Lodestone Cr.

Tanglewood Hill 1603 m

Blakeburn

Granite Creek

Roany Creek

W China Creek Rd.

China Creek Rd.

Borden Rd.

NAGAN-
KAMEEN

Tulameen River

Lodestone Lake

Lodestone Mountain 1801 m

Blakeburn

Rd.

Princeton

5,480,000 mN

Dear Mountain 1807 m

Newton Creek

Badger Creek

Findlay Creek

Lamont Creek

Dalby Creek

Old Blackmine Rd.

Wrights Rd.

Blackmine Rd.

Stevenson Rd.

Creek Rd.

Allenby Rd.

Sutter Creek

Squakin Creek

Arrastra Creek

French Creek

OKANAGAN-
SIMILKAMEEN

Whipsaw Creek Ecological Reserve

Forest

Crowsnest Hwy.

3

1

Tulameen River

Chisholm Cr.

650,000 m E | A | B | 660,000 m E | 67 | C | 670,000 m E | D | 680,000 m E | E

Mount Kennedy 1158 m

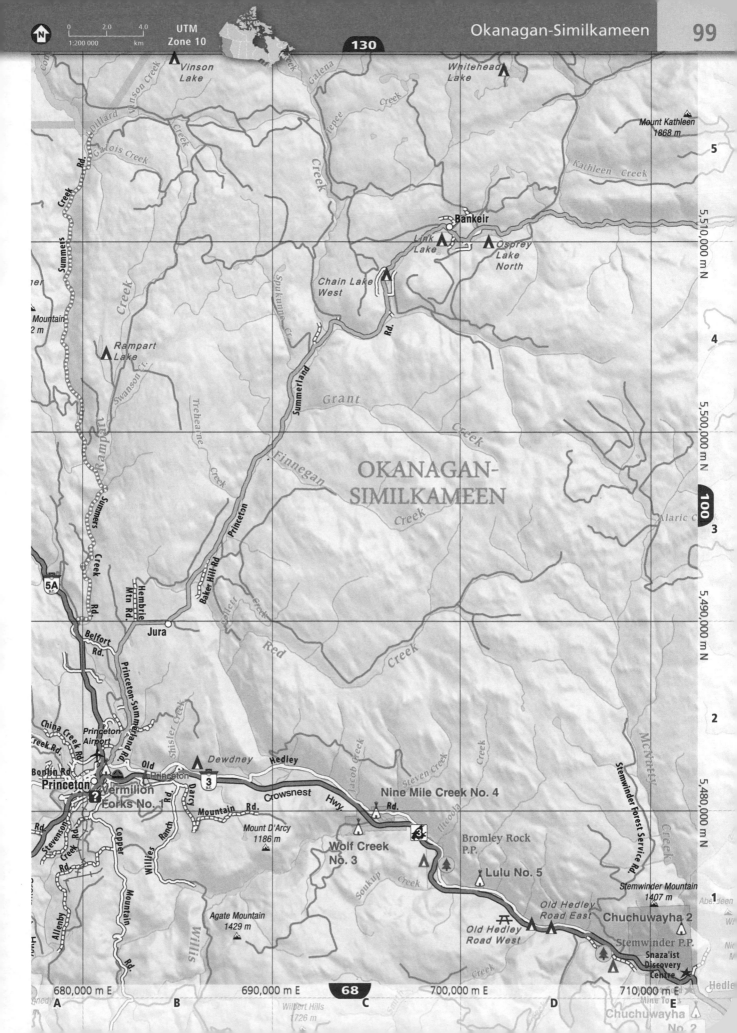

UTM
Zone 10

1:200 000

km

130

Vinson
Lake

Whitehead
Lake

Mount Kathleen
1868 m

Kathleen   Creek

5

Bankeir

Link
Lake

Osprey
Lake
North

5,510,000 m N

Chain Lake
West

Summerland

Grant

Rd.

4

Rampart
Lake

5,500,000 m N

100

Grant

Creek

**OKANAGAN-
SIMILKAMEEN**

Alaric Cr.

3

Finnegan

Creek

Princeton

5,490,000 m N

5A
B.C.

Hembrie
Mtn. Rd.

Baker Hill Rd.

Gillett   Creek

Belfort
Rd.

Jura

Red

Creek

2

Princeton
Airport

China Creek Rd.

Creek Rd.

Dewdney

Hedley

McNulleY

Stemwinder Forest Service Rd.

5,480,000 m N

Bonnie Rd.

Princeton

Old
Princeton

3
B.C.

Jacob Creek

Steven Creek

Nine Mile Creek No. 4

Creek

Vermilion
Forks No.

Darcy

Crowsnest

Hwy

Rd.

Stevenson
Rd.

Mountain   Rd.

Willies Ranch

Mount D'Arcy
1186 m

Copper

3

Tuloola

Wolf Creek
No. 3

Bromley Rock
P.P.

Lulu No. 5

Stemwinder Mountain
1407 m

1

Rd.

Creek

Shisler Creek

Soukup   Creek

Old Hedley
Road East

Chuchuwayha 2

Allenby

Mountain

Rd.

Agate Mountain
1429 m

Old Hedley
Road West

Stemwinder P.P.

Snaza'ist
Discovery
Centre

A   **B**   **68**   **C**   **D**   **E**

Wilbert Hills
1726 m

Chuchuwayha
No. 2

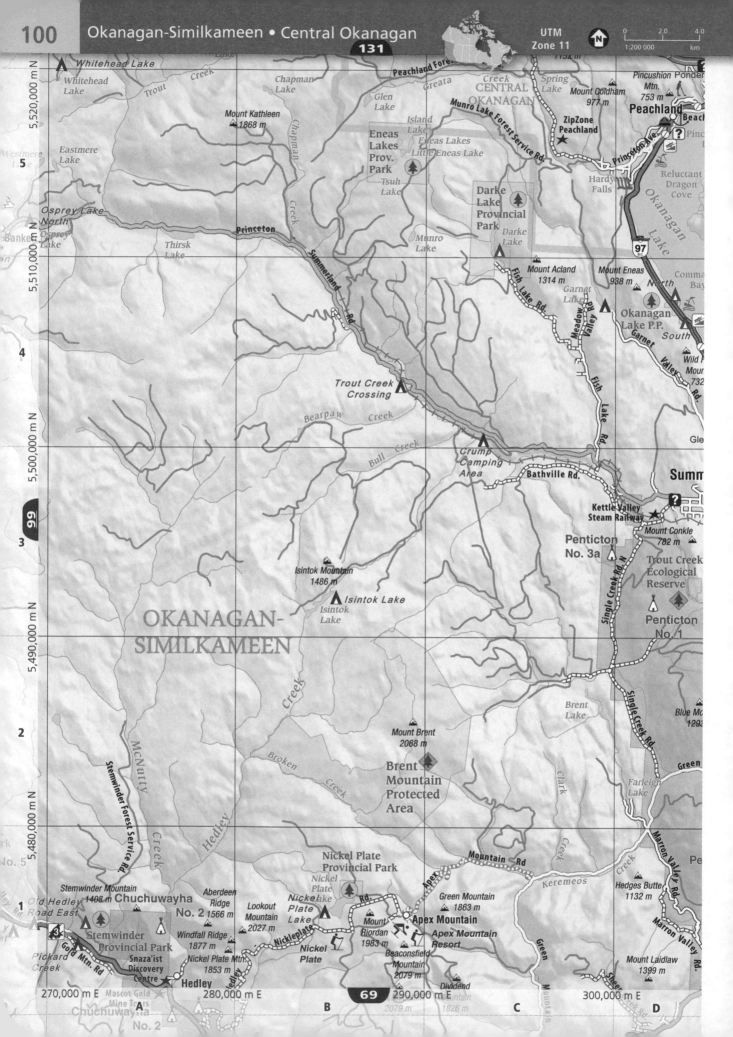

CENTRAL
OKANAGAN

Whitehead Lake

Whitehead
Lake

Eastmere
Lake

Westmere
L ake

Osprey Lake
North
Osprey
Lake

Banker
n

Trout

Creek

Chapman
Lake

Mount Kathleen
▲ 1868 m

Chapman

Creek

Glen
Lake

Greata

Peachland Fore

Creek

Spring
Lake

Mount Coldham
977 m

Pincushion Ponder
Mtn.
753 m

Peachland

Island
Lake

Eneas
Lakes
Prov.
Park

Eneas Lakes
Little Eneas Lake

Tsuh
Lake

Thirsk
Lake

Princeton

Summerland

Rd.

Munro
Lake

Munro Lake Forest Service Rd.

ZipZone
Peachland

Darke
Lake
Provincial
Park

Darke
Lake

Mount Acland
1314 m

Mount Eneas
938 m

Garnet
Lake

Fish Lake Rd.

Meadow

Fish

Lake

Rd.

Valley

Rd.

Hardy
Falls

Reluctant
Dragon
Cove

Okanagan

Lake

97
B.C.

Okanagan
Lake P.P.

North

South

Comma
Bay

Garnet

Valley

Wild
Moun
732

Trout Creek
Crossing

Bearpaw

Creek

Bull

Creek

Crump
Camping
Area

Bathville Rd.

Kettle Valley
Steam Railway

Mount Conkle
782 m

Summ

Penticton
No. 3a

Single Creek Rd. N

Trout Creek
Ecological
Reserve

Isintok Mountain
1486 m

Isintok Lake

Isintok
Lake

Penticton
No. 1

OKANAGAN-
SIMILKAMEEN

Creek

Brent
Lake

Clark

Farleigh
Lake

Blue Mo
1293

Green

McNutty

Stemwinder Forest Service Rd.

Creek

Hedley

Broken

Creek

Mount Brent
2068 m

Brent
Mountain
Protected
Area

Single Creek Rd.

Marron Valley Rd.

Stemwinder Mountain
1408 m   Chuchuwayha
No. 2

Aberdeen
Ridge
1566 m

Lookout
Mountain
2027 m

Nickel Plate
Provincial Park

Nickel
Plate
Rd.

Nickel
Plate
Lake

Mountain

Rd.

Keremeos

Creek

Hedges Butte
1132 m

Old Hedley
Road East

Stemwinder
Provincial Park

Snaza'ist
Discovery
Centre

Gold Mtn. Rd.

Pickard
Creek

Windfall Ridge
1877 m

Nickleplate

Nickel Plate Mtn.
1853 m

Hedley

Nickel
Plate

Mount
Riordan
1983 m

Beaconsfield
Mountain
2079 m

Apex

Apex Mountain

Green Mountain
1863 m

Apex Mountain
Resort

Green

Mountain

Mount Laidlaw
1399 m

Sheer

Marron Valley

Rd.

270,000 m E

Mascot Gold
Mine Trails

Chuchuwayha
No. 2

280,000 m E

Nickel
Plate

69

Dividend
Mountain
1826 m

290,000 m E

300,000 m E

Pe

A   B   C   D

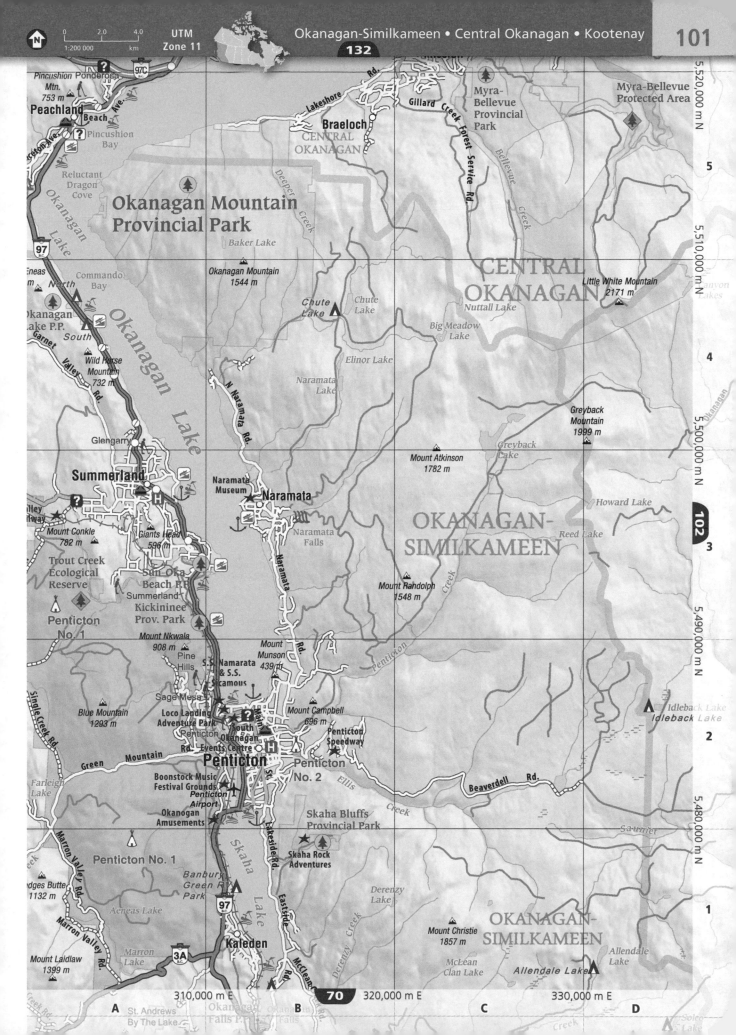

N

| 0 | 2.0 | 4.0 |
1:200 000   km

UTM
Zone 11

132

Okanagan-Similkameen • Central Okanagan • Kootenay

101

Pincushion Ponderosa
Mtn.
753 m

Peachland

Beach

97C

Pincushion
Bay

Reluctant
Dragon Cove

Okanagan
Lake

97
B.C.

Okanagan Mountain
Provincial Park

Baker Lake

Lakeshore Rd.

Braeloch

CENTRAL
OKANAGAN

Gillard Creek Forest Service Rd.

Myra-
Bellevue
Provincial
Park

Myra-Bellevue
Protected Area

Bellevue Creek

5,520,000 m N

5

5,510,000 m N

Eneas

North

Commando
Bay

Okanagan
Lake P.P.

South

Garnet Valley Rd.

Wild Horse
Mountain
732 m

Glengarry

Summerland

Mount Conkle
782 m

Valley Railway

Giants Head
596 m

Sun-Oka
Beach P.P.

Summerland
Kickininee
Prov. Park

Penticton
No. 1

Mount Nkwala
908 m

Pine
Hills

Sage Mesa

S.S. Namarata
& S.S.
Sicamous

Okanagan Mountain
1544 m

Chute
Lake

Chute
Lake

Elinor Lake

Naramata
Lake

N Naramata Rd.

Naramata
Museum

Naramata

Naramata

Naramata
Falls

CENTRAL
OKANAGAN

Nuttall Lake

Big Meadow
Lake

Little White Mountain
2171 m

Greyback
Mountain
1999 m

Greyback
Lake

Mount Atkinson
1782 m

Howard Lake

Reed Lake

OKANAGAN-
SIMILKAMEEN

Mount Rahdolph
1548 m

Okanagan Lake

5,500,000 m N

4

102

3

5,490,000 m N

Blue Mountain
1293 m

Loco Landing
Adventure Park

South
Penticton

Okanagan
Rd.   Events Centre

Penticton

Boonstock Music
Festival Grounds

Penticton
Airport

Okanogan
Amusements

Single Creek Rd.

Green Mountain Rd.

Farleigh
Lake

Marron Valley Rd.

Penticton No. 1

Bridges Butte
1132 m

Aeneas Lake

Mount Laidlaw
1399 m

Marron Valley Rd.

Marron
Lake

3A
B.C.

Kaleden

97
B.C.

Mount Munson
439 m

Mount Campbell
696 m

Penticton
Speedway

Penticton
No. 2

Ellis Creek

Skaha Bluffs
Provincial Park

Skaha Rock
Adventures

Banbury
Green Rv
Park

Skaha
Lake

Lakeside Rd.

Eastside Rd.

Derenzy Creek

McClear Rd.

Beaverdell Rd.

Saunier

Derenzy
Lake

Mount Christie
1857 m

McLean
Clan Lake

Idleback Lake
Idleback Lake

Penticton Creek

OKANAGAN-
SIMILKAMEEN

Allendale
Lake

Allendale Lake

5,480,000 m N

2

1

St. Andrews
By The Lake

Okanagan
Falls P.P.

Okanagan
Falls

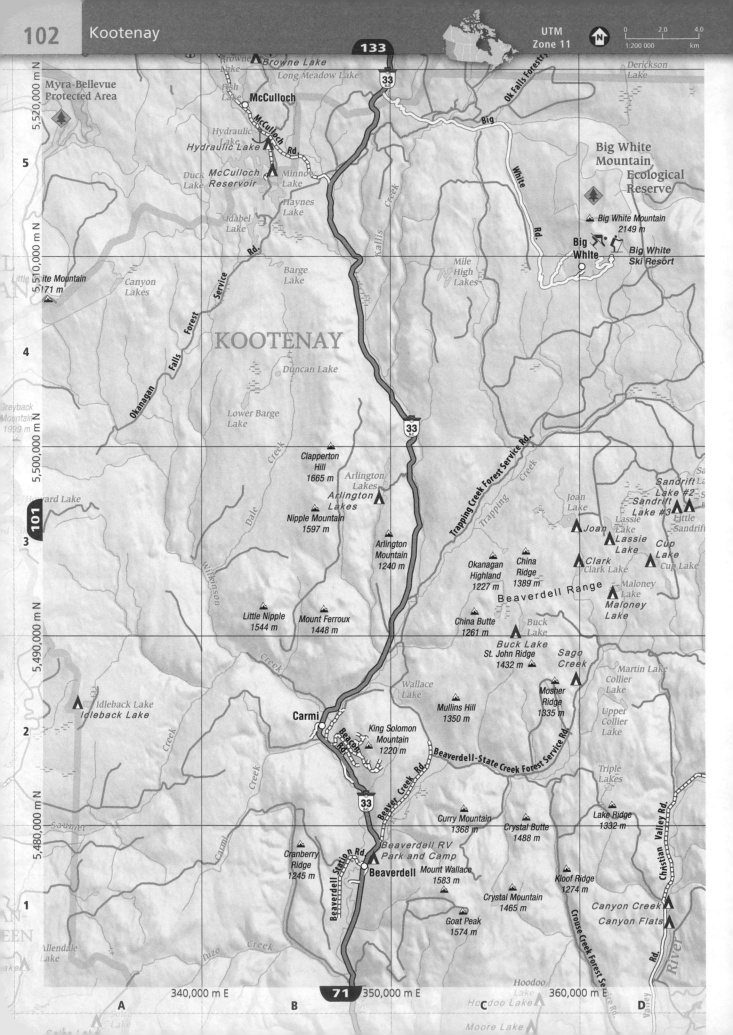

133

33
B.C.

Myra-Bellevue
Protected Area

Browne Lake

Browne Lake

Long Meadow Lake

Derickson Lake

Fish Lake

McCulloch

Ok Falls Forestry

Big

McCulloch Rd.

Hydraulic Lake

Hydraulic Lake

White

Big White Mountain Ecological Reserve

Duck Lake

McCulloch Reservoir

Minnow Lake

Big White Mountain
2149 m

Haynes Lake

Rd.

Big White

Idabel Lake

Kallis

Mile High Lakes

Big White Ski Resort

Service

Barge Lake

Little White Mountain
5171 m

Canyon Lakes

Creek

4

Forest

KOOTENAY

Duncan Lake

Falls

33
B.C.

Lower Barge Lake

Okanagan

Greyback Mountain
1999 m

Clapperton Hill
1665 m

Creek

Arlington Lakes

Sandrift Lake

Howard Lake

101

Dale

Arlington Lakes

Nipple Mountain
1597 m

Trapping Creek Forest Service Rd.

Creek

Joan Lake

Sandrift Lake #2

Sandrift Lake #3

3

Trapping

Joan

Little Sandrift

Arlington Mountain
1240 m

Lassie Lake

Wilkinson

Okanagan Highland
1227 m

China Ridge
1389 m

Clark

Lassie Lake

Cup Lake

Clark Lake

Cup Lake

Little Nipple
1544 m

Mount Ferroux
1448 m

China Butte
1261 m

Beaverdell Range

Maloney Lake

Maloney Lake

Creek

Buck Lake

Buck Lake

Sago Creek

Martin Lake

Idleback Lake

St. John Ridge
1432 m

Collier Lake

Idleback Lake

Wallace Lake

Mosher Ridge
1335 m

Upper Collier Lake

Creek

Mullins Hill
1350 m

2

Carmi

King Solomon Mountain
1220 m

Beaverdell-State Creek Forest Service Rd.

Triple Lakes

Beaver

Rd.

Creek

Beaver Creek Rd.

Lake Ridge
1332 m

Saunier

33
B.C.

Curry Mountain
1368 m

Crystal Butte
1488 m

Christian Valley Rd.

Cranberry Ridge
1245 m

Beaverdell RV Park and Camp

Beaverdell Station Rd.

Carmi

Beaverdell

Mount Wallace
1583 m

Kloof Ridge
1274 m

Crouse Creek Forest Service Rd.

1

Crystal Mountain
1465 m

Canyon Creek

Canyon Flats

Allendale Lake

Goat Peak
1574 m

River

Creek

Tuzo

Creek

Hoodoo Lake

71

Hoodoo Lake

Moore Lake

340,000 m E   **A**   350,000 m E   **B**   360,000 m E   **D**

5,520,000 m N

5

5,510,000 m N

5,500,000 m N

5,490,000 m N

5,480,000 m N

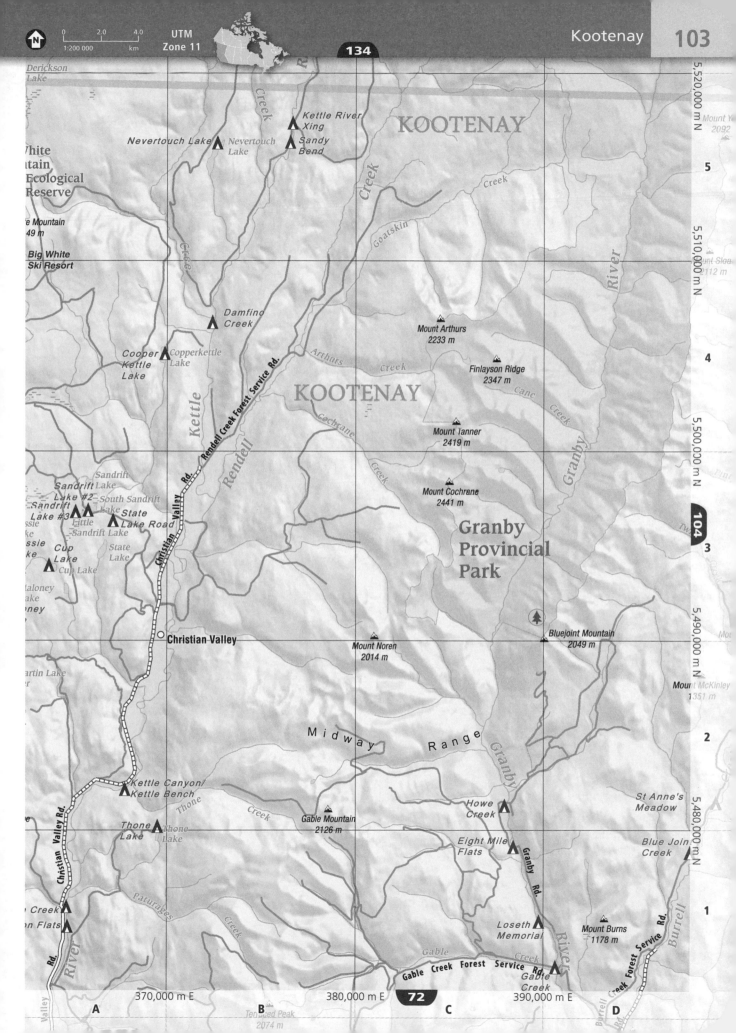

N

0   2.0   4.0
1:200 000   km

UTM
Zone 11

134

KOOTENAY

Derickson
Lake

Mount Ye
2092

Creek

5,520,000 m N

5

Kettle River
Xing
Sandy
Bend

Nevertouch Lake
Nevertouch
Lake

Creek

Creek

White
Mountain
Ecological
Reserve

Goatskin

5,510,000 m N

Mount Sloa
2112 m

e Mountain
49 m

Big White
Ski Resort

Damfino
Creek

Mount Arthurs
2233 m

River

4

Cooper
Kettle
Lake

Copperkettle
Lake

Arthurs

Finlayson Ridge
2347 m

Canc

Creek

Creek

KOOTENAY

Kettle

Rendell Creek Forest Service Rd.

Cochrane

Mount Tanner
2419 m

Granby

5,500,000 m N

Sandrift
Lake

Sandrift
Lake #2
South Sandrift
Lake
State
Lake Road

Rendell

Creek

Mount Cochrane
2441 m

Christian Valley

Sandrift
Lake #3
Little
Sandrift Lake

ssie
e

Cup
Lake

State
Lake

Granby
Provincial
Park

104

3

ssie
e

Cup Lake

aloney
ake
ney
e

Rd.

Bluejoint Mountain
2049 m

5,490,000 m N

artin Lake

Christian Valley

Mount Noren
2014 m

Midway   Range

Mount McKinley
1351 m

Granby

2

5,480,000 m N

Christian Valley Rd.

Kettle Canyon/
Kettle Bench

Thone

Creek

Howe
Creek

St Anne's
Meadow

Thone
Lake

Thone
Lake

Gable Mountain
2126 m

Eight Mile
Flats

Granby

Blue Join
Creek

Burrell

Paturages

Creek

Granby

River

Mount Burns
1178 m

Creek

1

Creek
n Flats

Loseth
Memorial

Burrell Creek Forest Service Rd.

Rd.

River

Gable

Creek

Gable Creek Forest   Service   Rd.
Gable
Creek

72

370,000 m E

380,000 m E

390,000 m E

A

B

Ten ed Peak
2074 m

C

D

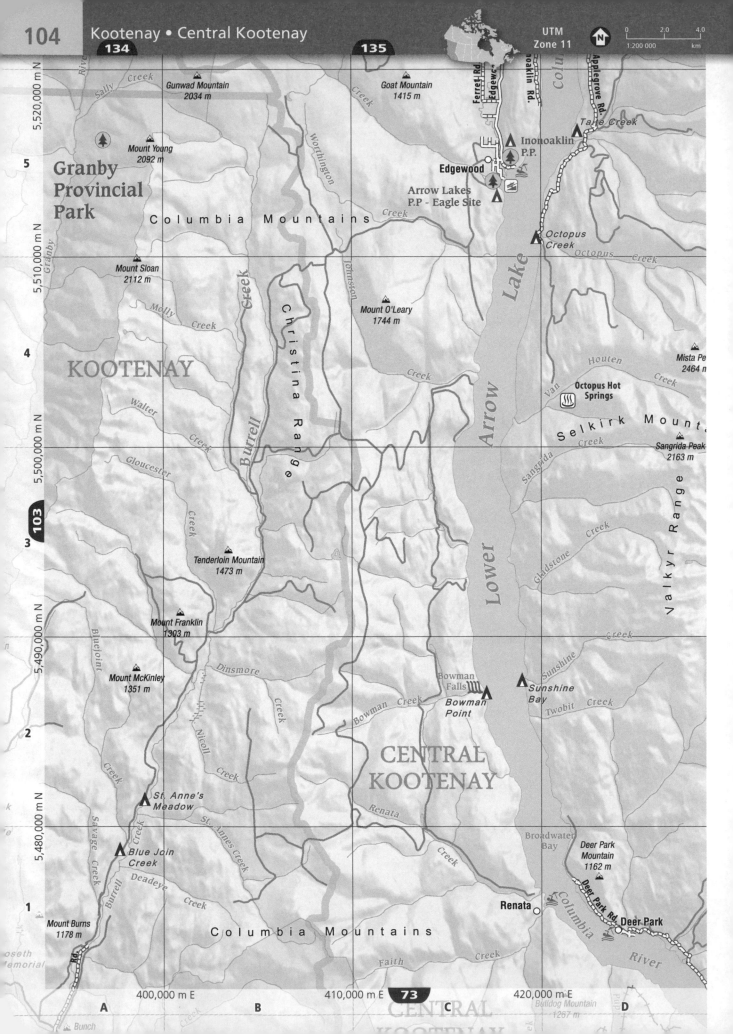

UTM
Zone 11

1:200 000

0   2.0   4.0
km

134

135

73

**Granby
Provincial
Park**

Gunwad Mountain
2034 m

Goat Mountain
1415 m

Sally Creek

River

Ferret Rd.

Edgewo

noaklin Rd.

Colu

Applegrove Rd.

Tarte Creek

Mount Young
2092 m

Worthington

Creek

Inonoaklin
P.P.

Edgewood

Arrow Lakes
P.P - Eagle Site

C o l u m b i a   M o u n t a i n s

Creek

Octopus
Creek

Octopus Creek

Mount Sloan
2112 m

Granby

Creek

Molly Creek

Burrell Creek

Christina Range

Johnson Creek

Mount O'Leary
1744 m

Lake

KOOTENAY

Walter Creek

Creek

Mista Pe
2464 m

Houten

Van

Creek

**Octopus Hot
Springs**

S e l k i r k   M o u n t

Gloucester

Creek

Sangrida

Creek

Arrow

Sangrida Peak
2163 m

103

Tenderloin Mountain
1473 m

Gladstone Creek

Lower

V a l k y r   R a n g e

Bluejoint

Creek

Mount Franklin
1303 m

Dinsmore

Creek

Bowman Creek

Creek

Mount McKinley
1351 m

Nicoll Creek

Bowman Falls

Bowman
Point

Sunshine
Bay

Sunshine

Twobit Creek

Creek

**CENTRAL
KOOTENAY**

St. Anne's
Meadow

St. Annes Creek

Renata Creek

Savage Creek

Blue Join
Creek

Creek

Broadwater
Bay

Deer Park
Mountain
1162 m

Burrell

Deadeye

Creek

Creek

Columbia

Deer Park Rd.

Renata

Mount Burns
1178 m

C o l u m b i a   M o u n t a i n s

Faith Creek

Creek

Deer Park

Rd.

oseth
emorial

River

Bunch

5,520,000 m N

5,510,000 m N

5,500,000 m N

5,490,000 m N

5,480,000 m N

5

4

3

2

1

400,000 m E

410,000 m E

420,000 m E

A

B

C

D

Bulldog Mountain
1267 m

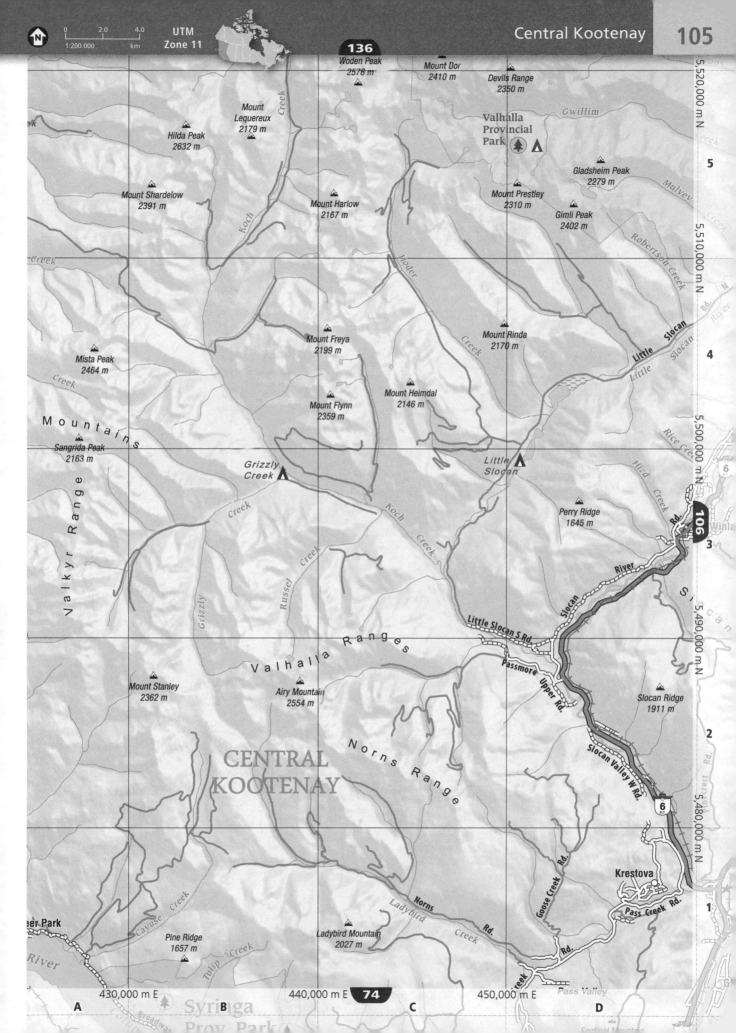

0 2.0 4.0
1:200 000 km
UTM
Zone 11

136

Woden Peak
2576 m

Mount Dor
2410 m

Devils Range
2350 m

Gwillim

Valhalla
Provincial
Park

Mount
Lequereux
2179 m

Hilda Peak
2632 m

Gladsheim Peak
2279 m

Mulvey

5

Mount Shardelow
2391 m

Mount Harlow
2167 m

Mount Prestley
2310 m

Gimli Peak
2402 m

Robertson Creek

Koch

Moder

Little Slocan

Little

River

N

Mista Peak
2464 m

Mount Freya
2199 m

Creek

Mount Rinda
2170 m

4

Creek

Mount Heimdal
2146 m

Rice Creek

Mountains

Mount Flynn
2359 m

Sangrida Peak
2163 m

Grizzly
Creek

Little
Slocan

Perry Ridge
1645 m

Hird Creek

6

106

Winla

Valkyr Range

Creek

Koch

Creek

River

Slocan

Slocan

3

Russel Creek

Grizzly

Little Slocan S Rd.

Passmore

Upper Rd.

Slocan Ridge
1911 m

Valhalla   Ranges

Mount Stanley
2362 m

Airy Mountain
2554 m

Slocan Valley W Rd.

Rd.

2

CENTRAL
KOOTENAY

Norns   Range

6
B.C.

Krestova

Goose Creek Rd.

Cayuse

Creek

Ladybird

Norns

Rd.

Pass Creek Rd.

1

er Park

River

Pine Ridge
1657 m

Tulip Creek

Creek

Ladybird Mountain
2027 m

Creek

Pass Valley

Pass Creek

430,000 m E

440,000 m E **74**

450,000 m E

A   Syringa   **B**   **C**   **D**

Prov. Park

5,520,000 m.N

5,510,000 m.N

5,500,000 m.N

5,490,000 m.N

5,480,000 m.N

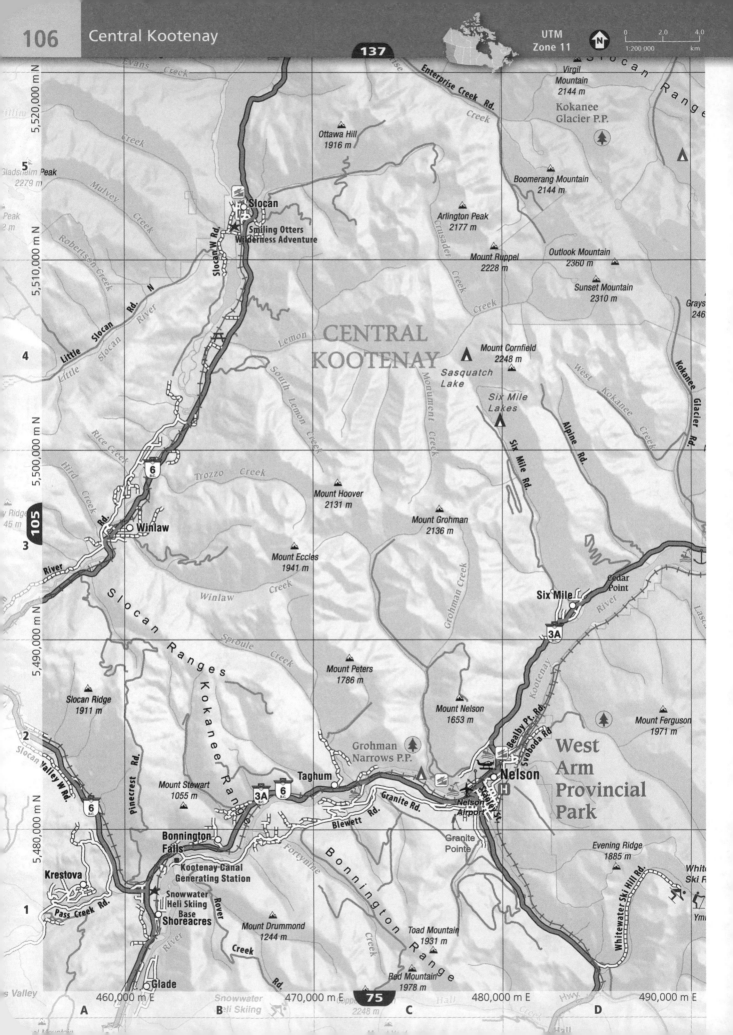

UTM
Zone 11

1:200 000

137

Virgil
Mountain
2144 m

Kokanee
Glacier P.P.

Enterprise Creek Rd.

Creek

Ottawa Hill
1916 m

Boomerang Mountain
2144 m

Gladsheim Peak
2279 m

Slocan

Smiling Otters
Wilderness Adventure

Arlington Peak
2177 m

Outlook Mountain
2360 m

Mount Ruppel
2228 m

Sunset Mountain
2310 m

Grays
246

Peak

Robertson Creek

Slocan W Rd.

Creek

Crusader

Creek

West

Mount Cornfield
2248 m

CENTRAL
KOOTENAY

Sasquatch
Lake

Kokanee

Little Slocan

Rd.

N

Slocan River

Lemon

Six Mile
Lakes

Kokanee
Glacier Rd.

Little Slocan

Creek

Glacier

Monument Creek

South Lemon Creek

Rice Creek

Alpine Rd.

Six Mile Rd.

Rd.

6
B.C.

Trozzo Creek

Mount Hoover
2131 m

Ridge
45 m

105

Mount Grohman
2136 m

Cedar
Point

Winlaw

Mount Eccles
1941 m

River

Six Mile

3A
B.C.

River

Winlaw

Creek

Grohman Creek

Slocan Ranges

Sproule Creek

Mount Peters
1786 m

Slocan Ridge
1911 m

Kootenay

Mount Nelson
1653 m

Bealby Pt. Rd.

West
Arm
Provincial
Park

Mount Ferguson
1971 m

Slocan Valley W Rd.

6
B.C.

Pinecrest Rd.

Grohman
Narrows P.P.

Svoboda Rd.

Kokanee Ranges

Mount Stewart
1055 m

Taghum

3A
B.C.

6
B.C.

Granite Rd.

Nelson

Nelson
Airport

Blewett Rd.

Evening Ridge
1885 m

Bonnington
Falls

Fortynine

Granite
Pointe

Whitewater Ski Hill Rd.

Krestova

Kootenay Canal
Generating Station

Bonnington Range

White
Ski R

Pass Creek Rd.

Snowwater
Heli Skiing
Base
Shoreacres

River

Toad Mountain
1931 m

Ymi

Mount Drummond
1244 m

Creek

Rd.

Creek

Glade

Red Mountain
1978 m

s Valley

460,000 m E

Snowwater
Heli Skiing

470,000 m E

75

2248 m

480,000 m E

490,000 m E

A
B
C
D

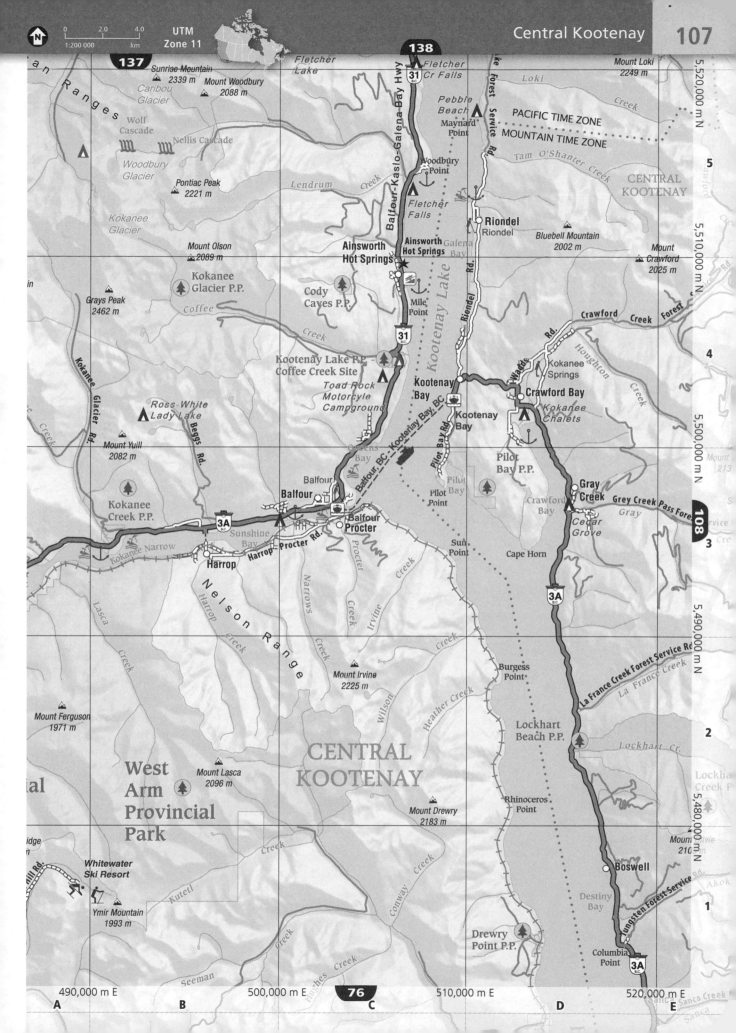

UTM Zone 11

1:200 000

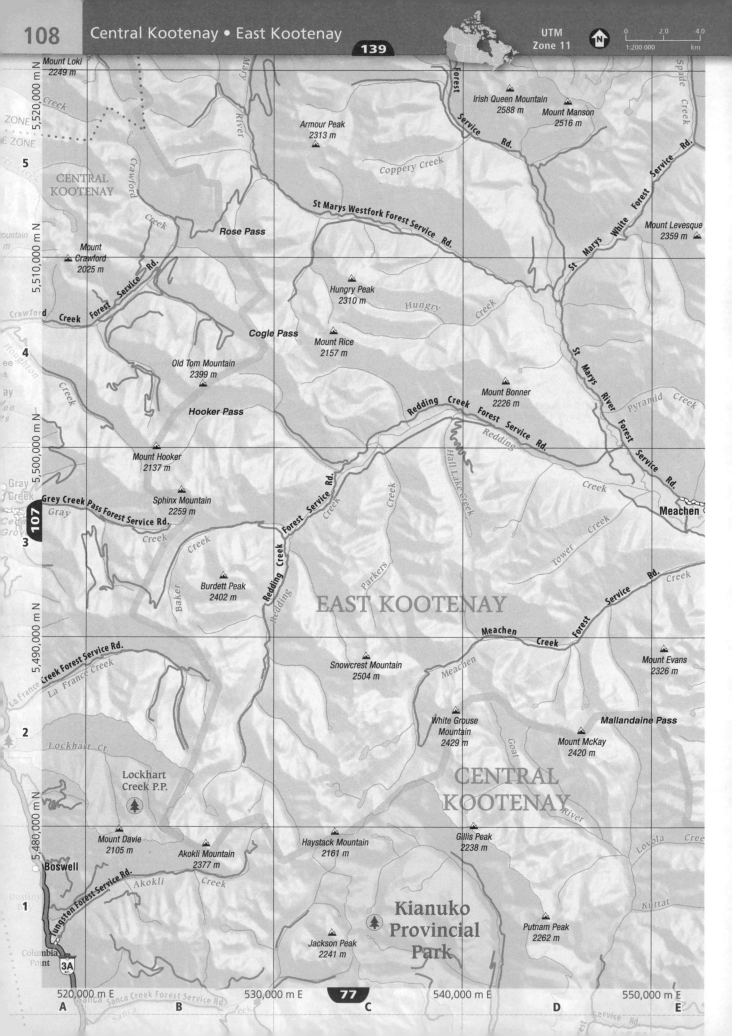

139

UTM
Zone 11

1:200 000

0   2.0   4.0
km

Mount Loki
2249 m

ZONE

E ZONE

5,520,000 m N

5

CENTRAL
KOOTENAY

Crawford Creek

Rose Pass

Mount
Crawford
2025 m

5,510,000 m N

Crawford Creek

Forest Service Rd.

Cogle Pass

Old Tom Mountain
2399 m

4

Hooker Pass

5,500,000 m N

Mount Hooker
2137 m

Sphinx Mountain
2259 m

Grey Creek Pass Forest Service Rd.

107

Gray Creek

3

Baker Creek

Burdett Peak
2402 m

Redding Creek

Redding

Irish Queen Mountain
2588 m

Mount Manson
2516 m

Forest Service Rd.

Coppery Creek

St Marys Westfork Forest Service Rd.

Hungry Peak
2310 m

Hungry Creek

Mount Rice
2157 m

Mount Bonner
2226 m

Redding Creek Forest Service Rd.

Redding

Hall Lake Creek

Forest Service Rd.

Parkers Creek

EAST KOOTENAY

St Marys White Forest Service Rd.

Mount Levesque
2359 m

St Marys

St Marys River Forest Service Rd.

Pyramid Creek

Creek

Tower Creek

Meachen

La France Creek Forest Service Rd.

La France Creek

5,490,000 m N

Snowcrest Mountain
2504 m

Meachen Creek

Meachen Creek

Forest Service Rd.

Mount Evans
2326 m

2

Lockhart Cr.

Lockhart
Creek P.P.

White Grouse
Mountain
2429 m

Mallandaine Pass

Mount McKay
2420 m

Goat

CENTRAL
KOOTENAY

River

5,480,000 m N

Mount Davie
2105 m

Boswell

Akokli Mountain
2377 m

Akokli Creek

Haystack Mountain
2161 m

Gillis Peak
2238 m

Lovola Creek

1

Destiny Bay

Tungsten Forest Service Rd.

Kianuko
Provincial
Park

Putnam Peak
2262 m

Kuttat

Columbia
Point

3A
B.C.

Jackson Peak
2241 m

Sanca Creek Forest Service Rd.

Sanca

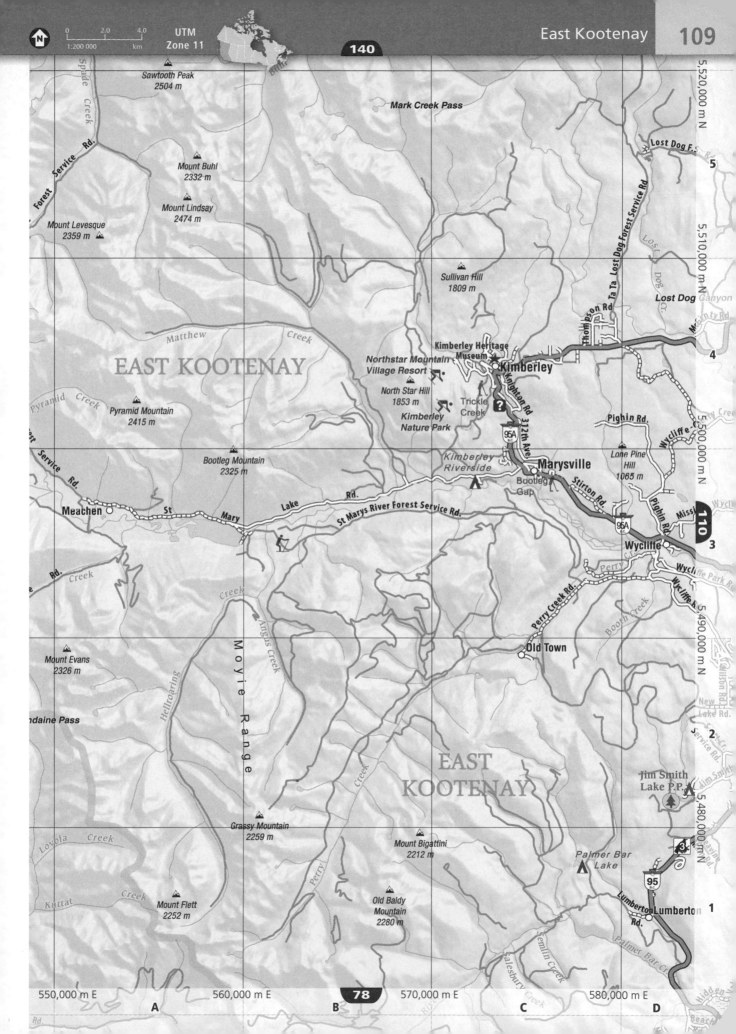

N

0   2,0   4,0
1:200 000   km

UTM
Zone 11

140

Sawtooth Peak
2504 m

Mark Creek Pass

Lost Dog F.S.

5,520,000 m N

Mount Buhl
2332 m

5

Mount Lindsay
2474 m

Lost
Dog
Cr.

Lost Dog Canyon

5,510,000 m N

Mount Levesque
2359 m

Matthew   Creek

Sullivan Hill
1809 m

Thompson Rd

McGinty Rd.

4

EAST KOOTENAY

Northstar Mountain
Village Resort

Kimberley Heritage
Museum

Kimberley

Pyramid Creek

Pyramid Mountain
2415 m

North Star Hill
1853 m

Kimberley
Nature Park

Trickle
Creek

?

Knighton Rd.

312th Ave.

Pighin Rd.

Wycliffe

5,500,000 m N

Lone Pine
Hill
1065 m

Bootleg Mountain
2325 m

Kimberley
Riverside

Marysville

95A

Service   Rd.

Meachen

St   Mary   Lake   Rd.

St Marys River Forest Service Rd.

Bootleg
Gap

Stirton Rd.

Pighin Rd.

95A

Missi

110

3

Wycliffe

Creek

Perry

Wycliffe Park Rd.

5,490,000 m N

Mount Evans
2326 m

Hellroaring

Moyie   Range

Angus Creek

Perry Creek Rd.

Old Town

Booth Creek

Wycliffe R.

ndaine Pass

New
Lake Rd.

2

EAST
KOOTENAY

Jim Smith
Lake P.P.

Lovola   Creek

Grassy Mountain
2259 m

Mount Bigattini
2212 m

Palmer Bar
Lake

3

5,480,000 m N

95

Kuttat

Creek

Mount Flett
2252 m

Perry

Old Baldy
Mountain
2280 m

Lumberton Lumberton
Rd.

1

550,000 m E   560,000 m E   570,000 m E   580,000 m E

78

Palmer Bar Cr.

A   B   C   D

UTM
Zone 11

1:200 000

140

141

Mount
Dingley
2113 m

Wild Horse
Hot Springs

Trail Cr.

Summit
Lake

Wasa
Lake P.P.

Wolf Creek Rd.

Torrent Rd.

Lewis Creek

Ta Ta
Creek

Wasa

Wasa Lake Park Dr.

Lazy Lake Rd.

Mount Ruault
2232 m

Mount Sneath
2438 m

Mount
Bill Nye
2071 m

Mount Haley
2620 m

Lost Dog F.S. Rd.

Lost Dog Canyon

McGinty Rd.

Lost Dog Cr.

Dog F.S. Rd.

93
B.C.

95A
B.C.

Lakit
Mountain
2147 m

Wildhorse River F.S. Rd.

Shepherd Gulch

Vertical
Mountain
1917 m

Boulder Cr.

Mather Creek

Mission Rd.

Ranch Rd.

Rd.

Sauqum Creek

Holmes Rd.

Lakit Creek Forest Service Rd.

F.S. Rd.

Lakit Lookout Rd.

Mount Lum
2302 m

Kootenay
I.R. No. 1

EAST
KOOTENAY

LD

Lone Peak
3684 m

Mount
Fisher
2846 m

Hughes Range

Mount
Patmore
2341 m

Thompson Rd.

Pighin Rd.

Lone Pine
Hill
1065 m

Wycliffe Cherry Creek Rd.

Mission
Rd.

Mission Wasa Low Rd.

St. Mary's

Buckman Rd.

Fort
Steele

Maus Creek Rd.

Horseshoe
Lake Camping

Khartoum Creek

Kootenay River

Hungary
2195

109

95A
B.C.

Wyccliffe

Mission- Wycliffe Rd.

Airport Access

Canadian
Rockies
Int'l Airport

Mission-Wycliffe Rd.

St. Mary River

Forty Steele-

Wildhorse Rd.

Eagle Hill Rd.

Fort Steele Rd.

Kelly Rd.

Fort Steele
Campground

Wardner-Fort Steele Rd.

The Steeple
2376 m

Wycliffe Park Rd.

Wycliffe Rd.

Pinghin Rd.

Perry Creek

North Creek

St.
Eugene

Casino
of the
Rockies

Shadow
Mountain

Menne Rd.

Mission Rd.

Mission
Hills

95
B.C.

3

Loopman Rd.

Isidore's Ranch
I.R. No.4

Norbury
Lake P.P.

Bull
Mount
222

Wildstone

Industrial Rd.

King St.

Theatre Rd.

Wilson Rd.

KIRK Rd.

New
Lake Rd.

Scott Cr.
Service Rd.

Canadian
Museum of
Rail Travel

Jim Smith Lake Rd.

Cranbrook

H

Cranbrook

2nd St. S

17th St. S

3

Crowsnest Hwy.

Mayook

Bull
River

Wardner-Fort Steele Rd.

Jim Smith
Lake P.P.

1st Ave. S

Spring Dr.

Silver

Peavine Main Rd.

Hidden Valley Rd.

49th St. S

Gold Creek Rd.

Mount
Baker
2103 m

Ha Ha Creek
F.S. Rd.

Haha Creek Rd.

Wardner
Lake P.P.

3

Palmer Bar
Lake

3

Lumberton Rd.

Lumberton

95
B.C.

Palmer Bar Creek

Cranbrook
Mountain
1980 m

Gold Creek Rd.

Wardner

Wardner- Kikomun

Kikomun

580,000 m E

590,000 m E

79

600,000 m E

610,000 m E

A

B

C

D

Moyie
Lake P.P.

Moyie Mountain
1953 m

5,520,000 m N

5,510,000 m N

5,500,000 m N

5,490,000 m N

5,480,000 m N

5

4

3

2

1

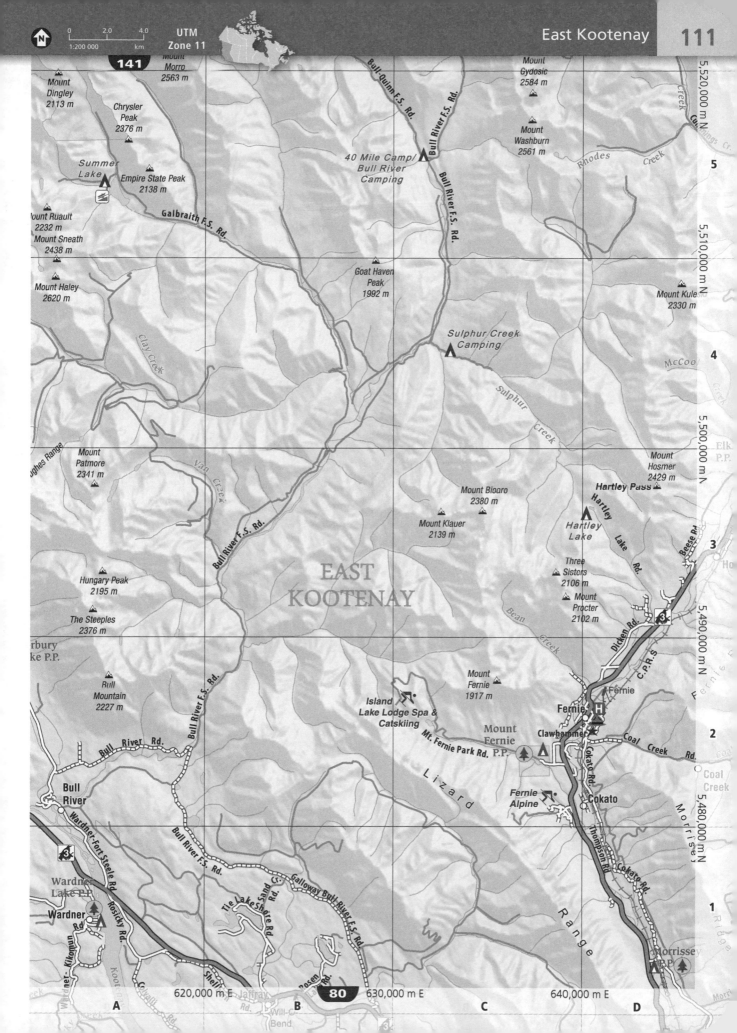

UTM
Zone 11

0   2.0   4.0
km
1:200 000

141
Mount
Morro
2563 m

Mount
Dingley
2113 m

Chrysler
Peak
2376 m

*Summer
Lake*

Empire State Peak
2138 m

Mount Ruault
2232 m

Mount Sneath
2438 m

Galbraith F.S. Rd.

Mount Haley
2620 m

Bull-Quinn F.S. Rd.

Bull River F.S. Rd.

Mount
Gydosic
2584 m

Mount
Washburn
2561 m

Rhodes   *Creek*

Cummings Cr.

40 Mile Camp/
Bull River
Camping

Bull River F.S. Rd.

Goat Haven
Peak
1992 m

Mount Kule
2330 m

Sulphur Creek
Camping

Sulphur   *Creek*

McCoo

Clay Creek

ughes Range

Mount
Patmore
2341 m

Van Creek

Bull River F.S. Rd.

Mount Bigaro
2380 m

Mount Klauer
2139 m

Mount
Hosmer
2429 m

Elk
P.P.

Hartley Pass

Hartley
Lake

Hartley Lake Rd.

Beese Rd.

Ho

EAST
KOOTENAY

Three
Sisters
2106 m

Mount
Procter
2102 m

3

Hungary Peak
2195 m

The Steeples
2376 m

Bean   *Creek*

Dicken Rd.

C.P.R.S

rbury
ke P.P.

Mount
Fernie
1917 m

Fernie

Fernie

H

Bull
Mountain
2227 m

Bull River F.S. Rd.

Island
Lake Lodge Spa &
Catskiing

Mount
Fernie
P.P.

Mt. Fernie Park Rd.

Clawhammer

Coal   *Creek*   *Rd.*

Coal
Creek

Bull   River   Rd.

**Bull
RIVER**

L i z a r d

Fernie
Alpine

Cokato

Cokato Rd.

Morrisey

Wardner-Fort Steele Rd.

Bull River F.S. Rd.

Thompson Rd.

3

*Wardner
Lake P.P.*

Wardner
Rd.

Rositky Rd.

Tie Lake Shore Rd.

Sand Cr.

Galloway Bull River F.S. Rd.

Range

Cokato Rd.

Morrisey
P.P.

Wardner - Kikomun

Koot

Galva

620,000 m E Jaffray

80

630,000 m E

640,000 m E

5,520,000 m N

5,510,000 m N

5,500,000 m N

5,490,000 m N

5,480,000 m N

5

4

3

2

1

A   B   C   D

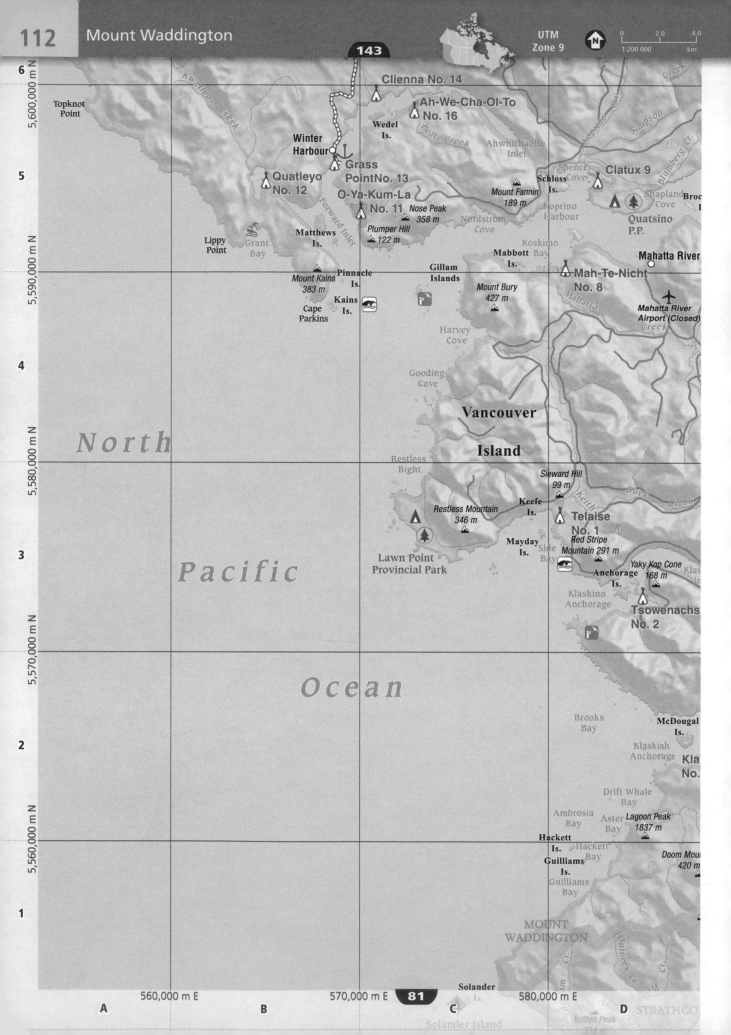

UTM
Zone 9

1:200 000

143

6

5,600,000 m N

Topknot
Point

Clienna No. 14

Ah-We-Cha-Ol-To
No. 16

Wedel
Is.

Ahwhichaoito
Inlet

Winter
Harbour

Grass
PointNo. 13

Schloss
Is.

Clatux 9

Spencer
Cove

5

Quatleyo
No. 12

O-Ya-Kum-La
No. 11

Mount Fannin
189 m

Nose Peak
358 m

Koprino
Harbour

Quatsino
P.P.

Shapland
Cove

Broc

Lippy
Point

Grant
Bay

Matthews
Is.

Plumper Hill
122 m

Nordstrom
Cove

Koskimo
Bay

Mabbott
Is.

Mahatta River

Mount Kains
383 m

Pinnacle
Is.

Gillam
Islands

Mount Bury
427 m

Mah-Te-Nicht
No. 8

Cape
Parkins

Kains
Is.

Harvey
Cove

Mahatta River
Airport (Closed)

5,590,000 m N

4

Gooding
Cove

North

5,580,000 m N

Restless
Bight

Vancouver

Island

Sieward Hill
99 m

Keefe
Is.

Pacific

Restless Mountain
346 m

Telaise
No. 1

Red Stripe
Mountain 291 m

Mayday
Is.

Side
Bay

Yaky Kop Cone
168 m

3

Lawn Point
Provincial Park

Anchorage
Is.

Klas

Klaskino
Anchorage

Tsowenachs
No. 2

5,570,000 m N

Ocean

Brooks
Bay

McDougal
Is.

2

Klaskish
Anchorage

Kla
No.

Drift Whale
Bay

5,560,000 m N

Ambrosia
Bay

Aster
Bay

Lagoon Peak
1837 m

Hackett
Is.

Hackett
Bay

Doom Mou
420 m

Guilliams
Is.

Guilliams
Bay

1

MOUNT
WADDINGTON

Solander
Is.

81

Solander Island

STRATHCO

Button Peak

560,000 m E

570,000 m E

580,000 m E

A

B

C

D

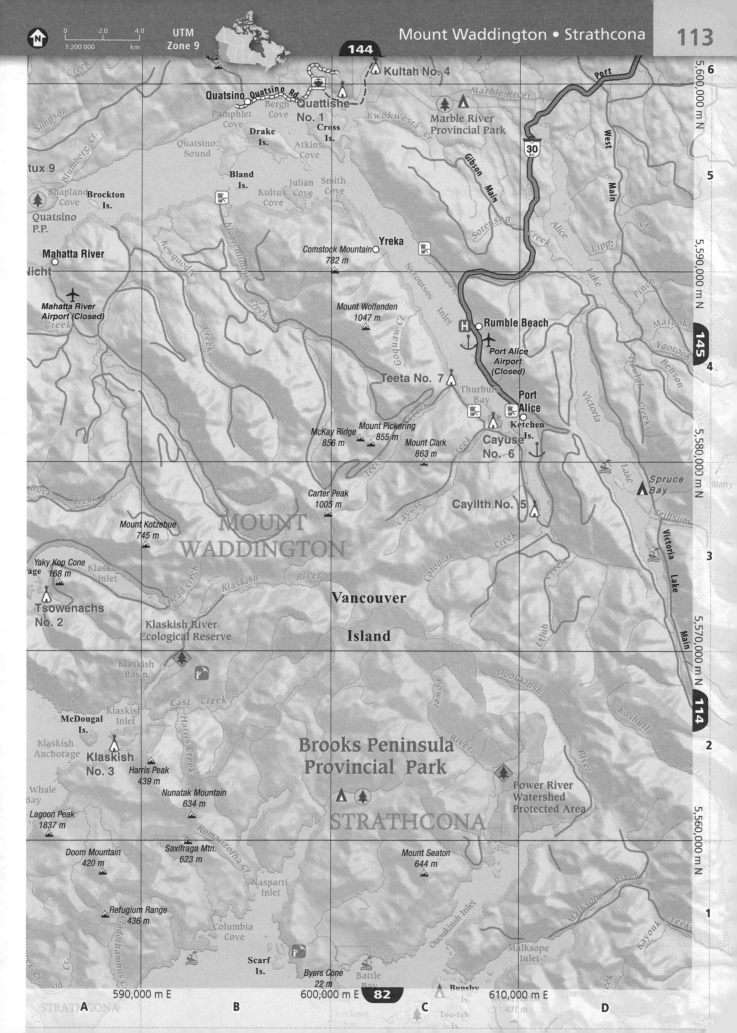

N

0   2.0   4.0
1:200 000   km

UTM
Zone 9

144

Kultah No. 4

5,600,000 m N   6

Quatsino Quatsino Rd.
Pamphlet
Cove
Bergh
Cove
Quattishe—
No. 1
Drake
Is.
Cross
Is.
Atkins
Cove

Kwokwesta Cr.

Marble River

30
B.C.

Port

West
Main

Marble River
Provincial Park

Quatsino
Sound

Bland
Is.
Kultus
Cove
Julian
Cove
Smith
Cove

5   5,590,000 m N

Gibson Main

Sorenson Creek

Alice

Lippy Cr.

Brockton
Is.

Shapland
Cove

Quatsino
P.P.

Yreka

Comstock Mountain
782 m

Nerousos Inlet

Malook
Cr.

145

Mahatta River

Nicht

Mahatta River
Airport (Closed)

Mount Wolfenden
1047 m

Rumble Beach

H

Port Alice
Airport
(Closed)

Yootook

Benson Creek

Flewker Creek

4   5,580,000 m N

Teeta No. 7

Thurbur
Bay

Port
Alice

Victoria

McKay Ridge
856 m
Mount Pickering
855 m
Mount Clark
863 m

Ketchen
Is.

Cayuse
No. 6

Lake

Spruce
Bay

Merry

Carter Peak
1005 m

Cayuse Creek

Cayilth No. 5

Tethsum

Victoria Lake

Mount Kotzebue
745 m

MOUNT
WADDINGTON

114

3   5,570,000 m N

Yaky Kop Cone
rage   168 m

Klaskino
Inlet

Head Creek

Klaskish   River

Klaskish

Vancouver

Quotkiush

Tsowenachs
No. 2

Klaskish River
Ecological Reserve

Klaskish
Basin

East   Creek

Island

Power   River

Utiuh Creek

Kashutl

McDougal
Is.

Klaskish
Inlet

Brooks Peninsula
Provincial Park

2   5,560,000 m N

Klaskish
Anchorage

Klaskish
No. 3

Harris Peak
439 m

Harris Creek

Whale
Bay

Nunatak Mountain
634 m

River

Power River
Watershed
Protected Area

Lagoon Peak
1837 m

Romatzo na Cr.

STRATHCONA

Doom Mountain
420 m

Saxifraga Mtn.
623 m

Mount Seaton
644 m

Malksope River

Nasparti
Inlet

Refugium Range
436 m

Columbia
Cove

Malksope
Inlet

Kayouk Creek

1   5,560,000 m N

Cladothamnus Cr.

Scarf
Is.

Byers Cone
22 m

Battle
Bay

82

Bunsby

Ououkinsh Inlet

STRATHCONA

A

590,000 m E   **B**

600,000 m E   **C**

Too-tah
Is.

610,000 m E   **D**

UTM
Zone 9

1:200 000

km

145

19
BC

**MOUNT
WADDINGTON**

**Vancouver
Island**

STRATHCONA

113

82

83

Yootook Cr
Tlewial Creek
Benson River

Spruce
Bay

Raging
River
Falls

Rainier Creek

Merry Widow Mountain
1208 m

Teilisum

Victoria Lake

Main

Blue Ox Creek

Kashutl River

Karmutzen Range

Killpala

Karmutzen Mountain
1164 m

Tlakwa

Storey Creek

Nimpkish Lake
Provincial Park

Nimp

Kinm

Tlakwa Mountain
1132 m

Atluck

Creek

Kainum Mountain
1097 m

Main

Pinder Creek

Snowsaddle Mountain
1072 m

Tahsish

Mount Renwick
920 m

Pinder Peak
1127 m

Kauwinch River

Garibaldi Peaks
929 m

Creek

Kwois

Tahsish-Kwois
Provincial Park

River

Wood
Cove

Monteith
Bay

Easy
Inlet

Kashutl
Inlet

Hankin
Cove

Kayouk Creek

False Ears
700 m

Artlish River

Artlish
Provinci

Tahsish
Inlet

Christine
Is.

Jansen
Bay

Chamiss Cr.

Werner
Bay

Yaku
Bay

Slate Mountain
696 m

Fair

Main

River

Clanninick Creek
Ecological Reserve

Chamiss
Bay

Chamiss
Bay

Moketas
Is.

Karouk
Is.

Fair Harbour

Fair
Harbour

Kaouk

Rowland

Creek

St. Pauls Dome
301 m

Kyuquot
Seaplane
Base

McKay
Cove

Surprise
Is.

Chutsis
Is.

Hohoae
Is.

Dixie
Cove

Copp
Is.

Dixie Cove Marine
Provincial Park

Family Humps
516 m

Harold Hill
194 m

quot

Walters
Is.

Barter
Cove

Amos
Is.

Whiteley
Is.

Centre
Cove

Amai Inlet

Amai

Creek

Kamils
Is.

Cachalot
Inlet

Eliza Ears
797 m

Oclucje
No. 7

Union
Is.

Kyuquot Hill
64 m

Volcanic
Cove

Stone Nipples
869 m

Ship Peak
620 m

Anvil

Narrowgut

Creek

Nuchatl

Racoon
Point

McLean

83

Thomson
Is.

Rugged Point
Marine P.P.

Remarkable Cone

Savey
No. 15

A
B
C
D

1
2
3
4
5
6

5,540,000 m N
5,550,000 m N
5,560,000 m N
5,570,000 m N
5,580,000 m N

620,000 m E
630,000 m E
640,000 m E

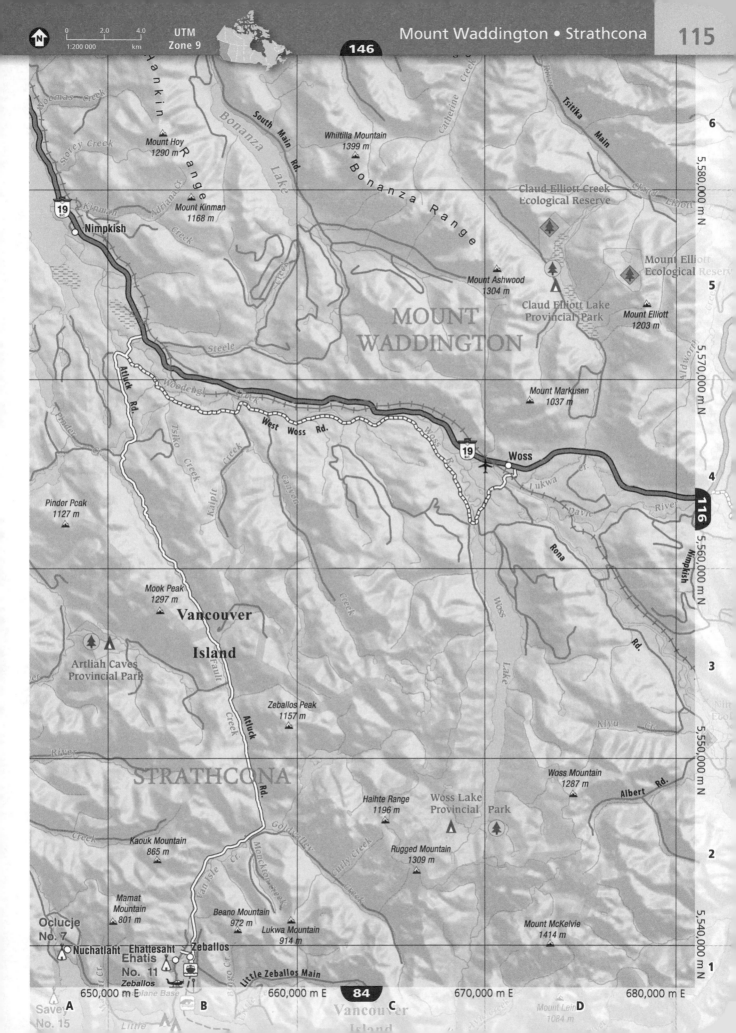

146

UTM
Zone 9

0   2.0   4.0
km
1:200 000

Kooomas Creek

Hankin Range

Bonanza Lake

South Main Rd.

Storey Creek

Mount Hoy
1290 m

Adriana Cr.

Mount Kinman
1168 m

Kinman Creek

19
B.C.

Nimpkish

Whiltilla Mountain
1399 m

Bonanza Range

Catherine Creek

Tsitika Main

5,580,000 m N   6

Claud Elliott Creek
Ecological Reserve

Mount Ashwood
1304 m

Claud Elliott Lake
Provincial Park

Mount Elliott
Ecological Reserve

Mount Elliott
1203 m

Aldworth

5,570,000 m N   5

MOUNT
WADDINGTON

Steele

Atluck Rd.

Woodengl

Tsiko Creek

Kalpit Creek

West Woss Rd.

Canyon

Woss

Mount Markusen
1037 m

19
B.C.

Woss

Lukwa Cr.

Davie River

116

Nimpkish

5,560,000 m N   4

Pinder Peak
1127 m

Pinder Creek

Rona

Woss Rd.

Mook Peak
1297 m

Vancouver

Island

Fault Creek

Woss Lake

Kiyu Cr.

Nitinat Cool

5,550,000 m N   3

Artliah Caves
Provincial Park

Atluck Creek

Zeballos Peak
1157 m

STRATHCONA

Atluck Rd.

Goldvalley

Monckton Creek

River

Kaouk Mountain
865 m

Van Isle Cr.

Haihte Range
1196 m

Curly Creek

Woss Lake
Provincial Park

Rugged Mountain
1309 m

Woss Mountain
1287 m

Albert Rd.

2

Mamat
Mountain
801 m

Beano Mountain
972 m

Lukwa Mountain
914 m

Mount McKelvie
1414 m

5,540,000 m N   1

Oclucje
No. 7

Nuchatlaht

Ehattesaht
Ehatis
No. 11
Zeballos

Zeballos

Little Zeballos Main

Bingo Cr.

650,000 m E

660,000 m E   84   670,000 m E

680,000 m E

Savey
No. 15

Little

A   B

Vancouver
Island   C   D

Mount Lein
1084 m

UTM
Zone 9

1:200 000

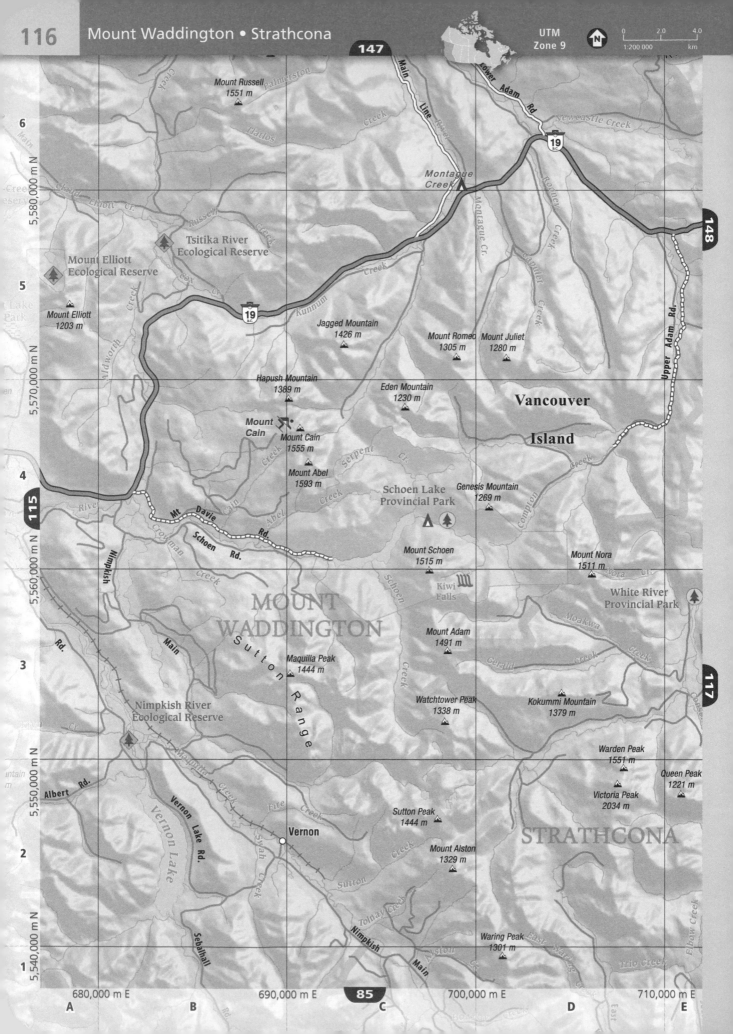

147

148

115

117

85

Mount Russell
1551 m

Montague
Creek

19
B.C.

Tsitika River
Ecological Reserve

Mount Elliott
Ecological Reserve

Mount Elliott
1203 m

19
B.C.

Jagged Mountain
1426 m

Mount Romeo
1305 m

Mount Juliet
1280 m

Hapush Mountain
1389 m

Eden Mountain
1230 m

Vancouver

Island

Mount
Cain

Mount Cain
1555 m

Mount Abel
1593 m

Schoen Lake
Provincial Park

Genesis Mountain
1269 m

Mount Schoen
1515 m

Mount Nora
1511 m

Kiwi
Falls

White River
Provincial Park

**MOUNT
WADDINGTON**

Mount Adam
1491 m

Maquilla Peak
1444 m

Sutton Range

Watchtower Peak
1338 m

Kokummi Mountain
1379 m

Nimpkish River
Ecological Reserve

Warden Peak
1551 m

Queen Peak
1221 m

Albert   Rd.

Victoria Peak
2034 m

Sutton Peak
1444 m

STRATHCONA

Vernon Lake Rd.

Vernon

Mount Alston
1329 m

Waring Peak
1301 m

680,000 m E

690,000 m E

700,000 m E

710,000 m E

5,580,000 m N

5,570,000 m N

5,560,000 m N

5,550,000 m N

5,540,000 m N

A B C D E

6

5

4

3

2

1

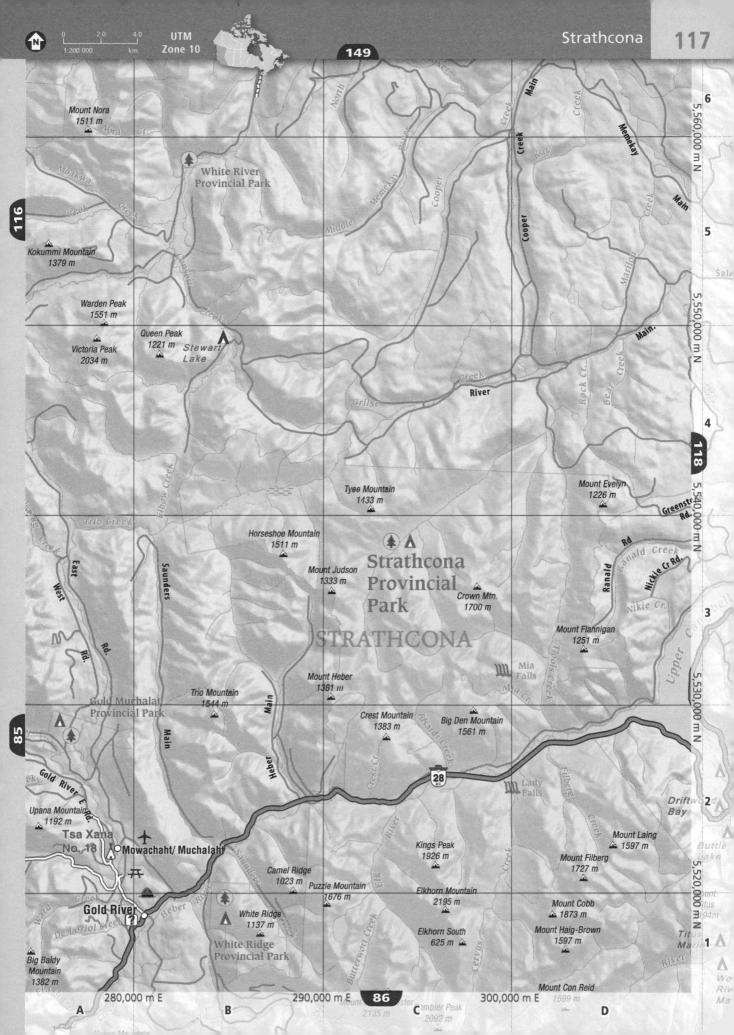

N

0   2.0   4.0   UTM
1:200 000   km   Zone 10

149

SOUTH

116

118

85

86

Mount Nora
1511 m

White River
Provincial Park

Kokummi Mountain
1379 m

Moakwa Creek

Cassedi Creek

Warden Peak
1551 m

Queen Peak
1221 m

Victoria Peak
2034 m

Stewart
Lake

Elbow Creek

Grilse

Creek

River

Trio Creek

Horseshoe Mountain
1511 m

Tyee Mountain
1433 m

Mount Judson
1333 m

Saunders

Strathcona
Provincial
Park

STRATHCONA

Crown Mtn.
1700 m

Mount Evelyn
1226 m

Greenst
Rd.

Ranald

Ranald Creek

Nickle Cr Rd.

Nikle Cr.

Mount Flannigan
1251 m

Tlools Creek

Mia
Falls

Mia Cr.

Upper Campbell

Mount Heber
1381 m

Trio Mountain
1544 m

Gold Muchalat
Provincial Park

Main

Heber

Main

Crest Mountain
1383 m

Crest Cr

Big Den Mountain
1561 m

Idsardi Creek

28
BC

Lady
Falls

Filberg Creek

Driftwood
Bay

Buttle
Lake

Upana Mountain
1192 m

Gold River E Rd.

Tsa Xana
No. 18

Mowachaht/ Muchalaht

Gold River

Saunders River

Camel Ridge
1023 m

Puzzle Mountain
1676 m

Elk River

Kings Peak
1926 m

Elkhorn Mountain
2195 m

Mount Laing
1597 m

Mount Filberg
1727 m

Mount Cobb
1873 m

White Ridge
1137 m

White Ridge
Provincial Park

Butterwort Creek

Cervus Creek

Elkhorn South
625 m

Mount Haig-Brown
1597 m

Big Baldy
Mountain
1382 m

De Loriol Creek

Mount Con Reid
1599 m

Gambier Peak
2092 m

Mount
Titus
494 m

Titus
Mari

River

Wo
Riv
Ma

280,000 m E   290,000 m E   300,000 m E

A   B   C   D

5,560,000 m N   6

5,550,000 m N   5

5,540,000 m N   4

5,530,000 m N   3

5,520,000 m N   2

1

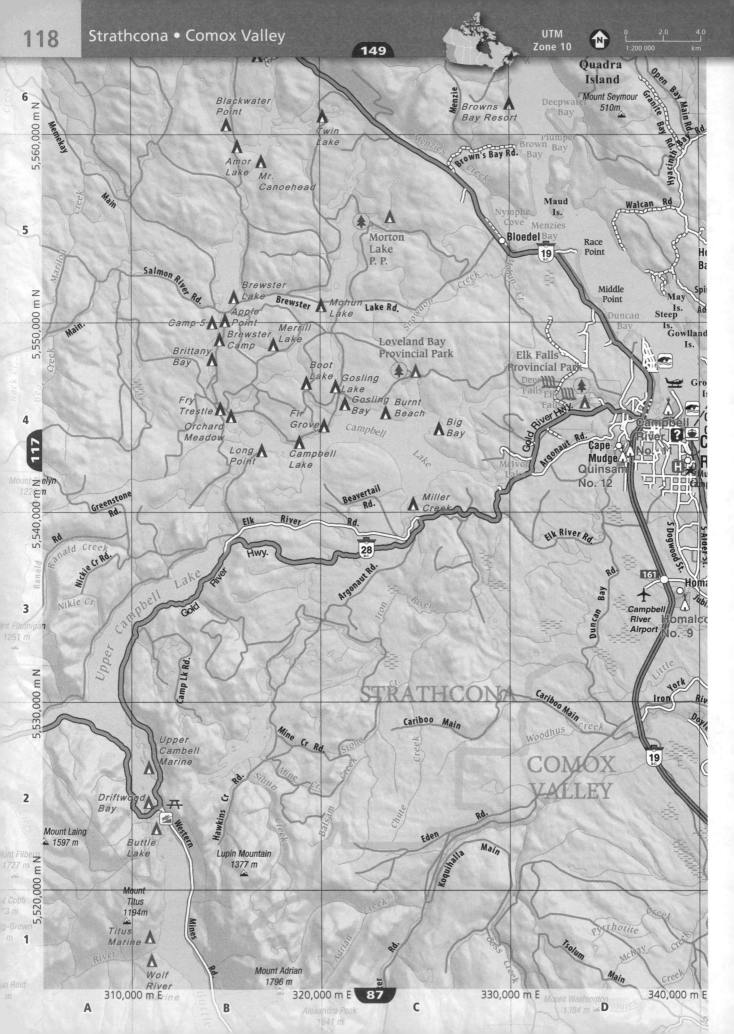

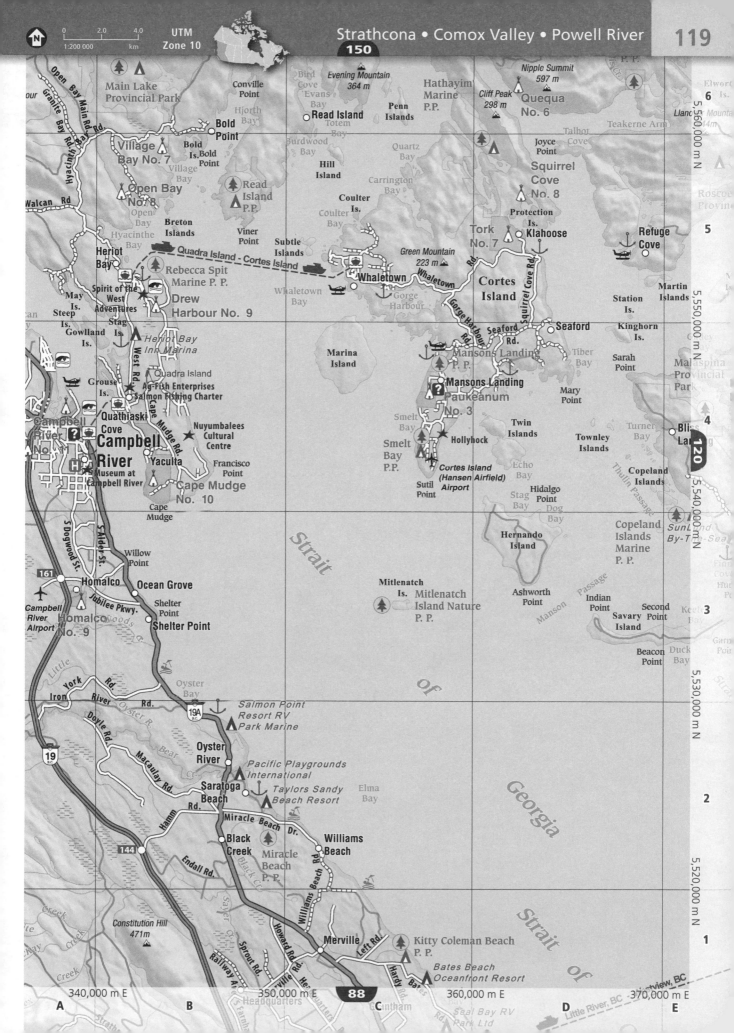

UTM
Zone 10

1:200 000

150

120

88

Main Lake
Provincial Park
Conville
Point
Bird
Cove
Evans
Bay
Evening Mountain
364 m
Hathayim
Marine
P.P.
Nipple Summit
597 m
Cliff Peak
298 m
Quequa
No. 6
Read Island
Penn
Islands
Hjorth
Bay
Totem
Bay
Bold
Point
Bold
Is.
Bold
Point
Burdwood
Bay
Quartz
Bay
Joyce
Point
Teakerne Arm
Village
Bay No. 7
Village
Bay
Hill
Island
Carrington
Bay
Squirrel
Cove
No. 8
Talbot
Cove
Open Bay
No. 8
Read
Island
P.P.
Coulter
Is.
Protection
Is.
Refuge
Cove
Breton
Islands
Viner
Point
Coulter
Bay
Tork
No. 7
Klahoose
Heriot
Bay
Hyacinthe
Bay
Quadra Island - Cortes Island
Subtle
Islands
Green Mountain
223 m
Martin
Islands
May
Is.
Spirit of the
West
Adventures
Rebecca Spit
Marine P. P.
Drew
Harbour No. 9
Whaletown
Whaletown
Cortes
Island
Station
Is.
Kinghorn
Is.
Steep
Is.
Gowlland
Is.
Stag
Is.
Heriot Bay
Inn Marina
West Rd.
Whaletown Bay
Gorge
Harbour
Seaford
Rd.
Seaford
Sarah
Point
Grouse
Is.
Quadra Island
Ag-Fish Enterprises
Salmon Fishing Charter
Marina
Island
Mansons Landing
P. P.
Tiber
Bay
Campbell
River
No. 1
Quathiaski
Cove
Nuyumbalees
Cultural
Centre
Mansons Landing
Paukeanum
No. 3
Mary
Point
Campbell
River
Yaculta
Francisco
Point
Smelt
Bay
Twin
Islands
Townley
Islands
Turner
Bay
Bliss
Landing
Museum at
Campbell River
Cape Mudge
No. 10
Smelt
Bay
P.P.
Hollyhock
Cortes Island
(Hansen Airfield)
Airport
Echo
Bay
Copeland
Islands
Cape
Mudge
Sutil
Point
Hidalgo
Point
Stag
Bay
Dog
Bay
Copeland
Islands
Marine
P. P.
SunLund
By-The-Sea
Willow
Point
Hernando
Island
S Dogwood St.
S Alder St.
Ocean Grove
Mitlenatch
Is.
Mitlenatch
Island Nature
P. P.
Ashworth
Point
Indian
Point
Second
Point
Homalco
Shelter
Point
Savary
Island
Campbell
River
Airport
Homalco
No. 9
Jubilee Pkwy.
Shelter Point
Beacon
Point
Duck
Bay
York
Rd.
Iron
River
Rd.
Oyster
Bay
Salmon Point
Resort RV
Park Marine
Doyle Rd.
Oyster
River
Pacific Playgrounds
International
Elma
Bay
Macaulay Rd.
Saratoga
Beach
Taylors Sandy
Beach Resort
Miracle Beach Dr.
Hamm
Black
Creek
Williams
Beach
Miracle
Beach
P.P.
Endall Rd.
Constitution Hill
471m
Williams Beach Rd.
Merville
Kitty Coleman Beach
P. P.
Railway Ave.
Sprout Rd.
Howard Rd.
Bates Beach
Oceanfront Resort
Seal Bay RV
Park Ltd

340,000 m E
350,000 m E
360,000 m E
370,000 m E

5,560,000 m N
5,550,000 m N
5,540,000 m N
5,530,000 m N
5,520,000 m N

A   B   C   D   E

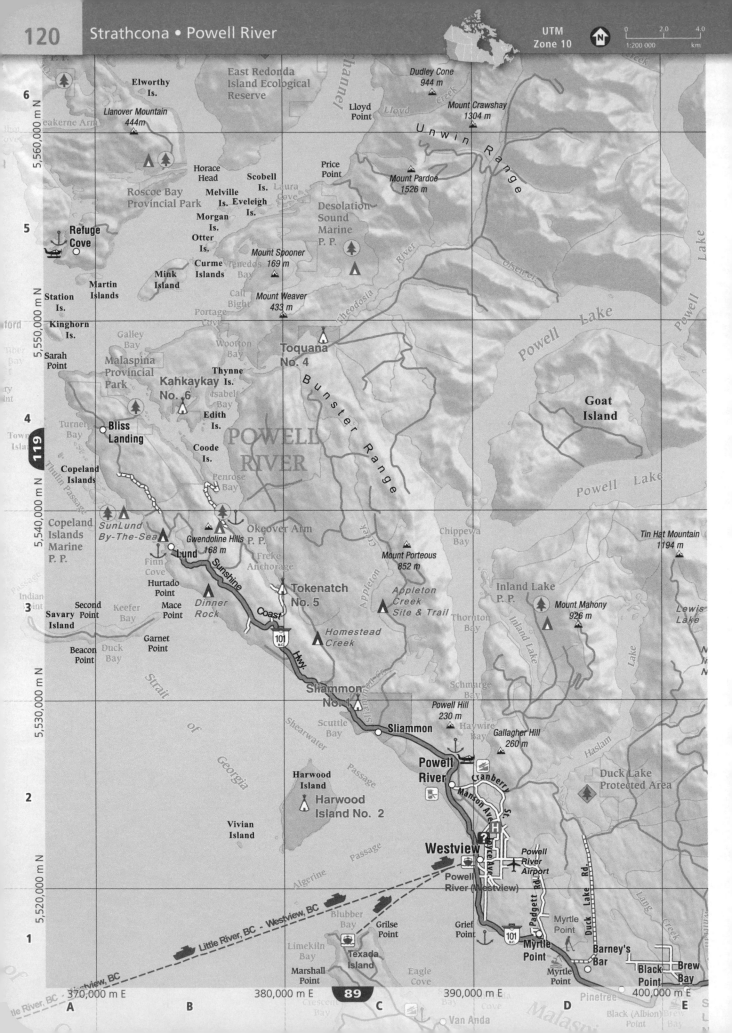

UTM Zone 10

1:200 000

0   2.0   4.0
km

E. P.

Elworthy Is.

Llanover Mountain
444m

East Redonda
Island Ecological
Reserve

Dudley Cone
944 m

Mount Crawshay
1304 m

Lloyd
Point

Unwin Range

6

5,560,000 m N

Roscoe Bay
Provincial Park

Horace
Head

Scobell
Is.

Melville
Is.

Price
Point

Mount Pardoe
1526 m

Eveleigh
Is.

Morgan
Is.

Otter
Is.

Curme
Islands

Mount Spooner
169 m

Desolation
Sound
Marine
P. P.

5

5,550,000 m N

Refuge
Cove

Martin
Islands

Mink
Island

Mount Weaver
433 m

Station
Is.

Kinghorn
Is.

Sarah
Point

Galley
Bay

Malaspina
Provincial
Park

Wootton
Bay

Toquana
No. 4

Goat
Island

Powell Lake

4

5,550,000 m N

Kahkaykay
No. 6

Thynne
Is.

Isabel
Bay

Edith
Is.

Bunster Range

POWELL
RIVER

119

Bliss
Landing

Coode
Is.

Penrose
Bay

Copeland
Islands

Okeover Arm
P. P.

Chippewa
Bay

Tin Hat Mountain
1194 m

Powell Lake

5,540,000 m N

Copeland
Islands
Marine
P. P.

SunLund
By-The-Sea

Gwendoline Hills
168 m

Freke
Anchorage

Mount Porteous
852 m

Inland Lake
P. P.

Mount Mahony
926 m

Lewis
Lake

Lund

Sunshine

Tokenatch
No. 5

Appleton
Creek
Site & Trail

3

Second
Savary Point
Island

Hurtado
Point

Mace
Point

Dinner
Rock

Coast

Homestead
Creek

Thornton
Bay

Inland Lake

Keefer
Bay

Garnet
Point

101
BC.

Hwy.

Beacon
Point

Duck
Bay

Indian
Point

Strait

Sliammon
No. 1

Schmarge
Bay

Haslam
Lake

5,530,000 m N

of

Georgia

Shearwater

Scuttle
Bay

Sliammon

Powell Hill
230 m

Haywire
Bay

Gallagher Hill
260 m

Duck Lake
Protected Area

2

Harwood
Island

Harwood
Island No. 2

Powell
River

Lake

Vivian
Island

Westview

Powell
River
Airport

Cranberry

Manson Ave.

St.

Duck Lake Rd.

5,520,000 m N

Algerine

Passage

Powell
River (Westview)

Myrtle
Point

Padgett Rd.

Barney's
Bar

1

Little River, BC - Westview, BC

Blubber
Bay

Grilse
Point

Grief
Point

101
BC.

Myrtle
Point

Black
Point

Brew
Bay

Limekiln
Bay

Texada
Island

Myrtle
Point

Lang

Marshall
Point

Eagle
Cove

Pinetree

Black (Albion)
Point

Westview, BC

370,000 m E

380,000 m E

89

390,000 m E

400,000 m E

Van Anda

Malasn

Crescent
Bay

A   B   C   D   E

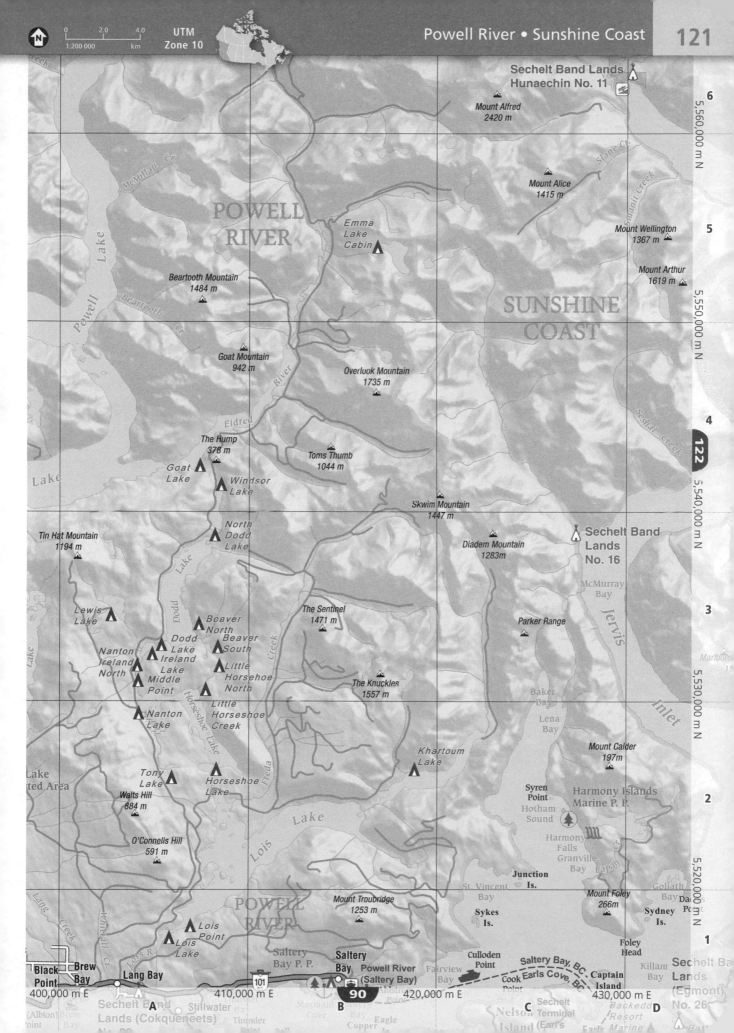

UTM Zone 10
1:200 000
0 2.0 4.0 km

POWELL RIVER

SUNSHINE COAST

Sechelt Band Lands
Hunaechin No. 11

Mount Alfred
2420 m

Mount Alice
1415 m

Mount Wellington
1367 m

Mount Arthur
1619 m

Emma Lake Cabin

Beartooth Mountain
1484 m

Goat Mountain
942 m

Overlook Mountain
1735 m

Eldred River

The Hump
378 m

Toms Thumb
1044 m

Goat Lake

Windsor Lake

Skwim Mountain
1447 m

Tin Hat Mountain
1194 m

North Dodd Lake

Diadem Mountain
1283m

Sechelt Band Lands No. 16

McMurray Bay

Lewis Lake

Beaver North

The Sentinel
1471 m

Parker Range

Jervis

Dodd Lake

Beaver South

Nanton North

Ireland Lake

Little Horseshoe North

The Knuckles
1557 m

Baker Bay

Middle Point

Little Horseshoe Creek

Lena Bay

Nanton Lake

Mount Calder
197m

Khartoum Lake

Tony Lake

Horseshoe Lake

Syren Point

Harmony Islands Marine P. P.

Walts Hill
884 m

Hotham Sound

O'Connells Hill
591 m

Harmony Falls

Granville Bay

Junction Is.

Lois Lake

St. Vincent Bay

Mount Troubridge
1253 m

Mount Foley
266m

Sydney Is.

POWELL RIVER

Sykes Is.

Foley Head

Lois Point

Lois Lake

Saltery Bay P. P.

Saltery Bay

Culloden Point

Captain Island

Black Point

Brew Bay

Lang Bay

101

Powell River (Saltery Bay)

Fairview Bay

Saltery Bay, BC.

Earls Cove, BC.

Cook Point

Sechelt Terminal

Sechelt Ba Lands (Egmont) No. 26

400,000 m E

410,000 m E

420,000 m E

430,000 m E

Sechelt B Lands (Cokqueneets)

Stillwater

Nelson Island

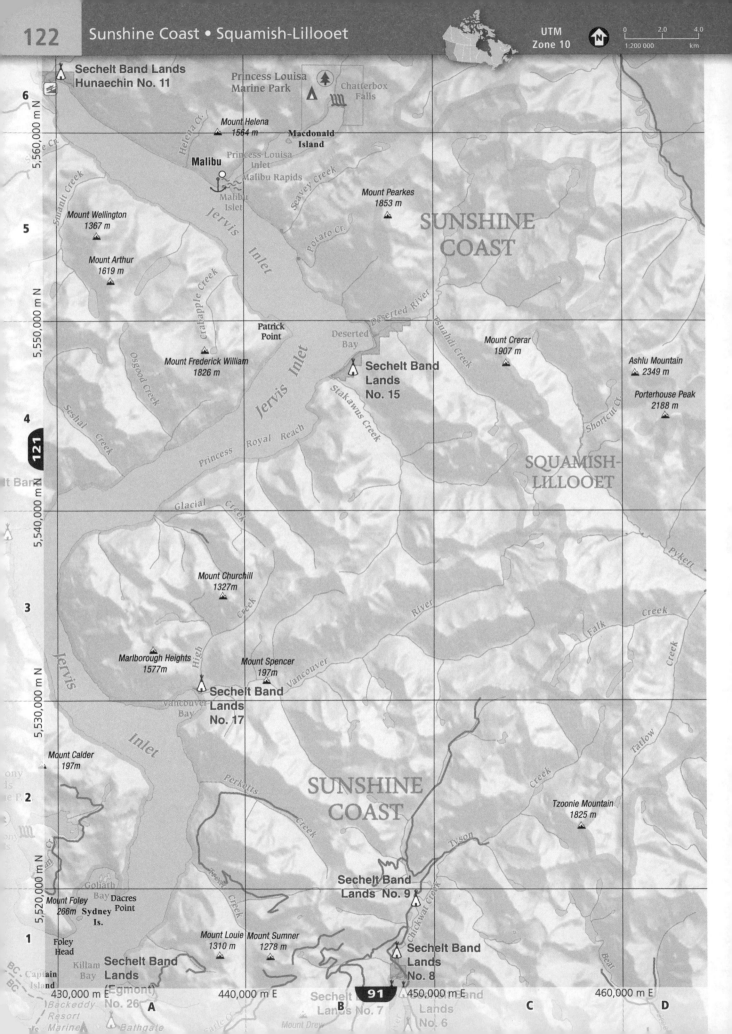

Sechelt Band Lands
Hunaechin No. 11

Princess Louisa
Marine Park

Chatterbox
Falls

Mount Helena
1564 m

Macdonald
Island

Princess Louisa
Inlet

Malibu

Malibu Rapids

Mount Pearkes
1853 m

**SUNSHINE
COAST**

Malibu
Islet

Helena Cr.

Seavey Creek

Squanit Creek

Mount Wellington
1367 m

Jervis

Potato Cr.

Mount Arthur
1619 m

Crabapple Creek

Deserted River

Osgood Creek

Patrick
Point

Deserted
Bay

Mount Crerar
1907 m

Ashlu Mountain
2349 m

Mount Frederick William
1826 m

Jervis Inlet

Sechelt Band
Lands
No. 15

Porterhouse Peak
2188 m

Seshal Creek

Inlet

Stakawus Creek

Tsuahdi Creek

**SQUAMISH-
LILLOOET**

Shortcut Cr.

121

Princess   Royal   Reach

Glacial   Creek

Pykett

High

Mount Churchill
1327m

Creek

River

Falk

Creek

Creek

Jervis

Marlborough Heights
1577m

Mount Spencer
197m

Vancouver

Sechelt Band
Lands
No. 17

Vancouver
Bay

Mount Calder
197m

Perketts

**SUNSHINE
COAST**

Creek

Tatlow

Creek

Tyson

Tzoonie Mountain
1825 m

Inlet

Sechelt Band
Lands No. 9

Chickwat Creek

Goliath
Bay

Dacres
Point

Mount Foley
266m Sydney
Is.

Foley
Head

Mount Louie
1310 m

Mount Sumner
1278 m

Bear

Sechelt Band
Lands
No. 8

Sechelt Band
Lands
(Egmont)

Killam
Bay

Captain
Island

BC.
BC.
BC.

No. 26

Backeddy
Resort
Marine

Sechelt
Lands No. 7

Mount Drew

Lands
No. 6

Bathgate

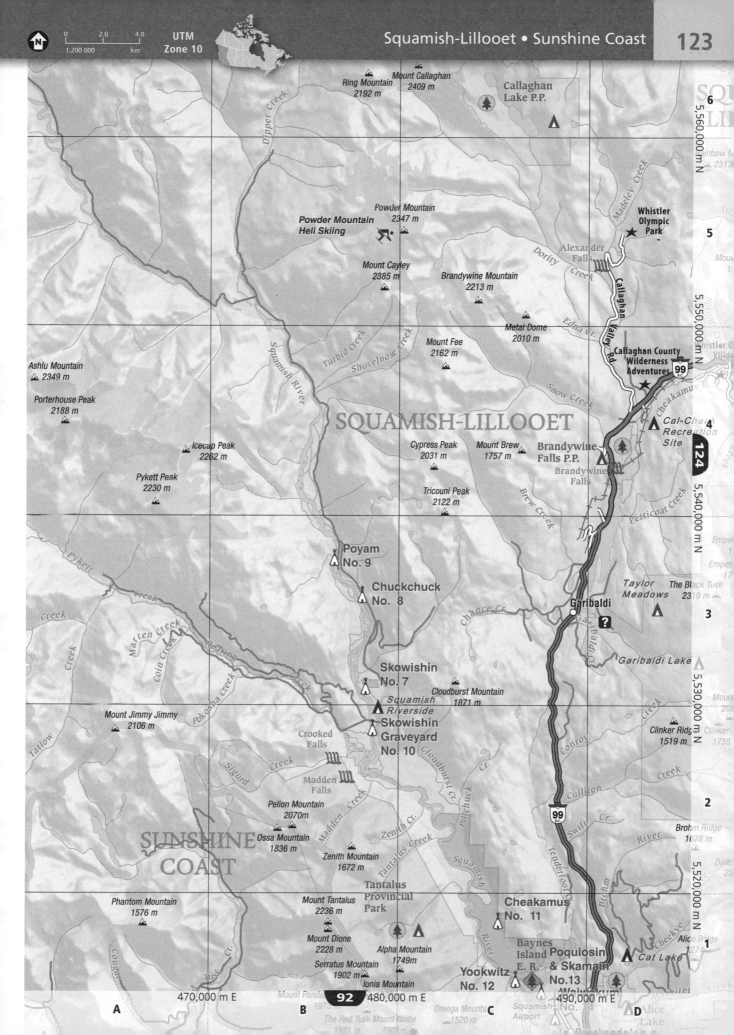

N

| 0 | 2.0 | 4.0 |
1:200 000   km

UTM
Zone 10

Squamish-Lillooet • Sunshine Coast

6
5,560,000 m N

Ring Mountain
2192 m

Mount Callaghan
2409 m

Callaghan
Lake P.P.

Madeley Creek

Rainbow M
2313 m

Powder Mountain
2347 m

Powder Mountain
Heli Skiing

Whistler
Olympic
Park

5

Dority Creek

Alexander
Falls

Mount Cayley
2385 m

Brandywine Mountain
2213 m

Callaghan Valley Rd.

Callaghan

5,550,000 m N

Metal Dome
2010 m

Edna Cr.

Callaghan County
Wilderness
Adventures

99
B.C.

Whistler
Villa

Ashlu Mountain
2349 m

Squamish River

Turbid Creek

Shovelnose Creek

Mount Fee
2162 m

Snow Creek

Cal-Cheat
Recreation
Site

4

Porterhouse Peak
2188 m

SQUAMISH-LILLOOET

124
B.C.

5,540,000 m N

Icecap Peak
2262 m

Cypress Peak
2031 m

Mount Brew
1757 m

Brandywine
Falls P.P.

Brandywine
Falls

Petticoat Creek

Pykett Peak
2230 m

Tricouni Peak
2122 m

Brew Creek

Emper

Empe
17

Pykett Creek

Poyam
No. 9

Chance Cr.

Taylor
Meadows

The Black Tusk
2319 m

3

Creek

Chuckchuck
No. 8

Garibaldi

?

Garibaldi Cr.

5,530,000 m N

Creek

Marten Creek

Coin Creek

Red Hing Creek

Pokosha Creek

Skowishin
No. 7

Cloudburst Mountain
1871 m

Garibaldi Lake

Mou
20

Mount Jimmy Jimmy
2106 m

Squamish
Riverside

Skowishin
Graveyard
No. 10

Conroy Creek

Clinker Ridge
1519 m

Clinker

Tatlow

Crooked
Falls

Sigurd Creek

Madden Falls

Cloudburst Cr.

Culliton

2

**SUNSHINE
COAST**

Pelion Mountain
2070m

Madden Creek

Zenith Cr.

Pilchuck Cr.

99
B.C.

Swift Cr.

Brohm Ridge
1678 m

Dalto

Ossa Mountain
1836 m

Zenith Mountain
1672 m

Tantalus Creek

Squamish

River

Tenderfoot Cr.

Brohm River

5,520,000 m N

Phantom Mountain
1576 m

Mount Tantalus
2236 m

Tantalus
Provincial
Park

Cheakamus
No. 11

Cheekye

Alice Ridge
127

1

Mount Dione
2228 m

Alpha Mountain
1749m

Baynes
Island
E. R.

Poquiosin
& Skamain
No.13

Cat Lake

Cougar Cr.

Serratus Mountain
1902 m

Ionia Mountain

Yookwitz
No. 12

Squamish
Airport

Tusk Cr.

Mount Panda

92

Omega Mounta
1520 m

Machir
Creek

Alice
Lake

The Red Tusk Mount Niobe
1921 m

470,000 m E   480,000 m E   490,000 m E

A   B   C   D

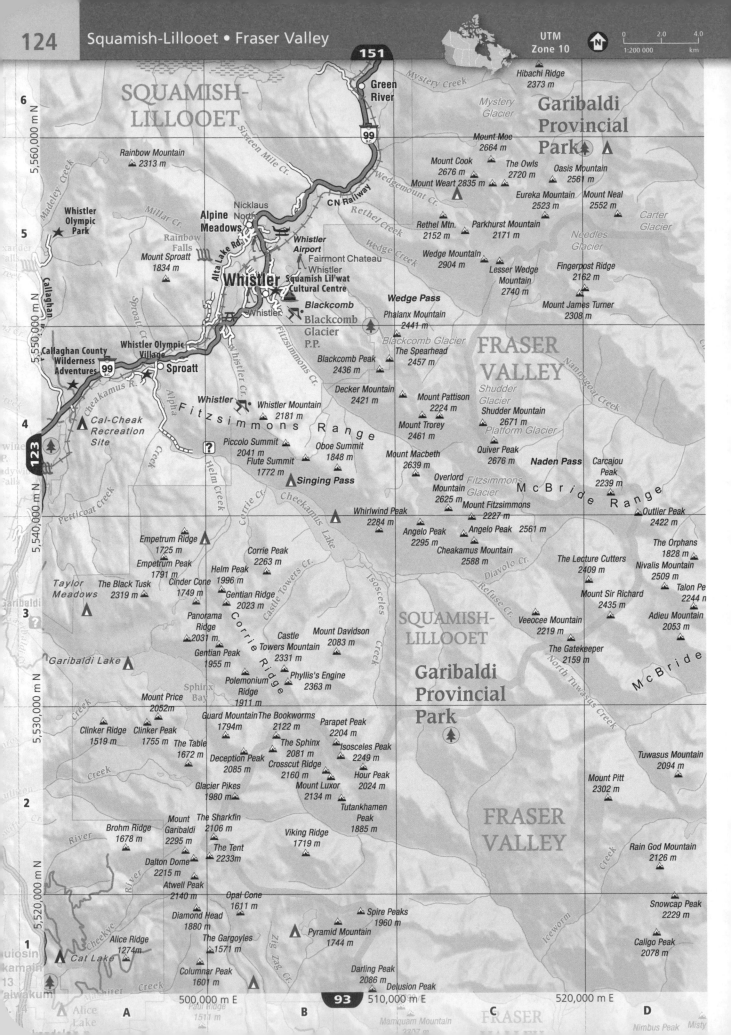

UTM
Zone 10

1:200 000

km

0   2.0   4.0

Hibachi Ridge
2373 m

SQUAMISH-LILLOOET

Mystery Creek

Mystery Glacier

Garibaldi Provincial Park

Mount Moe
2664 m

Green River

151

99
B.C.

Rainbow Mountain
2313 m

Sixteen Mile Cr.

Wedgemount Cr.

Mount Cook
2676 m

The Owls
2720 m

Oasis Mountain
2561 m

Mount Weart 2835 m

Eureka Mountain
2523 m

Mount Neal
2552 m

Whistler Olympic Park

Nicklaus North

Alpine Meadows

CN Railway

Rethel Creek

Rethel Mtn.
2152 m

Parkhurst Mountain
2171 m

Carter Glacier

Millar Cr.

Madeley Creek

Rainbow Falls

Mount Sproatt
1834 m

Whistler Airport

Wedge Creek

Wedge Mountain
2904 m

Needles Glacier

Alta Lake Rd.

Fairmont Chateau Whistler

Lesser Wedge Mountain
2740 m

Fingerpost Ridge
2162 m

Whistler

Squamish Lil'wat Cultural Centre

Callaghan Cr.

Whistler

Blackcomb

Wedge Pass

Mount James Turner
2308 m

Sproatt Cr.

Blackcomb Glacier P.P.

Phalanx Mountain
2441 m

Callaghan County Wilderness Adventures

Whistler Olympic Village

Sproatt

99
B.C.

Blackcomb Glacier

The Spearhead
2457 m

FRASER VALLEY

Nannegoat Creek

Cheakamus R.

Fitzsimmons Cr.

Blackcomb Peak
2436 m

Shudder Glacier

Shudder Mountain
2671 m

Cal-Cheak Recreation Site

123

Whistler Cr.

Whistler

Whistler Mountain
2181 m

Decker Mountain
2421 m

Mount Pattison
2224 m

Platform Glacier

Fitzsimmons Range

Mount Trorey
2461 m

Quiver Peak
2676 m

Naden Pass

Carcajou Peak
2239 m

Alpha Creek

Piccolo Summit
2041 m

Oboe Summit
1848 m

Mount Macbeth
2639 m

Helm Creek

Flute Summit
1772 m

Singing Pass

Overlord Mountain
2625 m

Fitzsimmons Glacier

Mount Fitzsimmons
2227 m

Outlier Peak
2422 m

M c B r i d e   R a n g e

Corrie Cr.

Cheakamus Lake

Whirlwind Peak
2284 m

Angelo Peak
2295 m

Angelo Peak 2561 m

The Orphans
1828 m

Petticoat Creek

Empetrum Ridge
1725 m

Corrie Peak
2263 m

Castle Towers Cr.

Diavolo Cr.

Cheakamus Mountain
2588 m

The Lecture Cutters
2409 m

Nivalis Mountain
2509 m

Taylor Meadows

Empetrum Peak
1791 m

Helm Peak
1996 m

Refuse Cr.

Talon Pe
2244 m

The Black Tusk
2319 m

Cinder Cone
1749 m

Gentian Ridge
2023 m

Isosceles Creek

Mount Sir Richard
2435 m

Adieu Mountain
2053 m

Panorama Ridge
2031 m

Corrie Ridge

Castle Towers Mountain
2331 m

Mount Davidson
2083 m

SQUAMISH-LILLOOET

Veeocee Mountain
2219 m

Garibaldi Lake

Gentian Peak
1955 m

Polemonium Ridge
1911 m

Phyllis's Engine
2363 m

Garibaldi Provincial Park

The Gatekeeper
2159 m

M c B r i d e

Sphinx Bay

North Tuwasus Creek

Mount Price
2052m

Guard Mountain
1794m

The Bookworms
2122 m

Parapet Peak
2204 m

Clinker Ridge
1519 m

Clinker Peak
1755 m

The Table
1672 m

The Sphinx
2081 m

Isosceles Peak
2249 m

Tuwasus Mountain
2094 m

Deception Peak
2085 m

Crosscut Ridge
2160 m

Hour Peak
2024 m

Mount Pitt
2302 m

Glacier Pikes
1980 m

Mount Luxor
2134 m

Tutankhamen Peak
1885 m

FRASER VALLEY

Brohm Ridge
1678 m

Mount Garibaldi
2295 m

The Sharkfin
2106 m

Viking Ridge
1719 m

Dalton Dome
2215 m

The Tent
2233m

Rain God Mountain
2126 m

Atwell Peak
2140 m

Opal Cone
1611 m

Spire Peaks
1960 m

Diamond Head
1880 m

Pyramid Mountain
1744 m

Snowcap Peak
2229 m

Zig Zag Cr.

Alice Ridge
1274m

Cat Lake

The Gargoyles
1571 m

Iceworm Creek

Caligo Peak
2078 m

Columnar Peak
1601 m

Darling Peak
2086 m

Delusion Peak

93

Alice Lake

Paul Ridge
1511 m

Mamquam Mountain

FRASER VALLEY

Nimbus Peak Misty

500 000 m E

510 000 m E

520 000 m E

A   B   C   D

N

0   2.0   4.0
1:200 000   km
UTM
Zone 10

Squamish Lillooet • Fraser Valley • Thompson-Nicola

152

125

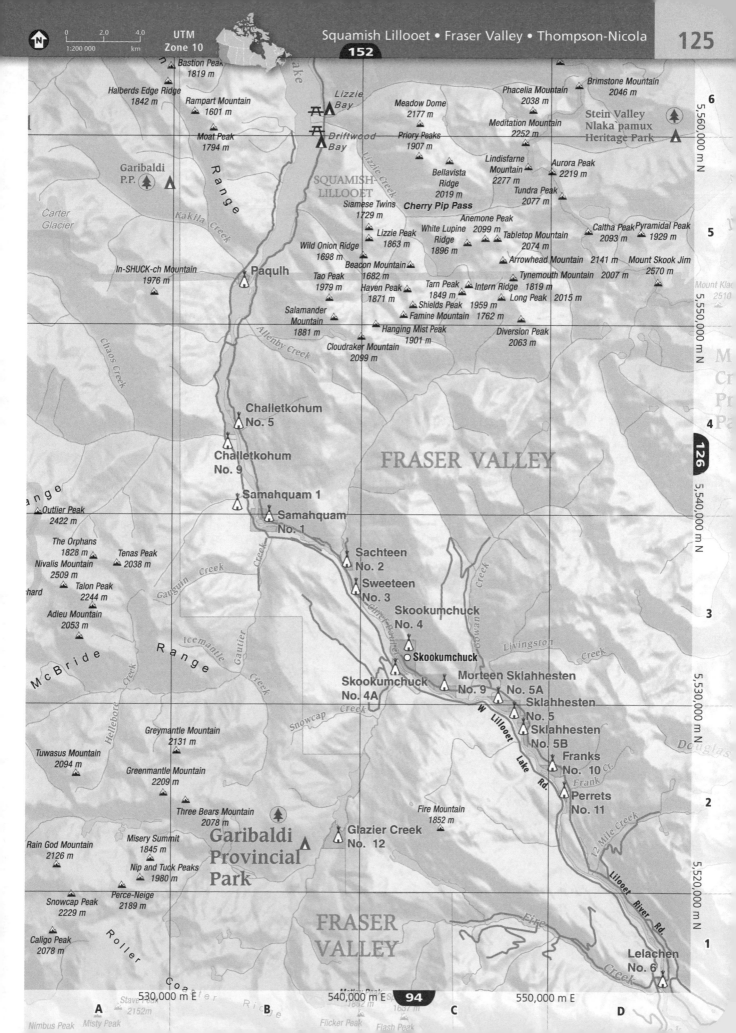

Bastion Peak
1819 m

Halberds Edge Ridge
1842 m

Rampart Mountain
1601 m

Lizzie
Bay

Driftwood
Bay

Meadow Dome
2177 m

Phacelia Mountain
2038 m

Brimstone Mountain
2046 m

Moat Peak
1794 m

Meditation Mountain
2252 m

Stein Valley
Nlaka`pamux
Heritage Park

Garibaldi
P.P.

SQUAMISH-
LILLOOET

Priory Peaks
1907 m

Lindisfarne
Mountain
2277 m

Aurora Peak
2219 m

Carter
Glacier

Kakila Creek

Bellavista
Ridge
2019 m

Cherry Pip Pass

Tundra Peak
2077 m

Siamese Twins
1729 m

Anemone Peak

Caltha Peak
2093 m

Pyramidal Peak
1929 m

In-SHUCK-ch Mountain
1976 m

Páqulh

Wild Onion Ridge
1698 m

Lizzie Peak
1863 m

White Lupine   2099 m
Ridge
1896 m

Tabletop Mountain
2074 m

Beacon Mountain
1682 m

Arrowhead Mountain   2141 m

Mount Skook Jim
2570 m

Tao Peak
1979 m

Haven Peak
1871 m

Tarn Peak
1849 m

Intern Ridge   1819 m

Tynemouth Mountain   2007 m

Mount Klac
2510

Salamander
Mountain
1881 m

Shields Peak   1959 m

Famine Mountain   1762 m

Long Peak   2015 m

M
Cr
Pr
Pa

Allenby Creek

Hanging Mist Peak
1901 m

Diversion Peak
2063 m

Cloudraker Mountain
2099 m

Chaos Creek

Challetkohum
No. 5

Challetkohum
No. 9

FRASER VALLEY

126

Range

Samahquam 1

Samahquam
No. 1

Outlier Peak
2422 m

The Orphans
1828 m

Tenas Peak
2038 m

Sachteen
No. 2

Nivalis Mountain
2509 m

Sweeteen
No. 3

hard

Talon Peak
2244 m

Skookumchuck
No. 4

Adieu Mountain
2053 m

Gauquin Creek

Gauthier Creek

Gowan Creek

Livingston Creek

Icemantle Creek

McBride

Range

Snowcap Creek

Skookumchuck

Skookumchuck
No. 4A

Morteen Sklahhesten
No. 9   No. 5A

Sklahhesten
No. 5

Greymantle Mountain
2131 m

W Lillooet Lake Rd.

Douglas

Tuwasus Mountain
2094 m

Greenmantle Mountain
2209 m

Sklahhesten
No. 5B

Franks
No. 10

Frank Cr.

Hellebore Creek

Three Bears Mountain
2078 m

Garibaldi
Provincial
Park

Fire Mountain
1852 m

Perrets
No. 11

Rain God Mountain
2126 m

Misery Summit
1845 m

Glazier Creek
No. 12

12 Mile Creek

Nip and Tuck Peaks
1980 m

Perce-Neige
2189 m

FRASER
VALLEY

Lillooet River Rd.

Snowcap Peak
2229 m

Caligo Peak
2078 m

Roller

Coast

Ridge

Fire Creek

Lelachen
No. 6

Stave Peak
2152m

530,000 m E

540,000 m E

94

550,000 m E

Nimbus Peak   Misty Peak

A

Flicker Peak

B

Flash Peak

C

D

6

5,560,000 m N

5

5,550,000 m N

4

5,540,000 m N

3

5,530,000 m N

2

5,520,000 m N

1

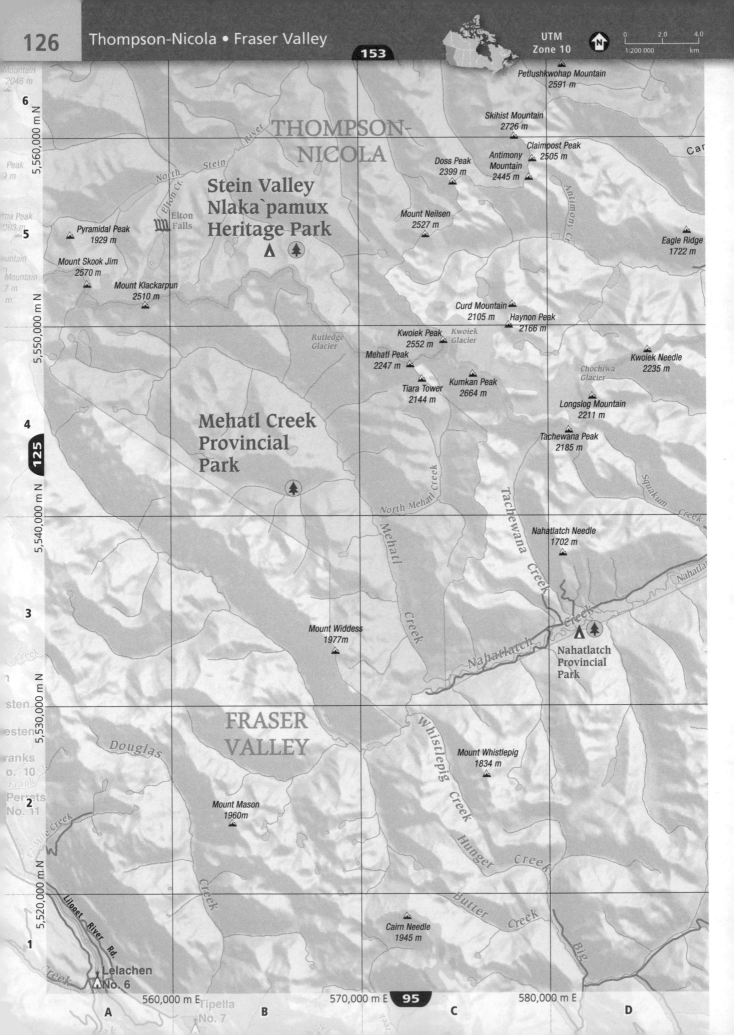

UTM
Zone 10

1:200 000

THOMPSON-
NICOLA

Petlushkwohap Mountain
2591 m

Skihist Mountain
2726 m

Claimpost Peak
2505 m

Doss Peak
2399 m

Antimony
Mountain
2445 m

**Stein Valley
Nlaka`pamux
Heritage Park**

Mount Neilsen
2527 m

Eagle Ridge
1722 m

Pyramidal Peak
1929 m

Mount Skook Jim
2570 m

Mount Klackarpun
2510 m

Curd Mountain
2105 m

Haynon Peak
2166 m

Rutledge
Glacier

Kwoiek Peak
2552 m

Kwoiek
Glacier

Kwoiek Needle
2235 m

Mehatl Peak
2247 m

Chochiwa
Glacier

Tiara Tower
2144 m

Kumkan Peak
2664 m

Longslog Mountain
2211 m

**Mehatl Creek
Provincial
Park**

Tachewana Peak
2185 m

North Mehatl Creek

Nahatlatch Needle
1702 m

Mehatl
Creek

Tachewana Creek

Squakum Creek

Mount Widdess
1977m

Nahatlatch
Creek

Nahatlatch
Provincial
Park

125

Whistlepig Creek

**FRASER
VALLEY**

Douglas

Mount Whistlepig
1834 m

Mount Mason
1960m

Hunger
Creek

Butter
Creek

Big

Cairn Needle
1945 m

Lelachen
No. 6

Lillooet River Rd.

Tipella
No. 7

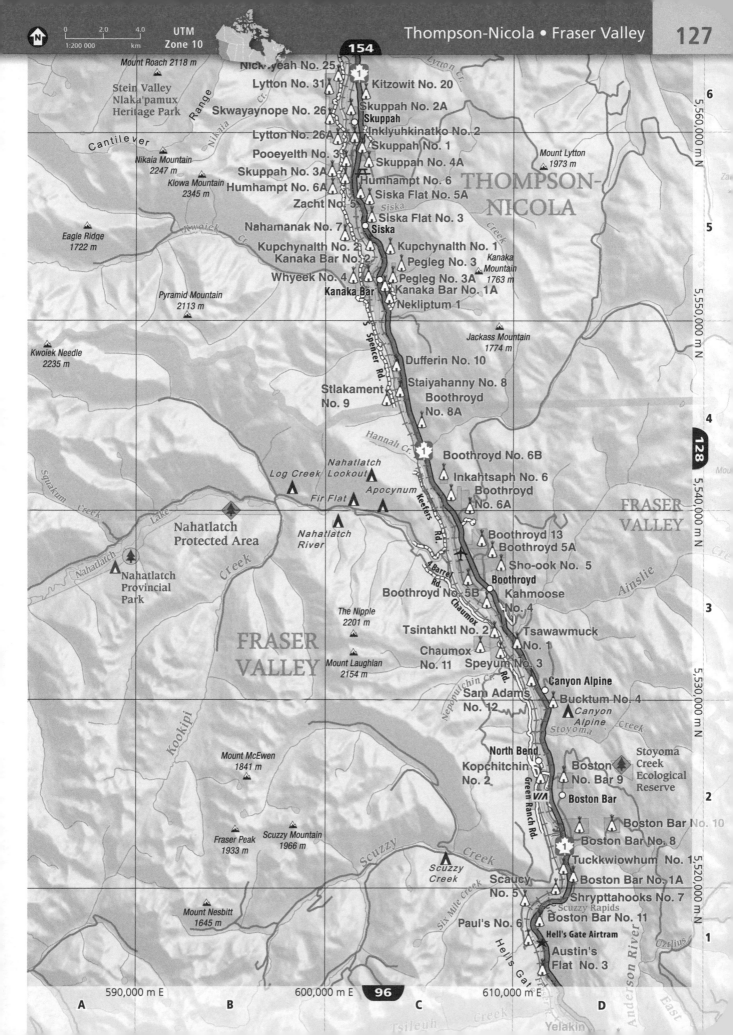

UTM
Zone 10

1:200 000

0   2.0   4.0
km

154

1

Nick.yeah No. 25

Lytton No. 31

Mount Roach 2118 m

Kitzowit No. 20

Skwayaynope No. 26

Skuppah No. 2A

Skuppah

Stein Valley
Nlaka'pamux
Heritage Park

Lytton No. 26A

Inklyuhkinatko No. 2

Skuppah No. 1

Pooeyelth No. 3

Skuppah No. 4A

Nikaia Mountain
2247 m

Skuppah No. 3A

Humhampt No. 6

Mount Lytton
1973 m

Klowa Mountain
2345 m

Humhampt No. 6A

Siska Flat No. 5A

THOMPSON-
NICOLA

Zacht No. 5

Siska

Nahamanak No. 7

Siska Flat No. 3

Siska

Eagle Ridge
1722 m

Kupchynalth No. 2

Kupchynalth No. 1

Kanaka Bar No. 2

Pegleg No. 3

Kanaka
Mountain
1763 m

Whyeek No. 4

Pegleg No. 3A

Pyramid Mountain
2113 m

Kanaka Bar

Kanaka Bar No. 1A

Nekliptum 1

Kwoiek Needle
2235 m

Jackass Mountain
1774 m

Dufferin No. 10

Staiyahanny No. 8

Stlakament
No. 9

Boothroyd
No. 8A

Hannah Cr.

1

Nahatlatch
Lookout

Boothroyd No. 6B

Log Creek

Inkahtsaph No. 6

128

Apocynum

Boothroyd
No. 6A

Fir Flat

Nahatlatch
Protected Area

Nahatlatch
River

FRASER
VALLEY

Boothroyd 13

Boothroyd 5A

Sho-ook No. 5

Nahatlatch
Provincial
Park

Boothroyd

Kahmoose
No. 4

The Nipple
2201 m

Boothroyd No. 5B

Tsintahktl No. 2

Tsawawmuck
No. 1

FRASER
VALLEY

Mount Laughlan
2154 m

Chaumox
No. 11

Speyum No. 3

Canyon Alpine

Mount McEwen
1841 m

Sam Adams
No. 12

Bucktum No. 4

Canyon
Alpine

Stoyoma

Stoyoma
Creek
Ecological
Reserve

North Bend

Kopchitchin
No. 2

Boston
No. Bar 9

Boston Bar

Boston Bar No. 10

Fraser Peak
1933 m

Scuzzy Mountain
1966 m

Boston Bar No. 8

Tuckkwiowhum No. 1

Mount Nesbitt
1645 m

Scuzzy
Creek

Scaucy
No. 5

Boston Bar No. 1A

Shrypttahooks No. 7

Scuzzy Rapids

Paul's No. 6

Boston Bar No. 11

Hell's Gate Airtram

Austin's
Flat No. 3

590,000 m E

600,000 m E

96

610,000 m E

A

B

C

D

5,560,000 m N

5,555,000 m N

5,550,000 m N

5,540,000 m N

5,530,000 m N

5,520,000 m N

6

5

4

3

2

1

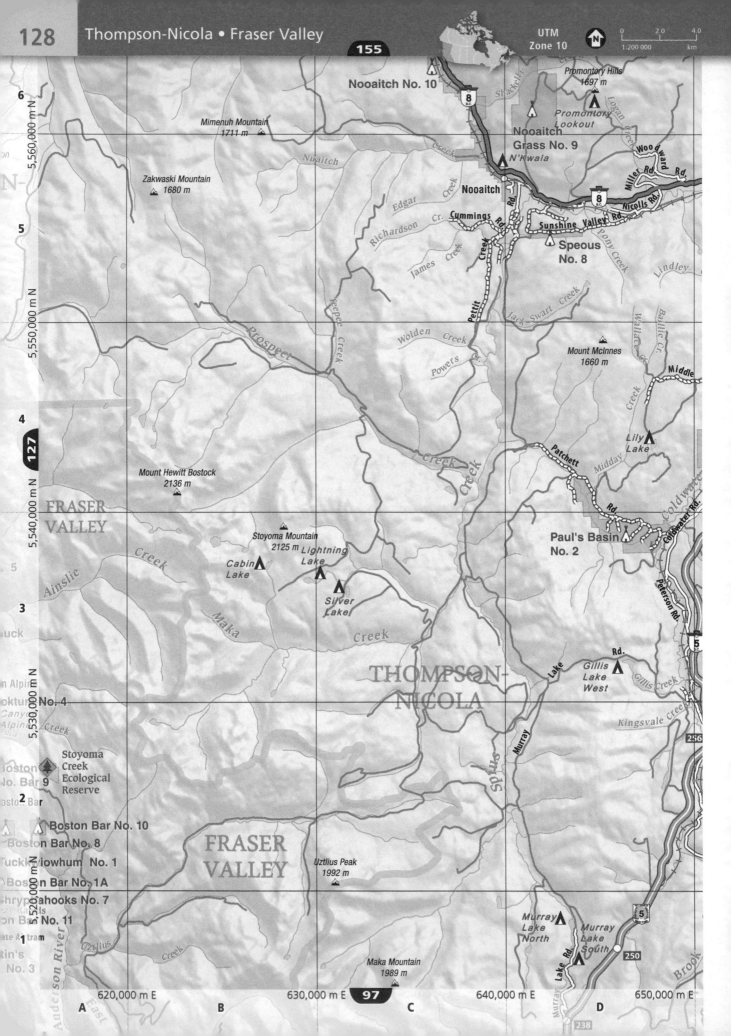

UTM
Zone 10

1:200 000

0   2.0   4.0
km

155

Nooaitch No. 10

8 B.C.

Promontory Hills
1697 m

Mimenuh Mountain
1711 m

Promontory
Lookout

Nooaitch
Grass No. 9

N'Kwala

Woodward

Miller Rd.

Rd.

Zakwaski Mountain
1680 m

Niaitch

Creek

Nooaitch

8 B.C.

Nicolls Rd.

Edgar

Creek

Cummings

Richardson Cr.

Sunshine Valley Rd.

Rd.

Pony Creek

Lindley

Speous
No. 8

Creek

James Creek

Prospect

Peepee

Creek

Pettit

Wolden Creek

Powers Cr.

Jack Swart Creek

Mount McInnes
1660 m

Wallace

Cr.

Baillie Cr.

Middle

Creek

**FRASER
VALLEY**

Creek

Creek

Patchett

Midday

Lily
Lake

5

Mount Hewitt Bostock
2136 m

Paul's Basin
No. 2

Coldwater Rd.

127

Stoyoma Mountain
2125 m

Cabin
Lake

Lightning
Lake

Ainslie

Creek

Silver
Lake

Peterson Rd.

Maka

Creek

**THOMPSON-
NICOLA**

Lake

Gillis
Lake
West

Rd.

Gillis Creek

5 B.C.

256

uck

No. 4

Murray

Kingsvale Creek

Alpine

Canyon

Alpine

Creek

Spius

Stoyoma
Creek
Ecological
Reserve

Boston
No. Bar 9

oston Bar

Boston Bar No. 10

Boston Bar No. 8

uck   iowhum No. 1

Boston Bar No. 1A

hryp ahooks No. 7

**FRASER
VALLEY**

Uztlius Peak
1992 m

Boston No. 11

tram

in's
No. 3

Uztlius

Creek

Murray
Lake
North

Murray
Lake
South

Murray Lake Rd.

5 B.C.

250

Maka Mountain
1989 m

Anderson River

East

97

238

Brook

620,000 m E   630,000 m E   640,000 m E   650,000 m E

A   B   C   D

5,560,000 m N

5,550,000 m N

5,540,000 m N

5,530,000 m N

5,520,000 m N

6

5

4

3

2

1

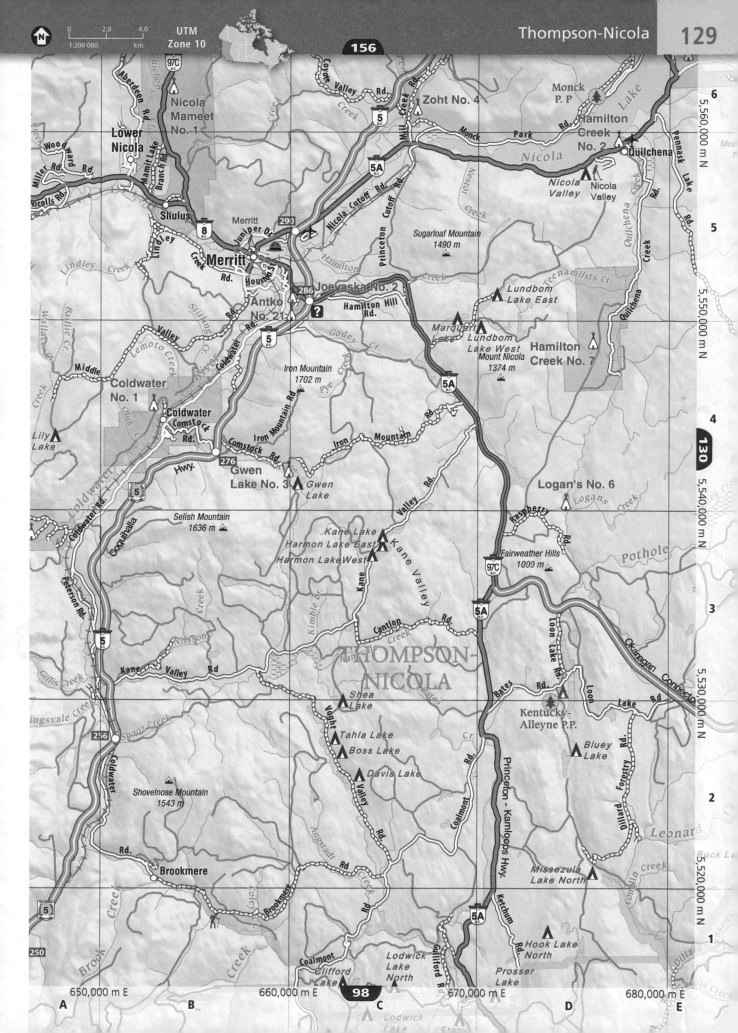

N

UTM
Zone 10

1:200 000

0   2.0   4.0
km

156

97C
B.C.

Nicola
Mameet
No. 1

Lower
Nicola

Woodward
Rd.

Miller Rd.

Nicolls Rd.

Aberdeen Rd.

Mamit Lake
Branch Rd.

Lindley Creek

Shulus

Lindley

Merritt
Juniper Dr.

8
B.C.

Merritt

290

Houston

Rd.

Antko
No. 21

286

5
B.C.

Coldwater Rd.

Lemoto Creek

Valley

Stirling Cr.

Middle

Coldwater
No. 1

Wallace Cr.

Baillie Cr.

Oluk Cr.

Lily
Lake

Coldwater
Comstock
Rd.

Comstock Rd.

276

Gwen
Lake No. 3

Hwy.

Iron Mountain Rd.

Iron
Mountain
Rd.

Iron Mountain
1702 m

Pye Creek

Godey Cr.

Iron   Mountain

Gwen
Lake

Coquihalla

Coldwater Rd.

5
B.C.

Selish Mountain
1636 m

Kane Cr.

Kimble Cr.

Kane Lake
Harmon Lake East
Harmon Lake West

Kane Valley

Valley

Rd.

Rd.

THOMPSON-
NICOLA

Kanwyk Creek

Cantlon
Creek

Peterson Rd.

Nilsson Cr.

5
B.C.

Kane   Valley   Rd

256

Gillis Creek

Kingsvale Creek

Coldwater

Spearing Creek

Shovelnose Mountain
1543 m

Shea
Lake

Voght

Tahla Lake

Boss Lake

Davis Lake

Voght   Valley

Rd.

Coldwater

Rd.

Brookmere

5
B.C.

250

Brook   Creek

Coldwater

Creek

Brookmere   Rd.

Coalmont
Clifford
Lake

98

Lodwick
Lake
North

Gulliford Rd.

Bates   Rd.

Coalmont

Rd.

Cr.

Zoht No. 4

Coyote
Valley   Rd.

Mill   Creek

Coyote   Creek

5
B.C.

Monck
Park

Monck
P. P.

Nicola   Lake

Hamilton
Creek
No. 2

Quilchena

Pennask Lake

5A
B.C.

Nicola Cutoff Rd.

Nicola   Cutoff   Rd.

Princeton   Cutoff   Rd.

Nestor   Creek

Nicola
Valley

Nicola
Valley

Sugarloaf Mountain
1490 m

Hamilton

Creek

Hamilton Hill
Rd.

Joeyaska No. 2

Lundbom
Lake East

Teenamilsts Cr.

Marquart
Lake

Lundbom
Lake West
Mount Nicola
1374 m

Quilchena   Creek

Hamilton
Creek No. 7

5A
B.C.

Logan's No. 6

Logans   Creek

Raspberry   Rd.

Fairweather Hills
1099 m

97C
B.C.

5A
B.C.

Loon   Lake   Rd.

Okanagan   Connector

Potole

Kentucky-
Alleyne P.P.

Loon   Lake   Rd.

Bluey
Lake

Leonard

Buck L.

Princeton - Kamloops Hwy.

Dillard   Forestry   Rd.

Conglin Creek

Missezula
Lake North

Ketchum

5A
B.C.

Hook Lake
North

Prosser
Lake

Lodwick
Lake

Story

130

5,560,000 m N

5,550,000 m N

5,540,000 m N

5,530,000 m N

5,520,000 m N

6

5

4

3

2

1

650,000 m E   660,000 m E   670,000 m E   680,000 m E

A   B   C   D   E

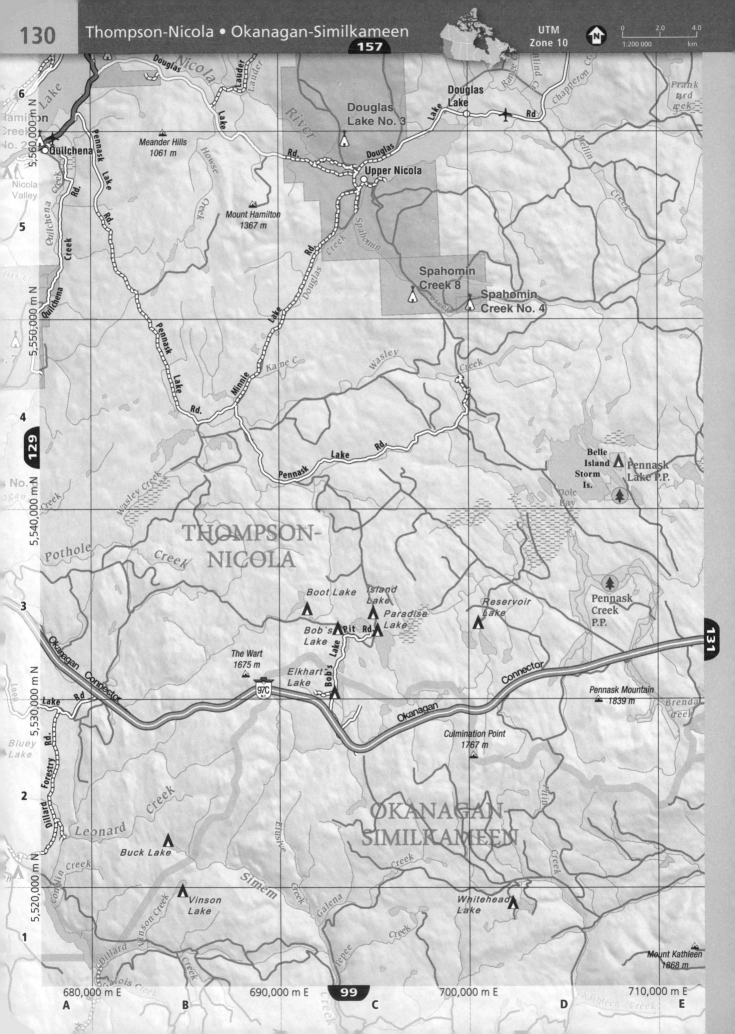

UTM
Zone 10

157

99

131

129

97C
B.C.

THOMPSON-
NICOLA

OKANAGAN
SIMILKAMEEN

Nicola
Valley

Quilchena

Meander Hills
1061 m

Mount Hamilton
1367 m

Douglas
Lake No. 3

Douglas
Lake

Upper Nicola

Spahomin
Creek 8

Spahomin
Creek No. 4

Belle
Island
Storm
Is.

Pennask
Lake P.P.

Pennask
Creek
P.P.

Dole
Bay

Reservoir
Lake

Boot Lake

Island
Lake

Paradise
Lake

Bob's
Lake

Pit Rd.

Bob's Lake

The Wart
1675 m

Elkhart
Lake

Okanagan Connector

Okanagan Connector

Pennask Mountain
1839 m

Culmination Point
1767 m

Bluey
Lake

Forestry Rd.

Dillard

Leonard Creek

Buck Lake

Vinson
Lake

Simem

Whitehead
Lake

Mount Kathleen
1868 m

680,000 m E

690,000 m E

700,000 m E

710,000 m E

5,560,000 m N

5,550,000 m N

5,540,000 m N

5,530,000 m N

5,520,000 m N

A B C D E

1 2 3 4 5 6

UTM
Zone 11

1:200 000

280,000 m E   290,000 m E   300,000 m E   310,000 m E

5,560,000 m N
5,550,000 m N
5,540,000 m N
5,530,000 m N
5,520,000 m N

6
5
4
3
2
1

130
132
158
100
101

A   B   C   D

Chapperon
Creek No. 6

Mount Chapperon
1774 m

Treadgold
Lake

Sandberg
Lake

Sandberg
Lake

CENTRAL
OKANAGAN

THOMPSON-
NICOLA

Stuart
Lake

Stuart
Lake

Shorts

Fintry Protected Area

Christie
Falls

Nicola

Beak

Creek

Roundtop Mountain
1726 m

Esperon
Lake

Loch
Drinkie

Mellin
Lake

River

Dorothy
Lake

Barton
Lake

Duo
Via Lake

Terrace
Mountain
1704 m

Barton Hill
1506 m

Dome Rock Mountain
1705 m

Big Horn
Lake

Rock
Lake

Old Dave
Lake

Mount Fileen
1664 m

Mount Sandberg
1782 m

Esperon Forest Service Rd.

kson Lake

use
datheume
Lake

Hatheume
Lake

Rat Lake

Tadpole Lake
Lake

Whiterocks Mountain
1807 m

nnask
ke P.P.

Eileen
Lake

Hatheume
ake South
son

Ellen Lake

Windy Lake

Raymer
Lake

West
Lake
Porcupine
Lake

Dobbin Lake
Islaht Lake

CENTRAL
OKANAGAN

Pinnacle
Lake

Windy Lake

Little
Windy
Lake

Cameron
Lake

Paynter
Lake

Lambly
Lake

Lambly
Lake

Mount
Swite
1499 m

Mount
Hayman
436 m

Mount Gottfriedsen
1794 m

Lacoma Creek

Lacoma
Lake

Trepanier
Prov.
Park

Jackpine Lake

Jackpine
Lake

Jack Pine Forest Service Rd.

Mount Last
1418 m

Carrot Mountain
1468 m

Hayman
Lake

Coquihalla

Highway

Trepanier

97C
B.C.

Crystal
Mountain

Tsinstikep

Brenda
Lake

Long
Lake

Macdonald
Lake

Walker

Brenda

Mount Clements
1492 m

Telemark Cross
Country
Ski Club

Glenrosa

Glenrosa

Mt.
Shannon
758 m

Shannon Lake Rd.

Peachland
Lake

Mines

Wilson Lake

Mount Wilson
1322 m

Silver
Lake

Jack Creek

Mount Miller
1075 m

Glenrosa
Rd.

Tsinstikeptum No. 9
Two Eagles

Westbank

West
Beac

Peachland
Lake

Headwater
Lakes

Rd.

Silver
Lake

Lookout Mountain
1152 m

Mount Law
1056 m

Mount Drought
939 m

ake

Crescent
Lake

Chapman
Lake

Glen
Lake

Peachland Forest Service Rd.

Greata

Creek

Spring
Lake

CENTRAL
OKANAGAN

Mount Goldham
977 m

Pincushion
Mtn.
753 m

Ponderosa

97C
B.C.

Mount Kathleen
1868 m

Eneas
Lakes
Prov.
Park

Island
Lake

Eneas Lakes
Little Eneas Lake

Munro Lake Forest Service

ZipZone
Peachland

Peachland

Beach

Pincushion
Bay

CEN
OKAN

Hardy

Reluctant
Dragon
Cove

Okanagan Mountain

UTM
Zone 11

1:200 000

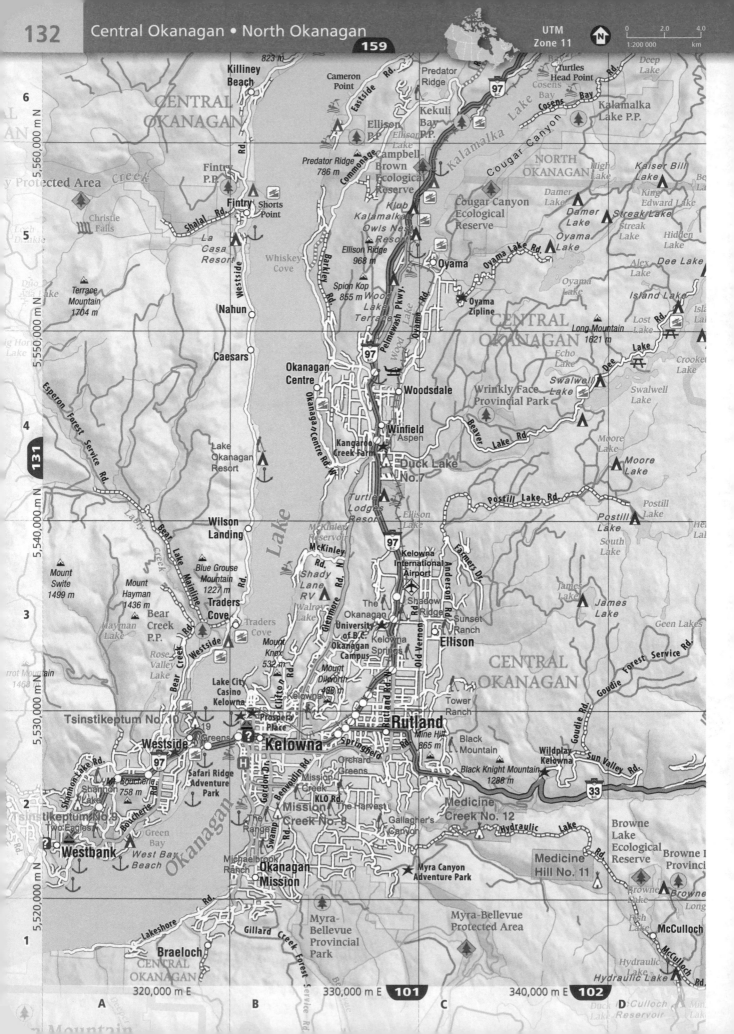

CENTRAL OKANAGAN

NORTH OKANAGAN

CENTRAL OKANAGAN

Killiney Beach

Cameron Point

Eastside Rd.

Predator Ridge

Turtles Head Point

Cosens Bay

Deep Lake

823 m

Predator Ridge 786 m

Commonage Rd.

Kekuli Bay P.P.

Kalamalka Lake P.P.

Kalamalka Lake

Cougar Canyon

Campbell-Brown Ecological Reserve

Klub Kalamalka

Owls Nest Resort

Cougar Canyon Ecological Reserve

Damer Lake

High Lake

Kaiser Bill Lake

King Edward Lake

Streak Lake

Ellison Ridge 968 m

Damer Lake

Oyama Lake

Streak Lake

Hidden Lake

Fintry P.P.

Fintry

Shorts Point

La Casa Resort

Whiskey Cove

Spion Kop 855 m

Wood Lake

Ellison P.P.

Oyama

Oyama Lake Rd.

Oyama Lake

Alex Lake

Dee Lake

Island Lake

Christie Falls

Terrace Mountain 1704 m

Westside Rd.

Barkley Rd.

Wood Lake Terrace

Pelmewash Pkwy.

Lost Lake

Island Lake

Nahun

Oyama Zipline

Long Mountain 1621 m

Dee Lake

Crooked Lake

Caesars

Okanagan Centre

Woodsdale

Wrinkly Face Provincial Park

Echo Lake

Swalwell Lake

Swalwell Lake

Okanagan Centre Rd. W.

Winfield

Aspen

Beaver Lake Rd.

Moore Lake

Lake Okanagan Resort

Kangaroo Creek Farm

Duck Lake No. 7

Moore Lake

Wilson Landing

Turtle Lodges Resort

Ellison Lake

Postill Lake Rd.

Postill Lake

Esperon Forest Service Rd.

Bear Lake Mainline

McKinley Reservoir

McKinley Rd.

South Lake

Mount Swite 1499 m

Blue Grouse Mountain 1227 m

Shady Lane RV

Kelowna International Airport

Farmers Dr.

James Lake

Mount Hayman 1436 m

Traders Cove

Walroy Lake

The Okanagan University of B.C. Okanagan Campus

Anderson Rd.

James Lake

Geen Lakes

Bear Creek P.P.

Hayman Lake

Rose Valley Lake

Westside Rd.

Mount Knox 532 m

Kelowna Springs

Shadow Ridge

Sunset Ranch

Goudie Forest Service Rd.

rrot Mountain 1468

Bear Creek

Clifton Rd.

Mount Dilworth 488 m

Old Vernon Rd.

Ellison

CENTRAL OKANAGAN

Lake City Casino Kelowna

Glenmore Rd.

Kelowna

Rutland Rd. N.

Tower Ranch

Tsinstikeptum No. 10

19

Greens

Prospera Place

Rutland

Mine Hill 865 m

Black Mountain

Goudie Rd.

Wildplay Kelowna

Sun Valley Rd.

Westside

97

Safari Ridge Adventure Park

Kelowna

Springfield

Black Knight Mountain 1288 m

33

Mt. Boucherie 758 m

Gordon Dr.

Benvoulin Rd.

Orchard Greens

Shannon Lake Rd.

Shannon Lake

Boucherie Rd.

Mission Creek

KLO Rd.

The Harvest

Medicine Creek No. 12

Hydraulic Lake

Browne Lake Ecological Reserve

Tsinstikeptum No. 9

Two Eagles

Green Bay

West Bay Beach

The Range

Swamp Rd.

Mission Creek No. 8

Gallagher's Canyon

Medicine Hill No. 11

Browne Provincial

Westbank

Michaelbrook Ranch

Okanagan Mission

Myra Canyon Adventure Park

Browne Lake

Browne

Okanagan Lake

Lakeshore Rd.

Gillard Creek Forest Service Rd.

Myra-Bellevue Protected Area

Fish Lake

Braeloch

Myra-Bellevue Provincial Park

McCulloch

CENTRAL OKANAGAN

320,000 m E

Bear Creek

330,000 m E

101

340,000 m E

102

Hydraulic Lake

McCulloch

Hydraulic Lake Rd.

A   B   C   D

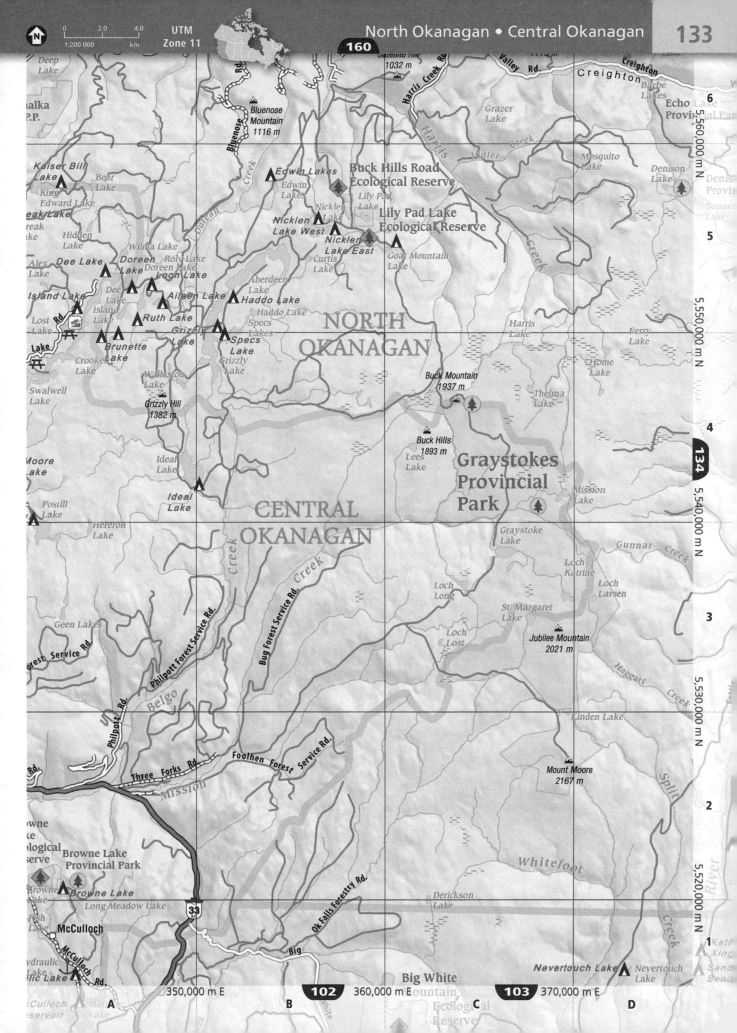

UTM
Zone 11

1:200 000

N

0   2.0   4.0
km

160

134

102

33

103

Deep
Lake

malka
P.P.

Bluenose
Mountain
1116 m

Satellite hill
1032 m

Valley Rd.

Creighton

Creighton

Echo Lake
Provincial Par

Denis
Provin

Bonne
Lake

Grazer
Lake

Mosquito
Lake

Denison
Lake

Kaiser Bill
Lake

Bear
Lake

King
Edward Lake

eak Lake

Hidden
Lake

Alex
Lake

Island Lake

Lost
Lake

Lake

Dee Lake

Wilma Lake

Doreen
Lake
Doreen Lake
Logn Lake

Roly Lake

Dee
Lake
Island
Lake

Ruth Lake

Brunette
Lake

Crooked
Lake

Aileen Lake

Grizzly
Lake

Wollaston
Lake

Swalwell
Lake

Grizzly Hill
1382 m

Moore
Lake

Postill
Lake

Edwin Lakes

Edwin
Lakes

Nicklen
Lake West

Nicklen
Lake East

Aberdeen
Lake

Haddo Lake

Haddo Lake

Specs
Lakes

Specs
Lake

Grizzly
Lake

Ideal
Lake

Ideal
Lake

Buck Hills Road
Ecological Reserve

Lily Pad
Lake

Lily Pad Lake
Ecological Reserve

Nicklen
Lake

Curtis
Lake

Goat Mountain
Lake

NORTH
OKANAGAN

Vidler

Creek

Harris

Harris
Lake

Ferry
Lake

Home
Lake

Thelma
Lake

Buck Mountain
1937 m

Buck Hills
1893 m

Lees
Lake

Graystokes
Provincial
Park

CENTRAL
OKANAGAN

Hereron
Lake

Geen Lakes

Forest Service Rd.

Philpott Forest Service Rd.

Philpott Rd.

Belgo

Bug Forest Service Rd.

Creek

Creek

Graystoke
Lake

Loch
Long

Loch
Lost

St. Margaret
Lake

Loch
Katrine

Loch
Larsen

Gunnar

Creek

Jubilee Mountain
2021 m

Rd.

Three Forks Rd.

Foalhen Forest Service Rd.

Mission

Linden Lake

Haggatt

Creek

Mount Moore
2167 m

Split

owne
ce
ological
serve

Browne Lake
Provincial Park

Browne

Browne Lake

Long Meadow Lake

McCulloch

Ok Falls Forestry Rd.

Big

Derickson
Lake

Whitefoot

River

Nevertouch Lake

Nevertouch
Lake

Ketl
Xing
Sand
Bend

Hydraulic
fic Lake

McCulloch

Rd.

Big White
Mountain
Ecological
Reserve

350,000 m E

360,000 m E

370,000 m E

5,560,000 m N

5,550,000 m N

5,540,000 m N

5,530,000 m N

5,520,000 m N

6

5

4

3

2

1

A

B

C

D

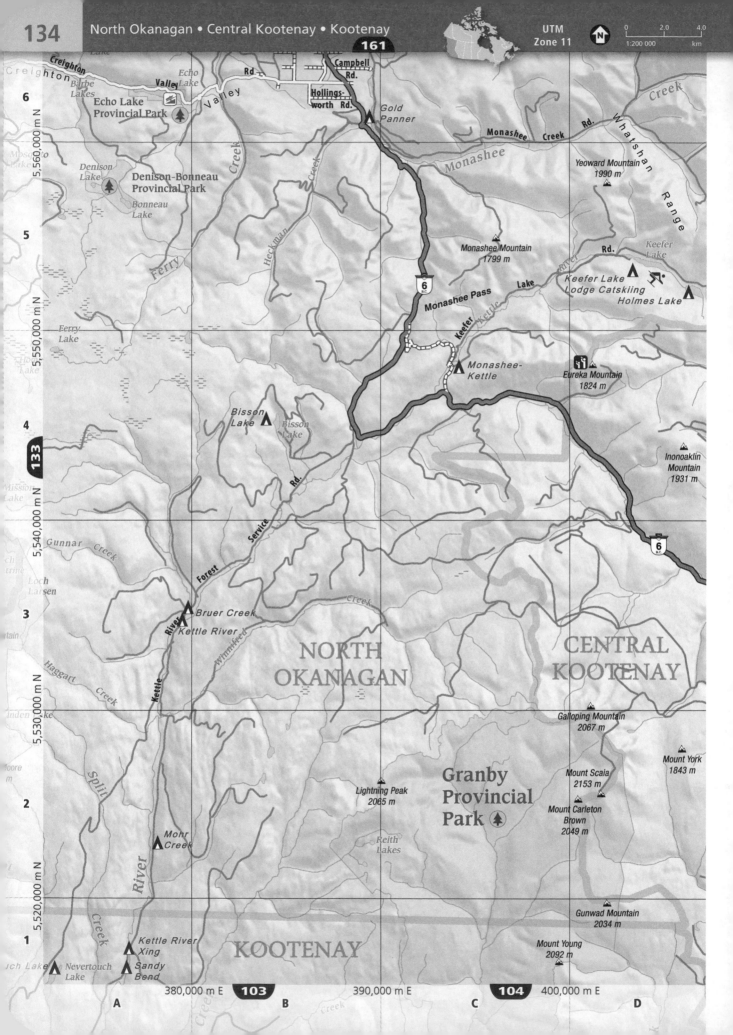

134

North Okanagan • Central Kootenay • Kootenay

161

UTM
Zone 11

N

1:200 000

0   2.0   4.0
km

Creighton
Creighton
Barbe
Lakes
Echo
Valley
Lake
Rd.
Campbell
Rd.
Gold
Panner
Monashee
Creek
Rd.
Whatshan
Range

Echo Lake
Provincial Park

Yeoward Mountain
1990 m

Mosquito
Lake

Denison
Lake

Denison-Bonneau
Provincial Park

Bonneau
Lake

Monashee Mountain
1799 m

Keefer
Lake

Keefer Lake
Lodge Catskiing
Holmes Lake

6
B.C.

Monashee Pass

Lake

Ferry
Lake

Heckman Creek

Ferry Creek

Keefer

Kettle

River

Monashee
Kettle

Eureka Mountain
1824 m

Kilgard
Lake

Bisson
Lake
Bisson
Lake

Inonoaklin
Mountain
1931 m

133

Mission
Lake

Rd.

Service

Gunnar Creek

Forest

6
B.C.

Loch
Larsen

Bruer Creek
Kettle River

Kettle River

Winnifred

Creek

**NORTH
OKANAGAN**

**CENTRAL
KOOTENAY**

Haggart

Creek

Galloping Mountain
2067 m

Linden Lake

Kettle

Mount York
1843 m

Mount Scaia
2153 m

Lightning Peak
2065 m

**Granby
Provincial
Park**

Mount Carleton
Brown
2049 m

Moore
m

Split

Mohr
Creek

Reith
Lakes

River

Gunwad Mountain
2034 m

Creek

Kettle River
Xing

Sandy
Bend

KOOTENAY

Mount Young
2092 m

Birch Lake

Nevertouch
Lake

380,000 m E

103

390,000 m E

104

400,000 m E

A   B   C   D

5,560,000 m N
5,550,000 m N
5,540,000 m N
5,530,000 m N
5,520,000 m N

6
5
4
3
2
1

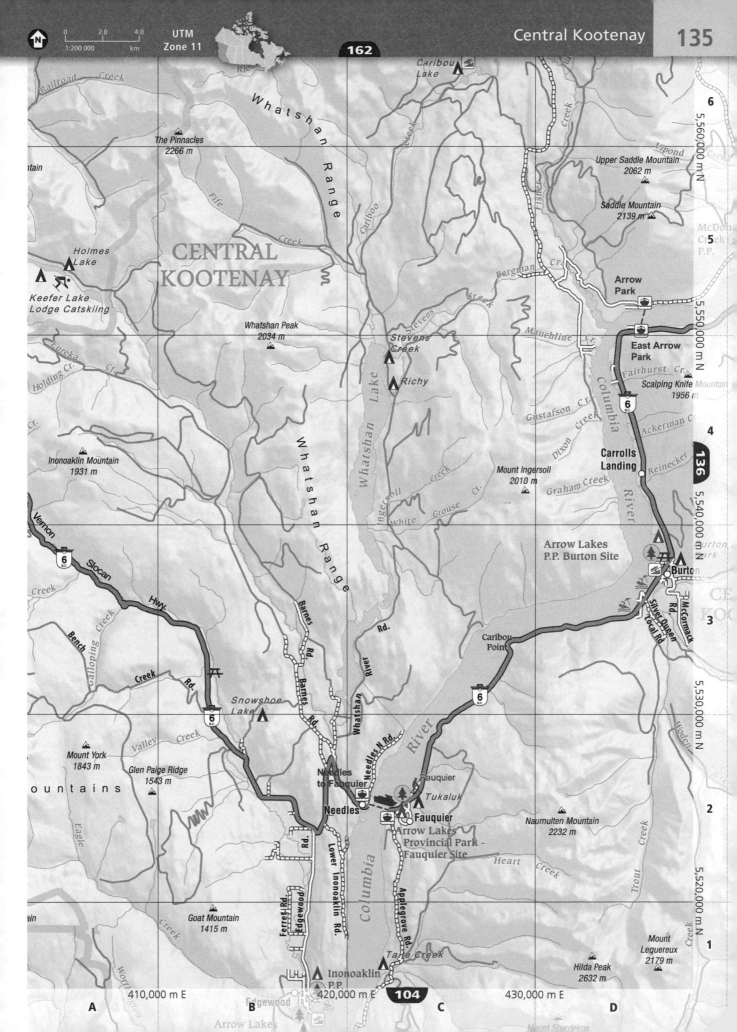

162

UTM
Zone 11

0   2.0   4.0
1:200 000   km

Caribou
Lake

6

5,560,000 m N

Upper Saddle Mountain
2062 m

The Pinnacles
2266 m

Saddle Mountain
2139 m

McDona
Creek
P.P.

5

CENTRAL
KOOTENAY

Holmes
Lake

Arrow
Park

Keefer Lake
Lodge Catskiing

East Arrow
Park

5,550,000 m N

Bergman   Cr.

Fairhurst   Cr.

Whatshan Peak
2034 m

Stevens
Creek

Scalping Knife
1956 m

Mauehline   Cr.

Eureka

Holding Cr.

Richy

6
B.C.

Mount Ingersoll

4

Gustafson   Cr.

Dixon   Creek

Ackerman   Cr.

Carrolls
Landing

136   5,540,000 m N

Inonoaklin Mountain
1931 m

Mount Ingersoll
2010 m

Graham Creek

Reinecker   Cr.

White   Grouse   Cr.

Arrow Lakes
P.P. Burton Site

Burton

Vernon

6
B.C.

Slocan   Hwy.

Arrow Lakes
P.P. Burton Site

Burton

Burton
Park

CE
KO

Galloping Creek

Bench   Creek   Rd.

Barnes   Rd.

Whatshan   River   Rd.

Rd.

Caribou
Point

Silver Queen Local Rd.

McCormack

3

Snowshoe
Lake

6
B.C.

Barnes   Rd.

6
B.C.

Valley   Creek

Mount York
1843 m

Glen Paige Ridge
1543 m

Eagle

Needles N Rd.

Needles
to Fauquier

Fauquier

Tukaluk

Naumulten Mountain
2232 m

5,530,000 m N

2

Needles

Fauquier

Arrow Lakes
Provincial Park -
Fauquier Site

Heart   Creek

Trout   Creek

Lower Inonoaklin Rd.

Columbia   River

Ferret Rd.

Edgewood Rd.

Applegrove Rd.

Goat Mountain
1415 m

Tahe Creek

Mount
Lequereux
2179 m

5,520,000 m N

1

Inonoaklin
P.P.

Hilda Peak
2632 m

Edgewood

104

410,000 m E

420,000 m E

430,000 m E

Arrow Lakes

Mount Sherdelow

A   B   C   D

UTM
Zone 11

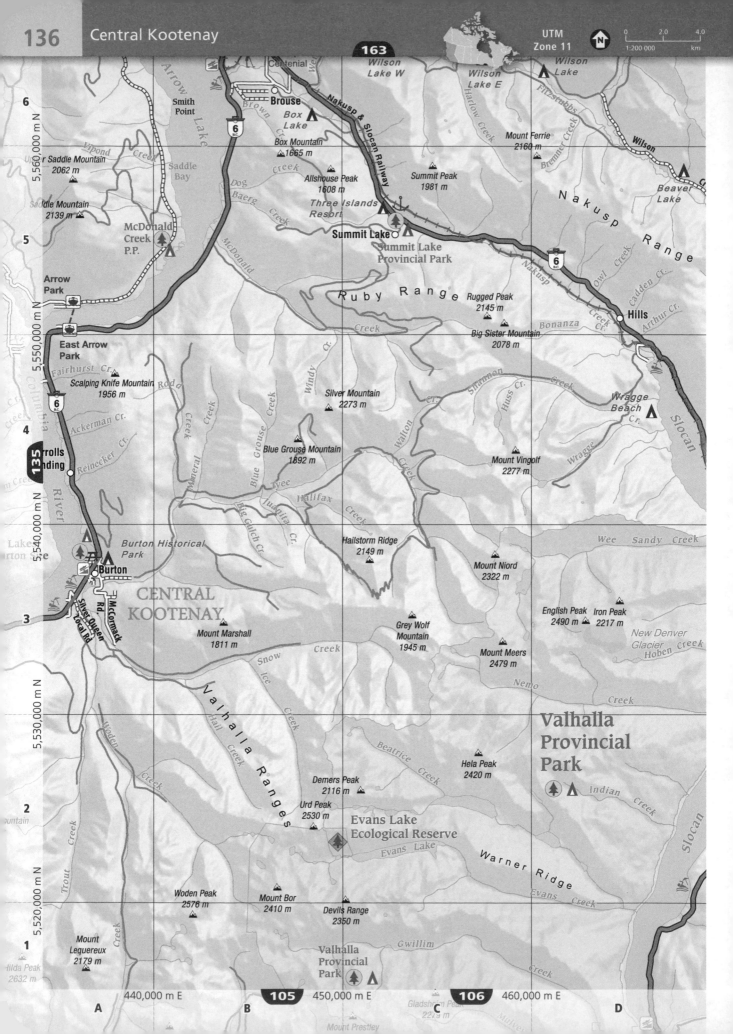

1:200 000

0   2.0   4.0
km

163

6 Smith Point

Centenial

Brouse

6 B.C.

Box Lake

Box Mountain
1665 m

Wilson Lake W

Wilson Lake E

Wilson Lake

Mount Ferrie
2160 m

Wilson

Nakusp Range

Beaver Lake

r Saddle Mountain
2062 m

Vipond Creek

Saddle Bay

Allshouse Peak
1608 m

Summit Peak
1981 m

ddle Mountain
2139 m

Dog Creek

Baerg Creek

Three Islands Resort

Summit Lake

Summit Lake Provincial Park

McDonald Creek P.P.

Arrow Park

East Arrow Park

Fairhurst Cr.

6 B.C.

135 rrolls nding

Scalping Knife Mountain
1956 m

Ackerman Cr.

Rodd Creek

Reinecker Cr.

Ruby Range

Nakusp Creek

6 B.C.

Rugged Peak
2145 m

Big Sister Mountain
2078 m

Owl Creek

Cadden Cr.

Hills

Arthur Cr.

Bonanza Creek

Silver Mountain
2273 m

Windy Cr.

Cr.

Walton Creek

Shannon Creek

Huss Cr.

Wragge Beach

Wragge Cr.

Slocan

Columbia River

Mineral Creek

Blue Grouse Creek

Blue Grouse Mountain
1892 m

Tyee Creek

Juanita Cr.

Halifax Creek

Mount Vingolf
2277 m

Wragge Creek

Lake rton Se

Burton Historical Park

Burton

CENTRAL KOOTENAY

Silver Queen Rd.

McCormack Local Rd.

Big Gulch Cr.

Mount Marshall
1811 m

Hailstorm Ridge
2149 m

Snow Creek

Grey Wolf Mountain
1945 m

Mount Niord
2322 m

Mount Meers
2479 m

English Peak
2490 m

Iron Peak
2217 m

New Denver Glacier

Hoben Creek

Wee Sandy Creek

Nemo Creek

Valhalla Provincial Park

Valhalla Ranges

Ice Creek

Hall Creek

Beatrice Creek

Demers Peak
2116 m

Urd Peak
2530 m

Evans Lake Ecological Reserve

Evans Lake

Hela Peak
2420 m

Indian Creek

Warner Ridge

Woden Creek

Trout Creek

untain

Woden Peak
2576 m

Mount Bor
2410 m

Devils Range
2350 m

Evans Creek

Slocan

Mount Lequereux
2179 m

ilda Peak
2632 m

Valhalla Provincial Park

Gwillim Creek

Gladsheim Peak
2279 m

Mount Prestley

5,560,000 m N   6
5,550,000 m N   5
5,540,000 m N   4
3
5,530,000 m N
5,520,000 m N   2
1

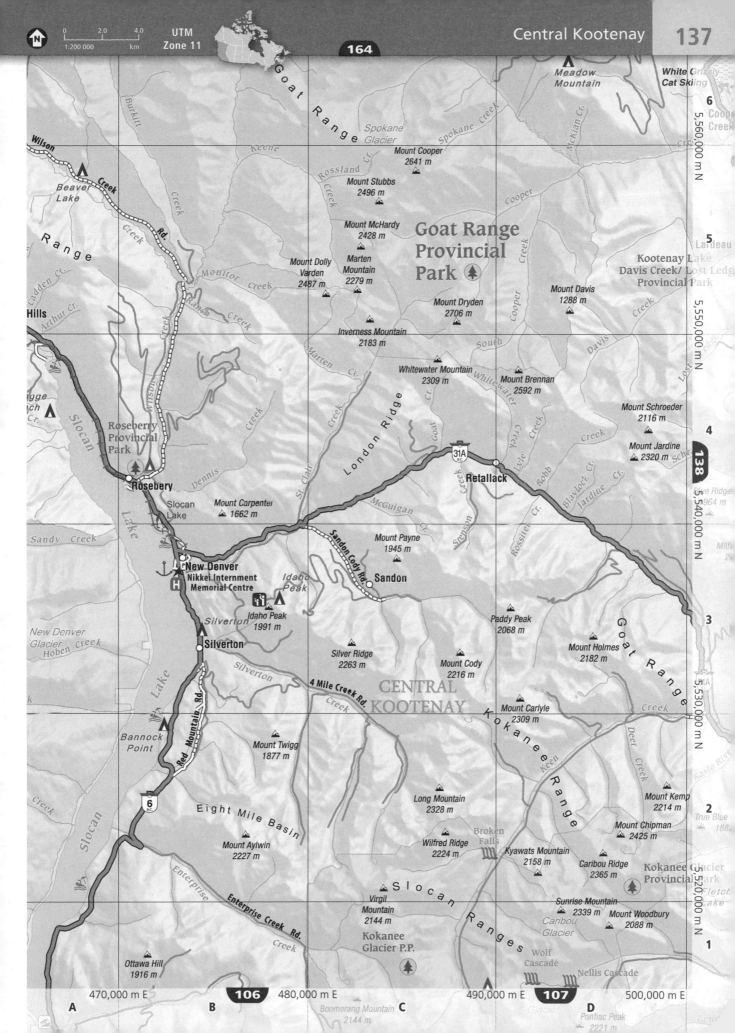

UTM
Zone 11
1:200 000
0 2.0 4.0
km

164

6

Goat Range

Wilson

Beaver
Lake

Burkitt

Creek

Keene

Spokane
Glacier

Spokane Creek

Mount Cooper
2641 m

Rossland

Mount Stubbs
2496 m

Cooper

White Grizzly
Cat Skiing

Meadow
Mountain

McKian Cr.

Cooper Cr.

5,560,000 m N

Range

Creek

Rd.

Cadden Cr.

Creek

Hills

Arthur Cr.

Monitor

Creek

Ranch

Mount McHardy
2428 m

Mount Dolly
Varden
2487 m

Marten
Mountain
2279 m

Goat Range
Provincial
Park

Mount Dryden
2706 m

Inverness Mountain
2183 m

Marten

Cr.

Cooper

Creek

Mount Davis
1288 m

Davis

Creek

Lardeau

Kootenay Lake
Davis Creek/ Lost Ledge
Provincial Park

5,550,000 m N

5

Ridge Ranch Cr.

Slocan

Roseberry
Provincial
Park

Rosebery

Creek

Dennis

Creek

Slocan
Lake

Mount Carpenter
1662 m

Sandy Creek

St. Clair Creek

London Ridge

Whitewater Mountain
2309 m

Goat

Cr.

Mount Brennan
2592 m

Whitewater

Creek

McGuigan

Cr.

31A
B.C.

Retallack

Lyle

Robb

Creek

Cr.

Rossiter Cr.

Blaylock Cr.

Jardine Cr.

Stenson Creek

Mount Schroeder
2116 m

Mount Jardine
2320 m

Schr

Blue Ridge
1964 m

138

5,540,000 m N

4

Lake

New Denver
Glacier

Hoben Creek

New Denver
Nikkei Internment
Memorial Centre
H

Idaho
Peak

Idaho Peak
1991 m

Silverton

Silverton

Silverton

Sandon Cody Rd.

Mount Payne
1945 m

Sandon

4 Mile Creek Rd.

Silver Ridge
2263 m

CENTRAL
KOOTENAY

Mount Cody
2216 m

Paddy Peak
2068 m

Mount Holmes
2182 m

Mount Carlyle
2309 m

Goat Range

Creek

5,530,000 m N

3

Slocan

Lake

Bannock
Point

Red Mountain Rd.

Mount Twigg
1877 m

Creek

Eight Mile Basin

Mount Aylwin
2227 m

6
B.C.

Enterprise

Enterprise Creek Rd.

Creek

Long Mountain
2328 m

Wilfred Ridge
2224 m

Broken
Falls

Kyawats Mountain
2158 m

Kokanee Range

Keen Creek

Mount Kemp
2214 m

Mount Chipman
2425 m

Caribou Ridge
2365 m

Deer Creek

Sunrise Mountain
2339 m

Caribou
Glacier

Mount Woodbury
2088 m

Kaslo River

True Blue
188

Milf
2

Kokanee Glacier
Provincial Park

Fletch
Lake

5,520,000 m N

2

Virgil
Mountain
2144 m

Kokanee
Glacier P.P.

Slocan Ranges

Wolf
Cascade

Nellis Cascade

Ottawa Hill
1916 m

470,000 m E

106

480,000 m E

Boomerang Mountain
2144 m

490,000 m E

107

Ponhac Peak
2221 m

500,000 m E

Leg

5,510,000 m N

1

A

B

C

D

UTM
Zone 11

1:200 000

165

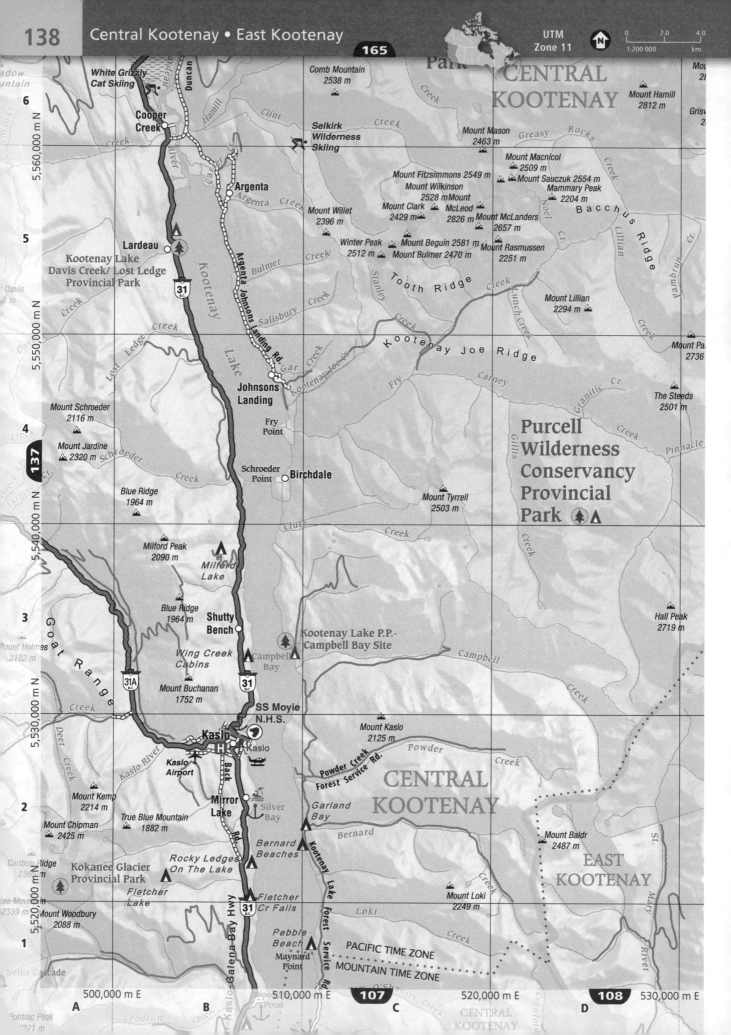

CENTRAL KOOTENAY

6

White Grizzly
Cat Skiing

Comb Mountain
2538 m

Mount Hamill
2812 m

Cooper
Creek

Selkirk
Wilderness
Skiing

Mount Mason
2463 m

Mount Macnicol
2509 m

5,560,000 m N

Argenta

Mount Fitzsimmons 2549 m
Mount Wilkinson
2528 m Mount
Mount Clark McLeod
2429 m 2826 m

Mount Sauczuk 2554 m
Mammary Peak
2204 m

Mount McLanders
2657 m

Bacchus Ridge

Mount Willet
2396 m

5

Lardeau

Winter Peak
2512 m

Mount Beguin 2581 m
Mount Bulmer 2470 m

Mount Rasmussen
2251 m

Kootenay Lake
Davis Creek/ Lost Ledge
Provincial Park

31
B.C.

Mount Lillian
2294 m

5,550,000 m N

Kootenay Joe Ridge

Mount Pa
2736

Johnsons
Landing

Tooth Ridge

137

Fry
Point

Mount Schroeder
2116 m

The Steeds
2501 m

4

Mount Jardine
2320 m

Purcell
Wilderness
Conservancy
Provincial
Park

Schroeder
Point Birchdale

Blue Ridge
1964 m

Mount Tyrrell
2503 m

Mount Holmes
2182 m

Milford Peak
2090 m

Milford
Lake

Hall Peak
2719 m

5,540,000 m N

3

Blue Ridge
1964 m

Shutty
Bench

Kootenay Lake P.P.-
Campbell Bay Site

Wing Creek
Cabins

Campbell
Bay

31A
B.C.

Mount Buchanan
1752 m

31
B.C.

5,530,000 m N

SS Moyie
N.H.S.

Goat Range

Kaslo

Mount Kaslo
2125 m

Kaslo

**CENTRAL
KOOTENAY**

Kaslo
Airport

Kaslo River

Powder Creek
Forest Service Rd.

Powder

Mount Kemp
2214 m

Mirror
Lake

Silver
Bay

Garland
Bay

Mount Baldr
2487 m

2

Mount Chipman
2425 m

True Blue Mountain
1882 m

Bernard
Beaches

Bernard

**EAST
KOOTENAY**

Caribou Ridge

Rocky Ledges
On The Lake

Kootenay Lake Forest Service Rd.

Mount Loki
2249 m

Kokanee Glacier
Provincial Park

Fletcher
Lake

Fletcher
Cr Falls

31
B.C.

5,520,000 m N

Mount Woodbury
2088 m

Kaslo-Galena Bay Hwy

Pebble
Beach

1

Maynard
Point

PACIFIC TIME ZONE

MOUNTAIN TIME ZONE

Nellis Cascade

500,000 m E

510,000 m E

107

520,000 m E

108

530,000 m E

A

B

C

D

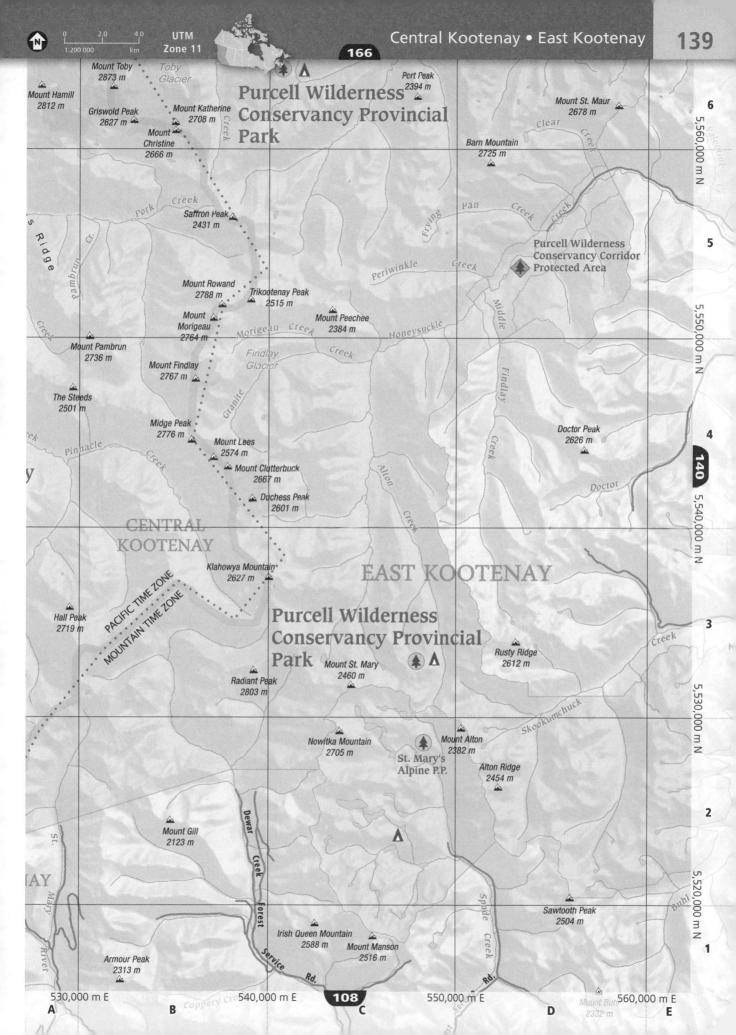

0   2.0   4.0
1:200 000   km

UTM
Zone 11

166

Mount Toby
2873 m

Toby Glacier

Mount Hamill
2812 m

Griswold Peak
2627 m

Mount Katherine
2708 m

Mount
Christine
2666 m

Port Peak
2394 m

**Purcell Wilderness
Conservancy Provincial
Park**

Mount St. Maur
2678 m

Clear Creek

6

Barn Mountain
2725 m

5,560,000 m N

Pork Creek

Saffron Peak
2431 m

Frying Pan Creek

Periwinkle Creek

**Purcell Wilderness
Conservancy Corridor
Protected Area**

5

5,550,000 m N

Pambrun Cr.

R i d g e

Mount Rowand
2788 m

Trikootenay Peak
2515 m

Mount
Morigeau
2764 m

Morigeau Creek

Mount Peechee
2384 m

Honeysuckle

Middle

Mount Pambrun
2736 m

Findlay Glacier

Creek

Findlay

The Steeds
2501 m

Granite

Creek

Doctor Peak
2626 m

4

140

5,540,000 m N

Pinnacle

Creek

Mount Findlay
2767 m

Midge Peak
2776 m

Mount Lees
2574 m

Mount Clutterbuck
2667 m

Duchess Peak
2601 m

Alton Creek

Doctor

**CENTRAL
KOOTENAY**

Klahowya Mountain
2627 m

EAST KOOTENAY

Creek

3

Hall Peak
2719 m

PACIFIC TIME ZONE

MOUNTAIN TIME ZONE

**Purcell Wilderness
Conservancy Provincial
Park**

Mount St. Mary
2460 m

Rusty Ridge
2612 m

5,530,000 m N

Radiant Peak
2803 m

Skookumchuck

Nowitka Mountain
2705 m

St. Mary's
Alpine P.P.

Mount Alton
2382 m

Alton Ridge
2454 m

St. Mary River

Mount Gill
2123 m

Dewar Creek

Spade Creek

Buhl

2

Sawtooth Peak
2504 m

5,520,000 m N

Forest

Irish Queen Mountain
2588 m

Mount Manson
2516 m

1

River

Armour Peak
2313 m

Service Rd.

Coppery Cree

108

Rd.

Mount Buhl
2332 m

530,000 m E

A

540,000 m E

B

C

550,000 m E

D

560,000 m E

E

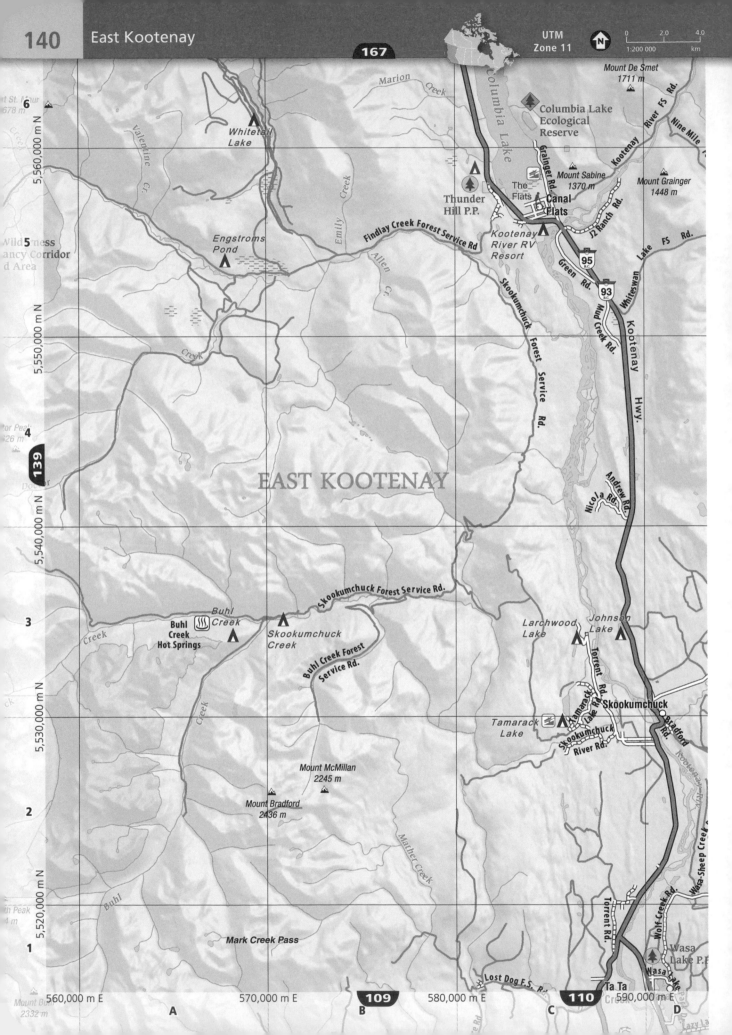

EAST KOOTENAY

Whitetail
Lake

Engstroms
Pond

Wilderness
ancy Corridor
d Area

Columbia Lake
Ecological
Reserve

Mount De Smet
1711 m

Thunder
Hill P.P.

The
Flats

Canal
Flats

Mount Sabine
1370 m

Mount Grainger
1448 m

Kootenay
River RV
Resort

Findlay Creek Forest Service Rd

J2 Ranch Rd.

Mud Creek Rd.

Green Rd.

Skookumchuck Forest Service Rd.

Kootenay Hwy.

Andrew Rd.

Nicola Rd.

Skookumchuck Forest Service Rd.

Larchwood
Lake

Johnson
Lake

Buhl
Creek

Buhl
Creek
Hot Springs

Skookumchuck
Creek

Buhl Creek Forest
Service Rd.

Torrent Rd.

Skookumchuck

Bradford
Rd.

Tamarack
Lake

Skookumchuck
River Rd.

Mount McMillan
2245 m

Mount Bradford
2436 m

Mather Creek

Creek

Buhl

Mark Creek Pass

Wolf Creek Rd.

Torrent Rd.

Wasa-Sheep Creek

Wasa
Lake P.P.

Lost Dog F.S. R

Ta Ta

Wasa Lake

Mount Buhl
2332 m

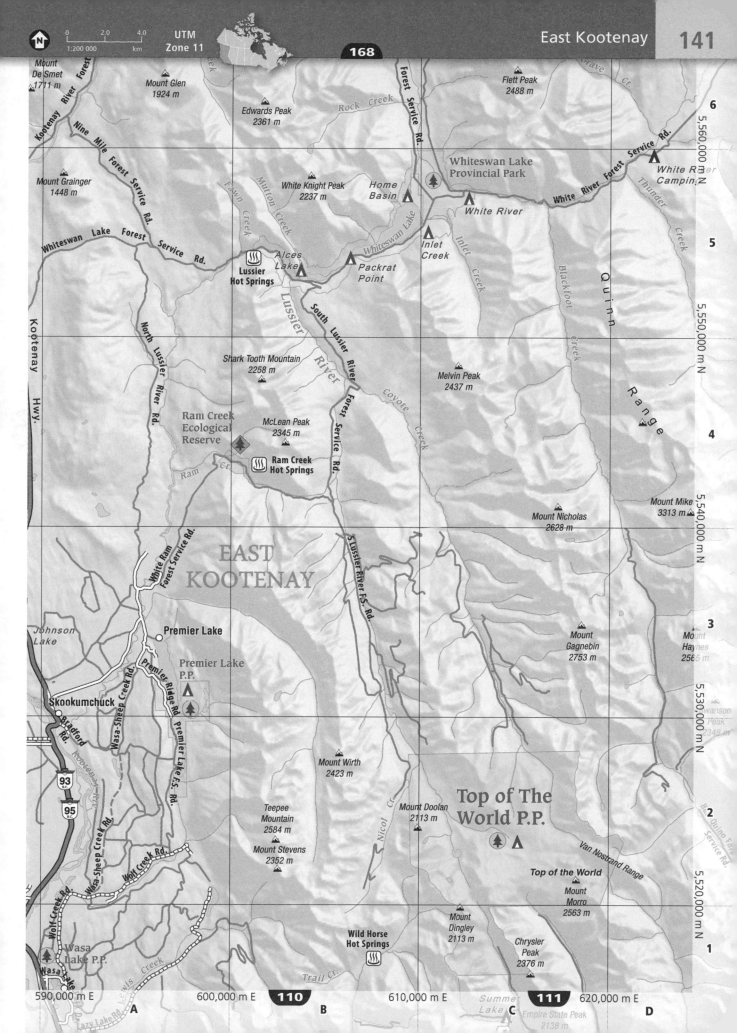

UTM
Zone 11

1:200 000

0   2.0   4.0
km

168

Mount De Smet 1711 m

Mount Glen 1924 m

Edwards Peak 2361 m

Rock Creek

Forest Service Rd.

Flett Peak 2488 m

White River Camping

6

5,560,000 m N

Kootenay River Forest

Nine Mile Forest Service Rd.

Mount Grainger 1448 m

Whiteswan Lake Forest Service Rd.

Fawn Creek

Mutton Creek

White Knight Peak 2237 m

Home Basin

Whiteswan Lake Provincial Park

White River

White River Forest Service Rd.

Thunder Creek

5

5,550,000 m N

Lussier Hot Springs

Alces Lake

Packrat Point

Whiteswan Lake

Inlet Creek

Inlet Creek

Blackfoot Creek

Q u i n n

R a n g e

North Lussier River Rd.

Kootenay Hwy.

Lussier River

South Lussier River

Forest Service Rd.

Coyote Creek

Shark Tooth Mountain 2258 m

Melvin Peak 2437 m

4

5,540,000 m N

Ram Creek Ecological Reserve

McLean Peak 2345 m

Ram Creek Hot Springs

Ram Cr.

Mount Nicholas 2628 m

Mount Mike 3313 m

White Ram Forest Service Rd.

EAST KOOTENAY

S Lussier River F.S. Rd.

Mount Gagnebin 2753 m

Mount Haynes 2565 m

3

5,530,000 m N

Johnson Lake

Premier Lake

Premier Lake P.P.

Premier Ridge Rd.

Premier Lake F.S. Rd.

Swanson Peak 2348 m

Skookumchuck

Bradford Rd.

Wasa-Sheep Creek Rd.

Mount Wirth 2423 m

Nicol Cr.

Mount Doolan 2113 m

Top of The World P.P.

Van Nostrand Range

2

5,520,000 m N

93 B.C.

95 B.C.

Kootenay River

Wasa-Sheep Creek Rd.

Wolf Creek Rd.

Teepee Mountain 2584 m

Mount Stevens 2352 m

Top of the World

Mount Morro 2563 m

Quinn Fa... Service Rd.

Wolf Creek Rd.

Wasa Lake P.P.

Wasa Lake

Lewis Creek

Trail Cr.

Wild Horse Hot Springs

Mount Dingley 2113 m

Chrysler Peak 2376 m

Summer Lake

Empire State Peak 2138 m

1

5,510,000 m N

590,000 m E

110

600,000 m E

610,000 m E

111

620,000 m E

A

B

C

D

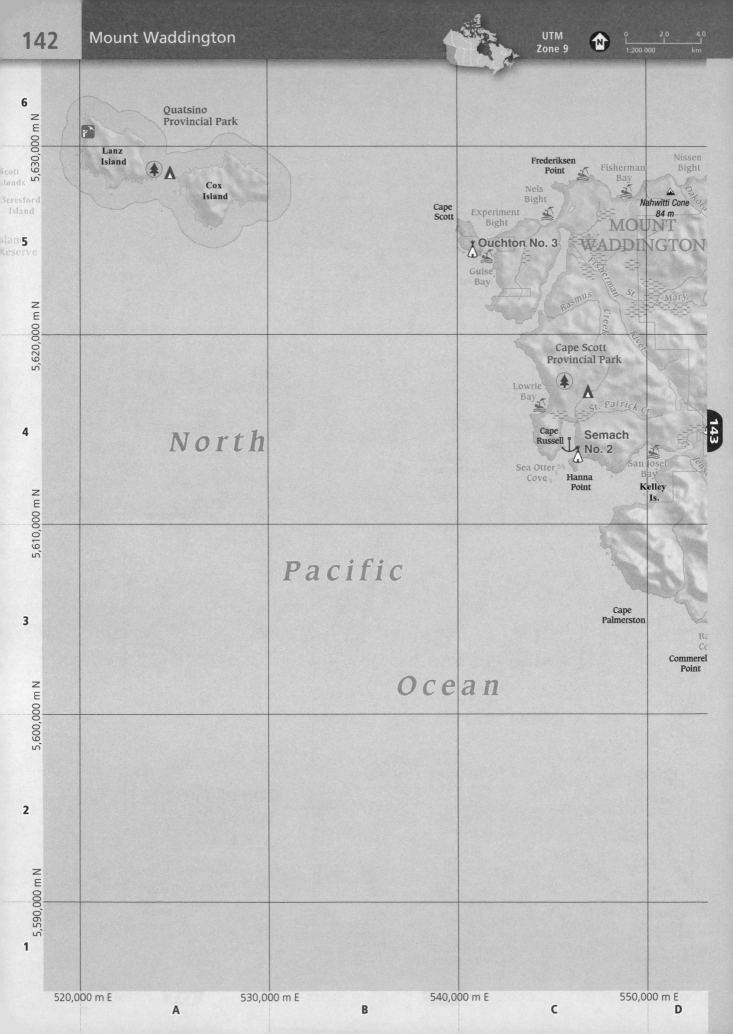

UTM
Zone 9

0   2.0   4.0
1:200 000   km

6

5,630,000 m N

Quatsino
Provincial Park

Lanz
Island

Scott
Islands

Beresford
Island

Island
Reserve

Cox
Island

Frederiksen
Point

Fisherman
Bay

Nissen
Bight

Nels
Bight

Nahwitti Cone
84 m

Dakota

Cape
Scott

Experiment
Bight

**MOUNT
WADDINGTON**

5

Ouchton No. 3

Guise
Bay

Fisherman

St.

Mary

Rasmus

Creek

River

5,620,000 m N

Cape Scott
Provincial Park

North

4

Lowrie
Bay

St. Patrick Cr.

Cape
Russell

Semach
No. 2

San Josef
Bay

Jensen

5,610,000 m N

Sea Otter
Cove

Hanna
Point

Kelley
Is.

143

Pacific

3

Cape
Palmerston

Ra
Co

Commerel
Point

5,600,000 m N

Ocean

2

5,590,000 m N

1

520,000 m E   **A**   530,000 m E   **B**   540,000 m E   **C**   550,000 m E   **D**

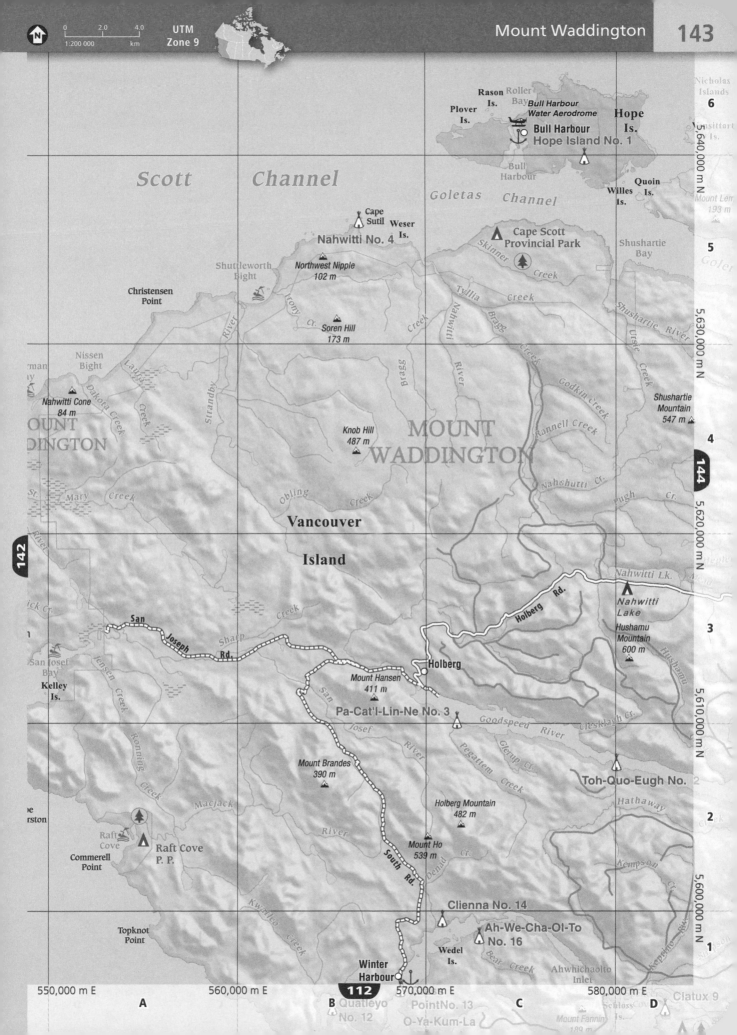

N

1:200 000

UTM
Zone 9

0   2.0   4.0
km

Nicholas
Islands

Scott   Channel

6

Rason
Is.

Roller
Bay

Plover
Is.

Bull Harbour
Water Aerodrome

Bull Harbour

Hope Island No. 1

Hope
Is.

Insittort
Is.

5,640,000 m N

Mount Len
193 m

Goletas   Channel

Bull
Harbour

Willes
Is.

Quoin
Is.

Golet

5

Cape
Sutil

Nahwitti No. 4

Weser
Is.

Skinner

Creek

Cape Scott
Provincial Park

Shushartie
Bay

5,630,000 m N

Shuttleworth
Bight

Northwest Nipple
102 m

Irony

Cr.

Tyllia

Creek

Nahwitti

Bragg

Creek

Shushartie   River

Ursye   Creek

Christensen
Point

Soren Hill
173 m

Creek

Bragg

River

Godkin Creek

Shushartie
Mountain
547 m

4

Nissen
Bight

Laura

Creek

MOUNT
WADDINGTON

Nahwitti Cone
84 m

Dakota Creek

Knob Hill
487 m

Rannell Creek

5,620,000 m N

144

Strandby

St.

Mary

Creek

Obling

Creek

Vancouver

Nahshutti   Cr.

Pugh

Cr.

142

River

Island

Nahwitti Lk.

5,620,000 m N

Nick Cr.

San

Joseph

Rd.

Sharp

Creek

Holberg

Rd.

Nahwitti
Lake

3

San Josef
Bay

Jensen

Creek

Holberg

Hushamu
Mountain
600 m

Hushamu

5,610,000 m N

Kelley
Is.

Mount Hansen
411 m

Pa-Cat'l-Lin-Ne No. 3

San

Goodspeed

River

Clesklagh Cr.

Ronning

Creek

Pegattem

Glerup   Cr.

Creek

Toh-Quo-Eugh No.

2

erston

Macjack

Mount Brandes
390 m

Josef

Holberg Mountain
482 m

Hathaway

5,600,000 m N

Raft
Cove

Raft Cove
P. P.

River

Mount Ho
539 m

Cr.

Denad

Kempson

Cr.

Commerell
Point

South   Rd.

Clienna No. 14

Topknot
Point

Kwatleo

Creek

Ah-We-Cha-Ol-To
No. 16

Bear   Creek

Ahwhichaolto

1

Wedel
Is.

Winter
Harbour

550,000 m E   560,000 m E   570,000 m E   580,000 m E

A   **B**   Quatleyo   Point No. 13   **C**   **D**   Clatux 9

No. 12

O-Ya-Kum-La

Mount Fannin

UTM
Zone 9

N

0   2.0   4.0
1:200 000
km

6

Nicholas
Islands

Hope
Is.
No. 1

Vansittart
Is.

Cascade
Harbour

Bright Is.

Joan
Is.

Philcox
Is.

Kent
Is.

Hosford
Is.

Robertson
Is.

Leading Hill
74 m

Ghost
Is.

Jeannette
Islands

Hedley
Islands

Redfern
Is.

Staples
Is.

McLeod
Is.

Mahpahkum No. 4

Quoin
Is.

Willes
Is.

Mount Lemon
193 m

Nigei Is.

Wakems
No. 6

Balaklava
Is.

Hurst
Is.

Harlequin
Bay

Wishart
Is.

Race
Is.

Deserters
Is.

Echo
Is.

5

Shushartie
Bay

Loquillilla
Cove

Goletas   Chanel

Gods Pocket
Marine P. P.

Port
Alexander

Glen-Gla-Ouch
No. 5

Crane
Is.

Bell
Island

Heard
Is.

Gordon
Is.

Namu, BC -
Prince Rupert, BC -
Bella Bella, BC

Duncan
Is.

Doyle
Is.

Port Hardy, BC

Shushartie River

Urge Creek

Phyl Cr.

Shushartie
Mountain
547 m

Songhees Cr.

Duval
Is.

Masterman
Islands

4

143

Georgie   Lake

Georgie
Lake

Great Bear
Nature Tours

Charlie
Islands

Peel
Is.

Nahwitti Lk.

Mead   Creek

Kains Lake

Jenkinson Creek

Tsulquate River

**MOUNT
WADDINGTON**

Tsulquate No. 4

Port Hardy

Agelessi
Adventure
Tours

Hardy
Bay

Port Hardy

The Seven Hills
155 m

Patrician
Cove

Hepler Creek

Holberg   Rd.

Glenlion Riv.

Jensen
Cove

Port Hardy
Seaplane Base

Shell Island
No. 3

Tho

Fort Ru

3

Nahwitti
Lake

Hushamu
Mountain
600 m

Husbamu

Kains Creek

Warokana   Creek

Nahwitti Mountain
528 m

Dick   Creek

Booth   Creek

Port Hardy
RV Resort

Quatse River
Regional Park

Downey Hills
218 m

Walden I.R.
No. 9

Byng Rd.

Fort
Rupert

Kippas
No. 2

Port
Airpo

145

Vancouver

Woodward Peak
297 m

Coal Harbour Rd.

Quatse River

Island

Pemberton Hills
575 m

Youghpan Creek

Bluebell Cr.

Hathaway   Creek

Toh-Quo-Eugh No. 2

Jules
Bay

Holberg
Inlet

Apple
Bay

Orr
Is.

Quatsino Subdivision No. 18

Port

Hardy

Washlawlis Cr.

2

Kempson Cr.

Simpson Cr.

Straggling
Islands

Nuknimish Cr.

**Coal
Harbour**

Coal
Harbour

Maquazneecht
Island No. 17

Rupert

Varney

Main

Inlet

Rupert

Poetkwaus Cr.

Mount Byng
425 m

Kultah No. 4

Marble River

Port

Main

West

1

Quatsino

Quatsino Rd.

Pamphlet
Cove

Bergh
Cove

Quattishe-
No. 1

Drake
Is.

Cross
Is.

Atkins
Cove

Kwokwesta Cr.

Marble River
Provincial Park

30

Quatsino
Sound

Julian   Smith

580,000 m E   **A**   590,000 m E   **B**   **113**   600,000 m E   **C**   610,000 m E   **D**

5,640,000 m N

5,630,000 m N

5,620,000 m N

5,610,000 m N

5,600,000 m N

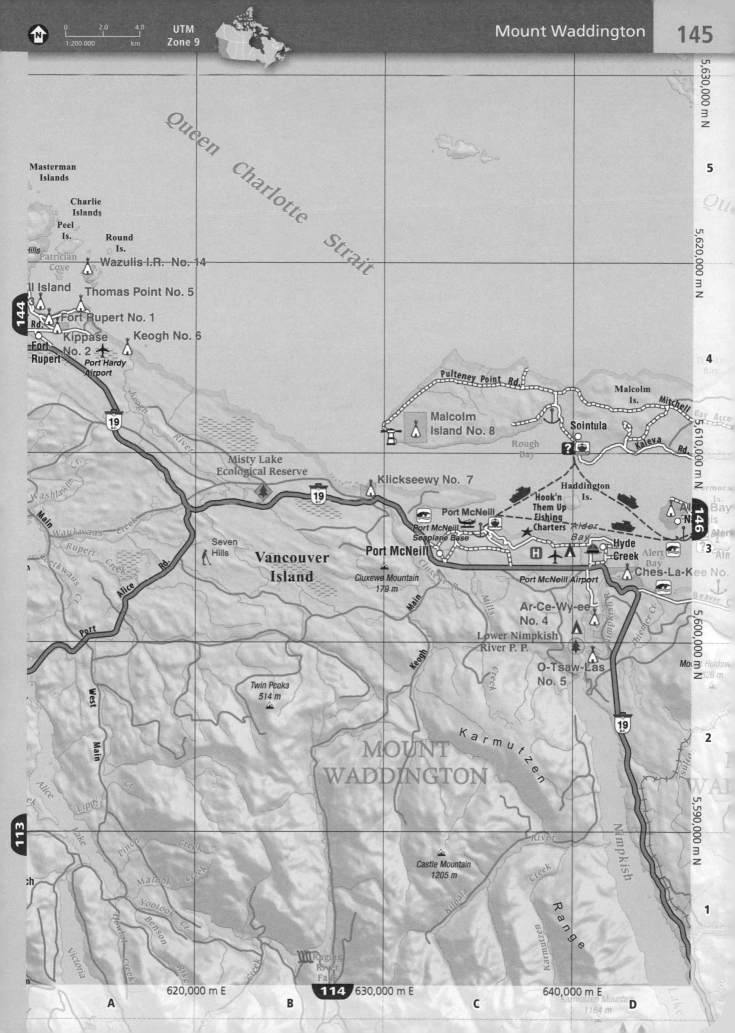

N

0   2.0   4.0
km
1:200 000

UTM
Zone 9

5,630,000 m N

Queen Charlotte Strait

5

Masterman
Islands

Charlie
Islands

Peel
Is.

Round
Is.

Hills

Patrician
Cove

Wazulis I.R. No. 14

5,620,000 m N

Qu

Thomas Point No. 5

ll Island

144

Fort Rupert No. 1

Rd.

Kippase
No. 2

Keogh No. 6

Fort
Rupert

Port Hardy
Airport

Keogh

River

Pulteney Point Rd.

Malcolm
Is.

Mitchell

Bay Acce

4

Sointula

Malcolm
Island No. 8

Kaleva

Rd.

19
B.C.

Rough
Bay

?

Misty Lake
Ecological Reserve

Klickseewy No. 7

Haddington
Is.

146

Washlawits

19
B.C.

Hook'n
Them Up
Fishing
Charters

Al
N

Bay

Ale

3

Main

Waukwaas

Creek

Rupert

Port McNeill

Alder

Bay

Alert
Bay

?

Seven
Hills

Port McNeill
Seaplane Base

Coetkwaus

Cr.

Alice

Vancouver
Island

Port McNeill

Ches-La-Kee No.

H

Port McNeill Airport

Hyde
Creek

Rd.

Cluxewe Mountain
179 m

Cluxewe R.

Beaver

Rhiemer Cr.

Port

Ar-Ce-Wy-ee
No. 4

Mount Holdsw
326 m

West

Main

Keogh

Mills

Creek

Lower Nimpkish
River P. P.

Nimpkish

5,600,000 m N

O-Tsaw-Las
No. 5

Twin Peaks
514 m

MOUNT

19
B.C.

113

WADDINGTON

Karmutzen

2

Alice

ek

Lippy

Pinch

Creek

Creek

Castle Mountain
1205 m

Kilpala

Range

Nimpkish

5,590,000 m N

WA

Malook

Creek

Creek

River

Creek

Yootook Cr.

Benson

Raging
River
Fa

Karmutzen Mountain

1

Victoria

Thewlet

620,000 m E

114 630,000 m E

640,000 m E

Karmutzen Mountain
1164 m

A   B   C   D

UTM
Zone 9

1:200 000

0   2.0   4.0
km

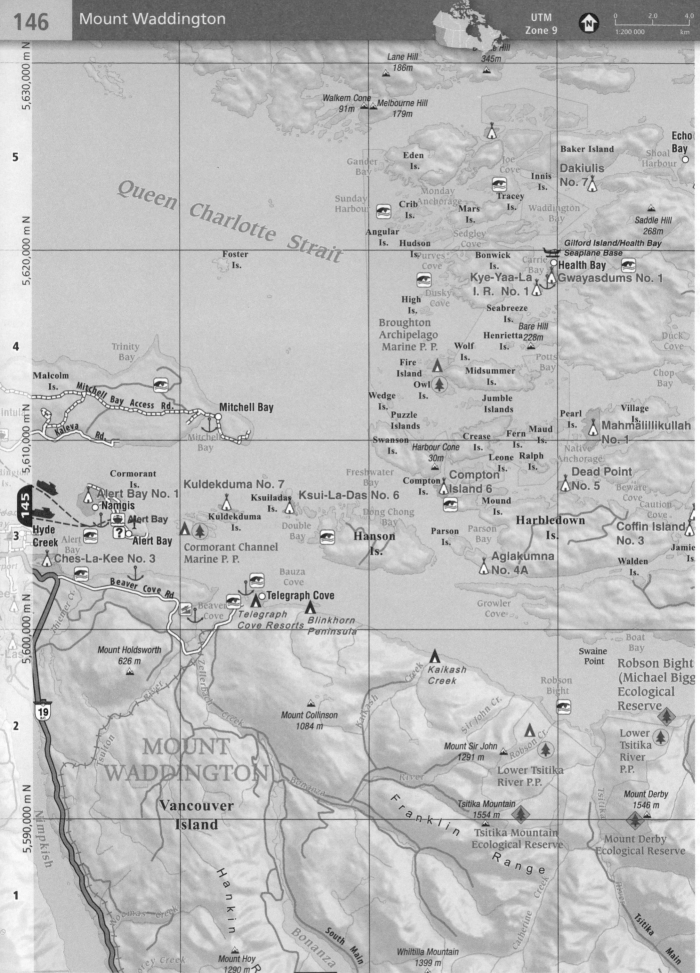

Lane Hill
186m

Walkem Cone
91m

Melbourne Hill
179m

345m

Echo
Bay

Baker Island

Shoal
Harbour

Dakiulis
No. 7

Saddle Hill
268m

Eden
Is.

Gander
Bay

Joe
Cove

Innis
Is.

Tracey
Is.

Waddington
Bay

Sunday
Harbour

Monday
Anchorage

Mars
Is.

Sedgley
Cove

Crib
Is.

Angular
Is.

Hudson
Is.

Curves
Cove

Bonwick
Is.

Carrie
Bay

Gilford Island/Health Bay
Seaplane Base

Health Bay

Foster
Is.

Kye-Yaa-La
I. R. No. 1

Gwayasdums No. 1

High
Is.

Dusky
Cove

Seabreeze
Is.

Duck
Cove

Broughton
Archipelago
Marine P. P.

Henrietta
Is.

Bare Hill
228m

Wolf
Is.

Chop
Bay

Trinity
Bay

Fire
Island

Midsummer
Is.

Potts
Bay

Malcolm
Is.

Mitchell Bay Access Rd.

Mitchell Bay

Wedge
Is.

Owl
Is.

Jumble
Islands

Kaleva   Rd.

Puzzle
Islands

Pearl
Is.

Village
Is.

Mahmalillikullah
No. 1

Mitchell
Bay

Swanson
Is.

Crease
Is.

Fern
Is.

Maud
Is.

Native
Anchorage

Harbour Cone
30m

Leone
Is.

Ralph
Is.

Cormorant
Is.

Kuldekduma No. 7

Ksui-La-Das No. 6

Freshwater
Bay

Compton
Is.

Compton
Island 6

Dead Point
No. 5

145

Alert Bay No. 1

Ksuiladas
Is.

Mound
Is.

Beware
Cove

Caution
Cove

Namgis

Kuldekduma
Is.

Dong Chong
Bay

Hyde
Creek

Alert Bay

Double
Bay

Parson
Is.

Parson
Bay

Harbledown
Is.

Coffin Island
No. 3

Jamie
Is.

Alert
Bay

Alert Bay

Hanson
Is.

Cormorant Channel
Marine P. P.

Aglakumna
No. 4A

Walden
Is.

Ches-La-Kee No. 3

Beaver Cove Rd.

Bauza
Cove

Growler
Cove

Boat
Bay

Telegraph Cove

Beaver
Cove

Swaine
Point

Robson Bight
(Michael Bigg
Ecological
Reserve

Telegraph
Cove Resorts

Blinkhorn
Peninsula

Robson
Bight

Mount Holdsworth
626 m

Kaikash
Creek

Lower
Tsitika
River
P.P.

19
B.C.

Zeilerbach Creek

Mount Collinson
1084 m

Mount Sir John
1291 m

Lower Tsitika
River P.P.

Mount Derby
1546 m

MOUNT
WADDINGTON

Tsikten Cr.

Franklin

Tsitika Mountain
1554 m

Mount Derby
Ecological Reserve

Vancouver
Island

Katkash Creek

Sir John Cr.

Robson Cr.

Range

Tsitika Mountain
Ecological Reserve

Tsitika River

Nimpkish

Tsulton River

Bonanza

Hankin

South Main

Franklin Creek

Catherine Creek

Tsitika
Main

1

Mount Hoy
1290 m

Whiltilla Mountain
1399 m

Butzen Mountain
1184 m

650,000 m E

115   660,000 m E

670,000 m E

A   B   C   D

Claud Elliott Creek
Ecological Reserve

5,630,000 m N

5,620,000 m N

5,610,000 m N

5,600,000 m N

5,590,000 m N

Queen Charlotte Strait

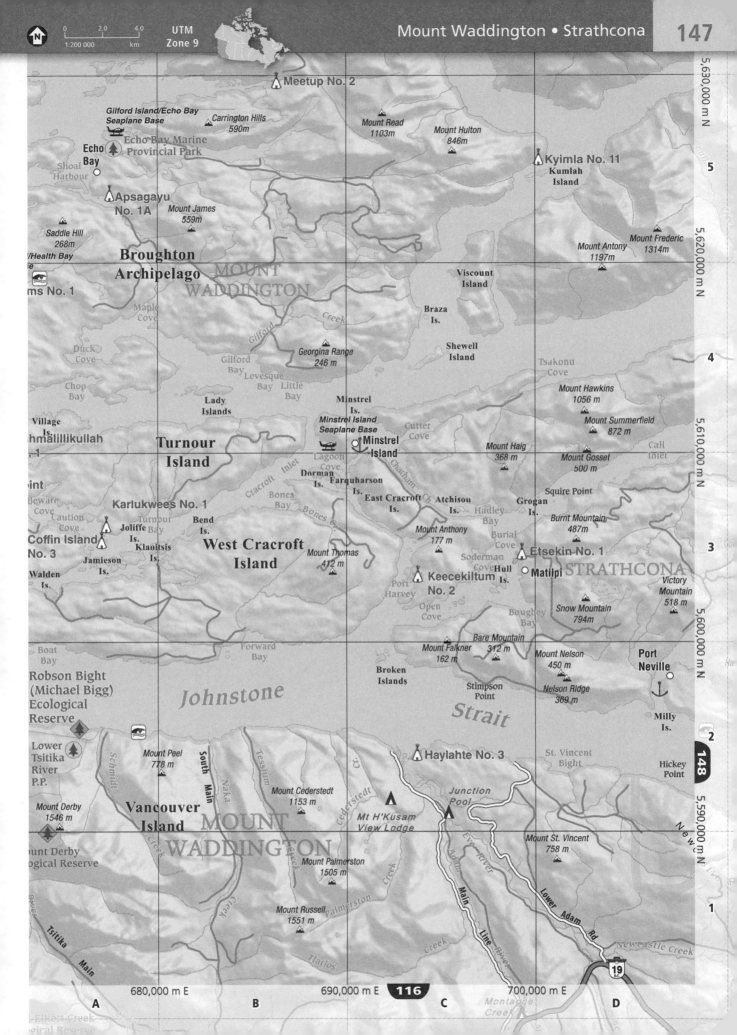

N

1:200 000

0   2.0   4.0
km

UTM
Zone 9

Meetup No. 2

Gilford Island/Echo Bay
Seaplane Base

Carrington Hills
590m

Mount Read
1103m

Mount Hulton
846m

Echo Bay Marine
Provincial Park

Echo
Bay

Kyimla No. 11

Kumlah
Island

Shoal
Harbour

Apsagayu
No. 1A

Mount James
559m

Mount Frederic
1314m

Saddle Hill
268m

Mount Antony
1197m

/Health Bay

Broughton
Archipelago

MOUNT
WADDINGTON

Viscount
Island

ms No. 1

Maple
Cove

Creek

Braza
Is.

Duck
Cove

Gilford

Shewell
Island

Tsakonu
Cove

Gilford
Bay

Georgina Range
246 m

Levesque
Bay

Little
Bay

Mount Hawkins
1056m

Chop
Bay

Lady
Islands

Minstrel
Is.

Mount Summerfield
872 m

Village
Is.
hmälillikullah

Minstrel Island
Seaplane Base

Cutter
Cove

Call
Inlet

Turnour
Island

Minstrel
Island

Mount Haig
368 m

Mount Gosset
500 m

Lagoon
Cove

Dorman
Is.

Farquharson
Is.

Chatham

int

Cracroft Inlet

Squire Point

Beware
Cove

Karlukwees No. 1

Bones
Bay

East Cracroft
Is.

Atchison
Is.

Grogan
Is.

Burnt Mountain
487m

Caution
Cove

Joliffe
Is.

Turnour
Bay

Bend
Is.

Hadley
Bay

Coffin Island
No. 3

Klaoitsis
Is.

West Cracroft
Island

Mount Thomas
412 m

Mount Anthony
177 m

Burial
Cove

Etsekin No. 1

STRATHCONA

Jamieson
Is.

Soderman
Cove

Hull
Is.

Matilpi

Walden
Is.

Keecekiltum
No. 2

Victory
Mountain
518 m

Port
Harvey

Snow Mountain
794m

Open
Cove

Boughey
Bay

Forward
Bay

Bare Mountain
312 m

Boat
Bay

Mount Falkner
162 m

Mount Nelson
450 m

Port
Neville

Robson Bight
(Michael Bigg)
Ecological
Reserve

Johnstone

Broken
Islands

Stimpson
Point

Nelson Ridge
369 m

Milly
Is.

Strait

St. Vincent
Bight

Lower
Tsitika
River
P.P.

Mount Peel
778 m

South
Main

Haylahte No. 3

Hickey
Point

Mount Derby
1546 m

Vancouver
Island

Tessium

Mount Cederstedt
1153 m

Junction
Pool

Mount St. Vincent
758 m

unt Derby
ogical Reserve

MOUNT
WADDINGTON

Schmidt

Naka

Cedersredt Cr.

Mt H'Kusam
View Lodge

Adam

Eve River

Lower Adam Rd

New

Mount Palmerston
1505 m

Line River

Mount Russell
1551 m

Palmerston Creek

Tlatlos
Creek

Montague
Creek

Newcastle Creek

19

Tsitika
Main

680,000 m E

690,000 m E 116

700,000 m E

A

B

C

D

5,630,000 m N

5

5,620,000 m N

4

5,610,000 m N

5,600,000 m N

3

148

2

5,590,000 m N

1

-Elkett Creek
gical Reserve

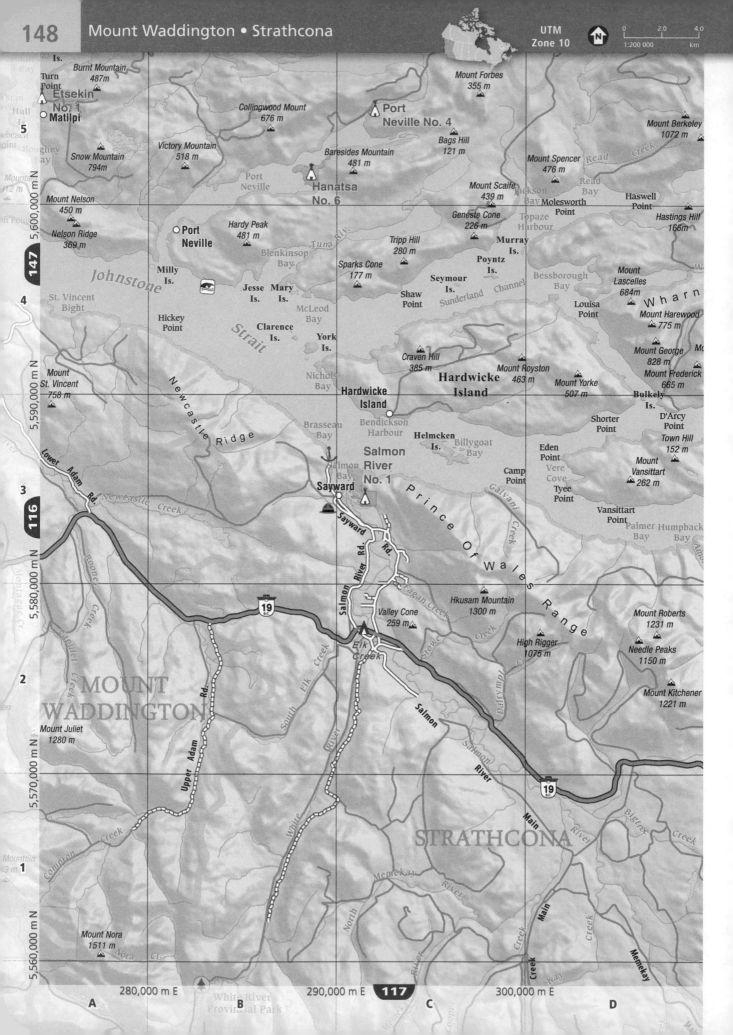

UTM
Zone 10

1:200 000

Turn Point
Etsekin No. 1
Matilpi

Burnt Mountain
487m

Collingwood Mount
676 m

Mount Forbes
355 m

Port Neville No. 4

Bags Hill
121 m

Mount Berkeley
1072 m

Mount Spencer
476 m

Snow Mountain
794m

Victory Mountain
518 m

Baresides Mountain
481 m

Mount Scaife
439 m

Read Bay

Haswell Point

Mount Nelson
450 m

Port Neville

Hanatsa No. 6

Geneste Cone
226 m

Molesworth Point

Hastings Hill
166 m

Nelson Ridge
369 m

Hardy Peak
481 m

Tripp Hill
280 m

Murray Is.

Topaze Harbour

Mount Lascelles
684m

Johnstone

Milly Is.

Blenkinsop Bay

Tuna Riv.

Sparks Cone
177 m

Poyntz Is.

Bessborough Bay

Wharn

Port Neville

Seymour Is.

Louisa Point

Mount Harewood
775 m

St. Vincent Bight

Jesse Is.

Mary Is.

McLeod Bay

Shaw Point

Sunderland Channel

Hickey Point

Clarence Is.

York Is.

Craven Hill
385 m

Hardwicke Island

Mount Royston
463 m

Mount Yorke
507 m

Mount George
828 m

Mount Frederick
665 m

Strait

Newcastle Ridge

Nichols Bay

Hardwicke Island

Mount Royston

Bulkely Is.

Mount St. Vincent
758 m

Brasseau Bay

Bendickson Harbour

Helmcken Is.

Billygoat Bay

Shorter Point

D'Arcy Point

Town Hill
152 m

Lower Adam Rd.

Salmon Bay

Salmon River No. 1

Eden Point

Camp Point

Vere Cove

Tyee Point

Mount Vansittart
262 m

Newcastle Creek

Sayward

Galvani Creek

Vansittart Point

Palmer Bay

Humpback Bay

Sayward Rd.

Salmon River Rd.

Prince Of Wales Range

MOUNT WADDINGTON

Roon Cr.

Caquilla Creek

Valley Cone
259 m

Fagan Creek

Hkusam Mountain
1300 m

Stowe Creek

Mount Roberts
1231 m

Mount Juliet
1280 m

Upper Adam Rd.

South Elk Creek

Elk Creek

High Rigger
1075 m

Needle Peaks
1150 m

Dalrymple Cr.

Salmon

Mount Kitchener
1221 m

White River

STRATHCONA

Salmon River

Main

Bigtree Creek

North River

Memekay River

Mount Nora
1511 m

Nora Cr.

Main

Creek

Kay Creek

Memekay

White River Provincial Park

280,000 m E

290,000 m E

300,000 m E

A   B   C   D

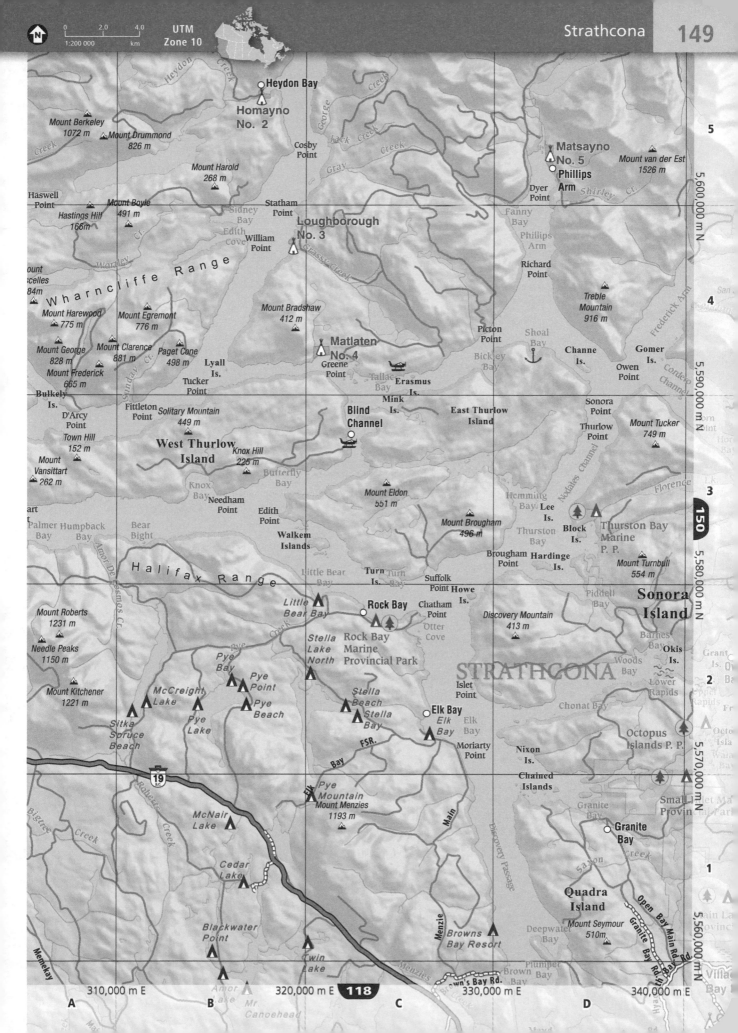

UTM
Zone 10

1:200 000

N

5

Mount Berkeley
1072 m

Mount Drummond
826 m

○ Heydon Bay

Homayno
No. 2

Matsayno
No. 5

Mount van der Est
1526 m

Cosby
Point

Phillips
Arm

Mount Harold
268 m

Dyer
Point

Haswell
Point

Mount Boyle
491 m

Statham
Point

Fanny
Bay

Hastings Hill
166m

Sidney
Bay

Loughborough
No. 3

Phillips
Arm

Edith
Cove

William
Point

Richard
Point

ount
scelles
84m

W h a r n c l i f f e   R a n g e

4

Mount Bradshaw
412 m

Treble
Mountain
916 m

Mount Harewood
775 m

Mount Egremont
776 m

Mount George
828 m

Mount Clarence
881 m

Paget Cone
498 m

Matlaten
No. 4

Picton
Point

Shoal
Bay

Channe
Is.

Gomer
Is.

Lyall
Is.

Greene
Point

Bickley
Bay

Owen
Point

Mount Frederick
665 m

Tucker
Point

Tallac
Bay

Erasmus
Is.

Bulkely
Is.

Fittleton
Point

Solitary Mountain
449 m

Mink
Is.

East Thurlow
Island

Sonora
Point

Mount Tucker
749 m

D'Arcy
Point

Blind
Channel

Thurlow
Point

Town Hill
152 m

West Thurlow
Island

Knox Hill
225 m

3

Mount
Vansittart
262 m

Knox
Bay

Butterfly
Bay

Mount Eldon
551 m

Hemming
Bay

Lee
Is.

Florence

Needham
Point

Block
Is.

Thurston Bay
Marine
P. P.

art

Palmer
Bay

Humpback
Bay

Bear
Bight

Edith
Point

Mount Brougham
496 m

Thurston
Bay

Mount Turnbull
554 m

H a l i f a x   R a n g e

Walkem
Islands

Brougham
Point

Hardinge
Is.

Piddell
Bay

Sonora
Island

Little Bear
Bay

Turn
Is.

Turn
Bay

Suffolk
Point

Howe
Is.

150

Mount Roberts
1231 m

Little
Bear Bay

Rock Bay

Chatham
Point

Discovery Mountain
413 m

Barnes
Bay

Okis
Is.

Grant
Is.

Needle Peaks
1150 m

Stella
Lake
North

Rock Bay
Marine
Provincial Park

Otter
Cove

S T R A T H C O N A

Woods
Bay

Lower
Rapids

Fr

2

Mount Kitchener
1221 m

McCreight
Lake

Pye
Bay

Pye
Point

Pye
Beach

Stella
Beach

Stella
Bay

Elk Bay

Islet
Point

Elk
Bay

Chonat Bay

Octopus
Islands P. P.

Octo
Isla
Wai
Bay

Sitka
Spruce
Beach

Pye
Lake

FSR.

Moriarty
Point

Nixon
Is.

Chained
Islands

Small
Provin

McNair
Lake

Pye
Mountain
Mount Menzies
1193 m

Main

Granite
Bay

Granite
Bay

1

Cedar
Lake

Quadra
Island

Mount Seymour
510m

Blackwater
Point

Menzie

Browns
Bay Resort

Deepwater
Bay

Twin
Lake

19

5,600,000 m N

5,590,000 m N

5,580,000 m N

5,570,000 m N

5,560,000 m N

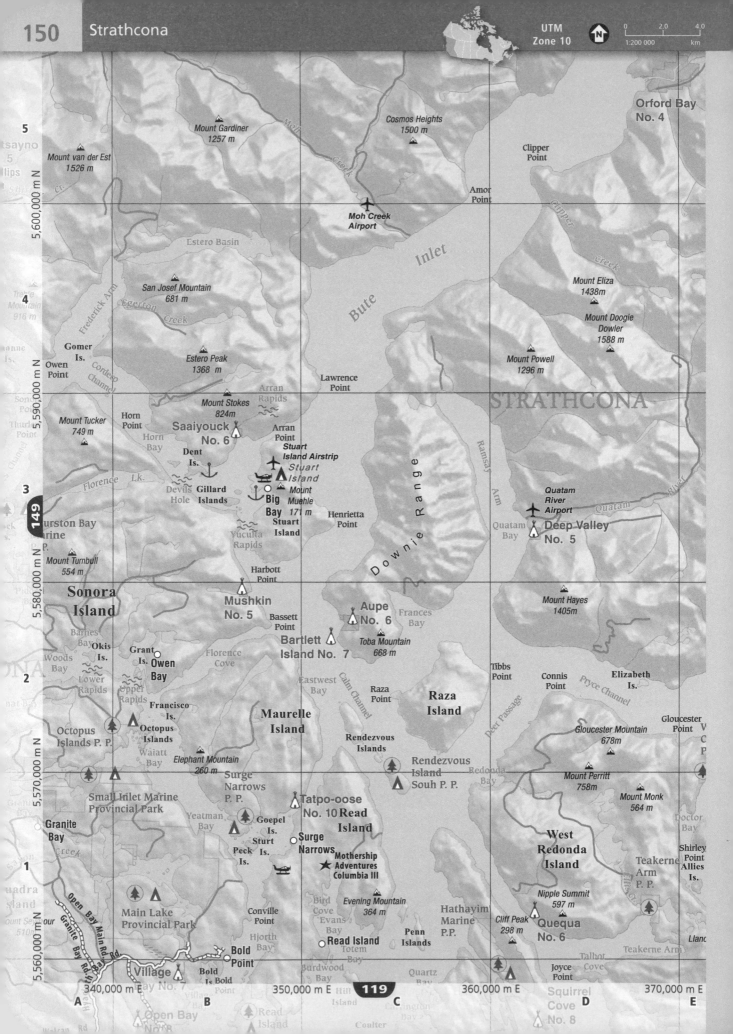

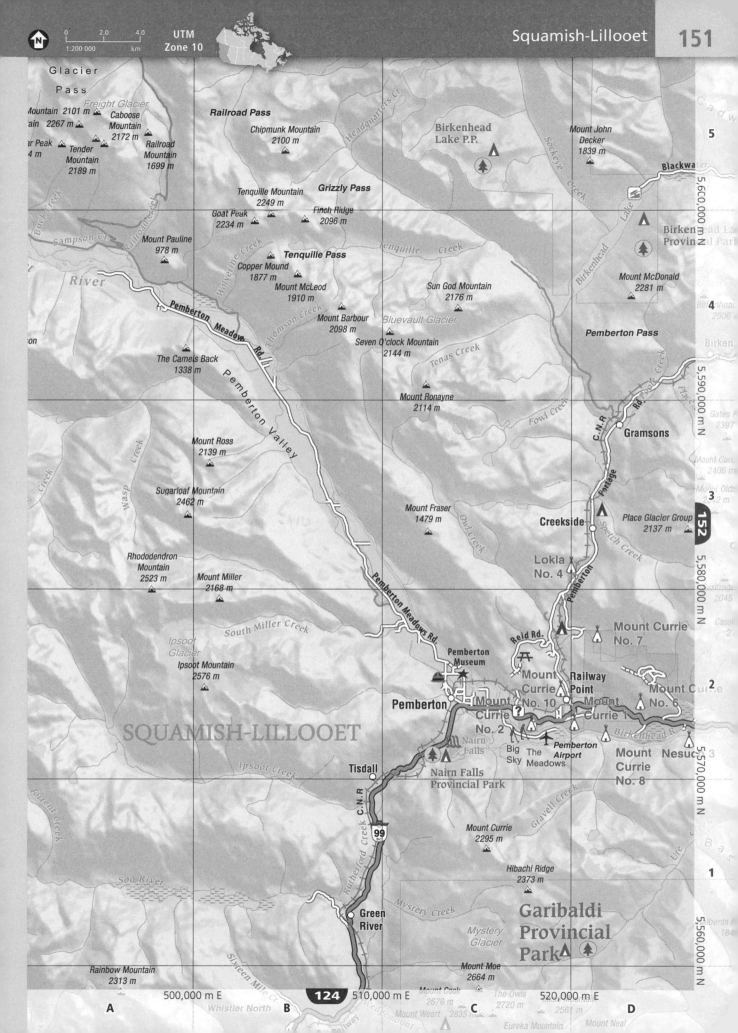

N

0   2.0   4.0
km
1:200 000
UTM
Zone 10

UTM

Glacier
Pass

Mountain 2101 m
ain 2267 m
Freight Glacier
Caboose
Mountain
2172 m
r Peak
4 m
Tender
Mountain
2189 m
Railroad
Mountain
1699 m

Railroad Pass

Chipmunk Mountain
2100 m

Birkenhead
Lake P.P.

Mount John
Decker
1839 m

Blackwa

Buck Creek
Railroadk

Sampson Cr

Tenquille Mountain
2249 m

Grizzly Pass

Finch Ridge
2096 m

Sockeye Creek

Birken
Provin
l Park

5

5,600,000 m N

Goat Peak
2234 m

Mount Pauline
978 m

Pemberton   Meadow

River

Rd

Wolverine Creek

Thomson Creek

Tenquille Pass

Copper Mound
1877 m
Mount McLeod
1910 m

Mount Barbour
2098 m

Tenquille   Creek

Sun God Mountain
2176 m

Bluevault Glacier

Seven O'clock Mountain
2144 m

Tenas Creek

Mount McDonald
2281 m

Pemberton Pass

Birken

Birkenhead   Lake

506

4

5,590,000 m N

Gates P
2397

The Camels Back
1338 m

Pemberton   Valley

Mount Ronayne
2114 m

Fowl Creek

C.N.R

Gramsons

Portage

Mount Garc
2406 m

Mount Olds
2 m

Wasp   Creek

Mount Ross
2139 m

Sugarloaf Mountain
2462 m

Mount Fraser
1479 m

Owl Creek

Creekside

Place Glacier Group
2137 m

152

3

5,580,000 m N

axfraxge
2045

Rhododendron
Mountain
2523 m

Mount Miller
2168 m

Pemberton   Meadows Rd.

Lokla
No. 4

Pemberton

Speich Creek

Mount Currie
No. 7

Cassi

South Miller Creek

Ipsoot
Glacier

Ipsoot Mountain
2576 m

Pemberton
Museum

Reid Rd.

Mount
Currie
No. 10
Railway
Point

Mount Currie
No. 6

2

5,570,000 m N

SQUAMISH-LILLOOET

Ipsoot Creek

Pemberton

Mount
Currie
No. 2

?

Mount
Currie 1

Birkenhead R.

Nairn
Falls

Tisdall

Nairn Falls
Provincial Park

Big
Sky
The
Meadows
Pemberton
Airport

Mount
Currie
No. 8

Nesuc

Mount Currie
2295 m

Gravell Creek

Torrent Creek

Rutherford Creek

C.N.R

99
BC

Green
River

Mystery Creek

Hibachi Ridge
2373 m

Ure
Bas

1

Soo River

Garibaldi
Provincial
Park

5,560,000 m N

Rainbow Mountain
2313 m

Sixteen Mile Cr

500,000 m E

124

510,000 m E

Whistler North

Mount Moe
2664 m

Mount Cook
2676 m

The Owls
2720 m

Mount Weart
2835 m

520,000 m E

Eureka Mountain
Mount Neal

A   B   C   D

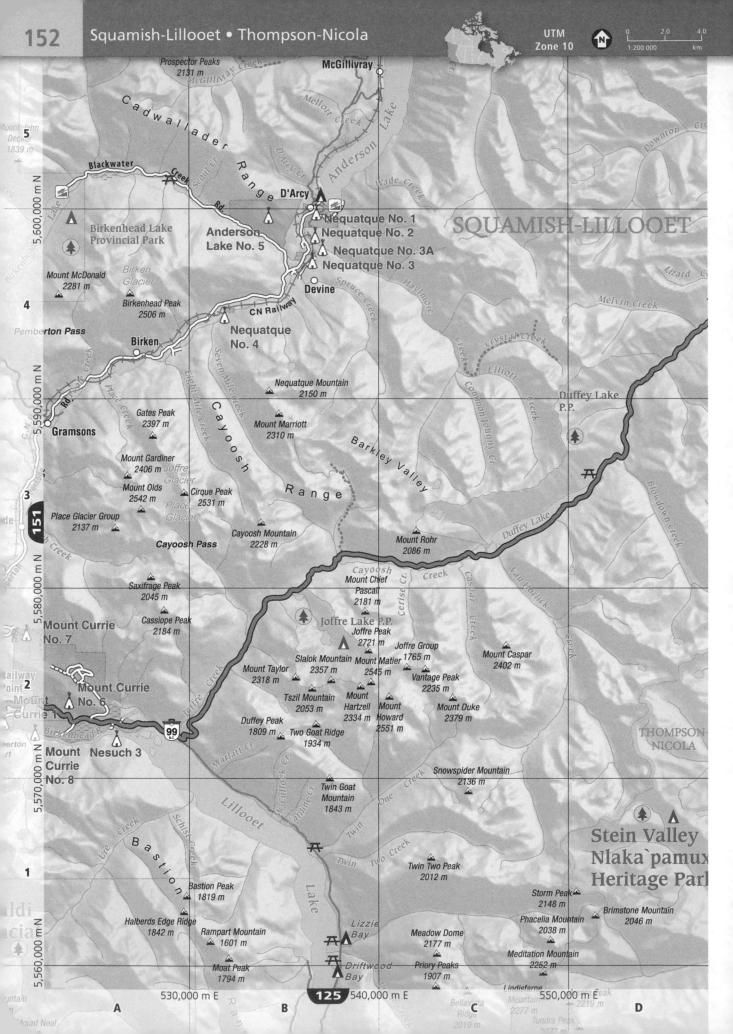

UTM
Zone 10

1:200 000

Prospector Peaks
2131 m

McGillivray

Cadwallader Range

Blackwater

Creek

D'Arcy

SQUAMISH-LILLOOET

Birkenhead Lake
Provincial Park

Anderson
Lake No. 5

Nequatque No. 1
Nequatque No. 2
Nequatque No. 3A
Nequatque No. 3

Mount McDonald
2281 m

Birken
Glacier

Devine

Birkenhead Peak
2506 m

CN Railway

Nequatque
No. 4

Pemberton Pass

Birken

Seven Mile Creek

Nequatque Mountain
2150 m

Duffey Lake
P.P.

Gramsons

Gates Peak
2397 m

Mount Marriott
2310 m

Melvin Creek

Crystal Creek

Elliott

Common Johnny Cr.

Mount Gardiner
2406 m

Joffre
Glacier

Barkley Valley

Mount Olds
2542 m

Cirque Peak
2531 m

Place
Glacier

Cayoosh

Place Glacier Group
2137 m

Cayoosh Mountain
2228 m

Range

Mount Rohr
2086 m

Duffey Lake

Blowdown Creek

Cayoosh Pass

Cayoosh

Creek

Saxifrage Peak
2045 m

Mount Chief
Pascall
2181 m

Caspar Creek

Van Horlick

Mount Currie
No. 7

Cassiope Peak
2184 m

Joffre Lake P.P.

Joffre Peak
2721 m

Joffre Group
1765 m

Mount Caspar
2402 m

Mount Taylor
2318 m

Slalok Mountain
2357 m

Mount Matier
2545 m

Vantage Peak
2235 m

Railway
Point

Mount Currie
No. 6

Tszil Mountain
2053 m

Mount
Hartzell
2334 m

Mount
Howard
2551 m

Mount Duke
2379 m

**THOMPSON-
NICOLA**

Mount
Currie 1

Duffey Peak
1809 m

Two Goat Ridge
1934 m

99
B.C.

Mount
Currie
No. 8

Nesuch 3

Lillooet

Snowspider Mountain
2136 m

Twin Goat
Mountain
1843 m

Twin
One
Creek

**Stein Valley
Nlaka`pamux
Heritage Park**

Bastion

McCullough Cr.

Catline Cr.

Twin
Two
Creek

Twin Two Peak
2012 m

Storm Peak
2148 m

Bastion Peak
1819 m

Brimstone Mountain
2046 m

Halberds Edge Ridge
1842 m

Rampart Mountain
1601 m

Lizzie
Bay

Meadow Dome
2177 m

Phacelia Mountain
2038 m

Meditation Mountain
2252 m

Moat Peak
1794 m

Driftwood
Bay

Priory Peaks
1907 m

Lindisfarne

125

530,000 m E

B

540,000 m E

C

550,000 m E

D

A

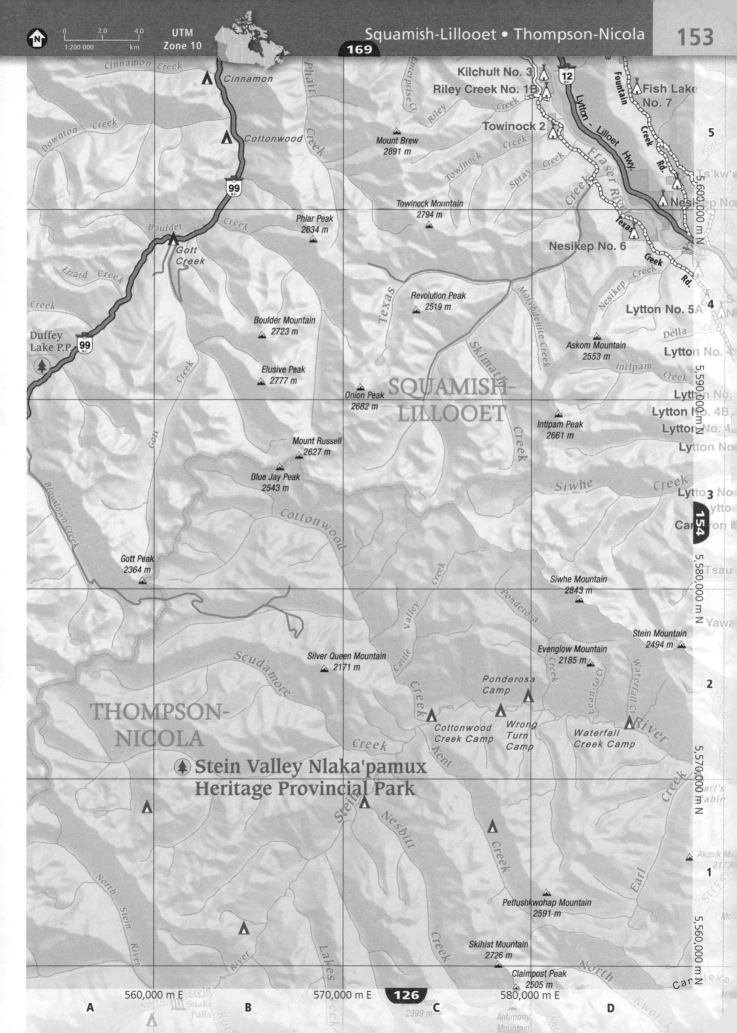

UTM
Zone 10
0   2.0   4.0
1:200 000   km

169

12

Cinnamon Creek
Cinnamon

Cottonwood

Phair Creek

Downton Creek

99 B.C.

Boulder Creek

Gott Creek

Lizard Creek

Creek

Duffey
Lake P.P.

99 B.C.

Gott Creek

Blowdown Creek

North Stein River

Kilchult No. 3
Riley Creek No. 1B

Enterprise Cr.
Riley Creek

Towinock Creek

Mount Brew
2891 m

Towinock 2

Towinock Mountain
2794 m

Spray Creek

Fountain

Lytton - Lilloet Hwy.

Fraser River

Fish Lake
No. 7

Creek Rd.

Ts'kw'a

5,600,000 m N

Nesikep No

Texas

Nesikep No. 6

Phiar Peak
2634 m

Texas Creek

Revolution Peak
2519 m

Molybdenite Creek

Nesikep Creek

Lytton No. 5A

Creek Rd.

Lytton No. 4

Boulder Mountain
2723 m

Elusive Peak
2777 m

Skimatch Creek

Askom Mountain
2553 m

Della

Lytton No. 4

Intlpam

Lytton No. 4B

Onion Peak
2682 m

SQUAMISH-
LILLOOET

Intlpam Peak
2661 m

Lytton No. 4.

Lytton No

Mount Russell
2627 m

Blue Jay Peak
2543 m

Siwhe Creek

Lytton 3

Lytton

154

Cayon

5,590,000 m N

5,580,000 m N

Cottonwood Creek

Gott Peak
2364 m

Siwhe Mountain
2843 m

Ponderosa Creek

Tsau

Yawa

Stein Mountain
2494 m

Silver Queen Mountain
2171 m

Scudamore Creek

Cattle Creek

Evenglow Mountain
2185 m

Learn to Cr.

Waterfall Creek

River

5,570,000 m N

THOMPSON-
NICOLA

Ponderosa
Camp

Kent Creek

Cottonwood
Creek Camp

Wrong
Turn
Camp

Waterfall
Creek Camp

Earl's Cabin

Stein Valley Nlaka'pamux
Heritage Provincial Park

Stein River

Nesbitt Creek

Creek

Earl Creek

Akasik M
2173

1

Petlushkwohap Mountain
2591 m

North Stein River

Skihist Mountain
2726 m

North Can

5,560,000 m N

Claimpost Peak
2505 m

kwoiek

560,000 m E

126

570,000 m E

580,000 m E

Stein
Snake
Falls

2399 m

Antimony
Mountain

A   B   C   D

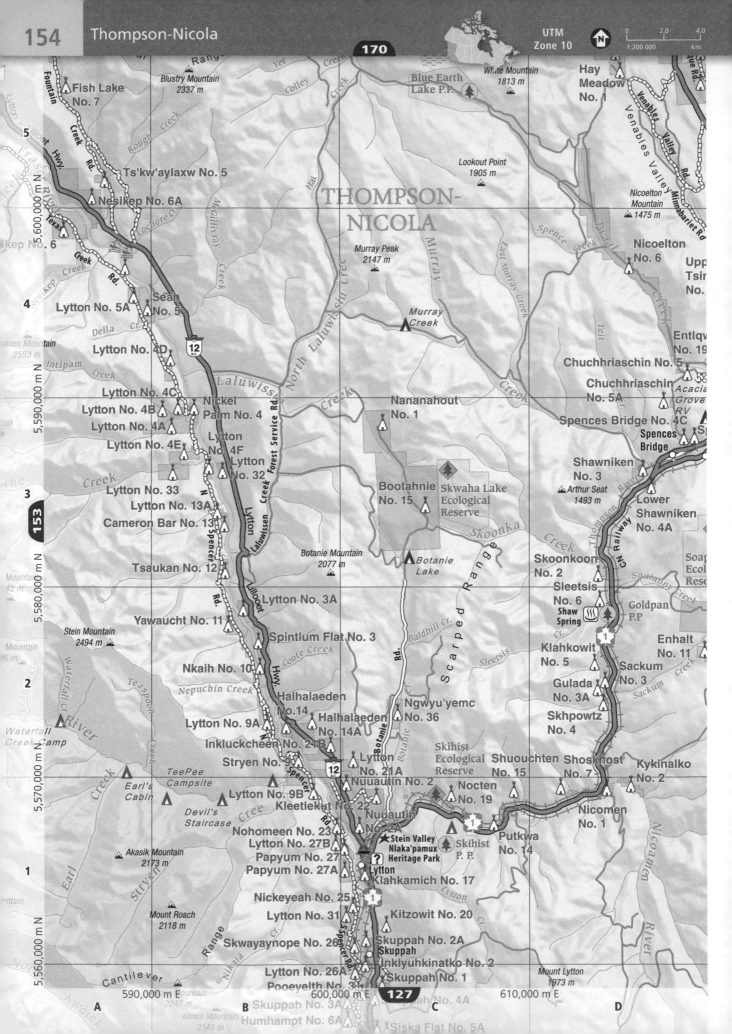

UTM
Zone 10

1:200 000

170

127

Fish Lake No. 7

Blustry Mountain 2337 m

Ts'kw'aylaxw No. 5

Nesikep No. 6A

ikep No. 6

Texas

Lytton No. 5A

Seah No. 5

Della

Lytton No. 4D

12 B.C.

skom Mountain 2553 m

Intlpam

Lytton No. 4C

Lytton No. 4B

Nickel Palm No. 4

Lytton No. 4A

Lytton No. 4E

Lytton No. 4F

Lytton No. 32

Lytton No. 33

Lytton No. 13A

Cameron Bar No. 13

Tsaukan No. 12

Peak

Creek

Lytton No. 3A

153

Stein Mountain 2494 m

Yawaucht No. 11

Spintlum Flat No. 3

Nkaih No. 10

Nepuchin Creek

Halhalaeden No.14

Halhalaeden No. 14A

Lytton No. 9A

Waterfall Creek Camp

Inkluckcheen No. 21B

Stryen No. 9

TeePee Campsite

Earl's Cabin

Lytton No. 9B

Devil's Staircase

Kleetlekut No. 22

Nohomeen No. 23

Nuuautin No. 2A

Akasik Mountain 2173 m

Lytton No. 27B

Papyum No. 27

Papyum No. 27A

Nickeyeah No. 25

Lytton
?

Stein Valley Nlaka'pamux Heritage Park

Klahkamich No. 17

Lytton No. 31

Mount Roach 2118 m

Skwayaynope No. 26

Kitzowit No. 20

Skuppah No. 2A

Skuppah

Inklyuhkinatko No. 2

Lytton No. 26A

Skuppah No. 1

Mount Lytton 1973 m

Pooeyelth No. 3

Cantilever

Mountain 2247 m

Skuppah No. 3A

Humhampt No. 6A

Klowa Mountain 2345 m

Siska Flat No. 5A

THOMPSON-NICOLA

White Mountain 1813 m

Blue Earth Lake P.P.

Hay Meadow No. 1

Venables Valley

Lookout Point 1905 m

Nicoelton Mountain 1475 m

Minnabariet Rd.

Murray Peak 2147 m

Murray Creek

Nicoelton No. 6

Upp Tsin No.

Entlqw No. 19

Chuchhriaschin No. 5

Chuchhriaschin No. 5A

Acacia Grove RV

Nananahout No. 1

Spences Bridge No. 4C

Spences Bridge

Sp

Bootahnie No. 15

Skwaha Lake Ecological Reserve

Shawniken No. 3

Arthur Seat 1493 m

Lower Shawniken No. 4A

Botanie Mountain 2077 m

Botanie Lake

Skoonkoon No. 2

Sleetsis No. 6

Shaw Spring

Goldpan P.P.

Enhalt No. 11

Klahkowit No. 5

Sackum No. 3

Gulada No. 3A

Skhpowtz No. 4

Skihist Ecological Reserve

Ngwyu'yemc No. 36

Shuouchten No. 15

Shoshnost No. 7

Kykinalko No. 2

Nocten No. 19

Lytton No. 21A

Nuuautin No. 2

Skihist P. P.

Putkwa No. 14

Nicomen No. 1

590,000 m E

600,000 m E

610,000 m E

A   **B**   **C**   **D**

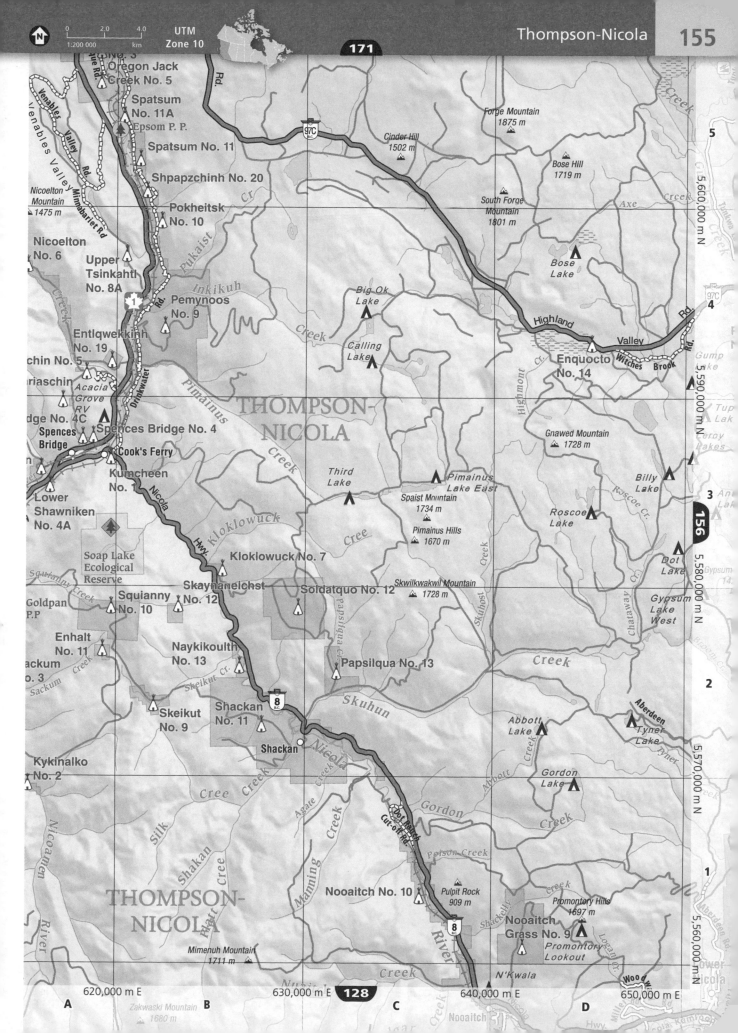

N

1:200 000

UTM Zone 10

0   2.0   4.0
km

171

97C B.C.

Forge Mountain 1875 m

Cinder Hill 1502 m

Bose Hill 1719 m

South Forge Mountain 1801 m

Axe Creek

Bose Lake

Big Ok Lake

Highland

Valley

Enquocto No. 14

Witches Brook

Calling Lake

Gnawed Mountain 1728 m

THOMPSON-NICOLA

Billy Lake

Third Lake

Pimainus Lake East

Spaist Mountain 1734 m

Roscoe Lake

Pimainus Hills 1670 m

Dot Lake

Skwilkwakwil Mountain 1728 m

Gypsum Lake West

Oregon Jack Creek No. 5

Spatsum No. 11A
Epsom P. P.

Spatsum No. 11

Shpapzchinh No. 20

Pokheitsk No. 10

Nicoelton Mountain 1475 m

Nicoelton No. 6

Upper Tsinkahtl No. 8A

Pemynoos No. 9

Entlqwekkinh No. 19

chin No. 5

riaschin

dge No. 4C

Acacia Grove RV

Spences Bridge No. 4

Spences Bridge

Cook's Ferry

Kumcheen No. 1

Lower Shawniken No. 4A

Soap Lake Ecological Reserve

Kloklowuck No. 7

Skaynanelchst No. 12

Soldatquo No. 12

Squianny No. 10

Goldpan P.P

Enhalt No. 11

ackum o. 3

Naykikoulth No. 13

Papsilqua No. 13

Skuhun

Abbott Lake

Aberdeen

Tyner Lake

Skeikut No. 9

Shackan No. 11

Shackan

8 B.C.

Gordon Lake

Kykinalko No. 2

Dot Ranch Cut-off Rd

Gordon

Poison Creek

THOMPSON-NICOLA

Nooaitch No. 10

Pulpit Rock 909 m

Promontory Hills 1697 m

Nooaitch Grass No. 9

Promontory Lookout

8 B.C.

Mimenuh Mountain 1711 m

N'Kwala

Zakwaski Mountain 1680 m

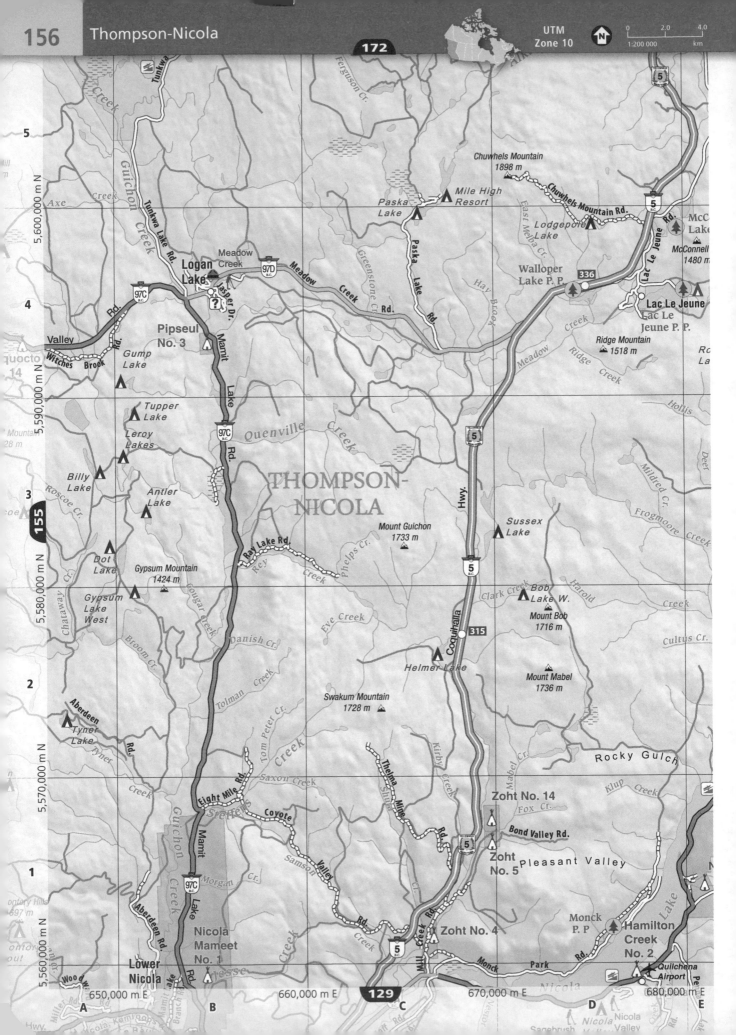

UTM
Zone 10

1:200 000

0   2.0   4.0
km

172

THOMPSON-
NICOLA

Chuwhels Mountain
1898 m

Chuwhels Mountain Rd.

Mile High
Resort

Paska
Lake

Lodgepole
Lake

Walloper
Lake P. P.

336

Lac Le Jeune

McC
Lake

McConnell
1480 m

Lac Le
Jeune P. P.

Meadow

Creek Rd.

Greenstone Cr.

Hay Brook

Ridge Mountain
1518 m

Ridge

Creek

Ro
La

Hollis

Logan
Lake

Meadow
Creek

97D

Meadow

Creek Rd.

97C

Jasper Dr.

?

Pipseul
No. 3

Manit

Lake

Rd.

Quenville Creek

5

Deer

Mildred Cr.

Frogmoore Creek

Valley

Rd.

Witches Brook

Gump
Lake

Tupper
Lake

Leroy
Lakes

97C

Billy
Lake

Antler
Lake

Mount Guichon
1733 m

Sussex
Lake

Roscoe Cr.

Ray Lake Rd.

Rey

Creek

Phelps Cr.

5

Clark Creek

Bob
Lake W.

Harold

Creek

Cultus Cr.

Dot
Lake

Gypsum Mountain
1424 m

Mount Bob
1716 m

Gypsum
Lake
West

Chataway Cr.

Cougar Creek

Broom Cr.

Danish Cr.

Eve Creek

Coquihalla

315

Helmer Lake

Mount Mabel
1736 m

Aberdeen

Tyner
Lake

Tolman

Creek

Tom Peter Cr.

Swakum Mountain
1728 m

Kirby Creek

Mabel Cr.

Rocky Gulch

Klup Creek

Tyner Rd.

Saxon Creek

Eight Mile Rd.

Coyote

Steffens

Thelma
Mine
Slough

Zoht No. 14

Fox Cr.

Bond Valley Rd.

5

Zoht
No. 5

Pleasant Valley

97C

Manit

Lake

Guichon Creek

Morgan Cr.

Aberdeen Rd.

Samson

Valley

Rd.

Creek

Rd.

5

Zoht No. 4

Monck
P. P

Hamilton
Creek
No. 2

Nicola
Mameet
No. 1

Jesse

Lower
Nicola

Mill Creek Rd.

Monck Park Rd.

Quilchena
Airport

Nicola

N
Nicola
Valley

129

5,600,000 m N

5,590,000 m N

5,580,000 m N

5,570,000 m N

5,560,000 m N

5

4

3

2

1

155

A   B   C   D   E

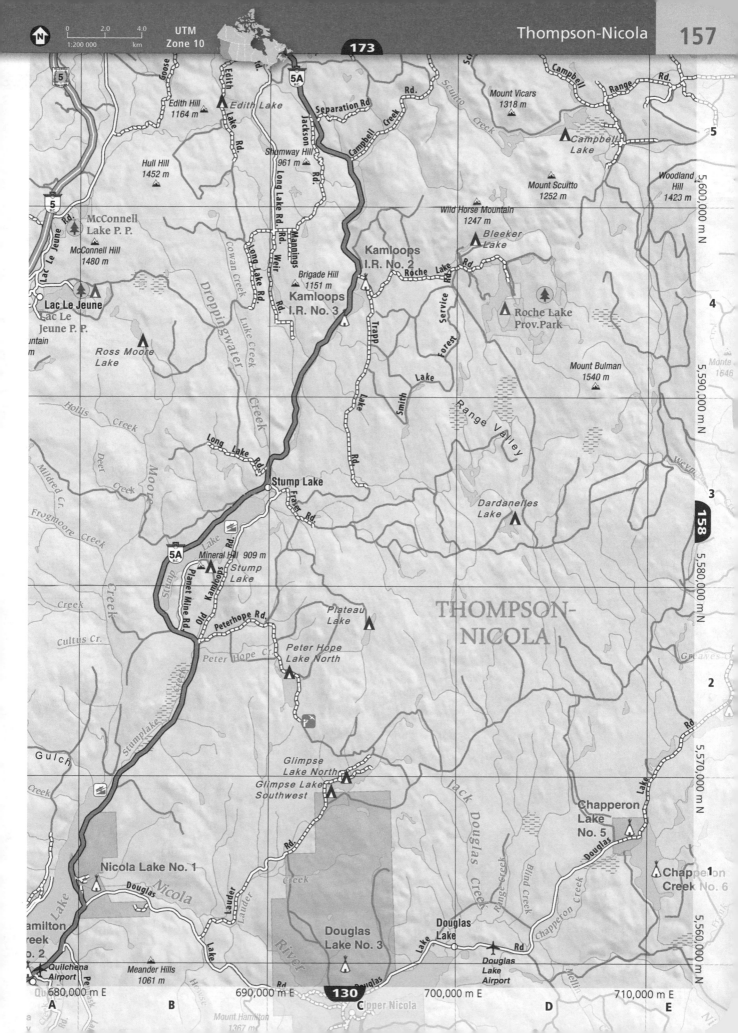

UTM
Zone 10
1:200 000
0   2.0   4.0
km

173

5A

5

5

5A

THOMPSON-NICOLA

Edith Hill
1164 m
Edith Lake

Separation Rd.

Mount Vicars
1318 m

Campbell
Lake

Hull Hill
1452 m

Shumway Hill
961 m

Campbell Creek

Mount Scuitto
1252 m

Woodland
Hill
1423 m

McConnell
Lake P. P.

McConnell Hill
1480 m

Wild Horse Mountain
1247 m

Bleeker
Lake

Roche Lake Rd.

Kamloops
I.R. No. 2

Lac Le Jeune

Lac Le
Jeune P. P.

Brigade Hill
1151 m

Kamloops
I.R. No. 3

Roche Lake
Prov.Park

Mount Bulman
1540 m

Monte
1646

Ross Moore
Lake

Trapp Lake

Smith Lake

Range Valley

Long Lake Rd.

Stump Lake

Dardanelles
Lake

158

Mineral Hill 909 m

Stump
Lake

Peterhope Rd.

Plateau
Lake

THOMPSON-
NICOLA

Greaves

Peter Hope Cr.

Peter Hope
Lake North

Glimpse
Lake North

Glimpse Lake
Southwest

Chapperon
Lake
No. 5

Nicola Lake No. 1

Douglas

Jack Douglas Creek

Chapperon
Creek No. 6

Douglas
Lake No. 3

Douglas
Lake

Douglas
Lake
Airport

amilton
reek
o. 2

Quilchena
Airport

Meander Hills
1061 m

130

Upper Nicola

Mount Hamilton
1367 m

680,000 m E   690,000 m E   700,000 m E   710,000 m E

A   B   C   D   E

5,600,000 m N

5,590,000 m N

5,580,000 m N

5,570,000 m N

5,560,000 m N

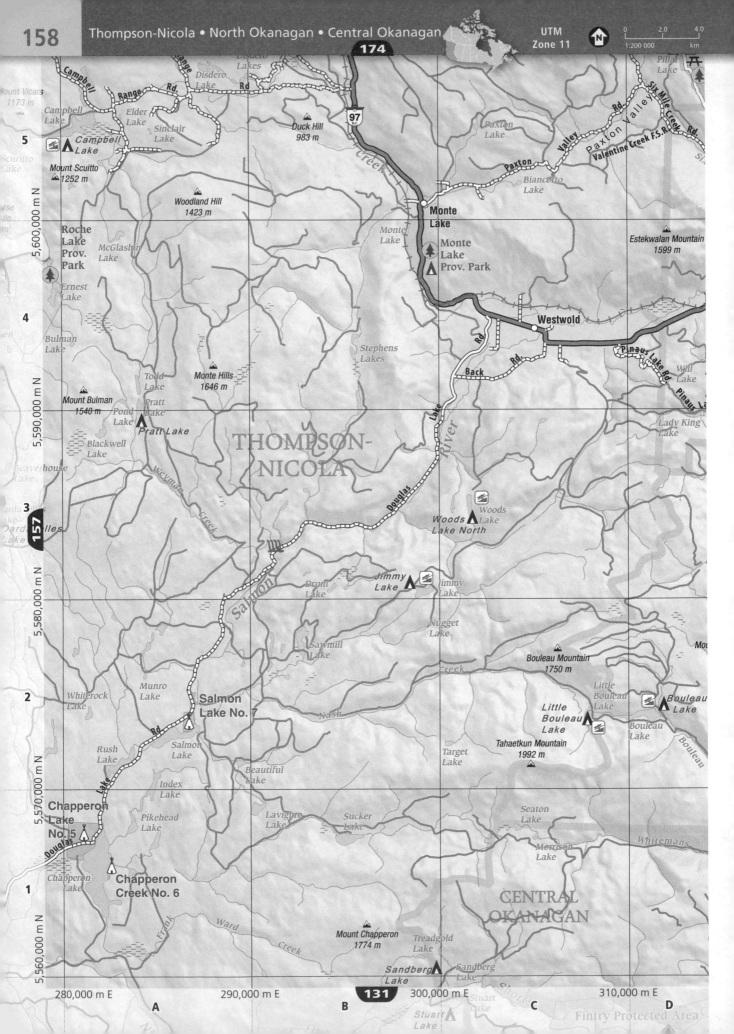

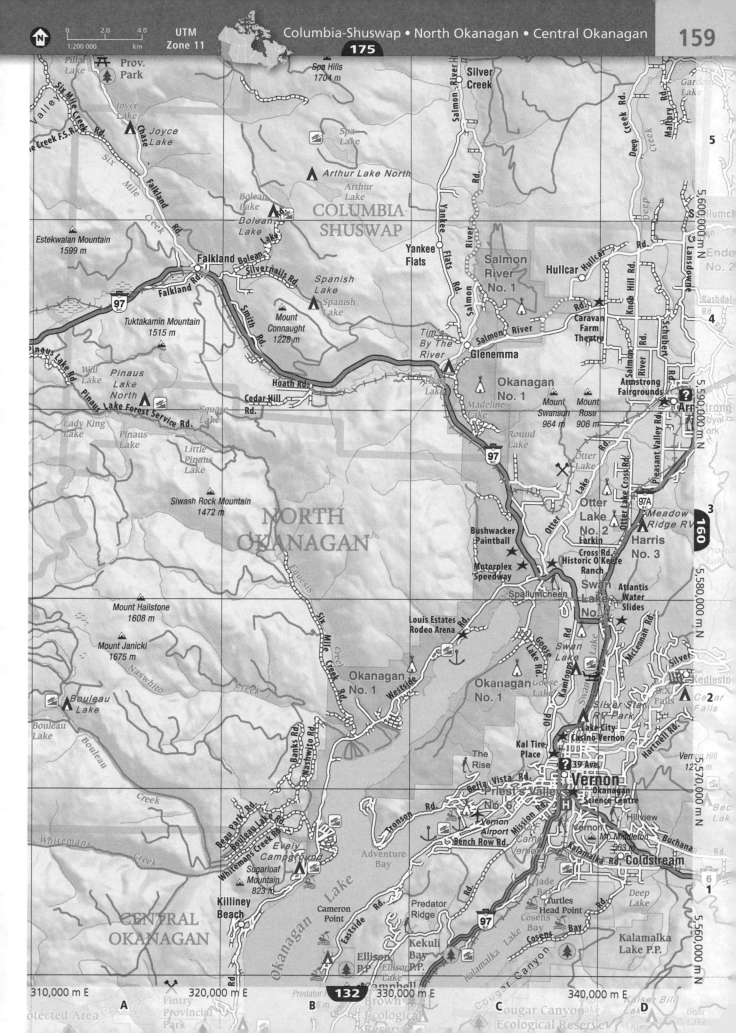

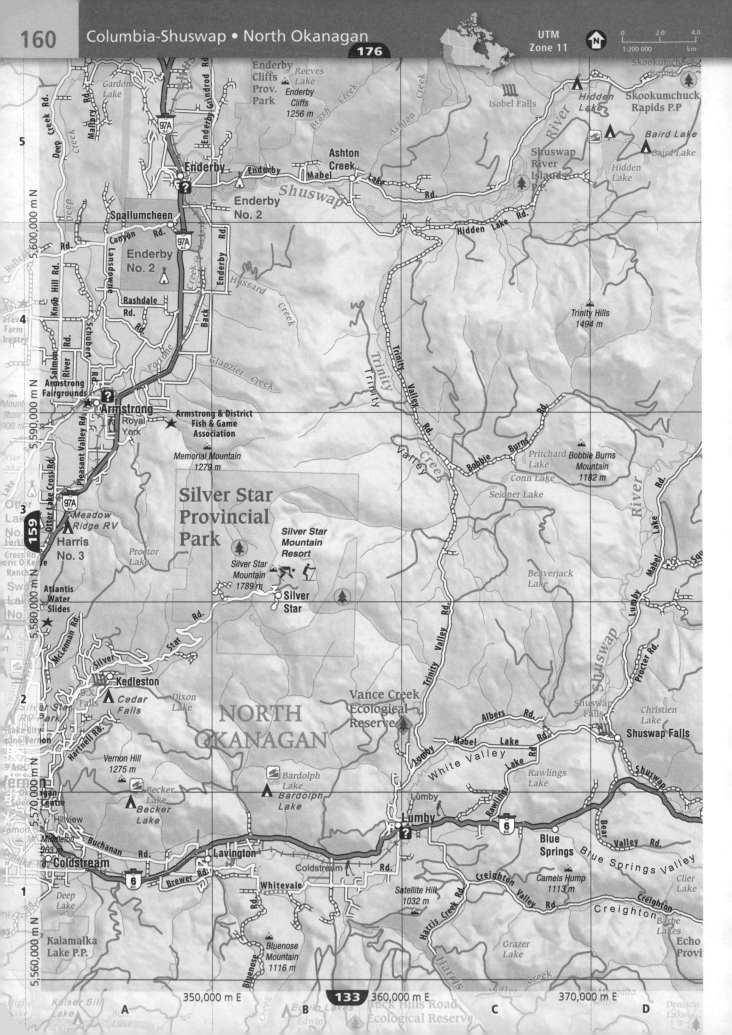

5

Gardom
Lake

Deep Creek Rd.

Mabry Rd.

97A
B.C.

Enderby
Cliffs
Prov.
Park

Enderby
Cliffs
1256 m

Reeves
Lake

Brash Creek

Ashton Creek

Isobel Falls

Hidden Lake

River

Skookumchuck
Rapids P.P

Baird Lake

Baird Lake

Hidden Lake

Enderby

Enderby

Mabel

Lake

Shuswap

Shuswap
River
Islands
P.P.

Spallumcheen

97A
B.C.

Canyon
Rd.

Enderby
No. 2

Enderby
No. 2

Lansdowne

Rashdale
Rd.

Schubert

Back

Enderby Rd.

Hyssard Creek

Hidden Lake Rd.

5,600,000 m N

4

Knob Hill Rd.

Salmon River Rd.

Rd.

Rd.

Glanzier Creek

For the

Trinity Valley Rd.

Trinity

Trinity Hills
1494 m

Armstrong
Fairgrounds

Armstrong

Royal
York

Pleasant Valley Rd.

Armstrong & District
Fish & Game
Association

Memorial Mountain
1279 m

Creek

Valley

Bobbie

Burns

Pritchard
Lake

Bobbie Burns
Mountain
1182 m

5,590,000 m N

3

159

97A
B.C.

Otter Lake Cross Rd.

Meadow
Ridge RV

Harris
No. 3

**Silver Star
Provincial
Park**

Proctor
Lake

Silver Star
Mountain
Resort

Silver Star
Mountain
1789 m

Conn Lake

Seidner Lake

River

Lake

Mabel

Rd.

Atlantis
Water
Slides

Silver
Star

Beaverjack
Lake

5,580,000 m N

Star

Rd.

Silver

Rd.

Trinity Valley Rd.

Shuswap

Lumby Rd.

Procter Rd.

2

Kedleston

B.X.
Falls

Cedar
Falls

Dixon
Lake

**NORTH
OKANAGAN**

Vance Creek
Ecological
Reserve

Albers

Rd.

Shuswap
Falls

Christien
Lake

Shuswap Falls

5,570,000 m N

Hartnell Rd.

Vernon Hill
1275 m

Becker
Lake

Becker
Lake

Bardolph
Lake

Bardolph
Lake

Lumby

Mabel

Lake

Rd.

White Valley

Lumby

Rawlings

Rawlings
Lake

Shuswap

1

Deep
Lake

Middleton

Coldstream

Buchanan

Rd.

Lavington

6
B.C.

Brewer Rd.

Whitevale

Coldstream

Rd.

Satellite Hill
1032 m

Lumby

6
B.C.

Creighton

Valley

Rd.

Camels Hump
1113 m

Blue
Springs

Bear

Valley

Rd.

Blue Springs Valley

Clier
Lake

Creighton

Creighton

Kalamalka
Lake P.P.

Bluenose
Mountain
1116 m

Grazer
Lake

Echo
Provi

5,600,000 m N

5,590,000 m N

5,580,000 m N

5,570,000 m N

5,560,000 m N

A   B   C   D

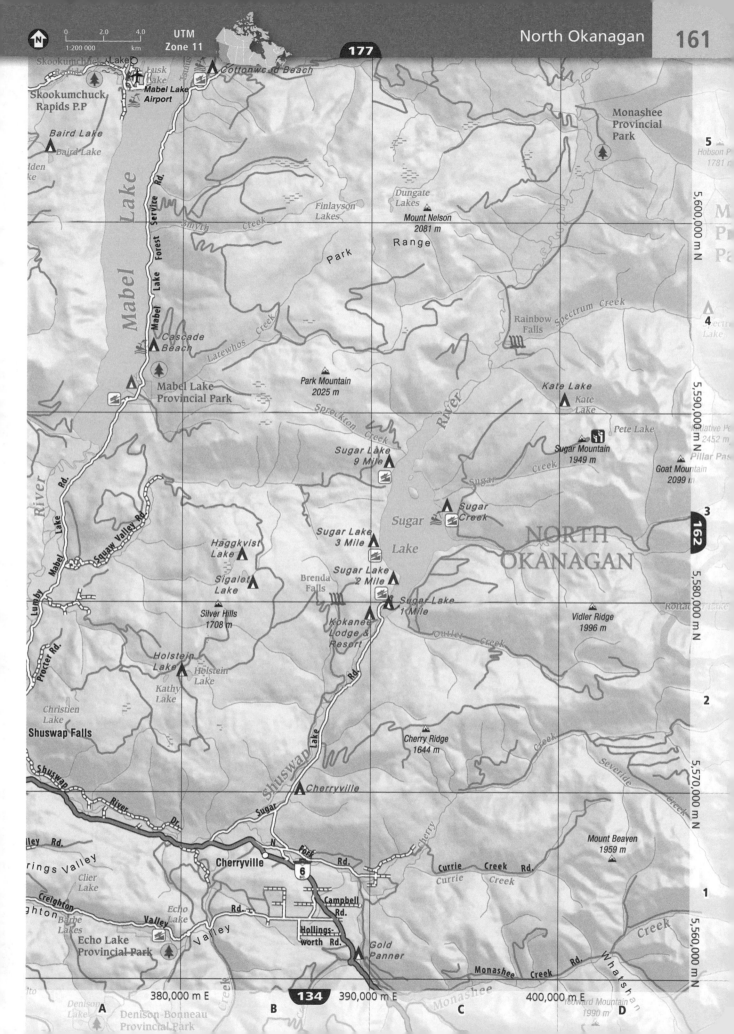

N

0 2.0 4.0
1:200 000   km

UTM
Zone 11

177

Skookumchuck Lake
Skookumchuck Rapids
Lusk Lake
Cottonwood Beach
Mabel Lake Airport
Skookumchuck Rapids P.P
Baird Lake
Baird Lake
olden ke

Monashee Provincial Park

Hobson P
1781 m

Mabel Lake

Mabel Lake Forest Service Rd.

Smyth   Creek

Finlayson Lakes

Dungate Lakes

Park   Range

Mount Nelson
2081 m

5,600,000 m N

M
P
Pa

5

Cascade Beach

Latewhos   Creek

Mabel Lake Provincial Park

Spreckron Creek

Park Mountain
2025 m

River

Rainbow Falls

Spectrum   Creek

Kate Lake

Kate Lake

ectra
Lake

5,590,000 m N

lative Pe
2452 m

Pillar Pas

4

Sugar Lake
9 Mile

Sugar Mountain
1949 m

Pete Lake

Goat Mountain
2099 m

River Rd.

Squaw Valley Rd.

Mabel Lake

Haggkvist Lake

Sugar Lake
3 Mile

Sugar   Creek

Sugar
Lake

Sugar Creek

NORTH
OKANAGAN

162

5,580,000 m N

3

Sigalet Lake

Brenda Falls

Sugar Lake
2 Mile

Lumby

Silver Hills
1708 m

Sugar Lake
1 Mile

Kokanee Lodge & Resort

Outlet   Creek

Vidler Ridge
1996 m

Ronald Lake

Procter Rd.

Holstein Lake

Holstein Lake

Kathy Lake

Rd.

2

Christien Lake

Shuswap Falls

Shuswap Lake

Cherry Ridge
1644 m

Creek

Severide

eek

5,570,000 m N

Shuswap

Shuswap   River

alley   Rd.

rings Valley

Clier Lake

ghton
Barbe Lakes

Sugar

Cherryville

Sugar

Fork

Cherryville

6
B.C.

Rd.

Mount Beaven
1959 m

Currie   Creek   Rd.

Currie   Creek

Cherry

1

Echo Lake

Valley

Rd.

Campbell Rd.

Echo Lake Provincial Park

Valley

Hollingsworth Rd.

Gold Panner

Monashee   Creek   Rd.

Whatshan

5,560,000 m N

Denison Lake

Denison-Bonneau Provincial Park

134

380,000 m E

B

390,000 m E

C

400,000 m E

Monashee

Howard Mountain
1990 m

D

A

5,560,000 m N

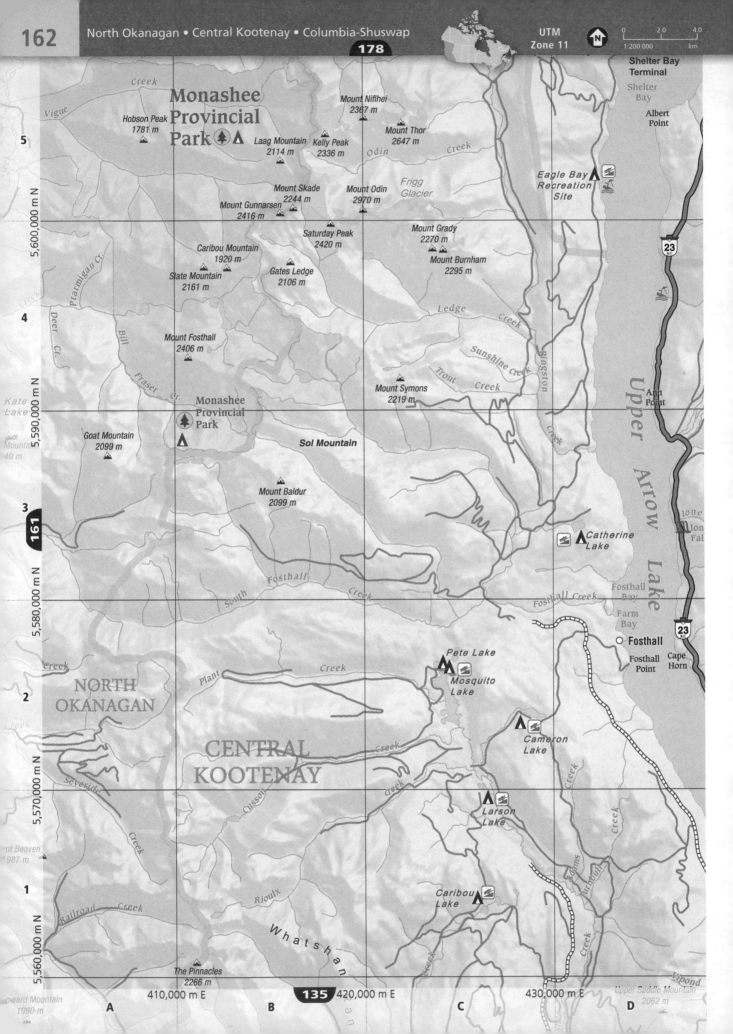

Shelter Bay
Terminal

Shelter
Bay

Albert
Point

Vigue   Creek

Mount Niflhei
2367 m

**Monashee
Provincial
Park**

Hobson Peak
1781 m

Laag Mountain
2114 m

Kelly Peak
2336 m

Mount Thor
2647 m

Odin   Creek

Eagle Bay
Recreation
Site

5

5,600,000 m N

Mount Skade
2244 m

Mount Odin
2970 m

Frigg
Glacier

Mount Gunnarsen
2416 m

Saturday Peak
2420 m

Mount Grady
2270 m

Caribou Mountain
1920 m

Gates Ledge
2106 m

Mount Burnham
2295 m

Slate Mountain
2161 m

Ledge   Creek

Ptarmigan Cr.

Kingston

4

5,590,000 m N

Mount Fosthall
2406 m

Sunshine Creek

Trout   Creek

Ann
Point

Mount Symons
2219 m

Upper   Arrow   Lake

Kate
Lake

Deer   Cr.

Bill

Fraser   Cr.

**Monashee
Provincial
Park**

Mountain
49 m

Goat Mountain
2099 m

Sol Mountain

Mount Baldur
2099 m

161

Catherine
Lake

lone
lone
Fall

3

5,580,000 m N

Fosthall
Bay

Farm
Bay

South   Fosthall   Creek

Fosthall Creek

Fosthall

Fosthall
Point

Cape
Horn

Pete Lake

**NORTH
OKANAGAN**

Plant   Creek

Mosquito
Lake

Creek

2

Creek

**CENTRAL
KOOTENAY**

Cameron
Lake

Severidge

Creek

Cussoi

Creek

Larson
Lake

5,570,000 m N

Adams

Turnbull

nt Beaven
987 m

Rioulx

Railroad   Creek

Caribou
Lake

1

5,560,000 m N

Whatshan

Creek

Vipond

oward Mountain
T 990 m

The Pinnacles
2266 m

Upper Saddle Mountain
2062 m

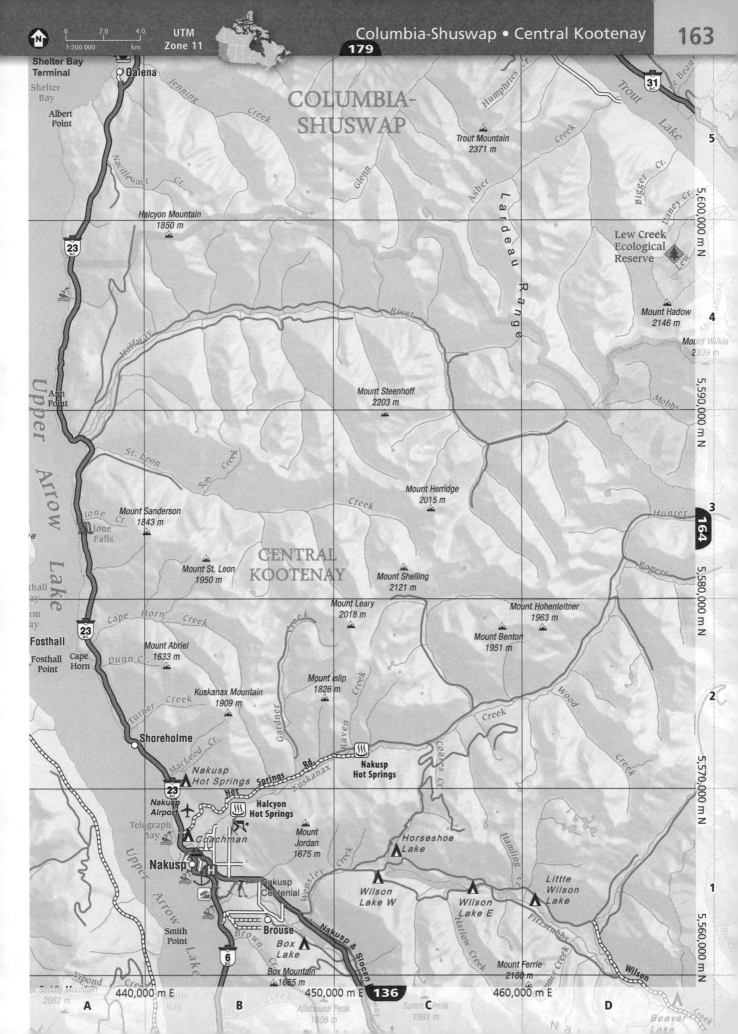

UTM
Zone 11

0 2.0 4.0
1:200 000   km

179

31
B.C.

COLUMBIA-
SHUSWAP

Shelter Bay
Terminal

Galena

Shelter
Bay

Albert
Point

Jenning Creek

Nacillewaet Cr.

Halcyon Mountain
1850 m

Trout Mountain
2371 m

Humphries Cr.

Creek

Bigger Cr.

Daney Cr.

Trout Lake

Lew Creek
Ecological
Reserve

Lew

5,600,000 m N

5

23
B.C.

Ann
Point

Upper Arrow Lake

Halfway

River

Lardeau Range

Asher

Mount Hadow
2146 m

Mount Wilkie
2339 m

4

5,590,000 m N

St. Leon

Mount Steenhoff
2203 m

Mobbs

Sob Creek

Mount Herridge
2015 m

Creek

Hunter

Rogers

164

3

5,580,000 m N

Fosthall

Mount Sanderson
1843 m

Ione Cr.

Ione
Falls

CENTRAL
KOOTENAY

Mount St. Leon
1950 m

Mount Shelling
2121 m

Mount Leary
2018 m

Mount Hohenleitner
1963 m

23
B.C.

Fosthall
Point

Cape
Horn

Cape Horn Creek

Mount Abriel
1633 m

Dunn Cr.

Mount Benton
1951 m

Kuskanax Mountain
1909 m

Turner Creek

Mount Islip
1826 m

Gardner

Raven Creek

Coates Cr.

Wood Creek

2

5,570,000 m N

Shoreholme

MacLeod Cr.

Nakusp
Hot Springs

Springs

Rd.

Kuskanax

Nakusp
Hot Springs

Creek

23
B.C.

Hot

Nakusp
Airport

Halcyon
Hot Springs

Telegraph
Bay

Coachman

Mount
Jordan
1675 m

Wensley Creek

Horseshoe
Lake

Hamling

Little
Wilson
Lake

Nakusp

H

Nakusp
Centenial

Wilson
Lake W

Wilson
Lake E

1

5,560,000 m N

Smith
Point

Upper Arrow Lake

Brouse

Box
Lake

Nakusp & Slocan

Harlow Creek

Fitzstubbs

6
B.C.

Box Mountain
1665 m

Mount Ferrie
2160 m

Wilson

Saddle Mountain
2062 m

Vipond Creek

440,000 m E

450,000 m E

136

Allishouse Peak
1608 m

Summit Peak
1981 m

460,000 m E

Beaver Lake

A

B

C

D

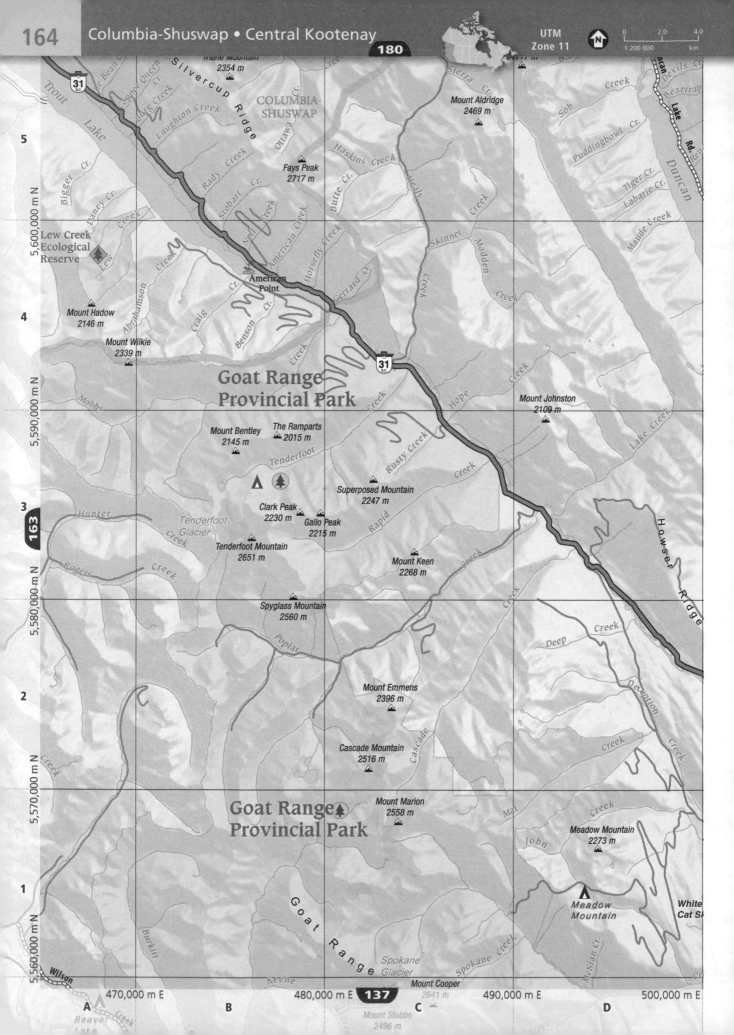

UTM
Zone 11
1:200 000

180

31
B.C

Mune Mountain
2354 m

COLUMBIA-SHUSWAP

Mount Aldridge
2469 m

Fays Peak
2717 m

5

5,600,000 m N

**Lew Creek
Ecological
Reserve**

**American
Point**

4

Mount Hadow
2146 m

Mount Wilkie
2339 m

31
B.C

Goat Range
Provincial Park

5,590,000 m N

Mount Johnston
2109 m

Mount Bentley
2145 m

The Ramparts
2015 m

Tenderfoot

Superposed Mountain
2247 m

3

163

*Tenderfoot
Glacier*

Clark Peak
2230 m

Gallo Peak
2215 m

Tenderfoot Mountain
2651 m

Mount Keen
2268 m

5,580,000 m N

Spyglass Mountain
2560 m

Mount Emmens
2396 m

2

Cascade Mountain
2516 m

Mount Marion
2558 m

Goat Range
Provincial Park

Meadow Mountain
2273 m

1

*Meadow
Mountain*

**White
Cat S**

5,560,000 m N

Wilson

*Spokane
Glacier*

Mount Cooper
2641 m

137

Mount Stubbs
2496 m

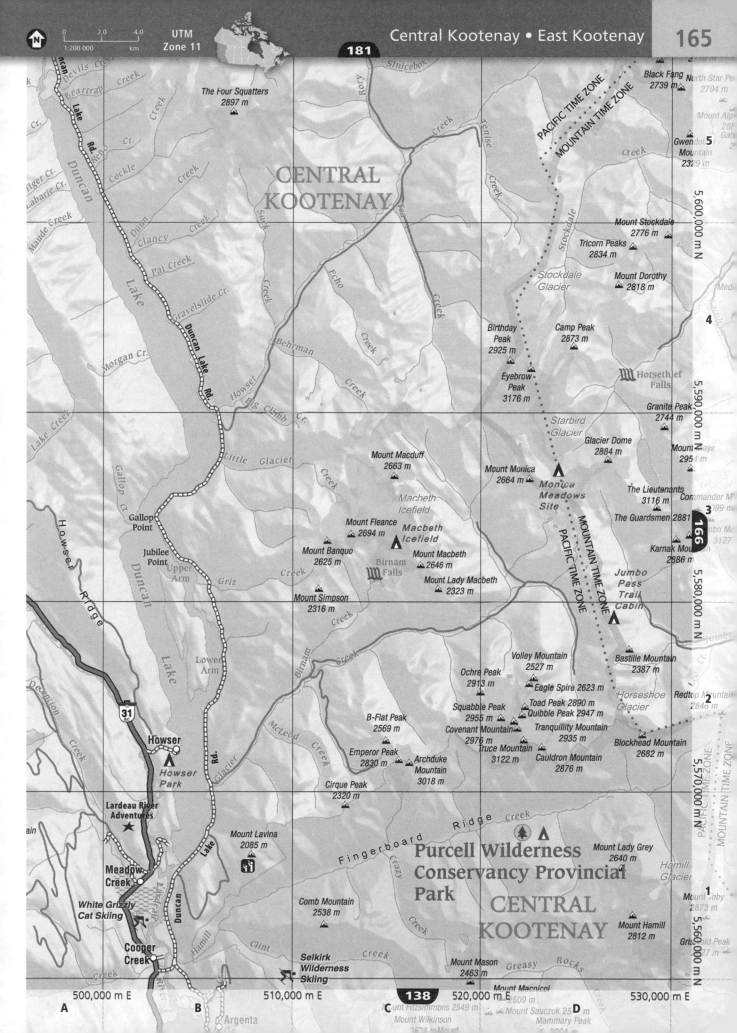

UTM
Zone 11

1:200 000

181

138

CENTRAL
KOOTENAY

PACIFIC TIME ZONE

MOUNTAIN TIME ZONE

Black Fang
2739 m

North Star Pe
2794 m

Mount Alpi
28t
Galt

Gwendolin
Mountain
2329 m

The Four Squatters
2897 m

Mount Stockdale
2776 m

Tricorn Peaks
2834 m

Stockdale
Glacier

Mount Dorothy
2818 m

Birthday
Peak
2925 m

Camp Peak
2873 m

Med

Eyebrow
Peak
3176 m

Horsethief
Falls

Granite Peak
2744 m

Starbird
Glacier

Mount Macduff
2663 m

Mount Monica
2664 m

Monica
Meadows
Site

Glacier Dome
2884 m

Mount
295

Jumbo
Glacier

Macbeth
Icefield

The Lieutenants
3116 m

Commander M
99 m

Mount Fleance
2694 m

Macbeth
Icefield

The Guardsmen 2881

Mount Banquo
2625 m

Mount Macbeth
2646 m

MOUNTAIN TIME ZONE

PACIFIC TIME ZONE

Karnak Mou
2886 m

mbo Glacier
3127

Birnam
Falls

Mount Lady Macbeth
2323 m

Jumbo
Pass
Trail
Cabin

Mount Simpson
2316 m

Upper
Arm

Gallop
Point

Jubilee
Point

Volley Mountain
2527 m

Bastille Mountain
2387 m

Lower
Arm

Ochre Peak
2913 m

Eagle Spire 2623 m

Horseshoe
Glacier

Redtop Mountain
2840 m

Squabble Peak
2955 m

Toad Peak 2890 m
Quibble Peak 2947 m

B-Flat Peak
2569 m

Covenant Mountain
2976 m

Tranquillity Mountain
2935 m

Blockhead Mountain
2682 m

Howser

Howser
Park

Emperor Peak
2830 m

Archduke
Mountain
3018 m

Truce Mountain
3122 m

Cauldron Mountain
2876 m

Cirque Peak
2320 m

Lardeau River
Adventures

Mount Lavina
2085 m

Fingerboard Ridge Creek

Purcell Wilderness
Conservancy Provincial
Park

Mount Lady Grey
2640 m

Hamill
Glacier

Meadow
Creek

CENTRAL
KOOTENAY

Mount Toby
2873 m

White Grizzly
Cat Skiing

Comb Mountain
2538 m

Mount Hamill
2812 m

Gris
27 m

old Peak

Cooper
Creek

Selkirk
Wilderness
Skiing

Mount Mason
2463 m

Greasy Rocks

Mount Macnicol
2509 m

500,000 m E

510,000 m E

520,000 m E

530,000 m E

Argenta

Mount Fitzsimmons 2549 m
Mount Wilkinson

Mount Sauczuk 25 m
Mammary Peak

A

B

C

D

166

5,600,000 m N

5,590,000 m N

5,580,000 m N

5,570,000 m N

5,560,000 m N

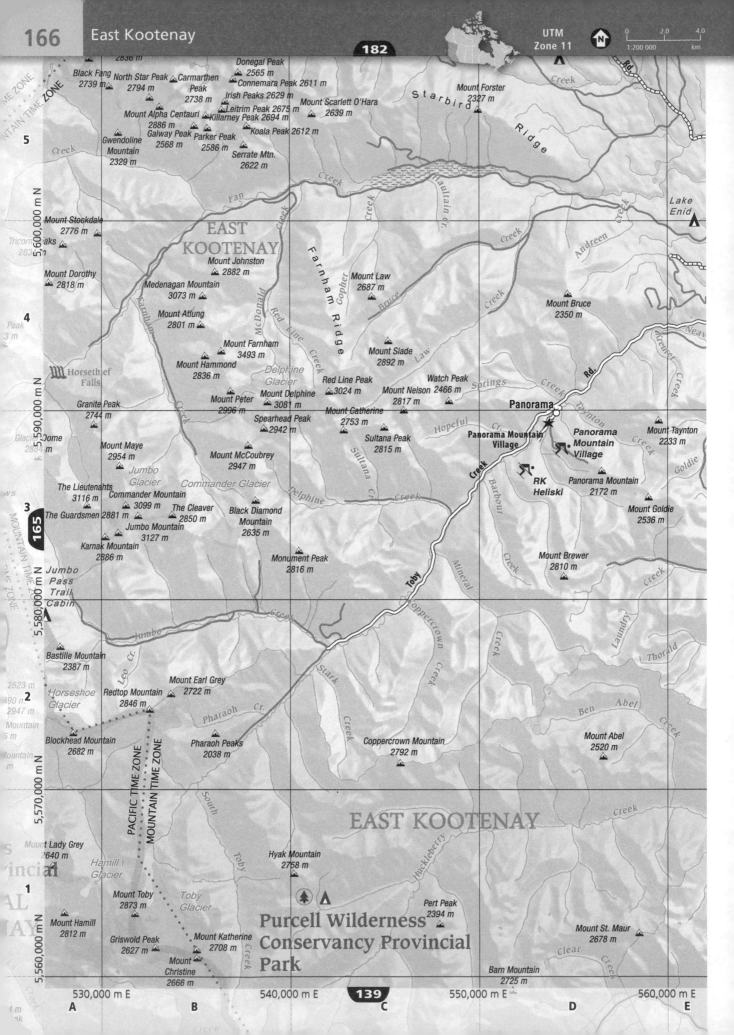

182

UTM
Zone 11

1:200 000

0   2.0   4.0

km

5

MOUNTAIN TIME ZONE

2836 m

Black Fang
2739 m

North Star Peak
2794 m

Carmarthen
Peak
2738 m

Donegal Peak
2565 m

Connemara Peak 2611 m

Irish Peaks 2629 m

Mount Scarlett O'Hara
2639 m

Mount Alpha Centauri
2886 m

Leitrim Peak 2675 m

Killarney Peak 2694 m

Galway Peak
2568 m

Parker Peak
2586 m

Koala Peak 2612 m

Gwendoline
Mountain
2329 m

Serrate Mtn.
2622 m

Starbird

Ridge

Mount Forster
2327 m

Lake
Enid

Creek

Haultain Cr.

Creek

Andreen

**EAST
KOOTENAY**

Mount Stockdale
2776 m

5,600,000 m N

Tricom Peaks
2836 m

Mount Dorothy
2818 m

Medenagan Mountain
3073 m

Mount Johnston
2882 m

Mount Law
2687 m

Mount Bruce
2350 m

Creek

Fan

Creek

Creek

Gopher

Farnham Ridge

Mount Atlung
2801 m

McDonald

Red Line Creek

Bruce

Law

Mount Slade
2892 m

Creek

Springs

Rd.

Krenel Creek

Neav

Peak
3 m

4

MOUNTAIN TIME ZONE

Mount Farnham
3493 m

Mount Hammond
2836 m

Horsethief
Falls

Delphine
Glacier

Mount Delphine
3081 m

Red Line Peak
3024 m

Watch Peak
2466 m

Mount Nelson
2817 m

Hopeful

Creek

Taynton

Panorama

Granite Peak
2744 m

Mount Peter
2996 m

Mount Catherine
2753 m

**Panorama Mountain
Village**

**Panorama
Mountain
Village**

Mount Taynton
2233 m

5,590,000 m N

Dome
2804 m

Spearhead Peak
2942 m

Mount Maye
2954 m

Mount McCoubrey
2947 m

Sultana Peak
2815 m

Sultana Cr.

Creek

Creek

Barbour

Creek

**RK
Heliski**

Panorama Mountain
2172 m

Mount Goldie
2536 m

Goldie

Jumbo
Glacier

Commander Glacier

3

165

The Lieutenahts
3116 m

The Guardsmen 2881 m

Commander Mountain
3099 m

The Cleaver
2850 m

Black Diamond
Mountain
2635 m

Delphine

Creek

Jumbo Mountain
3127 m

Karnak Mountain
2886 m

Monument Peak
2816 m

Mineral

Mount Brewer
2810 m

Jumbo
Pass
Trail
Cabin

5,580,000 m N

Creek

Toby

Coppercrown Creek

Laundry

Thorald

Bastille Mountain
2387 m

Jumbo Cr.

Creek

Leo Cr.

Stark

Creek

2

MOUNTAIN TIME ZONE

PACIFIC TIME ZONE

2623 m

390 n.

2947 m

Mountain
5 m

Horseshoe
Glacier

Redtop Mountain
2846 m

Mount Earl Grey
2722 m

Pharaoh
Cr.

Coppercrown Mountain
2792 m

Ben Abel

Mount Abel
2520 m

Creek

Mountain
m

Blockhead Mountain
2682 m

Pharaoh Peaks
2038 m

5,570,000 m N

South

Toby

Creek

Huckleberry

EAST KOOTENAY

Creek

1

Mount Lady Grey
2640 m

Hamill
Glacier

Hyak Mountain
2758 m

Pert Peak
2394 m

Mount St. Maur
2678 m

Mount Toby
2873 m

Toby
Glacier

Mount Hamill
2812 m

Griswold Peak
2627 m

Mount Katherine
2708 m

Mount
Christine
2666 m

**Purcell Wilderness
Conservancy Provincial
Park**

Barn Mountain
2725 m

Clear

Creek

5,560,000 m N

530,000 m E

540,000 m E

139

550,000 m E

560,000 m E

A   **B**   **C**   **D**   **E**

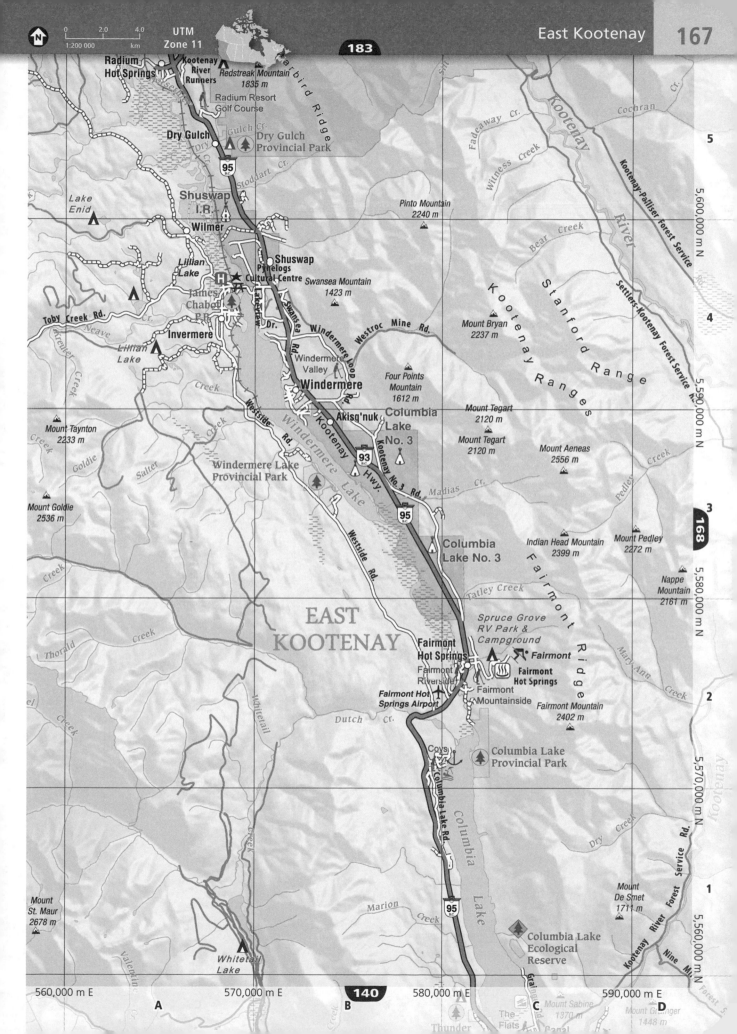

UTM
Zone 11

1:200 000

183

5

Radium
Hot Springs
Kootenay
River
Runners
Redstreak Mountain
1835 m
Radium Resort
Golf Course

Dry Gulch
Dry Gulch
Provincial Park

95

Shuswap
I.R.

Lake
Enid

Wilmer

Pinto Mountain
2240 m

Fadeaway Cr.

Witness Creek

Bear Creek

Kootenay

Kootenay-Palliser Forest Service

Settlers-Kootenay Forest Service

River

5,600,000 m N

Lillian
Lake

Shuswap
Pynelogs
Cultural Centre

Swansea Mountain
1423 m

James
Chabot
P.P.

Invermere

Lillian
Lake

Toby Creek Rd.

Windermere
Loop
Rd.

Windermere
Valley

Westroc Mine Rd.

Mount Bryan
2237 m

Kootenay Range

Stanford Range

Kootenay Ranges

4

5,590,000 m N

Windermere

Four Points
Mountain
1612 m

Mount Taynton
2233 m

Westside
Rd.

Windermere Lake
Provincial Park

Akisq'nuk

Columbia
Lake
No. 3

93

Kootenay No. 3 Rd.

95

Mount Tegart
2120 m

Mount Tegart
2120 m

Mount Aeneas
2556 m

Pedley Cr.

168

3

5,580,000 m N

Mount Goldie
2536 m

Goldie Creek

Salter Creek

Westside Rd.

Columbia
Lake No. 3

Madias Cr.

Indian Head Mountain
2399 m

Mount Pedley
2272 m

Nappe
Mountain
2161 m

Fairmont Ridge

EAST
KOOTENAY

Tatley Creek

Spruce Grove
RV Park &
Campground

Fairmont

Mary Ann Creek

2

5,570,000 m N

Thorald Creek

Fairmont
Hot Springs

Fairmont
Riverside

Fairmont Hot
Springs Airport

Fairmont
Hot Springs

Fairmont
Mountainside

Fairmont Mountain
2402 m

Whitetail Creek

Dutch Cr.

Coys

Columbia Lake Rd.

Columbia Lake
Provincial Park

Columbia Lake

Mount
St. Maur
2678 m

Whitetail
Lake

Marion Creek

95

Mount
De Smet
1711 m

Kootenay River Forest Service Rd.

Nine Mi.

1

5,560,000 m N

560,000 m E

A

140

570,000 m E

B

580,000 m E

Mount Sabine
1970 m

C

590,000 m E

Mount Granger
1448 m

D

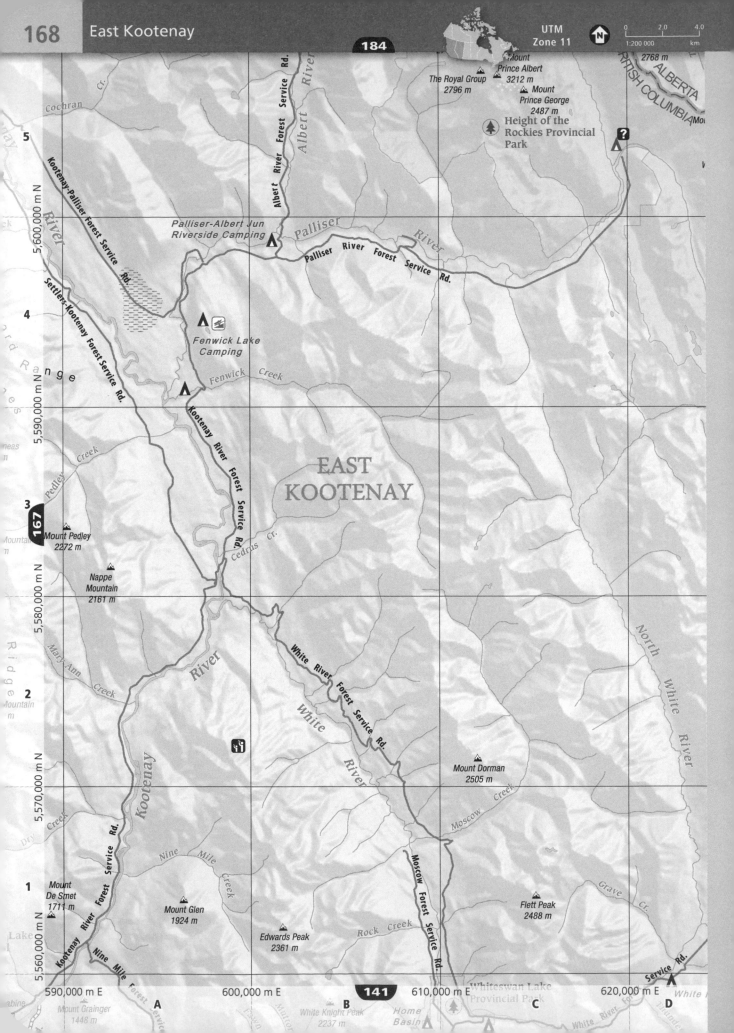

UTM
Zone 11

1:200 000

590,000 m E   600,000 m E   610,000 m E   620,000 m E

5,600,000 m N
5,590,000 m N
5,580,000 m N
5,570,000 m N
5,560,000 m N

**EAST
KOOTENAY**

The Royal Group
2796 m

Mount
Prince Albert
3212 m

Mount
Prince George
2487 m

2768 m

ALBERTA

BRITISH COLUMBIA

Height of the
Rockies Provincial
Park

Palliser-Albert Jun
Riverside Camping

Palliser   River   Forest   Service   Rd.

Albert   River   Forest   Service   Rd.

Kootenay-Palliser Forest Service Rd.

Settlers-Kootenay Forest Service Rd.

Fenwick Lake
Camping

Fenwick   Creek

Kootenay River Forest Service Rd.

Pedley   Creek

Mount Pedley
2272 m

Nappe
Mountain
2161 m

Cedrus   Cr.

White   River   Forest   Service   Rd.

White   River

North   White   River

Mary Ann   Creek

Kootenay   River

Mount Dorman
2505 m

Moscow   Creek

Moscow   Forest   Service   Rd.

Dry   Creek

Nine   Mile   Creek

Kootenay   River   Forest   Service   Rd.

Mount
De Smet
1711 m

Mount Glen
1924 m

Edwards Peak
2361 m

Rock   Creek

Flett Peak
2488 m

Grave   Cr.

Nine   Mile   Forest   Service

Mount Grainger
1448 m

White Knight Peak
2237 m

Home
Basin

Whiteswan Lake
Provincial Park

Service Rd.

White

Cochran   Cr.

Range

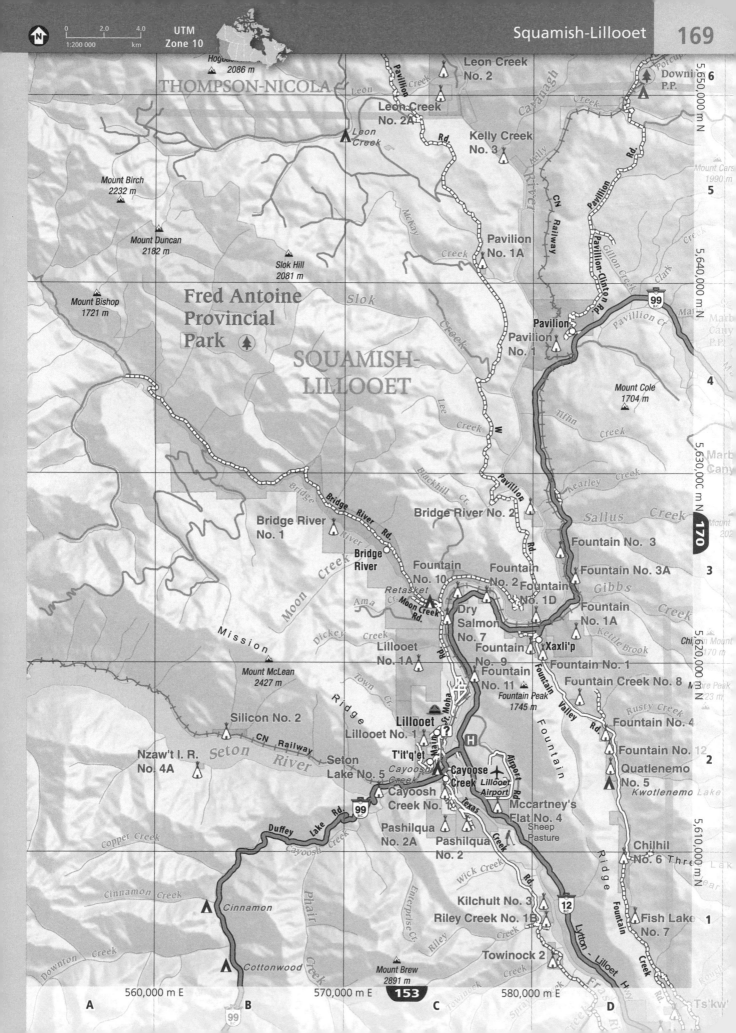

THOMPSON-NICOLA

Hogback 2086 m

Leon Creek No. 2

Leon Creek No. 2A

Leon Creek

Downing P.P.

Kelly Creek No. 3

Mount Birch 2232 m

Mount Duncan 2182 m

Slok Hill 2081 m

Pavilion No. 1A

Mount Cole 1704 m

Mount Bishop 1721 m

Fred Antoine Provincial Park

Pavilion

Pavilion No. 1

SQUAMISH-LILLOOET

Marb Cany P.P.

Bridge River No. 2

Fountain No. 3

Sallus Creek

Bridge River Rd.

Bridge River No. 1

Fountain No. 3A

Fountain No. 1D

Bridge River

Fountain No. 10

Fountain No. 2

Fountain No. 1A

Retasket Cr.

Moon Creek Rd.

Dry Salmon No. 7

Gibbs Creek

Kettle Brook

Lillooet No. 1A

Fountain No. 9

Xaxli'p

Fountain No. 1

Ama

Fountain No. 11

Fountain Creek No. 8

Mount McLean 2427 m

Fountain Peak 1745 m

Fountain No. 4

Silicon No. 2

Lillooet

Lillooet No. 1

Rusty Creek

Seton River

CN Railway

Seton Lake No. 5

T'it'q'et

Cayoosh Creek

Fountain No. 12

Nzaw't I. R. No. 4A

Cayoose Creek

Lillooet Airport

Quatlenemo No. 5

Kwotlenemo Lake

Cayoosh Creek No. 1

McCartney's Flat No. 4

Duffey Lake Rd.

Pashilqua No. 2A

Pashilqua No. 2

Sheep Pasture

Chilhil No. 6 Three

Cinnamon Creek

Cinnamon

Kilchult No. 3

Riley Creek No. 1B

Fish Lake No. 7

Cottonwood

Mount Brew 2891 m

Towinock 2

Lytton - Lillooet Hwy

Fraser R.

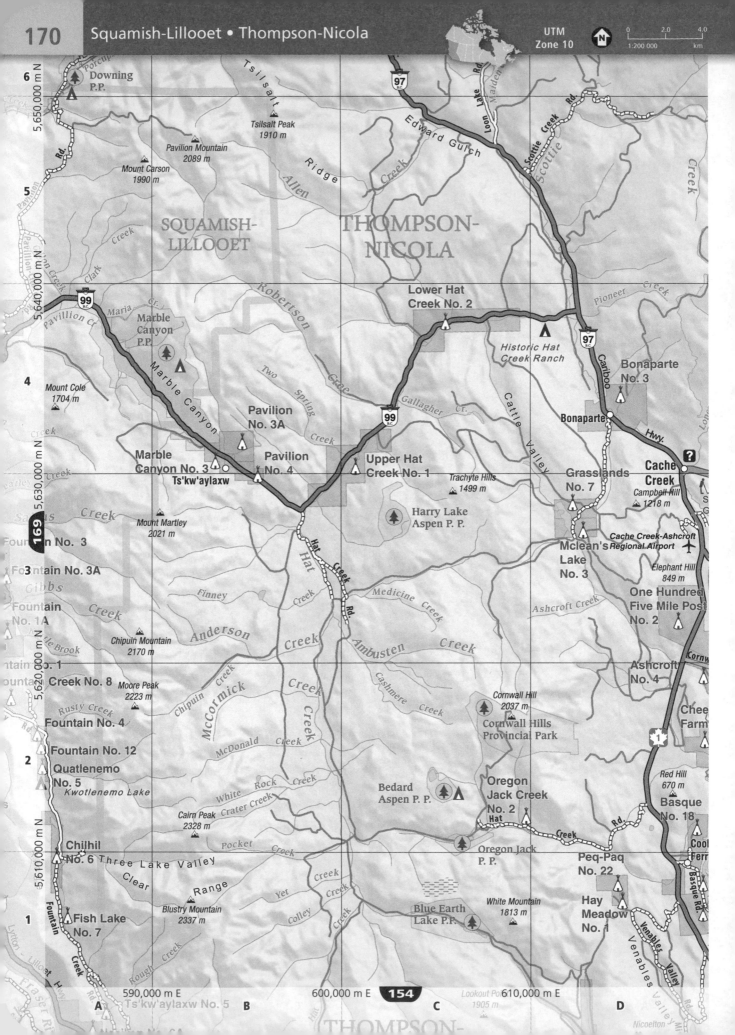

Downing
P.P.

Tsilsalt Peak
1910 m

Pavilion Mountain
2089 m

Mount Carson
1990 m

**SQUAMISH-
LILLOOET**

**THOMPSON-
NICOLA**

Lower Hat
Creek No. 2

Historic Hat
Creek Ranch

Bonaparte
No. 3

Mount Cole
1704 m

Marble
Canyon
P.P.

Pavilion
No. 3A

Bonaparte

Cache
Creek

Campbell Hill
1218 m

Marble
Canyon No. 3
Ts'kw'aylaxw

Pavilion
No. 4

Upper Hat
Creek No. 1

Trachyte Hills
1499 m

Grasslands
No. 7

Cache Creek-Ashcroft
Regional Airport

169

Mount Martley
2021 m

Harry Lake
Aspen P. P.

Mclean's
Lake
No. 3

Elephant Hill
849 m

Fountain No. 3

Fountain No. 3A

Gibbs

Fountain
No. 1A

Chipuin Mountain
2170 m

One Hundred
Five Mile Post
No. 2

Ashcroft
No. 4

Creek No. 8

Moore Peak
2223 m

Cornwall Hill
2037 m

Chee
Farm

Fountain No. 4

Fountain No. 12

Quatlenemo
No. 5

Kwotlenemo Lake

Cornwall Hills
Provincial Park

Cairn Peak
2328 m

Bedard
Aspen P. P.

Oregon
Jack Creek
No. 2

Red Hill
670 m

Basque
No. 18

Chilhil
No. 6

Three Lake Valley

Oregon Jack
P. P.

Peq-Paq
No. 22

Cool
Ferr

Blustry Mountain
2337 m

Blue Earth
Lake P.P.

White Mountain
1813 m

Hay
Meadow
No. 1

Fish Lake
No. 7

Lookout Po
1905 m

THOMPSON-

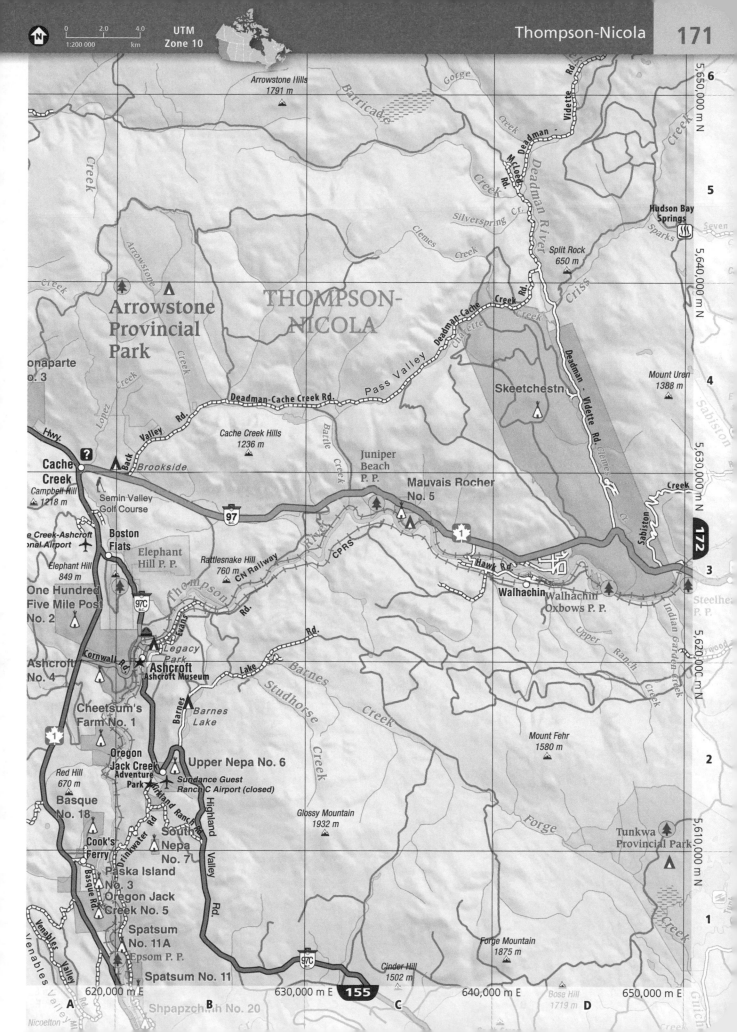

UTM
Zone 10

0   2.0   4.0
1:200 000   km

Arrowstone Hills
1791 m

Gorge

Barricade

Creek

Vidette Rd.

Deadman - McLoed

Rd.

Creek

Deadman River

Criss

Hudson Bay
Springs

Sparks

Seven

Silverspring Cr.

Split Rock
650 m

Mount Uren
1388 m

THOMPSON-
NICOLA

Clemes

Creek

Deadman-Cache

Creek

Rd.

Charette

Pass Valley

Deadman - Vidette Rd.

Clemes

Skeetchestn

Arrowstone
Provincial
Park

Creek

Arrowstone

Creek

Lopez

Creek

Deadman-Cache Creek Rd.

Battle

Creek

Cache Creek Hills
1236 m

Sabiston

Creek

Valley   Rd.

Brookside

Back

Juniper
Beach
P. P.

Mauvais Rocher
No. 5

Sabiston

Cr.

172

Creek

Cache
Creek

Campbell Hill
1218 m

Semin Valley
Golf Course

97
B.C.

River

CPRS

CN Railway

Hawk Rd.

e Creek-Ashcroft
onal Airport

Boston
Flats

Elephant
Hill P. P.

Rattlesnake Hill
760 m

Walhachin

Walhachin
Oxbows P. P.

Steelhe

P. P.

Elephant Hill
849 m

Thompson

Rd.

Evans

Rd.

Upper

Ranch

Indian Garden Creek

One Hundred
Five Mile Post
No. 2

97C
B.C.

Legacy
Park

Creek

Ashcroft
No. 4

Cornwall Rd.

Ashcroft
Ashcroft Museum

Lake

Barnes

Studhorse

Creek

Mount Fehr
1580 m

1

Cheetsum's
Farm No. 1

Barnes

Barnes
Lake

Red Hill
670 m

Oregon
Jack Creek
Adventure
Park

Upper Nepa No. 6

Sundance Guest
Ranch C Airport (closed)

Glossy Mountain
1932 m

Forge

Tunkwa
Provincial Park

Basque
No. 18

Drinkwater Rd.

Kirkland Ranch Rd.

South
Nepa
No. 7

Highland

Cook's
Ferry

Paska Island
No. 3

Oregon Jack
Creek No. 5

Valley

Rd.

Spatsum
No. 11A

Epsom P. P.

Venables Valley

Venables

Valley

Spatsum No. 11

Forge Mountain
1875 m

97C
B.C.

Cinder Hill
1502 m

Bose Hill
1719 m

155

Nicoelton

Shpapzchiih No. 20

620,000 m E

630,000 m E

640,000 m E

650,000 m E

5,650,000 m N

5,640,000 m N

5,630,000 m N

5,620,000 m N

5,610,000 m N

6

5

4

3

2

1

A   B   C   D

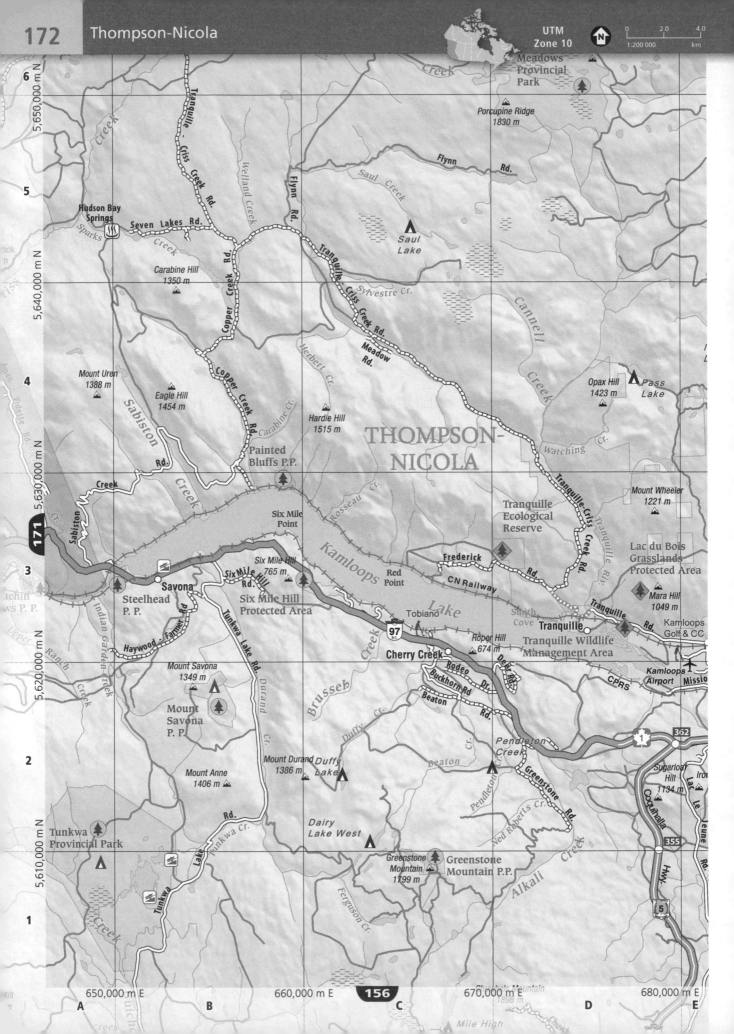

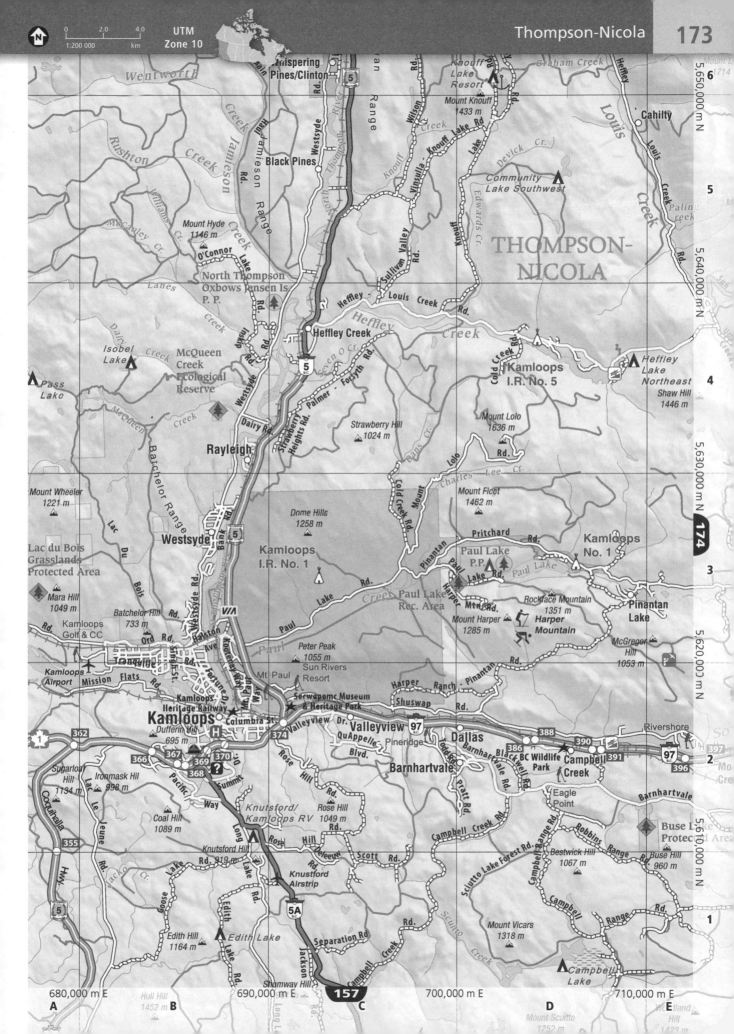

N

UTM
Zone 10

1:200 000

0   2.0   4.0
km

Wentworth

Whispering
Pines/Clinton

5

Knouff
Lake
Resort

Graham Creek

Heffley

Mount
1714

6

Rushton

Creek

Jamieson

Creek

Williams

Wilson

Knouff

Mount Knouff
1433 m

Knouff - Lake Rd.

Vinsulla -

Cahilty

Louis

Creek

Paling
reek

5

Black Pines

Westsyde

North Thompson

Rd.

Sullivan Valley

Sullivan

Cr.

Community
Lake Southwest

Devick

Cr.

THOMPSON-
NICOLA

Mount Hyde
1146 m

McCauley Cr.

O'Connor

North Thompson
Oxbows Jensen Is.
P. P.

Lanes

Creek

Heffley - Louis Creek

Rd.

Edwards Cr.

Knouff

5,650,000 m N

5,640,000 m N

Isobel
Lake

Creek

McQueen
Creek
Ecological
Reserve

Heffley Creek

5
B.C.

Heffley

Creek

Cold Creek

Kamloops
I.R. No. 5

Heffley
Lake
Northeast

Shaw Hill
1446 m

4

Pass
Lake

McQueen

Creek

Westside

Rd.

Insulp

Dairy Rd.

Strawberry
Heights Rd.

Palmer - Forsyth Rd.

Seven O Cr.

Strawberry Hill
1024 m

Dans. Cr.

Mount Lolo
1636 m

Rd.

Mount Wheeler
1221 m

Rayleigh

Lolo

Charles   Lee   Cr.

Mount Ficot
1462 m

5,630,000 m N

174

Lac du Bois
Grasslands
Protected Area

Batchelor Range

Lac

Du

Westsyde Rd.

Westsyde

5
B.C.

Bank Rd.

Kamloops
I.R. No. 1

Dome Hills
1258 m

Cold Creek Rd.

Mount

Pritchard

Paul Lake
P.P.

Rd.

Kamloops
No. 1

Mara Hill
1049 m

Bois

Batcholor Hill
733 m

Rd.

Lake

Creek

Rd.

Pinantan

Paul
Lake

Paul Lake
Rec. Area

Mtn. Rd.

Paul Lake

Rockface Mountain
1351 m

Pinantan
Lake

3

Kamloops
Golf & CC

Ord Rd.

Ralston

Singh St.

VIA

Paul

Creek

Paul

Peter Peak
1055 m

Mtn. Rd.

Mount Harper
1285 m

Harper
Mountain

McGregor
Hill
1053 m

5,620,003 m N

Rd.

Kamloops
Airport

Tranquille

Mission   Flats

Rd.

Kootenay Way

Fortune Dr.

Mt. Paul

Sun Rivers
Resort

Secwepemc Museum
& Heritage Park

Harper   Ranch - Pinantan

Shuswap

Rd.

2

Kamloops
Heritage Railway

Kamloops

1

362

Dufferin
695 m

366

367

370

369

368

H

Columbia St.

374

Valleyview

Pacific

Way

Summit

Dr.

QuAppelle
Blvd.

Valleyview

Pineridge

97
B.C.

Dallas

Barnhartvale Rd.

386

Black

388

BC Wildlife
Park

Todd Rd.

390

Campbell
Creek

391

Rivershore

97
B.C.

396

397

Mo
Cre

Sugarloaf
Hill
1134 m

Ironmask Hill
998 m

Coal Hill
1089 m

Pacific

Rose   Hill

Barnhartvale

Pratt Rd.

Bestwick Hill
1067 m

Campbell   Range Rd.

Eagle
Point

Barnhartvale

Buse Lake
Protect   Area

Buse Hill
960 m

1

355

5

Coquihalla

Lac Le Jeune Rd.

Goose Lake Rd.

Jacko

Cr.

Knutsford/
Kamloops RV

Knutsford Hill
Rd. 919 m

Edith

Lake Rd.

Rose Hill
1049 m

Rose   Hill   Rd.

Deleeuw

Scott   Rd.

Knutsford
Airstrip

5A
B.C.

Campbell   Creek   Rd.

Scutto Lake Forest Rd.

Robbins   Range

Campbell

Range   Rd.

1

Edith Hill
1164 m

Edith Lake

Separation Rd.

Shumway Hill

157

Jackson   Rd.

Campbell   Creek

Mount Vicars
1318 m

Scutto   Creek

Campbell
Lake

Mount Scuitto
1252 m

Wetland
Hill

680,000 m E

690,000 m E

700,000 m E

710,000 m E

A

B

C

D

E

5,610,000 m N

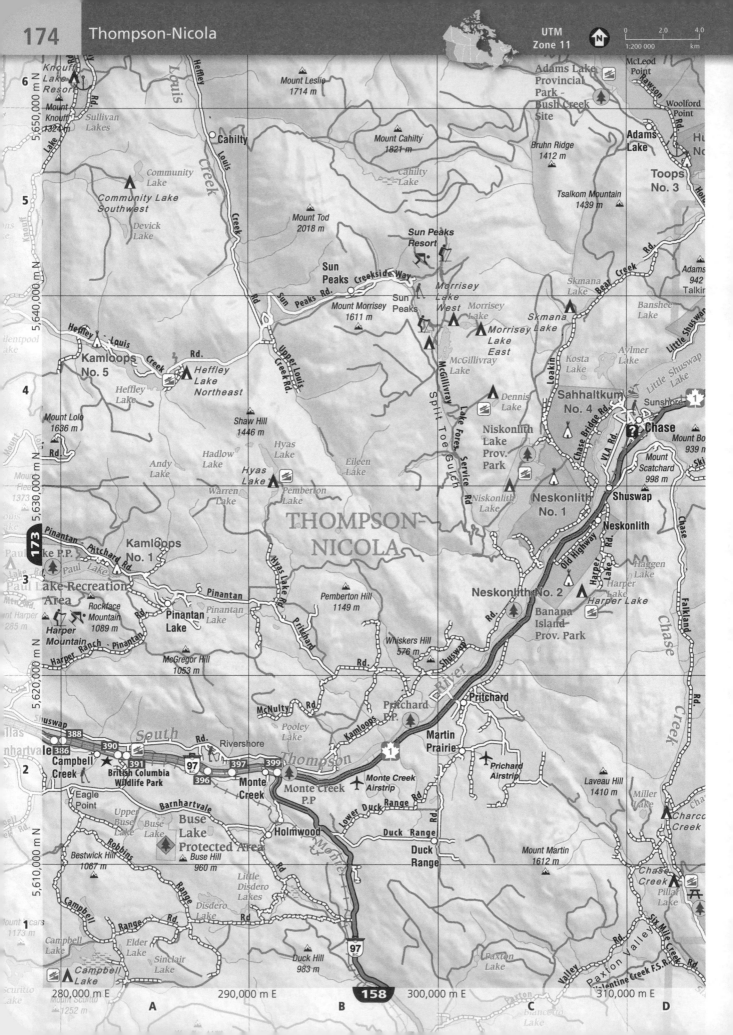

UTM
Zone 11

1:200 000

0   2.0   4.0
km

THOMPSON-NICOLA

Knouff Lake Resort
Mount Knouff 1324 m
Sullivan Lakes
Community Lake
Community Lake Southwest
Devick Lake
Mount Lolo 1636 m
Kamloops No. 5
Heffley Lake
Heffley Lake Northeast
Shaw Hill 1446 m
Andy Lake
Hadlow Lake
Hyas Lake
Warren Lake
Hyas Lake
Pemberton Lake
Eileen Lake

Cahilty
Mount Leslie 1714 m
Mount Cahilty 1821 m
Cahilty Lake
Mount Tod 2018 m
Sun Peaks Resort
Sun Peaks
Creekside Way
Mount Morrisey 1611 m
Sun Peaks
Morrisey Lake West
Morrisey Lake
Morrisey Lake East
McGillivray Lake
Dennis Lake

Adams Lake Provincial Park - Bush Creek Site
McLeod Point
Woolford Point
Rawson Point
Adams Lake
Toops No. 3
Bruhn Ridge 1412 m
Tsalkom Mountain 1439 m
Skmana Lake
Skmana Lake
Banshee Lake
Kosta Lake
Aylmer Lake
Little Shuswap Lake
Sunshore
Chase
Mount Scatchard 998 m

Niskonlith Lake Prov. Park
Sahhaltkum No. 4
Niskonlith Lake
Neskonlith No. 1
Shuswap
Neskonlith

Kamloops No. 1
Pinantan
Kamloops No. 1
Pinantan Lake
Pinantan
Pinantan Lake
McGregor Hill 1053 m
Pemberton Hill 1149 m
Whiskers Hill 576 m

Neskonlith No. 2
Banana Island Prov. Park
Harper Lake
Harper Lake
Haggen Lake

Paul Lake P.P.
Paul Lake
Paul Lake Recreation Area
Rockface Mountain 1089 m
Harper Mountain
Harper Ranch - Pinantan

McNulty
Pooley Lake
Pritchard
Pritchard P.P.
Pritchard
Martin Prairie

Campbell Creek
British Columbia Wildlife Park
Rivershore
Monte Creek
Monte Creek P.P
Monte Creek Airstrip
Prichard Airstrip
Laveau Hill 1410 m
Miller Lake

Eagle Point
Barnhartvale
Upper Buse Lake
Buse Lake
Buse Lake Protected Area
Buse Hill 960 m
Holmwood
Lower Duck Range
Duck Range
Duck Range
Mount Martin 1612 m

Bestwick Hill 1067 m
Robbins
Little Disdero Lakes
Disdero Lake

Campbell Lake
Elder Lake
Sinclair Lake
Duck Hill 983 m
Paxton Lake
Chase Creek
Pillar Lake
Charco Creek

173
158
97
388 390 391 396 397 399
97
1

280,000 m E   290,000 m E   300,000 m E   310,000 m E
A   B   C   D

6 N 5,650,000 m N
5 5,640,000 m N
4 5,630,000 m N
3 5,620,000 m N
2 5,610,000 m N
1

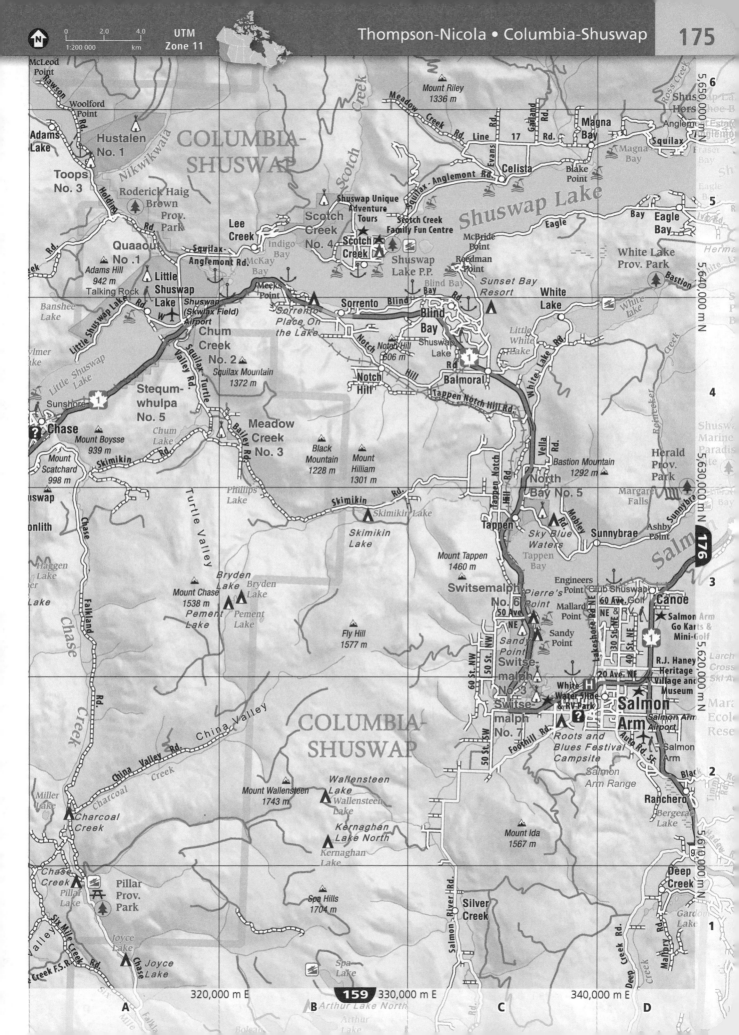

UTM
Zone 11

1:200 000

0   2.0   4.0
km

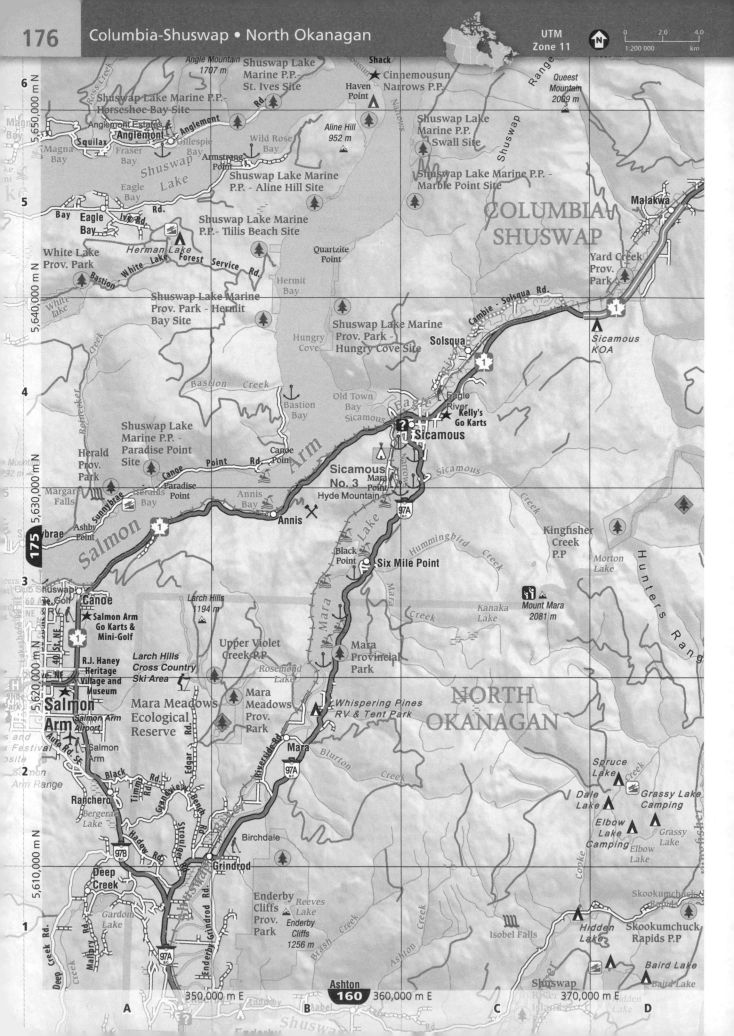

6

5,650,000 m N

Angle Mountain
1707 m

Shuswap Lake
Marine P.P.-
St. Ives Site

Shack

★ Cinnemousun
Narrows P.P.

Queest
Mountain
2009 m

Shuswap Lake Marine P.P.-
Horseshoe Bay Site

Haven
Point

Anglemont Estates

Anglemont

Anglemont

Squilax

Gillespie
Bay

Shuswap
Lake

Magna
Bay

Fraser
Bay

Armstrong
Point

Wild Rose
Bay

Aline Hill
952 m

Shuswap Lake
Marine P.P.-
Swall Site

Malakwa

5

5,640,000 m N

Eagle
Bay

Eagle
Bay

Ivy
Rd.

Shuswap Lake Marine
P.P.- Aline Hill Site

Shuswap Lake Marine P.P. -
Marble Point Site

**COLUMBIA-
SHUSWAP**

Yard Creek
Prov.
Park

White Lake
Prov. Park

Herman Lake
Forest

White Lake

Service
Rd.

Shuswap Lake Marine
P.P.- Tiilis Beach Site

Quartzite
Point

Cambie - Solsqua Rd.

Sicamous
KOA

Bastion

White
Lake

Shuswap Lake Marine
Prov. Park - Hermit
Bay Site

Hermit
Bay

Hungry
Cove

Shuswap Lake Marine
Prov. Park -
Hungry Cove Site

Solsqua

4

Creek

Bastion
Creek

Old Town
Bay
Sicamous

Bastion
Bay

Eagle
River
Kelly's
Go Karts

Sicamous

175

5,630,000 m N

Herald
Prov.
Park

Shuswap Lake
Marine P.P. -
Paradise Point
Site

Canoe
Point Rd.

Canoe
Point

Sicamous
No. 3

Hyde Mountain

Mara
Point

97A
B.C.

Kingfisher
Creek
P.P

Morton
Lake

Hunters Range

Margaret
Falls

Mountain
92 m

Sunnybrae

Heralds
Bay

Herald's
Point

Paradise
Point

Annis
Bay

Annis

Black
Point

Six Mile Point

Hummingbird

Creek

Mount Mara
2081 m

Ashby
Point

Salmon

Sunnybrae

3

5,620,000 m N

Club Shuswap
Golf
RV

Canoe

Larch Hills
1194 m

Mara
Creek

Kanaka
Lake

★ Salmon Arm
Go Karts &
Mini-Golf

R.J. Haney
Heritage
Village and
Museum

Larch Hills
Cross Country
Ski Area

Upper Violet
Creek P.P

Rosemond
Lake

Mara
Provincial
Park

**NORTH
OKANAGAN**

Salmon
Arm

Salmon Arm
Airport

Mara Meadows
Ecological
Reserve

Mara
Meadows
Prov.
Park

Whispering Pines
RV & Tent Park

Spruce
Lake

2

5,610,000 m N

Auto Rd. SE

Salmon
Arm
Range

Rancher

Black
Rd.

Timm
Rd.

Edgar
Rd.

Grandview Bench

Riverside Rd.

Shuswap River

Mara

97A
B.C.

Blurton

Creek

Dale
Lake

Grassy Lake
Camping

Bergeral
Lake

Birchdale

Elbow
Lake
Camping

Grassy
Lake

Deep Creek Rd.

Malibry
Rd.

Gardom
Lake

Deep
Creek

97B
B.C.

Hadow
Rd.

Grindrod

Enderby Grindrod Rd.

Grindrod
Rd.

Elbow
Lake

Skookumchuck
Rapids

1

Deep Creek Rd.

Creek

97A
B.C.

Enderby
Cliffs
Prov.
Park

Reeves
Lake

Enderby
Cliffs
1256 m

Brash Creek

Cooke Creek

Ashton Creek

Isobel Falls

Hidden
Lake

Skookumchuck
Rapids P.P

Shuswap
River

Baird Lake

Baird
Lake

Ashton
160

350,000 m E   360,000 m E   370,000 m E

A   **B**   **C**   **D**

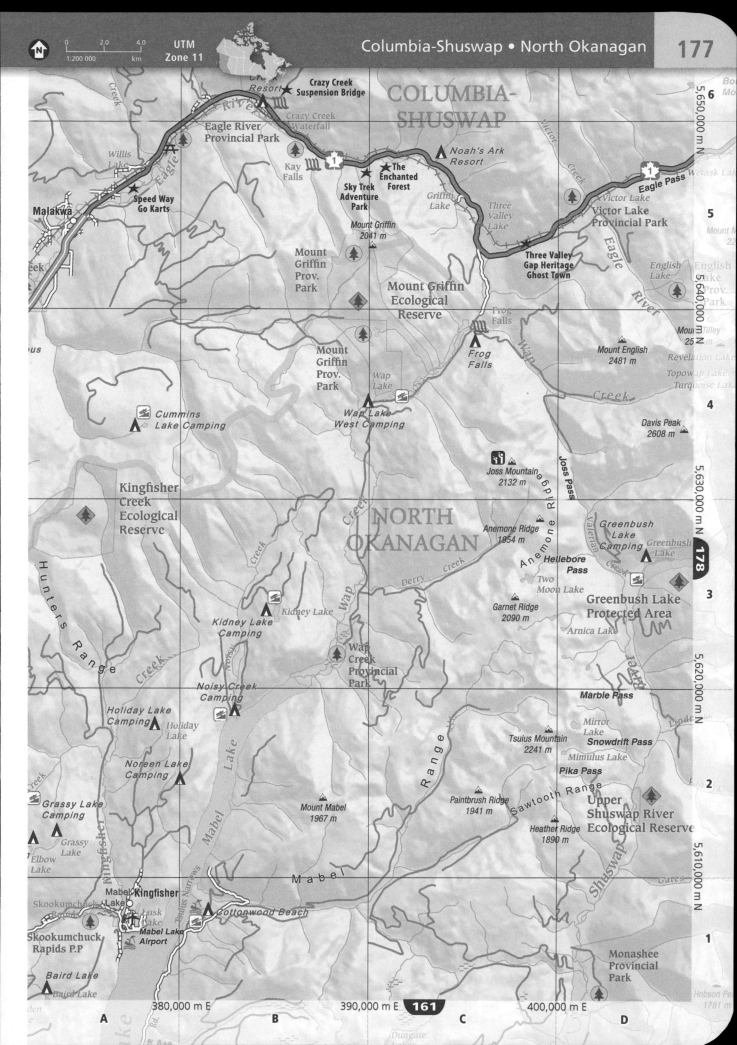

0   2.0   4.0
1:200 000   km
UTM
Zone 11

N

**COLUMBIA-
SHUSWAP**

6

Crazy Creek
Suspension Bridge

Crazy Creek
Waterfall

Eagle River
Provincial Park

Noah's Ark
Resort

Eagle Pass

Kay
Falls

Sky Trek
Adventure
Park

The
Enchanted
Forest

Griffin
Lake

Three
Valley
Lake

Victor Lake

Victor Lake
Provincial Park

5

Willis
Lake

Speed Way
Go Karts

Malakwa

Mount Griffin
2041 m

Mount
Griffin
Prov.
Park

Three Valley
Gap Heritage
Ghost Town

English
Lake

English
Lake
Prov.
Park

Mount M
22

5,640,000 m N

Mount Griffin
Ecological
Reserve

Frog
Falls

Mount English
2481 m

Mou
25

Tilley
m

Revelation Lake

Mount
Griffin
Prov.
Park

Frog
Falls

Wap
Lake

Topowap Lake
Turquoise Lake

Creek

4

Wap Lake
West Camping

Davis Peak
2608 m

Cummins
Lake Camping

Joss Mountain
2132 m

Joss Pass

Valerian

Greenbush
Lake
Camping

Greenbush
Lake

178

Kingfisher
Creek
Ecological
Reserve

**NORTH
OKANAGAN**

Anemone Ridge
1954 m

Anemone Ridge

Hellebore
Pass

3

Two
Moon Lake

Greenbush Lake
Protected Area

Derry   Creek

Garnet Ridge
2090 m

Arnica Lake

5,620,000 m N

Kidney Lake
Camping

Kidney Lake

Wap
Creek
Provincial
Park

Marble Pass

Noisy Creek
Camping

Mirror
Lake

Holiday Lake
Camping

Holiday
Lake

Tsuius Mountain
2241 m

Snowdrift Pass

Mimulus Lake

Noreen Lake
Camping

Pika Pass

Grassy Lake
Camping

Mount Mabel
1967 m

Paintbrush Ridge
1941 m

Sawtooth Range

Upper
Shuswap River
Ecological Reserve

Grassy
Lake

Heather Ridge
1890 m

Elbow
Lake

Mabel

Lake

Mabel

5,610,000 m N

Skookumchuck
Lake

Mabel Kingfisher

Lusk
Lake

Cottonwood Beach

Mabel Lake
Airport

Skookumchuck
Rapids P.P

Baird Lake

Monashee
Provincial
Park

1

Baird Lake

Hobson P
1781 m

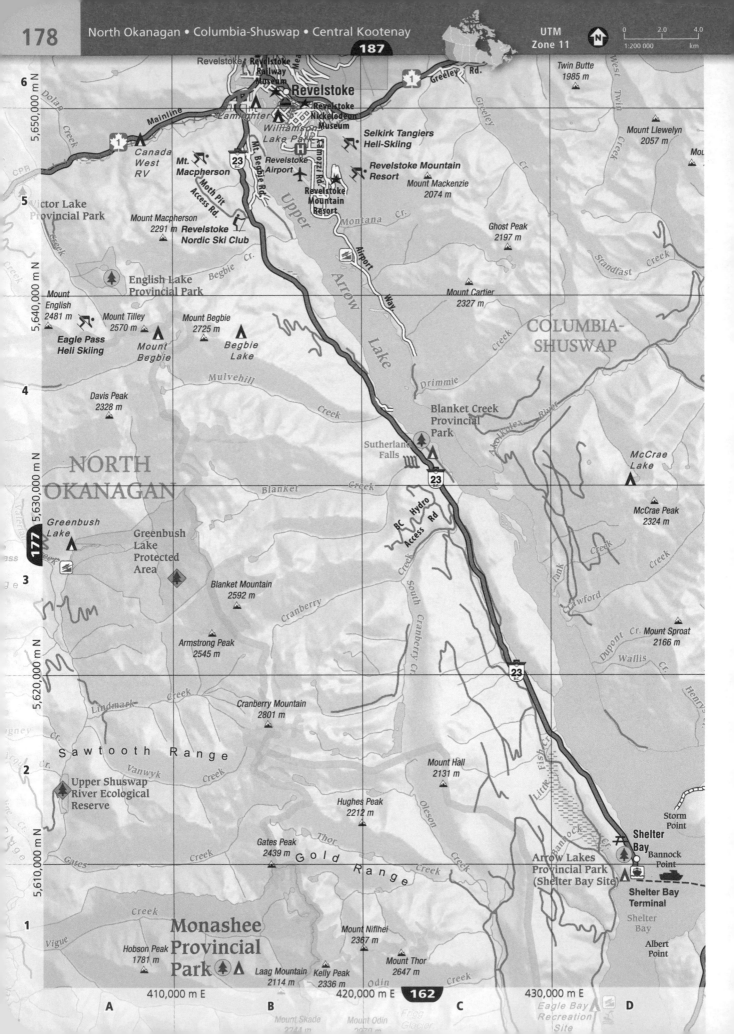

178

North Okanagan • Columbia-Shuswap • Central Kootenay

187

UTM
Zone 11

1:200 000

0   2.0   4.0
km

6

5,650,000 m N

CPR

Dolan Creek

Canada
West
RV

Mainline

Revelstoke
Revelstoke
Railway
Museum

Revelstoke

Revelstoke
Nickelodeun
Museum

Greeley Rd.

Twin Butte
1985 m

West Twin Creek

Mount Llewelyn
2057 m

Mou

5

5,640,000 m N

Victor Lake
Provincial Park

Mt.
Macpherson

Moth Pit
Access Rd.

Mt. Begbie Rd.

Revelstoke
Airport

23
BC

Williamson
Lake Park

Camozzi Rd.

Selkirk Tangiers
Heli-Skiing

Revelstoke Mountain
Resort

Mount Mackenzie
2074 m

Ghost Peak
2197 m

Standfast Creek

Mount Macpherson
2291 m

Revelstoke
Nordic Ski Club

Upper

Revelstoke
Mountain
Resort

Airport Way

Montana Cr.

Mount Cartier
2327 m

COLUMBIA-
SHUSWAP

4

5,630,000 m N

Mount
English
2481 m

Eagle Pass
Heli Skiing

Mount Tilley
2570 m

English Lake
Provincial Park

Begbie Cr.

Mount Begbie
2725 m

Mount
Begbie

Begbie
Lake

Mulvehill Creek

Arrow Lake

Drimmie Creek

Blanket Creek
Provincial
Park

Akolkolex River

McCrae
Lake

Davis Peak
2328 m

Sutherland
Falls

NORTH
OKANAGAN

Blanket Creek

23
BC

McCrae Peak
2324 m

177

Greenbush
Lake

Greenbush
Lake
Protected
Area

BC Hydro
Access Rd

South Cranberry Cr.

Frank Creek

Crawford

Cr. Mount Sproat
2166 m

3

5,630,000 m N

Blanket Mountain
2592 m

Cranberry Creek

Dupont Creek

Wallis

2

5,620,000 m N

Armstrong Peak
2545 m

Lindmark Creek

Sawtooth Range

Vanwyk Creek

Cranberry Mountain
2801 m

Upper Shuswap
River Ecological
Reserve

Mount Hall
2131 m

Oleson Creek

23
BC

Little Fisher Cr.

Bannock Creek

Storm
Point

2

5,610,000 m N

Hughes Peak
2212 m

Gates Peak
2439 m

Thor Creek

Gold Range

Shelter
Bay

Arrow Lakes
Provincial Park
(Shelter Bay Site)

Bannock
Point

Shelter Bay
Terminal

Shelter
Bay

1

Vigue Creek

Gates Creek

Monashee
Provincial
Park

Hobson Peak
1781 m

Laag Mountain
2114 m

Kelly Peak
2336 m

Mount Niflhei
2367 m

Odin Creek

Mount Thor
2647 m

Creek

Albert
Point

Eagle Bay
Recreation
Site

410,000 m E

420,000 m E

162

430,000 m E

Mount Skade

Mount Odin

Frigg Glacier

A   **B**   **C**   **D**

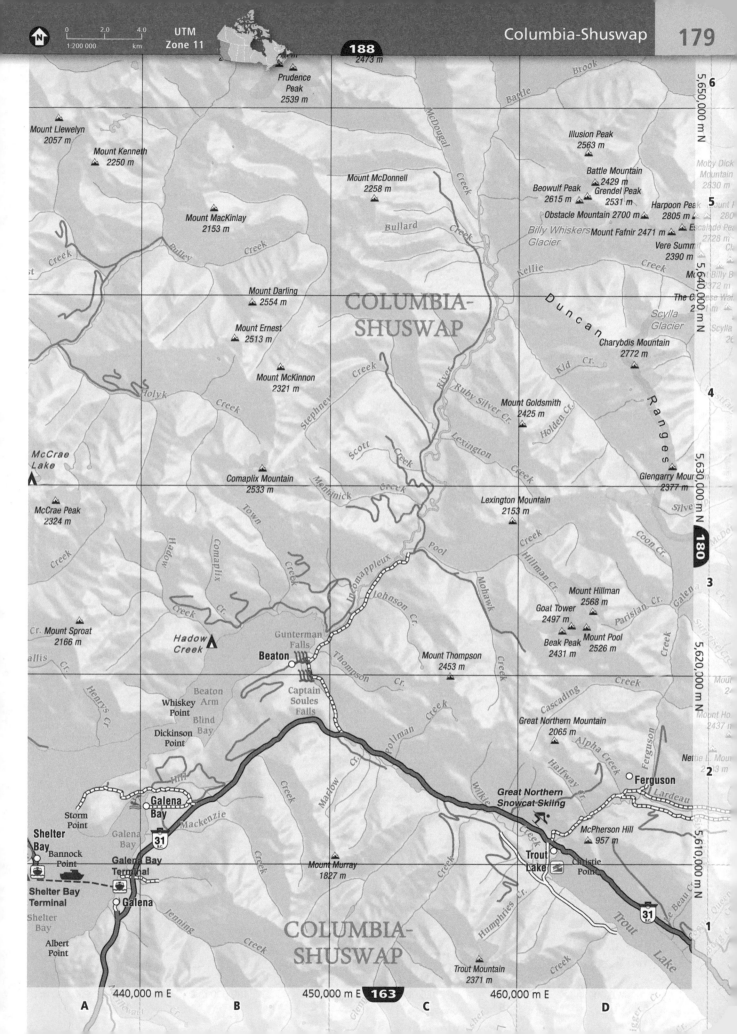

N

0   2.0   4.0
km
1:200 000
UTM
Zone 11

188

5,650,000 m N
6

Prudence
Peak
2539 m

2473 m

Illusion Peak
2563 m

Moby Dick
Mountain
2830 m

Mount Llewelyn
2057 m

Mount Kenneth
2250 m

Battle Mountain
2429 m
Beowulf Peak   Grendel Peak
2615 m   2531 m
Obstacle Mountain 2700 m

Harpoon Peak
2805 m

Mount Billy B
372 m

Escalade Pea
2728 m

Mount McDonnell
2258 m

Billy Whiskers
Glacier

Mount Fafnir 2471 m

5

Vere Summit
2390 m

5,640,000 m N

Mount MacKinlay
2153 m

Bullard

Kellie

The C

Scylla
Glacier

Scylla
2

Mount Darling
2554 m

COLUMBIA-
SHUSWAP

Duncan

Charybdis Mountain
2772 m

Kid   Cr.

Mount Ernest
2513 m

Creek

Ranges

4

Mount McKinnon
2321 m

Ruby Silver Cr.

Mount Goldsmith
2425 m

Holden Cr.

5,630,000 m N

McCrae
Lake

Scott

Comaplix Mountain
2533 m

Creek

Lexington

Creek

Glengarry Mour
2377 m

Silve

180

McCrae Peak
2324 m

Lexington Mountain
2153 m

Coon Cr.

Cr. Mount Sproat
2166 m

Town

Pool

Hillman Cr.

Mount Hillman
2568 m

Parisian

Cr.

Galena

3

Hadow
Creek

Gunterman
Falls

Mohawk

Goat Tower
2497 m

Mount Pool
2526 m

Beak Peak
2431 m

Beaton

Mount Thompson
2453 m

Thompson   Cr.

5,620,000 m N

Beaton
Arm

Captain
Soules
Falls

Cascading

Creek

Mour
24

Whiskey
Point

Blind
Bay

Great Northern Mountain
2065 m

Mount Ho
2437 m

Dickinson
Point

Pollman

Alpha Creek

Nettie L. Mou
13 m

2

Ferguson

Great Northern
Snowcat Skiing

Lardeau

Galena
Bay

Halfway

Storm
Point

Ferguson

Shelter
Bay

31
B.C.

McPherson Hill
957 m

Bannock
Point

Galena Bay
Terminal

Trout
Lake

Christie
Point

5,610,000 m N

Shelter Bay
Terminal

Galena

Mount Murray
1827 m

Shelter
Bay

COLUMBIA-
SHUSWAP

31
B.C.

1

Albert
Point

Trout Mountain
2371 m

440,000 m E

450,000 m E 163

460,000 m E

A   B   C   D

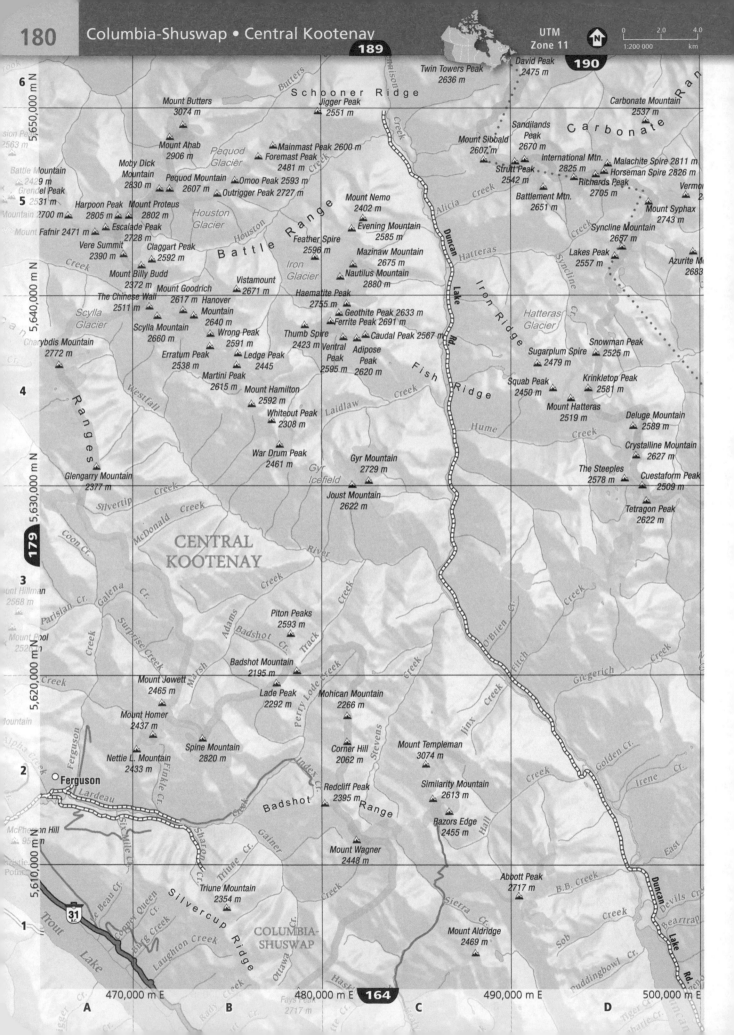

UTM
Zone 11

189

190

1:200 000 km

0   2.0   4.0

6

5,650,000 m N

Schooner Ridge

Twin Towers Peak
2636 m

David Peak
2475 m

Carbonate Mountain
2537 m

Carbonate

Mount Butters
3074 m

Jigger Peak
2551 m

Mount Sibbald
2607 m

Sandilands
Peak
2670 m

International Mtn.
2825 m

Malachite Spire 2811 m

Mount Ahab
2906 m

Mainmast Peak 2600 m

Strutt Peak
2542 m

Horseman Spire 2826 m

Moby Dick
Mountain
2830 m

Pequod
Glacier

Foremast Peak
2481 m

Richards Peak
2705 m

Vermo

Battlement Mtn.
2651 m

Pequod Mountain
2607 m

Omoo Peak 2593 m

Mount Syphax
2743 m

Harpoon Peak
2805 m

Mount Proteus
2802 m

Outrigger Peak 2727 m

Mount Nemo
2402 m

Syncline Mountain
2657 m

5

Mountain 2700 m

Escalade Peak
2728 m

Evening Mountain
2585 m

Lakes Peak
2557 m

Azurite M
2683

Mount Fafnir 2471 m

Vere Summit
2390 m

Houston
Glacier

Claggart Peak
2592 m

Feather Spire
2596 m

Mazinaw Mountain
2675 m

Mount Billy Budd
2372 m

Mount Goodrich
2617 m

Iron
Glacier

Nautilus Mountain
2880 m

Hatteras
Glacier

The Chinese Wall
2511 m

Hanover
Mountain
2640 m

Vistamount
2671 m

Haematite Peak
2755 m

Geothite Peak 2633 m

Scylla
Glacier

Scylla Mountain
2660 m

Wrong Peak
2591 m

Ferrite Peak 2691 m

Sugarplum Spire
2479 m

Snowman Peak
2525 m

Charybdis Mountain
2772 m

Erratum Peak
2538 m

Ledge Peak
2445

Thumb Spire
2423 m

Caudal Peak 2567 m

Ventral
Peak
2595 m

Adipose
Peak
2620 m

Squab Peak
2450 m

Krinkletop Peak
2581 m

Martini Peak
2615 m

Mount Hamilton
2592 m

Mount Hatteras
2519 m

Deluge Mountain
2589 m

4

Whiteout Peak
2308 m

Crystalline Mountain
2627 m

War Drum Peak
2461 m

Gyr Mountain
2729 m

The Steeples
2578 m

Cuestaform Peak
2509 m

5,630,000 m N

Glengarry Mountain
2377 m

Gyr
Icefield

Joust Mountain
2622 m

Tetragon Peak
2622 m

Ranges

179

CENTRAL
KOOTENAY

3

unt Hillman
2568 m

Piton Peaks
2593 m

Mount Pool
2523 m

Badshot Mountain
2195 m

Mount Jowett
2465 m

5,620,000 m N

Lade Peak
2292 m

Mohican Mountain
2266 m

Mount Homer
2437 m

Spine Mountain
2820 m

Corner Hill
2062 m

Mount Templeman
3074 m

2

Nettie L. Mountain
2433 m

Ferguson

Badshot

Redcliff Peak
2395 m

Range

Similarity Mountain
2613 m

McPherson Hill
932 m

Razors Edge
2455 m

5,610,000 m N

Mount Wagner
2448 m

Abbott Peak
2717 m

Triune Mountain
2354 m

Silvercup Ridge

COLUMBIA-
SHUSWAP

Mount Aldridge
2469 m

1

Trout Lake

31
B.C.

470,000 m E

480,000 m E

164

490,000 m E

500,000 m E

A   B   C   D

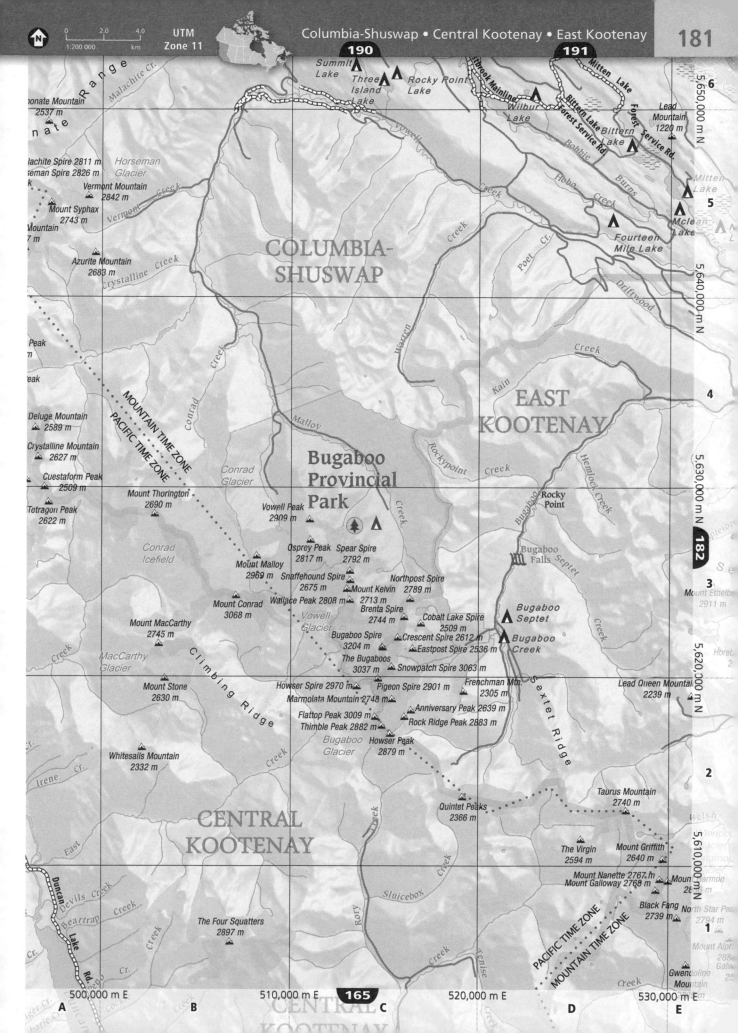

190   **191**

Range

Malachite Cr.

bonate Mountain
2537 m

Horseman
Glacier

Malachite Spire 2811 m
seman Spire 2826 m

Vermont Mountain
2842 m

Mount Syphax
2743 m

Mountain
7 m

Azurite Mountain
2683 m

Vermont Creek

Crystalline Creek

COLUMBIA-
SHUSWAP

Summit
Lake

Three
Island
Lake

Rocky Point
Lake

Wilbur
Lake

Bittern
Lake

Lead
Mountain
1220 m

Forest Service Rd.

Mitten
Lake

Mclean
Lake

Fourteen
Mile Lake

Hobo

Burns

Creek

Bobbie

Poet Cr.

Driftwood

5,650,000 m N

6

5,640,000 m N

5

Peak
m

eak

Deluge Mountain
2589 m

Crystalline Mountain
2627 m

Cuestaform Peak
2509 m

Tetragon Peak
2622 m

MOUNTAIN TIME ZONE
PACIFIC TIME ZONE

Conrad Creek

Conrad
Glacier

Conrad
Icefield

Mount Thorington
2690 m

Vowell Peak
2909 m

Mount Malloy
2969 m

Mount Conrad
3068 m

Mount MacCarthy
2745 m

MacCarthy
Glacier

Climbing Ridge

Bugaboo
Provincial
Park

Osprey Peak
2817 m

Spear Spire
2792 m

Snaffehound Spire
2675 m

Wallace Peak 2808 m

Vowell
Glacier

Mount Kelvin 2789 m
2713 m

Brenta Spire
2744 m

Bugaboo Spire
3204 m

The Bugaboos
3037 m

Northpost Spire

Cobalt Lake Spire
2509 m

Crescent Spire 2612 m

Eastpost Spire 2536 m

Snowpatch Spire 3063 m

Malloy

Rockypoint

Creek

Kain

EAST
KOOTENAY

Rocky
Point

Bugaboo
Falls

Bugaboo
Septet

Bugaboo
Creek

Hemlock Creek

Septet

4

5,630,000 m N

182

Mount Ethelbe
2911 m

3

5,620,000 m N

Mount Stone
2630 m

Howser Spire 2970 m

Marmolata Mountain 2748 m

Flattop Peak 3009 m

Thimble Peak 2882 m

Whitesails Mountain
2332 m

Pigeon Spire 2901 m

Anniversary Peak 2639 m

Rock Ridge Peak 2883 m

Bugaboo
Glacier

Howser Peak
2879 m

Frenchman Mtn.
2305 m

Sextet Ridge

Lead Queen Mountain
2239 m

Horel

2

Irene Cr.

Cr.

East

CENTRAL
KOOTENAY

Duncan

Devils Creek

Beartrap

Lake

Rd.

Creek

Cr.

The Four Squatters
2897 m

Creek

Rory

Sluicebox

Creek

Tenise

Quintet Peaks
2366 m

Taurus Mountain
2740 m

The Virgin
2594 m

Mount Griffith
2640 m

Mount Nanette 2767 m
Mount Galloway 2768 m

Black Fang
2739 m

PACIFIC TIME ZONE

MOUNTAIN TIME ZONE

Creek

welsh

Glacier

rramol
Glacier
armon
m

Mount
28 m

North Star Pea
2794 m

Mount Alp
288
Galw

Gwendoline
Mountain

5,610,000 m N

1

A   B   **165**   C   D   E

500,000 m E   510,000 m E   520,000 m E   530,000 m E

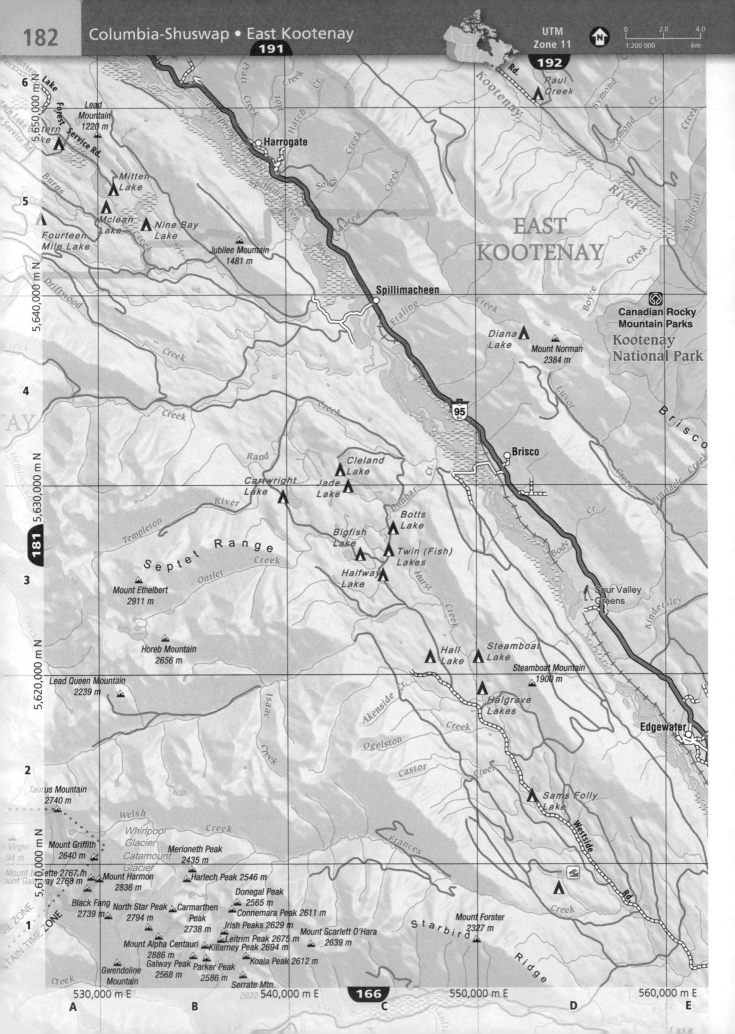

UTM
Zone 11

192

0   2.0   4.0
1:200 000   km

**EAST
KOOTENAY**

Canadian Rocky
Mountain Parks

**Kootenay
National Park**

Lead
Mountain
1220 m

Forest Service Rd.

Mitten
Lake

Harrogate

Mclean
Lake

Nine Bay
Lake

Fourteen
Mile Lake

Jubilee Mountain
1481 m

Driftwood

Spillimacheen

Diana
Lake

Mount Norman
2384 m

95
B.C.

Brisco

Cleland
Lake

Cartwright
Lake

Jade
Lake

Botts
Lake

Mount Ethelbert
2911 m

Septet   Range

River

Templeton

Outlet

Creek

Bigfish
Lake

Halfway
Lake

Twin (Fish)
Lakes

Spur Valley
Greens

Horeb Mountain
2656 m

Lead Queen Mountain
2239 m

Hall
Lake

Steamboat
Lake

Steamboat Mountain
1900 m

Halgrave
Lakes

Akenside

Ogelston

Castor

Edgewater

Taurus Mountain
2740 m

Welsh   Creek

Sams Folly
Lake

Whirlpool
Glacier
Catamount
Glacier

Merioneth Peak
2435 m

Mount Griffith
2640 m

Westside

Mount Nelson 2767 m
Mount Galway 2768 m

Mount Harmon
2836 m

Harlech Peak 2546 m

Black Fang
2739 m

North Star Peak
2794 m

Carmarthen
Peak
2738 m

Donegal Peak
2565 m

Connemara Peak 2611 m

Irish Peaks 2629 m

Mount Forster
2327 m

Starbird

Mount Alpha Centauri
2886 m

Leitrim Peak 2675 m

Killarney Peak 2694 m

Mount Scarlett O'Hara
2639 m

Koala Peak 2612 m

Gwendoline
Mountain

Galway Peak
2568 m

Parker Peak
2586 m

Serrate Mtn.
2622 m

Ridge

181

166

530,000 m E   540,000 m E   550,000 m E   560,000 m E

A   B   C   D   E

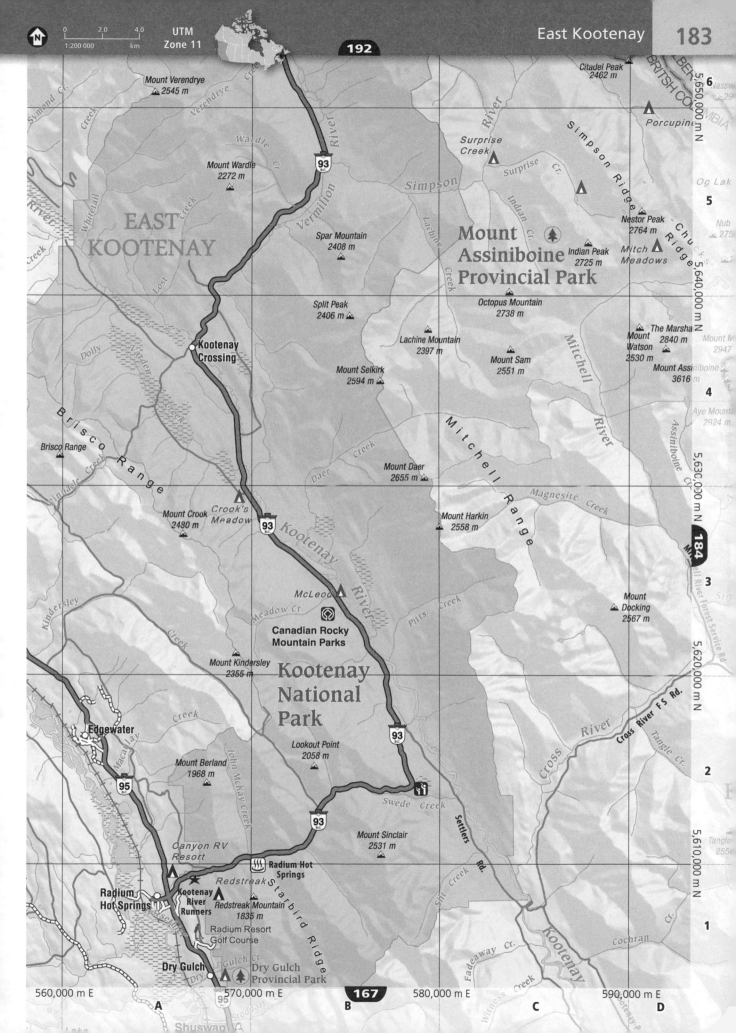

UTM
Zone 11
1:200 000

0   2.0   4.0
km

192

Citadel Peak
2462 m

BRITISH COLUMBIA

Mount Verendrye
▲ 2545 m

6

Porcupine

5,650,000 m N

Wardle Cr.

Vermilion River

93
B.C.

Mount Wardle
2272 m

Simpson River

Surprise
Creek
▲

Simpson Ridge

▲

Og Lak

EAST
KOOTENAY

Lost Creek

Spar Mountain
2408 m

Simpson

Lachine Cr.

Indian Cr.

Nestor Peak
2764 m

Mitch
Meadows

Chuck's Ridge

5,640,000 m N

Nub
275

5

Mount
Assiniboine
Provincial Park

Indian Peak
2725 m

Split Peak
2406 m ▲

Octopus Mountain
2738 m

The Marsha
2840 m

Mount M
2947

Dolly Varden Creek

Kootenay
Crossing

Lachine Mountain
2397 m

Mount Sam
2551 m

Mount
Watson
2530 m

Mount
Assiniboine
3616 m

Mount Selkirk
2594 m ▲

Mitchell River

4

5,630,000 m N

Aye Mounta
2924 m

Brisco Range

Brisco Range

Creek

Daer Creek

Mount Daer
2655 m ▲

Mitchell Range

Magnesite Creek

184

Pinnacle Creek

Mount Crook
2480 m

Crook's
Meadow
▲

93
B.C.

Kootenay River

Mount Harkin
2558 m ▲

Mount
Docking
2567 m ▲

SH

3

5,620,000 m N

Kindersley Creek

McLeod ▲

Meadow Cr.

Pitts Creek

Canadian Rocky
Mountain Parks

Mount Kindersley
2355 m

Kootenay
National
Park

Edgewater

Macaulay Creek

Mount Berland
1968 m

John McKay Creek

Lookout Point
2058 m

93
B.C.

Cross River FS Rd.

Cross River

Tangle Cr.

Tangle
2558

2

5,610,000 m N

95
B.C.

93
B.C.

Swede Creek

Settlers Rd.

Canyon RV
Resort

Radium Hot
Springs

Redstreak

Mount Sinclair
2531 m

Sin Creek Rd.

Radium
Hot Springs

Kootenay
River
Runners

Redstreak Mountain
1835 m

Starbird Ridge

Fadeaway Cr.

Kootenay

Cochran
Cr.

1

Radium Resort
Golf Course

Dry Gulch

Gulch Cr.

Dry Gulch
Provincial Park

Witness Creek

95

Shuswap

560,000 m E   A   570,000 m E   B   580,000 m E   C   590,000 m E   D

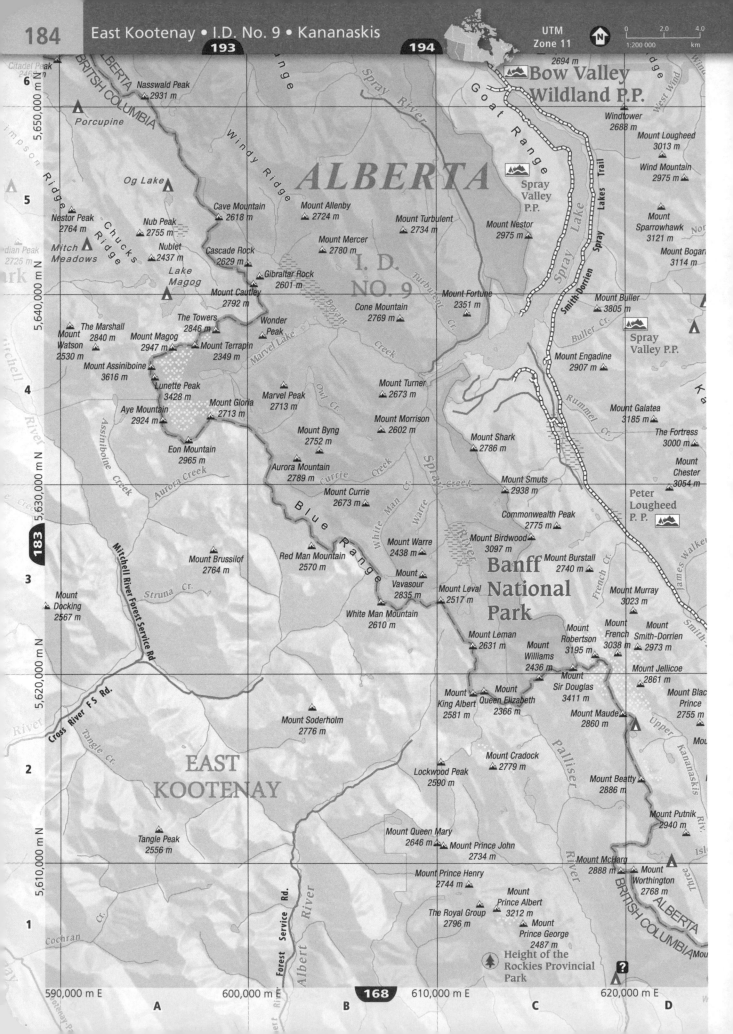

UTM
Zone 11
1:200 000

193   **194**

Citadel Peak
2446 m

Nasswald Peak
2931 m

ALBERTA

BRITISH COLUMBIA

Porcupine

Windy Ridge

Spray River

Goat Range

Bow Valley Wildland P.P.

2694 m

Windtower
2688 m

Mount Lougheed
3013 m

Og Lake

Cave Mountain
2618 m

Mount Allenby
2724 m

Mount Turbulent
2734 m

Spray Valley P.P.

Mount Nestor
2975 m

Wind Mountain
2975 m

Mount Sparrowhawk
3121 m

Nestor Peak
2764 m

Chucks Ridge

Nub Peak
2755 m

Nublet
2437 m

Mount Mercer
2780 m

I. D. NO. 9

Mount Bogart
3114 m

Indian Peak
2725 m

Mitch Meadows

Lake Magog

Cascade Rock
2629 m

Gibraltar Rock
2601 m

Cone Mountain
2769 m

Mount Fortune
2351 m

Smith-Dorrien

Spray Lake

Spray Lakes Trail

Mount Buller
3805 m

The Marshall
2840 m

Mount Cautley
2792 m

The Towers
2846 m

Wonder Peak

Mount Magog
2947 m

Mount Terrapin
2349 m

Marvel Lake

Bryant Creek

Buller Cr.

Spray Valley P.P.

Mount Watson
2530 m

Mount Assiniboine
3616 m

Lunette Peak
3428 m

Marvel Peak
2713 m

Owl Cr.

Mount Turner
2673 m

Mount Engadine
2907 m

Aye Mountain
2924 m

Mount Gloria
2713 m

Mount Morrison
2602 m

Mount Galatea
3185 m

Rummel Cr.

Assiniboine Creek

Eon Mountain
2965 m

Mount Byng
2752 m

Mount Shark
2786 m

The Fortress
3000 m

Aurora Creek

Aurora Mountain
2789 m

Currie Creek

White Man Cr.

Spray Creek

Mount Smuts
2938 m

Mount Chester
3054 m

Peter Lougheed P.P.

Mount Currie
2673 m

Mitchell River Forest Service Rd.

183

Mount Brussilof
2764 m

Blue Range

Red Man Mountain
2570 m

Commonwealth Peak
2775 m

Mount Birdwood
3097 m

Warre Cr.

Mount Burstall
2740 m

French Cr.

Mount Murray
3023 m

James Walker

Struna Cr.

Mount Docking
2567 m

Mount Vavasour
2835 m

Mount Leval
2517 m

Banff National Park

Mount Robertson
3195 m

Mount French
3038 m

Mount Smith-Dorrien
2973 m

Cross River FS Rd.

White Man Mountain
2610 m

Mount Leman
2631 m

Mount Williams
2436 m

Mount Jellicoe
2861 m

Mount Black Prince
2755 m

River

Mount Soderholm
2776 m

Mount King Albert
2581 m

Mount Queen Elizabeth
2366 m

Mount Sir Douglas
3411 m

Mount Maude
2860 m

Upper Kananaskis Riv.

Tangle Cr.

EAST KOOTENAY

Lockwood Peak
2590 m

Mount Cradock
2779 m

Palliser River

Mount Beatty
2886 m

Tangle Peak
2556 m

Mount Queen Mary
2646 m

Mount Prince John
2734 m

Mount Putnik
2940 m

Albert River

Mount Prince Henry
2744 m

Mount Prince Albert
3212 m

Mount McHarg
2888 m

Mount Worthington
2768 m

BRITISH COLUMBIA

ALBERTA

Cochran

The Royal Group
2796 m

Mount Prince George
2487 m

Height of the Rockies Provincial Park

Three Isl

Cross River FS Rd.

Forest Service Rd.

168

590,000 m E   600,000 m E   610,000 m E   620,000 m E

5,650,000 m N
5,640,000 m N
5,630,000 m N
5,620,000 m N
5,610,000 m N

6
5
4
3
2
1

A   B   C   D

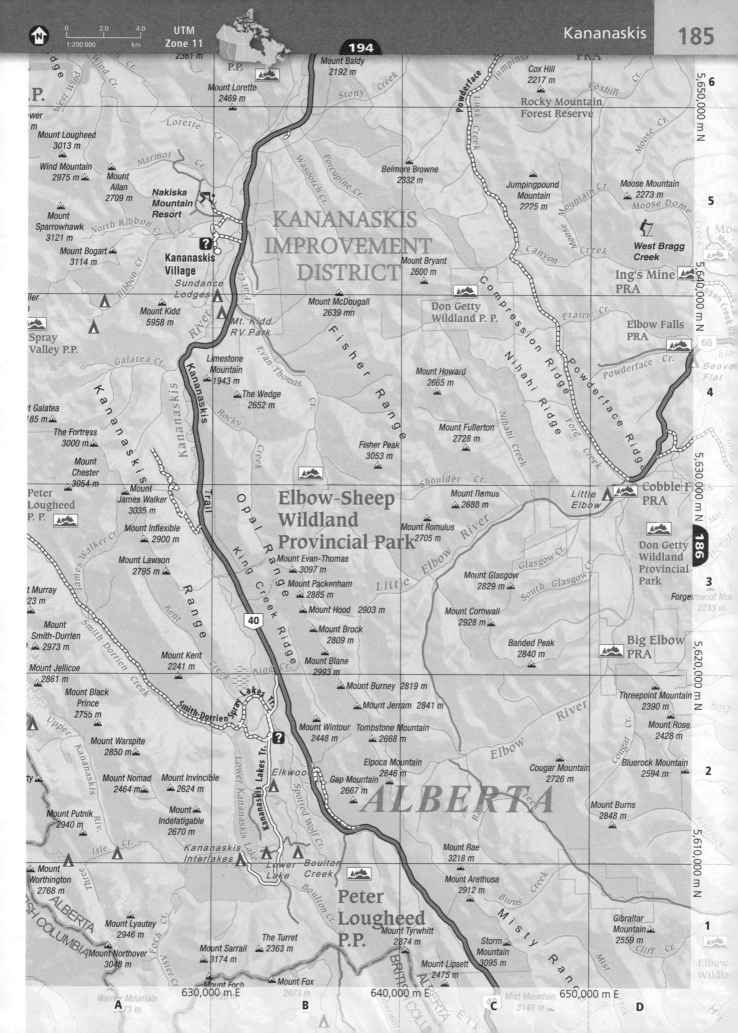

N

UTM
Zone 11

0   2.0   4.0
1:200 000   km

194

KANANASKIS IMPROVEMENT DISTRICT

Elbow-Sheep Wildland Provincial Park

Peter Lougheed P.P.

ALBERTA

Spray Valley P.P.

Peter Lougheed P. P.

Nakiska Mountain Resort

Kananaskis Village

Sundance Lodges

Mt. Kidd RV Park

Don Getty Wildland P. P.

West Bragg Creek

Ing's Mine PRA

Elbow Falls PRA

Cobble F PRA

Don Getty Wildland Provincial Park

Big Elbow PRA

Kananaskis Interlakes

Mount Baldy 2192 m

Mount Lorette 2469 m

Cox Hill 2217 m

Rocky Mountain Forest Reserve

Mount Lougheed 3013 m

Belmore Browne 2332 m

Jumpingpound Mountain 2225 m

Moose Mountain 2273 m

Wind Mountain 2975 m

Mount Allan 2709 m

Mount Sparrowhawk 3121 m

Mount Bryant 2600 m

Mount Bogart 3114 m

Mount McDougall 2639 mn

Mount Kidd 5958 m

Mount Howard 2665 m

Limestone Mountain 1943 m

The Wedge 2652 m

t Galatea 85 m

Mount Fullerton 2728 m

The Fortress 3000 m

Fisher Peak 3053 m

Mount Chester 3054 m

Mount Remus 2688 m

Mount James Walker 3035 m

Mount Romulus 2705 m

Mount Inflexible 2900 m

Mount Evan-Thomas 3097 m

Mount Glasgow 2829 m

Mount Lawson 2795 m

Mount Packenham 2885 m

Mount Cornwall 2928 m

t Murray 23 m

Mount Hood   2903 m

Mount Smith-Dorrien 2973 m

Mount Brock 2809 m

Banded Peak 2840 m

Mount Jellicoe 2861 m

Mount Kent 2241 m

Mount Blane 2993 m

Mount Black Prince 2755 m

Mount Burney 2819 m

Threepoint Mountain 2390 m

Mount Jerram 2841 m

Mount Rose 2428 m

Mount Warspite 2850 m

Mount Wintour 2448 m

Tombstone Mountain 2668 m

Mount Nomad 2464 m

Mount Invincible 2624 m

Elkwood

Elpoca Mountain 2846 m

Cougar Mountain 2726 m

Bluerock Mountain 2594 m

Mount Putnik 2940 m

Mount Indefatigable 2670 m

Gap Mountain 2667 m

Mount Burns 2848 m

Mount Worthington 2768 m

Lower Lake

Boulton Creek

Mount Rae 3218 m

Mount Lyautey 2946 m

Mount Arethusa 2912 m

Gibraltar Mountain 2559 m

Mount Northover 3048 m

The Turret 2363 m

Mount Tyrwhitt 2874 m

Mount Sarrail 3174 m

Storm Mountain 3095 m

Mount Lipsett 2475 m

Mount Foch

Mount Fox 2973 m

Mist Mountain 3140 m

Warrior Mountain

ALBERTA

BRITISH COLUMBIA

5,650,000 m N

5,640,000 m N

5,530,000 m N

5,620,000 m N

5,610,000 m N

630,000 m E

640,000 m E

650,000 m E

6

5

4

3

2

1

A   B   C   D

186

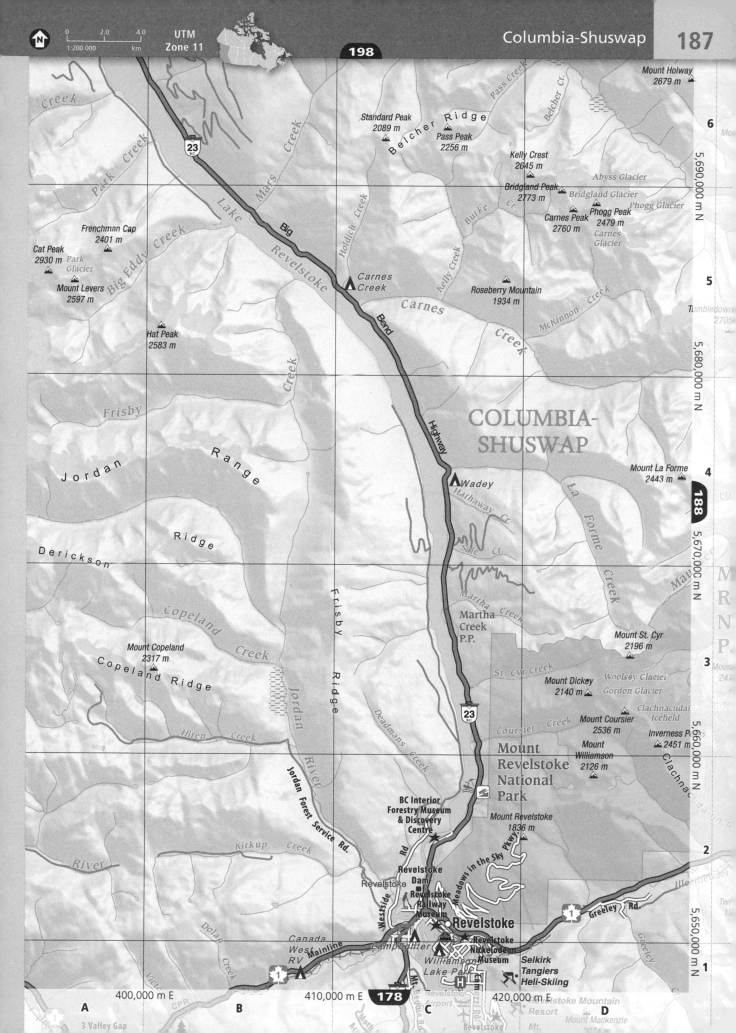

N

0   2.0   4.0
km
1:200 000

UTM
Zone 11

198

23
B.C.

Mount Holway
2679 m

Standard Peak
2089 m

Belcher Ridge

Pass Peak
2256 m

Kelly Crest
2645 m

Abyss Glacier

6

Bridgland Peak
2773 m

Bridgland Glacier

Phogg Glacier

Frenchman Cap
2401 m

Carnes Peak
2760 m

Phogg Peak
2479 m

Carnes
Glacier

5,690,000 m N

Cat Peak
2930 m

Park
Glacier

Big Eddy Creek

Lake

Revelstoke

Big

Mars Creek

Holdich Creek

Carnes
Creek

Burke Cr.

Kelly Creek

Roseberry Mountain
1934 m

Carnes

Creek

McKinnon Creek

Tumbledown
2705

5

Mount Levers
2597 m

Hat Peak
2583 m

Bend

Frisby

Jordan   Range

Ridge

Derickson

Copeland   Creek

Copeland Ridge

Mount Copeland
2317 m

Frisby   Ridge

Highway

COLUMBIA-
SHUSWAP

Wadey

Hathaway Cr.

Salle   Cr.

Martha   Creek

Martha
Creek
P.P.

La   Forme   Creek

Mount La Forme
2443 m

Mount St. Cyr
2196 m

Woolsey Glacier

Mount Dickey
2140 m

Gordon Glacier

St. Cyr Creek

Clachnacudainn
Icefield

Mount Coursier
2536 m

Mauvais

5,680,000 m N

5,670,000 m N

MRNP

Mour
247

188

4

3

Deadmans   Creek

Jordan   River

Jordan Forest Service Rd.

Kirkup   Creek

River

Dolan

Creek

Coursier   Creek

Mount
Revelstoke
National
Park

Mount Williamson
2126 m

Mount Revelstoke
1836 m

BC Interior
Forestry Museum
& Discovery
Centre

Meadows in the Sky Pkwy

Westside   Rd.

Revelstoke
Dam

Revelstoke
Railway
Museum

Canada
West
RV

Lamplighter

Canada West Mainline

1

1

Revelstoke

Revelstoke
Nickelodeon
Museum

Williamson
Lake Park

Selkirk
Tangiers
Heli-Skiing

Greeley   Rd.

Inverness Pass
2451 m

Clachnacudainn R.

5,660,000 m N

2

Greeley

5,650,000 m N

400,000 m E

A

178

B

410,000 m E

C

420,000 m E

D

23
B.C.

Mt. Begbie Rd.

3 Valley Gap

CPR

Victor

Revelstoke
Airport

Moth

Revelstoke Mountain
Resort

Mount Mackenzie

Revelstoke

Twi
19

H

1

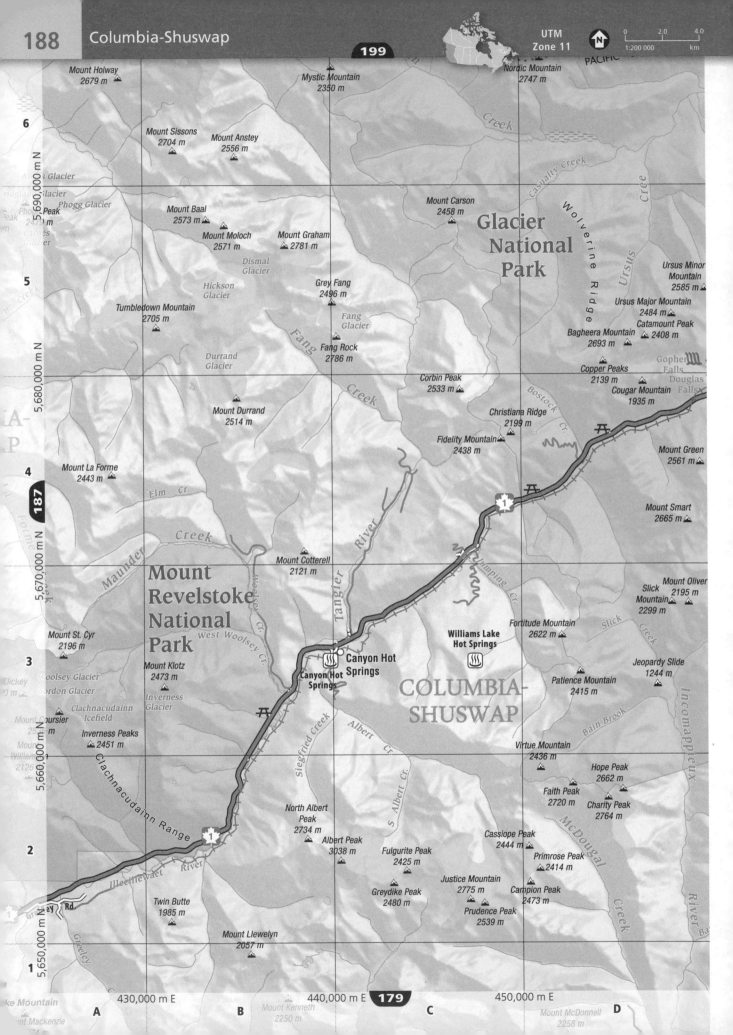

199

UTM
Zone 11
1:200 000

PACIFIC

0   2.0   4.0
km

Mount Holway
2679 m

Mystic Mountain
2350 m

Nordic Mountain
2747 m

Creek

Mount Sissons
2704 m

Mount Anstey
2556 m

Alpls Glacier

Phogg Glacier
Phogg Glacier
Peak

Carnes
Glacier

Mount Baal
2573 m

Mount Moloch
2571 m

Mount Graham
2781 m

Mount Carson
2458 m

Glacier
National
Park

Casualty Creek

Wolverine Ridge

Ursus

Creek

Dismal
Glacier

Hickson
Glacier

Grey Fang
2496 m

Ursus Minor
Mountain
2585 m

Tumbledown Mountain
2705 m

Fang
Glacier

Ursus Major Mountain
2484 m

Catamount Peak
2408 m

Durrand
Glacier

Fang Rock
2786 m

Bagheera Mountain
2693 m

Copper Peaks
2139 m

Gopher
Falls

Creek

Corbin Peak
2533 m

Cougar Mountain
1935 m

Douglas
Falls

Mount Durrand
2514 m

Christiana Ridge
2199 m

Bostock Cr.

Mount La Forme
2443 m

Fidelity Mountain
2438 m

Mount Green
2561 m

187

Elm   Cr.

Creek

Mount Cotterell
2121 m

River

Pumping Cr.

1

Mount Smart
2665 m

Maunder

Mount
Revelstoke
National
Park

Tangier

Slick
Mountain
2299 m

Mount Oliver
2195 m

Mount St. Cyr
2196 m

West Woolsey Cr.

Fortitude Mountain
2622 m

Slick   Creek

Dickey

Woolsey Glacier
Gordon Glacier

Mount Klotz
2473 m

Williams Lake
Hot Springs

Jeopardy Slide
1244 m

Mount Coursier

Clachnacudainn
Icefield

Inverness
Glacier

Canyon Hot
Springs

Patience Mountain
2415 m

Incomappleux

Mount
Williams
2126

Inverness Peaks
2451 m

Canyon Hot
Springs

COLUMBIA-
SHUSWAP

Bain Brook

Siegfried Creek

Albert Cr.

Virtue Mountain
2436 m

Hope Peak
2662 m

Clachnacudainn Range

1

S Albert Cr.

Faith Peak
2720 m

Charity Peak
2764 m

North Albert
Peak
2734 m

Cassiope Peak
2444 m

McDougal

Primrose Peak
2414 m

Albert Peak
3038 m

Fulgurite Peak
2425 m

Illecillewaet

River

Justice Mountain
2775 m

Campion Peak
2473 m

1

Greeley Rd.

Twin Butte
1985 m

Greydike Peak
2480 m

Prudence Peak
2539 m

Creek

River

ke Mountain

Greeley

Mount Llewelyn
2057 m

430,000 m E

440,000 m E

179

450,000 m E

t Mackenzie

Mount Kenneth
2250 m

Mount McDonnell
2258 m

A   B   C   D

5,690,000 m N
5,680,000 m N
5,670,000 m N
5,660,000 m N
5,650,000 m N

6   5   4   3   2   1

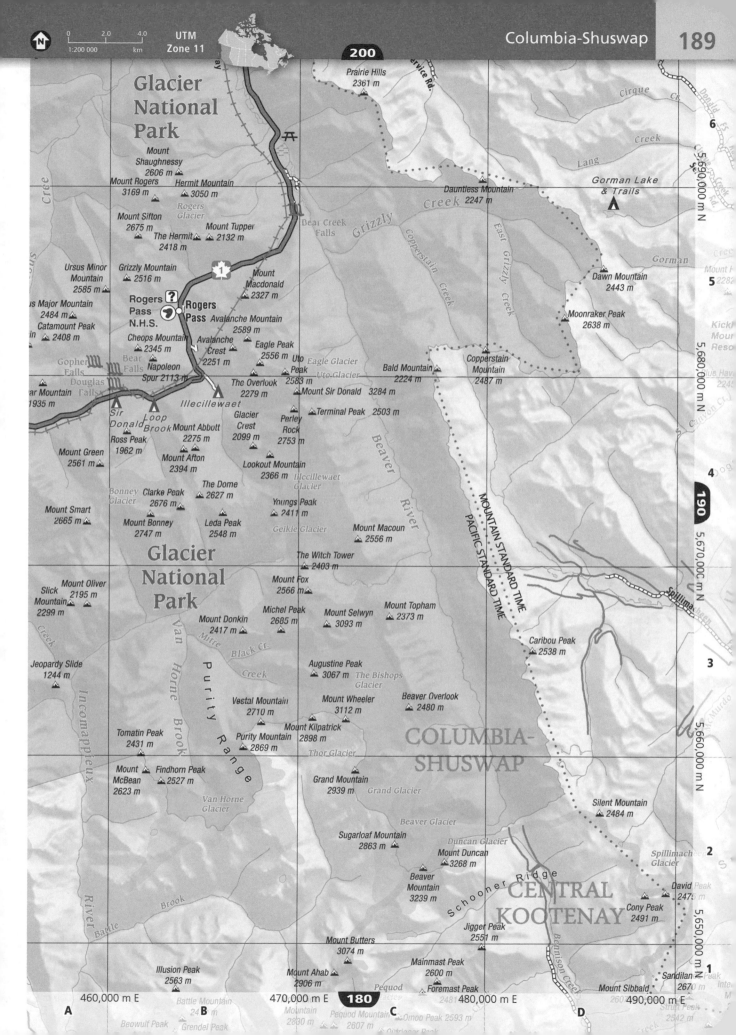

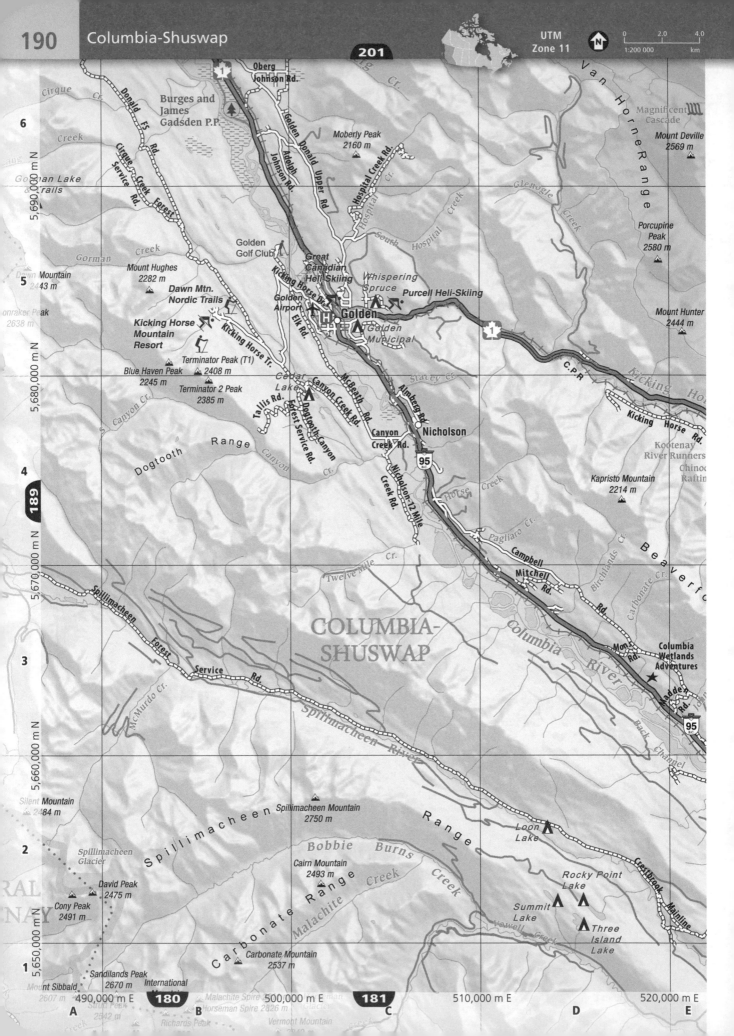

201

UTM
Zone 11

1:200 000

0   2.0   4.0
km

6

Cirque

Cirque Cr.

Creek

Donald FS. Rd.

Cirque Creek Forest Service Rd.

Gorman Lake & Trails

5,690,000 m N

Gorman Lake

Gorman Creek

Dawn Mountain
2443 m

Wonraker Peak
2638 m

5

Mount Hughes
2282 m

**Dawn Mtn.
Nordic Trails**

**Kicking Horse
Mountain
Resort**

Blue Haven Peak
2245 m

Terminator Peak (T1)
2408 m

Terminator 2 Peak
2385 m

5,680,000 m N

Tallis Rd.

Cedar Lake

Canyon Cr.

Dogtooth Canyon Forest Service Rd.

Canyon Creek Rd.

McBeath Rd.

Dogtooth   Range

Canyon

S. Canyon Cr.

4

189

5,670,000 m N

Spillimacheen

Oberg
Johnson Rd.

Golden Donald Upper Rd.

Adolph Johnson Rd.

Golden Golf Club

Kicking Horse Dr.

Golden
Airport

Golden

Kicking Horse Tr.

Elk Rd.

H

Golden
Municipal

Great
Canadian
Heli-Skiing

Whispering
Spruce

Purcell Heli-Skiing

Moberly Peak
2160 m

Hospital Creek Rd.

Hospital Cr.

South Hospital Creek

Stacey Cr.

Almberg Rd.

Nicholson

95
B.C.

Canyon
Creek Rd.

Nicholson-12 Mile Creek Rd.

Twelve Mile Cr.

Horse Creek

Pagliaro Cr.

Campbell

Mitchell Rd.

Van Horne Range

Magnificent
Cascade

Mount Deville
2569 m

Glenogle Creek

Porcupine
Peak
2580 m

Mount Hunter
2444 m

1

C.P.R.

Kicking Hor

Kicking Horse Rd.

Kootenay
River Runners

Chinoo
Rafti

Kapristo Mountain
2214 m

Birchlands Cr.

Carbonate Cr.

Beaverf

Columbia River

Mons Rd.

Columbia
Wetlands
Adventures

Maddex Rd.

95
B.C.

Back Channel

3

Service   Rd.

McMurdo Cr.

5,660,000 m N

Silent Mountain
2484 m

2

Spillimacheen
Glacier

David Peak
2475 m

Cony Peak
2491 m

Spillimacheen   Forest

Spillimacheen   River

Spillimacheen

COLUMBIA-
SHUSWAP

Spillimacheen Mountain
2750 m

Bobbie   Burns

Cairn Mountain
2493 m

Range

Creek

Malachite

Carbonate   Range   Creek

Range

Loon
Lake

Rocky Point
Lake

Summit
Lake

Three
Island
Lake

Volwell Creek

Crestbrook

Mainline

1

5,650,000 m N

Mount Sibbald
2607 m

Sandilands Peak
2670 m

International

Malachite Spire 2806 m

Horseman Spire 2826 m

Carbonate Mountain
2537 m

181

510,000 m E

520,000 m E

RAL
NAY

Richards Peak

Vermont Mountain

Still Peak
2642 m

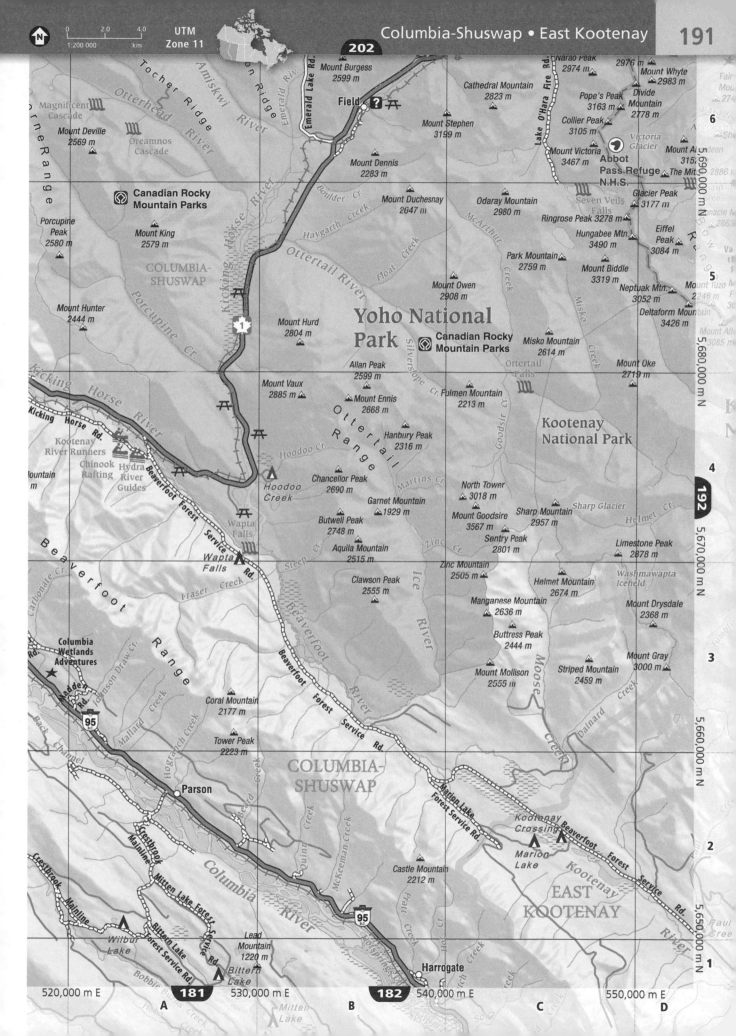

UTM
Zone 11

1:200 000

203

Banff National Park

◎ **Canadian Rocky Mountain Parks**

2976 m

Mount Whyte
2983 m

Fairview
Mountain
2744 m

Divide
Mountain
2778 m

Saddle Mountain 2433 m

Aberdeen Glacier

Sheol Mountain
2778 m

Mount Aberdeen
3152 m

The Mitre 2886 m

Glacier Peak
3177 m

Giant
Steps

Mount Temple
3543 m

Pinnacle Mountain
2863 m

Eiffel
Peak
3084 m

Tower of Babel
2103 m

Valley of
the Ten
Peaks ★

Consolation Lakes ★

Mount
Bowlen
3072 m

Mount Babel 3101 m

Neptuak Mtn.
3052 m

Mount Tuzo
2246 m

Mount
Perren
3051 m

Mount Fay
3234 m

Deltaform Mountain
3426 m

Mount Allen
3085 m

Mount
Little
3031 m

Quadra
Mountain
3041 m

Bident Mtn.
2807 m

Mount Bell
2910 m

Mount Oke
2719 m

Chimney Peak
2836 m

ALBERTA

Boom Cr.

Boom Mountain
2251 m

BRITISH COLUMBIA

Kootenay National Park

◎ **Canadian Rocky Mountain Parks**

Mount Whymper
2844 m

93

Vermillion Pass

The Continental Divide

Storm Mountain
3161 m

Marble Canyon

Marble

Stanley Peak
3155 m

Mount Ball
3311 m

The Paint Pots ★

Vermillion Peak
2622 m

Mount Haffner
2410 m

Mount Gray
3000 m

Numa
Falls

Isabelle Peak
2938 m

Mount Drysdale
2368 m

Limestone Peak
2878 m

Washmawapta
Icefield

I.D. NO. 9

Copper Mountain
2795 m

Castle Mountain
2766 m

1A

1

Castle Junction

50

Castle

Camp's Head
1675 m

Ink Pots ★

Johnston Canyon

1

Pilot Mountain
2934 m

Mount Brett
2984 m

Ball Range

Pharaoh Creek

Haiduk Peak
2641 m

Pharaoh Peaks
2548 m

Pharaoh Creek

Mount Avens
2819 m

Pulsatilla Mountain
2904 m

Block Mountain
2720 m

Protection Mountain
2767 m

Stuart Knob
2850 m

Helena Ridge

Protection Mountain

Panorama Ridge

Taylor Cr.

Windermere

Pkwy.

93

Altrude Creek

Banff

Foster Peak
3204 m

Numa Mountain
2720 m

Kootenay National Park

93

Twin Cairns
2434 m

Hawk Ridge

◎ **Canadian Rocky Mountain Parks**

★ **The Rock Wall**

EAST KOOTENAY

Paul Creek

Mount Verendrye
2545 m

Service Rd.

Paul Creek

191

Helmet Cr.

Ochre Creek

Tumbling Creek

Numa Cr.

Vermillion Range

Kootenay Hwy.

Vermilion Range

Floe Cr.

Serac Creek

Hawk Cr.

Redearth Cr.

Lost Horse Cr.

Verendrye Creek

Whitetail Cr.

Symond Cr.

Surprise

2272 m

5,690,000 m N
5,680,000 m N
5,670,000 m N
5,660,000 m N
5,650,000 m N

6
5
4
3
2
1

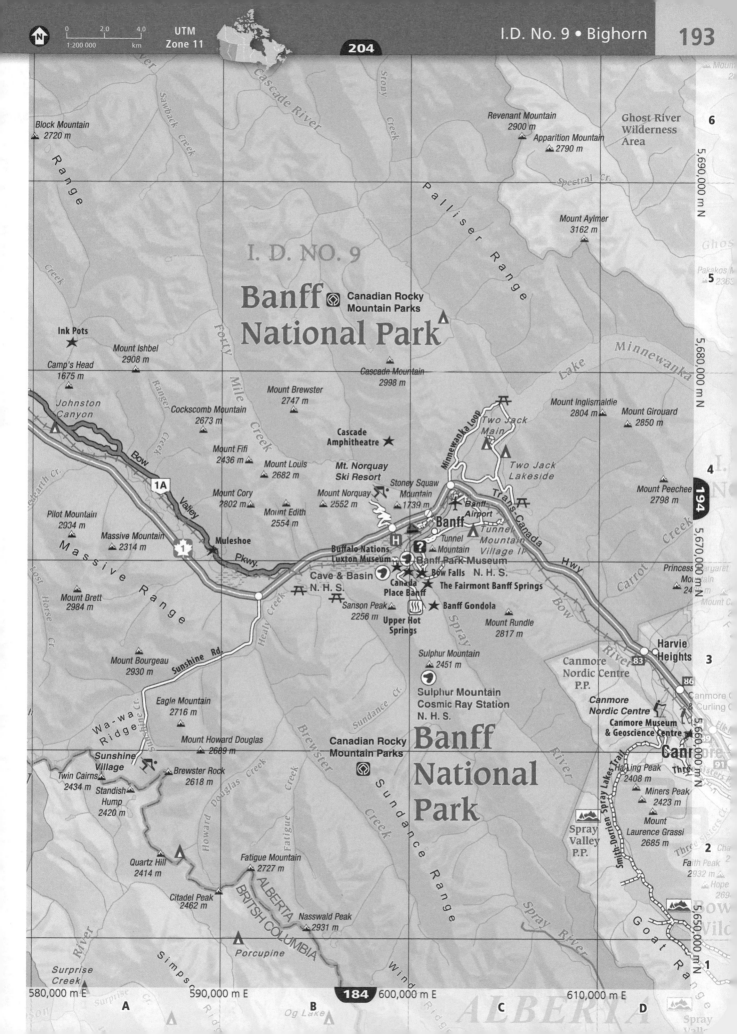

N

UTM
Zone 11

0   2.0   4.0
km
1:200 000

204

184

580,000 m E

590,000 m E

600,000 m E

610,000 m E

A   B   C   D

Block Mountain
2720 m

Revenant Mountain
2900 m

Apparition Mountain
2790 m

Ghost River
Wilderness
Area

6

5,690,000 m N

Mount Aylmer
3162 m

Pakakos M.
2363

5

I. D. NO. 9

Banff
National Park

Canadian Rocky
Mountain Parks

Lake Minnewanka

5,680,000 m N

Ink Pots

Mount Ishbel
2908 m

Camp's Head
1675 m

Cascade Mountain
2998 m

Mount Brewster
2747 m

Mount Inglismaldie
2804 m

Mount Girouard
2850 m

Johnston
Canyon

Cockscomb Mountain
2673 m

Cascade
Amphitheatre

Two Jack
Main

Two Jack
Lakeside

Mount Fifi
2436 m

Mount Louis
2682 m

Mt. Norquay
Ski Resort

Mount Norquay
2552 m

Stoney Squaw
Mountain
1739 m

Mount Peechee
2798 m

4

194

1A

Mount Cory
2802 m

Mount Edith
2554 m

Banff
Airport

Banff

Trans-Canada

5,670,000 m N

Pilot Mountain
2934 m

Massive Mountain
2314 m

Muleshoe

Buffalo Nations
Luxton Museum

Tunnel
Mountain
Village II

Hwy

Princess
Mou
24

1

Bow Valley Pkwy.

Banff Park Museum

Bow Falls   N. H. S.

Mount
Mount

Cave & Basin
N. H. S.

Canada
Place Banff

The Fairmont Banff Springs

Mount Brett
2984 m

Sanson Peak
2256 m

Banff Gondola

Upper Hot
Springs

Mount Rundle
2817 m

Harvie
Heights

83

Mount Bourgeau
2930 m

Sunshine Rd.

Sulphur Mountain
2451 m

Canmore
Nordic Centre
P.P.

86

Canmore
Curling

3

5,660,000 m N

Eagle Mountain
2716 m

Sulphur Mountain
Cosmic Ray Station
N. H. S.

Canmore
Nordic Centre

Canmore Museum
& Geoscience Centre

Can

Wa-wa
Ridge

Mount Howard Douglas
2689 m

Canadian Rocky
Mountain Parks

Banff
National
Park

Ha ling Peak
2408 m

Three

91

Sunshine
Village

Brewster Rock
2618 m

Miners Peak
2423 m

Twin Cairns
2434 m

Standish
Hump
2420 m

Mount
Laurence Grassi
2685 m

Spray
Valley
P.P.

Three Sisters P.

2

5,650,000 m N

Quartz Hill
2414 m

Fatigue Mountain
2727 m

Faith Peak
2932 m

Hope
269

Citadel Peak
2462 m

ALBERTA
BRITISH COLUMBIA

Nasswald Peak
2931 m

Bow
Wild

Surprise
Creek

Porcupine

ALBERTA

Spray
Valley

1

Og Lake

Spray River

Goat Range

Smith-Dorrien Spray Lakes Trail

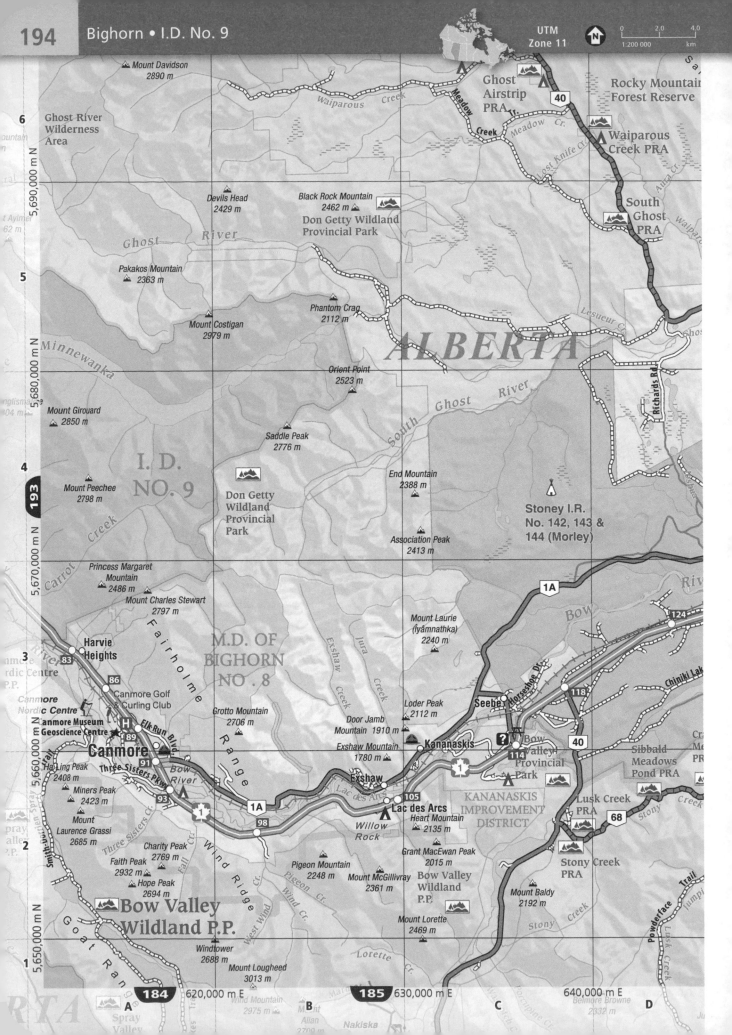

UTM
Zone 11

1:200 000

Mount Davidson
2890 m

**Ghost
Airstrip
PRA**

40

**Rocky Mountain
Forest Reserve**

6

**Ghost River
Wilderness
Area**

Waiparous Creek

Meadow Cr.

Lost Knife Cr.

**Waiparous
Creek PRA**

**South
Ghost
PRA**

Devils Head
2429 m

Black Rock Mountain
2462 m

**Don Getty Wildland
Provincial Park**

5,690,000 m N

t Aylmer
62 m

Ghost   **River**

Pakakos Mountain
2363 m

5

Mount Costigan
2979 m

Phantom Crag
2112 m

ALBERTA

Lesueur Cr.

5,680,000 m N

Minnewanka

Orient Point
2523 m

Mount Girouard
2850 m

nglisma
804 m

Saddle Peak
2776 m

South **Ghost** **River**

Richards Rd.

**I. D.
NO. 9**

**Don Getty
Wildland
Provincial
Park**

End Mountain
2388 m

4

Mount Peechee
2798 m

Association Peak
2413 m

**Stoney I.R.
No. 142, 143 &
144 (Morley)**

5,670,000 m N

Carrot   *Creek*

193

**Princess Margaret
Mountain**
2486 m

Mount Charles Stewart
2797 m

**Mount Laurie
(Îyâmnathka)**
2240 m

1A

124

Bow

Riv

Chiniki Lak

**Harvie
Heights**

85

Fairholme

**M.D. OF
BIGHORN
NO. 8**

Exshaw *Creek*

Jura *Creek*

**Mount Laurie
(Îyâmnathka)**
2240 m

3

nmore
ordic Centre
P.P.

86

**Canmore Golf
& Curling Club**

Grotto Mountain
2706 m

Loder Peak
2112 m

Seebe

Horseshoe Dr.

118

40

**Sibbald
Meadows
Pond PRA**

5,660,000 m N

Canmore
Nordic Centre

Elk Run Blvd.

89

H

**Door Jamb
Mountain 1910 m**

Kananaskis

?

**Bow
Valley
Provincial
Park**

Cra
Me
PR

Canmore Museum
Geoscience Centre

Canmore

91

**Bow
River**

Range

Exshaw Mountain
1780 m

1

114

Ha Ling Peak
2408 m

Three Sisters Pkwy

93

Exshaw

1

Lac des Arcs

**KANANASKIS
IMPROVEMENT
DISTRICT**

**Lusk Creek
PRA**

5,650,000 m N

Miners Peak
2423 m

1A

98

105

Lac des Arcs

Heart Mountain
2135 m

68

2

**Mount
Laurence Grassi**
2685 m

Three Sisters Cr.

Wind Ridge

Fall Cr.

Charity Peak
2769 m

Faith Peak
2932 m

Hope Peak
2694 m

Pigeon Mountain
2248 m

**Willow
Rock**

Pigeon Cr.

Mount McGillivray
2361 m

Grant MacEwan Peak
2015 m

**Bow Valley
Wildland
P.P.**

**Stony Creek
PRA**

Stony Creek

Powderface Trail

Mount Baldy
2192 m

spray
alley
P.P.

**Bow Valley
Wildland P.P.**

Goat Rang

West Wind Cr.

Mount Lorette
2469 m

1

Windtower
2688 m

Mount Lougheed
3013 m

Lorette *Cr.*

Belmore Browne

RTA

184

620,000 m E

Spray
Valley

A

Wind Mountain
2975 m

B

185

630,000 m E

Mount
Allan

Marg

Nakiska

C

640,000 m E

2332 m

D

Jumpin

Smith-Dorrien Spray Trail

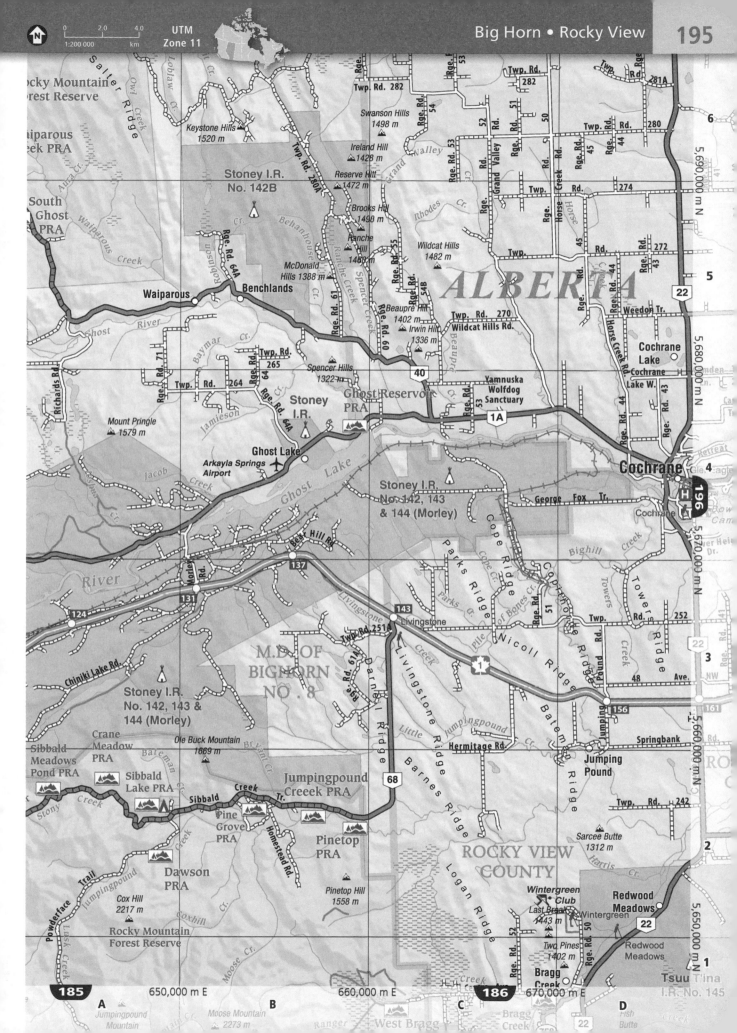

1:200 000

ROCKY VIEW COUNTY

Airdrie

Nose Creek
Valley Museum
Yankee Valley

Big Springs Rd.

Woodside

Cochrane
Lake

Big Hill
Springs
P. P.

Camden
Ln. 264
Carlson
Trail

Weedon Tr.

195

Cochrane

GlenEagles

Bow Riverside
Campground
Cochrane

River Heights
Dr.

Glenbow Ranch
Provincial Park

Bow River

Bearspaw Heights

Big Hill
1311 m

Bow Valley Trail

Spy Hill
1271 m

Stoney

Beddington

Nose Hill
Spring

Country

Crowchild

Nose Hill
1229 m

Nose Hill
Park

Nickle Arts
Museum

Calgary
Springbank
Airport

Calaway
Park

Calgary
West

Old
Banff
Coach
Rd.

Canada
Olympic
Park

Paskapoo
Slopes

Calgary

Confederation
Park

Devonian
Gardens

Glenbow
Museum

Springbank Rd.

Lower Springbank Rd.

Glencoe

Pinebrook

Wilhngdon
Hill
201 m

Cairn
Hill

Elbow
Springs

Shaganappi
Ave. SW

26 Ave. SW

Richmond St. SW

Military
Museums

Richmond
Green
Lakeview

Lougheed
House

Scotiabank
Saddledome

Elbow River

Glenmore Trail

Bonn Hill
1167 m

Earl
Grey

Heritage Park
Historical Village

Sarcee Butte
12 m

Redwood
Meadows

Bullhead Hill
1181 m

High Butte
1208 m

Cemetery
Hill
1134 m

Anderson Rd.

Redwood
Meadows

Tsuu T'ina
I.R. No. 14

Six Mile Coulee Rd.

Bullhead Rd.

Southland

186

680,000 m E   690,000 m E   700,000 m E

A   B   C   D

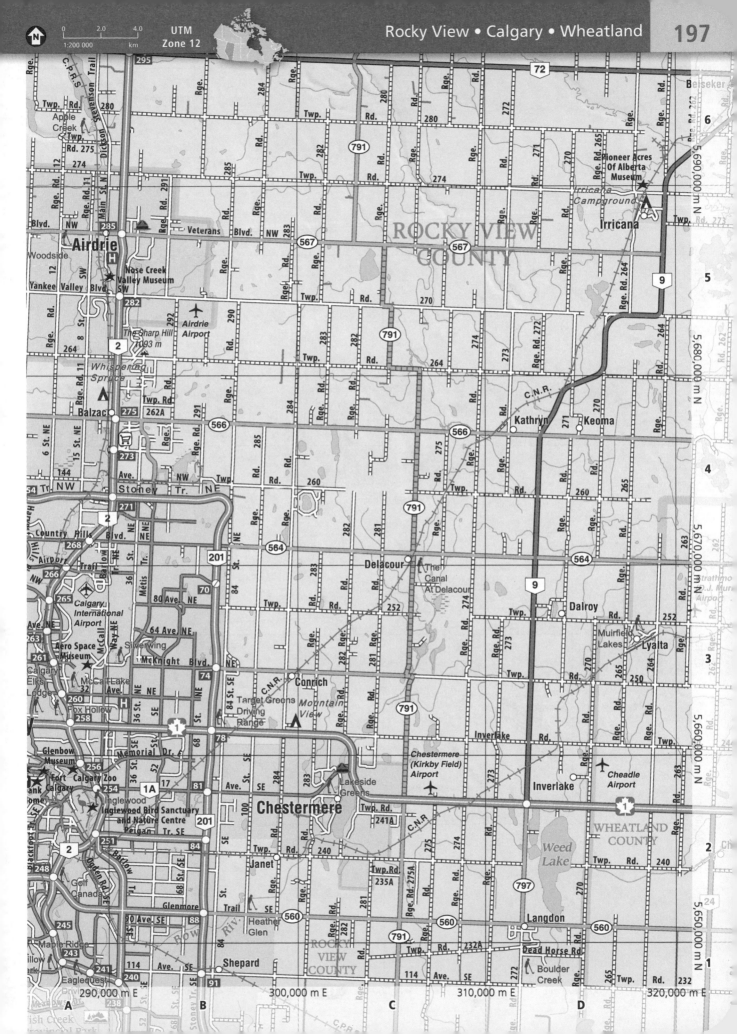

UTM
Zone 12
1:200 000
0   2.0   4.0
km

ROCKY VIEW COUNTY

Irricana
Pioneer Acres Of Alberta Museum
Irricana Campground
Kathryn
Keoma

Airdrie
Woodside
Yankee Valley Blvd.
Veterans Blvd. NW
Nose Creek Valley Museum
Airdrie Airport
The Sharp Hill 1093 m
Whispering Spruce
Balzac

Country Hills Blvd. NE
Calgary International Airport
Aero Space Museum
Silverwing
Calgary Elks Lodge
McCall Lake
Fox Hollow
Glenbow Museum
Fort Calgary
Calgary Zoo
Inglewood Bird Sanctuary and Nature Centre
Golf Canada
Maple Ridge
Eaglequest

Stoney Tr. NE
Metis Tr.
80 Ave. NE
64 Ave. NE
McKnight Blvd.
Memorial Dr.
Inglewood
Peigan Tr. SE
Glenmore Trail
90 Ave. SE

Delacour
The Canal At Delacour
Dalroy
Muirfield Lakes
Lyalta
Strathmore D.J. Airport

Conrich
Target Greens Driving Range
Mountain View
Chestermere (Kirkby Field) Airport
Lakeside Greens
Chestermere
Inverlake
Cheadle Airport

Janet
Heather Glen
Shepard
Langdon
Weed Lake

WHEATLAND COUNTY
ROCKY VIEW COUNTY
Boulder Creek
Dead Horse Rd.

Beiseker

290,000 m E   300,000 m E   310,000 m E   320,000 m E

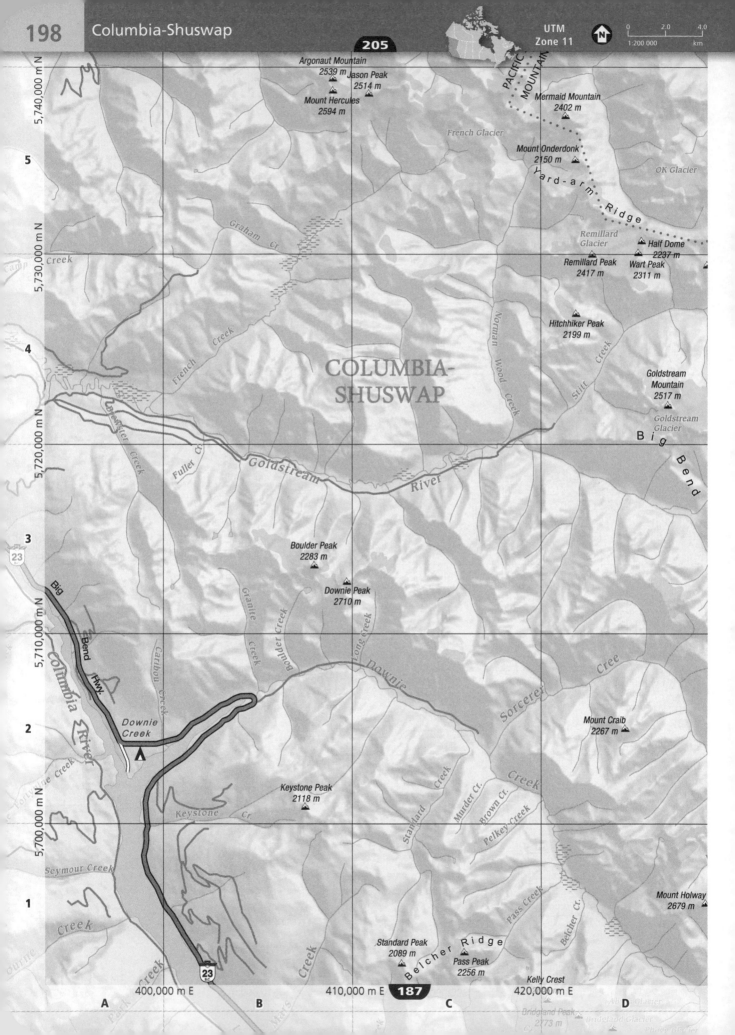

205

UTM
Zone 11

1:200 000

0   2.0   4.0
km

Argonaut Mountain
2539 m
Jason Peak
2514 m
Mount Hercules
2594 m

Mermaid Mountain
2402 m

French Glacier

PACIFIC MOUNTAIN

Mount Onderdonk
2150 m

OK Glacier

Yard-arm Ridge

Graham Cr.

Camp Creek

Remillard Glacier

Half Dome
2237 m

Remillard Peak
2417 m

Wart Peak
2311 m

French Creek

Norman Wood Creek

Hitchhiker Peak
2199 m

Stitt Creek

COLUMBIA-
SHUSWAP

Goldstream
Mountain
2517 m

Brewster Creek

Goldstream
Glacier

Big Bend

Fuller Cr.

Goldstream   River

Boulder Peak
2283 m

Granite Creek

Boulder Creek

Downie Peak
2710 m

Long Creek

Downie

Sorcerer   Creek

Mount Craib
2267 m

Big Bend Hwy.

Caribou Creek

Downie
Creek

Keystone Peak
2118 m

Standard Creek

Murder Cr.

Brown Cr.

Creek

Columbia River

Keystone   Cr.

Pelkey Creek

Pass Creek

Mount Holway
2679 m

Seymour Creek

Belcher Ct.

Tonkawatla Creek

Creek

Mars Creek

Standard Peak
2089 m

Belcher   Ridge

Pass Peak
2256 m

Kelly Crest

Bridgland Peak
2773 m

23

23
B.C.

187

400,000 m E

410,000 m E

420,000 m E

5,740,000 m N

5,730,000 m N

5,720,000 m N

5,710,000 m N

5,700,000 m N

5

4

3

2

1

A   B   C   D

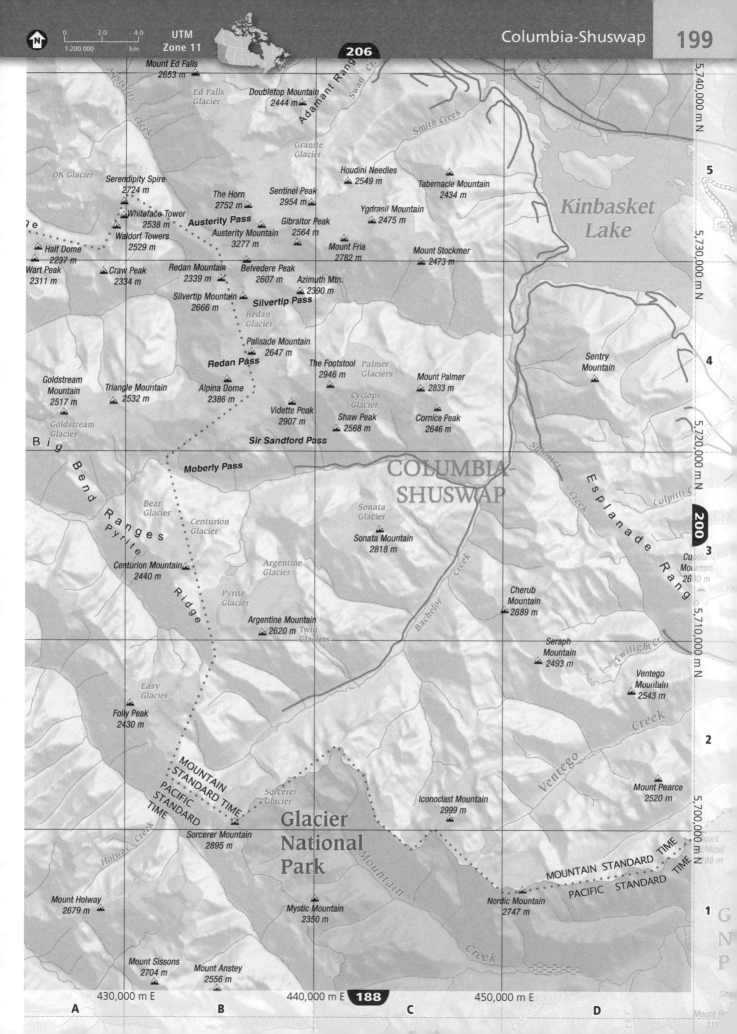

N
1:200 000
0   2.0   4.0
km
UTM
Zone 11

206

5,740,000 m N

Mount Ed Falls
2653 m

Ed Falls
Glacier

Doubletop Mountain
2444 m

Adamant Range

Swan Cr.

Smith Creek

Granite
Glacier

Houdini Needles
2549 m

Tabernacle Mountain
2434 m

**Kinbasket
Lake**

OK Glacier

5

Serendipity Spire
2724 m

The Horn
2752 m

Sentinel Peak
2954 m

Ygdrasil Mountain
2475 m

Whiteface Tower
2538 m

Austerity Pass

Gibraltor Peak
2564 m

Waldorf Towers
2529 m

Austerity Mountain
3277 m

Mount Fria
2782 m

Mount Stockmer
2473 m

5,730,000 m N

Half Dome
2237 m

Wart Peak
2311 m

Craw Peak
2334 m

Redan Mountain
2339 m

Belvedere Peak
2607 m

Azimuth Mtn.
2390 m

Silvertip Mountain
2666 m

Silvertip Pass

Redan
Glacier

Redan Pass

Palisade Mountain
2647 m

The Footstool
2946 m

Palmer
Glaciers

Mount Palmer
2833 m

Sentry
Mountain

Goldstream
Mountain
2517 m

Triangle Mountain
2532 m

Alpina Dome
2386 m

Vidette Peak
2907 m

Cyclops
Glacier

Shaw Peak
2568 m

Cornice Peak
2646 m

Goldstream
Glacier

B i g

Sir Sandford Pass

5,720,000 m N

Bend

Moberly Pass

**COLUMBIA-
SHUSWAP**

Esplanade Range

Colpitti C.

Ranges

Bear
Glacier

Centurion
Glacier

Sonata
Glacier

200

Pyrite

Sonata Mountain
2818 m

Cupola
Mountain
2600 m

3

Centurion Mountain
2440 m

Argentine
Glacier

Pyrite
Glacier

Bachelor

Cherub
Mountain
2889 m

Ridge

Argentine Mountain
2620 m

Twin
Glaciers

Creek

Seraph
Mountain
2493 m

Twilight Cr.

5,710,000 m N

Easy
Glacier

Ventego
Mountain
2543 m

Folly Peak
2430 m

Creek

Ventego

2

Mount Pearce
2520 m

**MOUNTAIN
STANDARD
TIME**

Sorcerer
Glacier

Iconoclast Mountain
2999 m

**PACIFIC
STANDARD
TIME**

**Glacier
National
Park**

Mountain

Mount
McNicoll
3188 m

5,700,000 m N

Sorcerer Mountain
2895 m

Holway Creek

MOUNTAIN STANDARD TIME

PACIFIC STANDARD TIME

Mount Holway
2679 m

Mystic Mountain
2350 m

Nordic Mountain
2747 m

1

G
N
P

Mount Sissons
2704 m

Mount Anstey
2556 m

Creek

Mount Br
311

430,000 m E

440,000 m E **188**

450,000 m E

A   B   C   D

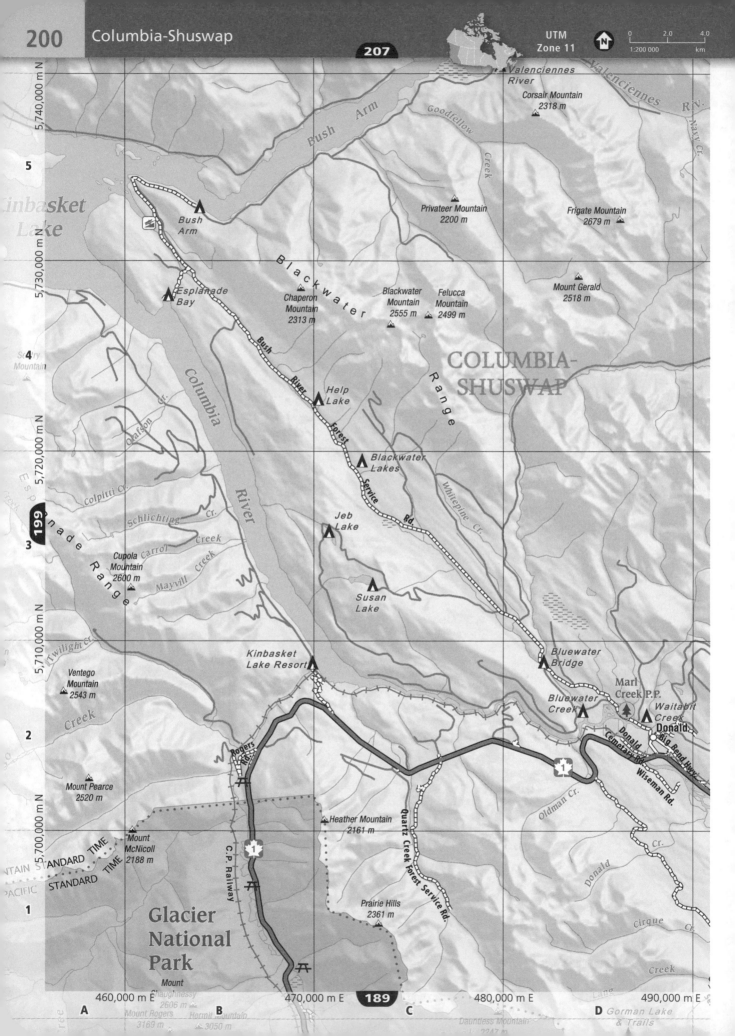

UTM
Zone 11

207

189

Valenciennes River

Corsair Mountain
2318 m

Privateer Mountain
2200 m

Frigate Mountain
2679 m

Bush Arm

Goodfellow Creek

Bush Arm

Blackwater

Chaperon Mountain
2313 m

Blackwater Mountain
2555 m

Felucca Mountain
2499 m

Mount Gerald
2518 m

Esplanade Bay

Columbia

Bush River

Help Lake

Forest

COLUMBIA-SHUSWAP

Range

Kinbasket Lake

Secory Mountain

Okafson Cr.

Colpitti Cr.

Schlichting Cr.

Carrol

Mayvill Creek

Creek

Blackwater Lakes

Service

Jeb Lake

Whitepine Cr.

199

Cupola Mountain
2600 m

Esplanade Range

River

Susan Lake

Rd.

Twilight Cr.

Ventego Mountain
2543 m

Kinbasket Lake Resort

Bluewater Bridge

Marl Creek P.P.

Creek

Rogers Rd.

Bluewater Creek

Waitabit Creek

Donald

Mount Pearce
2520 m

Donald

Cemetari Rd.

Big Bend Hwy.

Wiseman Rd.

1

Oldman Cr.

Mount McNicoll
2188 m

C.P. Railway

Heather Mountain
2161 m

Quartz Creek Forest Service Rd.

Donald

Cr.

STANDARD TIME

STANDARD

TIME

1

PACIFIC STANDARD

Glacier National Park

Prairie Hills
2361 m

Cirque

Creek

Mount
Chaughnessy
2606 m

Mount Rogers
3169 m

Hermit Mountain
3050 m

Dauntless Mountain

Gorman Lake & Trails

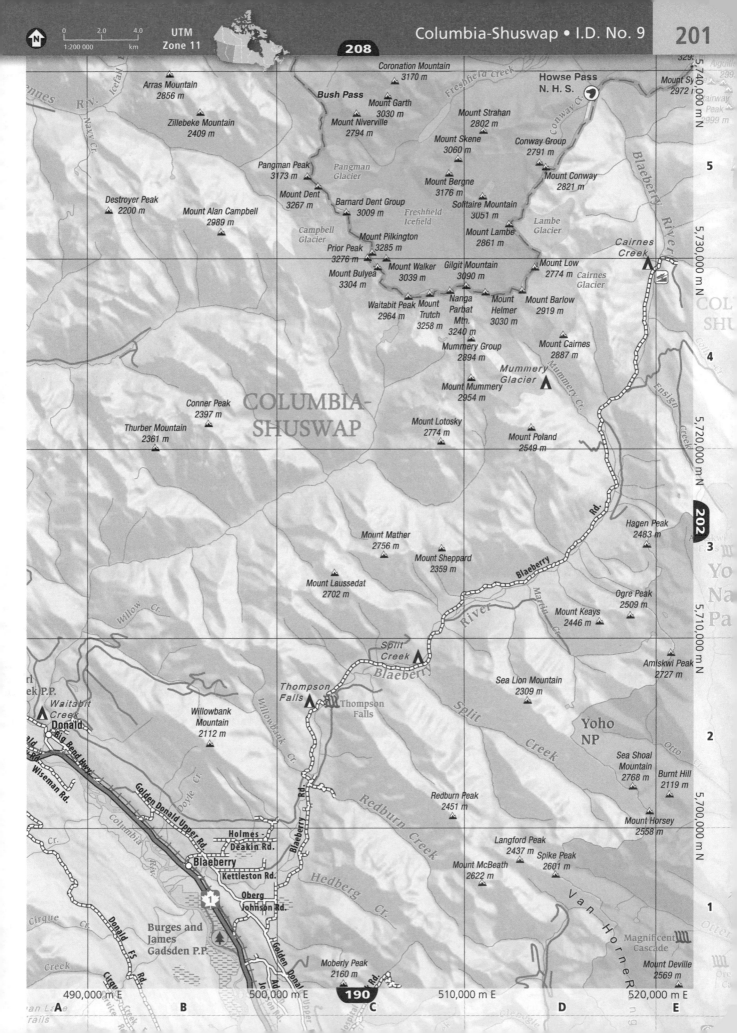

N

0   2.0   4.0
1:200 000   km

UTM
Zone 11

208

Coronation Mountain
3170 m

Arras Mountain
2856 m

Bush Pass

Mount Garth
3030 m

Mount Niverville
2794 m

Zillebeke Mountain
2409 m

Mount Strahan
2802 m

Howse Pass
N. H. S.

Mount Sy
2972 m

Pangman Peak
3173 m

Pangman
Glacier

Mount Skene
3060 m

Conway Group
2791 m

Mount Conway
2821 m

Destroyer Peak
2200 m

Mount Alan Campbell
2989 m

Mount Dent
3267 m

Barnard Dent Group
3009 m

Mount Bergne
3176 m

Freshfield
Icefield

Solitaire Mountain
3051 m

Campbell
Glacier

Mount Pilkington
3285 m

Mount Lambe
2861 m

Lambe
Glacier

Cairnes
Creek

Prior Peak
3276 m

Mount Walker
3039 m

Gilgit Mountain
3090 m

Mount Low
2774 m

Cairnes
Glacier

COL
SHU

Mount Bulyea
3304 m

Waitabit Peak
2964 m

Mount
Trutch
3258 m

Nanga
Parbat
Mtn.
3240 m

Mount
Helmer
3030 m

Mount Barlow
2919 m

Mummery Group
2894 m

Mount Cairnes
2887 m

Conner Peak
2397 m

COLUMBIA-
SHUSWAP

Mount Mummery
2954 m

Mummery
Glacier

Thurber Mountain
2361 m

Mount Lotosky
2774 m

Mount Poland
2549 m

Hagen Peak
2483 m

202

Mount Mather
2756 m

Mount Sheppard
2359 m

Blaeberry

Ogre Peak
2509 m

Mount Laussedat
2702 m

River

Mount Keays
2446 m

Yo
Na
Pa

Willow Cr.

Split
Creek

Blaeberry

Amiskwi Peak
2727 m

Thompson
Falls

Sea Lion Mountain
2309 m

Creek
P.P.

Waitabit
Creek

Willowbank
Mountain
2112 m

Thompson
Falls

Split

Yoho
NP

Donald

Willowbank Cr.

Sea Shoal
Mountain
2768 m

Burnt Hill
2119 m

Big Bend Hwy.

Wiseman Rd.

Golden Donald Upper Rd.

Holmes -
Deakin Rd.

Blaeberry Rd.

Redburn Peak
2451 m

Mount Horsey
2558 m

Doyle Cr.

Columbia

Blaeberry

Kettleston Rd.

Redburn Creek

Langford Peak
2437 m

Spike Peak
2601 m

Cr.

Oberg

Hedberg Cr.

Mount McBeath
2622 m

Van Horne Range

Johnson Rd.

1

Cirque

Cr.

Donald FS Rd.

Burges and
James
Gadsden P.P.

Golden Donald Upper Rd.

Moberly Peak
2160 m

Magnificent
Cascade

Mount Deville
2569 m

Creek

209

UTM
Zone 11

1:200 000

0   2.0   4.0
km

Pass

Aiguille Peak
2999 m
3295 m

Mount Synge
2972 m

Stairway
Peak
2999 m

Midway Peak
2771 m

Aries Peak
2647 m

Ebon Peak
2910 m

Breaker Mountain
2873 m

Capricorn
Glacier

Mount Patterson
3191 m

Parapet
Glacier

Mount Weed
3080 m

Conical Peak
2666 m

Mount Kentigern
2997 m

Silverhorn Mountain
2803 m

Marmot Mountain
2408 m

Mount Willingdon
3373 m

Clearwater
Mountain
2996 m

Observation Peak
3089 m

I.D.
NO. 9

Clearwater P.

Blaeberry River

Cairnes
Creek

COLUMBIA-
SHUSWAP

Barbette
Mountain
2855 m

Mistaya Mountain
2932 m

Caldron Peak
2909 m

Bow Pass

Bow
Summit

Cirque Peak
2866 m

Devon Mou
2912 m

Dolomite Pass

Pipeston

Collie Cr.

Ensign Creek

Trapper
Peak
2988m

Peyto Peak
2980 m

Mount
Jimmy Simpson
2839 m

Mount Thompson
2961 m

Bow Lake

Dolomite Peak
2998 m

Mosquito Mountain
2886 m

Mount Baker
3180 m

Mount Habel
2998 m

Portal Peak
2911 m

Bow Glacier
Falls

Crowfoot Mountain
3055 m

Noseeum Mountain
3002 m

Ayesha Peak
2798 m

Ayesha Glacier

Mount
Rhondda
2911 m

Bow
Glacier

St. Nicholas Peak
2284 m

Crowfoot
Glacier

Mosquito
Creek

Molar Pass

Mount Collie
2943 m

Mount Olive
3075 m

Vulture Glacier

Icefields

Molar
Glacier

Hagen Peak
2483 m

Mont des Poilus
2940 m

Mount Gordon
3002 m

Balfour Pass

Balfour Cr.

Hector Lake

Hector
Glacier

Amiskwi
Falls

Arete Peak
2794 m

Yoho Peak
2419 m

Diableret
Falls

Diableret
Glacier

Waputik
Mountains

Pulpit Peak
2542 m

Mount Hector
3394 m

Ogre Peak
2509 m

Yoho
National
Park

Glacier
des
Poilus

Fall of
the Waves

Mount Balfour
3284 m

Waputik
Icefield

Waputik
Glacier

t Keays
46 m

Isolated Peak
2845 m

Twin
Falls

Fairy
Glacier

Mount McArthur
3015 m

Amiskwi Peak
2727 m

Mount Pollinge
2816 m

Whaleback Mountain
2465 m

Angels
Falls

Laughing
Falls

Angels
Staircase Falls

Daly
Glacier

Mount Daly
3152 m

Kiwetinok Peak
2902 m

The Secretary-
Treasurer
2461 m

Point Lace
Falls

Takakkaw
Falls

Waputik Peak
2550 m

Yoho
NP

Mount Kerr
2863 m

The Vice President
3077 m

Takakkaw
Falls

Takakkaw
Falls

Mount Niles
2972 m

The President
3123 m

Whisky-jack
Falls

Sea Shoal
Mountain
2768 m

Burnt Hill
2119 m

Mount Carnarvon
3040 m

Michael Peak
2465 m

Mount Ogden
2455 m

Paget Peak
2560 m

Mount Bosworth
2771 m

Emerald Peak
2565 m

Wapta Mountain
2778 m

Mount Horsey
2558 m

Hamilton Spur
1943 m

Emerald
Lake
Lodge

Spiral
Tunnels

Kicking
Horse Pass
N.H.S.

Divide
Creek

Hamilton
Falls

Walcott Peak
2152 m

Mount Field
2253 m

Kicking
Horse

Mount
St. Piran
2649 m

Monarch

C.P. Railway

Narao Peak
2974 m

Mount Niblock
2976 m

Mount Whyte
2983 m

Tocher Ridge

Amiskwi River

Mount Burgess
2599 m

Cathedral Mountain
2823 m

Pope's Peak
3163 m

Divide
Mountain
2778 m

Magnificent
Cascade

Field

Collier Peak
3105 m

Mount Deville
2569 m

Oreamnos
Cascade

Mount Stephen
3199 m

Mount Victoria

Victoria
Glacier

Pass Refuge
N.H.S.

520,000 m E   530,000 m E   540,000 m E   550,000 m E

A   B   C   D   E

191

Canadian Rocky

Canadian Rocky

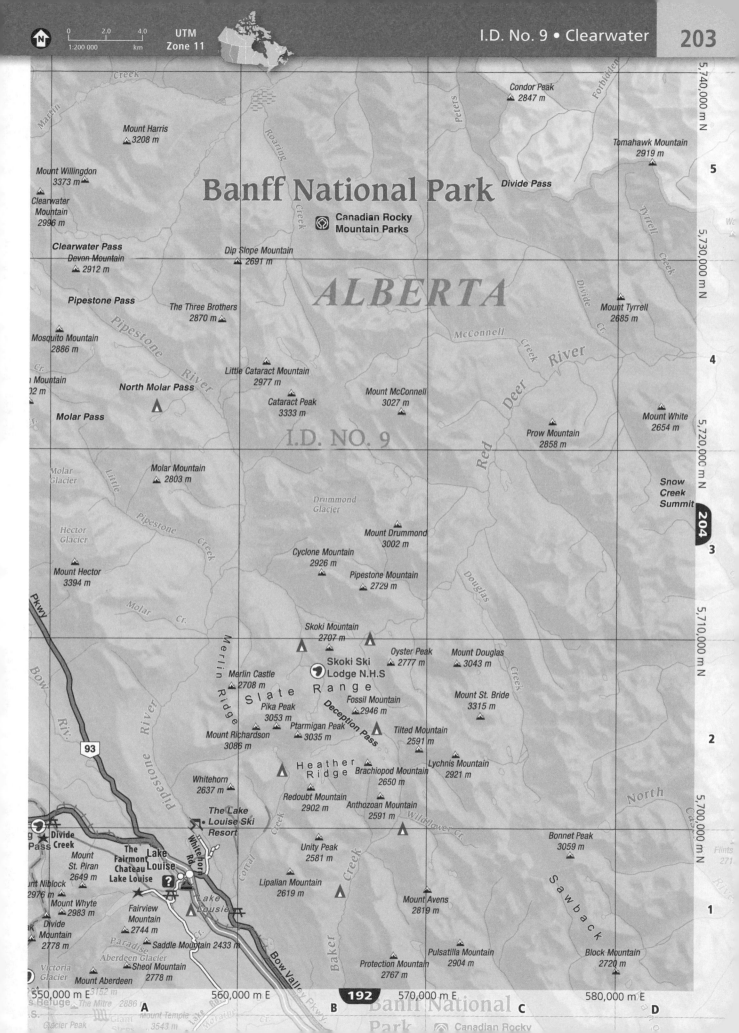

0   2.0   4.0
1:200 000   km

UTM
Zone 11

Creek

Condor Peak
2847 m

Peters

Forbidden

Banff National Park

Mount Harris
3208 m

Tomahawk Mountain
2919 m

Roaring

Divide Pass

Mount Willingdon
3373 m

Clearwater
Mountain
2996 m

Tyrrell

Canadian Rocky
Mountain Parks

Clearwater Pass

Dip Slope Mountain
2691 m

Devon Mountain
2912 m

ALBERTA

Creek

Divide

Mount Tyrrell
2685 m

Pipestone Pass

The Three Brothers
2870 m

McConnell

Cr.

Mosquito Mountain
2886 m

Pipestone

Little Cataract Mountain
2977 m

Mount McConnell
3027 m

Creek

River

Deer

02 m

Mountain

North Molar Pass

River

Cataract Peak
3333 m

I.D. NO. 9

Red

Prow Mountain
2858 m

Mount White
2654 m

Molar Pass

Molar
Glacier

Molar Mountain
2803 m

Drummond
Glacier

Snow
Creek
Summit

204

Little

Hector
Glacier

Pipestone

Creek

Mount Drummond
3002 m

Cyclone Mountain
2926 m

Douglas

Mount Hector
3394 m

Pipestone Mountain
2729 m

Molar   Cr.

Skoki Mountain
2707 m

Creek

Pkwy

Merlin Ridge

Slate   Range

Skoki Ski
Lodge N.H.S

Oyster Peak
2777 m

Mount Douglas
3043 m

Bow

Merlin Castle
2708 m

Pika Peak
3053 m

Fossil Mountain
2946 m

Mount St. Bride
3315 m

Riv.

93

Deception Pass

Ptarmigan Peak
3035 m

Tilted Mountain
2591 m

Mount Richardson
3086 m

Pipestone River

Heather
Ridge

Brachiopod Mountain
2650 m

Lychnis Mountain
2921 m

North

Whitehorn
2637 m

Redoubt Mountain
2902 m

Anthozoan Mountain
2591 m

Wildflower Cr.

g   Divide
Pass   Creek

The Lake
Louise Ski
Resort

Whitehorn Rd.

Bonnet Peak
3059 m

Flints
271

Mount
St. Piran
2649 m

The
Fairmont
Chateau
Lake Louise

Lake
Louise

Corral

Unity Peak
2581 m

Baker   Creek

Sawback

nt Niblock
2976 m

Mount Whyte
2983 m

?

Lake
Louise

Lipalian Mountain
2619 m

Mount Avens
2819 m

River

Divide
Mountain
2778 m

Fairview
Mountain
2744 m

Paradise

Saddle Mountain 2433 m

Aberdeen Glacier

Sheol Mountain
2778 m

Bow Valley Pkwy

Protection Mountain
2767 m

Pulsatilla Mountain
2904 m

Block Mountain
2720 m

Victoria
Glacier

Mount Aberdeen

3752 m

Refuge   The Mitre   2886 m

Glacier Peak

Mount Temple

3543 m

A   550,000 m E   560,000 m E   **B**   **192**   570,000 m E   **C**   580,000 m E   **D**

Banff National

Park   Canadian Rocky

5,740,000 m N

5

5,730,000 m N

4

5,720,000 m N

5,710,000 m N

3

5,700,000 m N

2

1

UTM
Zone 11

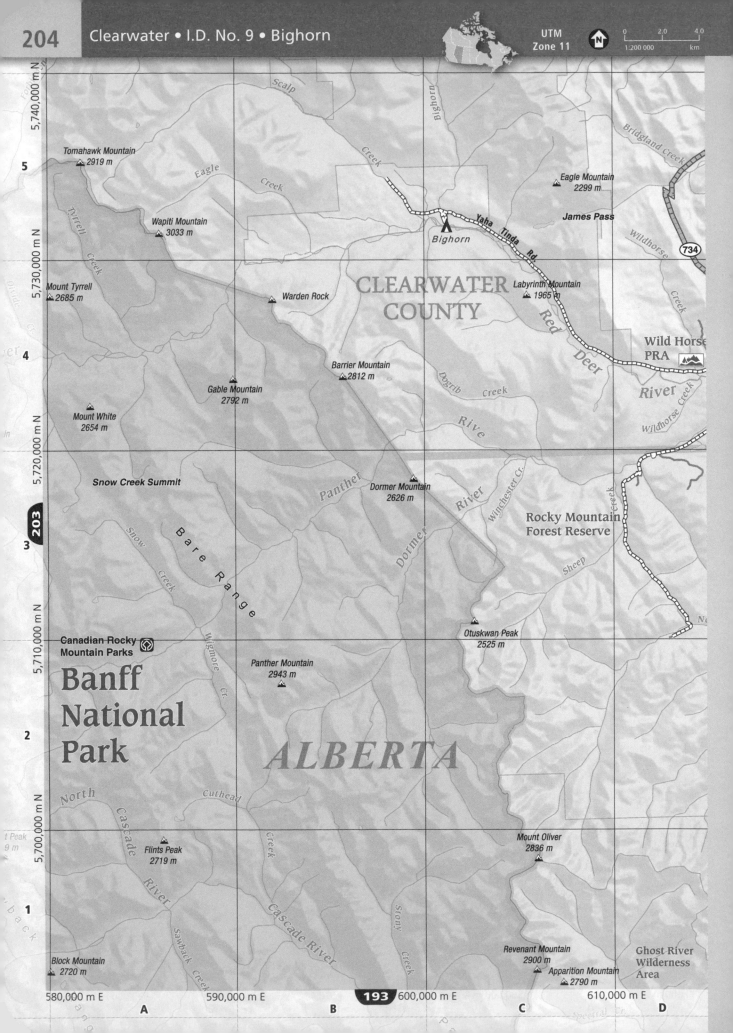

1:200 000

0   2.0   4.0
km

Tomahawk Mountain
▲ 2919 m

Eagle Creek

Eagle Mountain
▲ 2299 m

Bighorn Creek

James Pass

Bridgland Creek

Wapiti Mountain
▲ 3033 m

Scalp Creek

Yaha Tinda Rd.

Bighorn

Wildhorse Creek

734

Tyrrell Creek

Mount Tyrrell
▲ 2685 m

Warden Rock
▲

CLEARWATER
COUNTY

Labyrinth Mountain
▲ 1965 m

Red Deer River

Divide Cr.

Barrier Mountain
▲ 2812 m

Dogrib Creek

Wild Horse
PRA

Gable Mountain
▲ 2792 m

Rive

4

Mount White
▲ 2654 m

Wildhorse Creek

River

Snow Creek Summit

Panther Creek

Dormer Mountain
▲ 2626 m

Winchester Cr.

Creek

203

Bare Range

Snow Creek

Dormer River

Rocky Mountain
Forest Reserve

Sheep Creek

Canadian Rocky
Mountain Parks ⊚

Wigmore Cr.

Otuskwan Peak
▲ 2525 m

No

**Banff
National
Park**

Panther Mountain
▲ 2943 m

ALBERTA

North Cascade River

Cuthead Creek

t Peak
9 m

Mount Oliver
▲ 2836 m

Flints Peak
▲ 2719 m

Cascade River

Stony Creek

1

Block Mountain
▲ 2720 m

Sawback Creek

Cascade River

193

Revenant Mountain
2900 m
▲

Apparition Mountain
▲ 2790 m

Ghost River
Wilderness
Area

5,740,000 m N

5,730,000 m N

5,720,000 m N

5,710,000 m N

5,700,000 m N

5

4

3

2

1

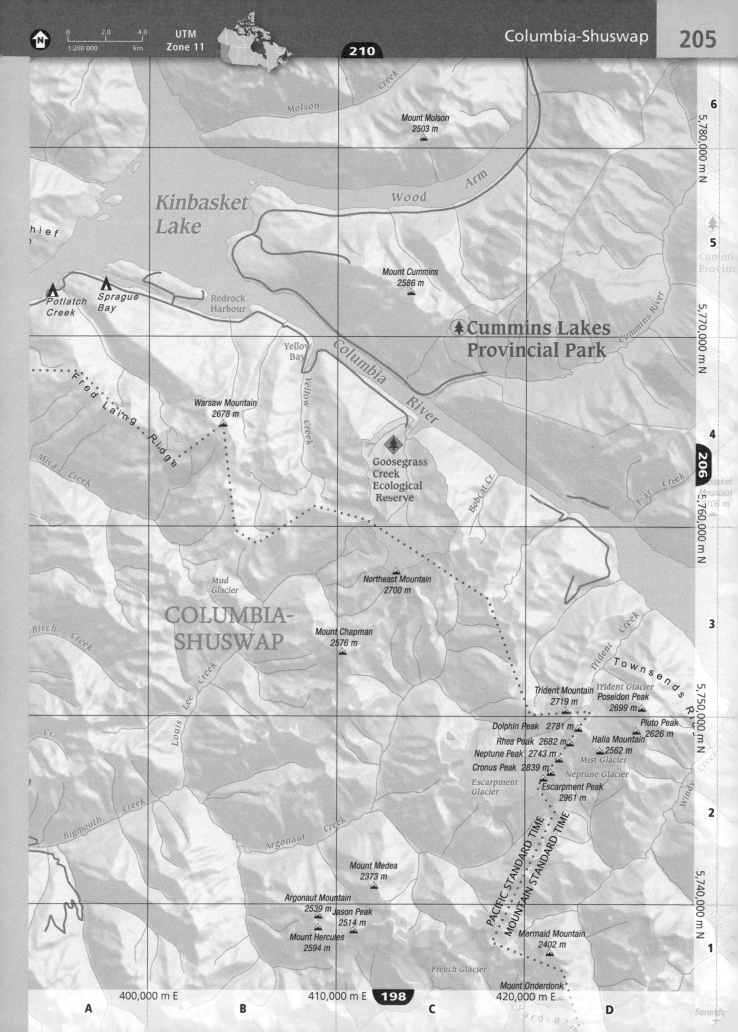

N

| 0 | 2.0 | 4.0 |
| 1:200 000 | | km |

UTM
Zone 11

210

6

5,780,000 m N

Kinbasket Lake

Wood **Arm**

Molson **Creek**

▲ Mount Molson
2503 m

5

5,770,000 m N

Cummi
Provinc

Mount Cummins
2503 m

hief
e

▲ Potlatch
Creek

▲ Sprague
Bay

Redrock
Harbour

Yellow
Bay

Columbia River

♠ **Cummins Lakes**
Provincial Park

Cummins River

Fred Laing Ridge

Warsaw Mountain
2678 m

Yellow Creek

4

5,760,000 m N

206

oosket
Mountain
106 m

Mica Creek

Goosegrass
Creek
Ecological
Reserve

Bobcat Cr.

Tsar Creek

COLUMBIA-
SHUSWAP

Mud
Glacier

Northeast Mountain
2700 m

Birch Creek

Louis Lee Creek

Mount Chapman
2576 m

Trident Creek

Townsends River

3

5,750,000 m N

Trident Mountain
2719 m ▲

Trident Glacier
Poseidon Peak
2699 m ▲

Dolphin Peak   2781 m ▲

Pluto Peak
2626 m

Rhea Peak   2682 m ▲

Halia Mountain
▲2562 m

Neptune Peak   2743 m ▲

Mist Glacier

Cronus Peak   2839 m ▲

Neptune Glacier

Escarpment
Glacier

Escarpment Peak
2961 m

Cr.

Bigmouth Creek

Argonaut Creek

PACIFIC STANDARD TIME

MOUNTAIN STANDARD TIME

Windy Creek

2

5,740,000 m N

Mount Medea
2373 m ▲

Argonaut Mountain
2539 m ▲

Jason Peak
2514 m ▲

Mount Hercules
2594 m ▲

Mermaid Mountain
2402 m ▲

French Glacier

Mount Onderdonk

1

CR. Glacier

Serendip

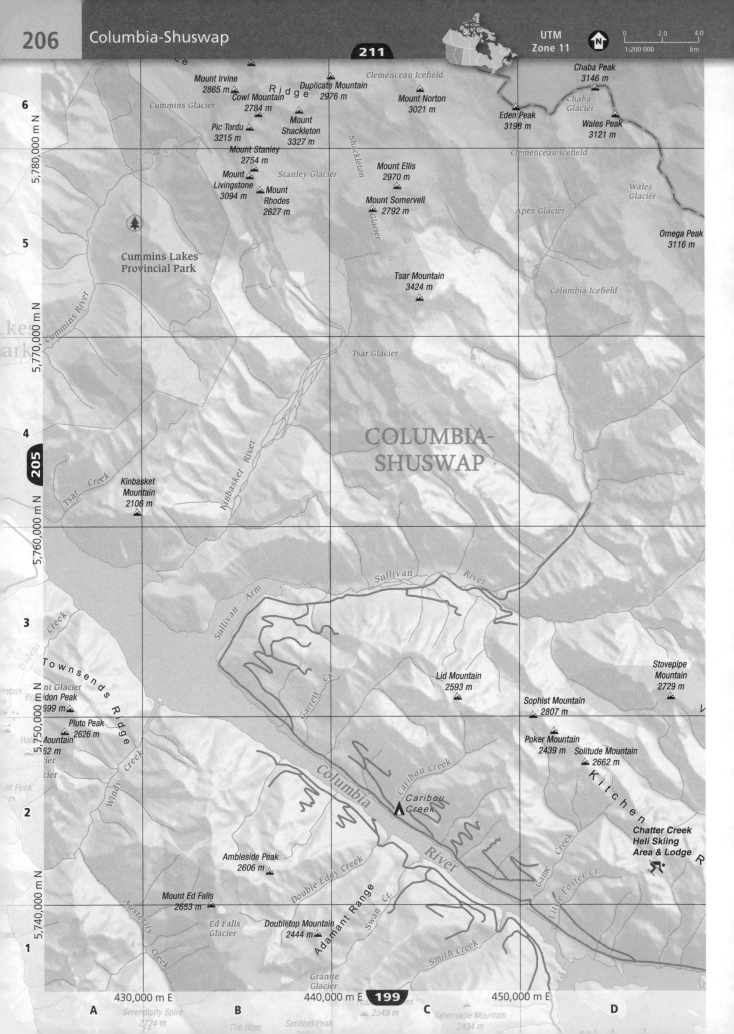

Chaba Peak
3146 m

Mount Irvine
2865 m

Duplicate Mountain
2976 m

Clemenceau Icefield

Chaba
Glacier

Cummins Glacier

Ridge

Cowl Mountain
2784 m

Mount Norton
3021 m

Eden Peak
3198 m

Wales Peak
3121 m

Pic Tordu
3215 m

Mount
Shackleton
3327 m

Mount Stanley
2754 m

Clemenceau Icefield

Shackleton

Mount
Livingstone
3094 m

Stanley Glacier

Mount
Rhodes
2627 m

Mount Ellis
2970 m

Wales
Glacier

Mount Somervell
2792 m

Apex Glacier

Glacier

Omega Peak
3116 m

Cummins Lakes
Provincial Park

Tsar Mountain
3424 m

Columbia Icefield

Cummins River

Tsar Glacier

COLUMBIA-
SHUSWAP

205

Tsar   Creek

Kinbasket
Mountain
2106 m

Kinbasket River

Sullivan   River

Trident

Creek

Townsends Ridge

Sullivan Arm

Garrett Cr.

Lid Mountain
2593 m

Stovepipe
Mountain
2729 m

nt Glacier
idon Peak
699 m

Sophist Mountain
2807 m

Kitchen

Pluto Peak
2626 m

Poker Mountain
2439 m   Solitude Mountain
2662 m

Hai
Mountain
62 m

Windy   Creek

Columbia

Caribou Creek

Caribou
Creek

Chatter Creek
Heli Skiing
Area & Lodge

Ambleside Peak
2606 m

River

Game   Creek

Little Foster Cr.

Mount Ed Falls
2653 m

Double Eddy Creek

Swan Cr.

Ed Falls
Glacier

Doubletop Mountain
2444 m

Adamant Range

Smith Creek

Aisicky   Creek

Granite
Glacier

199

430,000 m E   440,000 m E   450,000 m E

Serendipity Spire
2724 m

The Horn   Sentinel Peak   2549 m   Tabernacle Mountain
2434 m

A   B   C   D

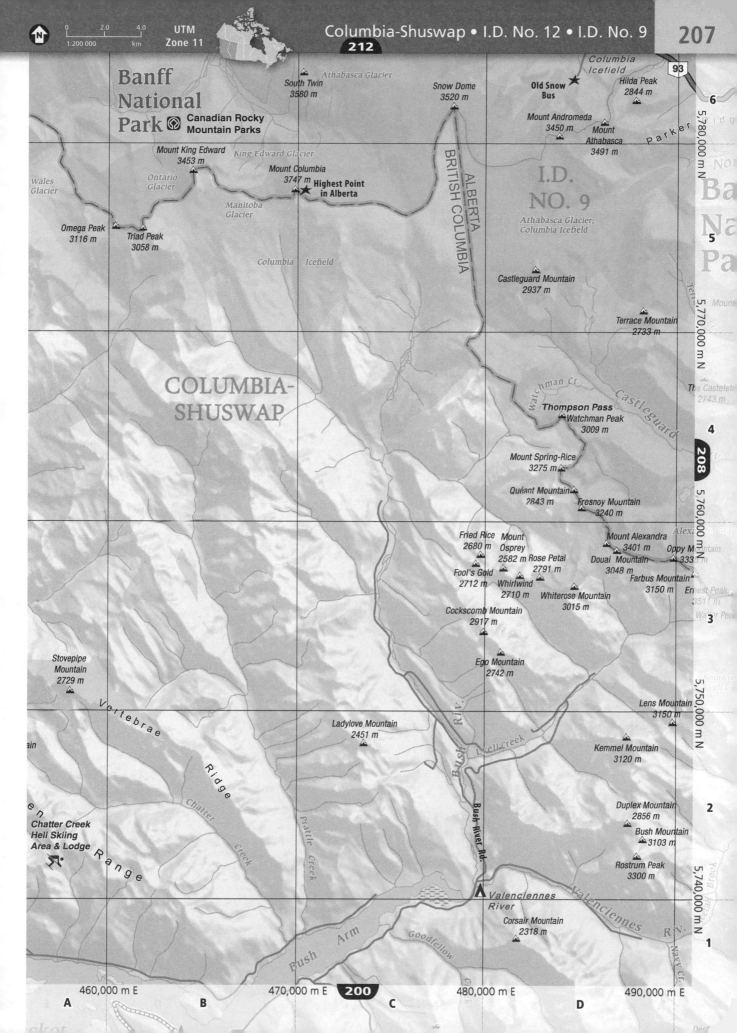

UTM
Zone 11

0   2.0   4.0
1:200 000   km

**Banff
National
Park** ◈ **Canadian Rocky
Mountain Parks**

South Twin
3580 m

Athabasca Glacier

Snow Dome
3520 m

Old Snow
Bus ★

Columbia
Icefield

93

Hilda Peak
2844 m

Mount King Edward
3453 m

King Edward Glacier

Mount Andromeda
3450 m

Mount
Athabasca
3491 m

Parker

Mount Columbia
3747 m ★ **Highest Point
in Alberta**

**I.D.
NO. 9**

Athabasca Glacier;
Columbia Icefield

No

Ba

Ontario
Glacier

Manitoba
Glacier

ALBERTA
BRITISH COLUMBIA

Wales
Glacier

Omega Peak
3116 m

Triad Peak
3058 m

Columbia   Icefield

Castleguard Mountain
2937 m

Mount

Na

Pa

Terrace Mountain
2733 m

Tе

The Castelets
2743 m

**COLUMBIA-
SHUSWAP**

Watchman Cr.

Castleguard

Thompson Pass
Watchman Peak
3009 m

208

Mount Spring-Rice
3275 m

Quéant Mountain
2843 m

Fresnoy Mountain
3240 m

Fried Rice
2680 m

Mount
Osprey
2582 m Rose Petal
2791 m

Mount Alexandra
3401 m

Alexa

Oppy M
3335 m

Douai Mountain
3048 m

Fool's Gold
2712 m

Whirlwind
2710 m

Whiterose Mountain
3015 m

Farbus Mountain
3150 m

Ernest Peak
3511 m
Wa er Pea

Cockscomb Mountain
2917 m

Stovepipe
Mountain
2729 m

Ego Mountain
2742 m

Lens Mountain
3150 m

V
e
r
t
e
b
r
a
e

Ladylove Mountain
2451 m

Bush River

Lyell Creek

Kemmel Mountain
3120 m

R
i
d
g
e

Chatter Creek

Pratله Creek

Bush River Rd.

Duplex Mountain
2856 m

Bush Mountain
3103 m

**Chatter Creek
Heli Skiing
Area & Lodge**

R
a
n
g
e

Rostrum Peak
3300 m

Valenciennes
River

Valenciennes

Bush
Arm

Goodfellow

Corsair Mountain
2318 m

Valenciennes R V

Navy Cr.

5,780,000 m N

5,770,000 m N

5,760,000 m N

5,750,000 m N

5,740,000 m N

6

5

4

3

2

1

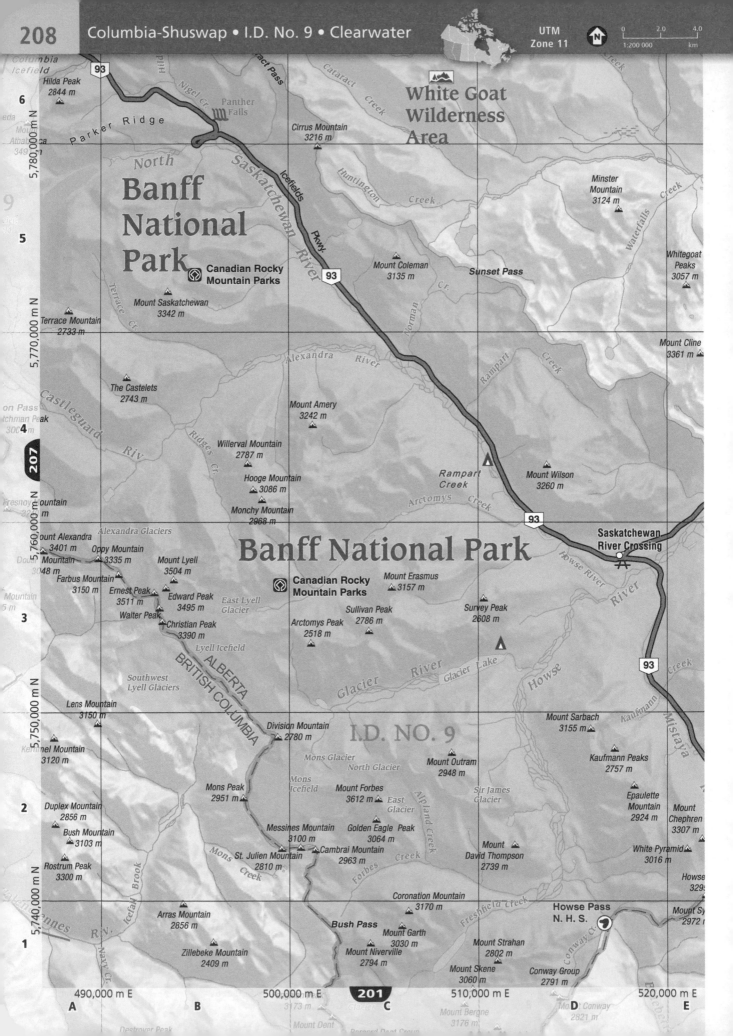

93

Hilda Peak
2844 m

Columbia
Icefield

Mount
Athabasca
3491 m

Cataract Pass

Nigel Cr.

Panther
Falls

Cirrus Mountain
3216 m

Cataract Creek

White Goat
Wilderness
Area

North

Parker Ridge

**Banff
National
Park**

Saskatchewan River

Icefields Pkwy.

Huntington Creek

Minster
Mountain
3124 m

Waterfalls Creek

93

Mount Coleman
3135 m

Sunset Pass

Whitegoat
Peaks
3057 m

Canadian Rocky
Mountain Parks

Mount Saskatchewan
3342 m

Terrace Mountain
2733 m

Terrace Cr.

Norman Cr.

Alexandra River

Mount Cline
3361 m

The Castelets
2743 m

Castleguard Riv

Castleguard

Mount Amery
3242 m

Ridges Cr.

Willerval Mountain
2787 m

Rampart Creek

Mount Wilson
3260 m

207

Hooge Mountain
3086 m

Fresnoy Mountain

Monchy Mountain
2968 m

Arctomys Creek

93

Alexandra Glaciers

Banff National Park

Saskatchewan
River Crossing

Mount Alexandra
3401 m

Oppy Mountain
3335 m

Dour Mountain
3048 m

Mount Lyell
3504 m

Canadian Rocky
Mountain Parks

Mount Erasmus
3157 m

Howse River

Farbus Mountain
3150 m

Ernest Peak
3511 m

Edward Peak
3495 m

East Lyell
Glacier

Sullivan Peak
2786 m

Survey Peak
2608 m

Mountain

Walter Peak

Christian Peak
3390 m

Arctomys Peak
2518 m

Lyell Icefield

ALBERTA
BRITISH COLUMBIA

Glacier River

Glacier Lake

Howse River

93

Kaufmann Creek

Lens Mountain
3150 m

Southwest
Lyell Glaciers

Division Mountain
2780 m

I.D. NO. 9

Mount Sarbach
3155 m

Kemmel Mountain
3120 m

Mons Glacier

North Glacier

Mount Outram
2948 m

Kaufmann Peaks
2757 m

Mistaya River

Duplex Mountain
2856 m

Mons
Icefield

Mons Peak
2951 m

Mount Forbes
3612 m

East
Glacier

Sir James
Glacier

Epaulette
Mountain
2924 m

Mount
Chephren
3307 m

Bush Mountain
3103 m

Messines Mountain
3100 m

St. Julien Mountain
2810 m

Golden Eagle Peak
3064 m

Cambrai Mountain
2963 m

Mount
David Thompson
2739 m

White Pyramid
3016 m

Rostrum Peak
3300 m

Mons Creek

Icefall Brook

Forbes Creek

Alpland Creek

Howse
3295 m

Coronation Mountain
3170 m

Freshfield Creek

Howse Pass
N. H. S.

Mount Sy
2972 m

Arras Mountain
2856 m

Bush Pass

Mount Garth
3030 m

Mount Niverville
2794 m

Mount Strahan
2802 m

Conway Cr.

Mount Conway
2821 m

Zillebeke Mountain
2409 m

Mount Skene
3060 m

Conway Group
2791 m

Mount Bergne
3176 m

Mount Dent

Destrover Peak

490,000 m E

500,000 m E

201

510,000 m E

520,000 m E

A   B   C   D   E

5,780,000 m N

5,770,000 m N

5,760,000 m N

5,750,000 m N

5,740,000 m N

6   5   4   3   2   1

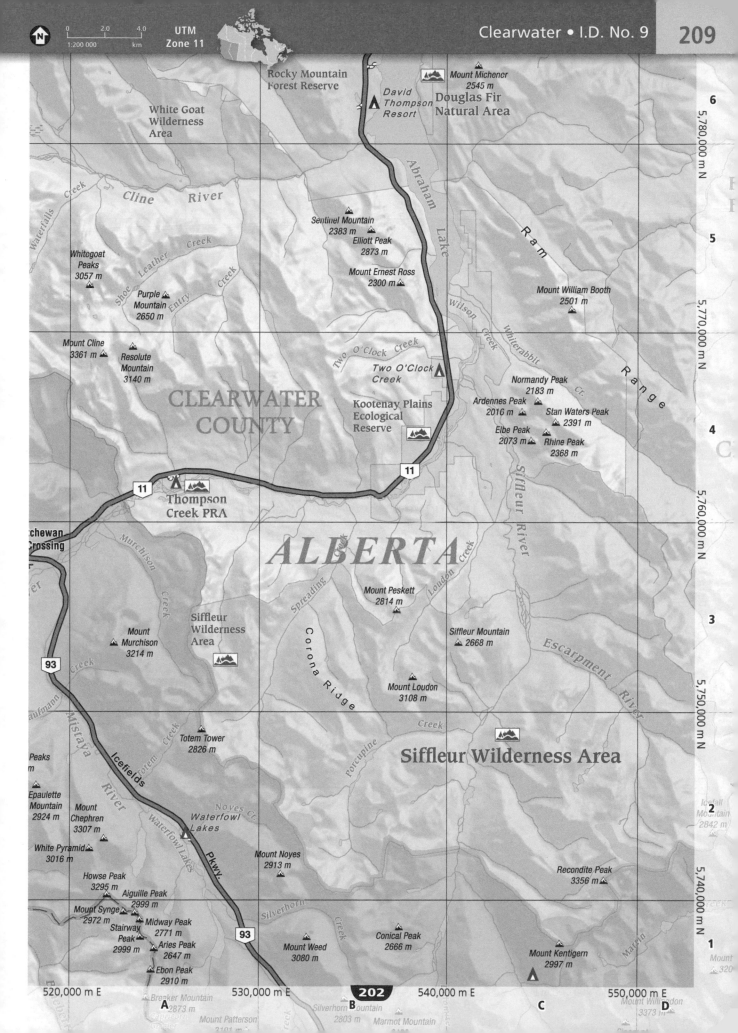

N

0   2.0   4.0
1:200 000   km

UTM
Zone 11

Rocky Mountain
Forest Reserve

Mount Michener
2545 m

David
Thompson
Resort

Douglas Fir
Natural Area

White Goat
Wilderness
Area

Waterfalls Creek

Cline   River

Creek

Shoe Leather

Whitegoat
Peaks
3057 m

Purple
Mountain
2650 m

Entry   Creek

Mount Cline
3361 m

Resolute
Mountain
3140 m

CLEARWATER
COUNTY

Abraham Lake

Ram

Sentinel Mountain
2383 m

Elliott Peak
2873 m

Mount Ernest Ross
2300 m

Two O'Clock   Creek

Two O'Clock
Creek

Kootenay Plains
Ecological
Reserve

Wilson   Creek

Whiterabbit   Cr.

Mount William Booth
2501 m

Normandy Peak
2183 m

Ardennes Peak
2016 m

Stan Waters Peak
2391 m

Elbe Peak
2073 m

Rhine Peak
2368 m

Range

Siffleur River

11

11

Thompson
Creek PRA

chewan
Crossing

r

93

Murchison   Creek

Kaufmann   Creek

ALBERTA

Siffleur
Wilderness
Area

Mount
Murchison
3214 m

Spreading   Creek

Corona   Ridge

Loudon   Creek

Mount Peskett
2814 m

Siffleur Mountain
2668 m

Escarpment   River

Mount Loudon
3108 m

Creek

Siffleur Wilderness Area

Porcupine

Totem   Creek

Totem Tower
2826 m

Peaks
m

Epaulette
Mountain
2924 m

Mount
Chephren
3307 m

White Pyramid
3016 m

Mistaya   River

Icefields

Waterfowl Lakes

Noyes   Cr.

Waterfowl
Lakes

Silverhorn

Mount Noyes
2913 m

Silverhorn   Creek

Recondite Peak
3356 m

Icefall
Mountain
2842 m

Howse Peak
3295 m

Aiguille Peak
2999 m

Mount Synge
2972 m

Stairway
Peak
2999 m

Midway Peak
2771 m

Aries Peak
2647 m

Ebon Peak
2910 m

Pkwy.

93

Mount Weed
3080 m

Conical Peak
2666 m

Mount Kentigern
2997 m

Mount
320

6

5

5,780,000 m N

5,770,000 m N

4

5,760,000 m N

3

5,750,000 m N

2

5,740,000 m N

1

520,000 m E

530,000 m E

202

540,000 m E

550,000 m E

A   Breaker Mountain   B   Silverhorn   C   D
2873 m   Mountain   Mount Willedon
2803 m   3373 m
Mount Patterson   Marmot Mountain
3101 m

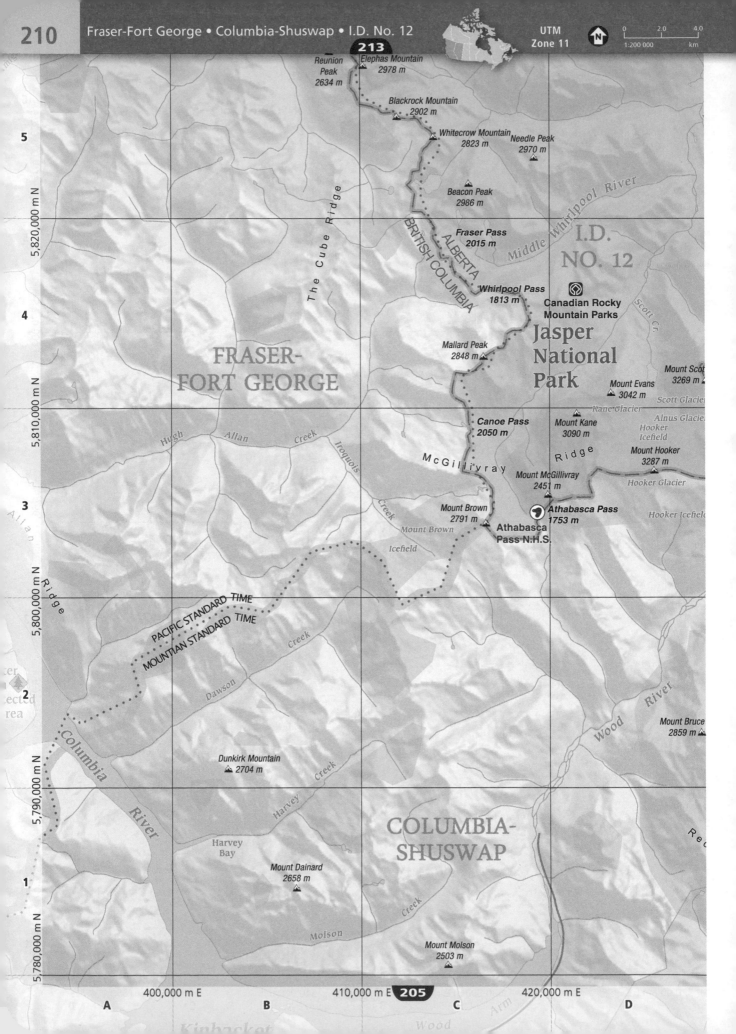

1:200 000

213

**FRASER-
FORT GEORGE**

**I.D.
NO. 12**

Canadian Rocky
Mountain Parks

**Jasper
National
Park**

Reunion
Peak
2634 m

Elephas Mountain
2978 m

Blackrock Mountain
2902 m

Whitecrow Mountain
2823 m

Needle Peak
2970 m

Beacon Peak
2986 m

Fraser Pass
2015 m

ALBERTA
BRITISH COLUMBIA

Middle Whirlpool River

Whirlpool Pass
1813 m

Mallard Peak
2848 m

Scott Cr.

Mount Scott
3269 m

Mount Evans
3042 m

Kane Glacier

Scott Glacier

Canoe Pass
2050 m

Mount Kane
3090 m

Alnus Glacier

Hooker
Icefield

Mount Hooker
3287 m

McGillivray

Ridge

Mount McGillivray
2451 m

Hooker Glacier

Mount Brown
2791 m

Athabasca Pass
1753 m

Athabasca
Pass N.H.S.

Hooker Icefield

Mount Brown
Icefield

The Cube Ridge

Hugh

Allan

Creek

Iroquois

Creek

PACIFIC STANDARD TIME

MOUNTIAN STANDARD TIME

Dawson

Creek

Allan Ridge

ter

ected
rea

Columbia

River

Mount Bruce
2859 m

Wood

River

Dunkirk Mountain
2704 m

Harvey

Creek

Harvey
Bay

Mount Dainard
2658 m

**COLUMBIA-
SHUSWAP**

Re

1

Molson

Creek

Mount Molson
2503 m

5,820,000 m N

5,810,000 m N

5,800,000 m N

5,790,000 m N

5,780,000 m N

Wood

Arm

Kinbasket

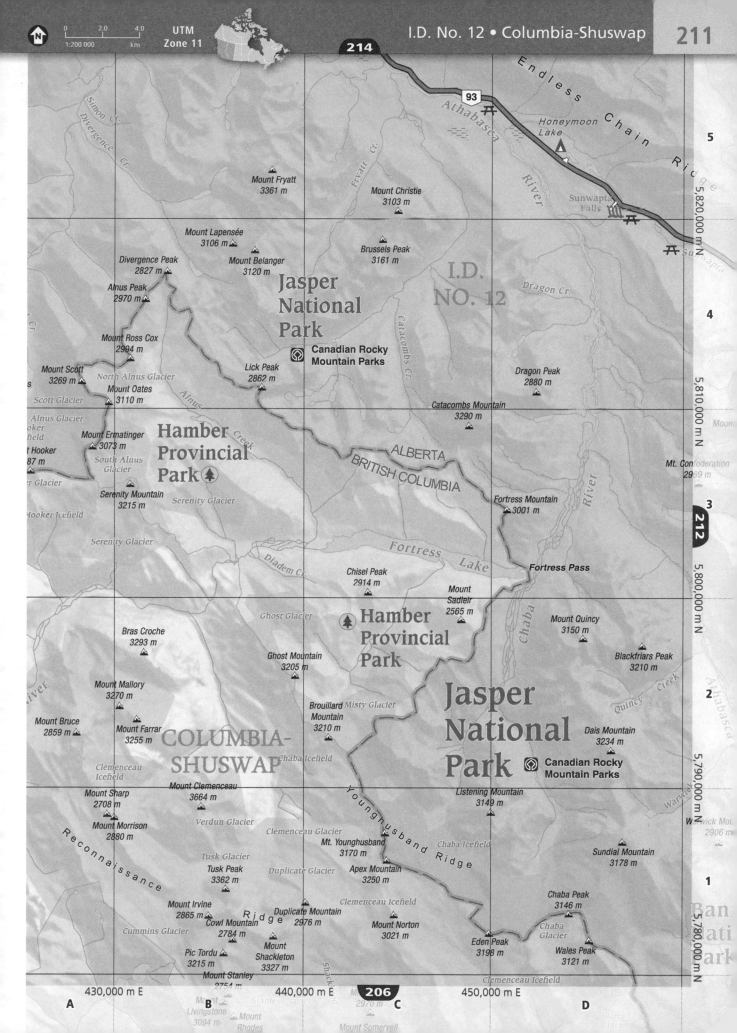

N

1:200 000

UTM
Zone 11

0   2.0   4.0
km

214

93

Endless Chain Ridge

Athabasca River

Honeymoon Lake

Sunwapta Falls

Sunwapta

5

5,820,000 m N

Mount Fryatt
3361 m

Mount Christie
3103 m

Fryatt Cr.

I.D.
NO. 12

Mount Lapensée
3106 m

Mount Belanger
3120 m

Brussels Peak
3161 m

Dragon Cr.

Divergence Peak
2827 m

Jasper
National
Park

4

Alnus Peak
2970 m

Dragon Peak
2880 m

Mount Ross Cox
2994 m

Catacombs Cr.

Lick Peak
2862 m

Canadian Rocky
Mountain Parks

5,810,000 m N

Mount Scott
3269 m

North Alnus Glacier

Catacombs Mountain
3290 m

Scott Glacier

Mount Oates
3110 m

Mount Con federation
2969 m

Alnus Glacier
Hooker
field

Mount Ermatinger
3073 m

Hamber
Provincial
Park ⌖

Alnus Creek

ALBERTA

BRITISH COLUMBIA

Fortress Mountain
3001 m

River

t Hooker
87 m

South Alnus
Glacier

3

212

r Glacier

Serenity Mountain
3215 m

Serenity Glacier

5,800,000 m N

Hooker Icefield

Serenity Glacier

Diadem Cr.

Fortress Lake

Fortress Pass

Chisel Peak
2914 m

Mount
Sadleir
2565 m

Mount Quincy
3150 m

Ghost Glacier

Hamber
Provincial
Park

Chaba

Bras Croche
3293 m

Ghost Mountain
3205 m

Blackfriars Peak
3210 m

Mount Mallory
3270 m

Quincy Creek

2

Mount Bruce
2859 m

Mount Farrar
3255 m

COLUMBIA-
SHUSWAP

Brouillard
Mountain
3210 m

Misty Glacier

Jasper
National
Park

Dais Mountain
3234 m

River

Chaba Icefield

Canadian Rocky
Mountain Parks

5,790,000 m N

Clemenceau
Icefield

Mount Clemenceau
3664 m

Listening Mountain
3149 m

W

Mount Sharp
2708 m

Verdun Glacier

Warwick Mou.
2906 m

Mount Morrison
2880 m

Clemenceau Glacier

Younghusband Ridge

Reconnaissance

Tusk Glacier

Mt. Younghusband
3170 m

Chaba Icefield

Sundial Mountain
3178 m

Tusk Peak
3362 m

Duplicate Glacier

Apex Mountain
3250 m

Ridge

Clemenceau Icefield

1

Mount Irvine
2865 m

Duplicate Mountain
2976 m

Chaba Peak
3146 m

Cummins Glacier

Cowl Mountain
2784 m

Mount Norton
3021 m

Chaba
Glacier

Ban
ati
Park

Pic Tordu
3215 m

Mount
Shackleton
3327 m

Eden Peak
3198 m

Wales Peak
3121 m

Mount Stanley
2754 m

Shack

Clemenceau Icefield

5,780,000 m N

430,000 m E

206

440,000 m E

450,000 m E

Mount
Livingstone
3094 m

Mount
Rhodes

Mount Somervell

Wales Mou.

A

B

C

D

UTM
Zone 11
1:200 000

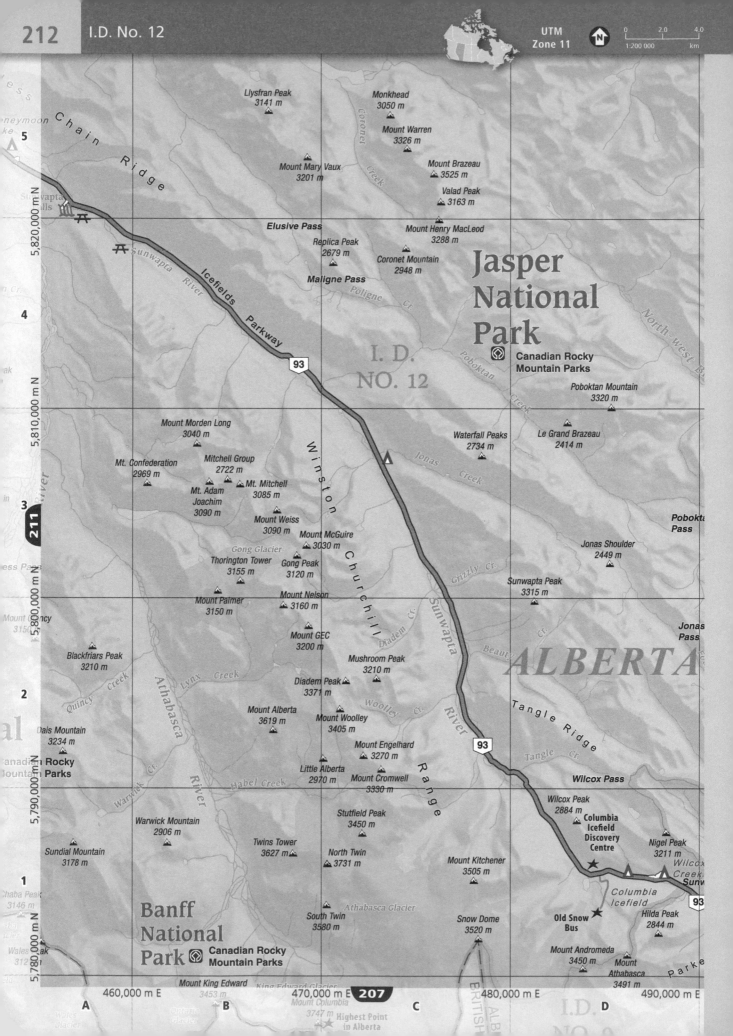

Llysfran Peak
3141 m

Monkhead
3050 m

Mount Warren
3326 m

Mount Mary Vaux
3201 m

Mount Brazeau
3525 m

Valad Peak
3163 m

Elusive Pass

Replica Peak
2679 m

Mount Henry MacLeod
3288 m

Coronet Mountain
2948 m

Maligne Pass

Jasper National Park

Canadian Rocky
Mountain Parks

I.D.
NO. 12

Poboktan Mountain
3320 m

Mount Morden Long
3040 m

Waterfall Peaks
2734 m

Le Grand Brazeau
2414 m

Mitchell Group
2722 m

Mt. Confederation
2969 m

Mt. Mitchell
3085 m

Poboktan
Pass

Mt. Adam
Joachim
3090 m

211

Mount Weiss
3090 m

Mount McGuire
3030 m

Gong Glacier

Jonas Shoulder
2449 m

Thorington Tower
3155 m

Gong Peak
3120 m

Sunwapta Peak
3315 m

Mount Palmer
3150 m

Mount Nelson
3160 m

Mount GEC
3200 m

Jonas
Pass

Blackfriars Peak
3210 m

Mushroom Peak
3210 m

ALBERTA

Diadem Peak
3371 m

Mount Alberta
3619 m

Mount Woolley
3405 m

Tangle Ridge

Dais Mountain
3234 m

Canadian Rocky
Mountain Parks

Mount Engelhard
3270 m

93

Wilcox Pass

Little Alberta
2970 m

Mount Cromwell
3330 m

Warwick Mountain
2906 m

Stutfield Peak
3450 m

Wilcox Peak
2884 m

Columbia
Icefield
Discovery
Centre

Twins Tower
3627 m

North Twin
3731 m

Sundial Mountain
3178 m

Nigel Peak
3211 m

Mount Kitchener
3505 m

Chaba Peak
3146 m

South Twin
3580 m

Athabasca Glacier

Snow Dome
3520 m

Old Snow
Bus

Columbia
Icefield

93

Hilda Peak
2844 m

Banff National Park

Canadian Rocky
Mountain Parks

Mount Andromeda
3450 m

Mount
Athabasca
3491 m

Wales Peak
3127

Mount King Edward
3453 m

King Edward Glacier

207

Mount Columbia
3747 m Highest Point
in Alberta

I.D.
NO. 9

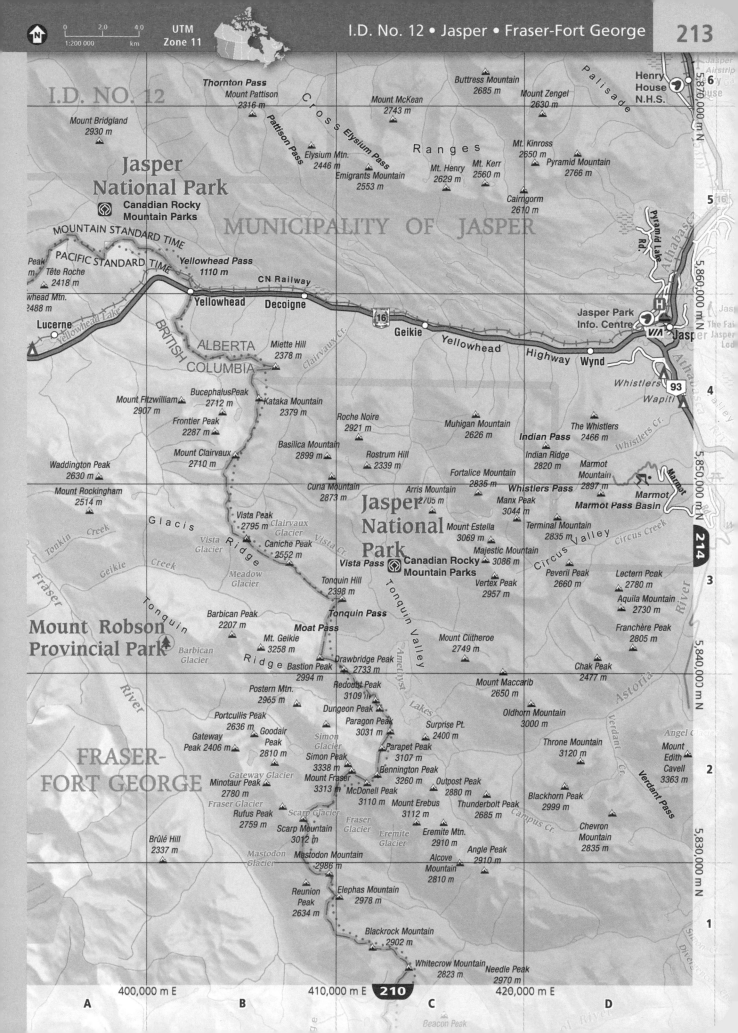

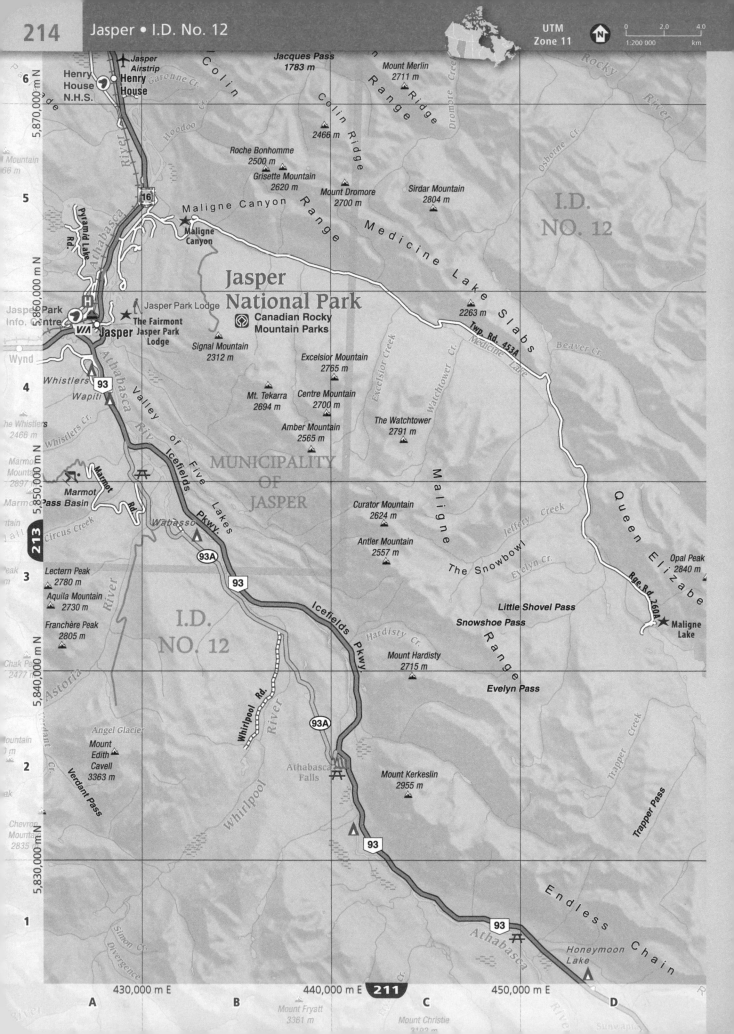

UTM
Zone 11

1:200 000

0   2.0   4.0
km

6

5,870,000 m N

Jasper
Airstrip

Henry
House
N.H.S.

Henry
House

Garonne Cr.

Colin

Hoodoo

Jacques Pass
1783 m

Mount Merlin
2711 m

Colin Ridge

Dromore Creek

Ridge

Rocky

River

5

Pyramid
Lake
Rd.

16

Athabasca River

Maligne Canyon

Roche Bonhomme
2500 m

Grisette Mountain
2620 m

2466 m

Mount Dromore
2700 m

Range

Sirdar Mountain
2804 m

Colin Ridge

Osborne Cr.

I.D.
NO. 12

Mountain
66 m

Malique
Canyon

Jasper
National Park

Jasper Park Lodge

Canadian Rocky
Mountain Parks

Medicine Lake Slabs

2263 m

Twp. Rd. 453A

Beaver Cr.

4

5,860,000 m N

Jasper Park
Info. Centre

H

VIA

Jasper

The Fairmont
Jasper Park
Lodge

Signal Mountain
2312 m

Excelsior Mountain
2765 m

Excelsior Creek

Watchtower Cr.

Medicine Lake

Wynd

Whistlers

93

Wapiti

Whistlers Cr.

Mt. Tekarra
2694 m

Centre Mountain
2700 m

Amber Mountain
2565 m

The Watchtower
2791 m

Maligne

Queen Elizabeth

The Whistlers
2466 m

5,850,000 m N

Marmot
Mountain
2897 m

Marmot

Marmot
Pass Basin

Marmot Rd.

Wabasso

MUNICIPALITY
OF
JASPER

Valley of Five Lakes

Curator Mountain
2624 m

Antler Mountain
2557 m

Jeffery Creek

Range

The Snowbowl

Evelyn Cr.

Rge. Rd. 260A

Opal Peak
2840 m

3

213

Circus Creek

Lectern Peak
2780 m

Aquila Mountain
2730 m

Franchère Peak
2805 m

Athabasca River

93A

93

Icefields Pkwy.

Little Shovel Pass

Snowshoe Pass

Maligne
Lake

Chak Peak
2477 m

I.D.
NO. 12

Icefields Pkwy.

Hardisty Cr.

Mount Hardisty
2715 m

Evelyn Pass

2

5,840,000 m N

Astoria River

Verdant Pass

Verdant Cr.

Mountain
0 m

Angel Glacier

Mount
Edith
Cavell
3363 m

Whirlpool Rd.

Whirlpool River

93A

Athabasca
Falls

Mount Kerkeslin
2955 m

Trapper Creek

Trapper Pass

Chevron
Mountain
2835 m

5,830,000 m N

Whirlpool River

93

Endless Chain

1

Simon Cr.

Divergence

Athabasca River

93

Honeymoon
Lake

Rocky River

A   B   C   D

Mount Fryatt
3361 m

Mount Christie
3103 m

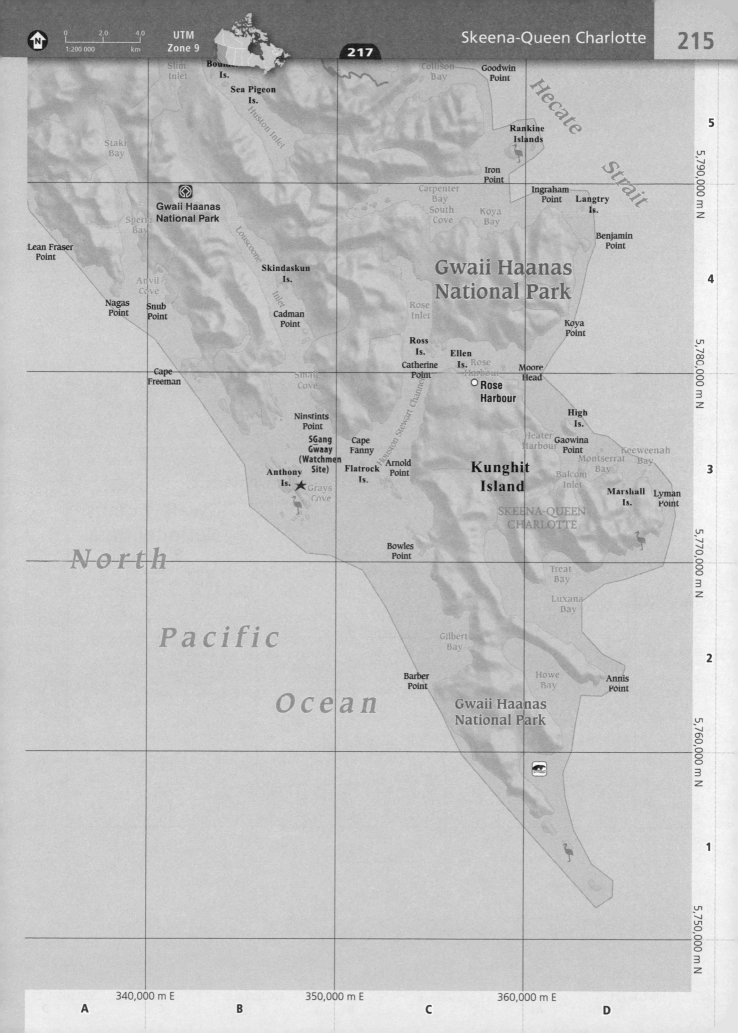

217

1:200 000

0 2.0 4.0
km

N

Hecate Strait

Slim Inlet

Boulton Is.

Sea Pigeon Is.

Collison Bay

Goodwin Point

Rankine Islands

Huston Inlet

Iron Point

Carpenter Bay South Cove

Koya Bay

Ingraham Point

Langtry Is.

Benjamin Point

Gwaii Haanas National Park

Staki Bay

Lean Fraser Point

Sperm Bay

Louscoone Inlet

Skindaskun Is.

Gwaii Haanas National Park

Rose Inlet

Koya Point

Anvil Cove

Nagas Point

Snub Point

Cadman Point

Ross Is.

Catherine Point

Ellen Is.

Rose Harbour

Moore Head

Cape Freeman

Small Cove

Ninstints Point

SGang Gwaay (Watchmen Site)

Anthony Is.

Grays Cove

○ **Rose Harbour**

High Is.

Heater Harbour

Gaowina Point

Montserrat Bay

Keeweenah Bay

Cape Fanny

Flatrock Is.

Arnold Point

Balcom Inlet

Kunghit Island

Marshall Is.

Lyman Point

Houston Stewart Channel

North

Bowles Point

SKEENA-QUEEN CHARLOTTE

Treat Bay

Luxana Bay

Pacific

Gilbert Bay

Ocean

Barber Point

Gwaii Haanas National Park

Howe Bay

Annis Point

219

220

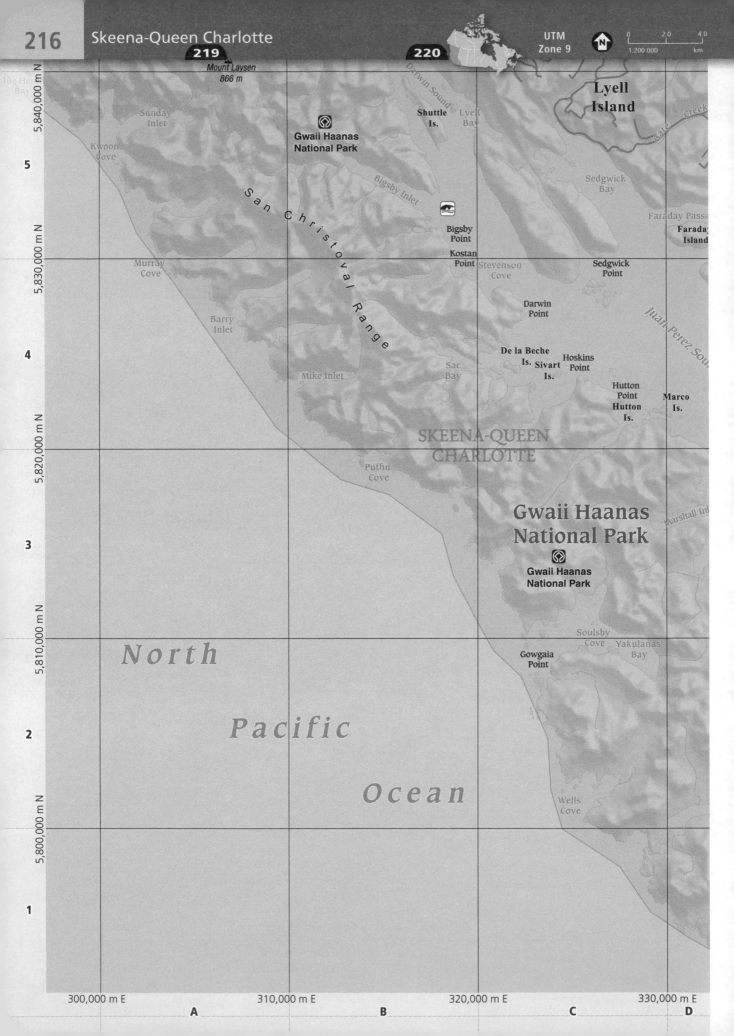

Mount Laysen
866 m

Shuttle
Is.

Lyell
Bay

Lyell
Island

Gate Creek

Darwin Sound

Gwaii Haanas
National Park

Sunday
Inlet

Kwoon
Cove

Jue Herr
Bay

Bigsby Inlet

Sedgwick
Bay

Faraday Passa

San Christoval Range

Bigsby
Point

Kostan
Point

Stevenson
Cove

Sedgwick
Point

Faraday
Island

Murray
Cove

Darwin
Point

Barry
Inlet

De la Beche
Is.

Sivart
Is.

Hoskins
Point

Juan Perez Sou

Mike Inlet

Sac
Bay

Hutton
Point
Hutton
Is.

Marco
Is.

SKEENA-QUEEN
CHARLOTTE

Puffin
Cove

Gwaii Haanas
National Park

Marshall Inl

Gwaii Haanas
National Park

Soulsby
Cove

Yakulanas
Bay

North

Gowgaia
Point

Pacific

Ocean

Wells
Cove

5,840,000 m N

5,830,000 m N

5,820,000 m N

5,810,000 m N

5,800,000 m N

5

4

3

2

1

300,000 m E

310,000 m E

320,000 m E

330,000 m E

A

B

C

D

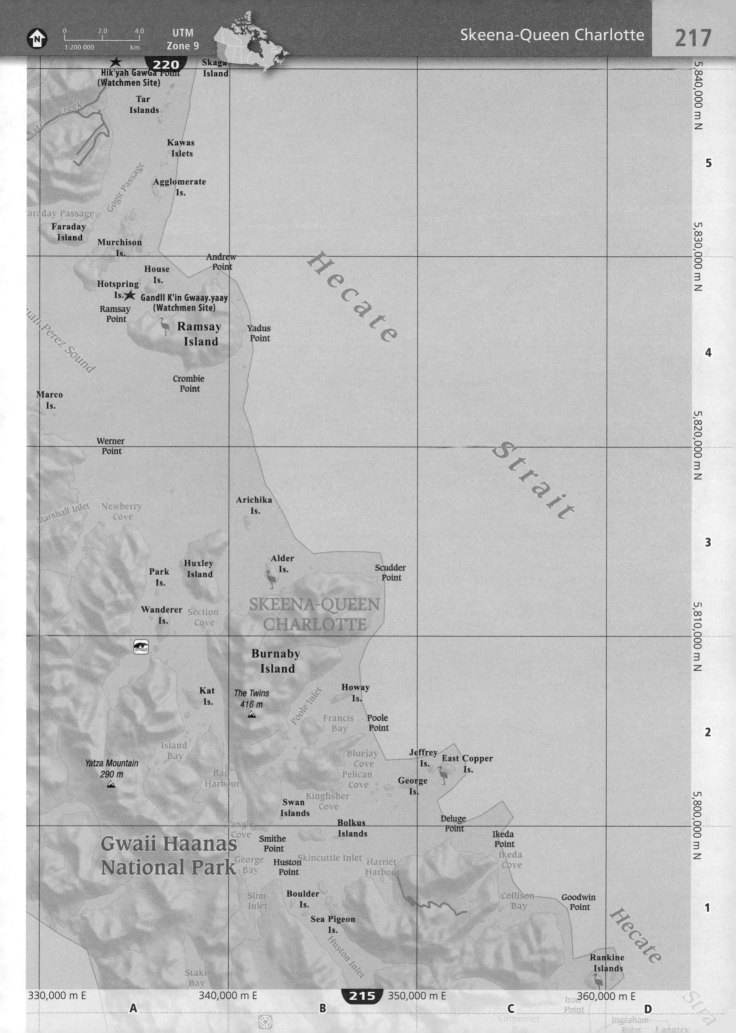

0   2.0   4.0
1:200 000   km

UTM
Zone 9

220

215

A   **B**   **C**   **D**

330,000 m E   340,000 m E   350,000 m E   360,000 m E

Hecate

Strait

Hecate

Sura

Skaga Island

★ Hik'yah GawGa Point
(Watchmen Site)

Tar Islands

Creek

Kawas Islets

Gogit Passage

Agglomerate Is.

Faraday Passage

Faraday Island

Murchison Is.

Andrew Point

House Is.

Hotspring Is. ★ **Gandll K'in Gwaay.yaay**
(Watchmen Site)

Ramsay Point

Ramsay Island

Juan Perez Sound

Yadus Point

Crombie Point

Marco Is.

Werner Point

Arichika Is.

Marshall Inlet

Newberry Cove

Alder Is.

Scudder Point

Huxley Island

Park Is.

SKEENA-QUEEN
CHARLOTTE

Wanderer Is.   Section Cove

Burnaby Island

Kat Is.   *The Twins*
△ 416 m

Poole Inlet

Howay Is.

Poole Point

Francis Bay

Island Bay

Bluejay Cove

Jeffrey Is.

East Copper Is.

Yatza Mountain
△ 290 m

Pelican Cove

George Is.

Bag Harbour

Kingfisher Cove

Swan Islands

Deluge Point

Bolkus Islands

Tangle Cove

Ikeda Point

Smithe Point

**Gwaii Haanas
National Park**

George Bay

Huston Point

Skincuttle Inlet

Harriet Harbour

Ikeda Cove

Slim Inlet

Boulder Is.

Collison Bay

Goodwin Point

Sea Pigeon Is.

Huston Inlet

Staki Bay

Rankine Islands

Iron Point

Carpenter Bay

Ingraham
Point   Langry

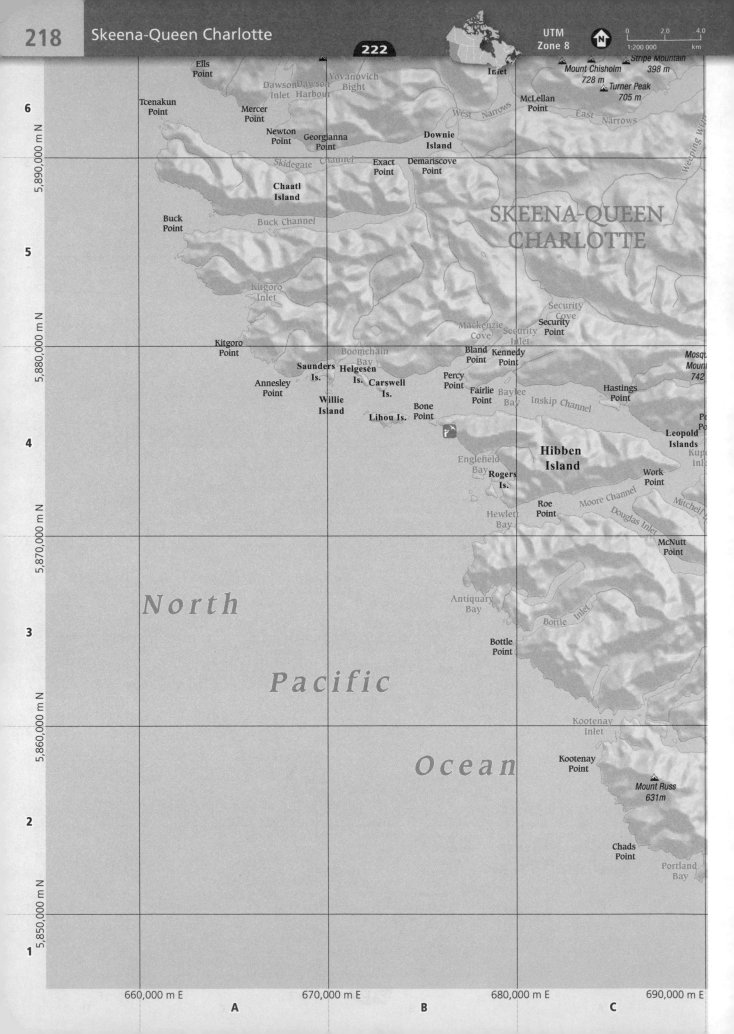

Ells
Point

Yovanovich
Bight

Inlet

Mount Chisholm
728 m

Stripe Mountain
398 m

Turner Peak
705 m

Tcenakun
Point

Dawson
Inlet

Dawson
Harbour

McLellan
Point

West Narrows

East
Narrows

Mercer
Point

Newton
Point

Georgianna
Point

Downie
Island

Weeping Will

5,890,000 m N

Skidegate Channel

Exact
Point

Demariscove
Point

Chaatl
Island

SKEENA-QUEEN
CHARLOTTE

Buck
Point

Buck Channel

5
Kitgoro
Inlet

Security
Cove

Kitgoro
Point

Mackenzie
Cove

Security
Point

Security
Inlet

Mosqu
Moun
742

5,880,000 m N

Saunders
Is.

Helgesen
Is.

Boomchain
Bay

Bland
Point

Kennedy
Point

Annesley
Point

Carswell
Is.

Percy
Point

Fairlie
Point

Baylee
Bay

Hastings
Point

Inskip Channel

Willie
Island

Lihou Is.

Bone
Point

Pe
Po

Leopold
Islands

Kupe
Inle

4
Englefield
Bay

Hibben
Island

Rogers
Is.

Work
Point

Mitchell

Roe
Point

Moore Channel

Hewlett
Bay

Douglas Inlet

5,870,000 m N

McNutt
Point

North

Antiquary
Bay

Bottle
Inlet

3
Bottle
Point

Pacific

5,860,000 m N

Kootenay
Inlet

Ocean

Kootenay
Point

Mount Russ
631m

2

Chads
Point

Portland
Bay

5,850,000 m N

1

660,000 m E   670,000 m E   680,000 m E   690,000 m E

A   B   C

6

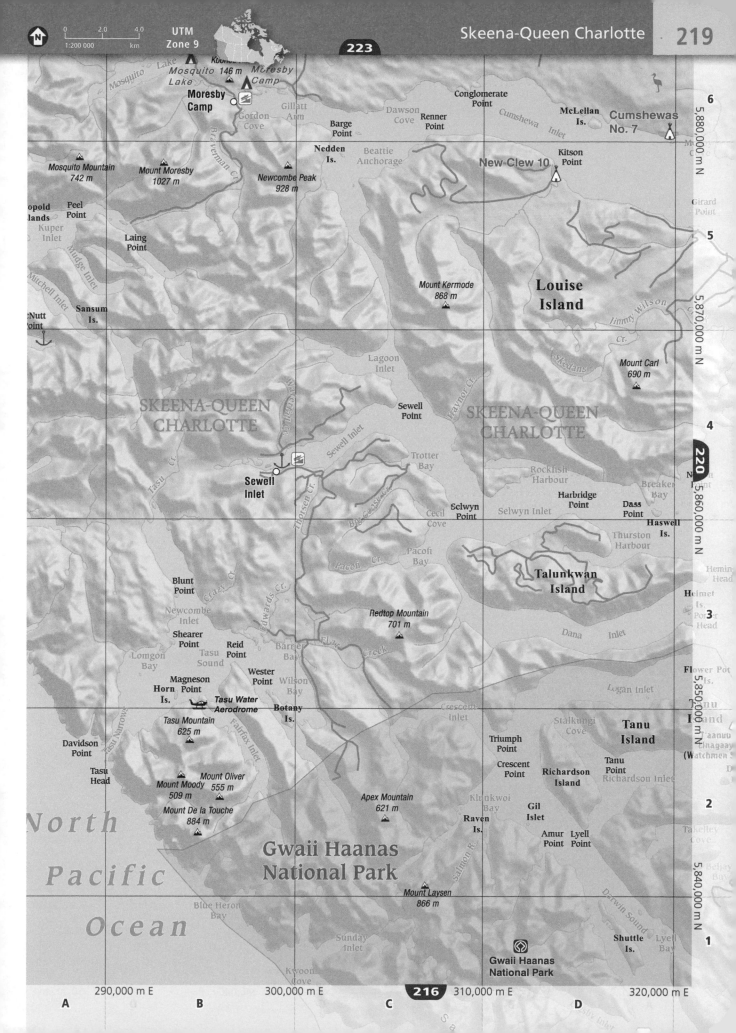

UTM
Zone 9

1:200 000

0   2.0   4.0
km

223

Kootenay Lake
Mosquito 146 m
Mosquito Lake
Moresby Camp

Moresby Camp

Gordon Cove

Braverman Cr.

Gillatt Arm

Dawson Cove

Renner Point

Conglomerate Point

McLellan Is.

Cumshewas No. 7

Cumshewa Inlet

Barge Point

Nedden Is.

Beattie Anchorage

New Clew 10

Kitson Point

Girard Point

Mosquito Mountain
742 m

Mount Moresby
1027 m

Newcombe Peak
928 m

Leopold Islands

Peel Point

Laing Point

Mudge Inlet

Kuper Inlet

Mitchell Inlet

McNutt Point

Sansum Is.

Mount Kermode
868 m

Louise Island

Jimmy Wilson Cr.

Mount Carl
690 m

Skedans

Lagoon Inlet

Sewell Point

Traynor Cr.

SKEENA-QUEEN CHARLOTTE

SKEENA-QUEEN CHARLOTTE

Waterfall Cr.

Tasu Cr.

Thorsen Cr.

Sewell Inlet

Sewell Inlet

Trotter Bay

Rockfish Harbour

Breaker Bay

North Point

220

Bigsby Inlet

Cecil Cove

Selwyn Point

Selwyn Inlet

Harbridge Point

Dass Point

Haswell Is.

Pacofi Cr.

Pacofi Bay

Thurston Harbour

Talunkwan Island

Hemlock Head

Blunt Point

Newcombe Inlet

Crazy Cr.

Edwards Cr.

Redtop Mountain
701 m

Dana Inlet

Helmet Is.

Porter Head

Shearer Point

Reid Point

Tasu Sound

Barney Bay

Flax Creek

Logan Inlet

Flower Pot Is.

Lomgon Bay

Wester Point

Wilson Bay

Crescent Inlet

Tanu Island

Magneson Point

Horn Is.

Tasu Water Aerodrome

Botany Is.

Stalkungi Cove

Tanu Island

T'aanuu Llnagaay (Watchmen S

Tasu Narrows

Davidson Point

Tasu Mountain
625 m

Fairfax Inlet

Triumph Point

Crescent Point

Richardson Island

Tanu Point

Richardson Inlet

Takelley Cove

Tasu Head

Mount Moody
509 m

Mount Oliver
555 m

Mount De la Touche
884 m

Apex Mountain
621 m

Klunkwoi Bay

Salmon R.

Gil Islet

Raven Is.

Amur Point

Lyell Point

Selby Bay

North Pacific

Gwaii Haanas National Park

Ocean

Blue Heron Bay

Mount Laysen
866 m

Darwin Sound

Shuttle Is.

Lyell Bay

Sunday Inlet

Kwoon Cove

Gwaii Haanas National Park

290,000 m E   300,000 m E   310,000 m E   320,000 m E

A   B   C   D

UTM
Zone 9

1:200 000

0   2.0   4.0
km

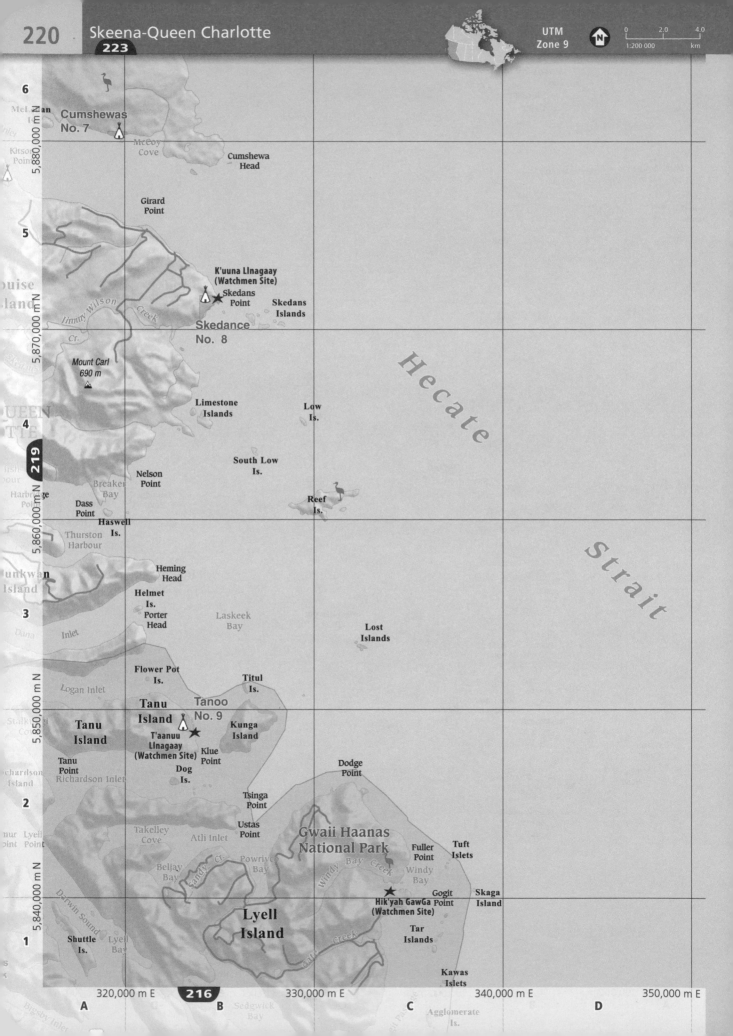

6

Mel**an**
Is.

Kitson
Point

Cumshewas
No. 7

McCoy
Cove

Cumshewa
Head

5,880,000 m N

Girard
Point

5

uise
land

Jimmy Wilson   Creek

Cr.

5,870,000 m N

K'uuna Llnagaay
(Watchmen Site)
Skedans
Point   Skedans
Islands

Skedance
No. 8

Mount Carl
690 m

Hecate

QUEEN
TTE

219

4

Limestone
Islands

Low
Is.

5,870,000 m N

South Low
Is.

Nelson
Point

Breaker
Bay

Reef
Is.

Dass
Point

Harbr**ge**
Po**t**

Haswell
Is.

Thurston
Harbour

5,860,000 m N

Strait

unkwan
Island

Heming
Head

Duna

Inlet

Helmet
Is.
Porter
Head

Laskeek
Bay

Lost
Islands

3

Logan Inlet

Flower Pot
Is.

Titul
Is.

Tanu
Island

Tanoo
No. 9

5,850,000 m N

Stalk**g**
Co**e**

Tanu
Island

T'aanuu
Llnagaay
(Watchmen Site)

Kunga
Island

Klue
Point

chardson
Island

Tanu
Point

Dog
Is.

Richardson Inlet

Dodge
Point

Tsinga
Point

2

nur Lyell
oint Point

Takelley
Cove

Atli Inlet

Ustas
Point

Gwaii Haanas
National Park

Fuller
Point

Tuft
Islets

Beljay
Bay

Sandy   Cr.

Powrivet
Bay

Windy Bay   Creek

Windy
Bay

5,840,000 m N

Darwin Sound

Hik'yah GawGa
(Watchmen Site)

Gogit
Point

Skaga
Island

Lyell
Island

1

Shuttle
Is.

Lyell
Bay

Gate   Creek

Tar
Islands

Kawas
Islets

Bigsby Inlet

Sedgwick
Bay

Agglomerate
Is.

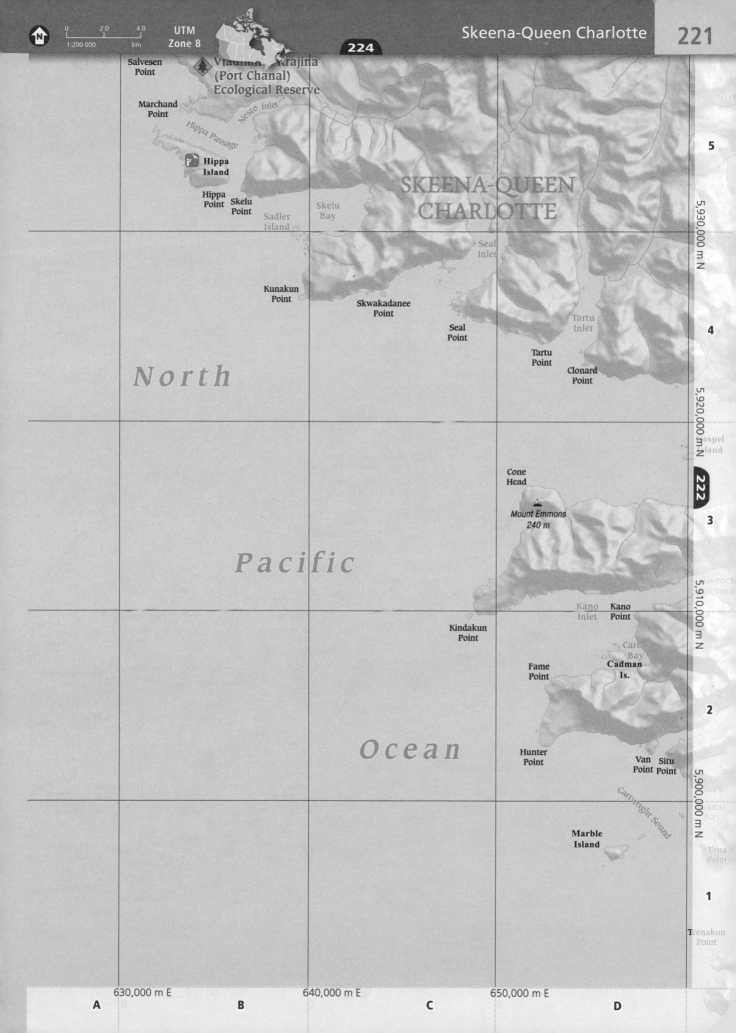

N

0   2.0   4.0
1:200 000   km

UTM
Zone 8

224

5,930,000 m N

5,920,000 m N

5,910,000 m N

5,900,000 m N

5

4

3

222

2

1

Salvesen
Point

Vladimir Krajina
(Port Chanal)
Ecological Reserve

Marchand
Point

Nesto Inlet

Hippa Passage

Hippa
Island

Hippa
Point

Skelu
Point

Sadler
Island

Skelu
Bay

SKEENA-QUEEN
CHARLOTTE

Seal
Inlet

Kunakun
Point

Skwakadanee
Point

Seal
Point

Tartu
Inlet

Tartu
Point

Clonard
Point

North

Gospel
Island

Cone
Head

Mount Emmons
240 m

Pacific

Govench
Pethora

Kano
Inlet

Kano
Point

Kindakun
Point

Carew
Bay

Fame
Point

Cadman
Is.

Ocean

Hunter
Point

Van
Point

Situ
Point

Cartwright Sound

Dudal
Bay

Marble
Island

Tana
Point

Tcenakun
Point

630,000 m E

640,000 m E

650,000 m E

A   B   C   D

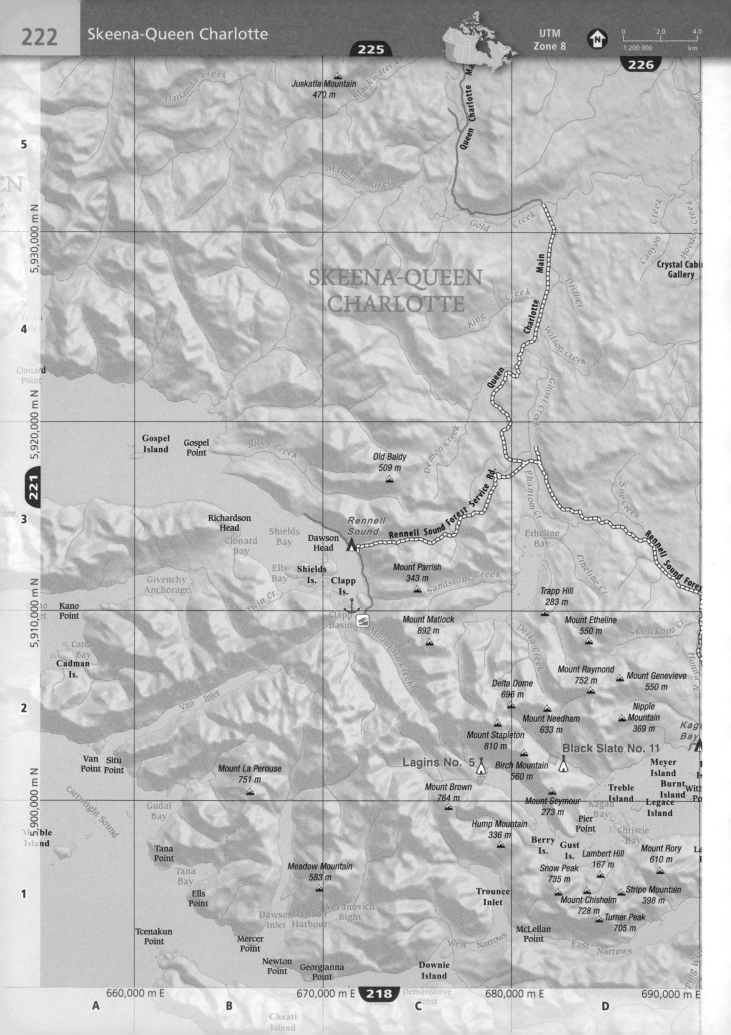

225

226

221

218

SKEENA-QUEEN
CHARLOTTE

Juskatla Mountain
470 m

Datlaman Creek

Blackwater Cr.

Queen Charlotte Ma

Mamin River

Marmin River

Gold Creek

Crystal Cabin
Gallery

King Creek

Charlotte
Main

Dallic Cr.

Wilson Creek

Queen

Ghost Creek

Canyon Creek

Hoodoo Creek

Tartu
Inlet

Clonard
Point

Gospel
Island

Gospel
Point

Riley Creek

Old Baldy
509 m

Demon Creek

Rennell Sound Forest Service Rd.

Phantom Cr.

Sue Creek

Rennell Sound Fore

Richardson
Head

Shields
Bay

Dawson
Head

Rennell
Sound

Etheline
Bay

Etheline Cr.

Skowkona Cr.

Clonard
Bay

Ells
Bay

Shields
Is.

Clapp
Is.

Mount Parrish
343 m

Sandstone Creek

Trapp Hill
283 m

Givenchy
Anchorage

Twin Cr.

Clapp
Basin

Mount Matlock
892 m

Mount Etheline
550 m

Delta Creek

Honna R.

Kano
Point

Carew
Bay

Mountain Creek

Mount Raymond
752 m

Mount Genevieve
550 m

Cadman
Is.

Van Inlet

Delta Dome
696 m

Mount Needham
633 m

Nipple
Mountain
369 m

Kaga
Bay

Mount Stapleton
810 m

Black Slate No. 11

Van
Point

Situ
Point

Mount La Perouse
751 m

Lagins No. 5

Birch Mountain
560 m

Meyer
Island

Cartwright Sound

Gudal
Bay

Mount Brown
764 m

Mount Seymour
273 m

Kagan
Bay

Treble
Island

Burnt
Island

With
Po

Pier
Point

Legace
Island

Marble
Island

Hump Mountain
336 m

Berry
Is.

Gust
Is.

Christie
Bay

Tana
Point

Tana
Bay

Meadow Mountain
583 m

Snow Peak
735 m

Lambert Hill
167 m

Mount Rory
610 m

Le

Ells
Point

Trounce
Inlet

Stripe Mountain
398 m

Tcenakun
Point

Dawson
Inlet

Dawson
Harbour

Yovanovich
Bight

Mount Chisholm
728 m

Turner Peak
705 m

McLellan
Point

Mercer
Point

Newton
Point

Georgianna
Point

Downie
Island

West Narrows

East
Narrows

5,930,000 m N

5,920,000 m N

5,910,000 m N

5,900,000 m N

A   B   C   D

Chaatl
Island

Demariscove
Point

N

0   2.0   4.0
1:200 000   km

UTM
Zone 9

226
16
16

Crystal Cabin
Gallery

Graham
Island

Survey Cr.

Lawn
Point

Lawn Hill
76 m

Lawn Cr.
Lawnhill

Halibut
Bight

Skaigha
No. 2

Dead Tree
Point

Miller   Cr.

Skowcona Mountain
△ 471 m

Yellowhead   Hwy.

16
16

Hecate Strait

Prince Rupert, BC - Skidegate, BC

Double Mountain
407 m

Stony Peak
164 m

Skidegate
No. 1

Skidegate

Spit
Point

Sandspit
Airport

Sandspit

The
Bunkhouse

Queen
Charlotte

Oceanview Dr.

Spirit
Lake

Haida Heritage Centre
At Kay Llnagaay

Rooney
Bay

Torrens
Is.

Jewell
Is.

Onward
Point

Gillatt
Is.

Shingle
Bay

Cape
Chroustscheff

Haida
Point

Skidegate
Landing

Queen Charlotte
City Seaplane Base

Lina
Island

Balch
Islands

Belle
Point

Skidegate
Inlet

Alliford Bay
Seaplane Base

16

Mount Poole
347 m

Blaine Cr.

Copper Bay Rd.

Copper
Bay

Sheldens
Bay

Dogfish
Bay

Khrana 4

Transit
Island

Alliford
Bay

Maude Channel

Maude
Island

Honna River

Weathered
Point

Leconide
Point

Fannin
Bay

Whiteaves
Bay

Sandilands
Island

MacMillan Cr.

Haans Cr.

Kaste
No. 6

Spur 20C

Deena Mainline

Deena No. 3

Alford Bay Rd.

Cumshewa Mountain
613 m

SKEENA-QUEEN
CHARLOTTE

Skidegate   Lake

Gray
Bay

Gray
Point

220

Moresby
Island

Mosquito Lake

Koohoo Hill
146 m

Mosquito
Lake

Moresby
Camp

Moresby
Camp

Gordon
Cove

Gillatt
Arm

Conglomerate
Point

McLellan
Is.

Cumshewas
No. 7

Barge
Point

Dawson
Cove

Renner
Point

Cumshewa Inlet

McEoy
Cove

Braeverna Cr.

Mount Moresby
1027 m

Newcombe Peak
928 m

Nedden

Beattie
Anchorage

219

Slew 10

Kitson
Point

Mount
Moresby

5,920,000 m N

5,910,000 m N

5,900,000 m N

5,890,000 m N

5,880,000 m N

5

4

3

2

1

290,000 m E   300,000 m E   310,000 m E   320,000 m E

A   B   C   D

227

UTM
Zone 8

N

0   2.0   4.0
1:200 000   km

6 N
5,980,000 m N

Conspicuous Cone
357 m

Stanley Creek

Fra...
Po...

Naden
No. 10

Morgan
Point

Dalton
Point

ope
int

Frederick
Island

Peril
Bay

Susk
No. 17

Haines Creek

Kose No

Davidson Creek

Ellis
Point

5

Kennecott
Point

Omega Mountain
211 m

Cave Creek

5,970,000 m N

Joseph Creek

Ingraham
Bay

Eden Lake

Cr...

4

SKEENA-QUEEN
CHARLOTTE

5,960,000 m N

Tiahn No. 27

Tian
Head

Otard
Bay

Tian
Bay

Tian
Islets

Beavis
Point

McIntosh
Point

Fortier Hill
536 m

Ironside Mountain
782 m

3

North

Chanal
Point

Turner
Point

Solide
Brock Islands
Islands

Port
Louis

Virgalias
Cove

Louis
Point

Tingley
Cove

Kiokathli
Inlet

5,950,000 m N

Pacific

Hosu
Cove

Gillian
Point

Vladimir J. Krajina
(Port Chanal)
Ecological Reserve

Dinan Creek

2

Ocean

Athlow
Bay

Notch
Point

Hughes
Point

Salvesen
Island

Freeman
Island

Cameron Range
740 m

Mace Creek

Port Chanal

Goose Empire
Co...Anchorage

5,940,000 m N

Salvesen
Point

Vladimir J. Krajina
(Port Chanal)
Ecological Reserve

1

Marchand
Point

Nesto Inlet

Hippa Passage

620,000 m E

A

630,000 m E

221

Ippa
Is...Bad

640,000 m E

C

650,000 m E

D

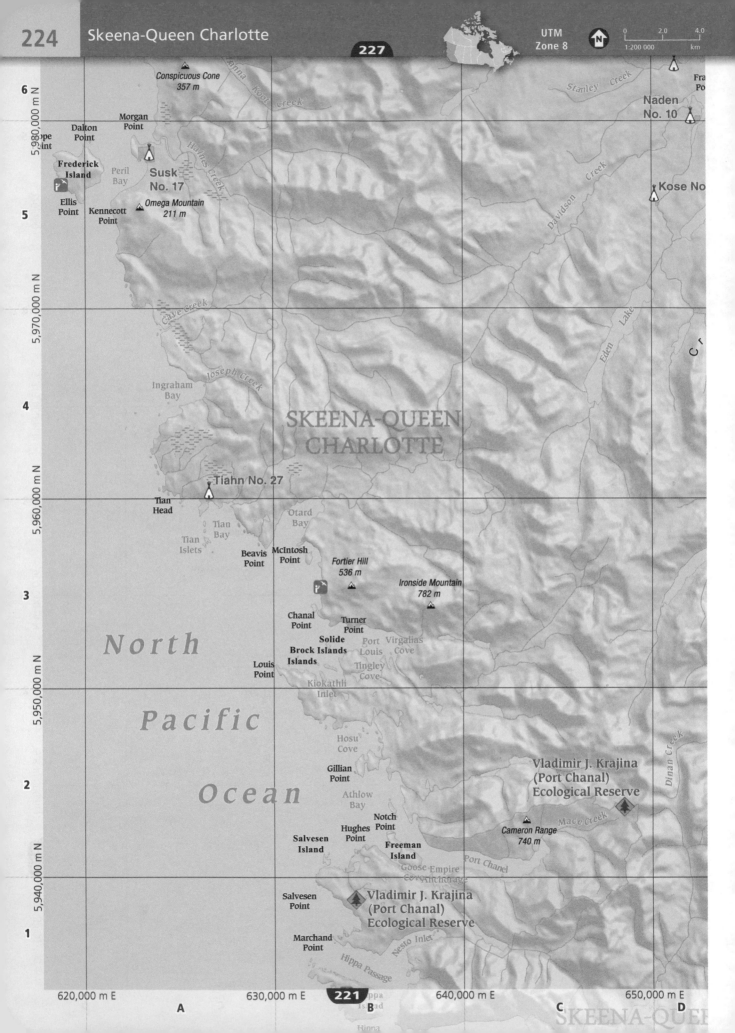

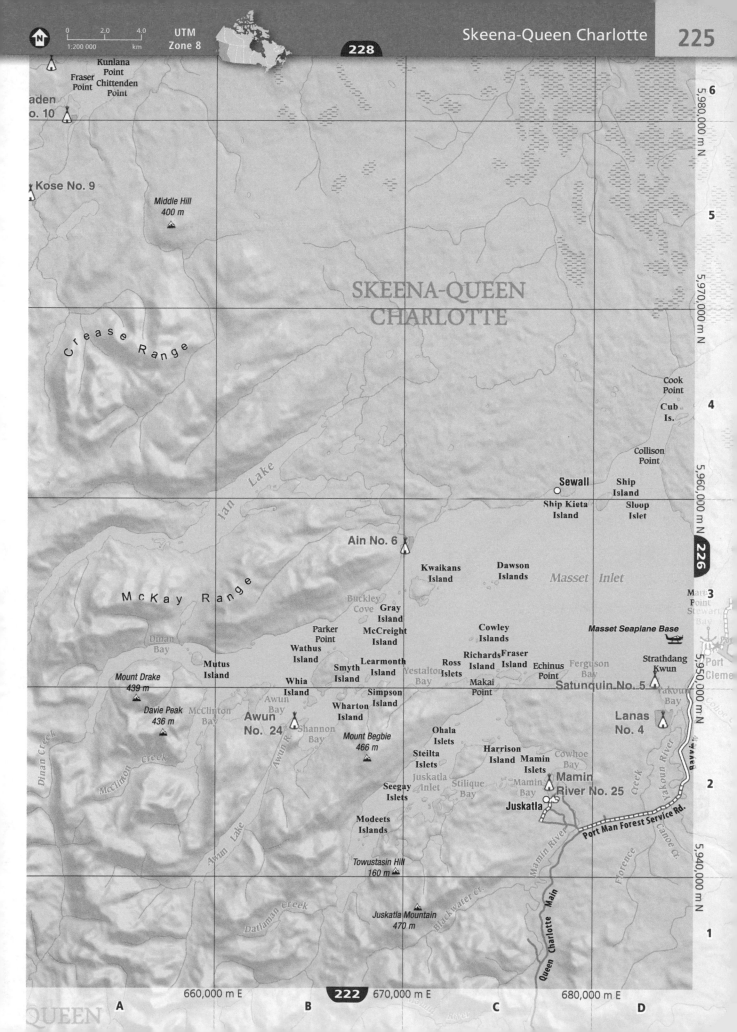

N

| 0 | 2.0 | 4.0 |
1:200 000 km

UTM
Zone 8

228

228

Kunlana
Point
Fraser   Chittenden
Point   Point

aden
o. 10

Kose No. 9

Middle Hill
400 m

Crease Range

SKEENA-QUEEN
CHARLOTTE

Cook
Point

Cub
Is.

Collison
Point

Ian Lake

Sewall   Ship
Island

Ship Kieta   Sloop
Island   Islet

Ain No. 6

Kwaikans   Dawson
Island   Islands

Masset   Inlet

226

226

McKay Range

Buckley
Cove   Gray
Island

Parker   McCreight
Point   Island

Cowley
Islands

Masset Seaplane Base

Mart
Point
Stewart
Bay

Dinan
Bay

Wathus
Island

Richards Fraser
Island   Island Echinus
Point   Ferguson
Bay

Strathdang
Kwun

Port
Cleme

Mutus
Island

Smyth
Island

Learmonth
Island

Ross
Islets

Yestalton
Bay

Makai
Point

Satunquin No. 5

Mount Drake
439 m

Whia
Island

Simpson
Island

Davie Peak
436 m

McClinton
Bay

Awun
Bay

Wharton
Island

Lanas
No. 4

akoun
Bay

Awun
No. 24

Shannon
Bay

Mount Begbie
466 m

Ohala
Islets

Harrison
Island Mamin
Islets

Cowhoe
Bay

Dinan Creek

McClinton Creek

Steilta
Islets

Juskatla
Inlet

Stilique
Bay

Mamin
Bay

Mamin
River No. 25

Seegay
Islets

Juskatla

Modeets
Islands

Port Man Forest Service Rd.

Mamin River

Florence Creek

Canoe Cr.

Awun Lake

Towustasin Hill
160 m

Datlaman Creek

Juskatla Mountain
470 m

Blackwater Cr.

Queen Charlotte Main

QUEEN

660,000 m E   **222**   670,000 m E   680,000 m E

222

A   B   C   D

6
5
4
3
2
1

5,980,000 m N
5,970,000 m N
5,960,000 m N
5,950,000 m N
5,940,000 m N

229

UTM
Zone 9

0   2.0   4.0
1:200 000
km

6

5,970,000 m N

Pure Lake
Provincial Park

Allan
Point

Hogan
Point

Nadu Riv.

Eagle Hill
53m

Cook
Point

**Cub
Island**

5

Otter

Creek

Collison
Point

5,960,000 m N

*Ship
Island*

*Sloop
Island*

225

Martin
Point

*Kumdis
Bay*

*Stewart
Bay*

**Naikoon
Provincial
Park**

Cape Ball

River

Cape
Ball

4

*Masset
Seaplane
Base*

**Port
Clements**

Copp creek

H e c a t e
S t r a i t

nquiry

Strathdang
Kwun

*Naikoun
Bay*

16

5,950,000 m N

16

Kumdis Creek

Mayer River

Bayview Dr.

Canoe Creek

*anas
o. 4*

Yellowhead   Hwy.

★ Pesuta
Shipwreck

3

est Service Rd.

Canoe

Creek

*Misty
Meadows*

?

**SKEENA-QUEEN
CHARLOTTE**

Tlell

Prince Rupert, BC - Skidegate, BC

2

222

5,930,000 m N

Canyon Creek

Hoodoo Creek

Blackbear Cr.

**Graham
Island**

★ **Crystal Cabin
Gallery**

16

1

16

Lawn
Point

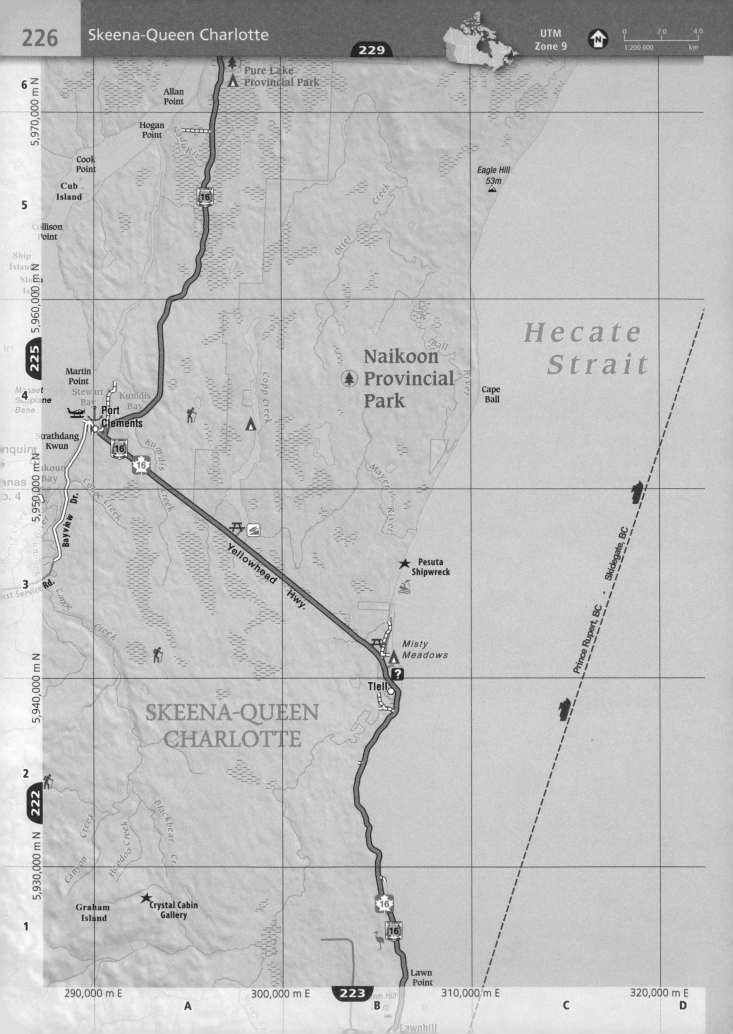

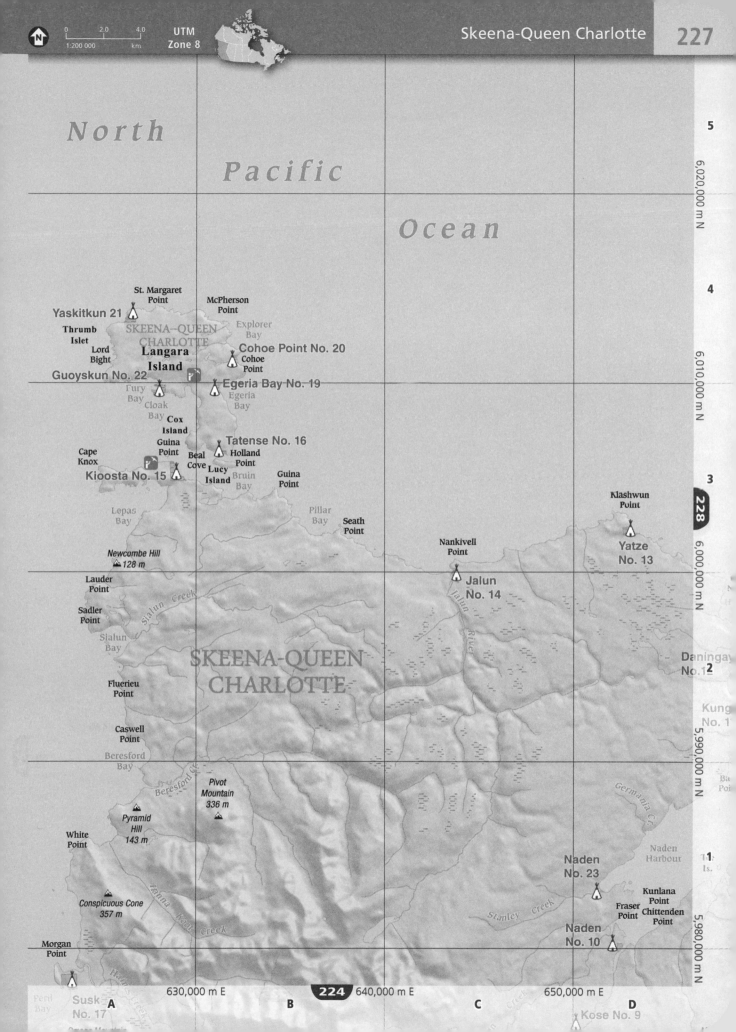

UTM
Zone 8

1:200 000

0 2.0 4.0
km

North

Pacific

Ocean

St. Margaret
Point

McPherson
Point

Yaskitkun 21

Thrumb
Islet

SKEENA–QUEEN
CHARLOTTE

Explorer
Bay

Cohoe Point No. 20

Lord
Bight

**Langara
Island**

Cohoe
Point

Guoyskun No. 22

Fury
Bay

Egeria Bay No. 19

Cloak
Bay

Egeria
Bay

Cox
Island

Guina
Point

Tatense No. 16

Cape
Knox

Beal
Cove

Holland
Point

Kioosta No. 15

Lucy
Island

Bruin
Bay

Guina
Point

Lepas
Bay

Pillar
Bay

Seath
Point

Klashwun
Point

Newcombe Hill
128 m

Nankivell
Point

**Yatze
No. 13**

Lauder
Point

**Jalun
No. 14**

Sadler
Point

Sialun
Creek

Sialun
Bay

SKEENA-QUEEN
CHARLOTTE

Jalun
River

Daningay
No. 12

Fluerieu
Point

Kung
No. 1

Caswell
Point

Beresford
Bay

Ba
Poi

Beresford Cr.

Pivot
Mountain
336 m

Germania Cr.

White
Point

Pyramid
Hill
143 m

Naden
Harbour

Naden
Is.

**Naden
No. 23**

Conspicuous Cone
357 m

Kunlana
Point

Stanley Creek

Fraser
Point

Chittenden
Point

Morgan
Point

**Naden
No. 10**

Feril
Bay

Susk
No. 17

630,000 m E

224 640,000 m E

650,000 m E

Kose No. 9

5

6,020,000 m N

4

6,010,000 m N

3

228 6,000,000 m N

2

5,990,000 m N

1

5,980,000 m N

A

B

C

D

UTM
Zone 8

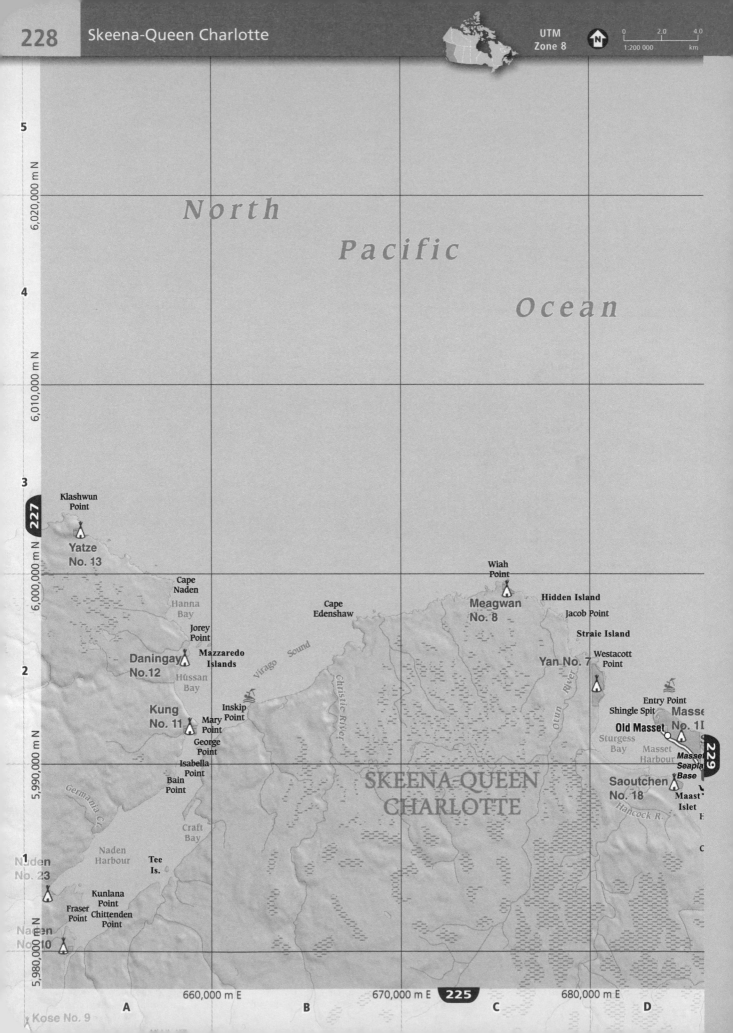

1:200 000

0　2.0　4.0
km

North

Pacific

Ocean

5

6,020,000 m N

4

6,010,000 m N

3

227

Klashwun
Point

**Yatze
No. 13**

6,000,000 m N

Cape
Naden

Hanna
Bay

Wiah
Point

**Meagwan
No. 8**

Hidden Island

Jacob Point

Cape
Edenshaw

Straie Island

Jorey
Point

Daningay
No.12

**Mazzaredo
Islands**

Virago Sound

**Westacott
Point**

Yan No. 7

2

Hussan
Bay

Christie River

Entry Point

**Kung
No. 11**

Inskip
Point

Shingle Spit

Masse
No. 1I

Mary
Point

Old Masset

229

George
Point

Sturgess
Bay

Masset
Harbour

Oun River

Isabella
Point

Masse
Seapla
Base

Bain
Point

**SKEENA-QUEEN
CHARLOTTE**

**Saoutchen
No. 18**

5,990,000 m N

Germania Cr

Maast
Islet

Craft
Bay

Hancock R.

1

**Naden
No. 23**

Naden
Harbour

Tee
Is.

Kunlana
Point

Fraser
Point

Chittenden
Point

Naden
No.10

5,980,000 m N

Kose No. 9

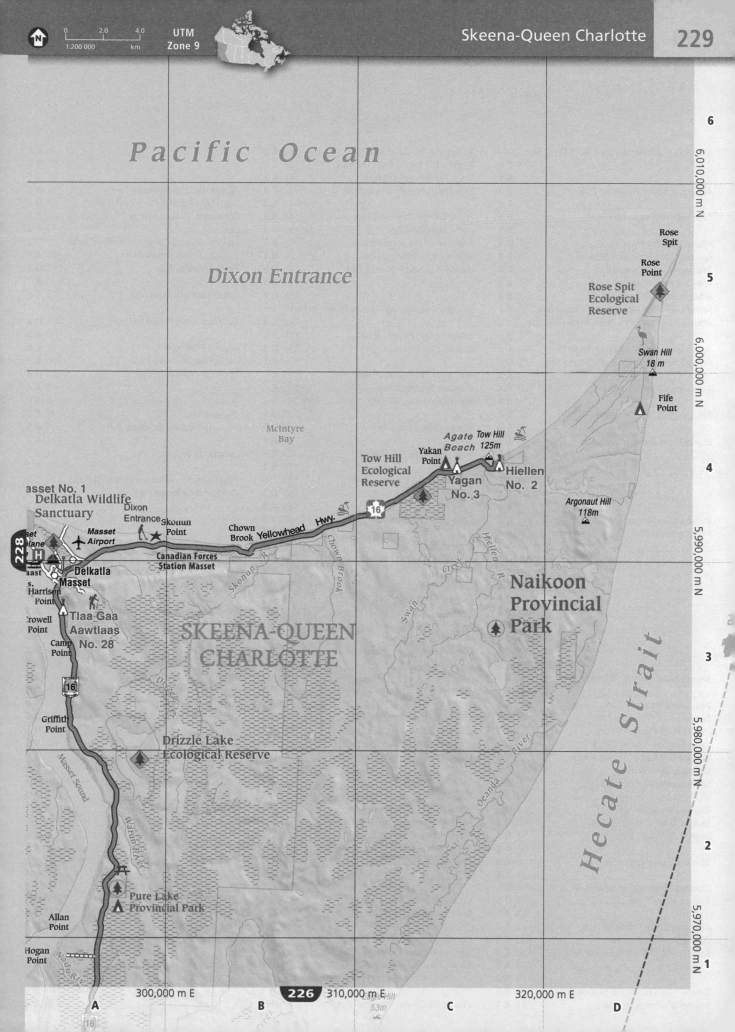

N

| 0 | 2.0 | 4.0 |
1:200 000   km

UTM
Zone 9

6

6,010,000 m N

Pacific Ocean

Dixon Entrance

Rose
Spit

5

Rose
Point

Rose Spit
Ecological
Reserve

6,000,000 m N

Swan Hill
18 m

McIntyre
Bay

Fife
Point

Tow Hill
125m

4

Agate
Beach

Yakan
Point

Tow Hill
Ecological
Reserve

Hiellen
No. 2

Yagan
No. 3

Masset No. 1
Delkatla Wildlife
Sanctuary

Dixon
Entrance   Skonun
Point

16

5,990,000 m N

Chown
Brook   Yellowhead   Hwy.

Masset
Airport

Argonaut Hill
118m

Masset
Plane

Canadian Forces
Station Masset

228

H

Delkatla
Masset

Naikoon
Provincial
Park

Harrison
Point

Crowell
Point

Tlaa Gaa
Aawtlaas
No. 28

SKEENA-QUEEN
CHARLOTTE

Camp
Point

Hecate Strait

16

3

5,980,000 m N

Griffith
Point

Drizzle Lake
Ecological Reserve

Massel Sound

2

Pure Lake
Provincial Park

Allan
Point

5,970,000 m N

Hogan
Point

1

300,000 m E

226   310,000 m E

320,000 m E

A   B   C   D

16

Park Listings

Golf Course Listing

Points of Interest

Using the **Community Index**

The Index

- In the community index, information is presented in the following order: **community name**, regional district abbreviation, **page number** and **grid reference**.
- A grid reference is a letter-number combination (e.g. C 5) that refers to the index grid on each page.

The Maps

- Each map is divided by an index grid with columns identified by the letters A through E and rows identified 1 through 7.
- To use the grid reference, identify where the appropriate row and column meet and search within this space for the required object.
- Adjacent map pages are indicated by the small red tabs around the frame of the map.

Abbreviations

Idaho _____ (ID)
Montana _____ (MT)
Washington _____ (WA)

Community Index

A

Abbotsford	63	D 2
	64	A 2
Aberdeen (WA)	52	C 6
	63	C 2
Acme (WA)	52	D 2
	53	A 2
Adams Lake	174	D 5
	175	A 5
Agassiz	64	D 4
	65	A 4
Ahousat	55	A 5
Ainsworth Hot Springs	107	C 5
Airdrie	196	D 5
	197	B 5
Aldergrove	63	B 2
Alderwood Manor (WA)	30	D 5
	31	A 5
	36	D 1
	37	A 1
Alert Bay	146	A 3
Allison Lake	98	D 4
Alpine Meadows	124	B 5
	26	D 1
	27	A 1
Anacortes (WA)	43	A 4
Anglemont	175	D 5
	176	A 5
Anmore	62	B 5
Annis	176	B 3
Apex Mountain	69	C 6
	100	C 1
Argenta	138	B 5
Arlington (WA)	37	B 5
Armstrong	159	D 4
	160	A 4
Ashcroft	171	B 2
Ashton Creek	160	B 5
	176	B 1

B

Bainbridge Island (WA)	30	B 3
Balfour	107	C 3
Balmoral	175	C 4
Balzac	196	D 4
	197	A 4
Bamfield	46	B 4
Banff	193	C 4
Bangor (WA)	29	D 4
Bankeir	99	C 5
	100	A 5
Barney's Bar	89	D 5
	90	A 5
	120	D 1
	121	A 1
Barnhartvale	173	C 2
	174	A 2
Baynes Lake	80	B 4
Bear Creek	96	B 2
Beaton	179	B 3
Beaux Arts Village (WA)	31	B 3
Beaverdell	102	C 1
Beiseker	197	E 6
Belcarra	62	B 5
	29	C 1
Bellevue (WA)	31	B 3
Bellingham (WA)	52	B 2
Benchlands	195	B 5
Big Bay	150	B 3
Big White	102	D 5
Birchdale	138	C 4
Birken	152	A 4
Black Creek	119	B 2
Black Pines	173	C 5
Black Point	89	D 5
	90	A 5
	120	D 1
	121	A 1
Blaeberry	201	B 1
Blakeburn	98	C 2
Blind Bay	175	C 4
Blind Channel	149	C 3
Bliss Landing	119	E 4
	120	B 4
Bloedel	118	D 5
Blowhole	84	C 4
Blue Springs	160	C 1
Blueberry Creek	74	D 4
Blyn (WA)	35	A 3
Boat Basin	54	B 4
Bold Point	119	B 6
	150	B 1
Bonaparte	170	D 4
Bonaparte	171	A 4
Bonnington Falls	106	B 1
Boothroyd	127	D 3
Boston Bar	127	D 2
	128	A 2
Boston Flats	171	B 3
Boswell	107	D 1
	108	A 1
Bothell (WA)	31	B 5
Bowser	89	B 1
Brackendale	92	D 5
	93	A 5
Braeloch	101	C 5
	132	B 1
Bragg Creek	186	B 5
	195	C 1
Bremerton (WA)	30	A 2
Brew Bay	89	E 5
	90	A 5
	120	E 1
	121	A 1
Bridesville	71	B 2
Bridge River	169	C 3
Brier (WA)	30	D 5
	31	A 5
Brilliant	74	D 5
Brinnon (WA)	29	B 4
Brisco	182	D 4
Britannia Beach	92	C 3
Brookmere	129	B 2
Brookswood	62	D 2
	63	A 2
Brouse	136	B 6
	163	B 1
Buckley Bay	88	D 2
	89	A 2
Bull River	110	D 2
	111	A 2
Bull Harbour	143	C 6
Burien (WA)	30	C 1
Burnaby	62	B 4
Burrard	62	B 5
Burton	135	D 3
	136	A 3

C

Cache Creek	170	D 4
	171	A 4
Caesars	132	A 4
Cahilty	173	E 5
	174	A 5
Calgary	196	D 3
	197	A 3
Campbell Creek	173	D 2
	174	A 2
Campbell River	118	E 4
	119	B 4
Canal Flats	140	C 5
Canmore	193	D 3
	194	A 3
Canoe	175	D 3
	176	A 3
Canyon	77	D 2
Canyon Alpine	127	D 3
	128	A 3
Canyon Hot Springs	188	C 3
Cape Mudge	118	D 4
Carmi	102	B 2
Carnation (WA)	31	D 3
Carrolls Landing	135	D 4
	136	A 4
	73	C 2
Cassidy	60	A 2
	59	D 2
Castle Junction	192	C 5
Castlegar	74	D 5
Caulfeild	61	C 5
Cawston	69	C 4
Caycuse	47	D 4
	48	A 4
Cayoose Creek	169	C 2
Cedar	60	A 3
Ceepeecee	84	C 4
Celista	175	C 5
Chamiss Bay	114	B 2
Chase	174	D 4
	175	A 4
Cheam View	65	B 4
Chemainus	49	A 6
	49	B 4
	60	A 2
Cherry Creek	57	E 5
	58	B 5
	172	C 3
Cherryville	161	B 1
Chestermere	197	C 2
Chilliwack	64	C 3

Using the **Road Index**

The Index

- In the road index, information is presented in the following order: road name, regional district abbreviation, **page number** and **grid reference**.
- A grid reference is a letter-number combination (e.g. C 5) that refers to the index grid on each page.

The Maps

- Each map is divided by an index grid with columns identified by the letters A through E and rows identified 1 through 7.
- To use the grid reference, identify where the appropriate row and column meet and search within this space for the required object.
- Adjacent map pages are indicated by the small red tabs around the frame of the map.

Abbreviations

Alberni-Clayoquot _____ (AC)	Fraser- Fort George _____ (FFG)	Mountain View County _____ (C-MV)
Bighorn No. 8 _____ (MD-8)	Glacier _____ (GL)	Municipality of Jasper _____ (JAS)
Calgary _____ (CAL)	Greater Vancouver _____ (GV)	Nanaimo _____ (NA)
Capital _____ (CA)	I.D. No. 4 _____ (ID-4)	North Okanagan _____ (NO)
Cardston County _____ (C-CAR)	I.D. No. 9 _____ (ID-9)	Okanagan Similkameen _____ (OS)
Central Kootenay _____ (CK)	I.D. No. 12 _____ (ID-12)	Powell River _____ (PR)
Central Okanagan _____ (CO)	I.D. No. 15 _____ (ID-15)	Rocky View County _____ (C-RV)
Clearwater County _____ (C-CL)	Idaho _____ (ID)	Skeena-Queen-Charlotte _____ (SQC)
Columbia - Shuswap _____ (CS)	Kananaskis Improvement District (ID-KAN)	Squamish-Lillooet _____ (SL)
Comox Valley _____ (COV)	Kneehill County _____ (C-KNE)	Strathcona _____ (ST)
Cowichan Valley _____ (CV)	Kootenay _____ (KO)	Sunshine Coast _____ (SC)
Crowsnest Pass _____ (CRO)	MD Foothills No. 31 _____ (MD-31)	Thompson-Nicola _____ (TN)
East Kootenay _____ (EK)	MD of Pincher Creek No. 9 _____ (MD-9)	Washington _____ (WA)
Flathead _____ (FL)	Montana _____ (MT)	Wheatland County _____ (C-WHE)
Fraser Valley _____ (FV)	Mount Waddington _____ (MW)	Yellowhead County _____ (C-YEL)

Road Index

Numbered Roads

0 Ave. (FV)	52 C 5		197 A 4	36	D 1	68 Ave. (GV)	62 C 3
	63 C 1	15th Ave. NE (WA)	30 D 4		37 A 1	68 St. (GV)	62 A 3
0 Ave. (GV)	52 A 5		37 A 6	36th St. (CK)	77 D 2	68 St. NE (CAL)	197 B 3
	63 A 1		44 A 1	37 St. SW (CAL)	196 D 1-2	68 St. SE (CAL)	197 B 1
1 Ave.NW (C-RV)	197 A 5	15th Ave. NW (WA)	30 C 4	38th St. (CK)	77 C 2	68th Ave. NW (WA)	36 D 6
1st Ave. (FV)	64 C 3	16 Ave. (GV)	51 C 6	39 Ave. (NO)	159 C 2		43 D 1
1st Ave. S (EK)	110 A 2		52 B 6	40 Ave. (GV)	62 C-D 2	69 St. NW (CAL)	196 C 4
2nd St. (KO)	72 B 2		62 C-D 2		63 A 2	69 St. SW (CAL)	196 C 2
2nd St. S (EK)	110 B 2		63 A-B 2	40 St. NE (CS)	175 D 3	69th Ave. SE (WA)	37 B 2
3rd Ave. NE (WA)	36 D 5-6		31 B 2	40 St. NE (CS)	176 A 3	72 Ave. (GV)	62 B 3
	37 A 5-6	17 Ave. SE (CAL)	197 B 2	43rd Ave. SE (WA)	37 B 3		62 D 3
	43 D 1	17 Ave. SW (CAL)	196 D 2	45th St. S (EK)	110 B 2		63 A 3
	44 A 1	17th St. S (EK)	110 B 2	48 Ave. NW (C-RV)	195 D 3	72 St. (GV)	62 A 2
4 Barrel Rd. (FV)	127 C 3	20 Ave. (GV)	51 C 6	48 Ave. NW (CAL)	196 A 3	76th Ave. NW (WA)	43 C 1
4 Mile Creek Rd. (CK)	137 C 3		62 C 2	49th St. S (EK)	110 B 2	80 Ave. (GV)	62 B, D 3
4th Ave. S (WA)	30 D 2	20 Ave. NE (CS)	175 D 3	50 Ave. NE (CS)	175 C 3		63 A 3
4th St. (WA)	37 B 4		176 A 3	50 St. NW (CS)	175 C 3	80th Ave. NW (WA)	36 C 6
4th St. NW (CAL)	196 C 4	20th St. (CK)	77 C 2		175 C 2		43 C 1
5th Ave. (FV)	65 D 6	24 Ave. (GV)	62 C 2	52 St. (GV)	50 D 6		29 D 1
	96 D 1	24 Ave. (GV)	63 B 2		61 D 2		30 A 1
6 St. NE (CAL)	196 D 4	24 St. SW (CAL)	197 A 5		62 A 2	83rd Ave. NE (WA)	37 B 4
	197 A 4	24th Ave. NW (WA)	30 C 4	52 St. (WA)	51 A 6	84 Ave. (GV)	62 B 3
6th St. (GV)	62 B 4	24th St. (CK)	77 C 2	52 St. SE (CAL)	197 B 1, 3		63 B 3
7th Ave. S (EK)	110 A 2	27th Ave. NE (WA)	37 A 4	56 Ave. (GV)	63 B 2	84 St. NE (CAL)	197 B 4
8 Ave. (GV)	51 D 5	28 Ave. (GV)	61 D 2	56th St. (GV)	50 D 6	84 St. SE (CAL)	197 B 2-3
	52 A 5		62 A 2		61 D 2		31 A 1
	62 D 1	30 St. NE (CS)	175 D 3		62 A 2	84th St. NE (WA)	37 C 4
	63 A 1		176 A 3	56th St. (WA)	51 A 6	85 St. NW (CAL)	196 C 4
8 St. SW (CAL)	197 A 5	32 Ave. (GV)	62 C-D 2	58 Ave. (FV)	63 C 2	85 St. SW (CAL)	196 C 2
8th Ave. NW (WA)	30 C 5		63 A 2	60 Ave. (GV)	62 C 3	85th St (WA)	30 C 4
9th St. S (EK)	110 B 2	32 Ave. NE (CAL)	197 B 3	60 Ave. NE (CS)	175 D 3	87th St. (OS)	70 B 2
10th Ave. (GV)	62 B 4	33 Ave. SW (CAL)	196 D 2		176 A 3	88 Ave. (GV)	62 B, D 3
12 Mile Coulee Rd. (C-RV)	196 C 4	35th Ave. NE (WA)	30 D 4	60 St. NW (CS)	175 C 3	88 St. (GV)	62 B 2
12th St. (GV)	62 B 4		31 A 4	60th St. SE (WA)	37 B 3	92 Ave. (GV)	62 B 3
14 St. NW (CAL)	196 D 3-4	35th Ave. SW (WA)	30 C 2	64 Ave. (GV)	62 C 3	96 Ave. (GV)	62 B, D 3
14 St. SW (CAL)	196 D 2	36 St. NE (CAL)	197 B 3-4		63 A 3		63 A 3
15 St. NE (CAL)	196 D 4	36 St. SE (CAL)	197 B 2	64 Ave. NE (CAL)	197 B 3	96 St. (GV)	62 B 2
		36th Ave. W (WA)	30 D 5	64 St. (GV)	62 A 2	99th Ave. NE (WA)	37 B 4
			31 A 5	67th Ave. NE (WA)	37 B 4-5	100 Ave. (GV)	62 B-C 3